THE BEST OF THE BEST OF Uncle John's BATHROOM READER

By the
Bathroom Readers' Institute

Bathroom Readers' Press
Ashland, Oregon

THE BEST OF THE BEST OF
UNCLE JOHN'S BATHROOM READER®

Articles in this Best Of edition have been included from the following books:
Uncle John's Ultimate Bathroom Reader © 1996; *Uncle John's Giant 10th Anniversary
Bathroom Reader* © 1997; *Uncle John's Great Big Bathroom Reader* © 1998; *Uncle
John's Absolutely Absorbing Bathroom Reader* © 1999; *Uncle John's All-Purpose Extra
Strength Bathroom Reader* © 2000; *Uncle John's Supremely Satisfying Bathroom Reader*
© 2001; *Uncle John's Bathroom Reader Plunges Into History* © 2001; *Uncle John's
Ahh-Inspiring Bathroom Reader* © 2002; *Uncle John's Bathroom Reader Plunges Into
the Universe* © 2002; *Uncle John's Unstoppable Bathroom Reader* © 2003; *Uncle John's
Bathroom Reader Plunges Into Great Lives* © 2003; *Uncle John's Colossal Collection of
Quotable Quotes* © 2004; *Uncle John's Slightly Irregular Bathroom Reader* © 2004;
Uncle John's Bathroom Reader Plunges Into the Presidency © 2004; *Uncle John's
Presents Mom's Bathtub Reader* © 2004; *Uncle John's Fast-Acting Long-Lasting
Bathroom Reader* © 2005; *Uncle John's Bathroom Reader Tees Off on Golf* © 2005;
Uncle John's Bathroom Reader Plunges Into Hollywood © 2005; *Uncle John's Curiously
Compelling Bathroom Reader* © 2006; *Uncle John's Bathroom Reader Wonderful World
of Odd* © 2006; *Uncle John's Tales to Inspire* © 2006; *Uncle John's Bathroom Reader
Extraordinary Book of Facts* © 2006; *Uncle John's Quintessential Collection of Notable
Quotables for Every Conceivable Occasion* © 2006; *Uncle John's Bathroom Reader
Plunges Into Music* © 2007; *Uncle John's Bathroom Reader Plunges Into National
Parks* © 2007; *Uncle John's Bathroom Reader Takes a Swing at Baseball* © 2008;
Uncle John's Triumphant 20th Anniversary Bathroom Reader © 2007.

For information, write:
The Bathroom Readers' Institute, P.O. Box 1117, Ashland, OR 97520
www.bathroomreader.com • 888-488-4642

Cover design by Michael Brunsfeld, San Rafael, CA (*Brunsfeldo@comcast.net*)

ISBN-13: 978-1-59223-912-2 / ISBN-10: 1-59223-912-9

Library of Congress Cataloging-in-Publication Data
The best of the best of Uncle John's bathroom reader / [by the Bathroom Readers'
Institute].
    p. cm.
ISBN 978-1-59223-912-2 (pbk.)
1. American wit and humor. 2. Curiosities and wonders. I. Bathroom Readers'
Institute (Ashland, Or.) II. Title: Uncle John's bathroom reader.
  PN6165.B47 2008
  818'.5402—dc22

                                                                2008018103

Printed in the United States of America
Fourth Printing: April 2011
4 5 6 7 8 15 14 13 12 11

THANK YOU!

*The Bathroom Readers' Institute sincerely thanks the people
whose advice and assistance made this book possible.*

Gordon Javna

Amy Miller

Jay Newman

Brian Boone

John Dollison

Thom Little

Julia Papps

JoAnn Padgett

Melinda Allman

Michael Brunsfeld

Angela Kern

Malcolm Hillgartner

Jahnna Beecham

The Three Jeffs

Sue Steiner

Stephanie Spadaccini

John Scalzi

Art Montague

Larry Kelp

Sydney Stanley

Scarab Media

Lisa Meyers

David Cully

Ginger Winters

Monica Maestas

Lilian Nordland

Sarah Rosenberg

Kent, Mary & Sue

Mom & Dad

(Mr.) Mustard Press

Steven Style Group

John Javna

Eddie Deezen

Julie Bégin

Elise Gochberg

Publishers Group West

Al "The Brain" MacDougall

Paddy Laidley

Raincoast Books

Laurel Graziano

Porter the Wonder Dog

Thomas Crapper

*...and the many writers,
editors, and other contributors
who have helped make
Uncle John the bathroom
fixture he is today.*

CONTENTS

Because the BRI understands your reading needs, we've
divided the contents by length as well as subject.

Short—a quick read

Medium—2 to 3 pages

Long—for those extended visits, when something
a little more involved is required

* Extended—for those leg-numbing experiences

INTRODUCTION

Welcome to what we modestly consider the very best *Bathroom Reader*...ever! If you're new to our series, then this is the perfect way to get acquainted with the Bathroom Readers' Institute, a dedicated team of trivia hounds founded by Uncle John in 1987. Since then, we've created an immense "movement" that's still being felt the world over.

As some of you longtime readers know, we did a *Best of* edition in 1995. For that one, we only had seven books to choose from. But since then we've been busy. How busy? Well, this second *Best of* (which makes an excellent companion to the first one) contains our favorite selections from more than 25 *Bathroom Readers*! So we were able to carefully pick and choose the pinnacle of what our book series has to offer. There really are some amazing stories in here. For example...

• The harrowing tale of the jumbo jet that became a jumbo glider

• The deadly legacy of the miniscule mosquito

• Two men you've never heard of: one who caused the most environmental damage ever, and another who saved a billion lives

• Super spies, luxurious bomb shelters, and the top secret U.S. plans to invade Canada

• The strange fate of Ted Williams's head, a spike through Phineas Gage's head, and how to cook a shrunken head

• Sharks with lights, the "Body Farm," and the "Suicide Song"

• Plus the best of the best of dumb crooks, strange lawsuits, court transquips, flubbed headlines, word and phrase origins, and more.

As you sit proudly with the most absorbing collection of bathroom reading ever to grace our pages, we want to thank you for being the best group of fans that any book series could hope for.

And as always, *Go with the Flow!*

> —Uncle John, the BRI staff,
> and Porter the Wonderdog

YOU'RE MY INSPIRATION

*It's always interesting to find out where the architects of
pop culture get their ideas. These may surprise you.*

GOLLUM. Andy Serkis provided the voice and movements
for the character in the *Lord of the Rings* films. He based
the voice on the sound of his cat coughing up a hairball.
Special effects artists modeled Gollum's wiry, bony frame on punk
rocker Iggy Pop.

THE CHEVROLET INSIGNIA. In 1913 Billy Durant, founder
of General Motors, liked the wallpaper pattern in a Paris hotel so
much that he ripped off a piece and brought it back to Detroit to
copy as the symbol for his new Chevrolet car.

WILE E. COYOTE AND ROAD RUNNER. Looney Tunes
animator Chuck Jones created the pair in 1948. The idea was
sparked by a passage from Mark Twain's 1872 book *Roughing It*,
about Twain's travels through the Wild West as a young man. In
the passage, Twain noted that the "coyotes are starving and would
chase a roadrunner."

VULCAN HAND SALUTE. Leonard Nimoy invented this for
Mr. Spock during the filming of a *Star Trek* episode. The gesture
was borrowed from the Jewish High Holiday services. The
Kohanim (priests) bless the congregation by extending "the
palms of both hands...with thumbs outstretched and the middle
and ring fingers parted." Nimoy used the same gesture, only with
one hand.

STEVIE RAY VAUGHAN. One of Vaughan's first influences
was blues guitarist Buddy Guy. Yet while Vaughan went on to
fame in the 1980s, Guy fell on hard times and nearly quit the
business...until one day when Guy heard Vaughan's playing. He
was so amazed that he decided to pick up his own guitar
again...unaware that the man who inspired him to return to
music was the same man that he inspired to start playing in the
first place.

Original name of New York's Park Avenue: 4th Avenue (until they built Central Park).

COURT TRANSQUIPS

The verdict is in: Court transcripts make great bathroom reading.
These were actually said—word for word—in a court of law.

Q: What gear were you in at the moment of impact?
A: Gucci sweats and Reeboks.

Q: Did you blow your horn or anything?
A: After the accident?
Q: Before the accident.
A: Sure, I played for ten years. I even went to school for it.

Q: Doctor, how many autopsies have you performed on dead people?
A: All my autopsies have been performed on dead people.

Q: Then Tommy Lee pulled out a gun and shot James in the fracas?
A: No sir, just above it.

"How far apart were the vehicles at the time of the collision?"

Q: Doctor, will you take a look at those X-rays and tell us something about the injury?
A: Let's see, which side am I testifying for?

Q: How was your first marriage terminated?
A: By death.
Q: And by whose death was it terminated?

Q: When he went, had you gone and had she, if she wanted to and were able, for the time being excluding all the restraints on her not to go, gone also, would he have brought you, meaning you and she, with him to the station?
D.A.: Objection. That question should be taken out and shot.

"Were you alone or by yourself?"

Q: Doctor, as a result of your examination of the plaintiff, is the young lady pregnant?
A: The young lady is pregnant, but not as a result of my examination.

Q: You say you're innocent, yet five people swore they saw you steal a watch.
A: Your Honor, I can produce 500 people who *didn't* see me steal it!

"You don't know what it was, and you didn't know what it looked like, but can you describe it?"

Q: How did you get here today?
A: I had a friend bring me.
Q: The friend's name?
A: We call him Fifi.
Q: To his face?

A two-hour movie uses about two miles of film.

RANDOM ORIGINS

Once again, the BRI asks—and answers—the question: where did this stuff come from?

AEROSOL CANS
In 1943 the U.S. Agriculture Department came up with an aerosol bug bomb. It used liquid gas inside steel cans to help WWII soldiers fight malaria-causing insects (malaria was taking a heavy toll on the troops). By 1947, civilians could buy bug bombs, too, but they were heavy "grenadelike" things. Two years later, Robert H. Abplanalp developed a special "seven-part leakproof" valve that allowed him to use lightweight aluminum instead of heavy steel, creating the modern spray can.

RESTAURANTS
The oldest ancestor of the restaurant is the tavern, which dates back to the Middle Ages. Typically taverns served one meal at a fixed hour each day, usually consisting of only one dish. According to French food historians, it wasn't until 1765 that someone came up with the idea of giving customers a *choice* of things to eat. A Parisian soup vendor named Monsieur Boulanger is said to have offered his customers poultry, eggs, and other dishes, but it was his soups, also known as "restoratives" or *restaurants* in French, that gave this new type of eatery its name.

HAMSTERS
The natural habitat of Golden or Syrian hamsters, as the pet variety is known, is limited to one area: the desert outside the city of Aleppo, Syria. (Their name in the local Arabic dialect translates to "saddlebags," thanks to the pouches in their mouths that they use to store food.) In 1930 a zoologist named Israel Aharoni found a nest containing a female and a litter of 11 babies in the desert and brought them back to his lab at the Hebrew University of Jerusalem. The mother died on the trip home; so did seven of her babies. Virtually all of the millions of domesticated Golden hamsters in the world are descended from the four that survived.

Hair is the second-fastest growing tissue in the body. The fastest: bone marrow.

FLUBBED HEADLINES

These are 100% honest-to-goodness headlines.
Can you figure out what they were trying to say?

Home Depot Purchases Wallpaper, Blinds Retailers

Nude Scene Done Tastefully in Radio Play

WOMAN NOT INJURED BY COOKIE

PECAN SCAB DISEASE CAUSING NUTS TO FALL OFF

Doctor Testifies in Horse Suit

LANSING RESIDENTS CAN DROP OFF TREES

Astronomers See Colorful Gas Clouds Bubble Out of Uranus

NATION SPLIT ON BUSH AS UNITER OR DIVIDER

Hillary Clinton on Welfare

Depp's* Chocolate Factory *Has Tasty Opening

Child's Stool Great For Use In Garden

Fried Chicken Cooked in Microwave Wins Trip

DEAD EXPECTED TO RISE

Deer Kill 130,000

Textron Inc. makes offer to screw company stockholders

Factory Orders Dip

Dr. Fuchs off to the Antarctic

School taxpayers revolting

North Korean Leader Names Ancient Frog "Ancient Frog"

STUD TIRES OUT

HELICOPTER POWERED BY HUMAN FLIES

Trees can break wind

Cockroach Slain, Husband Badly Hurt

TWO SISTERS REUNITED AFTER 18 YEARS AT CHECKOUT COUNTER

UTAH GIRL DOES WELL IN DOG SHOWS

Panda Mating Fails, Veterinarian Takes Over

Mercury boils at 674.11°F.

OOPS!

Everyone's amused by tales of outrageous blunders—probably because it's comforting to know that someone's screwing up even worse than we are. So go ahead and feel superior for a few minutes.

ASHES TO ASHES

"In 1990 the Wilkinsons, a family in Sussex, England, received what they thought was a gift package of herbs from Australian relatives. They stirred the contents into a traditional Christmas pudding, ate half of it, and put the remainder in the refrigerator.

"Soon thereafter, as a member of the family relates, 'We heard from Auntie Sheila that Uncle Eric had died, and had we received his ashes for burial in Britain.' Shocked, the Wilkinsons quickly summoned a vicar to bless, and bury, Uncle Eric's leftovers."

—*The Wall Street Journal*

BORDER CROSSING

"If you closely examine a map of South Dakota, you'll see that the man-made western border of the state has a slight bump in it as it runs north-south. When the territory was being surveyed, the boundary was set to fall on the 27th meridian west from Washington, D.C. As the surveyors working down from the north met those coming up from the south, they missed each other by a few miles. This error remains on every map to this day."

—*Oops*, by Paul Smith

UNPLUGGED

"In 1978 workers were sent to dredge a murky stretch of the Chesterfield-Stockwith Canal in England. Their task was to remove all the rubbish and leave the canal clear....They were disturbed during their teabreak by a policeman who said he was investigating a giant whirlpool in the canal. When they got back, however, the whirlpool had gone...and so had a 1½-mile stretch of the canal. A flotilla of irate holidaymakers were stranded on their boats in brown sludge.

Cost effective? It costs 8/10 of a cent to mint a penny.

"Among the first pieces of junk the workers had hauled out had been the 200-year-old plug that ensured the canal's continued existence. 'We didn't know there was a plug,' said one bewildered workman. All the records had been lost in a fire during the war."

—*The Book of Heroic Failures*

A PAIR OF BIRDBRAINS

"Each evening, birdlover Neil Symmons stood in his backyard in Devon, England, hooting like an owl—and one night, an owl called back to him. For a year, the man and his feathered friend hooted back and forth. Symmons even kept a log of their 'conversations.'

"Just as Symmons thought he was on the verge of a breakthrough in interspecies communication, his wife had a chat with next-door neighbor Wendy Cornes. 'My husband spends his night in the garden calling out to owls,' said Mrs. Symmons.

"'That's odd,' Mrs. Cornes replied. 'So does my Fred.'

"And then it dawned on them."

—"The Edge," *The Oregonian*

JUST DO IT

"In December 1998 a company had to erase an embarrassing mistake it made on pencils bearing an anti-drug message. The pencils carried the slogan: 'Too Cool To Do Drugs.' But a sharp-eyed fourth-grader in northern New York noticed when the pencils are sharpened, the message turns into 'Cool To Do Drugs' then simply 'Do Drugs.'

"'We're actually a little embarrassed that we didn't notice that sooner,' spokeswoman Darlene Clair told reporters."

—Associated Press

A FINE BOUQUET?

"Wine merchant William Sokolin had paid $300,000 for a 1787 bottle of Châteaux Margaux once owned by Thomas Jefferson. He presented it before a group of 300 wine collectors at Manhattan's Four Seasons restaurant in 1989, hoping that one of them might offer $519,000 for it. Before bidders could get out their checkbooks, he dropped the bottle and broke it."

—*Oops!,* by Smith and Decter

In Canada and the northern U.S., milk is sold in plastic bags as well as in jugs.

HAIR'S TO YOU

*Hair's a page of long, luxurious
facts…so cut loose.*

• How many hairs on your head? If you're blond, about 150,000. Brunette, 100,000. Redhead, 60,000.

• There are 550 hairs in the average eyebrow.

• About 10 percent of men and 30 percent of women shave solely with an electric razor.

• There are about 15,500 hairs in an average beard.

• Women start shaving at a slightly younger age than men do.

• Half of Caucasian men go bald. Eighteen percent of African American men do.

• American Indians rarely go bald.

• Hair is unique to mammals.

• Fifty percent of Americans have gray hair by the time they're 50 years old.

• Number of hair follicles on an average adult: 5 million.

• City dwellers have longer, thicker, denser nose hairs than country folks do.

• The older you get, the slower your hair grows.

• Cutting hair does not influence its growth.

• Hair covers the whole human body, except for the soles of the feet, the palms, mucous membranes, and lips.

• The average life span of a human hair: three to seven years.

• Your hair is as strong as aluminum.

• Women shave an area nine times as large as men do.

• Medical studies show that intelligent people have more copper and zinc in their hair.

Meat Loaf is a vegetarian.

FAMILIAR PHRASES

*We'd never try double-cross you, so we had to include some
of our favorite phrase origins (and this is no red herring).
Here they are, just in the nick of time....*

RED HERRING

Meaning: Distraction; diversionary tactic

Origin: When herring is smoked, it changes from silvery gray to brownish red and gives off a strong smell. Hunters use red herrings to train dogs to follow a scent...and, by dragging a red herring across the trail, they can also throw a dog off a scent.

EASY AS PIE

Meaning: Simple to complete

Origin: This phrase came from New Zealand, by way of Australia, in the 1920s. When someone was good at something, they were considered "pie at it" or "pie on it." For example, a good climber was "pie at climbing." Although the modern phrase is associated with pie (the dessert), it is actually derived from the Maori word *pai*, which means "good."

DOUBLE-CROSS

Meaning: Betray

Origin: Comes from boxing and describes a fixed fight. If a fighter deliberately loses, he "crosses up" the people who have bet on him to win; if he wins, he "crosses up" the people paying him to lose. Someone is betrayed no matter how the fight turns out; hence the name double-cross.

IN THE NICK OF TIME

Meaning: Without a second to spare

Origin: Even into the 18th century, some businessmen still kept track of transactions and time by carving notches—or nicks—on a "tally stick." One arriving just before the next nick was carved would save the next day's interest...just in the nick of time.

Frightening fact: *Phobatrivaphobia* is a fear of trivia about phobias.

WHAT A DOLL!

Here are five of the more unusual
dolls sold in America in recent years.

THUGGIES

Introduced in the summer of 1993, Thuggies came with something that no dolls had ever had before—criminal records. There were 17 different characters, with names like "Motorcycle Meany," "Dickie the Dealer," "Bonnie Ann Bribe," and "Mikey Milk 'em." They were outlaw bikers, dope pushers, white-collar criminals, even "check-kiting congressmen."

But despite their "personal histories," the dolls were designed to *discourage* crime, not encourage it. Each one came packaged in a prison cell and had its own rehabilitation program. Children were supposed to set them on the straight-and-narrow. (Bonnie Ann Bribe, for example, doing time for trying to bribe her way through school, had to read to senior citizens one hour a day.) The dolls even came with a gold star to wear when they successfully completed rehab.

"It works, believe me," Carolyn Clark, co-founder of Thuggies, Inc., told reporters. "It's not going to turn the kid into a criminal. It lets them know that they can correct this kind of behavior."

TONY THE TATTOOED MAN

Comes with tattoos and a "tattoo gun," that kids can use to apply the tattoos to the doll or to themselves. Additional tattoos— including "brains, boogers, bugged-out eyes and other anatomical atrocities"—are sold separately.

BABY THINK IT OVER

Like Thuggies, Baby Think It Over was designed to teach kids a lesson—in this case, "Don't get pregnant." The dolls are issued to junior-high and high school students so they can experience what it's really like to have a baby. Each doll weighs 10 pounds, and contains electronics that make it cry "at random, but realistic, intervals, simulating a baby's sleeping and waking patterns to its

First actor to appear on the cover of *Time* magazine: Charlie Chaplin, in 1925.

demand for food," says Rick Jurmain, who invented the doll with his wife, Mary.

Like a real baby, there's no way to stop the doll from crying once it starts except by "feeding" it, which is done by inserting a special key into the baby's back, turning it, and holding the baby in place with pressure for as long as 15 minutes. The key is attached to the "parent's" arm with a tamper-proof hospital bracelet, which prevents them from handing off the responsibility to someone else. And the teenagers have to respond quickly— once the baby starts crying, a timer inside the baby records how long it cries. It also records any shaking, drops, or harsh handling that takes place. If the crying baby is left unattended for longer than two minutes, the timer registers that as neglect.

There's also a "drug-addicted" version that's more irritable, has a "higher pitch, a warbling cry," and a body tremor. Priced at $200 apiece, Baby Think It Overs are sold as instructional aids, not toys.

RHOGIT-RHOGIT

Sexual abstinence is simply not an option for Rhogit-Rhogit. "Elegant, intellectual, and extremely sexy, Rhogit-Rhogit will seduce you with his male prowess, his animal sexuality, his vision, and his depth," says the sales catalog from BillyBoy Toys, the Paris company that manufactures it. "He feels equally comfortable in butch, tough-boy clothes as he does in the most avant-garde French and Italian designer clothes and the most utterly formal attire."

Rhogit-Rhogit also has a male sidekick, Zhdrick, who, according to the catalog "is, perhaps, the most sophisticated, sensual, and provocatively sexual doll ever made." The dolls retail for $1,000 apiece, which includes one designer outfit and one condom. If you want wigs, jeans, lassos, boots, underwear, top hats, or other accessories from the company's "Boy Stuff" collection, you have to pay extra. (A lot extra—outfits run $600 to $900 apiece.)

TALKING STIMPY DOLL

From the cartoon series, *Ren & Stimpy*. "Yank the hairball in Stimpy's throat and he talks. Squeeze his leg and he makes 'rude underleg noises.'" Recommended for "ages 4 and up."

The average U.S. teenage girl owns seven pairs of jeans.

QUOTES...AND THEIR CONSEQUENCES

*When a public figure puts his foot in his
mouth, the whole world is listening.*

Speaker: George H. W. Bush

Quote: "Just as Poland had a rebellion against totalitarianism, I am rebelling against broccoli, and I refuse to give ground. I do not like broccoli and I haven't liked it since I was a little kid and my mother made me eat it. Now I'm president of the United States and I'm not going to eat any more broccoli."

Consequences: Needless to say, the broccoli industry was upset. Broccoli, it seemed, had become Public Enemy Number One. After it was banned at the White House, some schools dropped it from their menu. At home, many of the nation's children followed suit and boycotted broccoli at the dinner table. Result: broccoli sales fell significantly in 1990.

It wasn't only the broccoli industry that was miffed—nutrition advocates blasted the president for sending a message to kids that vegetables were bad. Bush didn't help his case when he appointed pork rinds as the official snack on Air Force One (where broccoli was also banned).

To protest the president's position, broccoli growers from around the country sent tons of the vegetable to the White House. Bush stayed far away from the cases and ordered them delivered to various food banks and shelters in the Washington, D.C. area. As the 1990s rolled on, broccoli was found to help prevent cancer; it is currently making a comeback.

Speaker: NBA star Kevin Garnett

Quote: "This is it. It's for all the marbles. I'm sitting in the house loading up the pump, I'm loading up the Uzis, I've got a couple of M-16s, couple of nines, couple of joints with some silencers on them, couple of grenades, got a missile launcher. I'm ready for war."

"Facts do not cease to exist because they are ignored." —Aldous Huxley

Background: One of professional basketball's best players, the star forward with the Minnesota Timberwolves at the time, said this the day before a deciding playoff game against the Sacramento Kings. While such a comment might not be noticed in other years, this was said in May of 2004 while U.S. troops were mired in a bloody war in Iraq and Afghanistan.

Consequences: Families with sons and daughters serving in the war were irate. The NBA and Minnesota Timberwolves received a barrage of complaints demanding an apology, which Garnett swiftly gave: "Sincerely, I apologize for my comments earlier," he said. "I'm a young man and I understand when I'm appropriate, and this is totally inappropriate. I was totally thinking about basketball, not reality." No argument there. The flak died down after Garnett's lengthy apology, and Wolves' coach Flip Saunders had to remind his team to concentrate on basketball and not their star player's taunts to the press.

But Kings center Brad Miller, one of Garnett's biggest rivals, wouldn't let it go and added his own brand of ammunition to the mix: "I'm bringing my shotgun, my bow and arrow, my four-wheel drive truck, and four wheelers and run over him." In the end, Miller's shotgun was no match for Garnett's Uzis—the Wolves won.

Speaker: Paul Newman

Quote: "24 hours in a day, 24 beers in a case. Coincidence? I think not."

Consequences: Although this witty remark has often been attributed to the famous actor, salad dressing maker, and racecar driver, Newman never said it. Nevertheless, the quote has taken on a life of its own, especially at Princeton University in New Jersey. Every April 24, some of the rowdier students participate in "Newman's Day." Their goal: to drink one beer an hour for an entire day— while attending all of their classes. When Newman found out that such an event was named in his honor, he did not feel honored. He called on the university to "bring an end to this tradition." Princeton officials responded by saying that it was not a sanctioned event—they've been trying to stop it for years. So Newman and the university joined forces in 2004 to call on students to forgo Newman's Day. Although the event still happened, its numbers were reportedly down from previous years.

Population of North Pole, Alaska: 2,183.

Sad Irony: Newman's own son Scott died of a drug overdose at age 28, prompting his father to create the Scott Newman Center in 1980, a nonprofit organization "dedicated to the prevention of substance abuse through education."

Speaker: Hillary Clinton

Quote: "I'm not sitting here like some little woman standing by my man like Tammy Wynette."

Background: "Stand By Your Man," a country music classic recorded in 1968, was Wynette's biggest hit. Its simple lyrics basically say that if a woman truly loves her man, then she'll remain loyal when he goes a little wayward, " 'Cause after all, he's just a man."

During the 1992 presidential campaign, Bill and Hillary Clinton appeared on CBS' *60 Minutes*. Hillary made the comment after being asked about Bill's alleged affair with Gennifer Flowers.

Consequences: The comment did well for establishing Hillary Clinton as a strong, modern woman, but Tammy Wynette was infuriated. She fumed that the statement had "offended every true country music fan and every person who has made it on their own with no one to take them to a White House." It even served as fodder for country music DJs to label the Clintons as "country music-hating liberals." Not good press in an election year.

Clinton apologized profusely, saying that she meant no disrespect, and Wynette accepted. (She could have even thanked Clinton—all of the press put her name back in the headlines and gave new life to a 25-year-old song.) To show there was no bad blood, Wynette later performed "Stand By Your Man" at a Clinton fundraiser. And in the end, Hillary did stand by her man.

*   *   *

THE PRICE OF FAME

"People still think of me as a cartoonist, but the only thing I lift a pen or pencil for these days is to sign a contract, a check, or an autograph."

—**Walt Disney**

The vocabulary of the average person consists of 5,000 to 6,000 words.

MOVIE REVIEW HAIKU

*The classic Japanese poetry form—three lines of 5, 7,
and 5 syllables each—collides with pop culture.*

Planet of the Apes
Like *Batman*—great sets,
Bad plots, and promised sequels.
Damn them all to Hell!

Duck Soup
A fine collection
Of skits destined to inspire
The great Bugs Bunny.

2001: A Space Odyssey
Great special effects,
Without help from computers!
(Except HAL, of course.)

Apocalypse Now
Brilliant filmmaking
Overly long indulgence
Don't get off the boat

Erin Brockovich
Julia Roberts
Is Erin Brockovich in
Erin Brockovich!

The Matrix Revolutions
Directors, take note:
Franchise isn't everything.
Just let it die. Please.

March of the Penguins
An interesting
And exciting adventure
—if you're a penguin.

Cast Away
Made fire? Big deal.
Girlfriend dumped you anyway.
Stop talking to balls.

The Sixth Sense
One of those movies
I'd have rather seen before
I saw the preview.

American Pie
Rated R: No one
Over 17 allowed
Without teenager.

Airplane
"Surely you are not
Critiquing this!" "I am. And
Don't call me Shirley."

Forrest Gump
Mama always said,
"Stupid is as Stupid does."
Stupid rakes it in.

My Big Fat Greek Wedding
My big fat romance
Disguised as a really long
Windex commercial.

Groundhog Day
You will want to see
This movie several times.
Uh, sorry. Bad joke.

Actress Mary Pickford, nicknamed "America's Sweetheart," was Canadian.

THE WORLD'S (UN)LUCKIEST MAN

Is he lucky…or unlucky? You decide.

THE SELAK ZONE

On a cold January day in 1962, a Croatian music teacher named Frane Selak was traveling from Sarajevo to Dubrovnik by train. Well, that's where he *thought* he was going. Little did he know that he was actually about to embark upon a strange 40-year odyssey marked by freak accidents and near-death experiences.

• The train carrying Selak in 1962 inexplicably jumped the tracks and plunged into an icy river, killing 17 passengers. Selak managed to swim back to shore, suffering hypothermia, shock, bruises, and a broken arm, but very happy to be alive.

• One year later, Selak was on a plane traveling from Zagreb to Rijeka when a door blew off the plane and he was sucked out of the aircraft. A few minutes later the plane crashed; 19 people were killed. But Selak woke up in a hospital—he'd been found in a haystack and had only minor injuries.

• In 1966 he was riding on a bus that went off the road and into a river. Four people were killed—but not Selak. He suffered only cuts and bruises.

• In 1970 he was driving along when his car suddenly caught fire. He managed to stop and get out just before the fuel tank exploded and engulfed the car in flames.

• In 1973 a faulty fuel pump sprayed gas all over the engine of another of Selak's cars while he was driving it, blowing flames through the air vents. His only injury: he lost most of his hair. His friends started calling him "Lucky."

• In 1995 he was hit by a city bus in Zagreb but received only minor injuries.

• In 1996 he was driving on a mountain road when he turned a

Melon is from the Greek word for apple.

corner and saw a truck coming straight at him. He drove the car through a guardrail, jumped out, landed in a tree—and watched his car explode 300 feet below.

BAD NEWS (AND GOOD NEWS) TRAVELS FAST

By this time he was starting to get an international reputation for his amazing knack for survival. "You could look at it two ways," Selak said. "I am either the world's unluckiest man or the luckiest. I prefer to believe the latter."

How does the story of Frane Selak end? Luckily, of course. In June 2003, at the age of 74, Selak bought his first lottery ticket in 40 years...and won more than $1 million. "I am going to enjoy my life now," he said. "I feel like I have been reborn. I know God was watching over me all these years." He told reporters that he planned to buy a house, a car, and a speedboat, and to marry his girlfriend. (He'd been married four times before and reflected, "My marriages were disasters, too.")

Update: In 2004 Selak was hired to star in an Australian TV commercial for Doritos. At first he accepted the job, but then changed his mind and refused to fly to Sydney for the filming. Reason: He said he didn't want to test his luck.

*　　*　　*

BACKWARD TOWN NAMES

The names of dozens of U.S. cities come from other words spelled backward. Most were forced to do it after realizing that the town name they wanted was already taken. Others have quirkier origins.

• **Enola, South Carolina.** Originally named "Alone," but residents began to feel too isolated.

• **Nikep, Maryland.** Changed because it kept getting Pekin, Indiana's, mail by mistake.

• **Adaven, Nevada.** America's only city with its state's name spelled backward. It's a palindrome!

• **Tensed, Idaho.** Named for a missionary named DeSmet, the name was reversed when it was discovered there was already a DeSmet, Idaho. The town submitted their new name, Temsed, to Washington, D.C., but a clerical error resulted in the misspelling.

APOCALYPSE AGAIN

Most families vacation in Florida because of the warm weather and abundance of theme parks. You can shake hands with Mickey Mouse at Disney World, feed the dolphins at SeaWorld…and duck and cover in New Vietnam. Well, at least that was the idea.

BACKGROUND
In 1975 Reverend Carl McIntire, a New Jersey fundamentalist preacher and pro-Vietnam War activist, began construction on what was to be "New Vietnam." Spread out over 300 acres of land in Cape Canaveral, Florida, McIntire and his partner, former Green Beret Giles Pace, envisioned a theme park where people could get a glimpse of the Vietnam War.

What would the theme park look like? Here are a few of the attractions McIntire planned:

• **Sampan ride.** A *sampan* is an Asian sailboat. Tourists would take a sampan ride around a moat that encircled a recreated Vietnamese village with a neighboring Special Forces camp.

• **Special Forces camp.** The camp would be made up of simple concrete barracks displaying weapons "used by the Commies in Vietnam." Around the barracks would be trenches and mortar bunkers complete with sandbag walls and fake machine guns.

• **The perimeter.** The camp would be surrounded with row upon row of barbed wire, *punji* stakes, and fake Claymore mines to add to the atmosphere. "We'll have a recording, broadcasting a fire-fight, mortars exploding, bullets flying, Vietnamese screaming," McIntire explained, while hired GIs shoot blanks at the enemy. Visitors would be encouraged to take cover in the barracks or station themselves behind a machine gun and get in on the action.

• **A Vietnamese village.** The village would be made up of 16 thatched huts and four concrete upper-class Vietnamese homes that would double as retail shops and snack bars serving traditional Vietnamese cuisine. So after working up an appetite manning the machine guns, park visitors could stop in for a bowl of rice and noodles. The village was to be completely authentic, with irrigated

---

That little statue on the grill of every Rolls Royce car has a name: "Spirit of Ecstasy."

paddies, water buffalo, cows, chickens, ducks, and palm trees.

• **Vietnamese people.** Vietnamese people—real refugees from the real war—would travel through the village in traditional outfits and make New Vietnam come to life. McIntire planned this as a make-work program for Vietnamese refugees arriving in Florida at the end of the war. "Every penny will go back to the Vietnamese. The Bible says love your neighbor."

"They'll work anywhere for a paycheck," Pace commented. "And this will be work that won't be in competition with anyone else. There's nothing offensive about it."

INTO THE MORASS

The idea bombed and the park was never completed. Vietnamese refugees, having just experienced the horrors of a real war, weren't about to participate in a fake one. "My wife won't walk around that village in a costume like Mickey Mouse," refugee Cong Nguyen Binh told reporters. "We want to forget. We want to live here like you. We don't want any more war."

*   *   *

MISNOMERS

• The rare **red** coral of the Mediterranean is actually **blue.**

• The **gray** whale is actually **black.**

• Whale**bone** is actually made of **baleen,** a material from the whales' upper jaws.

• The Atlantic **salmon** is actually a member of the **trout** family.

• **Heart**burn is actually pyrosis, caused by the presence of gastric secretions, called reflux, in the lower **esophagus.**

• The Caspian **Sea** and the Dead **Sea** are both actually **lakes.**

• The horseshoe **crab** is more closely related to **spiders** and **scorpions** than crabs.

• The Douglas **fir** is actually a **pine** tree.

• A **steel**-jacketed bullet is actually made of **brass.**

• **Riptides** are actually **currents.**

Eh? HEARING AID SALES ROSE 40% WHEN PRESIDENT REAGAN GOT HIS.

THE 6 SIMPLE MACHINES

Uncle John first learned about simple machines in third grade. Being a fan of anything that's simple, he never forgot them (or his third-grade teacher, Mrs. Sigler). Can these machines actually be the basis for all tools?

TOOLING AROUND

Have you ever tried to lift a 200-pound lawnmower two feet off the ground and put it in the back of a pickup truck? Few people could do it. But from time to time it has to be done, and one way to make the job easier is by using a ramp, or *inclined plane*. An inclined plane is an example of what engineers call a "simple machine," one that requires the application of only a single force—in this case, you pushing the mower—to work.

By pushing the object up the inclined plane instead of lifting it straight up, the amount of strength, or force, required to get the mower into the truck is reduced. But there's a trade-off: You have to apply that reduced force over a greater distance to do the job. If the ramp is 10 feet long, for example, you have to push the mower a distance of 10 feet instead of lifting it straight up just 2 feet onto the truck. This trade-off—applying less force over a greater distance to accomplish tasks that would otherwise be difficult or impossible—is the physical principle behind all simple machines.

The inclined plane is only one type of simple machine—there are five more: the lever, the wedge, the screw, the wheel and axle (which work together), and the pulley. Believe it or not, all complex mechanical machines—bicycles, automobiles, cranes, power drills, toasters, you name it—are nothing more than different combinations of some or all of these six simple machines.

THE WEDGE

A wedge isn't much more than a moving inclined plane—it's so similar, in fact, that some experts consider wedges and inclined planes the same thing. One common example of a wedge is a cutting blade. Take the head of an axe: Its wedge shape converts a small force applied over a long distance—that of the axe head entering the piece of wood—into a force powerful enough to split a piece of wood into two pieces. If the tip of the axe head travels half an inch into the wood, its wedge shape drives the wood apart only a fraction of that distance, but it does so with tremendous force, enough to eventually split the wood in two. Try doing that with your bare hands!

The blades of virtually all cutting tools—knives, scissors, can openers, and even electric razors—operate on the same principle, as do zippers, plows, and even the keys to your house. If you examine the serrated edge of your house key, you'll see that it isn't much more than a series of wedges of different heights that lift the pins inside the lock to the precise height needed to turn the lock and open the door. The wedges on the key are double-sided, so that the key can be removed from the lock after it has performed its task.

THE SCREW

A screw may not look much like either a wedge or an inclined plane, but it's pretty much the same thing. It's an inclined plane wrapped in a spiral around a cylinder or shaft. You have to turn a screw several times, using a small amount of force, to drive it a tiny distance into a piece of wood, a task that would otherwise require great force.

THE LEVER

Like the inclined plane, the lever makes it possible to lift things that would otherwise be too heavy for humans to lift. The lever consists of a rod or bar that rests on a point or a supporting object called a *fulcrum*. If you've ever used a claw hammer to pull a nail out of a piece of board, you've used a lever. By applying a small force over a great distance, in this case the distance your hand on the handle travels as you pry the nail out of the wood, the lever converts this into a strong force applied over a short distance. Your hand will travel several inches, but the claw pulls the nail only an inch or so out of the wood. Bottle openers are levers, so are nutcrackers and even wheelbarrows—by lifting the handles of a wheelbarrow a foot or so off the ground, you're able to lift a heavy load near the wheel and push it where you want it to go. The handles of a pair of scissors are levers that magnify the force of the wedge-shaped blades. That's an example of a *complex* machine: a combination of simple machines (levers and wedges) that work together to perform a given task.

Found in a shark's belly in 1941: 3 belts, 9 shoes, 14 stockings, and 43 buttons.

THE WHEEL AND AXLE

One simple example of a wheel and axle is a screwdriver. In this case the handle is the wheel and the shaft is the axle, and, just as with the other machines, it gets its advantage by sacrificing distance for force. When you turn the handle of the screwdriver a full revolution, the shaft has also gone a full revolution—but it's traveled a much shorter distance. And the force it exerts over that distance is several times greater than the force you exerted over the handle's longer distance, allowing you to turn a screw into a wall. Other examples of wheel-and-axle machines that you use commonly: doorknobs, faucets, windmills, and the steering wheel in your car.

THE PULLEY

A single pulley can enable you to change the direction of the force that you use to do work. For example, if you want to lift something off the ground without a pulley, you have to lift upwards. But if you have a pulley attached to the ceiling and a rope running through it that's attached to the object you're trying to lift, by pulling the rope down you can lift the object up.

Using multiple pulleys together in a single device called a *block and tackle* allows you to lift objects heavier than your own weight, something that would be impossible with only one pulley, since you'd lift yourself off the ground instead of lifting the object. The block and tackle does this by distributing the weight of the object over multiple sections of rope—if the block and tackle contains four pulleys, for example, each length of rope will support 1/4 the weight of the object. If the object weighs 200 pounds, each of the four sections of rope is supporting 50 pounds of weight, and you only have to apply 50 pounds of force to lift the object...but you'll have to apply it over a greater distance, by pulling four times as much rope as you would have using only a single pulley. For every foot you want to raise the object off the ground, you will have to pull four feet of rope. As with all the other simple machines, you're applying a smaller force (your own strength) over a greater distance (four feet of rope instead of one) to get the same amount of work done (lifting a heavy object off the ground).

SPEAKING "TOURIST"

Here at the BRI, we have nothing but respect for park rangers. Not only do they brave bears, avalanches, and forest fires, they cope with a little-understood phenomenon called "tourists." Here are some of the silliest comments and questions park rangers have received from tourists at U.S. and Canadian national parks.

"How far is Banff from Canada?"

"At what elevation does an elk become a moose?"

"Where does Alberta end and Canada begin?"

"Do you have a glacier at this visitor center?"

"Is this a map I'm looking at?"

"We had no trouble finding the park entrances, but where are the exits?"

"The coyotes made too much noise last night and kept me awake. Please eradicate those annoying animals."

"How many miles of undiscovered caves are there?"

"Are you allowed to stay overnight in the camp-grounds?"

"Are the national parks natural or man-made?"

"Where does Bigfoot live?"

"Is there anything to see around here besides the scenery?"

"How come all of the war battles were fought in national parks?"

"When do they turn off the waterfalls?"

"Is this island completely surrounded by water?"

At Glacier National Park:

Tourist: How did these rocks get here?

Ranger: They were brought down by a glacier.

Tourist: But I don't see any glacier.

Ranger: Really? I guess it's gone back for more rocks.

THE WAY OF THE HOBO

Have you ever dreamed of hopping on a freight train and living off the land? Trust Uncle John, it's not as glamorous as it sounds. But just in case you do, here's a starter course.

HOBO HIERARCHY

What's the difference between a hobo, a tramp, and a bum?

Hobo: A migratory worker (the most respected of the three). Hoboes are resourceful, self-reliant vagabonds who take on temporary work to earn a few dollars before moving on. Some experts think the word *hobo* comes from *hoe boys*, which is what farmers in the 1880s called their seasonal migrant workers. Others say it's shorthand for the phrase *homeward bound*, used to describe destitute Civil War veterans who took years to work their way home.

Tramp: A migratory nonworker. A tramp simply likes the vagabond life—he's never looking for a job.

Bum: The lowest of the low; a worthless loafer who stays in one place and would rather beg than work for goods or services.

HOBO LINGO

Accommodation car: The caboose of a train

Banjo: A small portable frying pan

Big House: Prison

Bindle stick: A small bundle of belongings tied up in a scarf, handkerchief, or blanket hung from a walking stick

Bull: A railroad cop (also called a "cinder dick")

Cannonball: A fast train

Chuck a dummy: Pretend to faint

Cover with the moon: Sleep out in the open

Cow crate: A railroad stock car

Crums: Lice (also called "gray backs" and "seam squirrels")

Doggin' it: Traveling by bus

Easy mark: A hobo sign, or "mark," that identifies a person or place where one can get food and a place to stay overnight

---

Food fights? Most arguments in the home take place in the kitchen.

Honey dipping: Working with a shovel in a sewer

Hot: A hobo wanted by the law

Knowledge box: A schoolhouse, where hobos sometimes sleep

Moniker: Nickname

Road kid: A young hobo who apprentices himself to an older hobo in order to learn the ways of the road

Rum dum: A drunkard

Snipes: Other people's cigarette butts (O.P.C.B.); "snipe hunting" is to go looking for butts

Spear biscuits: To look for food in garbage cans

Yegg: The lowest form of hobo—he steals from other hobos

HOBO ROAD SIGNS

Wherever they went, hobos left simple drawings, or "marks," chalked on fence posts, barns, and railroad buildings. These signs were a secret code giving fellow knights of the road helpful tips or warnings.

"Angel food" found here—you have to sit through a sermon to get it.

The people who live here are rich (a silk hat and a pile of gold).

This homeowner has a gun—run!

Be prepared to defend yourself.

Beware of the "bone polisher" (a mean dog).

Townspeople don't want you here—keep moving!

It's safe to camp here.

Handcuffs—police around here don't like hoboes.

Can you taste them? The secret recipe for Dr Pepper is said to contain 23 fruit flavors.

THEY WENT THATAWAY

Sometimes the circumstances of a famous person's death are as interesting as their lives. Take these folks, for example.

GEORGE WASHINGTON

Claim to Fame: First President of the United States

How He Died: He was bled to death by doctors who were treating him for a cold

Postmortem: On December 12, 1799, Washington, 67, went horseback riding for five hours in a snowstorm. When he returned home he ate dinner without changing his clothes and went to bed. Not surprisingly, he woke up feeling hoarse and complaining of a sore throat. But he refused to take any medicine. "You know I never take anything for a cold," he told an assistant. "Let it go as it came."

Washington felt even worse the next day. He allowed the estate supervisor at Mount Vernon (a skilled veterinarian, he was the best person on hand for the job) to bleed him. In those days people thought the best way to treat an illness was by removing the "dirty" blood that supposedly contained whatever was making the patient sick. In reality, it only weakened the patient, making it harder to fight off the original illness.

That didn't work, so three doctors were called. First, they dehydrated Washington by administering laxatives and emetics (chemicals that induce vomiting). Then they bled the former president three more times. In all, the veterinarian and the doctors drained 32 ounces of Washington's blood, weakening him severely. He died a few hours later while taking his own pulse.

L. RON HUBBARD

Claim to Fame: Science-fiction writer and founder of the Church of Scientology

How He Died: No one knows for sure.

Postmortem: Hubbard founded his church in 1952. The larger it grew and the more money it collected from followers, the more controversial it became. A British court condemned Scientology

---

A running tiger can cover about 30 feet in a single stride.

as "immoral, socially obnoxious, corrupt, sinister and dangerous;" a Los Angeles court denounced it as "schizophrenic and paranoid."

Hubbard had a lot of enemies in law-enforcement agencies in the U.S., and the IRS suspected him of skimming millions in church funds. For a time he avoided prosecutors by sailing around the Mediterranean, and from 1976 to 1979 he lived in hiding in small desert towns in Southern California. Then in 1980 he vanished. He didn't resurface until January 25, 1986, when someone called a funeral home in San Luis Obispo, California, and instructed them to pick up a body from a ranch about 20 miles north of town. The corpse was identified as Lafayette Ronald Hubbard.

The FBI's fingerprint files confirmed that the man really was Hubbard. The official cause of death: a cerebral hemorrhage. But a "certificate of religious belief" filed on behalf of Hubbard prevented the coroner from conducting an autopsy, so we'll never really know.

JOHN DENVER

Claim to Fame: A singer and songwriter, Denver shot to fame in the 1970s with hits like "Rocky Mountain High" and "Take Me Home, Country Road."

How He Died: He crashed his own airplane.

Postmortem: Denver was a lifelong aviation buff and an experienced pilot. He learned to fly from his father, an ex-Air Force pilot who made his living training pilots to fly Lear Jets.

Denver had just bought an aerobatic plane known as a Long-EZ shortly before the crash and was still getting used to flying it. According to the report released by the National Transportation Safety Board, he needed an extra seatback cushion for his feet to reach the foot pedals, but when he used the cushion he had trouble reaching the fuel tank selector handle located behind his left shoulder. The NTSB speculates that he took off without enough fuel. When one of his tanks ran dry and the engine lost power, Denver accidentally stepped on the right rudder pedal while reaching over his left shoulder with his right arm to switch to the other fuel tank, and crashed the plane into the sea.

Final Irony: Denver's first big success came in 1967, when he wrote the Peter, Paul, and Mary hit "Leaving on a Jet Plane."

First all-female fire department: Ashville, New York, in 1943.

WHY ASK WHY?

Sometimes answers are irrelevant—it's the question that counts. Take a moment to ponder these cosmic queries.

"How come aspirins are packed in childproof containers, but bullets just come in a box?"
—Jay Leno

"Why do they bother saying raw sewage? Do some people cook the stuff?"
—George Carlin

"Why do they call it rush hour when nothing moves?"
—Robins Williams (as Mork)

"Do Lipton employees take coffee breaks?"
—Steven Wright

"Why can we remember the tiniest detail that has happened to us, and not remember how many times we have told it to the same person."
—Francois, Duc de la Rochefoucauld

"Should not the Society of Indexers be known as 'Indexers, Society of, The'?"
—Keith Waterhouse

"If women can sleep their way to the top, how come they aren't there?"
—Ellen Goodman

"Why does a slight tax increase cost you $200 and a substantial tax cut save you 38¢?"
—Peg Bracken

"Can a blue man sing the whites?"
—Algis Juodikis

"What are perfect strangers? Do they have perfect hair? Do they dress perfectly?"
—Ellen Degeneres

"If sex is such a natural phenomenon, how come there are so many books on how to do it?"
—Bette Midler

"Murder is a crime. Writing about it isn't. Sex is not a crime, but writing about it is. Why?"
—Larry Flynt

"At the ballet you see girls dancing on their tiptoes. Why don't they just get taller girls?"
—Greg Ray

"If bankers can count, how come they always have ten windows and two tellers?"
—Milton Berle

Cereal trivia: The marshmallows in Lucky Charms cereal are technically known as "marbits."

BAD MUSICALS

Plenty of weird concepts make it to the Broadway stage. Some are really successful. Not these.

MUSICAL: *Rockabye Hamlet* (1976)
TOTAL PERFORMANCES: 7
STORY: Adolescent angst and rebellion are major themes in rock music—and in Shakespeare's *Hamlet*. So that would make Hamlet the perfect inspiration for a rock musical, right? Wrong. Originally written as a radio play (under the title *Kronberg: 1582*), *Rockabye Hamlet* hit Broadway in 1976 with hundreds of flashing lights and an onstage band. Writers followed Shakespeare's storyline but abandoned his dialogue. They opted instead for lines like the one Laertes sings to Polonius: "Good son, you return to France/Keep your divinity inside your pants."
Notable Song: "The Rosencrantz and Guildenstern Boogie."

MUSICAL: *Bring Back Birdie* (1981)
TOTAL PERFORMANCES: 4
STORY: A sequel to the 1961 hit *Bye Bye Birdie*. In the original, teen idol Conrad Birdie sings a farewell concert and kisses a lucky girl before joining the military (it was inspired by Elvis Presley being drafted in the 1950s). *Bring Back Birdie* takes place 20 years later and couldn't have been farther from the real Elvis story— Birdie has settled down as mayor of a small town when somebody talks him into making a comeback. The only problem: audiences didn't come back.
Notable Moment: One night during the show's brief run, when actor Donald O'Connor forgot the words to a song, he told the band, "You sing it. I hate this song anyway," and walked off stage.

MUSICAL: *Via Galactica* (1972)
TOTAL PERFORMANCES: 7
STORY: A band of hippies (led by Raul Julia) travel through outer space on an asteroid in the year 2972, searching for an uninhabited planet on which to settle "New Jerusalem." The weightlessness of space was simulated by actors jumping on trampolines

---

Q: What was the Lone Ranger's name? (Hint: his first name isn't Lone.) A: John Reid.

for the entire show. A rock score would have suited the 1970s counterculture themes, but for some reason songwriters Christopher Gore and Galt McDermot chose country music.

Notable Name: The original title for the show was *Up!*, but producers changed it because it was being staged at the Uris Theatre and the marquee would have read *"Up! Uris."*

MUSICAL: *Carrie* (1988)
TOTAL PERFORMANCES: 5

STORY: Based on Stephen King's gory novel about a telekinetic teenager who kills everybody at her high school prom, *Carrie* was full of bad taste and bad ideas. It's regarded by many critics as the biggest flop (it lost $8 million) and worst musical of all time:

• *Newsday* called *Carrie* "stupendously, fabulously terrible. Ineptly conceived, sleazy, irrational from moment to moment, it stretches way beyond bad to mythic lousiness."

• *The Washington Post* likened it to "a reproduction of 'The Last Supper' made entirely out of broken bottles. You can't help marveling at the lengths to which someone went to make it."

Notable Songs: Carrie's mother sings about being sexually molested in "I Remember How Those Boys Could Dance," and Carrie serenades a hairbrush in "I'm Not Alone."

MUSICAL: *Breakfast at Tiffany's* (1966)
TOTAL PERFORMANCES: 0 (Closed in previews)

STORY: It had the highest advance sales of any show in 1966, primarily because of its cast—TV stars Mary Tyler Moore and Richard Chamberlain—but also because audiences expected a light, bouncy stage version of the popular movie. Unfortunately, they got a musical more like Truman Capote's original novella: dark and tragic. After a disastrous trial run, playwright Edward Albee was hired to rewrite the script. He did little to improve it, removing nearly all the jokes and making Moore's character a figment of Chamberlain's imagination. Audiences were so confused that they openly talked to and questioned the actors on stage. The show ran for four preview performances before producer David Merrick announced he was closing it immediately to save theatergoers from "an excruciatingly boring evening."

SHOCKING!

The electrifying tale of Shenandoah National Park ranger Roy Sullivan, who was struck by lightning seven times in 35 years…and lived to tell about them all.

STRIKE #1 (1942): While on duty in one of Shenandoah's fire lookout towers, Sullivan took his first hit. The lightning bolt hit his leg, and he lost a nail on his big toe.

STRIKE #2 (1969): This time, he was driving on a country road. The lightning hit his truck, knocked him out, and singed off his eyebrows.

STRIKE #3 (1970): People started calling Sullivan the "human lightning rod" after the third strike, which injured his shoulder.

STRIKE #4 (1972): He took this hit while on duty at one of Shenandoah's ranger stations. The lightning set his hair on fire, so Sullivan started carrying a bucket of water around with him—just in case he needed to put out a blaze (on himself or otherwise).

STRIKE #5 (1973): The bucket came in handy—this one also set his hair on fire. It also knocked him out of his car and blew off one of his shoes.

STRIKE #6 (1974): Lightning hit Sullivan at a park campground, and he injured his ankle.

STRIKE #7 (1977): This might have been his most dangerous strike. The lightning hit him while he was fishing and burned his stomach and chest, requiring a hospital stay. (He recovered.)

Honorable Mention: Sullivan's wife was also hit by lightning once while she and Roy were hanging up clothes on a line in their backyard.

MOTHERS OF INVENTION

There have always been women inventors—even if they've been overlooked in history books. Here are a few you may not have heard of.

LAURA SCUDDER

Invention: Potato chip bag

Background: Before a Southern California businesswoman named Laura Scudder came along in the mid-1920s, potato chips were sold in bulk in large barrels. When you bought chips at the store, the grocer scooped them out of the barrel and into an ordinary paper bag. If you got your chips from the bottom of the barrel, they were usually broken and stale.

It was Laura Scudder who hit on the idea of taking wax paper and ironing it on three sides to make a bag, then filling it with potato chips and ironing the fourth side to make an airtight pouch that would keep the chips fresh until they were eaten. Scudder's self-serve, stay-fresh bags were instrumental in turning potato chips from an occasional treat into a snack food staple.

MARTHA COSTON

Invention: Signal flare

Background: Martha Hunt was only 14 when she eloped with a Philadelphia engineer named Benjamin Coston...and only 21 when he died bankrupt in 1848, leaving her destitute with four small children. Not long after his death she found something interesting among his possessions: a prototype for a signal flare. She hoped that if it worked, she could patent it and use it to restore her family's fortunes.

But it didn't—so Martha started over from scratch, and spent nearly 10 years perfecting a system of red, white, and green "Pyrotechnic Night Signals" that would enable naval ships to communicate by color codes over great distances at night. (Remember, this was before the invention of two-way radio.) The U.S. Navy bought hundreds of sets of flares and used them extensively during the Civil War. They are credited with helping maintain the Union blockade of Confederate ports, and also with saving the lives of countless shipwreck victims after the war.

Mark Twain received a patent for "improved suspenders" in 1871.

PAGE 42

Here's one of our all-time favorite pages.

Elvis Presley died at **42**.

The angle at which light reflects off water to create a rainbow is **42** degrees.

The city of Jerusalem covers an area of **42** square miles.

The Torah (the holy book of Judaism) is broken into columns, each of which always has exactly **42** lines.

Fox Mulder (*The X-Files*) lives in apartment number **42**.

There are **42** decks on the *Enterprise* NCC1701-D (the *Next Generation* ship).

The only number retired by every major-league baseball team is Jackie Robinson's **42**.

A Wonderbra consists of **42** individual parts.

There are **42** Oreo cookies in a 1-pound package.

"The beast was given a mouth uttering proud boasts and blasphemies, and it was given authority to act for **42** months." —*Revelation 13:5*

In *Romeo and Juliet*, Juliet sleeps for **42** hours.

The right arm of the Statue of Liberty is **42** feet long.

Jimi Hendrix and Jerry Garcia were born in 1942.

The number of dots on a pair of dice: **42**.

Dogs have a total of **42** teeth over their lifetimes.

In *The Catcher in the Rye*, Holden Caufield lies and says that he is **42**.

The world-record jump by a kangaroo is **42** feet.

The natural vibration frequency of white mouse DNA: **42**.

The natural vibration frequency of human DNA: **42**.

There were **42** generations from Abraham to Jesus Christ.

And most important:
According to Douglas Adams's *The Hitchhiker's Guide to the Galaxy*, "the meaning of life, the universe, and everything" is the number **42**.

SNEAKY CORPORATIONS

Powerful corporations often set up fake "institutes" and programs that sound like independent foundations promoting the public good—when in fact they're just the opposite. Here are four examples.

VERY INCONVENIENT

The documentary film *An Inconvenient Truth* received a lot of attention and attracted huge audiences when it was released in May 2006. The film argues that global warming caused by industrial pollution is slowly altering the Earth's climate and melting the polar ice caps, and will eventually flood major cities and leave the planet uninhabitable.

But shortly after the movie came out, "public service" commercials began appearing on TV, calling global warming a myth and claiming that carbon dioxide—a byproduct of industrial pollution and automobile emissions (and the "villain" of the movie)—is actually not a pollutant at all, because "plants breathe it." They went on to say that industrial waste is not only harmless, it's essential to life.

So who made the "public service" ads? A think tank called the Competitive Enterprise Institute, whose members are almost exclusively oil and automobile companies, including Exxon, Arco, Ford, Texaco, and General Motors.

CHEMICALS ARE COOL!

In 1997 students in hundreds of high schools across America got a few hours off from class to attend "Chem TV." Supposedly designed to get kids excited about chemistry and science, it was a traveling multimedia extravaganza featuring loud music, videos, lasers, games, skits, dancers, free T-shirts, a huge set with giant TV screens, and a cast of enthusiastic young performers.

Educational? Sort of. Chem TV (meant to sound like "MTV") said it was about *chemistry*, but it was really about the *chemical industry*. It was part of a million-dollar public relations campaign by Dow Chemical—one of the world's biggest polluters—to help change its image. Dow had a controversial history: It supplied

---

"Death would be a beautiful place if it looks like Brad Pitt." —Carmen Electra

napalm and Agent Orange to the government during the Vietnam War, and lawsuits over faulty breast implants nearly bankrupted the company in 1995.

Critics charged that the Chem TV presentations were misleading (in one example, an actor took off his clothes to demonstrate that "your entire body is made of chemicals"). Chem TV didn't differentiate between a *chemical* (a man-made, often toxic combination of ingredients) and an *organic compound* (molecules that fuse together naturally—like water). Despite the criticism, the program toured schools for three years and won numerous awards. (And it was tax exempt because it was "educational.")

INDEPENDENT THOUGHT
In May 1998, the federal government filed a lawsuit against Microsoft, accusing the software giant of monopolistic behavior. In June 1999, the Independent Institute, a California-based legal think tank, ran full-page ads in the *New York Times* and *Washington Post* that staunchly defended Microsoft. In the form of an open letter (signed by 240 "economists"), it stated that prosecuting Microsoft would hurt consumers and weaken the economy. What exactly is the "Independent Institute"? It's not independent at all. Though its mission statement says it is "dedicated to the highest standards of independent scholarly inquiry," in 1998 it had exactly one source of funding: Microsoft.

JUNK FOOD = FITNESS
The American Council for Fitness and Nutrition was formed in 2003 to combat the United States' growing obesity problem. At least that's what they said. Shortly after its formation, the Council held a press conference to announce its latest findings: Contrary to numerous government and medical studies, they reported, too much fast food and vending machines filled with junk food did *not* make children fat.

Turns out the ACFN's interest in childhood obesity is purely business related. The ACFN is actually a lobbying group…for snack-food makers and fast-food restaurants. Its members include Pizza Hut, Taco Bell, Sara Lee, Pepsi, Nestle, McDonald's, Hershey, Coca-Cola, and the Sugar Association.

World's first speed limit: England, 1903. (20 mph.)

WAR PLAN RED

When this bizarre story surfaced a few years ago, it reminded us of this quote, attributed to Warren G. Harding: "I can take care of my enemies all right. But my damn friends—they're the ones that keep me walking the floors nights."

NORTHERN EXPOSURE

If you had to invade another country, how would you do it? Believe it or not, the United States military spent a lot of time pondering that question in the late 1920s, when it came up with a plan to invade its closest neighbor, Canada.

There was certainly a precedent for the two nations battling it out. The Continental Army invaded Canada during the American Revolution, and the U.S. Army made repeated incursions during the War of 1812. In 1839 the state of Maine only narrowly avoided a shooting war with the province of New Brunswick over a border dispute. Then, in 1866, about 800 Irish-American members of a group called the Fenian Brotherhood tried to occupy part of Canada for the purpose of using it as a bargaining chip to force Great Britain to grant independence to Ireland. (They were quickly driven back across the U.S. border.)

That last invasion had an upside for Canadians: It convinced the last holdouts in the independent provinces of New Brunswick, Nova Scotia, Ontario, and Quebec that they'd be better able to defend themselves against the *next* invasion if they banded together to form the Dominion of Canada, which they did on July 1, 1867.

TO THE DRAWING BOARD

Of course, these skirmishes paled in comparison to World War I, which raged from 1914 to 1918. That war, which was precipitated by the assassination of Archduke Ferdinand of Austria, caught most of the belligerents by surprise. It also lasted longer and was far more costly in blood and treasure than anyone ever dreamed a war could be. None of the nations that fought in it wanted to be caught off guard again; many began planning for whatever war might be lurking around the corner. The American military drafted a whole series of color-coded war plans to cover just about every conceivable scenario: War Plan Black was a plan for war with Germany;

Most people who are allergic to cats aren't allergic to cat fur, cat dander, cat saliva, or cat urine...

War Plan Orange dealt with Japan, a rapidly growing power in the Pacific. Other colors included Green (Mexico), Gold (France), Brown (The Philippines), and Yellow (China). There was even a War Plan Indigo, in case the United States had to invade Iceland, and a War Plan White that dealt with civil unrest within America's own borders.

SEEING RED

War Plan Red was America's plan for going to war with the British Empire, in the unlikely event that Britain (code name: Red) decided to "eliminate [the United States] as an economic and commercial rival." Since Canada (code name: Crimson) was part of the Empire and shared a 5,527-mile border with the U.S., much of the plan dealt with invading Canada and knocking it out of action before the British could use it as a staging ground for attacks on the U.S.

Here's how an invasion of Canada would have gone:

• The United States (code name: Blue) would attack and occupy Halifax, Nova Scotia, Canada's largest Atlantic port. The attack would deny Britain access to the rail and road links it would need to land troops in Canada and disperse them across the country.

• Next, the U.S. Army would attack across the border along three fronts: Troops would attack from either Vermont or New York to occupy Montreal and Quebec City; from Michigan into Ontario; and from North Dakota into Manitoba. Meanwhile, the U.S. Navy would take control of the Great Lakes. The effects of these attacks would be to seize Canada's industrial heartland while preventing similar attacks on America, and to further disrupt the movement of Canadian troops from one part of the country to another.

• Troops would cross from Washington into British Columbia and seize Vancouver, Canada's largest Pacific port. The U.S. Navy would blockade the port of Prince Rupert, 460 miles to the north.

Once the crisis passed and relations between America, Canada, and Great Britain returned to normal, the U.S. troops would be withdrawn from Canadian territory, right? No—"Blue intentions are to hold in perpetuity all Crimson and Red territory gained," the military planners wrote. "The policy will be to prepare the provinces and territories of Crimson and Red to become states and territories of the Blue union upon the declaration of peace."

...they are actually allergic to *sebum*, a fatty substance secreted by the cat's sebaceous glands.

THE FOG OF WAR(S)

So how seriously was the United States considering invading Canada? In all probability, not very. War Plan Red doesn't go into nearly as much detail as War Plan Black (Germany) or War Plan Orange (Japan), which military planners correctly assumed were much more significant threats. The intent of the other color-coded plans may have been to make war plans involving Germany and Japan seem less controversial. Why the subterfuge? After the horrors of World War I, in which nearly 10 million soldiers died, many people concluded that planning for wars only made them more likely.

The U.S. military didn't feel this way, of course, and one way they may have gotten around public opinion was to come up with all kinds of improbable war plans to make the *real* plans more palatable. A public that would not have tolerated the idea of the preparing for war with Germany and Japan would be less alarmed by the idea of the United States preparing for war with Germany, Japan, Canada, Iceland, Jamaica, Monaco, and Andorra.

WHAT'S GOOD FOR THE GOOSE...

Any sting Canadians may have felt when War Plan Red was declassified in 1974 was offset by the knowledge that Canada had drafted its own plans for invading the United States, and had done so several years before War Plan Red was approved in 1930. "Defense Scheme No. 1," as it was called, was created in 1921 by James Sutherland "Buster" Brown, Canada's director of military operations and intelligence. In many respects it was the opposite of War Plan Red: In the event that an American attack was imminent, Canadian forces would strike first, attacking and occupying key cities such as Albany, Minneapolis, and Seattle.

Unlike with War Plan Red, these cities wouldn't be annexed or even occupied for any longer than was absolutely necessary. The idea was to knock the U.S. off balance, then retreat back into Canada, blowing up bridges and destroying roads and railroads along the way in the hope of delaying the inevitable American counterattack until British reinforcements arrived. The plan received mixed reviews from the Canadian military: One general called it a "fantastic desperate plan that just might have worked"; other officers thought Brown was nuts. It remained on the books until 1928, when it was scrapped as impractical.

What'd they use before that? The English alphabet is about 700 years old.

AMAZING COINCIDENCES

*Over the years, we've found dozens of stories
about amazing coincidences. Here are
two of Uncle John's favorites.*

MESSAGE IN A BOTTLE

Charles Coghlan was born on Prince Edward Island, Canada, in 1841. He became a successful stage actor and toured the world, but the island was always his home. In 1899, during an appearance on Galveston Island, Texas, he fell ill and died, and was buried in a Galveston cemetery. On September 8, 1900, a hurricane struck Galveston, washing away most of the town and swamping all the cemeteries. Seven years later, a fishermen from Prince Edward Island noticed a large box in the water. He towed it to shore, chipped off the barnacles, and discovered the coffin of Charles Coghlan, beloved native son. It had floated into the Gulf of Mexico, been caught by the West Indian current, carried into the Gulf Stream, and deposited on shore only a few miles from his birthplace.

THE LONG WAY HOME

Actor Anthony Hopkins, while playing a role in a movie based on a book called *The Girl from Petrovka* by George Feifer, looked all over London for a copy of the book but was unable to find one. Later that day he was waiting in a subway station for his train when he noticed someone had left a book on a bench. Picking it up, Hopkins found it was... *The Girl from Petrovka*. Two years later Hopkins was filming another movie in Vienna when he was visited on the set by author George Feifer. Feifer complained that he no longer had even a single copy of his own book because he'd loaned his last one to a friend who had lost it somewhere in London. Feifer added that it was particularly annoying because he had written notes in the margins. Hopkins, incredulous, handed Feifer the copy he had found in the subway station. It was the same book.

Holy molar! In its lifetime, an alligator will go through as many as 3,000 teeth.

Q&A: ASK THE EXPERTS

Everyone's got a question or two they'd like answered.
Here are a few of those questions, with answers
from some of the nation's top trivia experts.

PICK A BALL OF COTTON

Q: *Should you toss out the cotton after opening a bottle of pills?*
A: Yes. "The cotton keeps the pills from breaking in transit, but once you open the bottle, it can attract moisture and thus damage the pills or become contaminated." (From *Davies Gazette*, a newsletter from Davies Medical Center in San Francisco)

MERRY XRISTOS

Q: *Why is the word Christmas abbreviated as "Xmas"?*
A: "Because the Greek letter *x* is the first letter of the Greek word for Christ, Xristos. The word *Xmas*, meaning 'Christ's Mass,' was commonly used in Europe by the 16th century. It was not an attempt to take *Christ* out of *Christmas*." (From *The Book of Answers*, by Barbara Berliner)

POL POSITION

Q: *How did "left" and "right" come to represent the ends of the political spectrum?*
A: "According to the *Oxford English Dictionary*: 'This use originated in the French National Assembly of 1789, in which the nobles as a body took the position of honor on the President's right, and the Third Estate sat on his left. The significance of these positions, which was at first merely ceremonial, soon became political.'" (From *Return of the Straight Dope*, by Cecil Adams)

TONGUE TWISTERS?

Q: *Why do people sometimes stick out their tongues when they're concentrating on a hard job?*
A: "When you need to concentrate on something—say, a word problem—you are using the part of the brain also used for processing motor input. Ever see people slow down when they're thinking

of something difficult while walking? It's caused by the two activities fighting for the same bit of brain to process them. By biting your lip or sticking your tongue out, you're keeping your head rigid and suspending motor activity, and hence, minimizing interference." (From *The Last Word 2*, by the *New Scientist* magazine)

TASTES LIKE...SPLEEN?

Q: *What's really in a hot dog?*

A: "All manufacturers must list their ingredients on the label. 'Beef,' 'pork,' 'chicken,' 'turkey,' etc. can only be used if the meat comes from the muscle tissue of the animal. If you see the words 'meat by-products' or 'variety meats,' the hot dog may contain snouts, stomachs, hearts, tongues, lips, spleens, etc. Frankfurters once contained only beef and pork but now can legally contain sheep, goat, and up to 15% chicken. Hot dogs are made by grinding the meat with water, seasoning, sweeteners, preservatives, salt, and binders." (From *Why Does Popcorn Pop?* by Don Voorhees)

HOT, BUT NOT

Q: *Why do people sweat when they eat really spicy food?*

A: "Spicy foods, such as chili peppers, contain a chemical that stimulates the same nerve endings in the mouth as a rise in temperature does. The nerves don't know what caused the stimulation; they just send a message to the brain telling it that the temperature near the face has risen. The brain reacts by activating cooling mechanisms around the face, and one of these mechanisms is perspiration." (From *Ever Wonder Why?*, by Douglas B. Smith)

A HAIR OF A DIFFERENT COLOR

Q: *Why does hair turn gray?*

A: "Gray (or white) is the base color of hair. Pigment cells located at the base of each hair follicle produce the natural dominant color of our youth. However, as a person grows older, more and more of these pigment cells die and color is lost from individual hairs. The result is that a person's hair gradually begins to show more and more gray. "The whole process may take between 10 and 20 years—rarely does a person's entire collection of individual hairs (which can number in the hundreds of thousands) go gray overnight." (From *How Things Work*, by Louis Bloomfield)

I'M SORRY

With our sincerest regrets, we're very sorry to bring you this collection of some of the funniest and strangest apologies ever uttered.

"We apologize for the error in last week's paper in which we stated that Mr. Arnold Dogbody was a defective in the police force. We meant, of course, that Mr. Dogbody is a detective in the police farce."
—*Ely Standard* (U.K.)

"My family and I are deeply sorry for all that Vice President Cheney and his family have had to go through this past week."
—**Harry Whittington, Washington lawyer, after Dick Cheney shot *him* in the face**

"In previous issues of this newspaper, we may have given the impression that the people of France were snail swallowing, garlic munching surrender-monkeys whose women never bother to shave their armpits. We now realise that the French football team can stop the Portuguese from getting to the World Cup Final. We apologise profusely to France. *Vive la France!*"
—*Daily Star* (U.K.), **after France beat the U.K.'s rival, Portugal, in the 2006 World Cup semifinals**

"I am so terribly sorry for urinating outside of a public place in your city. It was not a very intelligent thing to do."
—**a man charged with public urination in Fond du Lac, Wisconsin, where all offenders now have to write letters of public apology**

"I'm sorry I bet on baseball."
—**Pete Rose, written on 300 baseballs that he then priced at $1,000 each**

"Oh, goodness, I regret it, it was a mistake! I'm solely responsible for it, and I'm very, very sorry. It was a mistake, I was wrong, it's my fault, and I'm very, very sorry to hurt anyone."
—**Sen. George Allen (R–VA), after referring to an Indian-American constituent as a "macaca"**

"We ate everything but his boots."
—**part of an apology from the Navatusila tribe of Fiji, who killed and ate a British missionary in 1867, to the missionary's descendants**

WHAT'S IN A NAME?

*Product names don't necessarily reflect the product,
but rather the image that manufacturers want to
project. Were you fooled by these?*

CORINTHIAN LEATHER

Sounds Like: Fancy leather from some exotic place in Europe—specifically, the Greek city of Corinth. The phrase "rich Corinthian leather" was made famous by actor Ricardo Montalban, in ads for Chrysler's luxury Cordoba in the 1970s. (The seats were covered with it.)

The Truth: There's no such thing as Corinthian leather. The term was made up by Chrysler's ad agency. The leather reportedly came from New Jersey.

HÄAGEN DAZS

Sounds Like: An imported Scandinavian product.

The Truth: It was created by Ruben Mattus, a Polish immigrant who sold ice cream in New York City, who used what the *New York Times* called the "Vichyssoise Strategy":

> Vichyssoise is a native New Yorker. Created at the Ritz Carlton in 1917, it masqueraded as a French soup and enjoyed enormous success. When Mattus created his ice cream, he used the same tactic....He was not the first to think Americans would be willing to pay more for a better product. But he was the first to understand that they would be more likely to do so if they thought it was foreign. So he made up a ridiculous, impossible to pronounce name, [and] printed a map of Scandinavia on the carton.

The ice cream was actually made in Teaneck, New Jersey.

JELL-O PUDDING POPS

Sounds Like: There's pudding in the pops.

The Truth: There isn't. Family secret: One of Uncle John's relatives was involved with test-marketing the product several decades ago. When John asked him about it, he laughed, "Our research shows people think that if it says 'pudding' on the label, it's better quality or better for you. They're wrong. It's really the same."

World's highest fast-food restaurant: McDonald's in La Paz, Bolivia, at 11,000 ft. above sea level.

Anyway, we suppose that's why they still sell it with "pudding" on the label.

PACIFIC RIDGE PALE ALE, *"brewed in Northern California"*

Sounds Like: A small independent brewer in Northern California. The flyer says:

> Brewmasters Gery Eckman [and] Mitch Steele...always wanted to brew a special ale in Northern California just for California beer drinkers...so they created Pacific Ridge Pale Ale. It's produced in limited quantities, using fresh Cascade hops from the Pacific Northwest, two-row and caramel malts and a special ale yeast for a rich copper color. ...Handcrafted only at the Fairfield brewhouse.

The Truth: In tiny letters on the bottle, it says: "Specialty Brewing group of Anheuser-Busch, Inc., Fairfield, California."

SWEET 'N LOW SODA

Sounds Like: The drink was sweetened with nothing but Sweet 'n Low.

The Truth: As Bruce Nash and Allan Zullo write in *The Misfortune 500*, "MBC Beverage Inc., which licensed the Sweet 'N Low name...discovered that consumers wanted the natural sweetener NutraSweet rather than the artificial saccharine of Sweet 'N Low. So they sweetened Sweet 'N Low soda with NutraSweet, a Sweet 'N Low *competitor*."

DAVE'S CIGARETTES

Sounds Like: "A folksy brand of cigarette, produced by a down-to-earth, tractor-driving guy named Dave for ordinary people who work hard and make an honest living." According to humorist Dave Barry, here's the story sent to the media when the cigarettes were introduced in 1996:

> Down in Concord, N.C., there's a guy named Dave. He lives in the heart of tobacco farmland. Dave enjoys lots of land, plenty of freedom and his yellow '57 pickup truck. Dave was fed up with cheap, fast-burning smokes. Instead of just getting mad, he did something about it...Dave's Tobacco Company was born.

The Truth: Dave's was a creation of America's biggest cigarette corporation, Philip Morris, whose ad agency unapologetically called the story a "piece of fictional imagery."

SUPERGLUE FACTS

Some sticky trivia from Uncle John's
Extraordinary Book of Facts.

HOLD TIGHT

• Known technically as *ethyl-gel cyanoacrylate*, Superglue is so strong that a single square-inch bond can lift a ton of weight.

• Superglue doesn't stick to the bottle because it needs moisture to set, and there is no water in the bottle.

• Cyanoacrylate products are a $325-million-a-year industry. Approximately 90 percent of U.S. homes have at least one tube.

• During the Vietnam War tubes of superglue were put in U.S. soldiers' first-aid kits to help seal wounds. Special kinds of superglue are now used in hospitals worldwide, reducing the need for sutures, stitches, and staples. (It doesn't work on deep wounds or on wounds where the skin does a lot of stretching, such as over joints.)

• Superglue is now used in forensic detection. When investigators open a foil packet of ethyl-gel cyanoacrylate, the fumes settle on skin oils left behind in human fingerprints, turning the invisible smears into visible marks.

TIPS FOR USING SUPERGLUE

• A little dab'll do ya. Superglue bonds best when it's used at the rate of one drop per square inch. More than that requires a much longer bonding period, which may result in a weaker bond.

• If you're gluing two flat surfaces together, rough them up with sandpaper first. That'll give the glue more surface area to bond to. But make sure you blow off any dusty residue first.

• Glued your fingers together? Use nail polish remover. Don't have any? Try warm, soapy water and a little patience. Your sweat and natural skin oils will eventually loosen the bond.

TURKMENBASHI

*After the USSR broke up in 1991, the Soviet Republic
of Turkmenistan became an independent nation but
had no identity of its own. Enter Turkmenbashi.*

BACKGROUND
Turkmenistan had been under the control of Russia for
more than a quarter century when it was declared part of
the Soviet Union in 1924. In 1991, after the fall of Communism
and the USSR, the country found itself independent for the first
time in a hundred years. The new president, Saparmurat Niyazov,
was the obvious successor—he'd been the Communist Party's
puppet governor since 1985. But easing a country of five million
people into a new era of self-sufficiency and autonomy was not the
highest item on Niyazov's agenda. He was more concerned that
decades of Soviet control had left Turkmenistan with no national
identity. So, in 1993, Niyazov took it upon himself to create the
country in a new image: his own.

First he took the name *Turkmenbashi* (Leader of All Ethnic
Turkmen) and declared himself President for Life. Until his death
in 2006, he undertook scores of self-aggrandizing—and bizarre—
measures to make Turkmenistan a very unique place:

• The airport in the capital city of Ashgabat was renamed…
Turkmenbashi.

• Dozens of streets and schools across the country are now called…
Turkmenbashi.

• In 1998 a 670-pound meteorite landed in Turkmenistan. Scientists named it…Turkmenbashi.

• The name of the large port city Krasnovodsk was changed to…
Turkmenbashi.

• The new president also renamed the months. January is now
called…Turkmenbashi. April is called Gurbansoltan edzhe, after
his mother. (Bread, once called *chorek*, is now also called *gurbansoltan edzhe*.)

• The image of Turkmenbashi's face is used as the logo of all three

---

In Turkmenistan, *Uncle John's Bathroom Reader* is called *Turkmenbashi's Turkmenbashi Reader.*

state-run TV stations, and is legally required to appear on every clock and watch face as well as on every bottle of Turkmenbashi brand vodka.

• In 2001 Turkmenbashi wrote a book—a combination of poetry, revisionist history, and moral guidelines—called *Ruhnama* (Persian for "Book of the Soul"). It is now required to be prominently displayed in all bookstores and government offices, and next to the Koran in mosques. Memorization of the book is required to graduate from school and to get a state job or even a driver's license. Schoolchildren spend one entire day every week reading it. Since all Soviet-era books have been banned, most Turkmen libraries have only *Ruhnama* and other books written by Turkmenbashi. In 2006 Turkmenbashi made reading *Ruhnama* a requirement for entry into heaven.

• There's a 30-foot *Ruhnama* in Ashgabat, not far from a 50-foot solid-gold statue of Turkmenbashi.

• Not surprisingly, Turkmenbashi recently "won" the Magtymguly International Prize, honoring the best pro-Turkmen poetry, which is awarded by…Turkmenbashi himself.

MORE STRANGE ACTS OF TURKMENBASHI

• In 2004 Turkmenbashi banned newscasters from wearing makeup. Why? He said he couldn't tell the male and female news readers apart and that made him uncomfortable.

• After he quit smoking in 1997, he banned smoking for everybody else, too (but only in public places).

• In 2006, to mark Turkmenistan's independence day, Turkmenbashi gave each female resident a gift of 200,000 *manat* (about $38).

• He banned gold tooth caps and gold teeth, and suggested that tooth preservation could be more easily accomplished by chewing on bones.

• In 2000 he ordered that a giant lake be created in the desert along with a huge forest of cedar trees, which, he said, would help to moderate Turkmenistan's climate.

• In 2004 he ordered that a giant ice palace be built in the middle of that same desert, the Karakum—the hottest location in central Asia. If it's ever built, it will include a zoo with penguins.

Who owned the last cow to be kept at the White House? William Howard Taft (1909–1913).

BOOMERANG!

*Okay, let's throw this history of the boomerang
out there and see where it goes...OW!*

GET BACK

It ranks right up there with the kangaroo and the koala as being a quintessential Australian icon: the simple and fascinating device known as the boomerang. Believed by aviation experts to be the earliest heavier-than-air flying device made by humans, it has been part of Australian Aboriginal culture for thousands of years. Its invention may very well have been an accident.

Archaeological evidence suggests that Australian Aboriginals used "throwing sticks" for hunting at least as early as 15,000 years ago. They were long, thin, bladelike weapons specifically designed to fly as far and as *straight* as possible. So how did they end up with one that returned to the thrower? One theory is that some ancient hunter made a throwing stick that was shorter and lighter than usual and from a piece of wood with a pronounced curve in it, features that caused it to fly in a circular path back toward the point of origin. That made it relatively useless as a weapon, being difficult to throw accurately and too light to do serious damage to an animal. So why are they still around? Probably because they were simply fun to throw and catch. Whatever the reason, the boomerang was invented in southeastern Australia at least 10,000 years ago, and over the centuries became an integral part of aboriginal cultures throughout the southern part of the continent.

EARLY AEROSPACE ENGINEERS

What makes a boomerang return to its thrower? The laws of aerodynamics—applied sideways. A boomerang, with its V-shape, is basically two small wings joined together. They are shaped like airplane wings, with one flat side and one curved side. On an airplane the curved side is the top of the wing. As it moves through the air, the laws of aerodynamics cause air pressure to build up on the flat side, creating *lift* that pushes up on the bottom of the wing. The faster the wing moves through the air, the more lift it generates.

The village of Josefsberg, Italy, is in complete shadow 91 days of the year.

Because a boomerang spins like a propeller while it flies forward, at any given moment one of the two wings is moving in the direction of the flight. That means it's moving through the air faster than the other wing and, therefore, creating more lift. Since a boomerang is thrown to fly vertically, rather than horizontally like an airplane, the lift pushes it to the side rather than up. It keeps pushing as it continues to fly, sending it on a curved trajectory which—if you know how to throw it correctly—will send it all the way back to you.

BOOMERANG FACTS

• Throwing sticks weren't unique to Australia—ancient examples have been found all around the world. Several were even discovered in the tomb of King Tut. Evidence shows, however, that only in Australia was one developed that actually returned to the thrower.

• There were more than 500 languages spoken by different tribal groups in Australia when Europeans arrived, and there were many different names for the returning throwing stick. *Boomerang* comes from a word in the Dharuk language of the Turuwal people, from the area around what is now Sydney.

• Joe Timbery, an Aboriginal designer, thrower, and boomerang champion, was world-renowned among boomerang fans. In 1954 he even demonstrated his skills for Queen Elizabeth. Among his feats that day: having 10 boomerangs in the air simultaneously, and catching every one.

• In the 1960s boomerangs found their way into the world of competitive sports. Every two years, international teams compete for the Boomerang World Cup. (2004 winner: Germany.)

• Manual Schultz of Switzerland holds the world record for the longest throw with a full return: 780 feet.

• In 1993 John Gorski of Avon, Ohio, threw a boomerang that caught a thermal updraft—and flew up to an elevation of 600 feet. It stayed aloft for 17 minutes...before Gorski caught it again.

• Traditional warning to new boomerangers: "Remember—you are the target!"

Can ewe believe this? The first dice were made from sheep ankle bones.

ZAPPA'S LAW & OTHER FACTS OF LIFE

You know Murphy's Law: "If something can go wrong, it will." Here are some other immutable laws of the universe to consider.

Zappa's Law: "There are two things on Earth that are universal: hydrogen and stupidity."

The Murphy Philosophy: "Smile. Tomorrow will be worse."

Baruch's Observation: "If all you have is a hammer, everything looks like a nail."

Lowe's Law: "Success always occurs in private, and failure in full public view."

Todd's Law: "All things being equal, you lose."

Thompson's Theorem: "When the going gets weird, the weird turn pro."

Vac's Conundrum: "When you dial a wrong number, you never get a busy signal."

The Golden Rule of Arts and Sciences: "Whoever has the gold makes the rules."

The Unspeakable Law: "As soon as you mention something…

- if it's good, it goes away.
- if it's bad, it happens."

Green's Law of Debate: "Anything is possible if you don't know what you're talking about."

Hecht's Law: "There is no time like the present to procrastinate."

Sdeyries's Dilemma: "If you hit two keys on the typewriter, the one you don't want hits the paper."

The Queue Principle: "The longer you wait in line, the greater the likelihood that you are standing in the wrong line."

Johnson's Law: "If you miss one issue of any magazine, it will be the issue that contained the article, story or installment you were most anxious to read."

Issawi's Law of Progress: "A shortcut is the longest distance between two points."

Ginsberg's Theorem: "**1.** You can't win. **2.** You can't break even. **3.** You can't even quit the game."

Q. Which city has the lowest divorce rate on Earth? A. Vatican City (0.00 per 1,000 residents).

Perkins's Postulate: "The bigger they are, the harder they hit."

Johnson and Laird's Law: "A toothache tends to start on Saturday night."

The Salary Axiom: "The pay raise is just large enough to increase your taxes and just small enough to have no effect on your take-home pay."

Hutchin's Law: "You can't out-talk a man who knows what he's talking about."

Wellington's Law of Command: "The cream rises to the top. So does the scum."

Todd's Two Political Principles:

1. "No matter what they're telling you, they're not telling you the whole truth."

2. "No matter what they're talking about, they're talking about money."

Kirby's Comment on Committees: "A committee is the only life form with 12 stomachs and no brain."

Harrison's Postulate: "For every action, there is an equal and opposite criticism."

Murphy's Paradox: "Doing it the hard way is always easier."

*   *   *

RANDOM WORD ORIGINS

BUTTERFLY

Meaning: An insect

Origin: "The most generally accepted theory of how this insect got its name is a once-held notion that if you leave butter or milk uncovered in a kitchen, butterflies will land on it…and eat it. Another possibility is that the word is a reference to the color of the insects' excrement." (From *Dictionary of Word Origins*, by John Ayto)

GENUINE

Meaning: Real, not fake

Origin: "Originally meant 'placed on the knees.' In Ancient Rome, a father legally claimed his new child by sitting in front of his family and placing his child on his knee." (From *Etymologically Speaking*, by Steven Morgan Friedman)

A falling squirrel will use its tail as a parachute.

FAMOUS FOR 15 MINUTES

Here are some of the most memorable entries from our popular feature based on Andy Warhol's prophetic comment that "in the future, everyone will be famous for 15 minutes."

THE STAR: Jessica McClure, an 18-month-old infant in Midland, Texas.

THE HEADLINE: *All's Well that Ends Well in Texas Well*

WHAT HAPPENED: In 1987 McClure fell 22 feet down a well while playing in the backyard of her aunt's home. It was only eight inches in diameter and rescuers feared the well would collapse if they widened it. So they decided to dig another hole nearby and tunnel through solid rock to where Jessica was trapped.

After 58 hours, rescuers reached "Baby Jessica" and brought her to the surface. She had a severe cut on her forehead and gangrene on one foot that cost her her right little toe, but she was in remarkably good condition. The entire country watched the rescue unfold live on television. (At the time, it was the fourth-most-watched news story in television history.)

AFTERMATH: The McClure family was flooded with donations during and after the crisis. They used some of the money to buy a new house, then put the rest—an estimated $700,000 to $1 million—in a trust fund for Jessica to collect when she turns 25.

Baby Jessica, 22 years old in 2008, emerged from the experience unscathed (except for a few scars and the missing toe). Now a married college student, she doesn't even remember the incident which made her—according to a 2006 *USA Today* article—"one of the 25 people whose lives most moved Americans over the last quarter century."

THE STAR: Alvin Straight, a 73-year-old farmer

THE HEADLINE: *A Lawn Day's Journey: Laurens Man Mows Path to Fame*

WHAT HAPPENED: In the spring of 1994, Alvin Straight found out that his 80-year-old brother, Henry, had had a stroke. He hadn't seen Henry in seven years, and decided he'd better go

---

In 1912 the Giants and Yankees played a charity game to raise money for *Titanic* survivors.

see him "while I had the chance." The only problem: Alvin lived in Laurens, Iowa...and Henry lived 240 miles away in Mt. Zion, Wisconsin. Alvin didn't have a driver's license, didn't want anyone else to drive him, and wouldn't take public transportation. So he hitched a 10-foot trailer to his lawn tractor and started driving the back roads at 5 mph. It took him six weeks, and by the time he got to Mt. Zion, he was so sore "I could barely make it with two canes." CNN broadcast the story, making Straight an instant celebrity.

THE AFTERMATH: Bombarded with offers to appear on talk shows—with Letterman, Leno, etc.—he wouldn't go, because he refused to fly or take the train to either coast. Straight's story was chronicled in the critically acclaimed 1999 movie, *The Straight Story*, starring Richard Farnsworth as Alvin.

THE STAR: Joseph Hazelwood, captain of the Exxon *Valdez*

THE HEADLINE: *Captain's Career, and 1,500 miles of Alaskan Shoreline, Come to Oily End in Prince William Sound*

WHAT HAPPENED: On March 24, 1989, the Exxon *Valdez* oil tanker ran aground off the coast of Alaska, spilling 11 million gallons of oil over 10,000 square miles of water and 1,500 miles of shoreline. It was the worst oil spill in U.S. history. Hazelwood, who admitted to having consumed at least three drinks ashore before boarding the ship, had gone below and left his third mate and helmsman in charge of the ship. He was vilified by media all over the world as "a drunk who left his post."

THE AFTERMATH: Although he flunked the sobriety test administered 11 hours after the accident, Hazelwood was acquitted of operating a tanker while intoxicated. He was, however, convicted of misdemeanor negligence, fined $50,000, and sentenced to 1,000 hours of community service. He also had his captain's license suspended for nine months for leaving the bridge. Then he dropped out of the public eye. Although he was legally qualified to captain any ship on any ocean, he wasn't able to find work; no shipping company would risk the bad publicity. Instead, he worked as a lobster fisherman, boat transporter, and even as an instructor at New York's Maritime College, teaching students "how to stand watch on the bridge of a tanker."

Conspiracy? Sugar was first added to chewing gum in 1869...by a dentist.

THE OUTHOUSE DETECTIVES

*It's amazing what you can learn about people who lived
more than a century ago just by studying the junk they
disposed of in their outhouses. Still don't believe us?
Read on to find out what these privies reveal.*

MAGNUM P.U.
"Privy diggers" are hobbyists who dig up old outhouses
to collect the bottles and other objects that people
tossed down there, in some cases, more than 100 years ago. These
objects may be interesting in their own right, but they also shed
light on the daily lives of the people who dropped them there.
Some outhouse clues are subtler than others. See if you can figure
out what these outhouse discoveries may reveal about their original owners.

DISCOVERY: A child's doll, recovered completely intact

MYSTERY: Most items that are disposed of in an outhouse have
clearly been thrown away—they were garbage. It's unlikely that a
19th-century family would have thrown away an unbroken doll.
And yet it's not unusual to find perfectly intact dolls at the bottom of an outhouse. What are they doing down there?

THEORY: They ended up there by accident. "Lots of times, I
think, little girls went to the bathroom and accidentally dropped
their doll down there," says Michigan privy digger John Ozoga.
"Dad wouldn't go get it."

DISCOVERY: A wide variety of items recovered from a "two-
holer" (an outhouse with two holes to sit on instead of just one)

MYSTERY: Underneath one of the holes were perfume bottles,
pieces of china, and containers of Ruby Foam tooth powder.
Underneath the other hole: "I just found beer bottles piled up,"
Ozoga says. Why the difference?

THEORY: Two-holers, like modern public restrooms, were segregated according to sex. One side—in this case the side with the

---

Indonesia is the country with the most volcanoes...167 of which are active.

perfume bottles, china, and tooth powder—was for females; and the side with all the beer bottles was for males. Such a find may also provide insight into the family's attitude toward alcohol consumption: the outhouse was the only place where the men could enjoy a beer in peace.

DISCOVERY: Three bottles of Wilkerson's Teething Syrup, recovered from an outhouse in St. Charles, Missouri. (Teething syrup was used to help relieve a baby's teething pain.)

MYSTERY: What's remarkable about these bottles, privy diggers say, is that they are *never* found alone. "If you see one bottle in a privy hole, you'll see a lot of them," says privy digger David Beeler. Why?

THEORY: The syrup's active ingredient is opium, which is highly addictive. Babies who were given the syrup soon got hooked on the stuff, which meant that "parents had to keep on buying it to keep them from crying," Beeler explains.

DISCOVERY: Bottles, tin cans, and other brand-name items recovered from a 19th-century outhouse on Franklin Street in downtown Annapolis, Maryland. In the 19th century, that area was part of the African-American community.

MYSTERY: A surprisingly high percentage of the items recovered were national brands instead of local products. These findings correspond to other excavations of outhouses in the area, which suggests that African Americans used more national brands and fewer local brands than did white communities. Why?

THEORY: Anthropology professor Mark P. Leone, who directed the excavation, speculates that African Americans preferred national brands because the prices were set at the national level instead of by neighborhood grocers. By purchasing these brands, "they could avoid racism at the local grocery store, where shopkeepers might inflate prices or sell them substandard goods," he explains.

DISCOVERY: A "multitude" of Lydia Pinkham brand patent-medicine bottles, plus an entire set of gold-trimmed china dishes

MYSTERY: These items were recovered from an outhouse behind the 19th-century home of a wealthy Michigan family that was

---

Cold-blooded fact: It takes 35–60 minks to make a single coat.

excavated by John Ozoga in the 1990s. The bottles were clustered in a single layer, and the china dishes were found right on top of them. Why?

THEORY: The wife had fallen ill at a young age and died. Ozoga speculates that she was treated with the patent medicine. When she died, the family emptied the house of her belongings—including the entire set of china, which they threw down the hole in the outhouse—to avoid catching whatever it was that killed her.

*   *   *

TOILET TECH

A few high-tech inventions for our favorite room.

• **Flush Stopper.** A simple adhesive cover that "blinds" the electric eye of an automatic-flush toilet, so that it won't flush when little kids—who can be too small for the electric eye to "see"—are sitting on the toilet. "Our research shows that nearly 40% of all children develop some degree of stress associated with public restrooms due to a bad experience with an automatic-flush toilet," says inventor Jeffrey Kay.

• **Illuminated Commode Training Kit.** Teaches kids to find their own way to the bathroom at night. "Footsteps in a mat that glows in the dark show the way to the bathroom; a glow-in-the-dark ring surrounds the toilet, marking its presence as well as that of the toilet paper holder....It works equally well for people who have had too much alcohol."

• **The Zoë Toilet Seat.** Made by Toto USA, a division of Japanese plumbing fixture giant Toto. "This $699 wonder features a fan that sucks fumes through a deodorizing filter, a heated seat, and a remote-controlled bidet nozzle with three pressure settings. Push one button, and a whoosh of water masks your bathroom noises. Push another, and the seat cleans your bum with a spray of cool water and a jet of warm air. The Zoë has also been engineered with our SoftClose seat which eliminates annoying "toilet seat slam.""

• **The Geiger Toilet** was created by by Wolfgang Lehmann for the nuclear power industry. It tests nuclear plant workers' exposure to radiation by measuring the radioactivity of their urine.

Worldwide, Christmas has been celebrated on 135 different days of the year.

IRONIC, ISN'T IT?

There's nothing like a good dose of irony to put the problems of day-to-day life in proper perspective.

BEASTLY IRONY

• The crow population of Woodstock, Ontario, grew so large that residents started complaining to the city council about the noise. The council's solution: frequent bursts of noisy fireworks to scare the crows away.

• Tired of the other hunters who crowded into his favorite squirrel hunting grounds, in 1963 Pete Pickett strapped on some fake gorilla feet and tramped all over the place, hoping the prints would scare everyone else away. Instead, the footprints drew mobs of Bigfoot hunters.

IRONIC DEATHS

• English novelist Arnold Bennett died in Paris in 1931. Cause of death: He drank a glass of typhoid-infected water to demonstrate that Parisian water was perfectly safe to drink.

• In 1955 James Dean made an ad warning teens about driving too fast. ("The life you save may be mine," he said.) Shortly after, he died when his Porsche Spyder, going 86 mph, hit another car.

• In 1871 attorney Clement Vallandigham was demonstrating to a jury that the man his client was accused of shooting could have accidentally done it himself. Vallandigham took out a gun, held it as it was held at the scene of the crime, and pulled the trigger. The gun was loaded; he proved his point.

IRONY AND PUBLIC SAFETY

• In 1974 the Consumer Product Safety Commission ordered 80,000 buttons promoting toy safety. They said: "For Kids' Sake, Think Toy Safety." The buttons were recalled when the agency found out they had "sharp edges, parts a child could swallow, and were coated with toxic lead paint."

• According to *Industrial Machinery News*, an (unnamed) company with a five-year perfect safety record tried to demonstrate the

Donald Duck's "official" address: 1313 Webfoot Walk, Duckburg, Calisota.

importance of wearing safety goggles on-the-job by showing workers a graphic film containing footage of gory industrial accidents. Twenty-five people injured themselves while fleeing the screening room, 13 others passed out during the film, and another required seven stitches "after he cut his head falling off a chair while watching the film."

CRIMINAL IRONY

• Twenty-six-year-old Samuel Worlin Moore was arrested for attempted armed robbery in Long Beach, California. Witnesses were able to ID him because of the distinctive tattoo on his arm. It read "Not Guilty."

• The inmates at the prison in Concord, New Hampshire, spend their days making the state's license plates, which bear the motto LIVE FREE OR DIE.

GOVERNMENTAL IRONY

Florida's secretary of state, Katherine Harris, became famous during the 2000 presidential election as the person in charge of the disputed ballot count. In the 2004 local election in her hometown of Longboat Key, Florida, she was informed that her vote would not be counted because she had turned in an invalid ballot. (She forgot to sign it.)

ENVIRONMENTAL IRONY

In October 2005, Greenpeace's flagship, *Rainbow Warrior II*, was studying the effects of global warming on a fragile underwater coral reef in the Philippines when it accidentally ran aground on the reef, causing it significant damage. The environmental organization was fined 384,000 pesos ($6,800).

IRONY IN THE COURT

• In 2000 a branch fell off a tree in Nevada City, California, and struck a power line, cutting off power to the town for more than 30 minutes. The outage delayed the courtroom trial of the Pacific Gas & Electric Company, which was charged with "failing to trim vegetation around power lines."

• Love Your Neighbor Corp. of Michigan recently sued Love Thy Neighbor Fund of Florida for trademark infringement.

A group of hares is called a *down*. (A group of hairs is called a *wig*.)

LET'S DO A STUDY!

If you're worried that the really important things in life aren't being researched by our scientists, keep worrying.

• In 2003 researchers at Plymouth University in England studied primate intelligence by giving macaque monkeys a computer. They reported that the monkeys attacked the machine, threw feces at it, and, contrary to their hopes, failed to produce a single word.

• In 2001 scientists at Cambridge University studied kinetic energy, centrifugal force, and the coefficient of friction… to determine the least messy way to eat spaghetti.

• A 2001 study found that 60% of men in the Czech Republic do not buy their own underwear.

• Colorado State University scientists concluded that Western Civilization causes acne.

• In 1994 the Japanese meteorological agency concluded a seven-year study into whether or not earthquakes are caused by catfish wiggling their tails. (They're not.)

• So fish may not cause earthquakes, but a 2003 study carried out by scientists at Edinburgh University found that they do feel pain.

• Researchers at the University of Hungary in Budapest analyzed videos of the "Wave" at sporting events. Results: it almost always moves clockwise around the stadium, travels at about 40 feet per second, and the average width of a wave is 15 rows of seats.

• Researchers at Georgetown University found that caterpillars can "shoot" their feces a distance of 40 times their body length.

• In 2003 two scientists went to Antarctica to find the exact velocity by which penguins expel waste. Their report: "Pressures Produced When Penguins Pooh: Calculations on Avian Defecation."

• A 2002 study by the Department of Veterans Affairs Medical Center in Vermont found that studies are often misleading.

Geography fact: Brazil is larger than all 48 contiguous United States combined.

WHAT'S THE NUMBER FOR 911?

*Here's a collection of some of our favorite 911
calls. Believe it or not, they're all real.*

Recorded during a power outage.
Dispatcher: "911. Fire or emergency?"
Caller: "My power's out!"
Dispatcher: "Yes, sir, we're aware of that. Do you have an emergency?"
Caller: "No, I don't have a damn emergency. I just want to know if I'm going to be getting a rebate for the length of time I'm without power."
Dispatcher: "Uhhh, no, sir, you won't be charged for the electricity you *didn't* use."
Caller: "Well, that's more like it!"

Dispatcher: "911. What's the address of your emergency?"
Caller: "I need to know what I can do about someone who came into my home and put boogers on my wall."
Dispatcher: "Did you invite this person into your home?"
Caller: "Yes, but I didn't give him permission to put boogers on the walls."

Dispatcher: "911. What's the address of your emergency?"
Citizen: [no response]
Dispatcher: "911. What's the address of your emergency?"
Citizen [tentatively]: "Hello?"
Dispatcher: "Yes, this is 911, can I help you?"
Citizen: "You have the wrong number!"

Dispatcher: "911.What's the address of your emergency?"
Caller: "Can I give you my credit card number over the phone to pay on my warrant?"
Dispatcher: "What's the offense?"
Caller: "Credit card fraud."

Dispatcher: "911."
Caller: "Help! Help! Send the police! I been shot."
Dispatcher: "You said you've been shot?"
Caller: "I been shot!"
Dispatcher: "How many times were you shot?"
Caller: "This is the first time."

Forty percent of Americans have never visited the dentist.

Dispatcher: "911. What is your emergency?"

Male Caller: "You have got people working in the school right now. And they've been working all night long violating the noise code over here."

Dispatcher: "Sir, a noise complaint is not an emergency call. You'll have to call on the business line."

Male Caller: "Well how about if I shoot them, would it be an emergency then?"

Dispatcher: "Sure would."

Male Caller: "Alright."

Dispatcher: "911."

Male Caller: "I need a paramedic. Can you send one or do I have to call someone else?"

Dispatcher: "I'll take care of that, sir. Just calm down. What's the problem?"

Male Caller: "I saw a medical special on TV last night about a rare disease, and I think I have all the symptoms. My neighbor thinks I do, too."

Dispatcher: "911."

Female Caller: "I am trapped in my house."

Dispatcher: "Trapped? Is someone holding you there?"

Female Caller: "Someone? No. But there is a frog on the front porch."

Dispatcher: "A frog?"

Female Caller: "Yes, a frog."

Dispatcher: "Okay, but what is preventing you from leaving the house?"

Female Caller: "I told you. There is a frog on the porch and I am afraid of frogs."

Dispatcher: "And you don't have another door to the house?"

Female Caller: "No. There is only one door and I can't get out of the house with the frog sitting there."

Dispatcher: "Why don't you take a broom and sweep the frog off the porch?"

Female Caller: "I can't do that. I told you, I am afraid of frogs. He might get me."

Dispatcher: "Um…I'm not sure I can help you with this."

Dispatcher: "911. What is the location of your emergency?"

Caller: "Yes, I just wanted to let you know that I have some information that will help you to solve many of your cases."

Dispatcher [noting that the call originated from the state hospital]: "Okay, go ahead with that information."

Caller: "I am prepared to meet with the detectives and to reveal the true identity of Cinderella's stepmother."

Dispatcher: [Pause] "Okay."

In 1992, 30,000 Hawaiians signed a petition to change Maui's name… to Gilligan's Island.

THE CHEWING GUM KING

From Uncle John's Bathroom Reader Plunges Into Great
Lives, *meet the man who put the* chicle *in* Chiclets.

CHEWING THROUGH HISTORY

People have been chewing gum (and gumlike substances) since ancient times. The Greeks chewed *mastiche*, made from the resin of the mastic tree. The ancient Mayans first chewed *chicle*, the sap of the sapodilla tree, over 1,000 years ago. American Indians chewed the sap from spruce trees, and European settlers picked up the habit from them, adding beeswax to the sap. By the mid-1800s, people were chewing gum made from flavored and sweetened paraffin wax.

In 1870 amateur inventor Thomas Adams was discussing a business proposition with his houseguest, the infamous General Antonio Lopez de Santa Anna—the man responsible for the massacre at the Alamo 34 years earlier. Now Santa Anna was living in exile on New York's Staten Island and trying to raise money so he could build an army to march on Mexico City and seize power.

Santa Anna had a scheme to sell Mexican *chicle* to Americans, who he thought could use it as an additive to natural rubber to reduce its cost. At the time, natural rubber was extremely expensive, and if someone could figure out a way to reduce its cost, he figured, it could be worth millions. The general had brought a large quantity of chicle with him and wondered if Adams could do something with it.

MIXING IT UP

Adams spent more than a year fiddling with the substance, trying to make rain boots and toys—and failed every time. He was just about ready to throw out the entire batch when he remembered how much Santa Anna had enjoyed chewing it. He decided to mix up a batch of chicle gum in his kitchen that evening and give it a try. Result: Gum made from chicle was smoother, softer, and far superior in taste to the paraffin gums that were currently in vogue.

Communist leader Karl Marx once worked as a reporter for the *New York Daily Tribune*.

CHEWSY CUSTOMERS

Adams rolled the chicle gum into balls and wrapped them in colored tissue paper. He called his product "Adams New York Snapping and Stretching Gum" and visited drugstores in his neighborhood to see if they'd take it on consignment. Within days, so many orders had come in that Adams had to set up an operation to make the gum in large quantities. It eventually became impossible for him to keep up with all the orders, so he invented a chewing gum manufacturing machine, which he patented in 1871.

MILESTONES IN GUM

In 1875 Adams added licorice flavoring and called his new gum "Black Jack." It was the first flavored chicle gum on the market and the first gum to be offered in sticks. It was a winner—Black Jack was still being manufactured 100 years later.

In 1888 the company came up with another innovation when they introduced the first vending machines in the United States. Installed in New York City subway stations, they dispensed Black Jack and the company's new Tutti-Frutti gum. In 1899 Adams created a monopoly by merging the six largest chewing gum manufacturers into the American Chicle Company. One of the company's most famous products, Chiclets, was invented by a candy salesman who wrapped chicle in a hard candy shell. Chiclets became part of the American Chicle Company in 1914.

During World War II, the demand for chewing gum outstripped the chicle supply, so scientists developed new resins and synthetic gum bases as a substitute. Today, per capita consumption of chewing gum in the U.S. totals in excess of 195 million pounds a year. That works out to 175 sticks of gum per person per year.

POSTSCRIPT

Santa Anna never did profit from chicle sales or raise an army as he'd hoped, but he was allowed to return to Mexico shortly before his death in 1876. Thomas Adams died in 1905, and his sons ran the business until the American Chicle Company was acquired by Warner Lambert in 1960.

The first umbrella was invented by the ancient Egyptians...to shield the sun.

WHO'S GONNA WIN?

There are almost as many ways to predict who's going to be our next president as there are ballots. And believe it or not, some of these ways actually seem to work...kind of.

CRYSTAL BALL

Thousands of people make their living trying to predict the outcome of presidential elections. Journalists, pollsters, lobbyists, and political scientists all have a stake in it. The months leading up to an election are rife with speculation; everyone—academics and crackpots alike—trots out their sure-fire method to predict how it will all turn out. But you don't need to get out your tarot cards, bone up on economic indicators, or consult your astrological charts. We've got the answers right here.

IT'S THE HEIGHT, RIGHT?
The most common belief is that the taller candidate is the one to beat. In his 1965 book *Language on Vacation*, Dmitri Borgmann found that in the 19 U.S. presidential elections between 1888 and 1960, the taller candidate won the popular vote all but once, when 6'2" tall Franklin Roosevelt beat the taller Wendell Willkie (6'2½") in 1940. Psychologist John Gillis published *Too Tall, Too Small* in 1982 in which he claimed that the taller candidate won 80 percent of the 21 presidential elections from 1904 to 1984. Keep in mind that finding accurate data on the heights of the candidates, especially the losers, can be difficult; it may be best to back up your arsenal of predictive measures with a few more methods—even if in 8 of the last 10 elections, the taller candidate has won.

IT'S ALL IN A NAME?
Borgmann also had a hypothesis about the length of a candidate's name. Between 1876 and 1960, the candidate with the most letters in his last name won the popular vote 20 out of 22 times. (Maybe that's why the 2000 election—Gore vs. Bush—was so close.) But of course the winner of the popular vote is sometimes trumped by the winner of the electoral college, which happened

---

Thomas Jefferson once ate a tomato in public to prove it wasn't poisonous.

in the Tilden–Hayes contest of 1876 and the Cleveland–Harrison election of 1888. In recent years, the longer-named candidate has won only 3 out of 11 contests, so this theory doesn't seem to hold up anymore.

First names also seem to play into elections. Some observers point out that from FDR until Bill Clinton, a president with an unusual first name always followed a president with a common first name, and vice versa: Franklin, Harry, Dwight, John, Lyndon, Richard, Gerald, Jimmy, Ronald, George. But once again, the theory falls off in recent years (George, Bill, George).

IT'S THE ECONOMY, STUPID

Naturally, there are more serious ways to predict elections. Political scientist James Campbell demonstrates that a good way to predict our next president has been the growth rate (the percent change in the size of the economy) during April, May, and June of the election year. If the growth rate of the Gross Domestic Product (GDP—the combined value of all the spending in the country in a given year, plus the value of all exports minus the value of all imports) during this time is 2.6 percent or higher, the incumbent president or someone from his party will likely win. If the number is 1.5 percent or lower, then the incumbent party will probably lose. But what if the growth rate falls between these numbers? Then the future is murky. Since 1952 this method has predicted the outcome in every presidential contest but the one in 1968, when Vice President Hubert Humphrey lost to Richard Nixon. But political analysts say that outcome may have had more to do with the Vietnam War than the economy.

"GALLUP"ING TO THE WHITE HOUSE

The Gallup Poll has been calculating what they call the "President's Approval Rating" for more than 60 years, by asking the public whether they approve or disapprove of the way the president is handling his job. Emory University political scientist Alan Abramowitz has found that if the president's approval rating in mid-June of an election year is 51 percent or higher, he or his party will probably win. If his approval rating is 45 percent or lower, he or his party will probably lose. And once again anything between these numbers leaves us with an uncertain future. Since the mid-1950s, the Gallup approval rating has been perhaps the single best predictor of presidential election results, particularly in reelection years. Since 1952, the leader in the Gallup Poll taken between September 21 and 24 and between October 12 and October 16 has won every election. In the weeks between these crucial points and the November election, talking heads continue to analyze every blip in the percentage points. But it's invariably the Gallup Poll taken on those dates that predicts the outcome.

DIFFERENT SCHOOLS OF THOUGHT

Maybe all the pros should just pay attention to the amateurs when it comes to predicting election winners.

• According to the children's book publisher Scholastic, their polls of students from grades 1 through 12 have nailed the election outcomes for every presidential race for the past 50 years (except the close Kennedy–Nixon contest in 1960).

• BuyCostumes.com, a company specializing in—obviously— costume sales, has a unique method. Using the sales of Halloween masks depicting the two major candidates since 1980, the company has shown that mask sales correlate with the results of each election. In 1996 Bill Clinton's sales led Bob Dole's by 16 percent. In 2000 sales of the George W. Bush mask outpaced Al Gore's mask by 14 percent. In 2004 Bush outsold Kerry, 53% to 47%.

• Even what happens on a football field can predict who will sleep in the White House. For the past 15 elections, a win by the Washington Redskins in their last home game prior to Election Day has meant a win for the incumbent party; a loss at home means a loss for the incumbent party. The streak was broken in 2004 when the Redskins lost...but Bush won.

*   *   *

"If you were to go back in history and take every president, you'd find that the numerical value of each letter in their name was equally divisible into the year in which they were elected. By my calculations, our next president has to be named Yellnick McWawa."

—Cliff Clavin, *Cheers*

...Its presidential alums are the two Adamses, the two Roosevelts, and Kennedy.

SIGNS O' THE TIMES

Sometimes communication can be difficult...even in your native language. Here are actual signs posted across America.

At a maternity ward:
No Children Allowed

At a gas station:
We will sell gasoline to anyone in a glass container.

At a shop:
Our motto is to give our customers the lowest possible prices and workmanship.

In a cemetery:
Persons are prohibited from picking flowers from any but their own graves

At a dry cleaner:
38 years on the same spot

In the offices of a loan company:
Ask about our plans for owning your home.

In a restaurant:
Open 7 days a week and weekends

At a church:
Will the last person to leave please see that the perpetual light is extinguished.

In a clothing store:
Wonderful bargains for men with 16 and 17 necks

In a bookstore:
Rare, Out-of-Print, And Non-Existent Books

At a general store:
We buy junk and sell antiques

In a dry cleaner:
We do not tear your clothing with machinery. We do it carefully by hand.

At a convention:
For anyone who has children and doesn't know it, there is a daycare center on the 1st floor.

At a camera store:
One Hour Photos Ready In 20 Minutes

At a school basketball court:
Anyone caught hanging from the rim will be suspended.

At a drugstore:
Why be cheated elsewhere when you can come here?

If you're average, your feet hit the ground 7,000 times a day.

WORD GEOGRAPHY

A few common terms that were derived from the names of real places.

SUEDE
From: Sweden

Explanation: *Gants de Suede* is French for "gloves of Sweden." It was in Sweden that the first leather was buffed to a fine softness, and the French bought the *gants de Suede*. Suede now refers to the buffing processes—not to any particular kind of leather.

TURKEY
From: Turkey

Explanation: *Turk* means "strength" in Turkish. The turkey bird is a large European fowl named after the country of its origin. American colonists mistakenly thought a big bird they found in the New World was the same animal...so they called it a turkey.

MAYONNAISE
From: Port Mahon, Spain

Explanation: The *-aise* suffix is French for "native to" or "originating in." *Mahonnaise* was supposedly created to celebrate a 1756 French battle victory over the British on the Spanish isle of Port Mahon.

CHEAP
From: Cheapside, a market in London

Explanation: The Old English word was *ceap* (pronounced "keep"), which meant "to sell or barter." Because *Cheapside* was a major market where people went to barter for low prices, the word gradually took on a new pronunciation...and meaning.

COFFEE
From: Kaffa, Ethiopia

Explanation: According to legend, coffee beans were first discovered in the town of Kaffa. By the thirteenth century, the Kaffa beans had traveled, becoming *qahwah* in Arabia, *cafe* in Europe, and finally *coffee* in the New World.

Doctors, more than any other profession, are most likely to be late for a doctor's appointment.

COLOGNE
From: Cologne (Köln), Germany
Explanation: Scented water that was produced there beginning in 1709 was named for the city.

DENIM
From: Nimes, France
Explanation: The tough cloth used in jeans was also made in Nimes. It was called *serge di Nimes*—later shortened to *di Nimes*, which became *denim*.

SLAVE
From: Slavonia, Yugoslavia
Explanation: After large parts of Slavonia were subjugated by Europeans in the Middle Ages, a *slav* become synonymous with someone who lived in servitude. Eventually *Slav* became *slave*.

LIMERICK
From: Limerick, Ireland
Explanation: The town was popularly associated with humorous verses that had five lines, the first two rhyming with the last, the middle two rhyming with each other. The poems became an English fad in the mid-19th century, and people naturally identified them with the town's name.

HAMBURGER
From: Hamburg, Germany
Explanation: People in the immigration-port city of Hamburg—called Hamburgers—liked to eat raw meat with salt, pepper, and onion-juice seasoning, a treat brought to them via Russia that we call *steak tartare* today. A broiled version using chopped meat eventually became popular in America.

TURQUOISE
From: Turkey/Europe
Explanation: Another Turkish origin. Turquoise comes from a number of places, but was probably first imported to Europe from Turkey. So it was called *turquoise*, which means "Turkish stone."

Americans spend an estimated $10 billion a year on gambling and games of chance.

BEHIND THE BOOKS

*We can't identify the first book ever read in the bathroom,
but we have been able to find the stories behind
a few other publishing milestones.*

THE FANNIE FARMER COOKBOOK

Originally, cookbooks didn't give precise measurements for recipes—they just told readers to use a "pinch" of this, a "heaping spoonful" of that, and a "handful" of something else. Fannie Merrit Farmer, a domestic servant in the late 1850s, had no trouble following such recipes herself—but she found it almost impossible to give instructions to the young girl who helped her in the home where she worked. So she began rewriting the family's recipes using more precise measurements.

Forty years later, she had become the assistant principal of the prestigious Boston Cooking School. In 1896, she decided to publish her first book of "scientific" recipes, *The Fannie Farmer Cookbook*. Her publisher was so worried it wouldn't sell that he forced Farmer to pay for the printing costs herself. She did. It sold 4 million copies and permanently changed the way cookbooks are written.

DR. SPOCK'S BABY AND CHILD CARE

Dr. Benjamin Spock was a New York pediatrician with a background in psychology when Pocket Books approached him about writing a childcare book for new mothers. It wasn't the first time he'd gotten such an offer: in 1938 Doubleday had asked him to write a similar book, but he turned them down, saying he was inexperienced and wasn't sure he could write a good book. He almost rejected Pocket Books for the same reason—until the editor explained that it didn't *have* to be a very good book, "because at 25¢ a copy, we'll be able to sell a hundred thousand a year."

Feeling reassured, Spock accepted the offer and wrote *The Pocket Book of Baby and Child Care*. He began with the admonition "Trust yourself"—and wrote a book that was unlike any child-rearing book that had been written before. "The previous attitude in child-rearing books was, 'Look out, stupid, if you don't do as I

The term "hell on wheels" originally applied to the Union Pacific Railroad's saloon railcars.

say, you'll kill the baby,' " Spock recalls. "I leaned over backward not to be alarming and to be friendly with the parents."

His warm, supportive voice paid off; *The Pocket Book of Baby and Child Care* became the second-bestselling book in American history, second only to the Bible. It has sold an average of 1 million copies a year every year since it was published in 1946. Its impact on American culture has been profound. According to *The Paperback In America*: "For two generations of American parents, it has been the bible for coping with their newborns....A comparison of new mothers to the number of books sold during the baby boom's peak years—from 1946 to 1964, when nearly 75 million babies were born in the United States—put the estimate of 'Spock babies' at one in five, and that failed to account for the number of women who shared or borrowed the book or used it to raise more than one child."

THE COMPLETE BOOK OF RUNNING

Jim Fixx was a part-time author and full-time editor at *Horizon* magazine...until 1976, when his boss "suggested" he find another job. Fixx didn't want another magazine job, but all he knew how to do was write, and he had four kids to support. He'd been running for about eight years, and knew there was no book that gave practical advice for beginning runners, so he came up with an idea to make a quick $10,000—a "breezy, superficial" book called *The Lazy Athlete's Look Younger Be Thinner Feel Better & Live Longer Running Book*.

As it happened, one of the last things he did for *Horizon* magazine was meet with Pulitzer Prize-winning author Jerzy Kozinski. "As Kozinski and I sat talking in his studio in midtown Manhattan," Fixx recalled, "the conversation turned to my book."

> "You have a big job ahead of you," Kozinski said "To write a book like that, you have to read everything that's been written on the subject." Until then I hadn't thought of doing anything of the sort. All I wanted to do was get the book written quickly and collect my check. But I realized that Kozinski was right. The conversation turned a modest and easily manageable plan into a two-year obsession.

The Complete Book of Running came out in 1978. It immediately hit the bestseller list and became the bible of one of the biggest sports in America. Years later, Fixx died of a heart attack while jogging.

Caterpillars fast during the day.

IN DREAMS....

People have always been fascinated by dreams. What do they mean?
And on occasion, art, music, and even discoveries and inventions
have resulted directly from a dream. Here are some examples.

THE SEWING MACHINE

Elias Howe had been trying to invent a practical lock-stitch sewing machine for years, but had been unsuccessful. One night in the 1840s, he had a nightmare in which he was captured by a primitive tribe who were threatening to kill him with their spears. Curiously, all the spears had holes in them at the pointed ends. When Howe woke up, he realized that a needle with a hole at its tip—rather than at the base or middle (which is what he'd been working with)—was the solution to his problem.

DR. JEKYLL AND MR. HYDE

Since childhood, novelist Robert Louis Stevenson had always remembered his dreams and believed that they gave him inspiration for his writing. In 1884, he was in dire need of money and was trying to come up with a book. He had already spent two days racking his brains for a new plot when he had a nightmare about a man with a dual personality. In the dream, "Mr. Hyde" was being pursued for a crime he'd committed; he took a strange powder and changed into someone else as his pursuers watched. Stevenson screamed in his sleep, and his wife woke him. The next morning he began writing down *The Strange Case of Dr. Jekyll and Mr. Hyde.*

INSULIN

Frederick Banting, a Canadian doctor, had been doing research into the cause of diabetes, but had not come close to a cure. One night in 1920, he had a strange dream. When he awoke, he quickly wrote down a few words that he remembered: "Tie up the duct of the pancreas of a dog...wait for the glands to shrivel up...then cut it out, wash it...and filter the precipitation." This new approach to extracting the substance led to the isolation of the hormone now known as insulin, which has saved millions of diabetics' lives. Banting was knighted for his discovery.

Smallest town in the U.S.: Hove Mobile Park City, North Dakota, with a population of two.

LEAD SHOT

James Watt is remembered for inventing the steam engine, but he also came up with the process for making lead shot used in shotguns. This process was revealed to him in a dream. At the time, making the shot was costly and unpredictable—the lead was rolled into sheets by hand, then chopped into bits. Watt had the same dream each night for a week: He was walking along in a heavy rainstorm—but instead of rain, he was being showered with tiny pellets of lead, which he could see rolling around his feet. The dream haunted him; did it mean that molten lead falling through the air would harden into round pellets? He decided to experiment. He melted a few pounds of lead and tossed it out of the tower of a church that had a water-filled moat at its base. When he removed the lead from the water, he found that it *had* hardened into tiny globules. To this day, lead shot is made using this process.

THE BENZENE MOLECULE

Friedrich A. Kekule, a Belgian chemistry professor, had been working for some time to solve the structural riddle of the benzene molecule. One night while working late, he fell asleep on a chair and dreamed of atoms dancing before him, forming various patterns and structures. He saw long rows of atoms begin to twist like snakes until one of the snakes seized its own tail and began to whirl in a circle. Kekule woke up "as if by a flash of lightning" and began to work out the meaning of his dream image. His discovery of a closed ring with an atom of carbon and hydrogen at each point of a hexagon revolutionized organic chemistry.

THE MODERN IMAGE OF JESUS

Warner E. Sallman was an illustrator for religious magazines. In 1924 he needed a picture for a deadline the next day, but was coming up blank. Finally, he went to bed—then suddenly awoke with "a picture of the Christ in my mind's eye just as if it were on my drawing board." He quickly sketched a portrait of Jesus with long brown hair, blue eyes, a neatly trimmed beard, and a beatific look—which has now become the common image of Christ around the world. Since 1940, more than 500 million copies of Sallman's "Head of Christ" have been sold. It has been reproduced billions of times on calendars, lamps, posters, etc.

Chief, the U.S. Cavalry's last horse, died in 1968. He was 36.

GOSH, BATMAN...

The 1960s Batman TV series is well known for its campiness. But we've always liked the lessons on civics and citizenship Batman/Bruce Wayne gave to his ward, Robin/Dick Grayson. Here's some of Batman's choicest advice.

Robin: You can't get away from Batman that easy!
Batman: *Easily.*
Robin: *Easily.*
Batman: Good grammar is essential, Robin.

Batman: Better put five cents in the meter.
Robin: No policeman's going to give the Batmobile a ticket.
Batman: This money goes to building better roads. We all must do our part.

Dick: Gosh, economics is sure a dull subject.
Bruce: Oh, you must be jesting, Dick. Economics dull? The glamour, the romance of commerce. It's the very lifeblood of our society.

Dick: What's the use of learning French, anyway?
Bruce: Language is the key to world peace. If we all spoke each other's tongues, perhaps the scourge of war would be ended forever.
Dick: Gosh, Bruce, yes. I'll get these darn verbs if they kill me!

Batman: When you get a little older, you'll see how easy it is to become lured by the female of the species.
Robin: I guess you can never trust a woman.
Batman: You've made a hasty generalization, Robin. It's a bad habit to get into.

Robin: Gosh, Batman, those look like honest eyes.
Batman: Never trust the old chestnut, "Crooks have beady little eyes." It's false.

Bruce: Most Americans don't realize what we owe to the ancient Incas. Very few appreciate they gave us the white potato and many varieties of Indian corn.
Dick: Now whenever I eat mashed potatoes, I for one will think of the Incas.

Robin: We'd better hurry, Batman.
Batman: Not too fast, Robin. In good bat-climbing as in good driving, one must never sacrifice safety for speed.
Robin: Right again, Batman.

It takes a combine harvester 9 seconds to harvest enough wheat to make 70 loaves of bread.

LET'S TALK TURKEY

If you think radio talk shows get a lot of strange calls, take a look at some of the questions that the folks at the Butterball Turkey Talk-Line have fielded over the years.

DIAL "T" FOR TURKEY
If you bought a Butterball Turkey in the 1970s, it would have included a sheet of cooking instructions, just like they still do today. But people still called the company to complain when their birds didn't come out right, which made Butterball wonder if people even bothered to read and follow the instructions. Disappointing dinners make for poor repeat business, so in 1981 Butterball started printing a toll-free number on the packaging and inviting customers to call in with any cooking questions they might have.

In those days 800 numbers were fairly rare, and the idea of calling one to get free cooking advice was a novelty. The company wasn't sure that callers would get the concept or even understand that the long-distance call was free. But they hired six home economists, set them up with phones in the company's test kitchen, and waited to see if the phone would ring. They were flabbergasted when more than 11,000 people jammed the line during the holiday season, especially on Thanksgiving, when the company figured hardly anyone would bother to call. An American institution was born.

CLUELESS ON LINE 4

Today Butterball has an automated phone system and a Web site to handle the most frequently asked questions. Still, more than 100,000 people call in each year to talk to the 50 turkey experts who staff the phones from November 1 through December 25. The advent of cordless and cell phones has put the Talk-Line in even greater demand: People now call right from the dinner table to have someone talk them through the carving of the bird.

What's your favorite way to cook a turkey? Over the years, Butterball has tried to come up with cooking tips for every weird turkey fad that has come down the pike. In the early 1980s, they

Need a turkey tip? The number for the Turkey Talk-Line is 1-800-BUTTERBALL.

perfected a technique for cooking a turkey in the *microwave*—which, believe it or not, was the third-most popular question in those days. (By 1987 it had dropped all the way to #20.) Do you cook your turkey in a big brown paper bag? In a deep fryer? In a pillowcase smeared with butter? On a countertop rotisserie? The Butterball people won't always approve, but they will try to help.

DO TURKEYS HAVE BELLY BUTTONS?

Butterball has fielded some pretty bizarre questions over the past 25 years. Here are some favorites, along with the answers:

• **Should I remove the plastic wrap before I cook my turkey?** Yes.

• **I don't want to touch the giblets. Can I fish them out with a coat hanger?** Yes.

• **Can I poke holes all over the turkey and pour a can of beer over it to keep it moist?** You'll do more harm than good—the skin keeps the moisture in. Poking holes in it will dry it out.

• **Can you thaw a frozen turkey using an electric hair dryer? Or by wrapping it in an electric blanket? In the aquarium with my tropical fish? In the tub while the kids are having their bath?** No, no, no, and no. If you're in a hurry, thaw the turkey in the kitchen sink by immersing it in cold water. Allow half an hour per pound, and change the water every half hour.

• **How can I thaw 12 turkeys all at once?** The caller was cooking for a firehouse, so Butterball advised them to put them all in a clean trash can and hose them down with a firehose.

• **The family dog bit off a big piece of the turkey. Can the rest of it be saved?** Maybe. If the damage is localized, cut away the dog-eaten part of the bird and serve the rest. Disguise the maimed bird with garnishes, or carve it up out of view of your guests and serve the slices. The less your guests know, the better.

• **The family dog is *inside* the turkey and can't get out.** A few years back, Butterball really did get a call from the owner of a Chihuahua that climbed inside the raw bird while the owner's back was turned. The opening was big enough for the dog to get in, but not big enough for it to get back out. The turkey expert instructed the owner on how to enlarge the opening without injuring the dog.

For the record, turkeys do *not* have belly buttons.

(No word on whether the bird was eaten.) Butterball has also fielded calls from owners of gerbils and housecats. "I was told not to talk about that," one Talk-Line staffer told a reporter in 1997.

- **I need to drive two hours with my frozen turkey before I cook it. Will it stay frozen if I tie it to the luggage rack on the roof of my car?** The caller was from Minnesota, so the answer was yes. If you live in Florida, Hawaii, or Arizona, the answer is no.

- **I'm a truck driver. Can I cook the turkey on the engine block of my semi while I'm driving? If I drive faster, will it cook faster?** There've been cases in wartime where soldiers cooked turkeys using the heat from Jeep engines, but Butterball gives no advice on the subject.

- **I scrubbed my raw turkey with a toothbrush dipped in bleach for three hours. Is that enough to kill all the harmful bacteria?** The *heat of the oven* is what kills the bacteria; scrubbing the turkey with bleach makes it inedible. (In extreme cases like these, or anytime the Talk-Line staffers fear the bird has become unsafe to eat, they advise the cook to discard the bird, eat out, and try again next year. If the caller can't imagine Thanksgiving without turkey, they can get some turkey hot dogs.)

- **I didn't want to cook the whole turkey, so I cut it in half with a chainsaw. How do I get the chainsaw oil out of the turkey?** Toss the turkey and go get some hot dogs.

- **The turkey in my freezer is 23 years old. Is it safe to eat?** Butterball advised this caller that the bird was safe, but that it probably wouldn't taste very good. "That's what we thought," the caller told the Talk-Line. "We'll give it to the church."

MORE QUESTIONS FOR THE TALK-LINE

- How long does it take to thaw a fresh turkey?

- How long does it take to cook a turkey if I leave the oven door open the entire time? That was how my mom always did it.

- Does the turkey go in the oven feet first, or head first?

- Can I baste my turkey with suntan lotion?

- When does turkey hunting season start?

- How do I prepare a turkey for vegetarians?

The chattering sound made by monkeys is called *snuttering*.

AMAZING RESCUE

Here's a story from Uncle John's Tales to Inspire *about four courageous divers who risked life and limb to save a trapped whale...and were rewarded with the gift of a lifetime.*

TANGLED WEB

On the brisk Sunday morning of December 11, 2005, a crab fisherman spotted a heartbreaking sight off the coast of San Francisco: a 50-foot humpback whale trapped in a tangle of crab-pot lines. He immediately called for help, and within three hours the Marine Mammal Center had chartered a boat—normally used for whale-watching tours—and assembled a rescue team. As soon as they arrived on the scene, they assessed the situation. It didn't look good.

The female humpback was completely entangled in hundreds of yards of ropes that collectively weighed more than 1,000 pounds. To make matters worse, she'd already been struggling for hours to keep her blowhole above water, and they didn't know how much strength she had left. No whale that had been trapped like this off the west coast had ever survived. With time running out, the rescuers knew there was only one way to save her: dive in and start cutting the ropes one at a time.

INTO THE WATER

Four divers went in: James Moskito, Jason Russey, Ted Vivian, and Tim Young. Moskito was the first to reach the whale, and the first to understand the severity of the situation. More than 20 thick lines were wrapped tightly around her tail, flippers, torso, and mouth, all digging deep into her flesh. So, on top of everything else, the whale was losing blood. "I really didn't think we were going to be able to save her," Moskito later told the *San Francisco Chronicle*.

EASY DOES IT

The whale wasn't the only one at risk; her rescuers were in danger as well. They knew that even a small flip of the 50-ton animal's tail could kill any one of them. But once they got to work carefully

---

The cables on the Golden Gate Bridge contain 80,000 miles of steel wire.

cutting the ropes with large, curved knives, their fear quickly subsided. The men later said that they could somehow sense the whale knew they were there to help her. While they worked, she barely moved at all, just enough to stay afloat. At one point, Moskito found himself face to face with the animal as he cut the ropes from her mouth. "Her eye was there winking at me, watching me work. It was an epic moment of my life."

Finally, after more than an hour of nonstop cutting, the heavy ropes fell away and the humpback whale was able to move again. She immediately wriggled free of the few remaining lines and started out to sea.

THANK YOU

But then the whale did something unexpected. She swam in circles near the men, completing a few rotations. And then she swam right up to each of them and, one by one, gently nuzzled against them for a moment. "It felt to me like she was thanking us, knowing that she was free and that we'd helped her," Moskito recalled. "She stopped about a foot away from me, pushed me around a little bit and had some fun. It was amazing, unbelievable."

It was also fleeting—because a moment later, the humpback whale dove under the water...and was gone.

*　　*　　*

REAL CLASSIFIED ADS

Wanted: Cleaning and Janitorial help. Please leave mess.

Wanted: Desk clerk and housekeeping help at Best Western PLEASE NO PHONE CALLS!!! (760) 375-2311

Amana Washer. Owned by clean bachelor who seldom washed.

Used tombstone, perfect for someone named Homer Hendelbergenheinzel. One only.

For sale: Antique desk suitable for lady with thick legs and large drawers.

Dog for sale. Eats anything and is especially fond of children.

Shh! The word "listen" contains the same letters as the word "silent".

MYTH WORLD

Think you know everything about our home planet?
These items might surprise you as they debunk
some common myth-conceptions.

Myth: Mt. Everest is Earth's tallest mountain.
Fact: If you measure from the very bottom of the mountain to its peak, the world's tallest is Mauna Kea on the island of Hawaii. It rises 13,784 feet (4,201 m) above sea level, straight from the bottom of the sea. Of course the mountain would seem a lot taller if you could see all of it. But even though 18,000 feet (5,486 m) of the mountain is under the ocean, from its base to its height, Mauna Kea is over 31,000 feet (9,448 m) high. Mt. Everest's peak is a paltry 29,000 feet (8,839 m) high—above sea level.

Myth: The wettest spot on Earth is located in the South American rain forest. (That's why they call it the rain forest.)
Fact: Hawaii scores again. The wettest spot is on Mt. Waialeale on the island of Kauai. Waialeale is consistently drenched by rainfall at the rate of nearly 500 inches (1,270 cm) per year.

Myth: The driest spot on Earth is the Sahara desert.
Fact: The driest place on earth is in Chile. It's so dry in Calama, Chile, that 400 years went by without rain; the only source of moisture was the fog in the air. (A torrential rainstorm broke the 400-year dry spell in 1972, but the record remains intact.)

Myth: The Andes is the longest mountain range in the world.
Fact: Actually, the longest mountain range is underwater—in the Atlantic Ocean to be exact. The Mid-Atlantic Ridge runs 10,000 miles (16,093 km), all the way from Iceland to Antarctica.

Myth: Most of the world's plant life is in the dense jungles of Africa and South America.
Fact: The vast majority—85 percent, in fact—of the world's greenery is in the oceans.

The Pacific Ocean comprises 46% of the Earth's water area.

THE STRANGEST DISASTER OF THE 20TH CENTURY, PT. I

Here's the story of how scientists unlocked the secrets of the worst natural disaster in the history of the west African nation of Cameroon …and what they're doing to try and stop it from happening again.

THE DISCOVERY

On the morning of August 22, 1986, a man hopped onto his bicycle and began riding from Wum, a village in Cameroon, toward the village of Nyos. On the way he noticed an antelope lying dead next to the road. Why let it go to waste? The man tied the antelope onto his bicycle and continued on. A short distance later he noticed two dead rats, and further on, a dead dog and other dead animals. He wondered if they'd all been killed by a lightning strike—when lightning hits the ground it's not unusual for animals nearby to be killed by the shock.

Soon the man came upon a group of huts. He decided to see if anyone there knew what had happened to the animals. But as he walked up to the huts he was stunned to see dead bodies strewn everywhere. He didn't find a single person still alive—everyone in the huts was dead. The man threw down his bicycle and ran all the way back to Wum.

SOMETHING BIG

By the time the man got back to the village, the first survivors of whatever it was that had struck Nyos and other nearby villages were already stumbling into Wum. Many told tales of hearing an explosion or a rumbling noise in the distance, then smelling strange smells and passing out for as long as 36 hours before waking up to discover that everyone around them was dead.

Wum is in a remote part of Cameroon, so it took two days for a medical team to arrive in the area after local officials called the governor to report the strange occurrence. The doctors found a catastrophe far greater than they could have imagined: Overnight, something had killed nearly 1,800 people, plus more than 3,000 cattle and countless wild animals, birds, and insects—in short, every living creature for miles around.

The official death toll was recorded as 1,746 people, but that was only an estimate, because the survivors had already begun to bury victims in mass graves, and many terrified survivors had fled corpse-filled villages and were hiding in the forest. Whatever it was that killed so many people seemed to have disappeared without a trace just as quickly as it had come.

LOOKING FOR CLUES

What could have caused so many deaths in such a short span of time? When word of the disaster reached the outside world, scientists from France (Cameroon is a former French colony), the United States, and other countries arrived to help the country's own scientists figure out what had happened. The remains of the victims offered few clues. There was no evidence of bleeding, physical trauma, or disease, and no sign of exposure to radiation, chemical weapons, or poison gas. And there was no evidence of suffering or "death agony": The victims apparently just blacked out, fell over, and died.

One of the first important clues was the distribution of the victims across the landscape: The deaths had all occurred within about 12 miles of Lake Nyos, which some local tribes called the "bad lake." Legend had that that long ago, evil spirits had risen out of the lake and killed all the people living in a village at the water's edge.

Both the number of victims and the percentage of fatalities increased as the scientists got closer to the lake: In the outlying villages many people, especially those who had remained inside their homes, had survived, while in Nyos, which at less than two miles away was the closest village to the lake, only 6 of more than 800 villagers were still alive.

But it was the lake itself that provided the biggest and strangest clue of all: its normally clear blue waters had turned a deep, murky red. The scientists began to wonder if there was more to the legend of the "bad lake" than anyone had realized.

STILL LIFE

Lake Nyos is roughly one square mile in surface area and has a maximum depth of 690 feet. It's what's known as a "crater lake"—it formed when the crater of a long-extinct volcano filled with water. But was the volcano really extinct? Maybe an eruption was the culprit: Maybe the volcano beneath the lake had come back to life and in the process suddenly released enough poison gases to kill every living creature over a very wide area.

The theory was compelling but problematic: An eruption capable of releasing enough poison gas to kill that many people over that wide an area would have been very violent and accompanied by plenty of seismic activity. None of the eyewitnesses had mentioned earthquakes, and when the scientists checked with a seismic recording station 140 miles away, it showed no evidence of unusual activity on the evening of August 21. This was backed up by the fact that even in the hardest-hit villages, goods were still piled high on shelves in homes where every member of the household been killed. And the scientists noticed another mysterious clue: The oil lamps in these homes had all been extinguished, even the ones still filled with plenty of oil.

TESTING THE WATERS

The scientists began to test water samples taken from various depths in the lake. The red on the surface turned out to be dissolved iron—normally found on the bottom of the lake, not the top. Somehow the sediment at the bottom had been stirred up and the iron brought to the surface, where it turned the color of rust after coming into contact with oxygen.

The scientists also discovered unusually high levels of carbon dioxide (CO_2) dissolved or "in solution" in the water. Samples from as shallow as 50 feet deep contained so much CO_2 that when they were pulled to the surface, where the water pressure was lower, the dissolved CO_2 came bubbling out of solution—just as if someone had unscrewed the cap on a bottle of soda.

Plop, plop, fizz, fizz.
Oh, what an odd tale this is!
Part II of the story is on page 379.

Forks originally had two tines, and were known as "split spoons."

ODD JOBS IN THE CLOSING CREDITS

When you look at the list of a movie's crew, you'll see some strange job titles, like "key grip" and "best boy." What do those people actually do?

KEY GRIP. In movies, grips are the people who build the *rigging*—structures upon which lights are hung (but they don't touch the lights themselves—that's someone else's job). They are also the folks responsible for moving major set pieces. The key grip runs the crew of other grips, works with the director of photography, and coordinates with the gaffer (see below) to set up the scenes to be shot. A key grip sometimes acts as safety officer on a film set, making sure nothing explodes that's not supposed to, stunts are safely performed, and props are in working order.

GAFFER. The gaffer, sometimes credited as the chief lighting technician, is the head of a movie's electrical department, and it's his or her job to make sure all the lights are correctly placed for whatever scene is being shot. The gaffer works with the director of photography and the key grip to cover the scene and (if it's a big movie) has a staff of electricians to boss around. The name *gaffer* comes from an old English term meaning any man who is in charge of a group of hired hands.

CLAPPER LOADER. You know that thing they clap together at the beginning of a scene, with the number and take of the scene on it? That's a clapper (also known as a slate). The clapper loader is the person who snaps it together to make the clapping sound. He or she is also responsible for putting film stock into camera magazines. As digital film cameras become more commonplace, this task will probably change or be phased out.

FOCUS PULLER. Anyone who's fiddled with a camcorder knows how hard it is to keep everything in focus. Keeping all the

---

The title role of *Jerry Maguire*, played by Tom Cruise, was written for Tom Hanks....

shots clear is the focus puller's job on a film set. When the camera moves on a set, the focus puller will make tiny adjustments to the camera's focus with a device called a follow focus. The focus puller does this without actually looking through the camera lens (because the cameraperson is doing that). As you might expect, doing this with any measure of competence takes a fair amount of skill and practice.

DOLLY GRIP. The film camera used in making a movie is usually stationed on a movable rig called a *dolly*. The guy who moves the dolly around (and does the things required to make it move, like laying down track) is the dolly grip. Pushing a film camera around on a dolly is more complicated than it sounds, in no small part because the camera is actually running and filming scenes while the dolly is being pushed around the set. Before the shoot, the dolly grip has to confer with the camera crew to coordinate efforts so everything stays in focus and moves when and where it's supposed to.

FOLEY ARTIST. Most of the common sounds you hear in movies—glass breaking, leaves rustling, and doors opening—are actually added in later by people working in a room filled with special noise makers. These people are the Foley artists (named after Jack Foley, one of the earliest sound effects masters). Their noise-making implements don't often resemble what's supposed to be making noise on-screen: For example, clopping horses hooves are often imitated with coconut shells, which is parodied in the film *Monty Python and the Holy Grail*. In Hitchcock's 1960 film *Psycho*, Janet Leigh's demise was sonically replicated by a Foley artist stabbing a melon. Blaster fire in *Star Wars* (1977) was actually the sound of a hammer striking antenna tower wire.

BEST BOY. This can be the assistant to the head of either a film's lighting department or rigging department. The position's range of responsibilities depends upon the size of the crew, but they can include everything from making sure all lighting or rigging is satisfactorily placed, to hiring crew and handling negotiations. Best boys are not always boys (or men), although the position is usually credited as "Best Boy" regardless of gender.

FALSE ADVERTISING

*Americans tend to overlook an important side to our love affair
with celebrities—they're always trying to sell us something:
an idea, image, or product. And many of them don't
mind lying to us, either. Here are a few examples.*

FOR SALE: A Cherished Possession
In the early 1900s, Bat Masterson, legendary Wild West lawman, became a New York sports writer. Because he needed the money, he reluctantly agreed to sell his famous sixgun—the "gun that tamed the West."

The Truth: He actually bought old guns at pawnshops or junk stores, carved notches in them (one for each "kill"), and sold them to admirers for a tidy profit. Each time, he swore it was the authentic gun he'd used in Dodge City.

FOR SALE: An Intellectual Image
In 1961 an article in *Time* magazine helped convince Americans that they'd elected an exceptionally bright man as president. It reported that JFK had taken a course in something called "speed-reading" and could zip through an amazing 1,200 words a minute. It became common knowledge—and part of his mystique—that he could read a whole book in one sitting.

The Truth: The number was concocted by Kennedy and *Time* reporter Hugh Sidey. First, JFK told Sidey he could read 1,000 words a minute. Upon reflection, however, he decided that number sounded too low. "How about 1,200?" Sidey asked. "Okay," Kennedy replied. And that's what was printed. Actually, JFK never finished the speed-reading course he took and, at best, could read 800 wpm (still a lot, but not as impressive).

FOR SALE: A Folksy White House Tradition
It was a Yuletide tradition during the Reagan presidency: Gathering with reporters, the Great Communicator would ceremoniously light the National Christmas Tree on the Mall in Washington, D.C., by pushing a button from inside the White House.

What do French and African marigolds have in common? They both come from North America.

The Truth: The button wasn't connected to anything—a Park Service employee actually lit the tree. The press found out by accident in 1989, when President Bush went to the tree site and lit it in person. Bush's press secretary let it slip that, unlike the Reagan years, "that was the real thing." Cornered, he admitted that Reagan's button was a prop. "Then came the follow-up question," the *Washington Post* reported: "Were all the other buttons disconnected, too?"

FOR SALE: Ultimate Weirdness

In the 1980s, a number of strange stories about pop singer Michael Jackson were reported by the media—especially by the tabloids. The press reported, for example, that Jackson:

- had bought an oxygen chamber and was sleeping in it. The reason: he wanted to live to be 100.
- had offered to buy the remains of John Merrick, the "Elephant Man," for $500,000. (*Playboy* magazine jokingly responded that "descendants of the Elephant Man have offered $100,000 for the remains of Michael Jackson's nose.")
- was so obsessed with his chimp, Bubbles, that he was learning "monkey language" to communicate with him.

Even more than his music, the constant stream of reports on Jackson's weirdnesses made him a pervasive presence in pop culture. Everyone talked about him.

The Truth: The stories were all false—concocted, it turns out, by Jackson himself. According to one report, Jackson had "learned early how little truth means when seeking publicity" back when he was in the Jackson 5. In private, he even "began reading biographies of hokum-master P. T. Barnum for ideas."

*   *   *

PROCEED WITH CAUTION

- A black widow's poison is 15 times more powerful than rattlesnake venom.
- Black widows like warm, dark places, and in pre-indoor plumbing days, were "fond of hiding in outhouses, where they often spin webs across toilet seats."

It takes 720 peanuts to make a pound of peanut butter.

HUH?

Sometimes people combine two clichés that have nothing to do with each other—or just make up new clichés altogether. Well, if the shoe fits, take it to the cleaners.

"I've been up and down so many times that I feel as if I'm in a revolving door."
—**Cher**

"[John McCain] can't have it both ways. He can't take the high horse and then claim the low road."
—**George W. Bush**

"A zebra does not change its spots."
—**Al Gore**

"If you let that sort of thing go on, your bread and butter will be cut right out from under your feet."
—**Ernest Bevin, former British foreign minister**

"It's like an Alcatraz around my neck."
—**Thomas Menino, Boston mayor, on the shortage of parking spaces in his city**

"This isn't a man who is leaving with his head between his legs."
—**Dan Quayle, commenting on Chief of Staff John Sununu's resignation**

"That's just the tip of the ice cube."
—**Neil Hamilton, BBC**

"Mr. Milosevic has to be careful. The calendar is ticking."
—**Richard Haas, NBC News**

"Well, that was sure a cliff-dweller."
—**Wes Westrum, baseball coach, about a close game**

"We don't want to skim the cream off the crop here."
—**Gib Lewis, speaker of the Texas House**

"If you don't like the heat in the dressing room, get out of the kitchen."
—**Terry Venables**

"No one wants to say the sky is falling, but in this instance, I am afraid the emperor has no clothes. Despite Herculean efforts by the Council and Council staff, we are still only dealing with the tip of the iceberg."
—**Charles Millard, NYC councilman**

"If you don't know where you are going, you might wind up someplace else." —**Yogi Berra**

ROCKS ON THE GO

*They say that the desert can play tricks on you. If that's the case,
then California's Death Valley is the trickiest of them all.*

MOVE ON OVER
While traveling through the hot California desert in
1915, a mining prospector named Joseph Crook made a
startling discovery: Some rocks had trails in the hardened mud
behind them—as if they had slid across the desert floor all by
themselves. That portion of desert is now known as Racetrack
Playa in northwestern Death Valley National Park, and curious
people travel from great distances to witness one of nature's most
puzzling mysteries: the moving rocks of Death Valley.

HAPPY TRAILS

These otherwise ordinary rocks have been somehow transported
across the flat desert plain, leaving erratic trails. The stones come
in every size and shape, from pebbles to half-ton boulders. The
tracks they leave also vary. Some rocks travel only a few feet;
other trails go on for hundreds of yards. New tracks appear all the
time, with some of them crossing and looping, even doubling
back on themselves. Many rocks carve zigzag paths along the
ground, and some have even made complete circles. But there are
no footprints or tire tracks, nothing to reveal what force pushed
the rocks.

WEIRD SCIENCE

Some people contend that aliens are to blame, but geologists
have offered several theories, most of them having to do with
wind, rain, and even ice. But no one's ever come up with the
definitive explanation. Even recent GPS studies of the rocks
failed to pin down exactly why they move. The fact of the matter
is that Death Valley is the deepest hole in the Western Hemisphere and one of the warmest places on earth—and a literal
"hotbed" of odd geological phenomena. All scientists know for
sure is that the rocks do move—a lot. But to this day, no one has
ever seen one in motion.

George Washington took the oath of office as first president at Federal Hall in Manhattan.

HOW MOSQUITOES CHANGED HISTORY

From Uncle John's Bathroom Reader Plunges Into History, *here's the irritating story of how mosquitoes have been manipulating the course of human history since its very beginnings.*

1,600,000 B.C. Africa—Our ancestors take their first upright steps. Thanks to mosquitoes, they are already infected with malaria.

500 B.C. India—Brahmin priest Susruta deduces that mosquitoes are responsible for the spread of malaria. No one pays any attention for the next 2,400 years.

323 B.C. Babylon—Alexander the Great is felled by a mosquito and dies from malaria at the age of 33. His dream of a united Greek empire collapses within a few years, and widespread malarial infection contributes to the decline of Greek civilization.

A.D. 410 Rome—Marauding Visigoths finish off the Roman Empire, which was already weakened by malaria-spreading mosquito swarms in the low-lying areas surrounding the capital. Shortly afterward the conquest, Alaric, leader of the Visigoths, also dies of Malaria.

1593 Africa—Mosquitoes spread yellow fever and malaria to their relatives in the New World via the slave trade, setting the stage for epidemics that would decimate both colonial and aboriginal populations.

1658 England—Bitten by a mosquito, Oliver Cromwell dies of malaria, paving the way for the return of the British monarchy.

1690 Barbados—Mosquitoes spread yellow fever to halt a British expedition en route to attack the French in Canada.

1802 New Orleans—Napoleon sends troops to reinforce France's claim to Louisiana and put down a slave rebellion in Haiti. Of the 33,000 soldiers, 29,000 are killed by mosquito-borne yellow fever. Louisiana becomes part of the U.S.; Haiti becomes independent.

Paul McCartney wrote "When I'm 64" when he was 15.

1902 Stockholm—British army surgeon Dr. Ronald Ross receives the Nobel Prize for establishing the link between mosquito bites and malaria.

1905 Panama—Mosquitoes almost succeed in halting construction of the Panama Canal, as panicked workers flee a yellow fever epidemic.

1939 Colorado—DDT is tested and found to control mosquitoes and other insects. Mosquitoes eventually develop resistance to the chemical; humans and wildlife don't.

1942 Dutch East Indies—Japanese troops seize the islands that provide most of the world's quinine, the only reliable malaria medicine at the time, hoping mosquitoes will become their allies in fending off Allied forces. Nearly half a million U.S. troops in the East are hospitalized with malaria between 1942 and 1945.

1965–1975 Vietnam—Mosquitoes infect as many as 53 U.S. soldiers per thousand with malaria every day.

1995 Geneva—The World Health Organization (WHO) declares mosquito-born dengue fever a "world epidemic," while deaths from malaria rise to 2.5–3 million a year.

*   *   *

MORE BAD BUZZ

Besides malaria, dengue fever, and yellow fever, mosquitoes have often been in the news for a carrying a whole host of new and deadly blood-borne diseases.

Until 1999, West Nile virus, originating from the Nile River valley in Africa, had not previously been documented in the Western Hemisphere. The virus causes encephalitis, an inflammation of the brain, and can be transmitted by mosquitoes. West Nile was found in "overwintering" mosquitoes in the New York City area in early 2000, a sign that the virus was permanently established in the United States In 2000, 21 cases of the illness were reported, including two deaths in the New York City area.

By 2003, West Nile virus had spread to 45 states.

Monday is the only day of the week that has an anagram: dynamo.

GRANNY DUMPING

How do doctors, nurses, and other hospital workers deal with the stress of being exposed to illness and death on a daily basis? They come up with irreverent, occasionally morbid—and very funny—terms for what goes on in the hospital every day.

Blood Suckers: People who take blood samples, e.g., nurses or laboratory technicians

Gassers: Anesthetists

Rear Admiral: Proctologist

AGA: Acute Gravity Attack —the patient fell over

AGMI: Ain't Gonna Make It

Coffin Dodger: A patient the hospital staff thought was going to die, but didn't

Gone Camping: A patient in an oxygen tent

Shotgunning: Ordering lots of tests, in the hope that one of them will identify what is wrong with a patient

GPO: Good For Parts Only

D&D: Divorced and Desperate; someone who isn't sick but comes to the hospital because they need attention

CTD: Circling the drain, or close to death

Rule of Five: If more than five of the patient's orifices have tubes running out of them, they're CTD.

UBI: Unexplained Beer Injury

Pop Drop/Granny Dumping: Checking an elderly relative into an emergency room, just so you can go on vacation without them

ECU: "Eternal Care Unit" (deceased), as in: "He's gone to the ECU."

DBI: Dirt Bag Index—a mathematical formula: the number of a patient's tattoos times the number of missing teeth equals the number of days since they last bathed.

VIP: Very Intoxicated Person

Hand Them a Bible So They Can Study for the Final: They're going to die.

UNIVAC: Unusually Nasty Infection; Vultures Are Circling

Eating In: Feeding by way of an intravenous tube

GTTL: Gone To The Light (deceased)

Silver Bracelet Award: A patient brought in wearing handcuffs

---

Bathroom fact: The average water temperature for showers in the U.S. is 105°F.

THE BIRTH OF POST-ITS

Post-It Notes now seem like a logical and obvious product. In fact, you're probably so used to seeing Post-Its around your house or office that sometimes it's hard to imagine there was a time when they didn't exist. Actually, they began as a mistake, and almost didn't make it into the marketplace.

STICKIES

In 1964 a 3-M chemist named Spencer Silver was experimenting with a new adhesive. Out of curiosity, he added too much of a "reactant" chemical…and got a totally unexpected result: a milky white liquid that turned crystal-clear under pressure. He characterized it as "tacky" but not "aggressively adhesive."

He also found that it was "narcissistic"—i.e., it tended to stick to itself more than anything else. If you put it on one surface and stuck a piece of paper on it, either all or none of the adhesive would come off when you peeled off the paper.

Silver was intrigued with the stuff, but couldn't get his superiors at 3-M excited. So he wandered the hallways of the company giving demonstrations and presentations. He nearly had to beg 3-M to patent it.

Silver was sure there was a use for his adhesive—he just didn't know what it was. "Sometimes I was so angry because this new thing was so obviously unique," he says. "I'd tell myself, 'Why can't you think of a product? It's your job!'"

EUREKA

Finally, in 1974, someone came up with a problem to match Silver's solution. Every Sunday, Arthur Fry, another 3-M chemist, directed the choir in his church. He always marked songs in the hymnal with little scraps of paper. But one Sunday, while signaling the choir to stand, he fumbled his hymnal and all the bookmarks fell to the floor. As he frantically tried to find his place, he thought, "If only there was a way to get them to stick to the page." That's when he remembered seeing Silver's "now-it-sticks, now-it-doesn't" demonstration years earlier, And while the choir sang, he started thinking of situations where semi-sticky paper might be helpful.

The next morning, Fry rushed to work and tracked down some of Silver's adhesive. He found there were still problems to work out—like how to make sure the adhesive didn't come off on the document—and he worked with company chemists to solve them. Fry even created a machine in his basement that would make manufacturing easier by applying the adhesive in a continuous roll. When he was done, he found that the machine was bigger than his basement doorway...and it couldn't be disassembled without ruining it. So he knocked out a part of his basement wall.

NOT YET

Fry and his team began producing prototype Post-Its. As a form of informal marketing research, they distributed the sticky notes to offices around the building. They were a hit. "Once you start using them," one enthusiastic co-worker told him, "you can't stop."

Despite in-house success, the 3-M marketing department didn't believe Post-Its would sell. They kept asking: "Why would anybody buy this 'glorified scratch paper' for a dollar a package?" Their lack of enthusiasm showed up in test-marketing. It failed miserably.

STUCK ON YOU

Fry's boss couldn't believe that they wouldn't succeed if marketed properly. After all, they were using thousands of them at 3-M. The company decided to try a one-shot test-market blitz in Boise, Idaho. Their sales reps blanketed Boise with free samples and order forms. The result: a 90% reorder response from the companies that received samples—more than twice the 40% the company considered a success.

Post-Its went into full national distribution in 1980 and caught on across America. They've since become an international hit as well.

"The Post-It was a product that met an unperceived need," says Fry. "If you had asked somebody what they needed, they might have said a better paper clip. But give them a Post-It Note, and they immediately know what to do with it."

"Too bad 90% of the politicians give the other 10% a bad reputation." —Henry Kissinger

GRIDIRON FACTS

Uncle John's going long to bring you this page of football facts. Ready? Hut! Hut! Hike!

• The football huddle was invented at a university for the deaf...to keep the opposing team from seeing their hand signs.

• It takes 3,000 cows to supply the NFL with enough leather for a year's supply of footballs.

• John Heisman (of trophy fame) coined the word "hike" and split football games into four quarters.

• Top ticket price to the first Super Bowl, in 1967: $12. Top price in 2005: $500.

• Most successful high school football team in history: De La Salle Spartans of Concord, California. After more than 10 years and 151 wins, they lost to Washington's Bellevue Wolverines in September 2004.

• NFL great Vince Lombardi coined the phrase "game plan."

• Football has more rules than any other American sport.

• In 1888 Yale football coach Walter Camp fell ill. His wife coached for the entire season.

• Deion Sanders is the only man to play in the World Series and the Super Bowl.

• There is a 100 percent injury rate among professional football players.

• In the NFL, the host team must have 26 footballs inflated and ready for use.

• The L.A. Rams were the first football team to have emblems on their helmets.

• Nine of the 15 highest-rated television shows in history have been NFL championship games.

• So few Heisman Trophy winners have made it into the Pro Football Hall of Fame—only 8 (including O. J. Simpson)—that the prize has been called "the kiss of death" for college players.

THE BODY FARM

Ahh, Tennessee—home to Dollywood, Graceland, the Grand Ole Opry...and the world's creepiest research facility.

PUTRIFIED FOREST

The Anthropological Research Facility (ARF) of the University of Tennessee lies on three landscaped acres behind the UT Medical Center parking lot. Aside from the razor-wire fence, it looks like a lovely wooded park, complete with people lying on their backs enjoying a pleasant day in the sun. That is, until you smell the foul odor. A second glance tells you these sunbathers are not all on their backs: some are face down in the leaves; some are waist deep in the dirt. Others are encased in concrete or wrapped in plastic garbage bags or locked in car trunks. None of them seems to be enjoying anything. Why? They're all cadavers, planted by scientists from the University of Tennessee for the sole purpose of studying the decomposition of the human body.

Nicknamed "the Body Farm" by the FBI, this research facility develops and provides medical expertise to law enforcement professionals and medical examiners. It helps them pinpoint the exact time of death of a body—a critical part of any criminal investigation involving a cadaver.

DR. DEATH

ARF (or "BARF," as local critics call it) was founded in 1971 by forensic anthropologist Dr. William Bass. He had been asked to guess the age of a skeleton dug up on a piece of property once owned by a Confederate Army colonel named William Shy. Bass had examined some Civil War–era remains before, but they were mostly dust. Since this skeleton still had pieces of flesh attached to it, his analysis was able to determine that the person was a white male between 24 and 28 years old, who'd been dead about a year. Bass was correct about the race, gender, and age, but way off on the time of death. The skeleton, it turned out, belonged to William Shy himself, who was buried in 1864—107 years earlier. "I realized," Bass later recalled, "there was something here about decomposition we didn't know." He started the facility to help fill in the gaps.

Isuzu means "50 bells" in Japanese.

RIGOR MORTIS 101

The first corpses Bass and his team studied were bodies that had gone unclaimed at the morgue. At first they had four to five cadavers a year. Today all cadavers are donated by personal request and there's a waiting list. ARF researchers currently work with around 45 bodies a year.

"We go through the FBI reports and come up with the most common way a perpetrator will bury someone, and use these as our models," says Dr. Arpad Vass, a senior researcher at the facility. ARF scientists and graduate students then study the rate of *algor mortis*—the cooling of the body. The temperature of a corpse drops approximately 1°F per hour until it matches the temperature of the air around it—a useful clue for determining time of death. *Rigor mortis*—the stiffening of the body—generally starts a few hours after death and moves through the body, disappearing 48 hours later. If a body has been dead longer than three days, they look for other clues: What bugs have arrived to help with the decomposition? How old are the fly larvae? Are there beetles?

This process of *insect succession* (which species of insect feed on a decaying corpse, and in what order), as well as the effects of weather and climate on decomposition, are all closely monitored and measured. The scientists use this data to develop methods and instruments that accurately establish time of death. This expertise is shared with law enforcement agencies all over the world.

WHAT'S THAT SMELL?

Dr. Vass's research has shown that a body emits 450 chemicals at different stages of its decay. Each stage has a unique "bouquet," which Vass has given names such as *putrescine* and *cadaverine*. Using the same aroma scan technology used in the food and wine industry, one of his students is developing a handheld electronic "nose" for the FBI that will sniff out the time of death by identifying the presence of these different chemicals in a corpse.

Synthetic putrescine and cadaverine are now used to train "human remains dogs" (not to be confused with police dogs who search for escaped criminals). These dogs respond to the specific scent of death they've been trained to recognize, and they do it with amazing accuracy: They can tell their trainers whether a lake is concealing a corpse by sniffing the water's surface for minute bubbles of gas seeping from a rotting carcass underwater, and they can show police exactly where to dive to retrieve the body. The dogs can detect the faintest scent of a dead body on the ground, even if it was removed from the spot a year earlier.

Another researcher at ARF, Dr. Richard Jantz, has developed a computer program that can determine the gender, race, and height of an unknown skeleton. This software has been invaluable in helping forensic teams identify the victims of ethnic cleansing in Bosnia, Rwanda, and other war crime sites.

BREAKING IT DOWN

Warning: the following may require a strong stomach.

• Rigor mortis sets in just after death. The body stiffens, first at the jaws and neck. After 48 hours, the corpse relaxes and muscles sag.

• During the first 24 hours, the body cools at a rate of about 1°F per hour until it matches the temperature of the air around it. This is called *algor mortis*. Next, blood settles in the part of the body closest to the ground, turning the rest of the body pale.

• After two to three days, *putrefaction* is underway. The skin turns green and the body's enzymes start to eat through cell walls and the liquid inside leaks out. At this stage, fly larvae, or maggots, invade and start to eat the corpse's body fat. The maggots carry with them bacteria that settle in the abdomen, lungs, and skin.

• The bacteria feed on the liquid and release sulfur gas as a waste product. With nowhere to go, the gas causes the corpse to bloat and swell (and sometimes burst). By the end of the third day, the skin changes from green to purple to black. This stage is called *autolysis*, which means "self-digestion."

• Next is *skin slip*. As cells continue to break down, liquid continues to leak. After about a week, it builds up between layers of skin and loosens it, causing skin to start to peel off in large chunks.

• After two weeks, the fluid leaks from the nose and mouth. After three weeks, teeth and nails loosen; internal organs start to rupture.

• After about a month, the bacteria and enzymes have liquefied all body tissue until the corpse dissolves and sinks into the ground, leaving only the skeletal remains and what's called a *volatile fatty acid stain*. Sweet dreams...

Handyman hint: Keeping mothballs in your tool chest will help prevent rust.

PLITZ-PLATZ I WAS TAKING A BATH

As kids, we were all told that trains go "choo-choo" and cars go "beep beep." Check out the sounds they make in other languages.

AAH-CHOO!
Portuguese: Ah-chim!
German: Hat-chee!
Greek: Ap tsou!
Japanese: Hakshon!
Italian: Ekchee!

SPLASH!
Hindi: Dham!
Russian: Plyukh!
Danish: Plump!
Spanish: Chof!
Greek: Plitz-platz!

EENY-MEENY-MINY-MO
Arabic: Hadi-badi
Italian: Ambaraba chichicoco
Japanese: Hee-foo-mee-yo
Swedish: Ol-uh dol-uh doff
Polish: Ele mele dudki

CHOO-CHOO!
Chinese: Hong-lung, hong-lung
Danish: Fut fut!
Japanese: Shuppo-shuppo!
Swahili: Chuku-chuku!
Greek: Tsaf-tsouf!

ZZZZZZ...
Arabic: Kh-kh-kh...
Chinese: Hulu...
Italian: Ronf-ronf...
Japanese: Gah-gah...

UPSY-DAISY!
Arabic: Hop-pa!
Italian: Opp-la!
Japanese: Yoisho!
Russian: Nu davai!
Danish: Opse-dasse!

KITCHY-KITCHY-KOO!
Chinese: Gujee!
French: Gheely-gheely!
Greek: Ticki-ticki-ticki!
Swedish: Kille kille kille!

UH-OH!
Chinese: Zao le!
Italian: Ay-may!
Japanese: Ah-ah!
Swahili: Wee!
Swedish: Oy-oy!

BEEP BEEP!
Chinese: Dooo dooo!
Hindi: Pon-pon!
Spanish: Mock mock!
French: Puet puet!
Japanese: Boo boo!

CHUGALUG!
Arabic: Gur-gur-gur!
Hindi: Gat-gat!
Hebrew: Gloog gloog!
Russian: Bool-bool!
Chinese: Goo-doo, goo-doo!

American Indians spoke more than 133 different languages.

THAT '70s BATHROOM

Step into Uncle John's Groovy Time Machine and we'll travel back to the 1970s, when no bathroom was complete without...

RUBBER DUCKIES. After muppets Bert and Ernie first sang the song "Rubber Duckie" on *Sesame Street* in 1970 the little, yellow ducks became a bathroom fixture.

AQUA VELVA. "There's something about an Aqua Velva man," said the beautiful blond woman in the commercial, and millions of men believed her.

JOHNSON'S 'NO MORE TEARS' SHAMPOO. It hit the market in 1954, but it wasn't until the '70s that No More Tears became the best-selling American shampoo.

AN EARTH TONE BATHROOM SUITE. "Earth tones" were in. Green wasn't green—it was *avocado green*. Yellow wasn't yellow—it was *harvest gold*. Brown wasn't brown—it was *chocolate*. By today's standards, they're hard to look at (especially in combinations), but were all the rage in the 1970s.

FLOWER-SHAPED NON-SLIP BATH DECALS. The last remnants of the 1960s Flower Power fad ended up keeping people safe when getting in and out of the tub.

THE SHOWER MASSAGE. German company Hansgrohe introduced the first hand-held, adjustable showerhead, the *Selecta*, in 1968. Soon they were everywhere. In 1974 Teledyne came out with probably the most famous one, The Original Shower Massage.

A FUZZY TOILET SEAT COVER. Basically shag carpets on top of the toilet seat covers, they had one major drawback: when guys used the toilet, the thick cover would make the seat fall down...mid-stream, so to speak.

TIDY BOWL. In the 1970s, blue toilet water was clean toilet water. And then there was the Tidy Bowl Man, that little guy in the captain's suit in the boat inside the toilet tank.

AND TO READ? Sadly, there were no good books made especially for the bathroom...yet.

Bee stings are acidic, wasp stings are alkaline.

ANIMALS IN THE NEWS

Bad news got you down? Take a break from humanity.

HAIR CLUB FOR HEIFERS

Three Ohio livestock exhibitors were disqualified from the state fair for gluing hairpieces onto their prize-winning Holstein cows (to make their backs appear straighter). One judge got suspicious of the cows' appearance and ran his hand across their backs as they were leaving the show ring. When the hair came off in gluey clumps, officials disqualified Scott Long, Kreg Krebs, and Ken Krebs, and withheld the $335 prize. Using artificial enhancers is "unethical, and unfair to competitors who play by the rules," says Melanie Witt, an official with the Ohio Department of Agriculture.

RUN AWAY!

"Firemen in the eastern Ukrainian city of Donetsk fled a burning sauna in panic after mistaking a three-meter boa constrictor for a fire hose, the Itar-Tass news agency reported. The reptile, named Yasha by its owner, had succumbed to smoke and lost consciousness on the floor before the emergency workers arrived to tackle the blaze. A member of the startled fire crew eventually heeded pleas by the sauna staff to save the snake and dragged it to safety."

—*Mail & Guardian* (U.K.)

CAT-ASTROPHE

Bill Jenness got in trouble with the city of Whitman, Massachusetts, because of his cat—its poop was radioactive. The 11-year-old cat, Mitzi, was being treated for hyperthyroidism with radioiodine, which can make cats radioactive for weeks. The vet had warned Jenness that he had to limit his snuggling time with Mitzi, had to keep the cat away from children, and had to use gloves when flushing the cat's litter. But Jenness was afraid the litter would clog his septic system, so he put it in the garbage instead. After alarms at the local incinerator detected the radioactivity, workers found Mr. Jenness' mail nearby, and the city fined him $2,800 to clean up the radioactive scat.

WHALE OF A VACATION

In 2003 the Johnson family of Coventry, England, took a 10-day sailing vacation in Australia. But their trip came to a sudden end when a 10-ton humpback whale leapt out of the water and onto their 40-foot sailboat, damaging the rigging and pulling down the mast. "It's amazing no one was hurt or killed," 61-year-old Trevor Johnson told reporters. Total cost of chartering the boat: $238,000. (No word on whether the Johnsons got a refund.)

ELECTRIC COILS

On May 19, 2004, the entire nation of Honduras was plunged into darkness when a generator at the country's biggest hydroelectric plant failed. What caused a whole country to go dark? A boa constrictor slithered into a sensitive area of the power plant. The unlucky snake was electrocuted, and the resulting short circuit caused the emergency systems to shut down the entire plant, which shut down the country's electricity for about 15 minutes.

IT'S A SMELL WORLD

In an average month, trains operated by the West Japan Railway Company strike and kill 10 deer that wander onto railroad tracks. In 2003 the railroad decided to test a new kind of deer repellent on the rails—lion poop. Lions and deer are natural enemies, the thinking went, so the smell of the predator would keep the deer away. In August 2003, the railroad scrapped the experiment, not because it didn't work, but because it worked *too* well—the poop kept the deer away, but it smelled so bad that it kept everything else away too, including local residents. "The track really did stink," says railroad spokesperson Toshihiko Iwata. "We're experimenting with more environmentally friendly methods now."

MOOVY, BABY

In 2006 a woman in Lobez, Poland, was charged with "cultivating a narcotic" when police found marijuana plants on her property. The 55-year-old farmer defended herself by saying that it wasn't for humans—she was feeding the plants to her cow, which had been "skittish and unruly." She said that ever since she started feeding the cow the marijuana, it had been "calm as a lamb." She faces up to three years in jail.

BANKER FOR THE LITTLE GUY

A. P. Giannini was the first to challenge the unwritten rule that banks should only lend money to people who didn't need it.

TOUGH LESSON

Amadeo Pietro Giannini learned the value of a dollar the hard way: In 1877, when he was only seven years old, he saw his father killed in a fight with another man over exactly that amount—one dollar. The elder Giannini had been a farmer in California; he and his wife were both Italian immigrants. After his father's death, A. P.'s mother married Lorenzo Scatena, a local businessman who had recently entered the produce business. A. P. quit school at 14 to help his stepfather, who was so impressed by his stepson that he made him a partner in the business.

EARLY RETIREMENT

Giannini helped build his stepfather's produce business, and his reputation, by being fair and honest. And his work paid off—he did so well that he was able to retire at 31 by selling his half of the business to his employees. But his retirement didn't last long. When a group of San Francisco businessmen asked him to serve on the board of a small savings and loan located in the North Beach district—the heart of the Italian-American community—Giannini accepted.

In those days, most banks only loaned money to large businesses and people who were already wealthy. When Giannini couldn't convince the other members of the board to extend credit to hard-working poor people, he decided to start his own bank. So he lined up some investors and started what he called "The Bank of Italy" in a converted saloon. He even kept one of the bartenders on as an assistant teller.

The Bank of Italy was the first to offer home mortgages, auto loans, and installment credit. Giannini built his business by reaching out to local immigrants, even going door to door to explain his services to people who didn't know anything at all about banks.

Australian outlaw Ned Kelly wore a homemade suit of armor.

THINKING AHEAD

Just after the 1906 San Francisco earthquake, the fire that swept the city was getting a little too close to his bank, so Giannini borrowed a wagon, collected all his gold, currency, and records, and brought it all to his home. A few days later, while the other banks in town were still closed, he set up shop amid the rubble with a plank stretched across a couple of beer barrels serving as his desk. The loans he extended—in many cases based on little more than a handshake—helped rebuild the city.

That kind of foresight became one of Giannini's trademarks. Another was his willingness to work harder and longer than his competitors. Once, when he was riding his horse out of town to visit a farmer to close a deal, he saw another banker behind him on his way to the same farmer's house. Giannini took a shortcut, raced ahead, dismounted his horse, swam across a small pond, and ran the rest of the way to the farmhouse to get his contract signed before the other man arrived.

BRANCHING OUT

Because so many of his customers had to travel long distances to do business with him, Giannini decided to open a branch of his bank in San Jose in 1909. Then he started buying up other banks and opening new ones all over California and, eventually, in other major American cities.

In 1928 he purchased the Bank of America, an old and respected institution in New York City, and consolidated all of his banks under that name. He continued to open branches all over the U.S., making Bank of America the first nationwide bank. By 1945, it was the largest in the country.

TWICE AS NICE

Giannini was a social liberal in a conservative business, but most of his innovations, like loans to working people and installment payments, were sound business decisions that revolutionized the banking business and generated substantial profits for his shareholders. He also helped large and small businesses that were down on their luck or just getting started. His financial backing of the California wine and movie industries was instrumental in their growth. He created a motion-picture loan division and helped

Eugene O'Neill was expelled from Princeton for breaking a window in the president's office.

Charlie Chaplin, Douglas Fairbanks, D. W. Griffith, and Mary Pickford start United Artists. Giannini loaned Walt Disney $2 million when Disney went over budget on *Snow White*. The banker also is remembered for many visionary projects, including the financing of the construction of the Golden Gate Bridge.

Behind the scenes, he was also popular for his generosity to his employees. The profit-sharing and stock ownership plans he instituted for them cemented their loyalty, making the business even more successful.

MODEST MEANS

The man who tried to retire at 31 was still at the helm when he died in 1949, at the age of 79. His estate was valued at a relatively modest $500,000, because although he could have amassed a huge fortune in his lifetime, he was never interested in accumulating wealth and often didn't take a salary. He used most of the money he made to start foundations that funded scholarships and supported medical and agricultural research.

In 1999 *Time* magazine named Giannini one of the most important 100 persons of the 20th century—the only banker on the list.

"It's no use to decide what's going to happen unless you have the courage of your convictions. Many a brilliant idea has been lost because the man who dreamed it lacked the spunk or the spine to put it across"

—A. P. Giannini

*   *   *

BLIND JUSTICE

"Judge Claudia Jordan caused panic in her court in Denver when she passed a note to her clerk that read: 'Blind on the right side. May be falling. Please call someone.' The clerk rang for help. Informed that paramedics were on the way, the judge pointed to the sagging Venetian blinds on the right side of the room. 'I wanted someone from maintenance,' she said."

—*The Fortean Times*

The Mall of America in Bloomington, Minnesota, is the size of 78 football fields.

"I SPY"...AT
THE MOVIES

You probably know the kids' game "I spy, with my little eye..."
Well, moviemakers have been playing that game with each other
(and their actors) for years. Here are some in-jokes and gags
you can look for the next time you watch these films.

SCREAM (1996)
I Spy... Wes Craven, the film's director
Where to Find Him: He's the school janitor, wearing a
Freddy Krueger sweater from his *Nightmare on Elm Street* movie.

THE LOST WORLD: JURASSIC PARK (1997)
I Spy... Ads for some improbable new movies: *King Lear*, starring
Arnold Schwarzenegger; *Jach and the Behnstacks*, starring Robin
Williams; and *Tsunami Surprise*, with Tom Hanks's head attached
to a surfer's body
Where to Find Them: In the window of a video store.

THE ROCKY HORROR PICTURE SHOW (1975)
I Spy... Easter eggs
Where to Find Them: Various places during the movie. For
example, one is under Frank's throne, one is in a light fixture in
the main room, and you can see one when the group goes into an
elevator to the lab. What are they doing there? The film crew had
an Easter egg hunt on the set, but didn't find all the eggs...so they
show up in the film.

BACK TO THE FUTURE (1985)
I Spy... A nod to *The Rocky and Bullwinkle Show*
Where to Find It: The scene in which Marty (Michael J. Fox)
crashes into the farmer's barn. The farmer's name is Peabody; his
son is Sherman. Peabody and Sherman were the brilliant time-
traveling dog and his boy in the Jay Ward cartoon show.

America's oldest candy brand: NECCO wafers, sold since 1847.

THE RETURN OF THE KING (2003)

I Spy... Director Peter Jackson's arm

Where to Find It: In the tunnel of Shelob, when Sam's (Sean Astin) arm enters the frame and points the sword at the big spider, it's not Astin's arm, it's Jackson's.

HALLOWEEN (1978)

I Spy... William Shatner

Where to Find Him: On the psycho's face. The budget was so small, filmmakers couldn't afford to make a mask. So they bought a Captain Kirk mask, painted it white, and teased out the hair.

WHEN HARRY MET SALLY... (1989)

I Spy... Estelle Reiner, director Rob Reiner's mother

Where to Find Her: She's the woman who tells the waiter: "I'll have what she's having," when Meg Ryan fakes an orgasm in a restaurant.

FIGHT CLUB (1999)

I Spy...Starbucks coffee cups

Where to Find Them: In every shot, according to director David Fincher, who put the cups there to illustrate the pervasiveness of corporations in our society. "I don't have anything against Starbucks, per se," he says, "but do we need three on every corner?"

THE SHAWSHANK REDEMPTION (1994)

I Spy... A photograph of Morgan Freeman's son

Where to Find It: The parole papers that repeatedly receive a rejected stamp show a picture of Red (Morgan Freeman) when he was a young man. Morgan's son Alfonzo was used for the shot.

RESERVOIR DOGS (1992)

I Spy... A real-life act of revenge

Where to Find It: The scene in which actor Tim Roth shoots a woman. The actress was his dialogue coach...who had apparently made life difficult for him during filming. He insisted that she be cast in the role so he could "shoot" her.

Gail Borden (inventor of condensed milk) is buried beneath a headstone shaped like a milk can.

KURT'S QUOTES

Here are some thoughts from a man who dropped out of college because his professor told him his stories weren't any good. So what did Kurt Vonnegut do? He went on to become one of the 20th century's most celebrated novelists.

"I want to stay as close to the edge as I can without going over. Out on the edge you see all kinds of things you can't see from the center."

"People have to talk about something just to keep their voiceboxes in working order in case there's ever anything really meaningful to say."

"Just because some of us can read and write and do a little math, that doesn't mean we deserve to conquer the universe."

"I'd rather have written one episode of *Cheers* than anything I've written."

"We're terrible animals. I think that the Earth's immune system is trying to get rid of us, as well it should."

"I was taught that the human brain was the crowning glory of evolution so far, but I think it's a very poor scheme for survival."

"True terror is to wake up one morning and discover that your high school class is running the country."

"If you really want to disappoint your parents, and don't have the heart to be gay, go into the arts."

"Life is no way to treat an animal, not even a mouse."

"If you can do a half-assed job of anything, you're a one-eyed man in a kingdom of the blind."

"I still believe that peace and happiness can be worked out some way. I am a fool."

"Beware of the man who works hard to learn something, learns it, and finds himself no wiser than before."

"Laughter and tears are both responses to frustration and exhaustion. I myself prefer to laugh, since there is less cleaning up to do afterward."

"We are here on Earth to fart around. Don't let anybody tell you different." —Kurt Vonnegut

COMPUTER VIRUSES

Ever since computers first became affordable in the early 1980s, viruses have been a threat. They have cost individuals, companies, and governments billions in software, security, data replacement, and lost productivity. Here are some of the most infamous viruses to date.

ELK CLONER (1981)

Richard Skrenta, a 15-year-old high school freshman, gave his friends some disks of computer games. But there was a catch: the disks could only be used 49 times. On the 50th attempt, the screen went blank and this poem appeared:

It will get on all your disks. It will infiltrate your chips
Yes it's Cloner!
It will stick to you like glue. It will modify RAM too
Send in the Cloner!

What was intended as a prank turned out to be the first computer virus. Elk Cloner would hide in the computer's memory and then attach itself to the next disk inserted in the computer. Any other computer using *that* disk would then get infected in turn.

Hundreds of computers were damaged, and Elk Cloner hung around for years. But Skrenta was never punished—viruses were so new that they were not yet perceived as the crimes they are today.

MICHELANGELO (1992)

Technicians in New Zealand found this virus on a computer in late 1991, but there was no damage—the virus wasn't programmed to cause any destruction until the following March 6, the anniversary of Michelangelo's birthday. On that date it would make it look like the entire computer had been erased.

Only a handful of computers had the Michelangelo virus until January 1992, when a computer manufacturer accidentally shipped 500 infected PCs and another unwittingly distributed 900 infected floppy disks. Computer experts still didn't think it would spread very far, but then Reuters ran a story predicting that 25% of all American computers would be affected. Where'd they get that number? From anti-virus software manufacturers, who claimed Michelangelo would strike 20 million computers. When Doomsday

---

Frogs have no ribs.

arrived, though, the virus damaged only about 10,000 computers.

Michelangelo is still floating in cyberspace, yet despite being programmed to attack computers every March 6, there have been no reports of it doing any harm since 1992. But because of the frenzy it created, anti-virus software is now a billion-dollar industry. And whoever unleashed the virus was never caught.

LOVE BUG (2000)

In 2000, computer users received e-mails with the subject line "ILOVEYOU." When the recipient downloaded the accompanying attachment, the virus attacked the computer and sent itself to every e-mail addresses stored in the computer, starting a volatile chain reaction. Love Bug was first spotted in Asia but quickly spread worldwide. It disabled computers at the White House, the Pentagon, British Parliament, and many European e-mail servers. The damage was estimated at $10 billion.

Who did it? Police tracked down the culprits: Onel de Guzman and Reomel Ramones of the Philippines. But the Philippines had no laws against cyber crime, so despite the damage they caused, Guzman and Ramones went free. (Guzman was actually offered several computer programming jobs after he was cleared.)

The virus is now gone, but its method of distribution still lives: dozens of viruses have spread through e-mail with deceptive subject lines such as "You gotta read this," "Important! Read carefully," and even "How to protect yourself from the ILOVEYOU bug."

CODE RED (2001)

Using Microsoft's Internet server software, Code Red sent itself to e-mail addresses stored in the computers it infected, then flooded the Web with billions of megabytes of gobbledygook. Result: Web sites had text replaced with the phrase "hacked by Chinese."

Code Red's real goal: To infiltrate, flood, and shut down the White House Web site. That didn't happen, but other major sites such as AT&T, Hotmail, and Federal Express all fell prey to it. At its peak, Code Red was infecting 2,000 computers a minute. Total cost of lost data and productivity: $1.2 billion. (It was rumored that the virus was the work of the Chinese government as part of a secret computer hacking war with the United States.) To date, nobody has been arrested for creating or spreading Code Red.

The term "hacker" was coined at MIT in 1961.

BLASTER (2003)

Also known as Lovsan, Blaster wasn't technically a virus, it was a *worm*. A virus damages whatever computer is unlucky enough to accidentally cross its path, but a worm seeks out vulnerable computers and then infects them.

Blaster initially caused more headaches than harm. Once on a computer, it didn't delete information, it messed with the operating system. A message appeared, counting down 60 seconds until the computer would shut down and restart. This on-and-off cycle would go on forever. And if you shut off the computer manually, all data could be lost. But Blaster actually had a second, more devious goal: to shut down Microsoft's Web site. Microsoft fought back, successfully blocking Blaster from its site. Yet despite Microsoft's efforts, 500,000 computers lost data. And despite the offer of a $500,000 reward for information leading to the parties responsible for Blaster, their identities remain a secret.

MORE VIRUSES

PC-Write Trojan (1986). Infected computers while pretending to be a popular word-processing program.

Christmas Worm (1987). Hit IBM mainframes and replicated at a rate of 500,000 times per hour.

AIDS Trojan (1989). Disguised as an AIDS information program, it crippled hard drives then demanded money for the decoder information.

Little Black Book (1990). Synchronized viruses designed to infect AT&T's long distance switching system.

Tequila (1991). Swiss in origin, it was the first virus that could change itself to avoid detection in infected computers.

Chernobyl (1999). Programmed to delete hard drives on April 26, 1999, the 13th anniversary of the Chernobyl nuclear accident.

Melissa (1999). Infected computers via a fake Microsoft Word document sent by e-mail. Caused more than $80 million in damage. Its creator, David Smith, went to jail for 26 months.

Trojan.Xombe (2004). Posing as an official Windows upgrade message, stole personal information stored in computers.

MyDoom (2004). Shut down search engines like Yahoo! and Google.

King George III survived two assassination attempts...in one day.

SIMPLE SOLUTIONS

How often have you seen a clever solution to a difficult problem and said, "That's so obvious—I wish I'd thought of that!" Here are some simple, but brilliant, inventions that could change the world.

MONEYMAKER-PLUS

Problem: How can people irrigate crops in impoverished parts of the world? With electric pumps? Nope—electricity is often nonexistent, and where it is available it's too expensive for poor farmers.

Simple Solution: A foot-powered irrigation pump

Explanation: Approtec, a nonprofit company in Nairobi, Kenya, calls it the MoneyMaker-Plus. Working the pedals like a stair-climbing exercise machine, one person can pull water from a stream, a pond, or a well 20 feet deep, send it to sprinklers, and irrigate up to one and a half acres a day. In underdeveloped countries, such a device can be life-changing. As of 2002, Approtec estimates that 24,000 MoneyMaker-Plus pumps were in use, bringing an average of $1,400 a year more to people who previously earned less than $100 a year. The pumps helped create 16,000 new jobs and generate $30 million a year total in profits and wages. They're made from local materials (creating more jobs), they're easily repaired without special tools, they're lightweight for easy transport (25 pounds), and most importantly, they're affordable—they cost only $38.

ANTI–CELL PHONE SANDWICH

Problem: How can people effectively, cheaply—and legally—stop the ringing of cell phones in designated cell phone–free zones?

Simple Solution: Wall panels that jam cell phone signals

Explanation: Electronic jamming of cell phone transmissions is illegal in the United States, but Hideo Oka and fellow engineers at Japan's Iwate University figured out a way around that—they invented a nonelectronic method. The system consists of a layer of magnetic material (they use nickel zinc ferrite) sandwiched between two thin layers of wood. It looks like 3/8-inch wood pan-

---

Only two books in the Bible are named for women: Ruth and Esther.

eling. The nickel-zinc ferrite interferes with the electromagnetic waves that cell phones rely on. That means that theaters or restaurants or homeowners can use it to build "cell-free" zones. Oka believes he can find a way to manufacture the device with recycled materials, which would make it very affordable. Naturally, the cell phone industry isn't happy—observers say a legal battle is looming.

STAR

Problem: Arsenic in drinking water. Scientists say that naturally occurring contamination of groundwater in some developing countries causes as many as 200,000 deaths a year. How can people without access to high-tech filters or water-treatment plants make their water safe to drink?

Simple Solution: STAR, a patented—and remarkably cheap—filtration system

Explanation: In 2001, Xiaoguang Meng and George Korfiatis, scientists at the Stevens Institute of Technology, successfully tested a system that consisted of two buckets, some sand, and a tea-bag-sized packet of iron-based powder. This filter reduces arsenic levels in well water from 650 parts per billion (deadly) to 10ppb, the level recommended by the World Health Organization. Cost per family: $2 a year.

KENYA CERAMIC JIKO (KCJ)

Problem: In Kenya, most families use small metal charcoal-burning stoves—called *jikos*—for cooking. But they're terribly inefficient. And with the cost of wood and wood-based charcoal skyrocketing, how can people afford to cook for their families?

Simple Solution: The highly efficient Kenya Ceramic Jiko stove

Explanation: The KCJ is a small, hourglass-shaped metal stove with a ceramic lining in its top half. It uses up to 50% less fuel—saving the average family more than $60 a year. The manufacturer, KENGO (Kenya Energy and Environment Organization), has held workshops all over the country, demonstrating how the stoves work and even teaching villagers how to set up shops to make them. (Several women's groups make the ceramic linings.) The KCJ burns cleaner, reducing emissions, and costs only $3.

YODELING THE CLASSICS

*If you think the music your kids listen to is garbage, not so fast, Beethoven.
There's been music of questionable taste since the dawn of the record
industry. These bombs might not be musically entertaining,
but they are fun to read about. Here's a sample of
some of the weirdest albums ever made.*

LOU REED—*METAL MACHINE MUSIC*. In 1975 Reed
released this double LP consisting entirely of guitar feedback
and other ear-piercing electronic noise played back at various speeds. Recorded in his home on a four-track machine, Reed
claims the endless, monotonous noise is an avant-garde symphony.
(*Rolling Stone* called it "the tubular groaning of a galactic refrigerator.") It's rumored that Reed made the album in a hurry to fulfill a
recording contract. He disagrees. "I was serious about it," Reed
later said. "I was also really, really stoned."

JIMMY STURR—*POLKA DISCO*. In the 1970s, most young
people hated polka music, and their polka-loving grandparents
couldn't stand disco. Sturr, a polka musician, tried to unite the
two camps, but as it turns out, polka accordions and thumping
disco bass guitars don't mix very well.

MARY SCHNEIDER—*YODELING THE CLASSICS*.
Nicknamed "Australia's Queen of Yodeling," Schneider performs
well-known pieces of classical music, all yodeled. Rossini's "Barber
of Seville." Yodeled. Beethoven's "Minuet for Piano in G Major."
Yodeled. The "William Tell Overture." Yodeled.

HAVING FUN WITH ELVIS ON STAGE. In his later years,
Elvis Presley peppered his concert performances with all kinds of
odd patter—anecdotes and jokes, and the King going off on
bizarre tangents. His manager, Col. Tom Parker, found a loop-
hole in Presley's RCA Records contract that said *he* could keep
all the profits from any Presley album he released, as long as it
didn't contain Presley *singing*. Result: *Having Fun With Elvis on
Stage*—37 minutes of Presley's stage banter spliced together from

---

If a man with normal vision and a color-blind woman have children...

dozens of different shows. Parker marketed it as a "live" album, but it's really just Presley making wisecracks and comments, including "Look at all these things in my pants here," "I'm the NBC peacock," "Can I get a glass of water?" and "By the time this show is over, I'll have made a complete, total fool of myself." Presley also demonstrates the 11 different ways to pronounce "Memphis."

URBAN RENEWAL. On this tribute album, rappers and R&B singers perform the hits of one of their most beloved influences. Is it James Brown? George Clinton? Marvin Gaye? No—apparently, the real godfather of soul is soft-rock icon Phil Collins. Especially weird are the rapped versions of Collins's hits—Li'l Kim's "In the Air Tonite" and Ol' Dirty Bastard's "Sussudio."

THE TEMPLE CITY KAZOO ORCHESTRA—*SOME KAZOOS*. Pop and classical songs are played by large numbers of people with kazoos. The kazoo playlist includes "Stayin' Alive" by the Bee Gees, Led Zeppelin's "Whole Lotta Love," and "Also Sprach Zarathustra" (the theme from *2001: A Space Odyssey*).

THE ETHEL MERMAN DISCO ALBUM. Broadway star Merman was retired in 1979. Her show tunes and standards like "Everything's Coming Up Roses" weren't popular anymore, but disco was. Merman hated disco, but the 71-year-old agreed to make a disco album anyway. She knocked out new recordings of seven of her old Broadway classics in one afternoon. Producer Peter Matz then sped them up and added thumping disco beats. The album remains a favorite among kitsch enthusiasts.

FABIO AFTER DARK. In 1993 romance-novel cover model Fabio branched out by writing his own romance novels (*Pirate* and *Viking*), acting in margarine commercials, and recording this album. Interspersed with well-known love songs by the Stylistics, Billy Ocean, and Barry White, Fabio delivers rhyming monologues (backed by super-mellow saxophone music) about love and romance. "It's strange how I feel, everything seems so unreal," Fabio purrs in a very thick Italian accent. "There is no looking back, once you get a love attack."

I SCREAM, YOU SCREAM

We've uncovered a lot of food origins in the Bathroom
Readers. *Here's one of our favorite foods of all.*

ICE AGES

Which is oldest—ice cream, sherbet, or snow cones? As far as
anyone can tell, snow cones are the oldest: they date back at
least as far as Roman emperor Nero (37 A.D. to 68 A.D.), who
had snow brought down from mountaintops to cool his wine cel-
lars. On hot days he'd mix some of the extra snow with honey,
juices, and fruit pulps, and eat it as a snack.

Sherbet—which has more fruit and less milk or cream than ice
cream—came next. In the late 13th century, Marco Polo brought
a recipe for sherbet from China to Italy. Only a few people knew
about it. "Recipes [for sherbet] were secrets, closely guarded by
chefs to the wealthy," explains Charles Panati in *Extraordinary
Origins of Everyday Things.*

Historians estimate that sometime in the 16th century one of
these chefs—no one knows who—increased the milk content in
the recipe and reduced or eliminated the fruit entirely…inventing
ice cream in the process.

RICH DESSERT

Iced dessert remained an exclusive, upper-class treat for over a
century. "With refrigeration a costly ordeal of storing winter ice in
underground vaults for summer use," Panati says, "only the
wealthy tasted iced desserts." Then, in 1670, a Sicilian named
Francesco Procopio dei Coltelli opened Paris's first coffeehouse,
Cafe Procope. It was the first business ever to make ice cream
available to the general public.

This inspired other coffeehouses around Europe to do the same.
By the mid-17th century, ice cream could be found in most of the
continent's major cities…and by the end of the century, people
were addicted to it. Beethoven wrote from Vienna in 1794: "It is
very warm here….As winter is mild, ice is rare. The Viennese are
afraid that it will soon be impossible to have any ice cream."

ICE CREAM IN AMERICA

Meanwhile, ice cream had gotten a foothold in the New World. It was first brought over in 1690, and by 1777 it was being advertised in New York newspapers. Ice cream was popular with many of the Founding Fathers, including Alexander Hamilton, George Washington (who ran up a $200 ice cream tab with one New York merchant in the summer of 1790), and Thomas Jefferson (who had his own 18-step recipe for ice cream and is believed to be the first president to serve it at a state dinner). First Lady Dolly Madison's ice cream parties helped make ice cream fashionable among the new republic's upper crust.

CRANKING IT OUT

By the 1790s, ice cream was becoming more readily available in the United States, but it was still a rare treat due to the scarcity and high price of ice—and the difficulty in making it. Most ice cream was made using the "pot freezer" method: the ingredients sat in a pot that, in turn, sat in a larger pan of salt and ice. The whole thing had to be shaken up and down by one person, while another vigorously stirred the mixture.

   Over the next 50 years, two developments made ice cream an American staple:

1. In the early 1800s, "ice harvesting" of frozen northern rivers in winter months, combined with insulated icehouses that sprang up all over the country, made ice—and therefore ice cream—cheap for the first time. By 1810, ice cream was being sold by street vendors in nearly every major city in the United States.

2. In 1846, Nancy Johnson created the world's first hand-cranked ice cream freezer. With this invention, ice cream was both affordable and easy to make for the first time. By 1850, it was so common that *Godey's Lady's Book* could comment: "A party without it would be like a breakfast without bread."

WE ALL SCREAM

By 1900, electricity and mechanical refrigeration had given rise to a huge domestic ice cream industry. And it had become so closely identified with American culture that the people in charge of Ellis Island, determined to serve a "truly American dish" to arriving immigrants, served them ice cream at every meal.

IF YOU BUILD IT, THEY WILL COME

Some people call them roadside attractions; we call them tourist traps. Either way, it's an amazing phenomenon: There's nothing much to see there, nothing much to do there. Yet tourists go by the millions. Think we could get people to come to Uncle John's Bowl of Wonder?

WALL DRUG, Wall, South Dakota
Build It... One summer day in 1936, Dorothy and Ted Hustead had a brilliant idea: they put signs up along U.S. 16 advertising their struggling mom-and-pop drugstore. As an afterthought, they included an offer for free ice water. Wall Drug was situated 10 miles from the entrance to the South Dakota badlands, and on sweltering summer days before air conditioning, the suggestion of free ice water made rickety old Wall Drug seem like an oasis. When Ted got back from putting up the first sign, half a dozen cars were already parked in front of his store.

They'll Come: The Husteads knew they were on to something. Ted built an empire of billboards all over the United States, planting signs farther and farther away from his drugstore. There's now a sign in Amsterdam's train station (only 5,397 miles to Wall Drug); there's one at the Taj Mahal (10,728 miles to Wall Drug); and there's even one in Antarctica (only 10,645 miles to Wall Drug).

Today, Wall Drug is an enormous 50,000-square-foot tourist mecca with a 520-seat restaurant and countless specialty and souvenir shops; if it's hokey, odds are that Wall Drug sells it. They also have a collection of robots, including a singing gorilla and a mechanical Cowboy Orchestra. Wall Drug spends over $300,000 on billboards, but every cent of it pays off. The store lures in 20,000 visitors a day in the summer and grosses more than $11 million each year. And they still give away free ice water—5,000 glasses a day.

SOUTH OF THE BORDER, Dillon, South Carolina
Build It... Driving south on I-95 near the South Carolina border,

one object stands out from the landscape: a 200-foot-tall tower with a giant sombrero on top. The colossal hat is Sombrero Tower, centerpiece of the huge South of the Border tourist complex.

SOB, as the locals call it, began as a beer stand operated by a man named Alan Schafer. When Schafer noticed that his building supplies were being delivered to "Schafer Project: South of the [North Carolina] Border," a lightbulb lit up over his head and he decided his stand needed a Mexican theme.

They'll Come: Today, SOB sprawls over 135 acres and imports—and sells—$1.5 million worth of Mexican merchandise a year. It has a 300-room motel and five restaurants, including the Sombrero Room and Pedro's Casateria (a fast-food joint shaped like an antebellum mansion with a chicken on the roof). There's also Pedro's Rocket City (a fireworks shop), Golf of Mexico (miniature golf), and Pedro's Pleasure Dome spa. Incredibly, eight million people stop into SOB every year for a little slice of…Mexi-kitsch.

TREES OF MYSTERY, Klamath, California

Build It… When Carl Bruno first toured the towering redwood forests around the DeMartin ranch in 1931, he was awestruck by a handful of oddly deformed trees. Dollar signs in his eyes, Bruno snapped up the property and began luring in travelers to see trees shaped like pretzels and double helixes. He called his attraction Wonderland Park, and for the first 15 years of its existence, it did modest business—but something was missing…

They'll Come: He decided the park needed a 49-foot-tall statue of Paul Bunyan. In 1946 Bruno had the massive mythical logger installed near the highway and changed the park's name to Trees of Mystery. Business began to pick up. He added a companion piece, 35-feet-tall Babe the Blue Ox, in 1949. (When Babe was first introduced, he blew smoke out of his nostrils, which made small children run away screaming. The smoke was discontinued.)

Trees of Mystery prospered and is still open today. It recently added an aerial gondola ride, but the park is primarily a bunch of oddly shaped trees and a tunnel through a giant redwood. The gift shop, which sells cheesy souvenirs and wood carvings, has been hailed as "a model for other tourist attractions." The park was honored by *American Heritage* magazine as the best roadside attraction in 2001.

IT'S A WEIRD, WEIRD WORLD

Proof that truth really is stranger than fiction.

NOSING AROUND

"Ruth Clarke, 23, of London, England, underwent surgery to correct a lifelong breathing problem in 1981. She was presented with a tiddlywink, which doctors had removed from her nose. Clarke vaguely recalled losing the disk as a tot, but she didn't dream it was right under her nose all the time."

—*Encyclopedia Brown's Book of Strange Facts*

HERE I AM—ROCK YOU LIKE A HURRICANE!

"On the morning of September 21, 1938, a man in Westhampton Beach, New York, received a barometer in the mail. The needle was stuck on 'hurricane.' Thinking it was defective, he marched back to the Post Office and mailed the instrument back to the store from which he had purchased it. Later that day, the Great Hurricane of 1938 devastated the town...and much of the northeast. When the man finally returned to his home, it was gone."

—*Our Fascinating Earth*

ROCK YOUR WORLD

"For years, maps have shown that northern Germany's highest mountain, the Brocken, was 3,747 feet tall. But in 1998, more precise measurements revealed that the peak is only 3,741 feet tall. To avoid correcting the world's maps, a construction company trucked 19 tons of granite to the summit, stacking the rocks in a 6-foot pile."

—*The Oregonian*

NEXT COMES A STRAIGHTJACKET

"Despite 18 years working at a Florida fishing camp, Freddie Padgett was so terrified of water that he wore a life jacket to bed on

Boxer Jack Johnson invented the common household wrench.

stormy nights. Friends made fun of him, until a twister sucked him out of his RV while he was sleeping and dropped him into Lake Harney over a mile away. He suffered broken ribs and other injuries, but authorities say the life jacket probably saved his life."

—*The Skeptic*

A CASE OF COWLICK

PEREIRA, Colombia—"A Colombian hairdresser says he has found a way to lick baldness—literally. His offbeat scalp treatment involves a special tonic and massage—with a cow's tongue. 'I feel more manly, more attractive to women,' says customer Henry Gomez. 'My friends even say "What are you doing? You have more hair. You look younger."'"

—CNN *Fringe*

ROBBIN' HOOD

"In Australia, a man named Rob Banks, who was convicted of robbing banks, has been given a new trial because the judge said the jury may have been swayed by his name. This time he will be tried under an alias."

—"The Edge," *The Oregonian*

BRIDGE OVER DUBLIN WATER

"Irish hospital worker Willie Nugent decided he would raise money for charity by swimming across a river in downtown Dublin. There was only one problem: Nugent can't swim. So instead he crawled across a bridge, in movements 'resembling a breast stroke.'"

—Universal Press Syndicate

FAMILY FEUD

"Philip Buble, 44, was denied permission to bring his 'wife' into a main courtroom because she is a dog. Buble wanted the dog, who he calls Lady Buble, to sit with him in the courtroom while his father was being sentenced for attempted murder (the elder Buble tried to kill the younger Buble when he learned his son had married a dog). In Buble's plea to the court, he said, 'I'd like my significant other to attend by my side, as she was in the house during the attack, though not a witness to it, thank goodness.'"

—FHM

A turtle's shell is sensitive enough to feel a twig brush across it.

EXECUTIVE DECISIONS

They may be in positions of responsibility…they may be captains of industry…they may be among the world's most successful business people. But that doesn't mean they can't make really dumb decisions, just like the rest of us. Here are some classics.

SHOULD WE SIGN THEM UP?

Mike Smith and Dick Rowe, executives in charge of evaluating new talent for the London office of Decca Records.

Background: On December 13, 1961, Mike Smith traveled to Liverpool to watch a local rock 'n' roll band perform. He decided they had talent, and invited them to an audition on New Year's Day 1962. The group made the trip to London and spent two hours playing 15 different songs at the Decca studios. Then they went home and waited for an answer.

They waited for weeks.

Decision: Finally, Rowe told the band's manager that the label wasn't interested, because they sounded too much like a popular group called The Shadows. In one of the most famous of all rejection lines, he said: "Not to mince words, Mr. Epstein, but we don't like your boys' sound. Groups are out; four-piece groups with guitars particularly are finished."

Impact: The group was the Beatles, of course. They eventually signed with EMI Records, started a trend back to guitar bands, and ultimately became the most popular band of all time. Ironically, "Within two years, EMI's production facilities became so stretched that Decca helped them out in a reciprocal arrangement, to cope with the unprecedented demand for Beatles records."

SHOULD WE PUT OUR CANDY IN THAT KIDS' FILM?

John and Forrest Mars, Jr., owners of Mars Inc., makers of M&M's

Background: In 1981 Universal Studios called Mars and asked for permission to use M&M's in a new film they were making. This was (and is) a fairly common practice. Product placement deals

---

Thyme for a checkup? According to food researchers, thyme helps prevent tooth decay.

provide filmmakers with some extra cash or promotion opportunities. In this case, the director was looking for a cross-promotion. He'd use the M&M's, and Mars could help promote the movie.

Decision: The Mars brothers said "No."

Impact: The film was *E.T. The Extra-Terrestrial*, directed by Steven Spielberg. The M&M's were needed for a crucial scene: Elliot, the little boy who befriends the alien, uses candies to lure E.T. into his house.

Instead, Universal Studios went to Hersheys and cut a deal to use a new product called Reese's Pieces. Initial sales of Reese's Pieces had been light. But when *E.T.* became a top-grossing film—generating tremendous publicity for "E.T.'s favorite candy"—sales exploded. They tripled within two weeks and continued climbing for months afterward. "It was the biggest marketing coup in history," says Jack Dowd, the Hershey's executive who approved the movie tie-in. "We got immediate recognition for our product. We would normally have had to pay 15 or 20 million bucks for it."

HOW DO WE COME UP WITH SOME QUICK CASH?

Executives of 20th Century Fox's TV division (pre-Murdoch)

Background: No one at Fox expected much from M*A*S*H when it debuted on TV in 1972. Execs simply wanted to make a cheap series by using the M*A*S*H movie set again—so it was a surprise when it became Fox's only hit show. Three years later, the company was hard up for cash. When the M*A*S*H ratings started to slip after two of its stars left, Fox execs panicked.

Decision: They decided to raise cash by selling the syndication rights to the first seven seasons of M*A*S*H on a futures basis: local TV stations could pay in 1975 for shows they couldn't broadcast until October 1979—four years away. Fox made no guarantees that the show would still be popular; the $13,000 per episode was non-refundable. But enough local stations took the deal so that Fox made $25 million. They celebrated...

Impact: ...but prematurely. When M*A*S*H finally aired in syndication in 1979, it was still popular (in fact, it ranked #3 that year). It became one of the most successful syndicated shows ever, second only to *I Love Lucy*. Each of the original 168 episodes grossed over $1 million for local TV stations; Fox got nothing.

LOST ATTRACTIONS

As a kid growing up in New Jersey, Uncle John often went to Palisades Amusement Park. Then one day they announced they were tearing it down to build an apartment complex. Many areas have an attraction like that—it's an important part of the cultural landscape for decades...and then it's gone.

ATTRACTION: The Hippodrome
LOCATION: New York City
STORY: When it opened in 1905, it was called "the largest theater in the world." With a seating capacity of 5,300, only the biggest acts—in both size and popularity—performed there: Harry Houdini, diving horses, the circus, 500-person choirs. But the daily upkeep for such a mammoth theater, coupled with the cost of staging huge shows, forced a change. In 1923 it became a vaudeville theater and then, in 1928, it was sold to RKO and turned into a movie theater. It then became an opera house. Then a sports arena. The Hippodrome was finally torn down in 1939.
WHAT'S THERE NOW: An office building and parking garage.

ATTRACTION: Aquatarium
LOCATION: St. Petersburg, Florida
STORY: Housed in a 160-foot-tall transparent geodesic dome, the 17-acre Aquatarium opened in 1964. Tourists came from far and wide to visit this aquarium, which overlooked the Gulf of Mexico and was home to porpoises, sea lions, and pilot whales. But it rapidly started losing customers—and money—when the bigger and better Walt Disney World opened in nearby Orlando in 1971. In 1976 sharks were brought in and the site was renamed Shark World to capitalize on the popularity of *Jaws*, but it didn't help.
WHAT'S THERE NOW: Condominiums.

ATTRACTION: Pink and White Terraces
LOCATION: Lake Rotomahana, New Zealand
STORY: Called the eighth wonder of the world, the Terraces were once New Zealand's most popular and famous tourist attraction. They were two naturally occurring "staircases" of silica shelves that looked like pink and white marble. Each terrace (they were

---

2,200 people are quoted in *Bartlett's Familiar Quotations*. Only 164 are women.

two miles apart) was formed over thousands of years. Geysers spouted silica-laden hot water which flowed downhill and then crystallized into terraces as it cooled. But on June 10, 1886, a nearby volcano —Mount Tarawera—erupted, spewing lava, hot mud, and boulders. The eruption destroyed the village of Te Wairoa, killing 153 people, and the hot magma completely destroyed the terraces.
WHAT'S THERE NOW: Shapeless rock.

ATTRACTION: Jantzen Beach
LOCATION: Portland, Oregon
STORY: When it opened in 1928, this 123-acre amusement park on an island in the middle of the Columbia River was the largest in the United States. It housed a merry-go-round from the 1904 World's Fair, four swimming pools, a fun house, a train, and the Big Dipper—a huge wooden roller coaster. More than 30 million people visited "the Coney Island of the West" over its lifetime. But after World War II, attendance started to decline and continued steadily downward until the park finally closed in 1970.
WHAT'S THERE NOW: A shopping mall.

ATTRACTION: Palisades Amusement Park
LOCATION: Cliffside Park and Fort Lee, New Jersey
STORY: Built on steep cliffs on the west side of the Hudson River, it began in 1898 as a grassy park for picnics and recreation. In 1908 it was renamed Palisades Amusement Park and rides and attractions were added. It boasted a 400-by-600-foot saltwater pool ("world's largest"); the Cyclone, one of the biggest roller coasters in the country; and then in the 1950s, rock 'n' roll shows. Attendance grew during that period because of heavy advertising on TV and in comic books. (There was a hole in the fence behind the music stage kept open to let kids sneak in to avoid paying the 25-cent admission fee.) By 1967, the park had gotten *too* popular. The city of Cliffside Park was tired of park-related traffic, litter, and parking problems, so it rezoned the site for housing (it has great views of Manhattan). The park was shut down for good in 1971. Plans to retain the saltwater pool were scrapped when vandals destroyed it.
WHAT'S THERE NOW: High-rise apartment buildings.

It cost $3 million to build the *Titanic*...and $100 million to make the movie.

ATTRACTION: Crystal Palace
LOCATION: London, England
STORY: This massive 750,000 square foot structure originally housed the Great Exhibition of 1851, then was moved from Hyde Park to south London in 1854. Designed to evoke ancient Greek structures, the Crystal Palace featured dozens of columns, girders, and arches made of iron, and 900,000 square feet of glass. The building and surrounding grounds housed artwork and treasures from all over the world, including 250-foot-high fountains (requiring two water towers), gardens, and life-size replicas of dinosaurs. The coronation of King George V was held there, as was the annual English soccer championship. But after 1900, attendance started to dwindle. The Palace was closed on Sundays, the only day most Londoners had off from work. Then, in 1936, the Palace caught fire. The blaze was visible for miles. The building wasn't properly insured, so there wasn't enough to pay for rebuilding. All that was left were the water towers, later demolished during World War II out of fear Germany could use them to more easily locate London.
WHAT'S THERE NOW: A sports-arena complex.

ATTRACTION: Old Man of the Mountain
LOCATION: Cannon Mountain, New Hampshire
STORY: In 1805 surveyors Francis Whitcomb and Luke Brooks discovered this rock formation in the White Mountains of New Hampshire. Viewed from the correct angle, it had the appearance of a man's face. It jutted out 1,200 feet above Profile Lake and was estimated to be 40 feet tall and 25 feet wide. Nineteenth-century politician Daniel Webster and novelist Nathaniel Hawthorne wrote about the Old Man and helped make it a state icon. The Old Man graces New Hampshire's state quarter and a postage stamp. Signs of deterioration were first noted in 1906, and ever since, various methods—including cables and spikes—have been used to keep the face in place. But they didn't work. In 2003, the Old Man finally collapsed and crumbled.
WHAT'S THERE NOW: A rocky cliff. Viewfinders looking at the former landmark superimpose an image of the Old Man when it was intact to show visitors what it looked like.

The main cluster of riders in a bicycle race is called a *peloton*.

DUMBEST CROOKS

When we collected all of our dumb crook entries from the last 10 years, we had 46 pages' worth, proving there is no shortage of dimwits trying to outwit the law. Here are the dumbest and most head-scratching-est of them all.

IS THIS SEAT TAKEN?

"A thief in Munich, Germany, who stole a woman's World Cup ticket from her purse in 2006 was caught after he sat down to watch the game…next to the victim's husband. The unidentified 34-year-old numbskull mugged 42-year-old Eva Standmann while she was en route to the Munich stadium for the game between Brazil and Australia and came across the ticket in her bag. As he sat in what was supposed to be the woman's seat, he was met by her hubby, 43-year-old Berndt Standmann, who promptly notified stadium security and had the crook arrested."

—**Dumbcrooks.com**

STRONG ARMED

"The man on the witness stand in New Orleans was in obvious pain. Moving his right arm ever so slightly caused him to wince. He had injured his arm six months earlier in a job-related accident and was suing his former company for permanent disability. After a series of questions his client answered perfectly, his attorney asked the clincher, 'How high can you raise your arm right now?' Straining, the man slowly lifted his outstretched arm to shoulder level. 'And how far could you lift it before the accident?'

Without hesitation, the man proudly shot the same arm straight above his head, exclaiming, 'This high!' He was still holding his arm up when the judge slammed down his gavel and announced, 'Case dismissed!'"

—*Crimes and Misdumbmeanors*

HOT TIPS

"On several break-ins in Dade County, Florida, Ronald Bradley, 21, carefully wore gloves. But he wore golf gloves—the kind that left his fingertips naked. He was sent to prison for three years."

—*Sports Illustrated*

YOU REAP WHAT YOU SEW

"Los Angeles sheriff's deputies investigating the break-in of a sewing shop discovered the theft of a large industrial sewing machine, then noticed a thick thread snagged on the floor. They followed the thread out the door, down the alley, across the street, through a backyard, up some steps, and under a door. After kicking in the door, they discovered the sewing machine in the kitchen and nabbed three surprised thieves."

—*Maxim*

A LOST *THREE STOOGES* MOVIE?

"In August 1975, three men were on their way in to rob the Royal Bank of Scotland at Rothesay, when they got stuck in the revolving doors. They had to be helped free by the staff and, after thanking everyone, sheepishly left the building. A few minutes later they returned and announced their intention of robbing the bank, but none of the bank employees believed them. When they demanded £5,000, the head cashier laughed at them, convinced that it was a practical joke. Disheartened, the gang leader reduced his demand first to £500, then to £50 and ultimately to 50 pence. By this stage the cashier could barely control her laughter. Then one of the men jumped over the counter and fell awkwardly on the floor, clutching at his ankle. The other two attempted a getaway, but got trapped in the revolving doors for a second time, desperately pushing the wrong way."

—*The Incomplete Book of Failures*

IGNORING THE RULE OF THUMB

"A robbery at a Git-N-Go Convenience Store on the south side of Des Moines was called off for lack of convincing theatrics. 'Well, I could tell he didn't have a gun,' said Terry Cook, a clerk at the store. 'I knew it was his finger. I could see his thumb sticking out of his coat pocket.' The would-be robber, who acted tough and even inserted a harsh expletive in his demand for cash, wanted to argue. 'It is a gun,' he told Cook. 'No it isn't,' Cook replied. The frustrated suspect left the store but paused a moment in the parking lot, perhaps to go over in his mind the argument he'd just lost. He left the scene just before police arrived."

—*DribbleGlass.com*

First rock 'n' roll gold record: "Rock Around the Clock," by Bill Haley and the Comets, 1954.

MAKING *THE GODFATHER*, PART I

The Godfather is considered one of the best movies ever made— the American Film Institute ranks it #3, after Citizen Kane *and* Casablanca. *The story of how it got made is just as good.*

BOOKMAKER

In 1955 a pulp-fiction writer named Mario Puzo published his first novel, *The Dark Arena*, about an ex-GI and his German girlfriend who live in Germany after the end of World War II. The critics praised it, but it didn't sell very many copies.

It took Puzo nine years to finish his next novel, *The Fortunate Pilgrim*, which told the story of an Italian immigrant named Lucia Santa who lives in the Hell's Kitchen neighborhood of New York City. After two bad marriages, Lucia is raising her kids alone and worries about her daughter, who has become too Americanized, and her son, who is being pulled into the Mafia.

Today *The Fortunate Pilgrim* is widely considered a classic work of Italian American fiction; Puzo himself considered it the best book he ever wrote. But it sold as poorly as *The Dark Arena*— together the two books had earned Puzo only about $6,500. By then he was 45 years old, $20,000 in debt, and tired of being broke. He wanted his next novel to be a success. "I looked around and said...I'd better make some money," he recalled years later.

HIT MAN

Puzo figured that a story with an entire family of gangsters in it instead of only one would have more commercial appeal than *The Fortunate Pilgrim* had. He titled his third novel *Mafia*, and in a sign of how his fortunes were about to change, he received a $5,000 advance payment from the publisher. Then, after he'd completed only an outline and 114 pages, Paramount Pictures acquired the movie rights for $12,000 and agreed to pay an additional $50,000 if the movie actually got made.

Puzo's decision to pack his story with wiseguys paid off. *Mafia*, by now retitled *The Godfather*, was a publishing phenomenon. The most successful novel of the 1970s, it spent 67 weeks on the best-seller list and sold more than 21 million copies before it even made it to the big screen.

THE NUMBERS RACKET

Believe it or not, the success of the novel actually *hurt* its chances of becoming a decent film. Bestsellers appeal to movie studios because they have a guaranteed audience. But fans will come to the theater no matter what, so why spend extra money to get them there? Shortsighted studio executives are often tempted to maximize profits by spending as little on such movies as possible. At the time Paramount was in bad financial shape and its last Mafia film, *The Brotherhood*, starring Kirk Douglas, bombed. The studio couldn't afford another expensive mistake. It set the budget for *The Godfather* at $2 million, a miniscule figure even for the early 1970s.

Two million dollars wasn't enough money to make a decent film set in the present, let alone a period piece like *The Godfather*, which takes place from 1945 to 1955—and in Manhattan, one of the most expensive places in the country to shoot a film. To save on expenses, Paramount decided to move the story forward to the 1970s, and made plans to film it in a Midwestern city like Kansas City, or on the studio back lot instead of on actual New York streets. The title would still be *The Godfather*, but other than that the film would have very little in common with Puzo's novel.

Paramount signed Albert Ruddy, one of the co-creators of TV's *Hogan's Heroes*, to produce the film. Ruddy had produced only three motion pictures, and they'd all lost money, but what impressed the studio was that he had brought them in under budget. That was what Paramount was looking for in *The Godfather*—a critical flop that would nonetheless turn a quick profit because it had a built-in audience and would be filmed on the cheap.

NO, THANKS

By now it was clear in Hollywood that the studio was planning what was little more than a cinematic mugging of millions of fans of Puzo's novel. What director would want to work on something like that? It was enough to ruin a career. Ruddy approached several big directors about making the film but, of course, none were interested. So he turned to a hungry young director named Francis Ford Coppola.

He turned it down, too.

THE KID

In his short career, Coppola, then 31, had directed only four films (not including the nudie flicks he worked on while studying film at UCLA): *Dimentia 13*, a critical flop that bombed at the box office; *Finian's Rainbow*, another critical flop that bombed; *You're a Big Boy Now*, another critical flop that bombed; and *The Rain People* (starring James Caan and Robert Duvall), a critical *success* that bombed. With his track record, he couldn't afford to be too choosy, and yet when Albert Ruddy offered him *The Godfather* in the spring of 1970, Coppola picked up a copy of the book and read only as far as one particularly lurid scene early in the book before he dismissed the whole work as a piece of trash and told Ruddy to find someone else. (Have you read the book? It's the part where Sonny's mistress goes to a plastic surgeon to have her "plumbing" fixed and ends up having an affair with the doctor.)

AN OFFER HE COULDN'T REFUSE

Film buffs know that we have George Lucas to thank for *Star Wars*. We can thank him for *The Godfather*, too. In November 1969, Coppola had founded his own film company, American Zoetrope, and its first project was to turn his friend George's student film, *THX-1138*, into a feature-length movie. Today it's a cult classic, but it was such a dud when it was first released that it nearly forced American Zoetrope into bankruptcy. Coppola was so desperate to keep the studio's doors open that when Ruddy offered him the *Godfather* job a second time in late 1970, he agreed to at least give the novel another look.

This time Coppola read the book all the way through. He found more sections that he didn't like, but he was also captivated by the central story of the relationship between the Godfather, Don Corleone, and his three sons. He realized that if he could strip away the lurid parts and focus on the central characters, *The Godfather* had a shot at becoming a very good film.

Part II of the story is on page 317.

Long distance: A hippo's call can be heard from more than a mile away.

FABULOUS FOOD FLOPS

*Next time you see the hype for some amazing, "can't-miss"
food phenomenon, hold on to a healthy sense of
skepticism by remembering these duds.*

I HATE PEAS

If kids won't eat peas in their natural shape, why not mash them into a paste and make them look like French fries? Answer: Because, as one kid put it, "they still taste disgusting." Consumer researcher Robert McMath summed it up: "Kids said, 'A pea is a pea is a pea....I don't like peas. In fact, I hate peas, even if they're in the shape of French fries." I Hate Beans also flopped.

NESTEA'S TEA WHIZ

Would you give a "yellowish, carbonated, lemon-flavored drink" a name like 'Whiz'?

JUMPIN' JEMS

The soft drink equivalent of the lava lamp. Introduced in 1995 by Mistic Brands, it was supposed to have "jelly balls" floating in the liquid. A major flaw: The "jelly balls" settled to the bottom of the bottle. Consumers figured the product had gone bad and wouldn't touch it. "Even I didn't drink it," admitted Mistic's president.

YOU SAY TO-MA-TO, I SAY TO-BLAH-TO

In 1994 a small biotech company called Calgene got FDA approval for the first genetically engineered whole food to hit the stores in the United States—the *Flavr Savr* tomato. It was genetically altered to delay ripening, which allowed growers to keep the plant on the vine longer, shippers to keep it in the trucks longer, and grocers to keep it on shelves longer. It sounds good, but the tomatoes had problems: they didn't taste very good; crop yields were below expectations; and the machines used for packing them, built for still-green and firm tomatoes, mashed the Flavr Savrs to mush. After two years on the market, the original "Frankenfood" was pulled from stores. Calgene's loss: an estimated $150 million.

The first electric ovens were used in a Swiss hotel in 1889.

DINOS

After the success of Fruity Pebbles, in the early 1990s Post tried naming a cereal after the Flintstones' pet dinosaur. "A question that came up constantly," recalls a Post art director, "was 'We've got Cocoa Pebbles and Fruity Pebbles...so what flavor is Dino?'... It sounds like something Fred would be getting off his lawn instead of something you'd want to be eating."

KELLOGG'S CORN CRACKOS

From 1967, the box featured the Waker Upper Bird perched on a bowl of candy-coated twists. An internal company memo said: "It looks like a bird eating worms; who wants worms for breakfast?"

PUNCH CRUNCH

A 1975 spinoff of Cap'n Crunch. The screaming pink box featured Harry S., an exuberant hippo in a sailor suit, making goo-goo eyes at Cap'n Crunch. Many chain stores perceived the hippo as gay and refused to carry the cereal. Marveled one Quaker salesman: "How that one ever got through, I'll never understand."

GERBER SINGLES

This was Gerber Baby Food's attempt to sell food to adults. Launched in the 1970s, the line of gourmet entrees like sweet-and-sour pork and beef burgundy had two major problems: the food came in baby food–style jars, and the name "Singles" was a turnoff to customers who were lonely to begin with.

NO FURTHER EXPLANATION REQUIRED

See if you can figure out why these products bombed:

- Buffalo Chip chocolate cookies
- Mouth-So-Fresh Tongue Cleaner
- Gillette's For Oily Hair Shampoo
- Hagar the Horrible Cola
- Burns & Rickers freeze-dried vegetable chips
- Jell-O for Salads (available in celery, tomato, mixed-vegetable)
- Tunies (hot dogs made from tuna fish)

THANKSGIVING MYTHS

Historian Samuel Eliot Morison says that "more bunk has been written about Pilgrims than any other subjects except Columbus and John Paul Jones." After reading this, maybe you'll agree.

BACKGROUND
It's one of American history's most familiar scenes: A small group of Pilgrims prepare a huge November feast to give thanks for a bountiful harvest and show their appreciation to the Indians who helped them survive their first winter. Together, the Pilgrims and Indians solemnly sit down to a meal of turkey, pumpkin pie, and cranberries.

Just how accurate is this image of America's first Thanksgiving? Not very, it turns out. Here are some common misconceptions about the origin of one of our favorite holidays.

MYTH: The settlers at the first Thanksgiving were called Pilgrims.
THE TRUTH: They didn't even refer to *themselves* as Pilgrims— they called themselves "Saints." Early Americans applied the term "pilgrim" to *all* of the early colonists; it wasn't until the 20th century that it was used exclusively to describe the folks who landed on Plymouth Rock.

MYTH: It was a solemn, religious occasion.
THE TRUTH: Hardly. It was a three-day harvest festival that included drinking, gambling, athletic games, and even target shooting with English muskets (which, by the way, was intended as a friendly warning to the Indians that the Pilgrims were prepared to defend themselves).

MYTH: It took place in November.
THE TRUTH: It was some time between late September and the middle of October—after the harvest had been brought in. By November, says historian Richard Ehrlich, "the villagers were working to prepare for winter, salting and drying meat and making their houses as wind resistant as possible."

Every Thanksgiving, Americans consume 45 million turkeys—one for every 5½ U.S. citizens.

MYTH: The Pilgrims wore large hats with buckles on them.

THE TRUTH: None of the participants were dressed anything like the way they've been portrayed in art: the Pilgrims didn't dress in black, didn't wear buckles on their hats or shoes, and didn't wear tall hats. The 19th-century artists who painted them that way did so because they associated black clothing and buckles with being old-fashioned.

MYTH: They ate turkey.

THE TRUTH: The Pilgrims ate *deer*, not turkey. As Pilgrim Edward Winslow later wrote, "For three days we entertained and feasted, and [the Indians] went out and killd five deer, which they brought to the plantation." Winslow does mention that four Pilgrims went "fowling" or bird hunting, but neither he nor anyone else recorded which *kinds* of birds they actually hunted—so even if they did eat turkey, it was just a side dish. "The flashy part of the meal for the colonists was the venison, because it was new to them," says Carolyn Travers, director of research at Plimoth Plantation, a Pilgrim museum in Massachusetts. "Back in England, deer were on estates and people would be arrested for poaching if they killed these deer....The colonists mentioned venison over and over again in their letters back home." Other foods that may have been on the menu: cod, bass, clams, oysters, Indian corn, native berries and plums, all washed down with water, beer made from corn, and another drink the Pilgrims affectionately called "strong water."

A few things definitely *weren't* on the menu, including pumpkin pie—in those days, the Pilgrims boiled their pumpkin and ate it plain. And since the Pilgrims didn't yet have flour mills or cattle, there was no bread other than corn bread, and no beef, milk, or cheese. And the Pilgrims didn't eat any New England lobsters, either. Reason: They mistook them for large insects.

MYTH: The Pilgrims held a similar feast every year.

THE TRUTH: There's no evidence the Pilgrims celebrated again in 1622. They probably weren't in the mood—the harvest had been disappointing, and they were burdened with a new boatload of Pilgrims who had to be fed and housed through the winter.

McDonald's sells "McSpaghetti" in the Philippines and "McLak" salmon burgers in Norway.

MATH MNEMONICS

Even mathematicians mneed mnemonics to help them remember stuff. From Uncle John's Bathroom Reader Plunges into the Universe, *here are a few of their favorites.*

PREFIXES IN THE METRIC SYSTEM

Kilo, Hecta, Deca, Unit, Deci, Centi, Milli
- Kevin Had Ducked Under a Dark Creepy Monster
- Kids Have Doodled Upside-Down Converting Metrics
- King Hector Doesn't Usually Drink Cold Milk

Deci, Centi, Milli, Micro, Nano, Pico, Femto, Atto
- Dairy Cows Make Milk, Not Pink Fruit, Arthur

Tera, Giga, Mega, Milli, Micro, Nano, Pico, Femto, Atto
- To Go Metric Man Must Not Put Fools Aside

THE ASCENDING ORDER OF ROMAN NUMERALS

L, C, D, M = 50, 100, 500, 1000
- Lucky Cows Drink Milk
- Lucy Can't Drink Milk

TO REMEMBER WHAT AN ISOSCELES TRIANGLE IS

(*sung to the tune of "Oh Christmas Tree"*)

Isosceles, isosceles,
　　Two angles have
　　Equal degrees.

Isosceles, isosceles,
　　You look just like
　　A Christmas tree.

TO CALCULATE THE CIRCUMFERENCE OF A CIRCLE

　　If you cross a circle with a line,
　　Which hits the center and runs from spine to spine,
　　And the line's length is *d*,
　　The circumference will be *d* times 3.14159.

Some spiders produce threads that are stronger than a steel wire of the same size.

THE VALUE OF π (Pi)

(The number of letters in each word equal the numerals in Pi.)

3.14159265

• Now I know a super utterance to assist minds.

3.1415926

• May I have a large container of coffee?

3.14159265358979323846

• Sir, I send a rhyme excelling
  In sacred truth and rigid spelling,
  Numerical sprites elucidate
  For me the lexicon's dull weight.

THE SQUARE ROOT OF 2 = 1.414

• I wish I knew [the root of two].

*　　*　　*

MORE MNEAT MNEMONICS

The Taxonomic Classification for Humans

Eukarya, Metazoa, Chordata, Mammalia, Primata, Hominidae, Homo Sapiens

• Exotic Malaises Can Make People Hate Helping the Sick.

The Biological Groupings Used in Taxonomy

Domain, Kingdom, Phylum, Class, Order, Family, Genus, Species

• Danish Kings Possess Crowns Of Fine Gem Stones.
• Dandy King Phillip Came Over for Gene's Special Variety.
• Delighted Kings Play Cards On Fairly Good Soft Velvet.
• Drunken Kings Play Cards On Fat Girls' Stomachs.
• Destructive King Phillip Cuts Open Five Green Snakes.
• Dolphins, Kingfish, Pickerel, Catfish Over-Flowed God's Seas.

What are *gluons*, *leptons*, and *taus*? Some of the names for particles smaller than atoms.

MADE IN CHINA

Have you ever noticed that it seems like everything is made in China? Well, almost everything is made in China. Here's why. (And if you want to know what's not made in China, see page 531.)

IN THE RED

Prior to World War II, China was a major economic force, exporting huge amounts of raw goods (such as tea and rice) all over the world. When Mao Tse-Tung's Communist government assumed control of China in 1949, it took over all of the country's businesses. Not content with only exporting agricultural goods, Chairman Mao wanted China to become a major industrial power. So he implemented China's first "Five Year Plan" for economic development. Money, resources, and labor were all allocated by the government, which also set wages and prices. Even consumption of food and goods would be controlled through strict rationing.

Result: industry grew rapidly, but agricultural production suffered. The next Five Year Plan (1958) aimed to revive the agricultural sector to such heights that China could be completely self-sufficient. Farming output increased as planned, but the government neglected to update food storage and transportation technology. A huge grain crop went to waste and, coupled with huge floods from failed irrigation experiments, 30 million people in China starved to death between 1958 and 1961—the worst famine in recorded history.

After China publicly criticized the USSR for bowing to American pressure and removing missiles from Cuba during the Cuban Missile Crisis, the Soviet Union withdrew economic assistance in 1962. The rest of the world turned its back on China after it invaded India twice (1959 and 1962), suppressed a rebellion in Tibet (1959), and aided Vietnam in the Vietnam War. By 1970, China was almost completely alone. Self-sufficiency was the goal—but isolation was the result.

NIXON GOES TO CHINA

Conditions would begin to improve after President Richard Nixon's 1971 visit to Beijing. China agreed to re-establish ties with the United

States on the condition that American troops would leave Taiwan. (They had been stationed in the Chinese province since the Communist takeover.) Nixon agreed; tensions eased between China and the U.S.

OUT WITH THE OLD...

Chairman Mao died in 1976 and was replaced by the moderate Deng Xiaoping. Rejecting Mao's failed plans for self-sufficiency, Deng opened China to the world in 1980. To hasten modernization, the government encouraged foreign investment and invited western companies to bring their technology to China in the form of entire state-of-the-art Western factories. State-owned businesses remained the standard, but private ownership of companies became legal. Most revolutionary of all, the government took a capitalist approach to taxing businesses: it took a cut of the business' profits and allowed the remainder to be reinvested into the companies. The result of Deng's policies: China's industry grew at an annual rate of 11 percent in the 1980s and 17 percent in the 1990s, the fastest rate in the world at the time.

But here's what motivated American companies to open factories in China: cheap labor and lots of it. (As of 2002, the Chinese workforce was 762 million people.) China's large population creates huge demand (and competition) for jobs. This drives down wages, and they're made even lower by the government, which keeps pay rates low to control business costs. A worker in China earns about five percent of what a worker doing the same job in the United States would earn. Plus in China, there are no benefits, sick leave, or worker's compensation. China's labor laws are very relaxed: shifts can be 12 hours a day and most factories operate like sweatshops. One of the highest costs of doing business is labor, so low wages means products manufactured in China are unbeatably inexpensive, both to make and to buy.

WORLD DOMINATION

Today Western companies in almost every industry have factories in China. Even with the expense of moving overseas and constantly having to ship materials and goods to Chinese factories, the low wage rates (and lower taxes) still make it highly prof-

Some prehistoric dragonflies had wingspans as big as a hawk's.

itable. Economists estimate that as much as 90 percent of retail goods available in the United States were made in China.

• Some of the products: Apple computers, Avon cosmetics, Boeing airplanes, Clorox bleach, John Deere tractors, Dow chemicals, General Motors car parts, Hewlett-Packard printers, Johnson & Johnson first aid products, Mattel toys, Motorola cell phones, Toshiba televisions, Black & Decker drills, Intel microprocessors, Maytag appliances, Dell computers, Outboard Marine boats, Head & Shoulders shampoo, Rand McNally maps, Sony Play Stations, Serta mattresses, Sherwin-Williams paint, and Xerox copiers.

• Other companies use Chinese facilities to manufacture satellites, ships, trains, mining machinery, oil drilling equipment, power generators, plastics, pharmaceuticals, bicycles, sewing machines, metal knick-knacks, cement, coffee makers, shoes, and dishes.

• China produces more clothes than any other country. Its industry includes cotton, wool, linen, silk, and chemical fibers, as well as printing, dyeing, knitting, and automatic manufacture.

• China is the largest producer of steel in the world. From stainless steel to sheet metal to pipes, China passed Britain as the world's largest steel producer in the 1960s. The Chinese government increased industrial production so quickly by reassigning millions of farmers to crude backyard furnaces where they made steel from low-grade ore, scrap metal, and even household items.

• The world's six largest producers of American flags are all based in China. Most religious merchandise (like Virgin Mary statues, rosaries, and Buddha figurines) sold in the United States are made in China...a country with little religious freedom.

*   *   *

FLAMING IRONY

In 2002 firefighters were called to put out the flames at a factory in Neuruppin, Germany. What did the factory make? Fire extinguishers. But the fire extinguishers were filled with flame retardant at another facility...so at the time of the fire, none of them worked.

The *Palustris hefner* species of rabbit is named for Playboy mogul Hugh Hefner.

TRUE CONFESSIONS

A little bathroom pastime: Match the intimate revelation with the celebrity who said it. Inspired by Jon Winokur's book of quotes, True Confessions.

1. "Brain the size of a pea, I've got."

2. "I never wanted to be famous; I only wanted to be great."

3. "I learned the way a monkey learns—by watching its parents."

4. "If only I had a little humility, I would be perfect."

5. "The only reason they come to see me is that I know life is great—and they know I know it."

6. "It costs a lot of money to look this cheap."

7. "I look like a rock quarry that someone has dynamited."

8. "Sometimes, at the end of the day when I'm smiling and shaking hands, I want to kick them."

9. "I left high school a virgin."

10. "I never had a date in high school or in college."

11. "I'm not smart enough to lie."

12. "I'm at the age where food has taken the place of sex in my life. In fact, I've just had a mirror put over my kitchen table."

13. "I pretended to be somebody I wanted to be until I finally became that person. Or he became me."

14. "Sitting on the toilet peeing—that's where I have my most contemplative moments."

A. Tom Selleck

B. Cary Grant

C. Sally Jesse Raphael

D. Charles Bronson

E. Richard Nixon

F. Ronald Reagan

G. Madonna

H. Ray Charles

I. Princess Diana

J. Clark Gable

K. Dolly Parton

L. Prince Charles

M. Ted Turner

N. Rodney Dangerfield

ANSWERS: 1-I, 2-H, 3-L, 4-M, 5-J, 6-K, 7-D, 8-E, 9-A, 10-C, 11-F, 12-N, 13-B, 14-G

Maine is the only U.S. state with a one-syllable name.

RESCUED FROM THE TRASH

*In many Bathroom Readers, we've included a section called
"Lucky Finds" about the amazing things people have picked up
at flea markets and garage sales. Here's a variation on
the theme: pop-culture icons that almost got tossed
out with the garbage...and lost forever.*

CARRIE, *Stephen King's first novel*

Trash: In 1973 King, 24, was making $9,500 a year teaching high-school English and living in a trailer—a rented trailer—with his wife and two kids when he began work on *Carrie*. At the time, he was selling short stories to magazines just to make ends meet. "Carrie" started out as a short story, but the author couldn't finish it because it was "too realistic" and too focused on the "world of girls," which he didn't understand. "After six or eight pages," he said,

> I found myself in a high-school locker room with a bunch of screaming girls who were all throwing sanitary napkins and screaming "Plug it up!" at a poor, lost girl named Carrie White who had never heard of menstruation and thought she was bleeding to death.

Appalled by what he'd written, he threw the pages away.

Rescue: That night, as King's wife was emptying the wastebasket, she noticed the crumpled papers. "[She] got curious about what I'd been writing, I guess," he said. She thought it was great, and insisted that he finish it.

> I told her it was too long for the markets I'd been selling to, that it might turn out to be a short novel, even. She said, "Then write it." I protested that I knew almost nothing about girls. She said, "I do. I'll help you." She did, and for the last 28 years, she has.

Doubleday paid a meager $2,500 advance for the book, thinking it might be a sleeper. It wasn't—it was a blockbuster. *Carrie* became a nationwide bestseller, and was later made into a hit film. "The book's reception floored everyone, I think," King said, "except my wife."

Cost, in parts and labor, for an Academy Award Oscar statuette: about $300.

EMILY DICKINSON'S POEMS

Trash: Dickinson was a homebody and virtual recluse. She hid her writings from everyone, including family, and was so private that she asked her sister Lavinia to burn her letters, unopened packages, and manuscripts after she died. So when Emily passed away in 1886 at age 56, Lavinia respected her wishes.

After destroying hundreds of manuscripts and letters without reading them, Lavinia opened a bureau drawer and found more than 600 poems in one box, and hundreds more "totally unordered and in various stages of completion." Surprised by the discovery, she stopped to read some before burning them...and was astonished by the quality of the writing.

Rescue: Years later editor Mabel Loomis Todd recounted what happened next:

> Soon after Emily's death, Lavinia came to me, in late evening, actually trembling with excitement. She told me she had discovered a veritable treasure—quantities of Emily's poems which she had no instructions to destroy. She had already burned without examination hundreds of of manuscripts, and letters...carrying out her sister's expressed wishes but without intelligent discrimination. Later she bitterly regretted such inordinate haste. But these poems, she told me, must be printed at once.

Todd spent the next four years sorting and editing Dickinson's surviving letters and poems. The first volume of poems was published in November 1890, and sold out six printings in the first five months. Today, she is considered one of America's greatest poets.

JACKSON BROWNE'S CAREER

Trash: Browne was still an unknown singer in the late 1960s, when David Crosby, of Crosby, Stills, and Nash, urged him to send a demo tape to manager David Geffen. Browne did...and as Fred Goodman writes in *Mansion on the Hill*, "Geffen did exactly what most people in the entertainment industry do with unsolicited material from unknown performers—he threw it away without a listen."

Rescue: As luck would have it, Geffen's secretary happened to notice the 8 x 10 glossy that Browne had sent and thought he was attractive. Curious about how he sounded, she fished the recording out of the trash. Goodman writes:

"You know that record and that picture you threw out?" she asked Geffen the next day.

"You go through my garbage?" asked her boss.

"Well, he was so cute that I took it home. And he's very good. Listen to the record."

Geffen did…and took Browne on as a client. When he couldn't get anyone to sign Browne to a record contract, he started his own label, Asylum—and Browne became its first star. Browne then helped fill out the label's roster, turning it into a monster success by bringing Geffen acts like the Eagles and Linda Ronstadt. The "rescue" made Geffen a billionaire.

YOU BET YOUR LIFE, *a quiz show starring Groucho Marx*

Trash: *You Bet Your Life*—featuring hours of Groucho's comedy—was one of America's top 10 shows in the 1950s. But by 1973, it was off the air and long forgotten. In August of that year, the program's producer/creator, John Guedel, got a call from NBC:

> They asked me, "Would you like to have a set of films for your garage as mementos of the show?" I said, "What do you mean?" They said, "We're destroying them to make room in our warehouse in New Jersey." I said, "You're kidding. How many have you destroyed so far?" They said 15 of the 250 negatives. I said, "Stop! Right now! Let me talk to New York."

Rescue: Guedel immediately called NBC's top brass and made a deal to syndicate *You Bet Your Life* rather than destroy it. He approached several TV stations…but no one bought it. Finally he went to KTLA, Channel 5 in Los Angeles, and asked them to run the show as a favor to Groucho—so he wouldn't have to drag out his projector every time he wanted to watch it. They agreed and, to everyone's surprise, it was a hit. In fact, it was so popular that other stations signed up, sparking a Groucho fad. "The boom in Groucho-related merchandise exceeds the Davy Crockett craze of 20 years ago," a surprised Groucho told a reporter in the 1970s, "So now, they tell me, I'm a cult." Groucho died in 1977, but remains a pop icon.

*　　　*　　　*

"Hollywood is the place where they shoot too many pictures and not enough actors." —**Walter Winchell**

Which part of a map is the *ideo locator*? The part that says "YOU ARE HERE."

UNCLE JOHN'S PAGE OF LISTS

Lists pages are harder to put together than you might think. Here's one we're especially proud of, from our Absolutely Absorbing Bathroom Reader.

3 REAL EXCUSES USED IN COURT

1. "I was thrown from the car as it left the road. I was later found in a ditch by some stray cows."

2. "The indirect cause of the accident was a little guy in a small car with a big mouth."

3. "To avoid hitting the bumper of the car in front, I struck the pedestrian."

TOP 5 *BILLBOARD* SONGS ON APRIL 5, 1964

1. "Can't Buy Me Love" (The Beatles)

2. "Twist and Shout" (The Beatles)

3. "She Loves You" (The Beatles)

4. "I Want to Hold Your Hand" (The Beatles)

5. "Please Please Me" (The Beatles)

3 CELEBRITIES WHO SAY THEY'VE SEEN A UFO:

1. Muhammad Ali

2. Jimmy Carter

3. William Shatner

7 WEIRD PLACE NAMES

1. Peculiar, Missouri

2. Smut Eye, Alabama

3. Loudville, Massachusetts

4. Disco, Illinois

5. Yeehaw Junction, Florida

6. Slaughter Beach, Delaware

7. Humptulips, Washington

3 MEN KNOWN BY THEIR MIDDLE NAMES

1. James Paul McCartney

2. William Clark Gable

3. Ruiz Fidel Castro

5 MOST-HATED HOUSEHOLD CHORES

1. Washing dishes

2. Bathroom cleaning

3. Ironing

4. Vacuuming

5. Washing windows

—Gallup Poll

4 WORDS NOBODY USES ANYMORE

1. Podge ("to walk slowly and heavily")

2. Roinous ("mean and nasty")

3. Battologist ("someone who pointlessly repeats themselves")

4. Battologist ("someone who pointlessly repeats themselves")

3 MOST PRIZED AUTOGRAPHS

1. Shakespeare (6 are known to exist)

2. Christopher Columbus (8 exist)

3. Julius Caesar (none are known to exist)

Napoleon's favorite horse was named Marengo; George Washington's was named Lexington.

LUCKY LOHRKE

After 20 years of making Bathroom Readers, *we can't believe that we never heard this story before. It's one of the most amazing, tragic, and surreal tales in baseball—and American—history.*

BACKGROUND
Perhaps no one's ever deserved the nickname "Lucky" more than Jack Lohrke. As a ballplayer, he was a decent hitter and utility infielder for the Giants and Phillies from 1947 to '53. But Lohrke's most incredible achievement may have been just living long enough to play in the majors at all. Born in Los Angeles in 1924, he started playing minor league ball in 1942, when he was 18 years old. But then his life—along with those of thousands of other young men—was put on hold when he was called up to serve in World War II. And that's where this story begins.

BRUSH WITH DEATH #1: The Train
Riding on a troop train through California to ship off to war, Lohrke's railcar came off the tracks. Three men were killed in the horrific wreck while many of the survivors were severely burned by scalding water that rushed through the car. Lohrke walked away uninjured.

BRUSH WITH DEATH #2: The War
A year later, Lohrke survived the Battle of Normandy. Then he fought in the Battle of the Bulge, the deadliest campaign of World War II for American GIs, in which 19,000 U.S. servicemen were killed. On four separate occasions, the soldiers on either side of Lohrke were killed. Each time, he walked away uninjured.

BRUSH WITH DEATH #3: The Colonel's Seat
In 1945 Lohrke was sent home. Arriving in New Jersey, he boarded a plane for his flight back to California. Just as the plane was preparing to take off, a colonel marched onto the plane and took Lohrke's seat, forcing him to wait at the airport for the next transport. Less than an hour later, the plane crashed in Ohio. There were no survivors.

A record: 60.2% of the U.S. TV audience watched the last episode of M*A*S*H in 1983.

BRUSH WITH DEATH #4: The Phone Call

A year later, Lohrke was playing for the Double-A Spokane Indians in the Western International League. On a rainy day in June, the team's bus was negotiating Washington's Snoqualmie Pass through the Cascade Mountains on their way to a weekend series near Seattle. The Indians stopped for lunch at a diner in Ellensburg, and as they were preparing to get back on the bus, Lohrke was told he had a phone call. He thought that was odd, considering that he was in a small town in the mountains. But the team's owner had somehow tracked him down at the diner. And he had good news: Lohrke, who was on a hitting tear, had been promoted to the Triple-A San Diego Padres (then in the Pacific Coast League).

At first, Lohrke was ecstatic. But then he had to make a choice: Did he want to continue with the team to the Seattle area and take a train back to Spokane from there? Or could he make his way back home on his own? Lohrke thought about it...and chose to hitchhike directly back to Spokane. He bid his teammates farewell and watched them board the bus. About 30 minutes later, the bus skidded on the wet highway and crashed through a guardrail before tumbling 350 feet down into a ravine, where the gas tank exploded. Nine players were killed, eight of whom were recent war veterans. To this day, it remains one of the worst disasters in the history of American sports.

"I've often wondered how the Spokane owner knew we'd stop at that particular diner," Lohrke later said. "That was pure fate."

THE MIRACLE MAN

Although he was devastated by the loss of his teammates, Lohrke stuck with baseball and performed well enough in San Diego to make it the majors. As luck would have it, Lohrke was the third baseman on the 1951 New York Giants, the team that famously came back from a seemingly insurmountable deficit to win the National League pennant. Unfortunately, Lucky's off-the-field luck didn't show up in that year's World Series—he went hitless in a losing effort against the Yankees.

Lucky Lohrke retired from baseball in 1953 and, as of 2008, he's 84 years old and still very much alive.

GOOD GRIEF: THE *PEANUTS* STORY

Here's an inside look at the world's most popular comic strip and the man who created it.

BACKGROUND
To say that *Peanuts* is the most famous daily comic strip in the history of the art form is an understatement. Like Superman and Mickey Mouse, *Peanuts* transcended its medium and became woven into the fabric of society. Readers of all ages found something to connect with—Charlie Brown's perseverance in the face of one disappointment after another, Snoopy's cool, Lucy's crabbiness, or Linus's innocent wisdom. The sheer numbers *Peanuts* generated are still unmatched, nearly a decade after the strip came to an end: From 1950 to 1999, Charles Schulz wrote and drew 18,250 daily *Peanuts* strips. They appeared in 2,600 newspapers, reaching 355 million readers in 75 countries, and were translated into 21 different languages. Between the daily strips, the merchandising tie-ins, and the television specials, *Peanuts* is also a phenomenal moneymaker—at its peak, it earned more than $1 billion per year and made its creator, Charles M. Schulz, one of the richest entertainers in the world.

CRACKS IN THE ARMOR

So what *was* the appeal? For one, *Peanuts* was ahead of its time. *Doonesbury* creator Garry Trudeau, who grew up reading the strip, said, "*Peanuts* vibrated with '50s alienation. Everything about it was different. Edgy, unpredictable—it was the first Beat strip."

Early-1950s America was a time of prosperity: World War II had been won, the economy was strong, President Eisenhower encouraged good old American know-how for the construction of interstate highways and pristine neighborhoods. This optimism played out in popular movies, on television, and even in the comics. The few comic strips that featured children, like Ernie Bushmiller's *Nancy*, portrayed kids as innocent and…well, kidlike. In the movies, children routinely got into and out of cute adven-

---

A coffee tree yields only about a pound of coffee each year.

tures, never offering any great philosophical truths. And no one expected them to. Then, all of a sudden, here was a comic strip with a strange round-headed boy saying, "I don't feel the way I'm supposed to feel."

Statements like that reflected the painful truth that a lot of people *weren't* content. Treading a thin line between wholesome and subversive, Charlie Brown and his friends jumped off the page and connected with readers. Schulz tapped into something that kept people glued to *Peanuts'* extended storylines (something new to kid-oriented strips): they dealt more with pain than triumph.

The pain that emanated from the strip came straight from Schulz's own life. He once admitted, "I worry about almost all there is in life to worry about. And because I worry, Charlie Brown has to worry." Schulz also pointed to the strip's recurring themes: "All the loves are unrequited; all the baseball games are lost; all the test scores are D-minuses; the Great Pumpkin never comes; and the football is always pulled away." Schulz knew that for every winner out there, there were 10 more losers. They all want to win—to fit in—but most have to make do with what they end up with. The struggle to fit in had been a part of Schulz's life for as long as he could remember.

A BOY AND HIS DOG

Charles Monroe Schulz was born in Minneapolis, Minnesota, on November 26, 1922, to parents of German and Norwegian descent, and the family soon moved to nearby St. Paul. Daily newspaper comic strips were always a big part of his life (when he was two days old, an uncle gave him the nickname he carried for the rest of his life, "Sparky," after a horse called Sparkplug from the comic strip *Barney Google*).

In a way, reading *Peanuts* is like reading about Schulz's childhood. He owned a black-and-white dog named Spike that followed him around the neighborhood and ran onto the field during his baseball games. Just like Charlie Brown, Schulz flew his kites into the trees, liked to ice skate, went to summer camp reluctantly, and had a father who was a barber.

Also like Charlie Brown, Schulz was often teased by his friends, which led to a lifelong inferiority complex. Schulz's high marks in grammar school led to his being promoted from the third grade to the fifth grade, putting him in a classroom full of kids who were bigger, older, and more streetwise than he was. By the time he got to high school, Schulz suffered from bouts of depression.

But when he was alone, he found solace in reading and drawing comic strips. His first published drawing—at age 15—was a picture of Spike that he submitted to *Ripley's Believe It or Not!* Yet the drawings that Schulz submitted to his high-school yearbook were rejected. "I was a bland, stupid-looking kid who started off badly and failed at everything," he once said in an interview. Schulz never stopped drawing, though, and filled sketchbook after sketchbook with depictions of Popeye, Mickey Mouse, Donald Duck, and dozens more of his comic-strip heroes.

OFF TO WAR

After high school finally ended, Schulz dove straight into his dream. With his parents' support, he took a correspondence course at the St. Paul Art Instruction School. But his dreams were put on hold when he was drafted into the army and sent to Europe as a machine-gun squad leader. (On his only opportunity to shoot someone, his gun wasn't loaded. Fortunately, the German soldier surrendered.) Schulz's feelings of isolation only grew more intense during the war. He was still grieving for his mother, who had died in 1943, and he never really fit in with the other guys. Just as he had in high school, Schulz lost himself in his sketchbook. "The army taught me all I needed to know about loneliness," he said.

BACK TO THE DRAWING BOARD

Schulz returned to St. Paul in 1945 even more disillusioned, but he knew his path: cartooning. He went back to the Art Instruction School and asked them for a job as a correspondence-course instructor. They hired him. He soon landed a second job at a Catholic comic magazine called *Timeless Topix*, lettering their comics pages. While there, Schulz met a comic-strip artist named Frank Wing, who would become his mentor. Soon Schulz was drawing his own cartoons at *Timeless Topix*. His first: a single-panel cartoon with two kids sitting on a curb. "One kid," Schulz wrote, "is sitting on the curb with a baseball bat in his hands talking to a little girl, saying, 'I think I could learn to love you, Judy, if your batting average was a little higher.'" Wing saw the cartoon and told Schulz, "Sparky, I think you should draw more of those little kids. They're pretty good."

Around this time, Schulz discovered a classic comic strip called *Krazy Kat*, drawn by George Herriman. Without *Krazy Kat*, *Peanuts* might have been just another comic where the kids did kidlike things. But *Krazy Kat* was surreal—a cat, a mouse, and a dog living in a dreamlike world. They had childlike qualities countered by very advanced vocabularies. *Krazy Kat* demonstrated to Schulz that fantasy and grown-up language could be effective tools to describe not only the everyday lives of children, but of people in general. Even though he drew only kids from then on, Schulz's comic strips would be primarily targeted toward adults.

LI'L FOLKS

In 1947 Schulz sold his first newspaper cartoons—single-panel gags—to his hometown paper, the *St. Paul Pioneer Press*. Called *Li'l Folks*, it had no set cast of characters, but there was a kid he called Charlie Brown (borrowed from the name of an artist friend) and a dog that resembled Snoopy. While writing *Li'l Folks*, Schulz also sold 17 cartoons to the *Saturday Evening Post* from 1947 to 1950. Bolstered by these successes, he attempted to syndicate *Li'l Folks* in other newspapers, but couldn't get it picked up. Then in 1949 the *Pioneer Press* dropped *Li'l Folks*.

Rather than admit defeat, in 1950 Schulz shopped his best single-panel gag cartoons to United Features Syndicate in New York. They liked them…but thought they weren't original enough to stand out. So Schulz showed them a few four-panel comic strips he'd been working on. The syndicate loved them and asked Schulz to create "some definite characters." Energized, Schulz returned to St. Paul and started forming the characters that he would draw for the rest of his life.

For Part II of the Peanuts *story, go to page 349.*

*　　*　　*

There is only one beautiful child in the world, and
every mother has it.　　—Chinese proverb

STATE V. BIG HAIR

Names of actual court cases tried in the good old U.S. of A.

Friends of Kangaroo Rat v.
California Dept. of Corrections

U.S. v. Pipe on Head

United States of America v.
2,116 Boxes of Boned Beef,
Weighing Approximately
154,121 Pounds, and 541
Boxes of Offal, Weighing
Approximately 17,732 Pounds

Schmuck v. Dumm

Jones v.
God, Jesus, Others

Julius Goldman's Egg City v.
United States

Pam-To-Pee v.
United States

Klink v. Looney

United States ex rel.
Gerald Mayo v.
Satan and His Staff

Lexis-Nexis v. Beer

Muncher v.
Muncher

People v. Booger

Short v. Long

State of Indiana v.
Virtue

United States v.
$11,557.22 in U.S. Currency

Advance Whip & Novelty Co. v.
Benevolent Protective
Order of Elks

Fried v. Rice

United States v.
1,100 Machine Gun Receivers

Plough v. Fields

Frankenstein v.
Independent Roofing & Siding

Big v. Little

Ruff v. Ruff

State v. Big Hair

Hamburger v. Fry

I am the Beast Six Six Six of the
Lord of Hosts in Edmond Frank
MacGillevray, Jr., et. al. v.
Michigan State Police

Louisiana is the only state that still refers to the Napoleonic Code in its state law.

CRÈME *de la* CRUD

The best of the worst of the worst.

WORST HERSHEY FOOD PRODUCT
Beet Sherbet

Like many Americans, Milton Hershey, founder of the chocolate company, went on a vitamin kick in the early 1940s and started experimenting with vegetable juices. "It's much easier to drink raw vegetables than to eat raw vegetables," he explained. Surely vegetable juice sherbets were even better.

Hershey tested onion, carrot, and celery sherbets before concluding that beet sherbet tasted the "best" and adding it to the menu at the Hershey Hotel in Pennsylvania. Those brave few who ordered the stuff couldn't stomach it—it tasted terrible, which had completely escaped the man who gave us the Hershey bar. How'd that happen? Former CEO Samuel Hinkle blamed the cigars that Hershey, then in his mid-80s, had smoked for more than 60 years. "After smoking six, eight, ten cigars a day, Mr. Hershey had absolutely burned out his taste buds," Hinkle recalled. "He couldn't taste or smell a thing."

WORST CHOICE OF PROPS IN A LONDON PLAY
Real champagne, in a scene of the first (and last) performance of Ecarte *at the Old Globe Theatre*

Playwright Lord Newry was a stickler for authenticity, so when his 1870 play called for a picnic, he used a real picnic basket filled with roast chicken, pies, truffles...and several bottles of champagne, which the actors drank to the last drop. Leading lady Nita Nicotina was soon too drunk to remember her lines; her leading man kept track of his by shouting them out at the top of his lungs. That tired him out, so he laid down in the middle of the stage and fell fast asleep as the other actors worked around him, tripping over props and leaning against scenery that was not designed to support their weight.

By now the audience had lost its composure; when Nicotina walked out onstage at the beginning of the next scene wearing one

---

How do they know? Scientists say butterflies see in shades of green, red, and yellow.

red and one green boot, the audience lost itself in howling waves of laughter. That made her mad. "What are you laughing at, you beastly fools?" she screamed. "When you have done making idiots of yourselves, I will go on with this—*hiccup*—beastly play." She never got the chance—the audience laughed and booed the entire cast off the stage. (Except for the leading man, who was still asleep.)

WORST JOCKEY

Beltran de Osorio y Diez de Rivera, "Iron" Duke of Albuquerque

The duke developed an obsession with winning England's Grand National Steeplechase horse race when he was only eight years old, after receiving a film of the race as a birthday present. "I said then that I would win that race one day," the amateur rider recounted years later.

• On his first attempt in 1952, he fell from his horse; he woke up later in the hospital with a cracked vertebra.

• He tried again in 1963; bookies placed odds of 66–1 against him finishing the race still on his horse. (The duke fell from the horse.)

• He raced again in 1965, and fell from his horse after it collapsed underneath him, breaking his leg.

• In 1974, having just had 16 screws removed from a leg he'd broken after falling from the horse in another race, he fell while training for the Grand National and broke his collarbone. He recovered in time to compete (in a plaster cast) and actually managed to finish the race while still on his horse—the only time he ever would. He placed eighth.

• In 1976 the duke fell again during a race—this time he was trampled by the other horses and suffered seven broken ribs, several broken vertebrae, a broken wrist, a broken thigh, and a severe concussion, which left him in a coma for two days.

• He eventually recovered, but when he announced at the age of 57 that he was going to try again, race organizers pulled his license "for his own safety."

The Iron Duke never did win the Grand National, as he promised himself he would, but he did break another record—he broke more bones trying to win it than any jockey before or since.

First female national news anchor: Barbara Walters (1976).

BEHIND THE HITS

Here are a few "inside" stories about popular songs.

The Artist: The Beatles
The Song: "Yesterday" (1965)
The Story: This song just popped into Paul McCartney's head when he woke up one morning. He ran to the piano immediately and plunked out the tune so he wouldn't forget it. His sleepy-eyed lyrics: "Scrambled eggs… / Ooooh baby how I love your legs." It was only after people close to the band convinced them that the song had real potential that Paul rewrote the lyrics.

The Artist: Daryl Hall and John Oates
The Song: "Rich Girl" (1977)
The Story: Despite many years of hard work touring and recording, commercial success eluded Hall and Oates…until 1976, when Daryl Hall wrote this song. The inspiration: He'd always despised his girlfriend's ex-boyfriend, an obnoxious heir to a fast-food fortune who had had everything handed to him but appreciated nothing. Still, Hall thought "rich boy" might not sound right to record buyers, so he made the subject a "rich girl." The song was a breakthrough hit, going to #1 in March 1977. The group went on to sell 40 million albums and became the bestselling duo in music history.
Strange fact: Serial killer David Berkowitz, the Son of Sam, told reporters that his murders were partially motivated by "Rich Girl."

The Artist: Beck
The Song: "Loser" (1994)
The Story: One day, Beck was fooling around at producer Karl Stephenson's house. Beck started playing slide guitar, and Stephenson began recording. As Stephenson added a Public Enemy–style beat and a sample from Dr. John's "I Walk on Gilded Splinters," Beck attempted to freestyle rap—something he had never done before. Frustrated at his inability to rap, Beck began criticizing his own performance: "*Soy un perdedor*" ("I'm a loser" in Spanish). Beck wanted to scrap it, but Stephenson thought it was catchy. Stephenson was right—"Loser" made Beck a star.

Was he experienced? No—Jimi Hendrix never took a formal music lesson.

BUT WAIT!
THERE'S MORE!

If you buy this Bathroom Reader *right now for just $17.95, we'll include this amazing Book-O-Matic—free of charge! Here's the story of the Popeil family and their world of gadgets.*

YOURS FREE IF YOU ACT NOW!

Since the 1950s, the name Popeil has been synonymous with gadgets sold on television, in either breathless commercials for plastic food choppers or in 30-minute "infomercials" for spray-on hair. But Ron Popeil, the guy who sells the Showtime Rotisserie ("Set it…and…forget it") on TV, is actually a third-generation pitchman. His great-uncle, Nat Morris, started in Asbury Park, New Jersey, in the early 20th century. Like other pitchmen, Morris would set up a table at county fairs, carnivals, or along the beach and sell inexpensive items, usually kitchen utensils, to passersby. Morris was so successful at it that by the 1920s, he'd become wealthy enough to open his own metal kitchen products factory.

In 1932 Morris's nephew, Samuel Popeil, stepped in for a sick relative to demonstrate kitchen utensils at Macy's in New York City and discovered that he, too, had a natural ability for selling. Like Morris, Popeil became a master of "the pitch," honed over years of selling and performing product demonstrations at department stores, fairs, street corners, and boardwalks.

ISN'T THAT AMAZING!

Sam Popeil and his brother Raymond earned their living in the 1930s and '40s by selling products that were made at their Popeil Brothers factory. Eliminating the middleman associated with selling other companies' products meant more profits for the Popeil brothers. Raymond oversaw factory production and Sam came up with new gadgets, mostly graters and slicers that cost under a dollar. They gave the products names designed to evoke power and efficiency, like "Kitchen Magician" or "Slice-a-Way." These simple items were presented so enthusiastically by the Popeils that consumers bought them by the millions.

In Japan, apple farmers use turkeys to guard their orchards against monkeys.

In the late 1940s, the Popeil brothers fully embraced the plastics revolution. They sold plastic versions of common kitchen items such as breadboxes, flour sifters, cookie presses, and storage canisters. They were pleasing to the eye, looked modern, and were inexpensive to make.

AS SEEN ON TV

But as television took hold in the 1950s it threatened the Popeils' usual circuit of fairs, carnivals, and department store demonstrations. In 1956 the Grant Company, an early TV advertising agency based in Chicago, asked Popeil to sell the new Chop-O-Matic food chopper in a TV commercial. It would essentially be a four-minute, taped version of the Popeil's department store pitch.

But Grant didn't choose Sam or Raymond to appear in the ad. They picked Sam's 21-year-old son, Ron Popeil, to be the pitchman. (He'd spent the previous five years doing demonstrations of Popeil products around the Midwest.)

Despite good sales for the Chop-O-Matic, the Popeils weren't convinced of television's power. They went back to in-store demonstrations and made more Chop-O-Matic-like products, which they contracted other companies to sell on TV. They wouldn't make their own ad until 1961, for the Veg-O-Matic. On the strength of that TV ad (featuring Raymond Popeil), the product sold 11 million units. *That* convinced them.

Other Popeil Brothers items Americans couldn't live without:

• **Automatic Egg Turner** (1948). A metal spatula that could flip an egg or a pancake perfectly

• **Toastie Pie** (1950). A toasted-sandwich maker

• **Citrex Juicer** (1951). A tiny juicer that plugs into the fruit and allows the juice to pour into a glass

• **Plastic Plant Kit** (1957). Molds liquid plastic to make plastic plants, which were very exotic at the time

• **Chop-O-Matic** spawned these slicers, dicers, peelers, and mixers: **Dial-O-Matic** (1958), **The Amazing Veg-O-Matic** (1961), **Corn-O-Matic** (1964), **Mince-O-Matic Seven** (1965), **Peel-O-Matic** (1965), and **Whip-O-Matic** (1974).

The Popeils churned out new products and commercials well

into the 1970s. Their downfall: themselves. By being an early proponent of TV advertising, they actually demonstrated its lucrative potential to other companies, which drove up ad rates and commercial production costs. Meanwhile, the introduction of more sophisticated electric kitchen appliances was making their simple plastic and metal gadgets look cheap and dated. The Popeil Brothers company was sold in 1979; it was dissolved and liquidated within two years.

But there was still Ronco.

But wait, there's more! For the rest of the Popeil story, turn to page 339. Act now! Operators are standing by!

*   *   *

Here are some of Samuel Popeil's sure-fire sales tactics. (His son, Ron, uses many of the same methods on TV today.)

• Sales booths should be situated near makeup aisles or women's restrooms to ensure a receptive—and captive—audience.

• Get one or two people to stop and listen. That will pique the interest of others passing by.

• Tout the product's indispensability. Show how the item is a value because it performs multiple tasks. Memorize the spoken part of the pitch so you can deliver it flawlessly while you demonstrate the product. That will show how easy it is to use.

• Describe the product's usefulness repeatedly, using words like "magic," "fantastic," and "miracle." Ask rhetorical questions like "Isn't that amazing?" when demonstrating the product.

• Never reveal the price until the end of the pitch. This builds suspense. Say to the audience, "You're probably asking yourself what a product like this costs." Then give a high round number, like $40. Then say that the item is well worth that price, but right now it's much cheaper. Progressively move the price down: It's not $10; it's not $5. It's the low, low price of $3.98! To encourage immediate purchase, tell the crowd that "supplies are limited."

• But wait, there's more! Before allowing anyone to purchase it, suddenly introduce and demonstrate a smaller product, noting its "retail" value, and give it away for free with purchase.

Artist Paul Cézanne taught his parrot to say "Cézanne is a great painter."

NATURE'S REVENGE

*What happens when we mess around with nature, trying to
get it to do our bidding? Sometimes it works...but sometimes
nature gets even. Here are a few instances when people
intentionally introduced animals or plants into a
new environment—and regretted it.*

Import: English sparrows
Background: One hundred sparrows were brought from England
to Brooklyn, New York, in 1850. Reason: to control canker
worms that were killing trees in city parks.
Nature's Revenge: The sparrows did their job—for a while. Then
they got a taste for native insects, then they had a lot of babies, and
then they took off. By 1875 the sparrows had made it to San Francisco, stealing nesting sites from native birds and ravaging crops and
livestock feed along the way. In 1903 noted ornithologist W. L. Dawson said, "Without question the most deplorable event in the history
of American ornithology was the introduction of the English spar-
row." Today they number about 150 million in North America.
Note: They're not even sparrows—they're from the weaverbird family.

Import: Cane toads
Background: The cane toad can grow up to 10 inches long and
weigh as much as 4 pounds. Its croak is said to sound like a dog's
bark. This bizarre species is native to Central America but was
imported to Australia in 1935. Australian farmers wanted it to eat
two types of beetle that were damaging their sugarcane crop.
Nature's Revenge: Nobody seemed to notice that the cane toad
lives on the ground—so they were only able to eat beetles that fell
off the sugarcane. The experiment was a failure, then a disaster.
The toads feasted on other native insect species—many to the
point of extinction—and spread into neighboring habitats. They
are large enough to eat any insect, as well as frogs and other toads,
and have even been known to eat from dog and cat food bowls.
And, to make matters worse, they're poisonous. Whatever tries to
eat them dies—even if they only eat the tadpoles. The situation
continues to be dire: people who spot a cane toad are advised to
contact toad hotlines and Web sites.

Chew on this: What's a "winkle"? An edible sea snail.

Import: Rats
Background: In the 16th and 17th centuries, hoards of people were leaving Europe on ships bound for the New World. Tyranny, poverty, horrendous filth, and epidemics drove boatload after boatload of settlers across the Atlantic seeking wide-open spaces, better resources, more freedom, and less disease.
Nature's Revenge: The settlers found a pristine paradise—and quickly infested it with rats. Early ocean-crossing ships were famously rat-infested, the vermin often numbering more than the humans onboard. The adaptable rodent made itself at home and spread all over the continent. According to a study by Cornell University, by 1999 there were approximately a billion rats in the United States—on farms alone, and rats do an estimated $19 billion in economic damage every year.

Import: Rabbits, opossums, and stoats
Background: New Zealand's landscape had evolved for 60 to 80 million years with only four mammals—all bats. In this unique ecosystem, exceptionally unique flora and fauna, such as flightless birds, prospered. Then, in the early 1800s, Europeans arrived bringing sheep, pigs, and goats as livestock, as well as rabbits and opossums as game for sportsmen.
Nature's Revenge: Rabbits multiply...like rabbits. By 1894 more than 17 million rabbit pelts were being exported annually. While that made money for some, the rabbits' effect on the land, competing wildlife, and sheep farmers was devastating. The opossum did similar damage by eating massive amounts of native plant life in the exotic canopy.

Desperate farmers imported the stoat, a weasel-like creature that eats rabbits and opossums. That worked for a while, but birds, insects, and bats were easier for the stoats to catch. They quickly decimated bird populations, especially that of the kiwi. Thanks to the stoat, today several other species are either endangered or already extinct. New Zealand's government spends millions every year trying to stop the continuing rampage. And what of the stoat's intended targets, the rabbit and opossum? As of 2001, they were still the number one and number two pests in the country.

Rice-O-Roni: Italy produces the most rice of any country in Europe.

AMERICA'S FIRST REALITY TV SHOW

Survivor and The Real World *may seem innovative, but they owe a huge debt to a show that hasn't aired since 1973, despite being named one of the greatest shows of all time by* TV Guide. *Here's the story of the show that started it all.*

GET REAL

In 1971 a documentary film producer named Craig Gilbert came up with a novel idea for an educational TV show: film the lives of four American families in four different parts of the country—the West Coast, the Midwest, the South, and the East Coast. A different film crew would be assigned to each family and would film their lives for four straight weeks, from the moment the first person got up until the last person went to bed. Many hours of footage would be filmed, then it would be edited and condensed into four one-hour documentaries, one on each family. The documentaries would be broadcast on PBS.

Television programming was a lot different in those days—for years viewers had been fed a steady diet of decidedly *un*realistic family shows like *Ozzie and Harriet*, *Father Knows Best*, *The Waltons*, and *The Brady Bunch*. Gilbert figured viewers might be interested in a new aspect of American family life: reality.

FAMILY SECRETS

For the West Coast family, Gilbert chose the Louds, an upper middle-class family living in Santa Barbara, California—parents Bill and Pat, and their five teenage children: sons Lance, Kevin, and Grant, and daughters Delilah and Michele. "They basically said, 'How would you like to star in the greatest home movie ever made?'" Lance Loud remembered. "We didn't have to do anything, just be our little Southern California hick selves."

Gilbert hired two filmmakers, Susan and Alan Raymond, to film the family. Shortly after production got underway, he decided to dump the four-family concept and focus exclusively on the Louds—for a longer time period. To this day it is unclear whether

The mayfly's eggs take 3 years to hatch. Lifespan: about 6 hours.

Craig Gilbert knew it at the time, but the Louds' marriage was in serious trouble (thanks to Bill's philandering), and their son Lance, who lived in New York, was gay. The Louds had assumed that keeping their family secrets for four weeks wouldn't be that difficult; but now Gilbert was asking them for permission to film for months on end. Could they withstand this invasion of their privacy?

Bill and Pat thought it over…and decided to take a chance. "I thought I might get away with just saying, 'These are my children and my kitchen and my pool and my horses, over and out.'" Pat Loud recalled years later. "What naifs we were!"

OPEN HOUSE

Bill and Pat need not have worried about protecting Lance Loud's privacy—he was completely open about his sexuality, even when the film crew was present. He was the very first openly gay teenager ever shown on American television; for many viewers, he was the first out-of-the-closet homosexual they had ever seen.

As for the Louds' marital problems, they proved both impossible to hide and impossible to repair. As the weeks passed and Pat became more comfortable around the cameras, she began to open up about the problems she was having with Bill. Their marriage continued to deteriorate until finally, a few months into filming, Pat threw Bill out of the house. The Raymonds were there, and they captured it all on film.

12-STEP PROGRAM

By the time the Raymonds wrapped up production, they'd been filming the Louds for seven solid months. They had so much raw footage—more than 300 hours worth—that it took them the better part of two years to edit it down to the 12 one-hour episodes that would air as *An American Family* beginning in January 1973.

One of the reasons the Louds agreed to allow the film crew into their home in the first place was because they didn't think many people would ever see the finished product. This was a documentary, after all, and one being made for educational television at that. PBS wasn't even broadcast in Santa Barbara in 1971 (by 1973, it was); besides, Pat didn't watch much educational television and she didn't think anyone else would, either. "We erroneously believed the series would be a simply interminable home movie that no one in their right mind would watch for more than five minutes," she recalled in 2002. Lance Loud thought of the film as "a very odd, never-to-be-noticed project."

HITTING THE BIG TIME

But when *An American Family* finally hit the airwaves in January 1973, more than 10 million people tuned in, making it one of the most-watched series in PBS history. The viewers were there for episode 2, when Lance's sexuality was revealed; they were there for episode 9, when Pat Loud asked Bill for a divorce; and they stayed glued to their sets until the series came to an end in episode 12.

Overnight, the Louds became one of the most famous families in America. They were on the cover of *Newsweek* (underneath the banner "Broken Family"), they made the national television talk shows, appearing with Dick Cavett, Dinah Shore, Mike Douglas, and Phil Donahue, and their problems were discussed around the water coolers of every workplace in America. Everyone knew who they were.

ROUGH GOING

Today, more than 30 years later, the Louds may be remembered with fond nostalgia, but that wasn't the case in 1973. Many viewers were stunned by what they saw. The Louds were an upper middle-class family, more affluent than most of the viewers who watched them. Like the fictional TV families people were used to seeing on the tube, the Louds seemed to have it all: They lived in a big, beautiful house in sunny Southern California; they had steady, high-paying jobs; they had four cars, five beautiful children, three dogs, two cats, a horse, a swimming pool—seemingly everything that anyone could possibly want. So why weren't they happy? Why couldn't Bill and Pat save their marriage? Why was Lance Loud gay? What on Earth was *wrong* with these people?

Many viewers—not to mention pundits and TV critics—came to see Bill and Pat Loud as unfit parents and their family as the personification of everything that was wrong with American families in the early 1970s. *Newsweek* called the Louds "affluent zombies" and described the series as "a glimpse into the pit." *The New York Times Magazine* called Lance Loud a "flamboyant leech," the "evil flower of the family," and an "emotional dwarf."

Sounds worse than it is: The medical condition *epistaxisis* is...a nosebleed.

That wasn't at all how the Louds had expected to come across. "People were shocked, and we were shocked that they were shocked," Lance Loud remembered.

> We thought people would be on our side and sympathize with a family responding to all the different moods and trends of the times. But they didn't sympathize; they misunderstood, thinking that we were arrogant in our stupidity. They were totally wrong.

NO HOLLYWOOD ENDING

In the end, nearly everyone associated with the film ended up regretting ever getting involved. Bill and Pat accused the Raymonds of distorting their family life, zooming in on problems and controversies at the expense of everything else. "It seemed that the entire series was all about Lance being homosexual and my husband and I divorcing," Pat Loud says. "My other four children and their friends seemed to be of no real interest to the editors."

The Raymonds had their own regrets. Though they did make two more films about the Louds—in 1983 and 2003—they swore off making documentaries about any other family. "It was too brutal," Susan Raymond says. "We made films on policemen, on a prison warden, on a principal of a school—people who are public officials. But we didn't do anything on ordinary people or families. We didn't think they could handle that kind of scrutiny."

FINAL CHAPTER

After the show ended, Lance Loud spent several years as the lead singer of a punk rock band called the Mumps, but though his fame brought the band some notoriety, it also made it harder for them to be taken seriously. The Mumps broke up in 1980 and Lance returned to Southern California, where he worked as a freelance journalist, published in magazines like *The Advocate*, *Interview*, and *Vanity Fair*. He also abused intravenous drugs for nearly 20 years, which caused him to become infected with hepatitis. In 1987 he learned that he was HIV positive.

In late 2001, his health failing, Lance checked into an L.A. hospice and called the Raymonds to see if they would document his relationship with his family during this final phase of his life. They agreed. Why did Lance want to do it? Felled by years of unsafe sex

Cold comfort: Saint Lydwina is the patron saint of ice skating.

and drug addiction, he'd come to see his life as a cautionary tale. But he also wanted to show viewers that for all the problems the Louds had gone through, 30 years later they still loved each other and were close. "He could have asked for a priest or a minister, but he called for his filmmakers," Susan Raymond says.

Lance Loud died on December 22, 2001, at the age of 50—the same age his father was when *An American Family* premiered in 1973. *Lance Loud! A Death in an American Family* aired on PBS in January 2003.

After the original series ended, Pat Loud moved to New York and became a literary agent. She has since retired and now lives in Los Angeles. Bill Loud remarried in 1976; he is retired and also lives in Los Angeles. Kevin Loud lives with his family in Paradise Valley, Arizona; Grant, Delilah, and Michele Loud and their families all live in Los Angeles.

DUBIOUS ACHIEVERS

Alan and Susan Raymond, credited with filming the first-ever reality TV show, are still making documentaries…but they refuse to watch any of the shows their work has inspired. Anthropologist Margaret Mead predicted that *An American Family* would come to be seen "as important a moment in the history of human thought as the invention of the novel," but judging from the shows that have followed it—*The Real World, Big Brother,* and *The Osbournes* among them—it's a safe bet she was wrong.

"Like Frankenstein's monster, it's a mixed blessing to be considered someone who spawned this reality TV genre," Alan Raymond says. "I think it's a largely superficial, stupid genre of television programming that I don't think as a documentary filmmaker I take much pride in."

*   *   *

A Final Note. For all it cost them personally, how much money were the Louds paid for letting a crew film them for seven months? Not much. "The family received no compensation for their participation in the film," Pat Loud says. "The only money we got was a check for $400 to repair the kitchen where the gaffer's tape had pulled the paint off the walls."

Scientists say: An adult must taste a disliked food 10 times before learning to like it.

UNCLE JOHN'S STALL OF FAME

*We're always amazed by the creative ways people get involved
with bathrooms, toilets, toilet paper, etc. To honor them,
we've created Uncle John's Stall of Fame.*

Honoree: Donna Summer, pop singer
Notable Achievement: Writing a Top 10 song in the bathroom
True Story: At a posh hotel, Summer was washing her hands in the ladies' room. She mused to herself that the washroom attendant there had to work awfully hard for her money. It suddenly hit Summer that she had a song title. So she rushed into a stall and wrote lyrics for it. "She Works Hard for the Money" was an international hit that went to #3 on the *Billboard* chart.

Honoree: Jacob Feinzilberg, a San Jose, California, inventor
Notable Achievement: Inventing the ultimate port-a-potty
True Story: In 1993 Feinzilberg came up with the Inflate-a-Potty, a toilet so portable it can actually fit in a purse. It can be inflated in seconds and is used with an ordinary eight-gallon kitchen bag as a disposable liner. He came up with the idea for it at a picnic when his young daughter suddenly "heard nature's call and found no place to answer it."

Honoree: The City of Auckland, New Zealand
Notable Achievement: Converting sewage into parkland
True Story: Auckland has figured out a unique way to recycle the 60,000 tons of recycled biosolids (treated human waste) building up in its sewage-treatment facilities. They plan to fill up a 30,000-year-old volcano called Puketutu Island with the human waste and turn it into a regional park. Scheduled to last from 2011 until 2041, the dumping will cost around $25 million (including the price of building the park). Many local residents are understandably apprehensive about a mountain-sized poo park that could

---

The earliest known will was written in 2550 B.C.

potentially erupt, but Ian Smith, an Auckland University volcanologist, assures them that the volcano no longer poses any danger—and that the treated waste doesn't smell bad any more. "I think it is pretty safe," he said.

Honoree: Koko, the gorilla that knows American sign language
Notable Achievement: Being the first member of the ape family to master "potty talk"
True Story: In the late 1990s, Koko participated in a live Internet chat on America Online. According to one account, "When asked about her boyfriend, Koko replied, 'toilet.'"

Honorees: Officials at the Amsterdam International Airport in The Netherlands
Notable Achievement: Inventing a new "target game"
True Story: It's a simple but brilliant idea. In 1999 airport officials had workers etch the outline of a housefly into each urinal, near the drain. "Men aim at the fly, which limits splashing," says a spokesman. Since the installation, the flies have been credited with reducing "urinal floor spillage" by 80%.

Honoree: Lieutenant Governor Steve Windom of Alabama
Notable Achievement: Strategic use of a chamber pot to wear down his political enemies
True Story: In March 1999, Windom, a Republican, was presiding over the 35-member state legislature composed of 18 Democrats and 17 Republicans. During an important battle over Senate procedures, Windom feared that if he surrendered the gavel and left the chamber for even a minute, the Democrats would take control and his party would lose the fight. So the lieutenant governor decided he wouldn't even to go out to the bathroom until the battle was won.

"Anticipating the worst," one reporter wrote, "he brought a pitcher to the chamber and conducted business—both official and personal—from behind a large podium." Two days and two 15-hour marathon sessions later, the Democrats gave in and Windom won the battle. "It takes guts to be an effective lieutenant governor," he told reporters. "It also takes a bladder of steel."

A typical hurricane lasts nine days.

THE COFFEE LAWSUIT

The "McDonald's coffee case" is frequently cited as the definitive frivolous lawsuit. But it was actually a complex—and legitimate—tale of terrible injury, corporate indifference, personal greed…and millions of dollars.

BACKGROUND

On February 27, 1992, 79-year-old Stella Liebeck was riding in the passenger seat of her Ford Probe in Albuquerque, New Mexico (her grandson, Chris, was driving). The Liebecks went through a McDonald's drive-through and Stella ordered an 8-ounce cup of coffee. Then they parked the car so she could safely add cream and sugar. Liebeck put the cup between her knees and pulled the far side of the lid up to remove it…but she pulled too hard. Liebeck spilled the entire cup of coffee into her lap. She was wearing sweatpants, which quickly absorbed the coffee and held it against her skin, forming a puddle of hot liquid. Frantically, she removed her pants. It took her about 90 seconds, but it was too late: The coffee had already scalded her thighs, buttocks, and groin.

Liebeck was rushed to a hospital, where doctors diagnosed her with third-degree burns (the worst kind) on 6% of her body, and lesser burns on an additional 16% of her body. In total, nearly a quarter of her skin had been burned. Liebeck remained hospitalized for eight days while she underwent skin-graft surgery. She also endured two years of follow-up treatment.

THE CASE

In 1993 Liebeck asked McDonald's for $20,000 to cover her medical bills, blaming the company and its coffee for her injuries. McDonald's made a counteroffer: $800. Liebeck hired attorney Reed Morgan and formally sued McDonald's for $90,000, accusing the company of "gross negligence" for selling "unreasonably dangerous" and "defectively manufactured" coffee. McDonald's still wouldn't settle. Why not? Common sense dictates that a multibillion-dollar corporation would pay out a small amount to make the lawsuit—and the bad publicity—simply go away. But between 1982 and 1992, McDonald's had actually received more

---

than 700 complaints about the temperature of its coffee and had even been sued over it a few times. Every case had been thrown out of court for being frivolous; McDonald's thought Liebeck's suit would be no different.

THE POSITIONS

Liebeck and Morgan used those 700 complaints to argue that McDonald's had consistently sold dangerously hot coffee and "didn't care" about its customers. McDonald's brought in quality-control manager Christopher Appleton, who testified that the rate of complaint amounted to one per 24 million cups of coffee sold—not enough to necessitate a chain-wide change.

So how hot *was* the coffee? McDonald's internal documents—presented by Liebeck's side—showed that individual restaurants were required to serve coffee at 180° to 190°F (water boils at 212°). At 180°, coffee can cause a third-degree burn in only two seconds of contact. Morgan argued that coffee should be served no hotter than 140° and backed it up with evidence showing that other fast-food chains served their coffee at that temperature. McDonald's countered that the reason it served coffee at 180° was because drive-through customers were mostly travelers and commuters who wanted their coffee to remain hot for a long time.

THE FALLOUT

The jury found mostly in Liebeck's favor, but she didn't get millions. They found McDonald's 80% responsible for serving coffee it knew could cause burns and without a decent warning label. Liebeck was held 20% accountable for spilling the cup. She was awarded $160,000 in compensatory damages (80% of the $200,000 she sued for). Morgan suggested that punitive damages should amount to two days' worth of coffee revenues, and the jury agreed, awarding Liebeck that exact amount: $2.7 million. The judge reduced it to $480,000. Both sides appealed the verdict; the parties settled in 1994—nearly three years after the incident—for $600,000.

McDonald's also promised to reduce the temperature of its coffee to about 160°, which it did. But since 1994, McDonald's admits that it has slowly raised it back up to 180°, the same temperature that gave a 79-year-old woman burns on a quarter of her body. So sip carefully.

Surveys show: The most popular day for eating out is one's own birthday.

RATHERISMS

*Former anchorman Dan Rather may be known as a serious
journalist, but we love him for these odd phrases,
ad-libbed during election night coverage.*

"This race is hotter than a Times Square Rolex."

"The presidential race is swinging like Count Basie."

"This race is humming along like Ray Charles."

"Bush is sweeping through the South like a big wheel through a cotton field."

"In southern states, Bush beat Kerry like a rented mule."

"You know that old song: It's delightful, it's delicious, it's de-lovely for President Bush in most areas of the country."

"His lead is as thin as turnip soup."

"Keep in mind they are teetotally meetmortally convinced they have Ohio won."

"The re-election of Bill Clinton is as secure as a double-knot tied in wet rawhide."

"We don't know whether to wind a watch or bark at the moon."

"These returns are running like a squirrel in a cage."

"This race is as tight as a too-small bathing suit on a too-hot car ride back from the beach."

"Bush is sweeping through the South like a tornado through a trailer park."

"This race is as tight as the rusted lug nuts on a '55 Ford."

"This race is spandex-tight."

"This race is shakier than cafeteria Jell-O."

"When it comes to a race like this, I'm a long-distance runner and an all-day hunter."

"The Michigan Republican primary is tighter than Willie Nelson's headband."

"His lead is as thin as November ice."

"A lot of people in Washington could not be more surprised if Fidel Castro came loping through on the back of a hippopotamus this election night."

THE WORLD'S FIRST VIDEO GAME

*Ever heard of William Higinbotham? He's the guy
who invented the world's first video game. But he
never made a cent off his invention and hardly
anyone has heard of him. Uncle John thinks
it's time he got the credit he deserves.*

HOWDY, NEIGHBOR

How would you feel if a nuclear reactor came online
just down the street from your house? Would knowing
that it was just a "small" research reactor, dedicated to finding
"peaceful uses" for atomic energy, make you feel any better?
That's what happened in 1950 at the Brookhaven National
Laboratory in Long Island, New York.

Despite all of its public assurances, local residents were visibly concerned about the potential dangers of the new plant.
One way the facility tried to ease public fears was by hosting an
annual "Visitor's Day," so that members of the community could
look around and see for themselves what kinds of projects the
scientists were working on. There were cardboard displays with
blinking lights to look at, geiger counters and electronic circuits
to fiddle with, and dozens of black-and-white photos that
explained the different research projects underway at the lab.

In other words, Visitor's Day was pretty boring.

SOMETHING TO DO

In 1958 a Brookhaven physicist named William Higinbotham
decided to do something about it. Years earlier, Higinbotham
had designed the timing device used to detonate the first atomic bomb; now he set his mind to coming up with something
interesting for Visitor's Day. "I knew from past visitor's days
that people were not much interested in static exhibits," he
remembered. "So that year, I came up with an idea for a hands-on display."

FOLLOW THE BOUNCING BALL

Looking around the labs, Higinbotham found an electronic testing device called an oscilloscope, which has a cathode ray tube display similar to a TV picture tube. He also found an old analog computer (modern computers are digital, not analog) that he could hook up to the oscilloscope in such a way that a "ball" of light would bounce randomly around the screen.

"We found," Higinbotham remembered, "that we could make a game which would have a ball bouncing back and forth, sort of like a tennis game viewed from the side." The game he came up with looked kind of like this:

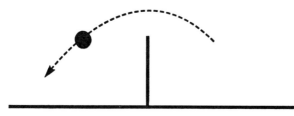

Two people played against one another using control boxes that had a "serve" button that hit the ball over the net, and a control knob that adjusted how high the ball was hit. And just as in real tennis, if you hit the ball into the net, it bounced back at you.

BEST IN SHOW

It took Higinbotham two hours to draw up the schematic diagram for "Tennis for Two," as he called it, and two weeks of tinkering to get it to work. When Visitor's Day came around and Higinbotham put it on a table with a bunch of other electrical equipment, it only took the visitors about five minutes to find it. Soon hundreds of people were crowding around it, some standing in line for more than an hour for a chance to play the game for a minute or two. They didn't learn much about the peaceful applications of nuclear energy that Visitor's Day in 1958. But they sure had fun playing that game.

Higinbotham didn't have an inkling as to the significance of what he'd done. "It never occurred to me that I was doing anything very exciting," he remembered. "The long line of people I thought wasn't because this was so great, but because all the rest of the things were so dull."

Seeing is believing: Frogs use their eyeballs to push food down their throat.

GAME OVER

So what happened to Higinbotham's video tennis game? He improved it for Visitor's Day 1959, letting people play Tennis for Two in Earth gravity, or low gravity like on the moon, or very high gravity like that found on Jupiter.

Then, when Visitor's Day was over, he took the video game apart and put the pieces away. He never brought them out again, never built another video game, and never patented his idea.

Willy Higinbotham would probably be completely forgotten today were it not for a lawsuit. When video games began taking off in the early 1970s, Magnavox and some other early manufacturers began fighting in court over which one of *them* had invented the games. A patent lawyer for one of Magnavox's competitors eventually learned of Higinbotham's story and brought the Great Man into court to prove that he, not Magnavox, was the true father of the video game.

OUCH!

In 2001 Americans spent more on video game systems and software—$9.4 billion—than they did going to the movies—$8.35 billion. What did Higinbotham, who died in 1994, have to show for it? Nothing. He never made a penny off his invention. Not that he could have—he worked for a government laboratory when he invented the game, so even if he had patented the idea, the U.S. government would have owned the patent.

"My kids complained about this," he joked, "And I keep saying, 'Kids, no matter what, I wouldn't have made any money.'"

*　　*　　*

SEA-ING THINGS

Dolphins sometimes play chase in long lines, like people doing a snake dance or snap-the-whip. Sailors, seeing this long line of something moving in the water, have sometimes reported seeing huge sea serpents.

It's easy to spot someone with *hexadectylism*: six fingers on one hand or six toes on one foot.

URBAN LEGENDS

Psst! Have you heard the story about the woman who ate the octopus eggs? Remember the BRI rule of thumb: If a story sounds true, but also seems too perfect to be true, it's probably an urban legend.

The Story: Firefighters cleaning up the scene of a California forest fire are shocked to find the charred remains of a scuba diver hanging from the limbs of a burnt tree. An autopsy reveals that the cause of death was massive internal injuries sustained from a fall. An investigation reveals that he was diving off a nearby coast on the day of the fire…and was scooped up into a bucket of seawater being carried by a firefighting helicopter.

The Truth: The story, which sometimes involves a fisherman still clutching his fishing pole, has been around since at least 1987. It falls into one of the most popular urban legend categories of all: "What a stupid/unusual way to die!" (It's even popular in France, which has also been cited as the location of the incident.)

The Story: A young woman who lives near a beach becomes pregnant but swears it's a mistake. It turns out that she accidentally swallowed microscopic octopus eggs while swimming and has a baby octopus growing inside her, spreading its tentacles to various parts of her body.

How It Spread: The story was first published in the *Boston Traveler* in the 1940s and is kept alive mainly in coastal towns.

The Truth: No medical records have ever been found to verify this story, but a fear of foreign bodies growing inside us keeps it afloat. Similar legends exist about eating pregnant cockroaches in fast food.

The Story: Two speeding semi trucks crash head on in a heavy fog. The drivers survive, but the two trucks are too smashed together to separate, so the towing company tows them to the junkyard in one piece. A few weeks later, junkyard workers notice a terrible smell coming from the wreck. They pry the cars apart…and discover a Volkswagen beetle with four passengers crushed flat in between the two trucks.

The Truth: Urban legends featuring small cars smashed by big

Ireland's longest place name: Muckanaghederdauhaulia ("pig marsh between two saltwater inlets").

vehicles are so numerous that they're practically a category by themselves. What keeps them alive is the general fear of meeting a similar fate.

The Story: Two young men are driving home from a party one rainy night and notice a beautiful young woman standing by the side of the road. She doesn't have a raincoat or umbrella, so they stop and offer her a ride. She accepts, and while they drive her to her house, one of the men gives her his jacket to wear.

About a block from the woman's house, they turn around to say something to her...but she is gone. They drive to her house anyway and knock on the door. The woman who answers tells them, "That was my daughter. She was killed two years ago on the same spot you picked her up. She does this all the time." The next day the young men look up the girl's obituary in the library. There it is—complete with a picture of the girl they picked up. Then they go to the cemetery...and find the jacket she borrowed resting on her tombstone.

The Truth: According to folklorist Richard Dorson, it predates the automobile. The story "is traced back to the 19th century," he writes, "in America, Italy, Ireland, Turkey, and China; with a horse and wagon picking up the benighted traveler." In the Hawaiian version, the girl hitches a ride on a rickshaw.

The Story: A few years before the 1991 Gulf War, Barbara Walters did a news story on gender roles in Kuwait in which she reported that Kuwaiti wives traditionally walk several paces behind their husbands. She returned to Kuwait after the war and noticed that women were now walking several paces *ahead* of their husbands. When Walters asked a Kuwaiti woman how so much social progress had been accomplished in so little time, the woman replied, "Land mines."

How It Spread: By word of mouth and e-mail, starting shortly after the end of the Gulf War.

The Truth: This is the latest version of a classic urban legend that has been around as long as landmines themselves. The subjects of the story—Kuwaitis, Korean and Vietnamese peasants, and in the case of World War II, nomads in North Africa—change to fit the circumstances of each new war.

LIFE IN A JAR

*One amazing woman in Poland—and four teens in
Kansas who tracked her down and told her story.*

SENDLER'S LIST

In 1999 a teacher at Uniontown High School in Kansas encouraged four students to do a project for a national History Day contest. Norm Conard told his 9th-grade students—Elizabeth Cambers, Megan Stewart, and Janice Underwood, and 11th-grader Sabrina Coons—that the project should reflect the classroom motto, "He who changes one person, changes the world entire." The quote is from the Jewish holy book the Talmud, and Conard suggested basing the project on the Holocaust.

He showed them a 1994 news clipping about "other Schindlers," people who, like Oskar Schindler (made famous in the film *Schindler's List*), had saved Jews from the Nazis during World War II. One of the people mentioned was a Polish woman named Irena Sendler, who was said to have saved 2,500 Jewish children from the Warsaw ghetto. Schindler had saved about 1,100 people. "We thought this had to be a mistake or something," said Conard. "Maybe this Sendler saved 250, but not 2,500. I mean, nobody had ever heard of this woman."

SEARCHING FOR IRENA

"We became obsessed with finding out everything we could about Irena," said 15-year-old Elizabeth Cambers. And they soon found out that the number was right. But how Irena Sendler had saved the children was almost unbelievable.

Sendler was a social worker in Warsaw when the Nazis invaded Poland in 1939. By 1940 they had created the Warsaw ghetto: 400,000 Jews were confined to an area one square mile in size. They were not allowed to leave, and conditions quickly became deplorable. Hundreds died every day from starvation or disease, and soon more were being sent to die in death camps. By 1942 more than 80,000 had perished.

Sendler, who was not Jewish, was sickened by what she saw... so she made a plan. She forged a pass from the Warsaw Epidemic

---

Surprising but true: The bottom of the Grand Canyon is above sea level.

Control Department and, starting in 1942, went into the ghetto every day. There she would ask parents to do the unthinkable: give their children to her so she could smuggle them out. It meant that the parents would probably never see them again, but for the children to stay, the stricken parents knew, was to let them die.

BURYING HOPE

At incredible risk to herself, Irena smuggled dozens of children out of the ghetto day after day. She took them right past the guards, showing fake documents and saying they were ill. Or she would put children in coffins, saying they were dead. Once out, she gave the children phony papers with new names and found Polish families to adopt them, or she placed them in orphanages. Some she hid in churches and convents.

But while she was saving the children, Sendler knew that she was taking them from their families, and from their own identities. So she made lists of all their real names and addresses and their new locations—in code—and put the lists into glass jars. Then she buried the jars beneath an apple tree in a neighbor's backyard, hoping that one day she could dig them up, find the children, and reunite them with their families.

On October 20, 1943, Irena Sendler was found out by the Nazis. She was imprisoned—and, because she was the only one who knew the location of the children and the jars, she was tortured. Gestapo agents broke both her feet and both her legs, but Sendler refused to tell them anything. She spent three months in prison, then was sentenced to death.

The girls were so moved by Sendler's story that they wrote a play about it entitled *Life in a Jar*. Elizabeth Cambers played "Jolanta," Irena's code name and the only name by which the children knew her, and Megan Stewart played a mother who must give up her children. They performed the play at school, then in local clubs and churches. People in the community were so moved by Sendler's story that the school district, which didn't have a single Jewish student, declared an official Irena Sendler Day. On top of that, the girls' work won them first prize in the National History Day contest for the state of Kansas. But the best was yet to come.

FINDING IRENA

The girls kept looking for more clues about Irena's life. They contacted the Jewish Foundation for the Righteous, an organization that honors non-Jews who risked their lives to save Jews during the Holocaust, to ask if they knew the location of Irena's grave. They didn't, they said, but they had something else: her address. Irena Sendler was alive.

Elizabeth, Megan, Janice, and Sabrina immediately wrote to Irena in Warsaw and told her about their project and play. Six weeks later they got an enthusiastic reply. "Your performance and work," Irena wrote, "is continuing the effort I started over fifty years ago."

Sendler also told them the rest of her story: She had been brutally tortured and sentenced to death by the Nazis when she refused to tell them where the children were. But the Polish underground came to her rescue, securing Irena's release by bribing a guard. She spent the rest of the war a fugitive.

After the war ended, Sendler immediately went back to her neighbor's house, dug up the jars, and began tracking down the children, hoping to reunite as many as possible with their parents. She was able to find many, but hundreds she could not—and most of the parents were dead.

WARSAW

In 2001 the students' dream came true when they traveled to Poland to meet the subject of their long study. Irena Sendler, by then 89 years old, took the girls in like granddaughters. "We ran up and hugged her and cried," said Elizabeth Cambers. "We told her she is our hero, but she said she doesn't think of herself that way. 'Heroes do extraordinary things,' she told us. She just did what she had to do."

The group was even able to meet some of the children, now in their 50s, who were saved by Irena (and by others who helped her, Irena was always quick to point out). One was Elzbieta Ficowska, rescued by Irena when she was five months old by being carried out in a carpenter's toolbox. They also met a Polish poet who was saved by Irena, who called the young women "rescuers of the rescuer" for bringing Irena's amazing story to the public. And to the public it went. The story of the students' visit to Irena in Warsaw and of their performance of *Life in a Jar* spread. When they returned home, the four young women were interviewed on radio and TV, and in newspapers and magazines worldwide.

The four original students have all graduated, but the Sendler Project, as it is now known, continues today with Mr. Conard and new students. *Life in a Jar* has been performed more than 170 times in the United States and Europe. They also have a Web site (irenasendler.org), through which they raise money for people like Sendler, who risked their lives to save others.

Irena Sendler, now 99, continues to correspond with the four girls (they've visited her twice more, the last time in 2005). She now lives in a nursing home in Warsaw and is being cared for, appropriately, by a woman she smuggled out of the Warsaw ghetto more than 60 years ago.

*   *   *

FROM THE BAD JOKE FILE

A man who wanted to achieve enlightenment made a pilgrimage to a Buddhist monastery high in the mountains. There he found the wisest monk and told him his goal. The monk replied, "To reach enlightenment, you must take a vow of silence for 10 years."

After 10 years of silent meditation, the monk said to the man, "You may now speak."

"My bed is too hard," said the man.

"You have not yet reached enlightenment," replied the monk. "You must not speak again for 10 years."

So the man remained silent for 10 more years, and then the monk came to him and said, "You may now speak."

"The food here is too cold," he said.

"You still have not yet reached enlightenment," said the monk.

So the man took another vow of silence. Ten years later—after 30 years of meditation—he was again allowed to speak.

"I quit," he said.

"Good," replied the monk. "All you do is complain, anyway."

Shocking news: There are about 500 species of fish capable of producing electricity.

THE WORST CITY IN AMERICA

Every city has something to be proud of—even the ones listed here. But some cities, despite their beauty, charm, or cultural importance, also have features of which they might be a little less proud. Here are a few cities with dubious distinctions.

• According to a survey by AutoVantage (an auto club like AAA), Miami, Florida, is the city with the rudest drivers.

• A Cornell University study determined that New York City has the lowest quality of housing. (The World Health Organization says that New York is also the noisiest city in the United States.)

• Because of high divorce and unemployment rates and consistently gloomy weather, the city statistics analyzing firm BestPlaces named Tacoma, Washington, the country's most stressful place to live.

• Breathe easy if you don't live in these places: Greenville, South Carolina (where residents suffer the most respiratory tract infections); Scranton, Pennsylvania (the worst city for asthma sufferers); and Tulsa, Oklahoma (the pollen capital of America).

• Based on the number of accidents and fatalities, the International Federation of Bike Messenger Associations named Boston the most dangerous place to ride a bike.

• Zero, a group dedicated to slowing population growth, determined what cities were the best and worst in which to raise children based on the quality of healthcare, education, public safety, transportation, the job market, and the natural environment. The best was Fargo, North Dakota; the worst was Newark, New Jersey.

• According to the National Coalition for the Homeless, Sarasota, Florida, is the city most hostile toward homeless people.

• *Forbes* magazine named Pittsburgh, PA, the worst city for single people. Reasons: expensive beer, few nightclubs, and not enough single people.

Iowa is bigger than Portugal.

- Worst traffic congestion: Los Angeles. (Not coincidentally, it also has the worst air pollution.)

- City with the bumpiest, most pothole-infested roads: Seattle.

- In 2007 *Men's Health* magazine analyzed various cities' obesity rates, eating habits, and other data, including how much time people spend exercising and sitting in traffic. Result: Las Vegas was judged the nation's "fattest city."

- The city with the most suicides per capita is Medford, Oregon.

- Decatur, Illinois, has the highest skin cancer fatality rate.

- America's most rat-infested city is Baltimore.

- New Orleans leads in both gun- and diabetes-related deaths per capita.

- Hallmark Cards calls El Paso, Texas, the city with the worst sense of humor, based on polls in which very few people said they considered themselves funny. (The city also has very low sales of Hallmark's humorous cards.)

- City with the highest percentage of lawyers: Washington, D.C. Nearly 2% of all residents are attorneys.

- According to the book *Cities Ranked and Rated*, the worst overall city in America is Modesto, California. The city scored a 0 on the book's 100-point scale for its high cost of living, high unemployment rate, lack of activities, and the highest car theft rate in the United States.

*   *   *

CAN'T WAKE THE DEAD?

"A fake wake organized by Donald Warren for his 80th birthday had to be cancelled...because he died for real the day before. Warren, of Verwood, Dorset, had even rented a coffin in which he was to lie, propped up to watch 'mourners.' But he died from a fatal heart attack. Family members were too upset to comment, but lifelong pal Mike Sharman, 78, said, 'Most of us think the arranging of the party brought on the attack.'"

—*The Sunday Mirror* (U.K.)

Q: What is *nikhedonia?* A: "The feeling of pleasure one gets from anticipating victory."

THE WILHELM SCREAM

Have you ever heard a sound effect in a film—a screeching eagle, a car crash, or a laughing crowd—that you swear you've heard before in other movies? You're probably right. Here's the story behind Hollywood's most famous "recycled" sound effect.

SOUNDS FAMILIAR

Like most American kids growing up in the 1950s, Ben Burtt went to the movies...*a lot*. Movie budgets were much smaller back then, and film studios reused whatever they could—props, sets, stock footage, sound effects, everything. If you watched and listened to the movies carefully, you might have noticed things you'd seen and heard in other movies.

Burtt noticed. He was good at picking out sounds—especially screams, and especially one scream in particular. "Every time someone died in a Warner Bros. movie, they'd scream this famous scream," he says.

By the 1970s, a grown-up Burtt was working in the movie business himself, as a sound designer—the guy who creates the sound effects. Years had passed, but he'd never forgotten that classic Warner Bros. scream. So when he got the chance, he decided to track down the original recording. It took a lot of digging, but he eventually found it on an old studio reel marked "Man Being Eaten by an Alligator." It turns out it had been recorded for the 1951 Warner Bros. western *Distant Drums* and used at least twice in that movie: once in a battle with some Indians, and then—of course—when a man is bitten and dragged underwater by an alligator.

A STAR IS BORN

No one could remember what actor had originally been hired to record the scream, so Burtt jokingly named it after a character in the 1953 movie, *Charge at Feather River*. The character, named Wilhelm, screams the scream after he is struck in the leg by an arrow. The "Wilhelm Scream" was used two more times in that film: once when a soldier is struck by a spear, and again when an Indian is stabbed and then rolls down a hill.

The Wilhelm Scream is now more than 50 years old, but if you

Top 5 causes of home accidents: stairs, glass doors, cutlery, jars, power tools (in that order).

heard it you'd probably recognize it, because Burtt, who's worked on almost every George Lucas film, uses it often—including in his Academy Award-winning sound design for *Star Wars*. "That scream gets in every picture I do, as a personal signature," he says.

So when you hear a Wilhelm Scream in a film, can you assume that Burtt did the sound effects? No—when other sound designers heard what he was doing, they started inserting the scream into their movies, too. Apparently, Burtt isn't the only person good at noticing reused sound effects, because movie buffs have caught on to what he is doing and discovered at least 66 films that use the Wilhelm Scream. A few examples:

AHHHHHHHHHEEEEEIIIIII!!!

Star Wars **(1977)** Just before Luke Skywalker and Princess Leia swing across the Death Star's chasm, a stormtrooper falls in.

The Empire Strikes Back **(1980)** 1) In the battle on the ice planet Hoth, a rebel soldier screams when his big satellite-dish laser gun is struck by laser fire and explodes. 2) As Han Solo is being frozen, Chewbacca knocks a stormtrooper off of the platform.

Return of the Jedi **(1983)** 1) In the desert scene, Luke slashes an enemy with his light saber. The victim screams as he falls into the Sarlac pit. 2) Later in the film, Han Solo knocks a man over a ledge. The man is Ben Burtt himself, making a cameo appearance—and that's him impersonating the Wilhelm Scream…with his own voice.

Batman Returns **(1992)** Batman punches a clown and knocks him out of the way. The clown screams.

Toy Story **(1995)** Buzz Lightyear screams when he gets knocked out of the bedroom window.

Titanic **(1997)** In the scene where the engine room is flooding, a crew member screams when he's hit with a jet of water.

Spaceballs **(1987)** Barf uses a section of tubes to reflect laser bolts back at three guards. The last one screams.

Lethal Weapon 4 **(1998)** A gunshot turns a terrorist's flame-thrower into a jet pack, and he flies into a gasoline truck.

Lord of the Rings: The Two Towers **(2002)** A soldier falls off the wall during the Battle of Helm's Deep…and lets out a Wilhelm.

THIS SIDE UP

The story of a slave who escaped in a most unusual way,
earning him freedom, fame…and a very odd nickname.

TRAVELING SHOW

In the 1850s, a American named Henry "Box" Brown toured England, speaking and sometimes singing to enthusiastic audiences. Part of his show was a panorama he'd created called "Mirror of Slavery," a moving scroll with scenes depicting slave life—scenes that he knew firsthand. The pictures also told the story of how he got his nickname.

A PROMISE BROKEN

Born into slavery in the United States, Brown was separated from his parents as a teenager and taken by his owner to Richmond, Virginia, to work in a tobacco factory. He worked hard and even earned a little money. He fell in love, got married, and had three children with his wife, Nancy.

Before he married, Henry asked his owner to promise never to sell Nancy or their children. The owner agreed, but a few years later changed his mind. Henry watched helplessly as his family was led away with ropes around their necks. They were being taken south, and he sensed—correctly—that he'd never see them again. After that, if Henry Brown decided that if his life was going to be worth living, it would have to be in freedom. So he worked out a bold plan, one that could easily kill him—even if it worked.

IN THE HANDS OF FATE

Henry Brown had a white friend, a carpenter, who built him a wooden crate, 3 feet long, 2½ feet deep and 2 feet wide. On the outside, the carpenter painted "THIS SIDE UP, WITH CARE." He addressed the box to a friend in Philadelphia, an abolitionist who was a member of the Underground Railroad. On March 23, 1849, Henry Brown folded up his 5-foot-8-inch, 200-pound self and squeezed inside the box. He later wrote, "I laid me down in my darkened home of three feet by two, and… resigned myself to my fate."

In a 1993 election, Canada's ruling Progressive Conservatives lost 153 of their 155 seats.

The carpenter nailed the box shut, left it for baggage handlers, and sent a telegraph to his contact in Philadelphia, saying that the box was on its way.

BOXED IN

Inside the box, Brown had a small leather bag of water and some crackers. Three tiny holes in the box let in some light and air. He carried a hand drill, but as it turned out, he didn't have enough room to use it even if he'd been suffocating.

Unfortunately, the baggage handlers didn't always pay attention to the words printed on the crate. The first handlers turned it upside down, so Brown was resting on his head. He was eventually tossed into a train's baggage car, where the box rolled over and he was right side up again.

DEFINITELY WRONG SIDE UP

The crate was next put on a steamboat, upside-down again. Henry described his body's reactions: "I...found to my dismay, that my eyes were almost swollen out of their sockets, and the veins on my temple seemed ready to burst. I made no noise, however, determining to obtain 'victory or death,' but endured the terrible pain, as well as I could, sustained under the whole by the thoughts of sweet liberty. About half an hour afterwards, I attempted again to lift my hands to my face, but I found I was not able to move them. A cold sweat now covered me from head to foot."

At that point, Brown thought he might die inside the box. But finally someone noticed the words on the outside and turned it over. The crate was next put on a wagon. Then it was thrown off, and landed upside down. "I seemed to be destined to escape on my head," Henry later commented.

He listened in terror as workmen argued over whether they could fit such a big crate onto the next train. But finally they picked it up and shoved it into the baggage car—this time, right side up.

ALL RIGHT INSIDE?

Twenty-seven hours after it was sent—and 350 miles from where it had started—Henry's box arrived in Philadelphia. After three more hours, a group of Underground Railroad members quietly picked it up at the station, put it on a wagon, and took it to a house. The people who crowded around the box were afraid to open it at first. Finally, someone knocked on the box and asked, "Is all right within?" to which Henry replied, "All right." Brown's new friends were overjoyed, and hurried to pry the box open. Brown got up, shook himself, and immediately fainted.

FREE AT LAST

He was free, and from that day on he was known as Henry "Box" Brown. He and a friend toured the free states with the box and the panorama, describing to audiences what a life of slavery was like. His book, *Narrative of Henry Box Brown*, was published later that year. But in 1850, the U.S. Congress passed the Fugitive Slave Act. Now, suspected slaves could be arrested in the Northern states and returned to their masters. Once again, Henry Brown was in danger.

MR. SHOWBIZ

So Henry Brown took his panorama to England and continued his antislavery lectures there. Later, around 1862, he began traveling with a show that included singers, dancers, and even ventriloquists. He was last heard of about 1864, living in freedom in Wales.

*   *   *

A RUNAWAY ON THE RUNWAY

In 2006 Terry and Susan Smith, along with their dog Poppy, were moving from England to Spain. "We were in our seats ready for takeoff and looking forward to our new life," said retired truck driver Terry, "when we suddenly saw Poppy on the runway." They screamed for the plane to stop, and spent the next hour attempting to catch and calm the terrified dog. Poppy had apparently chewed her way out of her travel crate before the hatch closed. The Smiths, including Poppy, took a later flight (at a cost of about $800).

From 1790 to 1800, the capital of the United States was Philadelphia.

COOL BILLIONS

*We could give you a billion reasons to read these
cool facts, but we don't have enough room.*

• If you had $1 billion and spent $1,000 a day, it would take 2,740 years to spend it.

• One billion people would fill roughly 305 Chicagos.

• It took until 1800 for the world's population to reach 1 billion, but only 130 years more for it to reach 2 billion—in 1930.

• One billion people lined up side by side would stretch for 568,200 miles.

• First magazine in history to sell a billion copies: *TV Guide*, in 1974.

• More than 1 billion people on Earth are between the ages of 15 and 24.

• One Styrofoam cup contains 1 billion molecules of CFCs (chlorofluorocarbons)—harmful to the earth's ozone layer.

• A single ragweed plant can release a billion grains of pollen.

• To cook 1 billion pounds of pasta, you'd need 2 billion gallons of water—enough to fill nearly 75,000 Olympic-size swimming pools.

• The ratio of billionaires to the rest of the U.S. population is 1 to 4.5 million.

• Nearly 1 billion Barbie dolls (including friends and family) have been sold since 1959. Placed head to toe, the dolls would circle the Earth more than three times.

• The first billion-dollar corporation in the U.S. emerged in 1901—United States Steel.

• One teaspoon of yogurt contains more than 1 billion live and active bacteria.

• The first year in which the U.S. national debt exceeded $1 billion was 1863.

• There are about 1 billion red blood cells in two to three drops of blood.

"A billion here, a billion there, and soon you're talking about real money." —Sen. Everett Dirksen

AMAZING LUCK

Sometimes we're blessed with it, sometimes we're cursed with it—dumb luck. Here are some examples of people who've lucked out...for better and for worse.

HEAVY SLEEPER

Keith Quick, 28, a homeless man in Omaha, Nebraska, climbed into a dumpster and went to sleep. Bad move—he happened to do it on garbage pickup day and was still sleeping when the garbage truck emptied the dumpster into its compactor and crushed it. Quick cried out for help but it wasn't until the trash had been compacted two or three more times that the garbage men finally heard him. The trash was compressed so tightly that it took firefighters more than an hour to dig him out. Incredibly, he suffered no serious injuries.

SEEING IS BELIEVING

In 1990, 14-year-old Lisa Reid went permanently blind as the result of a brain tumor. Then one night about 10 years later, she smacked her head on a coffee table as she was bending down to kiss her guide dog goodnight. When she woke up the next morning, 80% of the vision in her left eye had been restored. She celebrated the miracle "by telephoning her mother and reading aloud the health warning on a packet of cigarettes."

THAT SINKING FEELING

In 1829, four days out of Sydney, Australia, a heavy storm struck the vessel *Mermaid*, and drove it into a reef. All 22 on board jumped ship and swam to a large rock. After three days of waiting, another ship, the *Swiftsure*, found and rescued them. Five days later another storm struck. The *Swiftsure* was swept into a ridge and wrecked. Both crews escaped and waited for rescue on some nearby rocks. They were soon picked up by the schooner *Governor Ready*, which caught fire three hours later. Once again they abandoned ship, this time in lifeboats. Along came the cutter *Comet*, which had been blown off course by a storm. The crew of the *Comet* loaded the crews and passengers of all three vessels on

An adult turkey has about 3,500 feathers.

board. Five days later a storm snapped the *Comet's* mast, ripped her sails, and ruined her rudder. The *Comet's* crew loaded into the longboat, leaving the passengers to cling to floating bits of wreckage. After 18 hours passed the mail boat *Jupiter* came along and rescued everyone, only to hit a reef and sink two days later. Fortunately, the passenger vessel *City of Leeds* was nearby and picked up everyone, finally delivering them back to Sydney. The doomed voyage sank five ships, but incredibly, not a single life was lost.

BODY ARMOR

In June 2001, Dana Coldwell, 31, of Frankenmuth, Michigan, was mowing her lawn when the mower blade struck a 1½-inch-long nail and sent it hurtling toward her chest. The nail struck her on the right breast, but didn't pierce her heart—an injury that would probably have been fatal. Why? It was deflected by the "liquid-curved" Maidenform bust-enhancing bra she was wearing. "I almost didn't wear the bra, but a higher power told me to put it on," she says. "I don't know if I will be mowing the lawn after this, but if I do, I'll be wearing the bra."

GOOD THING THEY DIDN'T CLEAN UP

While visiting their sons in Nebraska, Larry and Leita Hatch stopped at a local Burger King. Larry bought a soft drink and when he peeled off the "Cash Is King" game sticker, he became the only $1 million winner in the entire country. (Wait, it gets better.) He stopped at a grocery store to make a copy of the ticket, but when he got to his son's house, he found he'd lost the original. So he went back to the grocery store—three hours later—and calmly picked up the ticket where it was lying…on the floor in the checkout line.

PICK ME A WINNER

Every year the Dearborn Heights Police Supervisors Association holds a raffle in Taylor, Michigan, and because it's a fundraiser for the police, they're careful to be sure everything is aboveboard. The prize for the 2001 raffle was a $20,000 Harley-Davidson Road King Classic; the winning ticket was to be picked by the 2000 winner, an autoworker named Tom Grochoki. There were 7,800 tickets in the barrel. Grochoki picked one, handed it to Lt. Karl Kapelczak, and went back to the crowd to hear the winner's name announced. The winner: Tom Grochoki.

The world's longest movie, *Cure For Insomnia* (1987), runs 85 hours.

MOUNT PELÉE

What's worse than a volcanic eruption in your town? A volcanic eruption in your town on Election Day. Here's one of the strangest events in the history of Western democracy.

ELECTION DAY POLITICS

One of the worst volcanic disasters in history was caused not by the eruption...but by politics.

Mount Pelée, on the island of Martinique in the Caribbean Sea, began smoking and shaking in late April 1902. The people of St. Pierre, the town at the base of the volcano, remembered that the volcano had rumbled years earlier, but since it had quieted down and was seemingly dormant, they weren't too concerned... at first.

But when scalding mud flows began pouring down the mountain and ashes fell faster than they could be swept away, many changed their minds and thought the town should be evacuated. As it happened, the city's elections were only a few days away. The mayor and the governor of the island were concerned about the growing popularity of a radical political party that stood for equal rights for all races and threatened the white supremacy of the island.

Mayor Fouche and Governor Mouttet refused to allow anything to delay the election even a single day. The editor of the paper was on their side and published articles by fictional "volcano experts" who had supposedly examined the situation and said there was no danger.

BLOWBACK

Soon the volcano became more violent. A giant mudslide wiped out the sugar mill on the edge of town, taking the workers with it, and a huge seismic wave spawned by undersea earthquakes wiped out the entire seafront district. People began packing to leave, but found the roads out of town blocked by soldiers sent by the governor. He was determined to prevent anyone from leaving before the election.

The Incas measured time by how long it took a potato to cook.

The people went to the local church and begged the bishop to intervene on their behalf, but he refused to go against the wishes of the state. At dawn on election day, Mount Pelée exploded. A colossal cloud of super-heated gasses, ash, and rock blew out of a notch in the crater, directly at the town four miles away, at a rate of 100 mph. Within three minutes, the entire population—including the mayor, governor, bishop, and newspaper editor—was dead. Even ships anchored offshore were set ablaze, killing crew members and passengers.

Only two people in the town survived. A black prisoner condemned to death for murdering a white man was to have been hanged that day, but the governor had granted him clemency in the hopes that it would give him some of the black vote. The prisoner was being held in an underground cell with one small window facing away from the volcano. He was horribly burned, but survived and later toured with the Barnum and Bailey Circus as a sideshow attraction.

The only other survivor was the town cobbler, a religious fanatic who had been hiding in his cellar, praying, when the mountain erupted. He, too, was terribly burned, and some reports say that he never regained his sanity after coming out of his cellar to find every single one of the townfolk—30,000 people in all—dead.

*　　*　　*

RIDICULOUS POLITICAL WORDS

- **Flugie:** A rule that helps only the rule maker.
- **Speechify:** To deliver a speech in a tedious way.
- **Bloviate:** To speechify pompously.
- **Roorback:** An invented rumor intended to smear an opponent.
- **Bafflegab:** Intentionally confusing jargon.
- **Gobbledygook:** Nonsensical explanation, bafflegab.
- **Snollygoster:** A politician who puts politics ahead of principle.
- **Boondoggle:** Wasteful or crooked government-funded project.
- **Mugwump:** A political maverick.

The phrase "to soft-pedal something" refers to the piano pedal used to mute the tone.

SPY HUNT: GRAY DECEIVER, PART I

Everyone loves a spy thriller—especially when it's real life. Here's an amazing tale that a BRI operative recently uncovered.

THE MOLE

In February 1994, FBI agents arrested a 30-year veteran of the CIA named Aldrich Ames. The charge: spying for the Soviet Union. In the nine years that Ames was an active spy, he exposed more than 100 sensitive operations and revealed the name of every CIA intelligence source in the Soviet Union. At least 10 of them were executed; many others were sent to prison. Ames was paid more than $2.5 million for his efforts and was promised another $1.9 million, making him the highest-paid double agent in history, not to mention one of the most damaging.

Yet as pleased as the FBI and the CIA were to have caught and convicted Ames (he received a life sentence), disturbing signs soon began to emerge that there might be one, and possibly even more moles hiding elsewhere in various U.S. intelligence agencies. Some secrets known to have been compromised couldn't be traced back to Ames—he simply didn't know about them.

So both the CIA and the FBI set up new mole-hunting teams and set to work looking for spies. The FBI gave the investigation the code name GRAYSUIT; each time a new suspect was identified they were given a code name with "GRAY" as a prefix. The new mole hunt dredged up two more relatively minor spies: an FBI agent named Earl Edwin Pitts and a CIA agent named Harold J. Nicholson. Both men were arrested in 1996 and sentenced to more than 20 years in prison.

BIG SECRETS

Neither arrest answered the question of who was responsible for giving the two biggest intelligence secrets to the Russians:

• **The Tunnel.** Someone told the Soviets about the secret eavesdropping tunnel that the FBI and the National Security Agency (NSA) had dug beneath the new Soviet embassy in Washington,

D.C. The tunnel program cost more than $100 million but never produced a single piece of useful intelligence, because the Russians were told of its existence in 1994—five years before they moved in.

• **The Spy.** As we told you in *Uncle John's Slightly Irregular Bathroom Reader*, in 1989 the FBI was hot on the trail of a senior U.S. diplomat named Felix Bloch, who was suspected of spying for the KGB. Someone tipped off his handler, a KGB spy named Reino Gikman. Gikman then tipped off Bloch, blowing the FBI's investigation before they could collect enough information to indict him. To date Bloch has never been charged with espionage.

MYSTERY MAN

Both the spy tunnel and the Bloch investigation were FBI operations, but early on the FBI concluded that the mole was more likely to be a CIA official, so that's where they focused their efforts.

For years tips had been coming in from U.S. sources in Russia, describing a spy who had a thing for "exotic dancers," sometimes liked to be paid in diamonds, and was said to make "dead drops" (leave packages and pick up money) in Nottoway Park in Vienna, Virginia. None of the Russian sources knew the man's identity—as far as anyone knew at the time, the man had never revealed his real name to his handlers or even told them which intelligence agency he worked for. Apparently he'd never met with his Russian handlers, either. No one even knew what he looked like.

THE MATRIX

One of the ways intelligence agencies hunt for spies is to make what is called a "matrix." They compile a list of all the intelligence secrets that have been betrayed, and then make a list of the people who had access to those secrets. Then, using whatever other clues they have, they try to rule suspects in or out. The FBI mole hunters used just such a matrix to narrow a list of 100 suspects down to seven and then down to just one: a CIA agent named Brian Kelley. They gave him the nickname GRAY DECEIVER.

Kelley specialized in exposing Soviet "illegals," spies who do not pose as diplomats and thus have no diplomatic immunity if they are caught. One illegal that Kelley had uncovered was Reino Gikman, the KGB agent who tipped off Felix Bloch. Kelley was a distinguished agent—he'd been awarded five medals for his work at the CIA, including one for the Felix Bloch case. But the FBI was now convinced that he'd been a spy all along. Uncovering Gikman and then warning him about Bloch was the perfect cover—who would ever suspect that a decorated CIA officer would blow his own case?

DIGGING DEEP

In late 1997 the FBI arranged for Kelley to be given a new assignment: to review the Felix Bloch files to see if any clues had been missed. The real purpose of the assignment was to isolate him and keep him at CIA headquarters, making it easier for FBI mole hunters to keep an eye on him until enough evidence was collected for him to be arrested.

In the meantime, the FBI placed Kelley on round-the-clock surveillance and secretly searched his home. They also tapped his phone lines, sifted through his garbage, searched his home computer, and planted listening devices all over the house. On one occasion they even tailed him all the way to Niagara Falls, only to lose him near the Canadian border. That suggested that Kelley was "dry cleaning"—taking evasive action to lose anyone who might be following him, so he could slip over the border into Canada, presumably to meet with his Russian handlers.

ONE TOUGH COOKIE

It was then that the mole hunters realized just how difficult it was going to be to catch Kelley red-handed. Sure, they knew about the dry cleaning incident at the border, and they also knew that Kelley shopped at a mall where SVR operatives had been seen in the past (the KGB was renamed the SVR after the collapse of the Soviet Union). But after all the bugging, searching, and garbage sifting, the only incriminating piece of physical evidence they were able to find was a single hand-drawn map of nearby Nottoway Park, with various times written at different locations on the map. To the mole hunters it could only be one thing: a map of various dead drops, complete with a schedule of different drop-off times. With the exception of the map, though, Kelley seemed to be an expert at erasing nearly every trace of his double life.

In fact, to the untrained eye, he didn't seem like a spy at all.

Who was the mole? Covertly flip to Part II on page 411.

Tough guy: A 100-pound cougar can take down an 800-pound elk.

RARE CONDITIONS

If you're like Uncle John, when you get an ailment—say, a cold—you ask yourself, "Why is it called a 'cold?'" If you get one of these odd diseases, you probably won't have to ask how it got its name.

• **MAPLE SYRUP URINE DISEASE.** An inherited metabolic disease that makes the urine and sweat smell like maple syrup.

• **KABUKI MAKEUP SYNDROME.** This birth defect causes facial features to distort, resembling the overpronounced and elongated made-up faces of Japanese Kabuki actors.

• **PRUNE-BELLY SYNDROME.** An absence of abdominal muscles gives the stomach a wrinkled, puckered look and a severe pot belly that stretches out grotesquely.

• **JUMPING FRENCHMAN.** An acquired condition first discovered in the 19th century among Canadian lumberjacks. Patients have extreme reactions to sudden noises or surprises: they flail their arms, jump in the air, cry, scream, and hit people.

• **HAIRY TONGUE.** Due to tobacco use or poor oral hygiene, the tiny hairs on the tongue grow to be several inches long and the tongue itself turns black.

• **FOREIGN ACCENT SYNDROME.** After a severe brain injury or stroke, a person begins speaking their native language with a foreign accent. English-speaking Americans might suddenly sound Russian, for example.

• **WANDERING SPLEEN.** The muscles that hold the spleen in position are missing or undeveloped, causing the spleen to "wander" around the lower abdomen and pelvic region.

• **ALICE-IN-WONDERLAND SYNDROME.** Vision is distorted, making objects appear much smaller than they actually are. For example, a house may appear to be the size of a shoebox or a cat may look no bigger than a mouse.

North Dakota is the only state in the U.S. never to have had an earthquake.

TOASTER FOODS

We wrote about how the toaster was invented back in BR #2—now here's the origin of America's two biggest-selling toaster foods.

EGGO WAFFLES

The *Eggo* name has probably been around longer than you think. It was coined in 1935, when three brothers—Frank, Tony, and Sam Dorsa—borrowed $35 to buy a waffle iron and started experimenting with waffle batter. When they got a batter they liked, they sold it to restaurants in Northern California. A fourth brother, George, suggested they call their product "Eggo" because "the batter has lots of eggs." In 1937, the company went public, and the brothers built a big waffle-batter factory in San Jose.

After World War II, when Americans began buying home freezers in record numbers, the Dorsas guessed there was a bigger market for frozen waffles than for waffle batter. So in 1950, they gambled and switched their entire production to ready-made waffles. Within a year, they were cranking out 10,000 an hour...and still couldn't keep up with demand. Kellogg's bought the company in 1968. Today, the brand controls an estimated 60% share of the $500 million frozen waffle industry.

POP-TARTS

The Pop-Tart story starts with dog food, not cereal...and not with Kellogg's but with its rival, Post. According to Steve Hymon, in the *Chicago Tribune*:

> In 1957, Post's pet-food division came out with Gaines Burgers [which] were a novel concept because the dog food was semi-moist but didn't have to be refrigerated—a convenience many humans coincidentally sought in their breakfast food.
>
> In 1963, the Post research and development department, using some of the same technology that made Gaines Burgers possible, figured out a way to keep fruit filling moist while inhibiting the growth of spoilage-causing bacteria. The obvious application: a fruit-filled pastry that could be shipped and stored without having to be refrigerated.

The Rolling Stones made their American TV debut on *The Red Skelton Show*.

On Feb. 16, 1964, Post unveiled its new product, Country Squares. The food industry oohed and aahed; the business press buzzed; grocers waited expectantly.

And waited.

Post blundered. It took so long to get its product to grocery stores that Kellogg's had had a chance to catch up. In just six months, Kellogg's created and test-marketed Pop-Tarts. People at Post knew they were sunk. Hymon goes on:

> The names given to the two products were one more indication of Kellogg's superior marketing savvy. Kellogg's appreciated that kids were the primary target audience for Pop-Tarts because they had yet to establish breakfast habits of their own. Post seems to have been more confused. As awful a name as Country Squares seems in 1994, it was arguably worse in 1964, when the word "square" was widely used to mean "nerdy." When paired with "country," it seemed to describe a food for middle-age rubes from the sticks.

POPPING OFF

The original Pop-Tarts came in four flavors: Strawberry, Blueberry, Brown Sugar, and Apple-Currant (which Kellogg's quickly changed to Apple-Berry when it realized most consumers didn't know what currants were). Kellogg's put its marketing muscle behind the new product, blitzing kid's TV shows with commercials featuring Milton the Toaster. By 1967, they had both created and locked up the $45 million toaster pastry market. The brand maintained a 75% market share into the 1990s, with $285 million in sales in 1990...and nearly $500 million by 1993.

What happened to Country Squares? Post changed the name to Post Toast-Em Pop-Ups, but it was too late. Post finally gave up in the early 1970s and sold the marketing rights to someone else.

TOASTER FLOPS. *Not every toaster food works. Here are some other ideas that bit the big one...and the reasons why.*

- **Downyflake Toaster Eggs.** Too weird.
- **Reddi-wip's Reddi Bacon.** Bacon fat dripped to the bottom of the toaster, creating a fire hazard.
- **Toaster Chicken Patties.** Same problem, with chicken fat.
- **Electric French Fries.** Stamped out in slab form, they "looked like a picket fence, tasted like a picket fence."

MISSED IT BY THAT MU...

How frustrating is it to work for so long on something only to see it fail right before the payoff? These people know.

THE GRAND SCHEME: A group of inmates at Kinross Correctional Facility in Michigan spent three months planning and implementing a daring escape. Because the prison was originally built as an Air Force barracks, the walls weren't fortified the way most modern prison walls are. All the cons had to do was break through eight inches of unreinforced concrete and then dig out about 50 feet of soft dirt. To start, one of the prisoners made a small hole in the back corner of his cell, where guards routinely look but seldom touch. (Authorities believe he may have used a dumbbell from the gym as a hammer.) Then each night he would dig a little more, keeping some of the dirt in the crescent-shaped tunnel and flushing the rest down the cell toilet (which caused clogs in the system that baffled prison administrators). By March 2007, the tunnel extended several feet beyond the outside fence. All they had left to do was dig "up" to freedom.

FOILED: During a routine check of the cell, one of the guards noticed something odd on the wall; he touched it and found the soft spot, prompting an immediate investigation...and the end of the escape plan. Although little information about the case was given to the press, one thing is known: Only one more night of digging and the prisoners would have made it.

THE GRAND SCHEME: For more than two years, John and Penny Adie, organizers of an annual classical music festival in England, had been working tirelessly to raise enough money to buy a Bösendorfer grand piano. Valued at £45,000 ($89,000) and made exclusively in Austria, Bösendorfers are the preferred piano of many of the world's greatest players. "They're the Stradivarius of the piano world," said John Adie. By April 2007, they had finally raised all the money they needed and they purchased the piano at a London auction. The only thing left to make their dream a reality was to deliver the Bösendorfer to the concert hall.

Silly rabbit! Trix are for dentists! When Trix cereal was introduced in 1954, it was 46.6% sugar.

FOILED: As the delivery workers were hauling "the Stradivarius of the piano world" up the walkway, 20 feet from their destination they lost control of the dolly...and John and Penny watched in horror as their prized piano fell eight feet off of a ledge and smashed discordantly onto the ground below. "It was a total loss," said John, noting that insurance would probably cover only half of what the piano is worth. "It's more than money that is the issue here," said John. "It was like seeing a priceless painting torn to shreds," Penny added.

GRAND SCHEME: Charles McKinley, a 25-year-old shipping clerk from Brooklyn, New York, wanted to fly home to see his parents in DeSoto, Texas, in 2003—but he couldn't afford a plane ticket. So he decided to use one of the big boxes from his workplace and ship *himself* home (with his employer unknowingly footing the bill). McKinley poked some holes in the box, then packed himself, some clothes, food, and his computer inside. An accomplice sealed the box and marked it "Computer Equipment." McKinley's two-day wild ride in a box took him on a shipping truck from Brooklyn to New Jersey, then on a plane to Buffalo, New York, which then flew him to Fort Wayne, Indiana, then (after changing planes) to Fort Worth, Texas, and finally on a truck to DeSoto, about 14 miles south of Dallas.

FOILED: As the driver was retrieving the "package" from the back of the delivery truck to bring it to McKinley's dad's house, he noticed a little slit in the top, and peeking through the slit was an eye looking up at him. The driver gasped. McKinley kicked open the side of the box, picked up all of his stuff, and calmly walked into the house. The driver called his boss, who then called the Feds, who came and arrested McKinley. He was charged as a stowaway, which is a federal offense. McKinley later revealed that just before the driver went to retrieve the box, he moved a piece of clothing that had been covering him so he could get a peek at the man. If McKinley had only waited one more minute for the driver to leave, he would have been home free.

*　　*　　*

Q: What time of day was Adam born?
A: A little before Eve.

Losing face: In ancient China, criminals caught robbing travelers had their noses cut off.

THE SECRET OF NANCY DREW

The most famous girl sleuth in history had her own secret for over 60 years: the identity of her creator.

THE MYSTERY

As every fan knows, the author of the Nancy Drew series is Carolyn Keene. She began writing about the girl detective in 1930 (debut adventure: *The Secret of the Old Clock*), and today her work is as popular as ever. There are more than 20 million Nancy Drew books currently in print, in 18 languages.

The only problem: There is no person named Carolyn Keene—the name was invented by a man named Edward Stratemeyer. For over 60 years it was assumed that his daughter, Harriet Stratemeyer Adams, really wrote the books. Then in 1968, a real-life amateur sleuth uncovered the whole truth.

THE CLUES

1. *It was Edward Stratemeyer who first conceived the broad outlines of Nancy Drew, the 16-year-old amateur detective, in 1930.*

• Stratemeyer started out writing "dime novels" in the 1890s. During the Spanish-American War, he invented a fantastically popular series of juvenile stories starring the Rover Boys. Then he created teenage scientist Tom Swift and the Bobbsey Twins.

• In 1906, he realized he couldn't write stories fast enough to keep up with demand. So he began hiring newspaper reporters to write books from his plot outlines, paying them between $50 and $250 per novel. They never got credit—Stratemeyer made them sign a contract giving up all rights to their work, renouncing royalties, and promising never to reveal their identities.

• Thus the Stratemeyer Syndicate was born. By the 1920s, the syndicate was producing and selling millions of books a year. They starred Baseball Joe, Dave Dashaway, Bomba the Jungle Boy, the Motor Girls, and many more. In 1927, Stratemeyer invented one of his most popular series, the Hardy Boys (and its "author," F. W. Dixon).

Alexander the Great introduced the eggplant to Europe.

• By the time of his death, Stratemeyer had developed more than 800 books for children and teenagers under 88 different pseudonyms. Just before he died in 1930, he came up with the idea that would be the Syndicate's biggest seller—Nancy Drew.

2. *Stratemeyer's daughter, Harriet, took over the Syndicate. She later said she found the first three Nancy Drew manuscripts among her father's possessions.*

• After graduating from Wellesley College in 1915, Adams went to work for her father—but not as a writer. Ironically, Stratemeyer didn't feel that women should work. "If they did," Adams recalled, "it was a disgrace and meant their fathers couldn't support them."

• Nevertheless, when Stratemeyer passed away in 1930, Adams and her sister took over the business. In the next 50 years, she outproduced her father, and is credited with writing 180 books and originating the plots for 1,200 others.

• Adams said that her father wrote the first three Nancy Drew books himself, and that in 1930, she found them, cleaned them up, and sent them off to be published. Then she took over the series and wrote the rest of them. Throughout her life, Adams was celebrated as the "real Carolyn Keene."

3. *But there was a disparity between Nancy Drew and Adams's other characters.*

• Nancy was independent, quick-thinking, in charge—a protofeminist; Adams's other creations, like the Dana Girls, were flat and conventional.

• Critics and fans were puzzled by this. In a long analysis of the Nancy Drew series in *The Horn Book*, for example, Anne Scott MacLeod concluded that

> What Harriet Adams achieved in Nancy Drew was, apparently, as accidental as it was monumental. "If I made Nancy liberated, I was unconscious of the fact," Mrs. Adams said in 1980. It is ungenerous, but entirely believable. Adams's portraits of other women [in her other books]...seem ample evidence that she was [not] a feminist.

MYSTERY SOLVED

Adams wasn't a feminist—but Mildred Wirt Benson was.

In 1968 Geoffrey S. Lapin, a Nancy Drew fan, tracked Benson

Baby giraffes can grow as much as 1 inch every two hours.

down in Toledo, Ohio. The 87-year-old had been working there as a reporter for 50 years—and was still writing a weekly column for the *Toledo Blade* called "On the Go with Millie Benson."

But back in 1930, she was a reporter for the *Des Moines Register*. Edward Stratemeyer approached her about writing the first Nancy Drew story. He gave her a one-paragraph outline and paid her $125. She produced *The Secret of the Old Clock*.

At first, Stratemeyer wasn't happy with the character Benson had created. He felt Nancy was too independent and bossy at a time when girls were supposed to be delicate and dependent on men. But he had a deadline, and sent the manuscript to the publisher anyway.

By 1934—four years after the first Nancy Drew story was published—the series had outsold every other children's book in existence. Girls loved Nancy because she showed that they could have experiences on an equal level with boys. Benson told a reporter later:

> I sort of liked the character from the beginning. Now that kind of woman is common, but then it was a new concept, though not to me. I just naturally thought that girls could do the things boys did.

THE REAL NANCY DREW

"Mrs. Benson's life has tended to resemble her heroine's," commented a critic in the *New York Times*. "A doctor's daughter, she was the first woman to get a master's degree in journalism from the University of Iowa. She was [also] an accomplished pilot who "made nine solo trips to Central America to study pre-Columbian archaeology."

Benson wrote 26 of the first 30 Nancy Drew books, but never revealed her identity. She didn't want a lawsuit from the Stratemeyer Syndicate and besides, she "didn't want to get pestered."

After being discovered by Lapin, Benson was elected to the Ohio Women's Hall of Fame in 1993 and was honored by the University of Iowa at the first Nancy Drew Conference the same year.

Did she enjoy the attention? Well, yes, she admitted to the *New York Times*, but added: "I'm so sick of Nancy Drew I could vomit."

King Henry VIII owned tennis shoes.

LAME EXCUSES

What's your excuse for not reading this page sooner?

Offender: Texas State Senator Bill Moore

Offense: Critics charged that he would personally profit from a bill he was backing.

Lame Excuse: "I'd just make a little bit of money. I wouldn't make a whole lot."

Offender: Demi Moore

Offense: She changed the ending of *The Scarlet Letter* from sad to happy.

Lame Excuse: "Not many people have read the book."

Offender: Edward G. Edwards

Offense: The Louisiana gubernatorial candidate suffered an embarrassing loss in a debate with his opponent shortly before the 1992 election.

Lame Excuse: "I deliberately fumbled around and didn't do as good as I could. I gave that guy a false sense of security and he fell for it hook, line, and sinker."

Offenders: Two operators at Dresden Nuclear Power Plant

Offense: They were caught sleeping on the job. John Hogan, the Commonwealth Edison supervisor of news information, explained it to reporters.

Lame Excuse: "It depends on your definition of 'asleep.' They weren't stretched out. They had their eyes closed. They were seated at their desks with their heads in a nodding position."

Offender: Ozzy Osbourne

Offense: The hard rocker bit the head off of a dead dove at a CBS Records meeting.

Lame Excuse: "I wanted them to remember me."

Offender: Jim Morrison

Offense: Revealing himself while on stage

Lame Excuse: "I just wanted to see what it looked like in the spotlight."

*   *   *

"It is better to offer no excuse than a bad one."

—**George Washington, in a letter to his niece Harriet Washington, October 30, 1791**

Keep trying! At last count, Ozzy Osbourne has been in rehab 14 times.

UNCLE JOHN'S TOY BOX

You can find some of the oddest things to play with in the BRI's toy box!

THE LIBRARIAN ACTION FIGURE—*With amazing push-button shooshing action!* This five-inch doll is based on a real librarian named Nancy Pearl. And she loves it. "It's a lovely idea and a lovely tribute to my chosen profession." But some librarians are less than thrilled with the "push-button shooshing action." Says one: "It's so stereotypical I could scream!"

BENIGN GIRL. Made in Taiwan, this hot-pink toy cell phone comes with a picture of a Barbie-esque doll on the "screen." Benign Girl's features are printed on the box: • BATTERY • OPERATED • CREATIVE • VARIOUS MUSIC. The instructions: "Beautiful girl, press any button!"

THE HORRIFIED B-MOVIE VICTIMS PLAYSET. Includes nine "victims," each about three inches tall. They come in various poses reacting to the horror of whatever monster is chasing them. (Monster not included.) *But the good news:* Any standard household item can be used as a substitute monster—a Chia pet, Mr. Potato Head, the cat, a vacuum cleaner...

JOHNNY REB CANNON. This early-1960s toy could never be released today. Not only did it feature a Confederate flag, the 30-inch cannon came with a ramrod and fired hard plastic cannonballs up to 35 feet. And then there's the jingle: "We'll all be gay when Johnny comes marching home!"

FLYING WITCH 2000 B.C. It looks like the makers of this toy confused B.C. with A.D. Why? Because this little green witch rides a big yellow rocket. Hung on a string and powered by a tiny propeller, the witch is supposed to fly in circles...on her rocket.

REMOTE-CONTROL FARTING BEAR. "He's cute, he's cuddly, and he's flatulent. There's nothing he likes more than to be in the arms of some poor, unsuspecting victim so he can let out a big, juicy one when you press the remote control!"

Little things mean a lot: 200 million atoms placed in a row would measure one inch.

THE REAL SPARTACUS

The true story of the slave who became the most feared man in the Roman Empire! A noble hero meets a black-hearted villain in battle! A rebel uprising! Romance, adventure, and a cast of thousands!

THRACE IS THE PLACE

As the movie *Spartacus* opens, the hero is sweaty and bedraggled, breaking up rocks. The voice-over tells us that he was the son of a slave, sold into slavery when he was 13.

Not exactly. The real Spartacus was a tribal warrior from the ancient region of Thrace, which is now part of Greece, Bulgaria, and Turkey. His tribe was probably conquered by the Roman army—history's a little unclear on this—because he became a Roman soldier. Then he deserted the army, was captured, was brought to Rome, and then was sold into slavery. The year: 73 B.C.

GOING, GOING, GONE

Unlike the movie, where Spartacus is a bachelor so he can fall in love with a beautiful slave girl, the real Spartacus was married by the time he became a slave. His wife, a priestess, was captured along with him. Legend has it that when they were together in the slave market, a snake coiled itself around Spartacus's face as he slept. His wife interpreted the snake as a lucky sign, an omen that her husband would become powerful. But soon afterward, both of them became the property of a man named Lentulus Batiates. Their new owner ran a gladiator school in Capua, near Mount Vesuvius.

GLADIATOR-IN-TRAINING

Some of Spartacus's fellow students at the imperial gladiator school were prisoners of war from northern Europe, while others were convicted criminals whose lives were spared because they were tough enough to qualify for gladiator training. The "school" was actually a prison, with plenty of opportunity to fight with other "students." The men were taught how to handle the gladiatorial weapons: fishing spears, chains, swords, nets, and lassos.

All across Rome, gladiators were big-name celebrities. Wealthy citizens decorated the walls of their villas with portraits of the greatest gladiators. Teenagers swooned over their favorites the way they do over pop stars today. In the ruins of Pompeii, archaeologists found love notes to gladiators that young girls had scribbled on public walls.

But Spartacus wasn't interested in fame. He reportedly told the others, "If we must fight, we might as well fight for freedom." One day they got their chance.

THE FIGHT FOR FREEDOM

Spartacus's words inspired 200 of his fellow gladiators to stage a revolt. Using knives and skewers from the school's kitchen, they fought their way out. About 80 managed to escape, including Spartacus and his wife. And in a twist that sounds like an unbelievable movie plot, as the gladiators ran through Capua, they found carts filled with gladiatorial weapons. The escapees swapped their kitchen tools for the real thing and fled.

Once the rebels made it to the countryside, they selected Spartacus as their leader. His first order of business was to lead his troops against the soldiers who'd followed them. The gladiators defeated their pursuers and traded up in weaponry again. Now they were equipped to handle nearly anything. They headed south toward Mount Vesuvius, plundering farms for food and freeing slaves. Most of the slaves were happy to join the ever-growing rebel band.

SNEAK ATTACK

Back in Capua, the local authorities called in the troops. With 3,000 Roman soldiers bearing down on them, Spartacus and company retreated up a narrow path that was the only access to Vesuvius. The rest of the mountain was too steep and slippery to climb. It looked like the Romans, who waited nonchalantly at the bottom, had them trapped.

At the top of Vesuvius, the rebels improvised rope ladders from vines and climbed down the other side. They had the perfect opportunity to sneak away, but Spartacus couldn't resist ambushing the Romans. The rebels stormed the rear of the Roman camp and captured it easily.

What? Sorry, I wasn't paying attention: *Aprosexia* is the inability to concentrate.

RAGGED ARMY

Though the Roman senate sent armies out to capture Spartacus, the best and strongest of Rome's fighting men were out conquering the rest of the world. The next two armies they assembled were thrown together piecemeal: an elderly man here, a dreg of society there. Spartacus and his men easily mowed them down.

Every victory brought Spartacus more fame—and more slaves to his side. Less than a year after the escape from Capua, the army of slaves totaled a whopping 70,000. The Roman senate became terrified that the rebels were going to head straight for Rome.

But that was the last thing Spartacus wanted. He knew only too well the power of Rome and was as frightened of the real Roman army as the senate was of him. So he started his troops north toward the Alps. But Spartacus had created a monster—his men didn't want to escape. They wanted to go on looting and plundering.

ENTER THE BLACK-HEARTED VILLAIN

Rome now had to enlist its best troops against Spartacus. The only problem was that the senate couldn't find a general to lead them: Possibly losing to a ragtag bunch of rebels was more indignity than most military men wanted to face.

But they found a volunteer in Marcus Crassus, who had been waiting for the right moment to step into the limelight. Crassus was the richest man in Rome, and one of the most unprincipled—in a city where corruption was already rampant. He'd made his money in various shady business, and is still famous for starting Rome's first fire brigade. But his firefighting method also had its profits—the property owner had to pay an exorbitant fee before his fire brigade would help them (and the fires were often set by Crassus's employees). This was the man charged with the task of leading 10 Roman legions against Spartacus.

A HARSH LESSON

Crassus was smart enough to know that Spartacus wanted to get far away from Rome. So he sent a lieutenant named Mummius with two legions and strict orders not to fight, but to provoke the rebels into marching north, where he would wait for them. But instead, Mummius attacked Spartacus's rebels…and was soundly defeated.

Alexander Hamilton wasn't born in the United States, but on the Caribbean island of Nevis.

Crassus was furious, and after Mummius retreated and returned with his men to camp, Crassus sentenced the defeated legions to the traditional Roman punishment, known as "decimation." The soldiers were divided into groups of 10, and each group drew lots to see which one of them would die. The unlucky ones-in-ten were executed in front of the whole army. This, Crassus felt, would inspire the men to obey orders next time.

THOSE WHO ARE ABOUT TO DIE...

The rebels didn't head north, as Crassus predicted, but instead turned toward the south. Crassus and his legions chased them all the way to the toe of the Italian boot, just across the water from the island of Sicily. The slaves stood with their backs to the sea, facing 50,000 of the best-trained soldiers in the world. To make things worse, Crassus had his men dig a ditch 37 miles long and 15 feet wide and deep. It cut the rebels off from any escape route but the sea. For extra insurance, the ditch was backed by a wall. The rebels managed to cross the ditch and tried to scale the wall, but were beaten back after losing more than 10,000 men. When Spartacus heard that another army was on its way to join Crassus, he led his men in one more desperate charge. This time the rebels made it over the wall and through enemy lines. But as they fled, the new army blocked their way. Spartacus decided to turn and fight.

DECISIONS, DECISIONS

In the long and bloody battle, Spartacus was killed, though his body was never found among the tens of thousands of dead. His followers fled to the mountains, pursued by Crassus. After one last battle, 6,000 slaves were captured. Crassus had them all crucified, their bodies spaced evenly along the road from Capua to Rome. No record has ever been found of the fate of Spartacus's wife.

Movie note: At the end of the film *Spartacus*, Spartacus survives the battle, leading to the inspiring scene where Crassus promises that he won't crucify the remaining men if someone will point out Spartacus. Of course, Kirk Douglas is about to speak up when the other men, one by one, stand up and shout "I'm Spartacus!" "I'm Spartacus!" According to Kirk Douglas, the slave army's cries were actually shouted by a crowd at a Michigan State (Spartans) vs. Notre Dame football game.

In 1839 Maine and New Brunswick, Canada, fought a bloodless "War of Pork and Beans."

THE INCREDIBLE SHRINKING HEADS

There have been many head-hunting cultures in the world—even the French had the guillotine—but only one made shrunken heads. Here's the story.

THE JIVARO

The Jivaro (pronounced "hee-var-o") tribes live deep in the jungles of Ecuador and Peru. They don't do it anymore as far as anyone knows, but as recently as 100 years ago they were ardent head shrinkers. The Jivaro tribes were constantly at war with other neighboring tribes (and with each other), and they collected the heads of their fallen enemies as war trophies. The head, once shrunk, was called *tsantsa* (pronounced "san-sah"). For the Jivaro the creation of tsantsa insured good luck and prevented the soul of the fallen enemy from seeking revenge.

As Western explorers came in increasing contact with the Jivaro tribes in the late 19th century, shrunken heads became a popular souvenir. Traders would barter guns, ammo, and other useful items for shrunken heads; this "arms-for-heads" trade caused the killing to climb rapidly, prompting the Peruvian and Ecuadorian governments to outlaw head shrinking in the early 1900s. If you buy a head today, it's guaranteed to be a fake.

THE JOY OF COOKING...HEADS

Here's the Jivaro recipe for a genuine shrunken head (don't try this at home): Peel skin and hair from skull; discard skull. Sew eye and mouth openings closed (trapping the soul inside, so that it won't haunt you). Turn inside out and scrape fat away using sharp knife. Add jungle herbs to a pot of water and bring to a boil; add head and simmer for one to two hours. Remove from water. Fill with hot stones, rolling constantly to prevent scorching. Repeat with successively smaller pebbles as the head shrinks. Mold facial features between each step. Hang over fire to dry. Polish with ashes. Moisturize with berries (prevents cracking). Sew neck hole closed. Trim hair to taste.

Grossest fact in this entire book: You inhale about 700,000 of your own skin flakes daily.

TITANIC COINCIDENCES

There's something almost mystical about the Titanic. *There are so many bizarre coincidences associated with it, you'd think it was an episode of* The Twilight Zone.

THE TITAN/TITANIC

In 1898 a short novel called *The Wreck of the Titan, or Futility,* by Morgan Robertson, was published in the United States. It told the story of the maiden voyage of an "unsinkable" luxury liner called the *Titan.*

Robertson described the boat in great detail. The *Titan,* he wrote, was 800 feet long, weighed 75,000 tons, had three propellers and 24 lifeboats, and was packed with rich passengers. Cruising at 25 knots, the *Titan's* hull was ripped apart when it hit an iceberg in April. Most of the passengers were lost because there weren't enough lifeboats. Robertson apparently claimed he'd written his book with the help of a psychic "astral writing partner."

Eerie Coincidence: Fourteen years later, the real-life *Titanic* took off on its maiden voyage. Like the fictional *Titan,* it was considered the largest and safest ship afloat. It was 882.5 feet long, weighed 66,000 tons, had three propellers and 22 lifeboats, and carried a full load of rich passengers. Late at night on April 14, 1912, sailing at 23 knots, the *Titanic* ran into an iceberg which tore a hole in its hull and upended the ship. More than 1,500 people drowned because there weren't enough lifeboats.

THE TITANIAN/TITANIC

In 1935 a "tramp steamer" called the *Titanian* was heading from England to Canada. On watch was a 23-year-old seaman named William Reeves. It was April, the month when the Titanic hit an iceberg and went down. As the *Reader's Digest Book of Amazing Facts* tells it:

Young Reeves brooded deeply on this. His watch was due to end at

---

One American in eight is considered poor, but one home in six has at least three cars or trucks.

midnight. This, he knew, was the time the *Titanic* had hit the iceberg. Then, as now, the sea had been calm. These thoughts swelled and took shape as omens...as he stood his lonely watch....He was scared to shout an alarm, fearing his shipmates' ridicule. But he was also scared not to.

Eerie Coincidence: All of a sudden, Reeves recalled the exact date of the *Titanic* accident—April 14, 1912—the day he had been born. That was enough to get him to act.

He shouted out a danger warning, and the helmsman rang the signal: engines full astern. The ship churned to a halt—just yards from a huge iceberg that towered menacingly out of the night.

More deadly icebergs crowded in around the tramp steamer, and it took nine days for icebreakers from Newfoundland to smash a way clear.

THE LUCKLESS TOWERS

Talk about coincidences! BRI member Andrew M. Borrok (hope we got that right—the fax is hard to read) submitted the following excerpt just as Uncle John was writing this piece. Obviously we had to include it. Thanks!

The stoker on the *Titanic* was named Frank Lucks Towers. Charles Pelegrino writes in his book, *Her Name, Titanic:*

Though he would survive this night (*Titanic*) without injury, his troubles were just beginning. In two years he'd be aboard the *Empress of Ireland* when it collided with another ship, opening up a hole in the *Empress'* side. (Note: it was the worst peacetime maritime disaster—over 2,000 lost.) It would be an usually hot night, and all the portholes would be open as she rolled onto her side in the St. Lawrence River. In minutes she would be gone—yet miraculously, Frank Towers was going to survive—virtually alone. He'd take his next job aboard the *Lusitania,* (sunk by German U-boats in 1915) and would be heard to shout "Now what!" when the torpedo struck. He'd swim to a lifeboat, vowing every stroke of the way to take up farming.

His story was destined to inspire a young writer to script a teleplay entitled *Lone Survivor.* The teleplay was so well received that it paved the way for a series. The writer's name was Rod Serling and the series became *The Twilight Zone.*

WHEN IN ROME...

Uncle John is fascinated by the international rules of etiquette (especially anything bathroom-related). Over the years he's picked up quite a few tidbits of advice to help you get by in foreign countries.

Argentina: People tend to stand very close. If you back away from someone, they'll assume you're shy and close the gap. Or they might just be offended by your rudeness.

Austria: Cut your food with a fork. To use a knife implies the food is tough and unappealing.

Brazil: Brazilian women can be romantically aggressive. It's not uncommon for a woman to send a note to a man in a restaurant asking for his phone number...even if he's with his wife or girlfriend.

Bulgaria: In this east-European country, shaking your head "no" actually means "yes." Nodding means "no."

Czech Republic: Raising your voice damages your credibility. You will be considered a buffoon.

Denmark: Never compliment other people's clothing. It's considered too intimate.

Australia: Don't say "g'day, mate" to an Australian. Avoid the temptation to talk about convicts (Australia was founded as a penal colony) or mention *Crocodile Dundee*. It's condescending.

Egypt: Don't add salt to a meal. It's insulting to the cook, implying that the food is unpalatable.

France: Bread will be waiting for you on the table in restaurants, but don't eat it until the main course arrives. It's not an appetizer—it's meant to accompany meals.

Singapore: Chewing gum, jaywalking, spitting, littering, and not flushing a public toilet are not only considered rude, they're also illegal...and you can be fined $500 per offense.

South Korea: If you want to get someone's attention, don't point and do the "come here" thing. Instead, extend your arm, palm down, and wiggle your fingers downward.

Hats off! Wearing a hat is considered disrespectful in Fiji.

Japan: It's considered rude to eat food on the street, especially if you're walking. Sit down to eat, even if it's a cup of coffee or an ice cream cone.

Italy: It's rude to get up to use the bathroom during a meal. Wait until the meal's over.

The Netherlands: Cafés and coffee shops aren't the same thing. Both sell food and both sell coffee, but "coffee shops" are also places where marijuana is sold and consumed.

Hungary: Never clink glasses. According to legend, 13 Hungarian generals were jailed by Austria in the 1848 revolution. Their Austrian captors clinked glasses at every meal, so Hungarians unofficially vowed to ban the practice for 150 years. Technically, the ban is now over, but it's still honored.

Finland: It's the home of Nokia, so cell phones are universal. But in public places, you must set your phone to "vibrate." If it rings in a theater, restaurant, library, or even at a sporting event, you will be asked to leave.

Poland: When dining at someone's home, thank them by saying *dziekuje* (jen-koo-yeh). But don't say it to a waiter in a restaurant unless you really mean it; in that context, it means "keep the change."

Sweden: If you touch something in a store or market, you're expected to buy it.

Thailand: Thailand is a Buddhist country, so all life is deemed precious there. Be careful not to step on spiders, and never swat at insects.

*   *   *

A RANDOM ORIGIN

On a 1976 Lynyrd Skynyrd live album, singer Ronnie Van Zant asks the audience, "What song is it you want to hear?" The audience demands "Free Bird!" and the band plays it. The tradition of shouting it at non-Skynyrd concerts started in Chicago in 1988. Disc jockey (and Lynyrd Skynyrd fan) Kevin Matthews instructed listeners to attend a Florence Henderson concert and shout out requests for "Free Bird" to torment the singer. Fans then started yelling the song at other unhip concerts, then at any concert at all.

Equal rights: By law, all tombstones in Norway must be the same height.

THE KING OF COTTON

When you hear the name Eli Whitney, you probably think of his invention, the cotton gin. But you may not realize how profoundly it (and his other inventions) changed the world. Here's the history they never taught you in school.

LOOKING FOR WORK

In 1792 a 27-year-old Massachusetts Yankee named Eli Whitney graduated from Yale University and landed a tutoring job in South Carolina. He was glad to get it—he needed the money to pay off his school debts. But when he arrived there he discovered that the job paid half of what he'd been promised, which meant he'd never be able to save any money. He turned the job down.

Suddenly he was jobless, penniless, and stranded in the South, hundreds of miles from home. But he'd made the trip from New York with a friend named Phineas Miller, who was escorting *his* employer, a widow named Mrs. Greene, back to Georgia. When Greene invited Whitney to spend a week at her plantation outside of Savannah, he gladly accepted. He had no place else to go.

Whitney repaid Mrs. Greene's generosity by designing an embroidery frame for her. Greene was impressed by the cleverness of the design, and it got her thinking. If Whitney was this clever, maybe he could solve a problem that plagued her and other planters—how to "gin," or remove the seeds from, cotton...without doing it by hand.

Upland cotton, the only kind that grew in the interior regions of the South, had seeds that were "covered with a kind of green coat resembling velvet," as Whitney put it. These fuzzy seeds stuck to the cotton fibers like Velcro. Removing them by hand required so much labor—one person could clean only about a pound of cotton per day—that upland cotton was essentially worthless.

MASS PRODUCTION

If a way could be found to remove the seeds more easily, upland cotton had the potential to become a very valuable export crop. Why? The Industrial Revolution had transformed the English textile industry (which turned the cotton into thread and the thread into cloth) into a monster and caused demand for cotton to soar.

As late as the 1730s, spinners and weavers made cloth just as they had for centuries: slowly and by hand. One person, sitting at a spinning wheel, could spin raw cotton into only one string of yarn at a time. It took 14 days to make a pound of yarn, which one or two weavers could then weave into a single piece of cloth.

In the mid-1700s, English inventions with colorful names like the flying shuttle (1733), the spinning jenny (1764), the water frame (1769), and the mule (1779), changed all that; so did the introduction of steam power in 1785. Now a single unskilled laborer—even a child or someone formerly thought too old to work—could tend machines that made hundreds and eventually thousands of strands of yarn at once, or that wove it into yards and yards of cloth, faster than the eye could see.

THE BIG BANG
Because of these inventions, the English textile industry's appetite for cotton became enormous and grew exponentially from year to year. In 1765 spinners and weavers in England had turned half a million pounds of cotton into cloth; by 1790 the new machines were consuming 28 million pounds of cotton per year, nearly all of it imported from other countries. As demand for raw cotton soared, it got harder and harder to find enough of it to feed all of the new machines.

How much of the imported raw cotton came from the American South? Almost none. As late as 1791, the year before Whitney arrived in Georgia, exports for the entire South totaled a few hundred bags at most. But not for long.

NO PROBLEM
So how long did it take Whitney to solve the problem that had vexed Southern planters for years? Ten days. It took several months to perfect the design, but after just 10 days, this Yankee, who'd landed at Greene's plantation purely by chance, managed to invent this revolutionary machine.

The design was so simple that it was a wonder nobody else had thought of it before. It consisted of a wooden roller with wire "teeth" that grabbed the cotton fibers and pulled them through a slotted iron screen. The slots in the screen were wide enough to let the teeth and the cotton fibers through, but they were too narrow for the seeds, which separated out and fell into a box.

A rapidly rotating brush then removed the cotton fibers from the teeth and flung them into a bin. This allowed the user to feed raw cotton into the machine indefinitely, without having to stop every few minutes to clean the teeth.

Using Whitney's cotton gin, in one day a laborer could clean as much as 10 pounds of upland cotton, which before would have taken 10 days to clean by hand. If a larger gin powered by water or a horse was used, a laborer could clean as much cotton in one day as would have taken more than *seven weeks* to clean by hand.

BRAVE NEW WORLD

Over the next several decades, Whitney's cotton gin transformed the South. Tens of thousands and eventually millions of acres of wilderness were cleared to make way for enormous cotton plantations. By 1810 U.S. exports of cotton to England had grown from almost nothing to 38 million pounds, making the South the largest supplier of cotton to that country.

And that was only the beginning. By the start of the Civil War, the Southern "cotton belt," as it came to be known, was exporting *920 million* pounds of cotton to England each year, more than 90% of its cotton imports. Cotton had become, as one historian described it, "the largest single source of America's growing wealth." Cotton was king.

THE CLOTHES ON YOUR BACK

But Whitney's invention had more far-reaching effects than increasing U.S. exports. The industrialization of cotton production vastly increased the supply of cotton cloth. That changed cotton from one of the most expensive fabrics on Earth to one of the cheapest—and in the process, it clothed the world.

Between 1785, the year that steam power was introduced to the textile industry, and the early 1860s, the price of cotton cloth fell by more than 99%. That's the equivalent of a price of Tommy Hilfiger jeans falling from $5,000 to $50.

In the past almost no one had been able to afford cotton, (how many $5,000 pairs of jeans could you afford?), and things like leather and wool made poor substitutes. (Don't believe it? Treat yourself to a pair of wool underpants and you'll see what we mean.) "Most of humanity," historian Paul Johnson writes in *A History of the American People*, "were unsuitably clothed in garments which were difficult to wash and therefore filthy."

Cheap, abundant cotton cloth changed that, too. "There is no instance in world history where the price of a product in potentially universal demand came down so fast," Johnson writes. "As a result, hundreds of millions of people, all over the world, were able to dress comfortably and cleanly at last."

CHAINS OF COTTON

There is yet another aspect to Eli Whitney's cotton gin—an ugly, inhuman side, that cast a shadow over all of the good it did. Many Americans think of Whitney's invention as an emancipator, a machine that freed the slaves from having to do the hand ginning of cotton. On the contrary, the rise of cotton cultivation in the South actually helped to entrench the institution of slavery, condemning millions of black Americans to its horrors just when many opponents of slavery thought it might finally be dying out.

Between 1775 and 1800 the price of slaves had fallen from about $100 per slave to $50, and abolitionists predicted that if the institution were left alone, it would die on its own. Or at the very least, as slavery weakened, it would become easier to abolish.

But the invention of the cotton gin changed everything. As the amount of acreage brought under cultivation in the South soared, so did the demand for slaves to work the plantations. Between 1800 and 1850, the price of a slave rose from $50 to as much as $1,000. Slavery, formerly thought to be in decline, quickly became integral to the new Southern economy.

As such, the leaders of the Southern states became increasingly militant in their determination to defend it and even expand it beyond the South. For a new generation of Southern leaders, the institution of slavery—because of the prosperity that came with it—was something to be defended, even to the death.

The cotton gin had made it happen...and made the Civil War inevitable.

Part II of the story of Eli Whitney starts on page 453.

Dolphins can hear underwater sounds from as far as 15 miles away.

THE CREEPIEST MOVIE EVER MADE

Can a dead person star in a movie? Well, if a star unexpectedly dies before film production is complete, what's the studio supposed to do—pass up a great opportunity for free publicity? Not a chance.

BIG TIME

In 1970 a filmmaker named Raymond Chow quit his job at Shaw Brothers Studios, Hong Kong's largest film studio at the time, and formed Golden Harvest Studios. Not long afterward he signed an up-and-coming young martial artist to play the lead in his first movie. The actor was Bruce Lee and the movie, *The Big Boss*, was his first feature-length kung fu film.

The Big Boss shattered Hong Kong box-office records when it premiered in 1971. Lee's follow-up film, *Fist of Fury*, was even more successful. His third film, *The Way of the Dragon*, did better still when it was released in 1972.

These three blockbusters put Golden Harvest on the map and helped introduce the Hong Kong film industry to the international market. In 1973 Golden Harvest became the first Hong Kong studio to partner with a major Hollywood studio when it collaborated with Warner Bros. on Lee's fourth and "final" film, *Enter the Dragon*. Today Golden Harvest is Hong Kong's largest and most successful movie studio. They owe much of their success to Bruce Lee.

THE CLONE WARS

When Lee died suddenly in July 1973, only four weeks before *Enter the Dragon* debuted on the silver screen, how did the studio honor him? By cashing in on the publicity surrounding his death, of course. And they weren't the only ones: Hong Kong studios flooded the market with Bruce Lee knock-off films as fast as they could make them—movies with titles like *New Fist of Fury*, *Bruce Lee Fights Back from the Grave*, *Exit the Dragon*, *Re-Enter the Dragon*, *Enter Another Dragon*, and *Enter the Fat Dragon*, starring kung fu copycats like Bruce Le, Bruce Li, Bruce Liang, and Dragon Lee.

Roman gladiators gave product endorsements.

UNFINISHED BUSINESS

But by far the strangest of these films was *Game of Death,* which Lee started but did not live to finish. The only parts that he completed were the fight scenes, including one with pro basketball player Kareem Abdul-Jabbar. There was no plot line in any of the finished scenes, but Golden Harvest plowed ahead anyway, taking just 11 minutes of the original fight footage and creating an entirely new movie around it, using a double to play Bruce Lee's character Billy Lo, a movie star who refuses to submit to gangsters who control the Hong Kong film industry.

PROBLEM SOLVING

How do you make a movie using a dead actor? Golden Harvest tackled the problem in a number of different ways:

• Lee's double was filmed in wide angle shots, from behind, or in the dark whenever possible.

• Reaction shots of the real Bruce Lee, recycled from his earlier films, were spliced into the scenes with Lee's double.

• In one scene they literally cut out a still photograph of Bruce Lee's head and pasted it on the screen over the double's head.

• In scenes where the double does show his face, he wears a large pair of dark sunglasses and sometimes even a fake moustache and beard. In other scenes he wears a motorcycle helmet with the darkened visor pulled down.

• The plot was written to explain the character's changed appearance: Early in the film a gangster tries to kill Billy Lo by shooting him in the face. Lo survives, but undergoes plastic surgery to repair the damage, and emerges from the hospital literally a new man.

SOME THANKS

Had Golden Harvest simply left it at that, *Game of Death* would hardly be worth anyone's while. But they didn't. When Billy Lo gets shot and is rushed to the hospital, he decides to fake his death and even arranges his funeral, so that his assailants won't know he's still alive and coming after them. Golden Harvest added this element to the plot to give them an excuse to incorporate footage of Bruce Lee's *actual funeral,* including close-up shots of the open casket as mourners file past. For a brief moment the camera even peeks inside the coffin, showing Lee's embalmed face—probably the only time in history that a movie star's cadaver appears in his own feature film.

TRAGIC COINCIDENCE

When the gangsters shoot Bruce Lee's character Billy Lo, they do it by sneaking onto the movie set where he's filming a gun battle and fill the gun with real bullets instead of blanks. Moments later, Billy is "accidentally" shot while filming the scene.

Fifteen years after *Game of Death* premiered, in March 1993, Bruce Lee's only son, 28-year-old Brandon Lee, died on the set of the movie *The Crow*. While filming a scene in which his character is shot and killed, the prop gun, supposed to be loaded only with blanks, was loaded with a real .44-caliber slug.

Police concluded it was an accident resulting from the film crew's negligence: Sometimes "dummy" bullets—real bullets with the gunpowder and primer removed—are used to make it look like a gun contains real bullets. On this occasion one of the dummy bullets apparently came apart inside the gun, and a slug remained lodged in the barrel. Nobody bothered to make sure the barrel was clear before blanks were loaded into the gun. When the gun was fired at Lee, the slug shot out and struck him in the lower abdomen. He died in surgery 12 hours later.

LESSON LEARNED

Game of Death was unfinished when Bruce Lee died and was later finished without him. Similarly, *The Crow* was unfinished when Brandon Lee died and was later finished without him, using computer-generated special effects. This time the Lee family approved, believing that Brandon would have wanted the film to be completed.

The footage of him being shot was left out. In fact, mindful of the way Bruce Lee's death had been exploited in *Game of Death*, the family had the footage destroyed. As a family spokesperson put it, "they didn't want it to fall into the wrong hands."

*   *   *

"If you love life, don't waste time—for time is what life is made of."
—**Bruce Lee**

DOG GIVES BIRTH TO KITTENS!

...and other great tabloid headlines.

ALIENS PASSING
GAS CAUSED HOLE IN
OZONE LAYER!
—*Weekly World News*

***KEY TO
HAPPINESS...YOUR
GRANNY'S ARMPITS!***
—*New York Post*

**I FOUND JESUS
UNDER MY WALLPAPER**
—*The Sun*

*NUDIST WELFARE MAN'S
MODEL WIFE FELL FOR CHI-
NESE HYPNOTIST FROM THE
CO-OP BACON FACTORY*
—*News of the World*

**HOTCAKES NO LONGER
SELLING WELL**
—*Weekly World News*

OATMEAL PLANT BLOWS
UP; OMAHA BURIED IN
ICKY GOO
—*National News Extra*

*MOST UFOs LOOK LIKE
REGULAR PLANES!*
—*Weekly World News*

*GIRL SCALPED BY BERSERK
TORTILLA-MAKING MACHINE*
—*National News Extra*

I THOUGHT MY WIFE WAS
CHEATING WITH KEVIN
COSTNER...BUT I FOUND HER
WITH PRINCE ANDREW!
—*The Star*

*FOUNTAIN OF YOUTH
FOUND IN NYC SUBWAY
TOILET*
—*Weekly World News*

**HUBBY SUES EX: "GIVE
ME BACK MY KIDNEY!"**
—*The Sun*

DA VINCI'S ROBOT COMES TO
LIFE AFTER 500 YEARS
—*Weekly World News*

ELVIS IS DEAD!
—*National Enquirer (2003)*

An adult male gorilla can bench press about 4,000 pounds.

UNCLE JOHN'S FLATULENCE HALL OF FAME

It used to be that no one talked about farts...now, it's no big deal.
You can't get away from it. Which is fine by us. Here we honor
people who have made an art out of passing gas. (By the way—
if this is your favorite part of the book, we recommend a
tome called Who Cut the Cheese?, *by Jim Dawson.)*

Honorees: Simon Brassell, Karen Chin, and Robert Harman
Notable Achievement: Finding a way to discuss dinosaur farts without making people laugh
True Story: In 1991, the three scientists published a paper proposing that millions of years' worth of dinosaur farts may have helped make the Earth more hospitable for humans and other mammals. How? The methane gas passed by dinosaurs during the Cretaceous period, they suggested, "may have been a contributor to global warming."

Honoree: King Louis XIV of France
Notable Achievement: Turning a fart into a compliment
True Story: "It is said," Frank O'Neil writes in *The Mammoth Book of Oddities*, "that Louis XIV expressed his admiration for the Duchess of Orleans, by doing her the honor of breaking wind in her presence."

Honoree: Randy Maresh, an employee at an Albertson's supermarket in Gresham, Oregon
Notable Achievement: Making someone so mad at his farting that they sued him
True Story: In the mid-1990s, Tom Morgan sued co-worker Randy Maresh for $100,000, claiming in court papers that Maresh "would continually and repeatedly seek out the plaintiff on the premises of Albertson's [supermarket] while plaintiff was engaged

---

Before he wrote *The Satanic Verses*, Salman Rushdie worked as an advertising copywriter.

in his employee duties. That defendant, after locating plaintiff, would position himself in the proximity of plaintiff so as to direct his 'gas' toward plaintiff, humiliating plaintiff and inflicting severe mental stress upon plaintiff." (In his written response to the suit, Maresh's lawyer argued that farts are "expressive behavior," and as such, are protected by the First Amendment.) No word on the outcome.

Honoree: Dr. Michael Levitt of Minneapolis, Minnesota
Notable Achievement: Inventing a Breathalyzer-type test that can detect a propensity for excessive farting
True Story: Dr. Levitt's test checks for elevated levels of hydrogen in a patient's breath. If it's there, the patient is likely to be gassy. (Not everyone is impressed with Dr. Levitt's scientific breakthrough: "If Levitt is checking his patients' breath for flatulence," Jeffrey Kluger writes in *Discover* magazine, "I wouldn't even ask how he'd propose to conduct dental work.")

Honoree: Canelos Indians of Ecuador
Notable Achievement: Turning a fart into a supernatural experience...and a free meal
True Story: "The Canelos Indians," Eric Rabkin writes in *It's a Gas*, "are particularly scared by their farts because they believe the soul escapes the body along with the smell. They have developed a ritual to counter this escape. When in a group someone breaks wind, one of the rest, the quickest, will clap him on the back three times and say, '*Uianza, uianza!*' The meaning of this word is unknown but it does signify a feast by that name which the person who farted is obliged to prepare....Alternatively, he can discharge his obligation by rewarding the clapper's kindness with three big clay vessels of manioc beer."

Honoree: Ned Lowenbach, assistant district attorney in Tuolumne County, California
Notable Achievement: Using farts as a legal strategy
True Story: In 1988 a defense attorney appealed his client's conviction, protesting that Lowenbach had disrupted trial proceedings by passing gas. "He farted about one hundred times," the attorney said. "He even lifted his leg a few times."

In German, a partypooper is called a *partymuffel.*

AMAZING ANIMALS: THE OPOSSUM

*When we saw the opossum on a list of wildlife that thrives
in cities, it made us curious about how it manages to
survive in such a hostile environment. Turns out that
this tough little critter is quite an amazing animal.*

OLD-TIMER

Of all the mammals on Earth, opossums are among the oldest. Fossil records show it going back more than 100 million years. Remarkably, the gray-and-white, pink-nosed, rat-tailed opossums we see in our backyards today are almost identical to the ones that walked around with the dinosaurs. They have survived that long with very few evolutionary changes.

The opossum is a *marsupial*, a primitive type of mammal distinguished by its unique reproductive system. It gives birth to embryos that develop into viable "pups" in an external pouch—like a kangaroo. There used to be thousands of species of marsupials in North America, but over tens of millions of years they migrated south, into what is now South America.

Continental drift prevented them from returning until fairly recently (less than eight million years ago) and by that time another type of mammal had evolved: *placental* mammals, which develop their young *inside* their bodies. Placental mammals dominated. Of all the South American marsupial species that could have survived in North America, only one did: the opossum.

SURVIVOR

The evolutionary cards are stacked against the opossum.

It's not fast: it has a top speed of 1.7 mph.

It's not large: adults range from 6 to 12 pounds.

It's not exceedingly smart: it has almost the smallest brain-to-body ratio of any land mammal.

It's not aggressive, nor well-suited for fighting to defend itself. So why is the primitive opossum the only marsupial that made it in

North America? Here are some features that helped opossums beat the odds:

• They'll eat anything. They can survive on worms, snails, insects, snakes, toads, birds, fruits, vegetables, or garbage. (They'll also eat cat food and dog food.)

• Opossums are unusually resistant to diseases, including rabies. They're also very resistant to snake venom—a dose of rattlesnake venom that would kill a horse barely affects an opossum.

• They have a prehensile (grasping) tail that they can use to gather branches and grass for nesting, climb trees, and escape predators.

• Opossums are the only animals besides primates that have an opposable thumb. It's on their hind feet, and they use it to grasp with, like humans do.

• Male opossums have another unique appendage: a forked penis. Females have a two-channel vagina, so everything has to line up correctly for successful mating. This means that the opossum can't crossbreed with other species, which is another reason it has changed so little over the eons.

PLAYING 'POSSUM

Another unique trait that plays a big part in the opossum's survival is its ability to "play dead." Is it playing? Not exactly.

When an opossum is threatened by an enemy, it doesn't have a lot to work with. It doesn't want to fight and avoids it at all costs. It hisses and growls, baring its mouthful of teeth—it has 50, the most of any land mammal. It will even emit a foul odor, vomit, or defecate to repel the enemy. Sometimes these strategies work.

But if the predator is really hungry and still a threat, the opossum has one more weapon. It passes out. It's not an act, it's an involuntary reaction to overwhelming danger. It goes into a coma or shocklike state: the heart rate drops drastically, the body temperature goes down, the tongue hangs out, and it drools. It is, for all appearances, dead. Why is that good? Most predators won't eat dead animals. They'll usually sniff around, then leave it alone.

After a while, as short as a minute or as long as six hours, the opossum will "wake up" and waddle on its way to survive another day, another week, and who knows, maybe another 100 million years.

I AM A ROCK

Everybody knows that Alcatraz (also known as "the
Rock") was a federal prison. But it wasn't always
just the dungeon of the notorious.

GOLDEN OPPORTUNITIES

When gold was discovered near San Francisco in 1848, word spread like a virus. Seemingly overnight, the sleepy western town turned into a full-fledged city. The population exploded from about 800 people in 1848 to 25,000 at the end of 1849. The federal government, which granted California statehood in 1850, saw the rising importance of the port of San Francisco and the need to defend it. Alcatraz Island—near the Golden Gate, the entrance to San Francisco Bay from the Pacific Ocean—was the perfect place for the main military installation.

The first order of business was building a lighthouse, the first on the Pacific shoreline; it was built between 1852 and 1853, stood 166 feet high, and could be seen from 14 miles away. The light became operational in 1854, and right away, lighthouse keepers found it unpleasant to work on the island. The isolation—Alcatraz is more than a mile from San Francisco, across the frigid, frequently choppy bay—made it a lonely and boring place to live.

Meanwhile, the military set to work converting the island to the first permanent fortification on the Pacific coast. They blasted off the top of the hills to create a plateau and installed 111 cannons around the island's perimeter. In 1864, the army added three gigantic cannons with 15-inch shells that weighed 440 pounds apiece. (Each of the cannons weighed 50,000 pounds.) The last line of defense for Alcatraz was a citadel, a fort in which soldiers could hunker down in the case of a prolonged siege. The citadel held four months' worth of supplies for 200 men. Work on the fort finished in 1859, just in time for the outbreak of the Civil War in 1861.

ALL QUIET ON THE WESTERN FRONT

Although San Francisco was the 12th-largest urban area in the

---

A hummingbird egg is the size of a Tic-Tac breath mint....

country in 1861, its distance from the main conflicts of the Civil War meant things at Alcatraz were fairly low key.

In March 1863, the Union government learned of a plot hatched in San Francisco to start up a Confederate privateering ship, which would loot and steal on behalf of the secessionist South. The ship, the *J.M. Chapman*, made it no farther than Alcatraz. The navy stopped the ship before it ever made it out of the bay. The privateers were arrested and brought to Alcatraz to be held until the end of the war.

By then, Alcatraz had been occasionally been used as a military prison, and continued that role through the Civil War. In 1861, four Navy sailors who refused to swear an oath of loyalty to the Union were held there. And just after President Lincoln was assassinated, 39 citizens who spoke positively about the president's death were hustled off to Alcatraz's basement as safekeeping against a possible riot or insurrection.

WE STILL KEEP BAD GUYS HERE

Alcatraz continued as a military installation after the end of the Civil War, but its buildings were showing their age. The government tried to modernize the island during the 1870s, but it quickly became apparent that Alcatraz's time as defender of the Pacific coast was petering out...less than two decades after it opened.

Alcatraz's biggest asset became its prison. Nineteen Hopis from Arizona were shipped there in 1895 for refusing to let their children attend public schools. In 1898 the prison was filled to capacity with detainees from the Spanish-American War. Finally, in 1907, Alcatraz officially became solely a military prison when the last remaining active army troops left the island.

BIGGER, BUT NOT BETTER

During its time as a military prison, Alcatraz underwent expansion. A new cell block was planned, but because it was going to be so tall that it would block the lighthouse, a new lighthouse had to be built, too. The new electric light opened in 1909. The new cell block accommodated 600 prisoners, and it was a minimum-security facility, in contrast to the supersecure federal prison that was the next (and most famous) occupant of Alcatraz.

But, as with the fort, the military prison didn't last long. It was expensive to maintain a facility on an island; everything had to be shipped over on boats. Alcatraz's biggest problem was that it had no freshwater source, so it was dependent on enormous cisterns that collected rainwater or water sent from shore. In 1933 the army gave the compound to the Federal Bureau of Prisons, leaving behind 32 unlucky prisoners who became the Rock's first inmates.

TO PRISON AND BEYOND

For the next 30 years, Alcatraz was the most notorious federal prison in the United States. Criminals from Al Capone to Robert Franklin Stroud (better known as the Birdman of Alcatraz) were incarcerated there. Escape attempts from Alcatraz are legendary— one (that of Frank Morris, who'd managed to escape from several other prisons before coming to Alcatraz) even inspired the film *Escape from Alcatraz*. Most inmates, though, served out their full sentences on the Rock. Attorney General Robert Kennedy closed the prison in 1963.

Nobody really knew what to do with Alcatraz after that. A number of proposals were suggested, but none took hold. For a while, it looked like the government might build a memorial to the United Nations, which had been established in San Francisco, but the State Department didn't like the idea of associating the UN with a former prison. The city tried to slate Alcatraz for commercial development, but San Franciscans didn't go for it. They wanted the National Park Service to take control of the place.

In the midst of the squabbling, on November 20, 1969, a group of 90 Native Americans landed on Alcatraz and announced they wanted to buy it for $24 worth of beads and red cloth, referring to the price paid to a local tribe for Manhattan Island in 1626. (They actually considered this a generous offer, because an 1868 treaty between the Sioux and the United States stated that ownership of "surplus land," which is how Alcatraz was classified, reverts to Native Americans.) The government wanted them off, but they refused to leave unless the government agreed to build a Native American cultural center and university.

The government had no such plans. Both sides dug in their heels, and there was no progress for a long time. The occupation became a *cause célèbre*. Jane Fonda and Ethel Kennedy visited, winning sympathy for the Native Americans. Hippies from San

Remember Longfellow? "Gitchee Gumee" was the Ojibwa name for Lake Superior.

Francisco moved in. Graffiti appeared everywhere. The occupiers announced that they would give tours to raise money for supplies, but the government countered by saying that anyone going to Alcatraz was trespassing and would be prosecuted. Neither side would budge.

But then the leader of the occupation, Richard Oakes, left the island in January 1970 after his daughter died in a fall. Without him, the movement foundered. Negotiations went nowhere, so the government tried to force the protesters from the island by cutting off the electricity and water delivery. Three days later, fires broke out. The lighthouse keeper's quarters, the warden's house, the prison doctor's home, and the social hall were destroyed. The government blamed the Indians for the fire; the Indians blamed undercover government agents. People moved off the island slowly but steadily. By June 1971, the occupiers numbered only 15. Eventually, federal marshals went to the island and removed the remaining Native Americans.

The National Park Service has been in charge of Alcatraz since 1972, and started giving public tours the following year. Today it's a popular tourist destination—more than 1 million visitors per year take the ferry ride to the island to see the remnants and ruins of its different eras. There's even a nighttime tour, which was recently voted the "Best Tour of the Bay Area."

*   *   *

CARS YOU'RE UNLIKELY TO SEE IN AMERICA
Believe it or not, all these model names are real:

Nissan Homy	Suzuki Mighty Boy
Toyota Deliboy	Toyota Urban Supporter
Honda Life Dunk	Daihatsu Naked
Volugrafo Bimbo	Honda Today Humming
Renault Twingo	Toyota Synus
Nissan Sunny California	Mitsubishi Lettuce
Isuzu Elf Van	Isuzu Begin Funk Box
Suzuki Cappuccino	Mazda Bongo Friendee

North America has the greatest diversity of freshwater mussels in the world—297 species.

FABULOUS FLOPS

*Some consumer products are popular the moment they hit
the market, while others never get off the ground.
Their only legacy is a few bathroom laughs.*

Cheese-Filtered Cigarettes. In 1963, a Wisconsin businessman looking for new ways to use local cheese had a brainstorm: If smoke can be used to flavor cheese, why can't cheese
be used to flavor smokes? According to the *Wall Street Journal*, University of Wisconsin chemists found that Parmesan and Romano
were the best filter cheeses, using "a combination of one-third charcoal and two-thirds cheese." The cigarette industry didn't bite.

Grubbies Sneakers. You've heard of pre-washed jeans. In 1966,
B.F. Goodrich came up with a similar idea: "pre-tattered" sneakers.
You didn't have to wait months for your sneakers to look beat-up.
With Grubbies, all you added was the foot odor.

Indoor Archery. In the early '60s, bowling was one of America's
hottest sports. Hoping to "do for archery what automatic pin-set-
ters have done for bowling," a number of entrepreneurs opened
"archery lanes," with automatic arrow-returns. They expected to
have thousands around the United States by 1970.

Look of Buttermilk/Touch of Buttermilk Shampoo. A 1970s
"health product." Were you supposed to eat it or wash with it?
Did you want to wash with it? Rubbing dairy products into their
hair didn't exactly conjure up images of cleanliness in the minds
of most consumers. "Touch of Yogurt Shampoo" also flopped.

Plastic Snow. Before snowmaking machines, how did ski resorts
keep people skiing during dry spells? In the mid-'60s, plastics
seemed like the answer. One resort spread tons of styrofoam pellets
on their ski runs; they quickly blew away. Another company
offered mats with nylon bristles, like Astroturf, and New Jersey's
Great Gorge ski area laid them out on its slopes. They worked
well...unless you fell down. "The bristles were needle-sharp and
everybody tore his pants," founder Jack Kurlander told reporters,
"There was blood, blood, blood. Boy were we embarrassed!"

When you correct for the weight difference, men are proportionately stronger than horses.

SPACED-OUT SPORTS

There's a fine line between stupid and surreal. This page has crossed that line, but was then called for a 15-yard encroachment penalty and had to swim back to second base until the goalie scored three free throws.

"We talked five times. I called him twice, and he called me twice."
—**Larry Bowa,
California Angels coach**

"I'll fight Lloyd Honeyghan for nothing if the price is right."
—**Marlon Starling**

"The Yankees, as I told you later, are in a slump."
—**Dizzy Dean**

"Okay, everyone, now inhale... and then dehale."
—**Maury Wills, Los Angeles
Dodgers captain**

"I don't think we learned a lesson. I think it was a learning experience for us."
—**Shaquille O'Neal**

"This is the earliest I've ever been late."
—**Yogi Berra**

"That picture was taken out of context."
—**Jeff Innis, MLB pitcher,
on an unflattering photo**

"I felt like the track came to us, but then it went beyond us."
—**Dale Earnhardt Jr.,
on the California Speedway**

"Good pitching will always stop good hitting, and vice-versa."
—**Casey Stengel**

"Football coaches have a way to get it done with what they give you. You're going to get it done. If you don't get it done, you don't have to worry about getting it done because you're done."
—**Paul Pasqualoni,
college football coach**

"It's a catch-21 situation."
—**Kevin Pietersen, cricket
player, on his withdrawal
from the A-squad**

"Sometimes even Superman gets a chink in his armor."
—**Steve Francis, NBA
player, on being injured**

"I think we're capable of going exactly as far as we go."
—**Chris Ford, NBA coach**

"I hate sports as rabidly as a person who likes sports hates common sense." —H. L. Mencken

"Randy Moss is like a beautiful woman who can't cook, doesn't want to clean, and doesn't want to take care of kids. You really don't want her, but she's so beautiful that you can't let her go. That's how Randy is."

—Deion Sanders,
NFL player

"I didn't know big guys had groins. I'm finding out today that I actually have one."
—Norman Hand, NFL player,
after straining his groin

"My mom was real happy. She was elated at everything, too."

—Steve Karsay, on being
the #1 pick in the
1990 baseball draft

"I've had marriages that have lasted shorter than this."
—John Daly, on a rain delay
at a golf tournament

"It really left a taste in my mouth."

—Vladimir Guerrero,
Anaheim Angels, after
being swept in the playoffs

"I don't want to shoot my mouth in my foot, but those are games we can win."
—Sherman Douglas,
NBA player

"On our team we got a lot of young guys and they always want to poke at you and tickle you and stuff and I really hate that."
—Eddy Curry, NBA player

"My most memorable Christmas memory was having all of my uncles and aunties out of prison for one Christmas, and that includes me. We had a lot of run-ins with the law, and to have us all out at one time was great."
—Caron Butler, NBA player

"We had lost four in a row, so it was very important to win this game. If we lose to Miami, it's like losing three games."

—Hakeem Olajuwon,
NBA player

"I've never seen anything like it. I'm not going to say it was a miracle, because that's crippled people getting up and walking, the blind seeing. But that's the closest thing to it I've ever seen."

—Larry Foote, on a
Pittsburgh Steelers playoff win

"Everybody in the room gets to punch you in the face."
—Tom Rossley, NFL coach,
on what happens if a
player's cell phone rings
during a team meeting

The traditional gift for a 44th wedding anniversary is…groceries.

SEQUOIA AND THE CHEROKEE ALPHABET

The story of a man who single-handedly brought the written word to his entire culture.

THE HEIGHT OF HUMAN ACHIEVEMENT

Most people accept written language as a given, but archaeologists believe writing was invented independently by only a few ancient cultures, and that almost every subsequent writing system was derived from these originals. That writing developed at all is a testament to human ingenuity.

So the fact that one man invented a completely original writing system in the early 19th century is pretty remarkable. What makes it even more remarkable is that he did it without ever having read or written a single word in any preexisting alphabet. The only language he had ever spoken was Cherokee. His name was Sequoia.

TAKING UP THE PEN

Few details of his life are known, but Sequoia is believed to have been born sometime between 1750 and 1775, a time when settlers from the growing region around Georgia, South Carolina, and Tennessee were beginning to threaten Cherokee independence. He was a part of the last generation of Cherokees to live freely in their ancestral homeland, the same generation that was eventually forced west over the infamous Trail of Tears. Recognizing that the European culture had an advantage in being able to communicate through writing, Sequoia became determined to level the playing field by devising a similar system for his own language.

Beginning in 1809, he created an 85-character system of syllables, which differed from the English alphabet in that the characters depicted full syllables instead of individual sounds. It took him 12 years. When he was finished, he had created a writing system still marveled at today for the ease with which it can be learned.

Charles Lindbergh once worked with Dr. Alexis Carrel on the design for an artificial heart.

Previously illiterate speakers of Cherokee were able to master it within a matter of weeks. And they could teach it to others just as quickly.

POWER OF THE PRESS

Sequoia introduced his syllabary in 1821. Within just five years, the Cherokees were operating what the Boston *Missionary Herald* described as:

> the first printing press ever owned and employed by any nation of the Aborigines of this Continent; the first effort at writing and printing in characters of their own; the first newspaper and the first book printed among themselves; the first editor, and the first well-organized system for securing a general diffusion of knowledge among the people.

But while some white settlers gloried in the "civilized" advancement of the Cherokee nation, others saw it as a threat —Indians who successfully adopted European ways would be more difficult to displace. In 1835, as the Cherokees were waging a legal battle to retain their homes, the state of Georgia seized the presses of their newspaper, The Cherokee Phoenix.

The Cherokees were forced west into "Indian Territory" (present-day Oklahoma) in 1838. Sequoia is believed to have moved there sometime before the last holdouts were rounded up. In 1844 the tribal government cast a new set of Cherokee type and began publication of a new newspaper, *The Cherokee Advocate*—which ran until 1906.

A LIVING LANGUAGE

The fact that the displaced Cherokees were able to conduct tribal business and publish information in their own language helped ensure the language's survival into the 21st century. Though classified by linguists as "imperiled," today Cherokee is among the healthiest of Native North American languages. It is still spoken by 22,000 people and is undergoing revitalization efforts aimed at increasing its usage.

Through his solitary efforts, made at a time when his entire culture was threatened with destruction, Sequoia helped his people to survive, and gave them a lasting voice.

Did they put skates on their barrels? Niagara Falls froze solid in the winter of 1925.

Here are some of the Cherokee symbols and their corresponding sounds:

Ꭰ	ah	Ꭿ	hi	Ꮍ	mu	Ꮀ	ho
Ꭱ	ay	Ꮪ	du	Ꮡ	su	Ꮉ	ma
Ꭲ	ee	Ꮈ	lv	Ꮥ	de	Ꮔ	nu
Ꭳ	oh	Ꮅ	li	Ꮆ	lo	Ꮛ	quv
Ꭴ	oo	Ꮎ	na	Ꮴ	tse	Ꮶ	tso
Ꭵ	uh	Ꮫ	dv	Ꮹ	wa	Ꮏ	hna
Ꭶ	ga	Ꮝ	s	Ꮾ	wv	Ꮩ	do
Ꭹ	gi	Ꮤ	ta	Ᏻ	yu	Ꮣ	da
Ꭺ	go	Ꮁ	hu	Ᏼ	yv	Ꮦ	te
Ꭼ	gv	Ꮷ	tsu	Ꮃ	la	Ꮗ	que
Ꭸ	ge	Ꮭ	tla	Ꮿ	ya	Ꮱ	tlu
Ꮧ	di	Ꮢ	sv	Ꮑ	ne	Ꮬ	dla

* * *

SOME FAVORITE FOREIGN PHRASES

KUSAT' SEBE LOKTI (Russian)
Translation: "[Don't] bite your elbows."
Meaning: Don't cry over spilled milk; don't get upset over things you can't control.

TRITTBRETTFAHRER (Germany)
Translation: "Running-board rider"
Meaning: Someone who benefits from someone else's hard work.

KINGO NO FUNI (Japan)
Translation: "Goldfish crap"
Meaning: A sycophant or hanger-on. (Sometimes when a goldfish does its business, the business remains attached to its rear end for a while before falling off.)

Nerd...or prodigy? Bill Gates started programming at the age of 13.

MY END IS NEAR

Uncle John predicts that his death will come...on the last day of his life. As creepy as it sounds, some people have actually been able to predict their deaths much more accurately than that. Take these folks...

ARNOLD SCHOENBERG

Claim to Fame: Austrian composer...and a man obsessed with the number 13

Prediction: Schoenberg was born on September 13, 1874 and believed he would probably die on the 13th as well. Which month and year? Probably, he decided, on a Friday the 13th, and most likely in 1951, when he was 76 (7 + 6 = 13).

What Happened: That year, July 13 fell on a Friday, and Schoenberg stayed in bed all day, awaiting death. Late that night, his wife went to his room to check on him and scold him for wasting the day so foolishly. When she opened the door, Schoenberg looked up at her, uttered the single word "harmony," and dropped dead. Time of death: 11:47 p.m. ...13 minutes before midnight.

FRANK BARANOWSKI

Claim to Fame: Host of *Mysteries Around Us,* a radio show that dealt with issues of the paranormal

Prediction: Early in January 2002, Baranowski announced to his listeners that he expected to die on January 19.

What Happened: As advertised, Baranowski became an eerily suitable topic for his own show by dying on January 19—exactly as he said he would. Cause of death: congestive heart failure. "It's like he just produced his last show," a co-worker told reporters.

DAVID FABRICIUS

Claim to Fame: German astronomer and Protestant minister

Prediction: For some reason, Fabricius became fixated on the idea that he would die on May 7, 1617. Rather than tempt fate, when the day came, Fabricius decided to play it safe and stay home.

What Happened: About two hours before midnight, he decided

Tablecloths originally served as big napkins: people wiped their hands and faces on them.

that the danger had passed. He stepped outside to get some air...and was promptly murdered by a man from his own church.

FELIPE GARZA, JR.

Claim to Fame: A 15-year-old high school student living in Patterson, California, in 1985

Prediction: Felipe had a crush on a classmate named Donna Ashlock, who had a degenerative heart disease and was only weeks away from death when Felipe's mother saw a newspaper article about her condition and read it to Felipe. "I remember his voice in the next room," Mrs. Garza remembered. "He said, 'I'm going to die, and I'm going to give my heart to Donna.'"

What Happened: Although Felipe seemed to be in perfect health, he died a few days later when a blood vessel in his brain suddenly burst. His family donated his heart to Donna the following day.

Final Chapter: Unfortunately, the ending was not a happy one. Donna's body rejected Felipe's heart a few years later, and she died in March 1989 before another suitable donor could be found. She and Felipe are buried in the same cemetery.

THE REVEREND FREDDIE ISAACS

Claim to Fame: Founder of the Reformed Apostolic Church in Cradock, South Africa

Prediction: In January 2002, Reverend Freddie told his followers that he would soon be "going home." He had received a message from the Lord to join Him in Heaven, he said, and God had set the date for Saturday, February 2. He had his grave dug in advance and even booked the town hall for the funeral, busing in hundreds of "mourners" from all over South Africa. He also went on a shopping spree of biblical proportions, sure that the Creator would take care of the bills after he was gone. "We will miss his earthly body," one church member told reporters, "but we know that he will be sitting at the right hand of the Father."

What Happened: February 2 came and went...and Freddie didn't die. A spokesperson explained to his enraged and humiliated followers that there had been a misunderstanding, saying, "His actual announcement was, 'I am going home.' That is why it is important for us to sit down and clarify certain words and terms, such as the difference between death and going home."

STRANGE LAWSUITS

These days, it seems that people will sue each other over practically anything. Here are some real-life examples of unusual legal battles.

THE PLAINTIFF: The Swedish government

THE DEFENDANT: Elisabeth Hallin, mother of a five-year-old boy named Brfxxccxxmnpccclllmmnprxvclmnckssqlbb11116 (which she pronounces "Albin")

THE LAWSUIT: For five years, the Hallins, who say they believe in the surrealist doctrine of "pataphysics," refused to give their son a name. Then Swedish tax officials informed them it was a legal requirement. They chose Brfxxccxxmnpccclllmmnprxvclmn-ckssqlbb11116—which was immediately rejected by the authorities. The couple insisted that the "typographically expressionistic" name was merely "an artistic creation," consistent with their pataphysical beliefs.

THE VERDICT: The government disagreed. The Hallins were fined 5000 kronor (about $735) and ordered to come up with a different name.

THE PLAINTIFF: Sharon Silver

THE DEFENDANT: Gerald Pfeffer, her ex-husband

THE LAWSUIT: After the couple divorced in 1985, Silver moved out of state. Pfeffer stayed in their St. Paul, Minnesota, home. In 1988 the reunion committee of Silver's high school class sent an "update" questionnaire to her old address. Pfeffer filled it out and returned it. A sample of his answers:

Current occupation: "Retired on third husband's divorce settlement."

Current interests / hobbies: "Night clubbing and partying. Looking for new and wealthier husbands."

Recent outrageous / unusual / interesting experience: "Going to W. Virginia on the job and having an affair with two different guys while my third husband was in Minnesota working two jobs."

The committee printed these (and other) answers in its newsletter. Silver sued for libel; her ex-husband argued that it was all true.

THE VERDICT: After three years of litigation, the case was settled out of court for $75,000—$50,000 from Gerald, $25,000 from the Harding High School Class of 1958. "Well, I thought they were pretty good answers at the time," Pfeffer commented afterward.

THE PLAINTIFF: John Cage Trust
THE DEFENDANT: Mike Batt, a British composer
THE LAWSUIT: In 1952 composer John Cage wrote a piece he called "4'33"." It was four minutes and 33 seconds of silence. In 2002 Batt included a track called "A One Minute Silence" on an album by his rock band The Planets, crediting it to "Batt/Cage." That's when Cage's estate came in—they accused Batt of copyright infringement.

Batt's response: "Has the world gone mad? I'm prepared to do time rather than pay out." Besides, he said, his piece was much better than Cage's because "I have been able to say in one minute what Cage could only say in four minutes and 33 seconds."
THE VERDICT: The suit ended with a six-figure out-of-court settlement. "We feel that honour has been settled," said Nicholas Riddle, Cage's publisher, "because the concept of a silent piece is a very valuable artistic concept."

THE PLAINTIFF: Lorene Bynum
THE DEFENDANTS: St. Mary's Hospital in Little Rock, Arkansas
THE LAWSUIT: In 1992 Bynum visited her husband, a patient at the hospital. She wanted to use the bathroom, but the toilet seat was dirty—and there wasn't enough toilet paper to spread out on it. So she took off her shoes and tried to go to the bathroom standing on the toilet seat. Unfortunately the seat was loose. Bynum fell, spraining her lower back. She sued the hospital for negligence.
THE VERDICT: A jury awarded Bynum $13,000. But the Arkansas Supreme Court overturned it, explaining, "The injuries resulted from her act of standing on the commode seat, which was neither designed nor intended to be used in that way."

WILD WEST TRIVIA

*Howdy, buckaroo. Saddle up and ride off into the sunset
with these honest-to-goodness Old West facts.*

- Billy the Kid's first crime? Stealing clothes from a Chinese laundry.

- In the Old West, more cowboys died crossing swollen rivers than during gunfights.

- Butch Cassidy was raised in a Mormon family.

- *Buckaroo* is the anglicized form of *vaquero*, the Spanish word for cowboy.

- Wild Bill Hickok had a brother. His nickname: Tame Bill.

- Two black aces and eights are called the "dead man's hand." It's what Wild Bill Hickok was holding when he was shot dead in the Number Ten Saloon in Deadwood, Dakota Territory.

- Jesse James issued his own press releases.

- The gunfight at the O.K. Corral lasted 30 seconds and left three bad guys dead and three good guys wounded.

- John Henry "Doc" Holliday was a doctor of dentistry.

- Billy the Kid was buried in a shirt five sizes too big.

- Legendary outlaw Johnny Ringo didn't die with his boots on—his killer made him take them off before shooting him.

- 1860 ad for Pony Express riders:

  Wanted: Young, skinny, wiry fellows not over 18. Must be expert riders willing to risk death daily. Orphans preferred.

- There were no ponies used in the Pony Express.

- Jesse James's father was a Baptist minister.

- The notorious Black Bart (Charles E. Bolton) robbed 27 Wells Fargo stagecoaches in his day; on his release from San Quentin prison, he disappeared and was never heard from again.

TOM SWIFTIES

This classic style of pun was originally invented in the 1920s. They're atrocious and corny, so of course we had to include them.

"Welcome to Grant's Tomb," Tom said cryptically.

"Smoking is not permitted in here," Tom fumed.

"I prefer to press my own clothes," Tom said ironically.

"It's the maid's night off," Tom said helplessly.

"You're burning the candle at both ends," Tom said wickedly.

"I hope I can still play the guitar," Tom fretted.

"They pulled the wool over my eyes," Tom said sheepishly.

"Someone removed the twos from this deck," Tom deduced.

"I haven't caught a fish all day!" Tom said, without debate.

"I memorized the whole thing," Tom wrote.

"A thousand thanks, Monsieur," said Tom mercifully.

"I'd love some Chinese soup," said Tom wantonly.

"I forgot what to buy," Tom said listlessly.

"I'll have to send that telegram again," Tom said remorsefully.

"The criminals were escorted downstairs," said Tom condescendingly.

"I got punched in the stomach three times," said Tom triumphantly.

"I was removed from office," said Tom disappointedly.

"Oh no! I dropped my toothpaste," said Tom, crestfallen.

"That's no purebred," Tom muttered.

"Measure twice before you cut," Tom remarked.

"Thanks for shredding the cheese," Tom said gratefully.

"That's the last time I'll pet a lion," Tom said offhandedly.

"...and you lose a few," concluded Tom winsomely.

THE LEADED GAS CONSPIRACY

It happens all the time. A product comes out and is found to be harmful, but they keep making it anyway. Here's the story of one of the most harmful products of all.

KNOCK KNOCK

In the early days of the automobile industry, gasoline motors were highly prone to engine knock, caused by low-octane fuel igniting too early in the engine's cylinders. It sounded like a sharp tapping or rattling, and that wasn't far off—the motor was rattling itself apart. At the same time, horsepower was lost because the fuel wasn't being burned efficiently, all of which made for a lot of very noisy and very sluggish automobiles. With thousands of new cars entering the road each year, something had to be done.

Luckily, there was an easy solution: grain alcohol. Internal combustion engines ran great on it, but it was too expensive to be the standard motor fuel by itself. Testing conducted for General Motors by Charles Kettering's Dayton Engineering Laboratories Company (DELCO) showed that alcohol raised the octane of gasoline—allowing for higher engine compression and eliminating knock. By 1921 a blend of 30 percent alcohol to 70 percent gasoline was the fuel of choice among most automotive engineers.

But later that year an engineer named Thomas Midgley, the DELCO engineer assigned to solve the problem, found a cheaper way to eliminate engine knock. While working under contract for General Motors, he added a small amount of tetraethyl lead to gasoline and discovered that it also did the trick. Even better, lead was much less expensive than grain alcohol. But Midgley's cost-cutting solution would come at a very high price.

HAZARDOUS MATERIAL

Lead is a neurotoxin that collects in the blood and bones of humans and damages the central nervous system. Overexposure can cause convulsions, blindness, hallucinations, and cancer—as well as coma and death. Its dangers have been known since at

---

Natural gas has no odor. The bad smell is added to alert you if there's a leak.

least 100 B.C., when Greek physicians described lead poisoning and noted the danger posed to workers by fumes from lead smelting operations. In Midgley's time, health risks associated with lead-based paint were so well documented that in 1920 the League of Nations proposed banning its use. But despite all the risks associated with lead, and ignoring the proven effectiveness of cleaner-burning alcohol/gasoline blends, in 1923 General Motors, DuPont, and Standard Oil formed the Ethyl Gasoline Company to produce and sell gas with a tetraethyl lead additive.

LET THE BATTLE BEGIN

Almost immediately, workers in leaded gasoline plants started showing signs of lead poisoning. By 1924 at least 15 workers had died from exposure before better ventilation was added to factories. The scientific community called for the banning of lead, labor unions called for safer working conditions, and the New York Board of Health banned sales of leaded gas in 1924. The Ethyl Company found itself at the center of a public health debate—and it was ready to fight.

When the U.S. Public Health Service held hearings on the matter the following year, Midgley testified: "So far as science knows at the present time, tetraethyl lead is the only material available that can bring about these [anti-knock] results."

Midgley was lying: science knew about alcohol blends. Midgley himself owned several patents on alcohol blends, and three years earlier he'd claimed that "alcohol is unquestionably the fuel of the future." Now he was saying lead was perfectly safe—pouring leaded gas over his hands and sniffing its fumes to prove his point. But Midgley left out another fact: he was suffering from lead poisoning and had been forced to take time off to recuperate in 1923.

INCONCLUSIVE

In the end, the Public Health Service recommended that a committee be formed to study the effects of leaded gas. Their report: "Owing to the incompleteness of the data, it is impossible to say definitely whether exposure to lead dust increases in garages where tetraethyl lead is used."

The Ethyl Company declared itself vindicated, and leaded gas was back on sale in 1926.

IT'S A CONSPIRACY!

If Midgley and Ethyl knew that lead was so harmful compared to the alternatives, why did they try to cover it up? Money. Because adding lead to gasoline was cheaper than adding alcohol, as long as Ethyl had control over the lead additive business, Ethyl controlled the entire gas industry...and would fight tooth and nail to keep it that way.

✔ Car dealers warned their customers about lead's dangers until 1927—when GM ordered their dealers to promote it.

✔ The following year the Lead Industries Association was formed to counter the negative publicity. The Ethyl Company—along with its parent companies, GM, DuPont, and Standard Oil—hired scientists willing to claim that lead couldn't be conclusively tied to illness.

✔ The Ethyl Company refused to sell to distributors who also carried alcohol blends.

✔ Because it was a national company, Ethyl was able to undercut the price of any independent filling station that tried to buck the system. During the Great Depression, people sought out the cheapest gas they could find—Ethyl made sure it was theirs.

Henry Ford called alcohol the "fuel of the future" (as had Midgley years before) and continued to make carburetors that would run on either gas or gas/alcohol blends until 1929. But by 1936 it no longer mattered: leaded gasoline accounted for 90 percent of the fuel sold in the United States, most of that produced by Ethyl.

CLEANING UP

In the 1950s, a geochemist from the California Institute of Technology named Clair Patterson (who was not on the Ethyl Company's payroll) hypothesized that atmospheric lead levels had increased drastically since leaded gas was introduced in 1923. His proof came from ice core samples taken from glaciers in Greenland. In areas where more snow falls than melts every year, ice builds up in layers that can be counted and studied (much like a tree's growth rings). By counting back through 40 years of annual snowfall and measuring the amount of lead in each layer, Patterson was able to show in a 1965 study that the high levels of atmospheric lead found in industrialized countries were a result of leaded gasoline use. Patterson's findings led to the Clean Air Act of 1970. A provision in the act required automakers to install catalytic converters in all new cars. Catalytic converters, it just so happened, are fouled and rendered useless by lead deposits.

The oil industry still continued to resist. With the infrastructure still in place to make—and profit from—leaded gas, they tried to sell as much of it as they could before it was phased out. For years industry "experts" insisted that precatalytic converter motors would be harmed by unleaded gas—which has since proven not to be the case.

Finally, in 1986, leaded gasoline was removed from American gas pumps for good, though it continues to be sold throughout the developing world, and was common in Eastern Europe until the European Union banned it in 2000. Today, alcohol blends are increasingly being used to boost octane and to meet improved emissions standards. Lead is being replaced by the very additive it replaced in the 1920s—alcohol.

THE WORLD'S MOST DANGEROUS MAN?

Leaded gas wasn't Midgley's only contribution to the modern world. After curing engine knock with tetraethyl lead, he turned his attention toward the development of a non-toxic, non-flammable refrigerant gas for use in refrigerator and air conditioner compressors. In 1928 he came up with *chlorofluorocarbons*, or CFCs—the chemical whose use is credited with creating the hole in the ozone layer. These two technological advances have led some to note that Thomas Midgley may have had a bigger impact on the environment than any other single organism in the history of the Earth.

What goes around... Midgley contracted polio in middle age and suffered partial paralysis. He died in 1944 when he was accidentally strangled by a contraption he had built to help himself in and out of bed.

*   *   *

"Men and nations behave wisely once they have exhausted all other alternatives."
                                                    —Abba Eban

---

Oberammergaueralpenkräuterdelikatessenfrühstückskäse is a type of cheese.

THE BIRTH OF THE DISHWASHER

We mentioned Josephine Cochrane briefly in our fourth Bathroom Reader, but we've wanted to tell the whole story for years. Thanks to her, most of us don't have to suffer through "dishpan hands."

DISH-RESPECT

What really is the mother of invention? When it comes to the invention of the dishwasher, necessity had nothing to do with it. It was chipped china.

Josephine Cochrane was a wealthy socialite from Shelbyville, Illinois. She gave a lot of dinner parties and was very proud of her china, which had been in the family since the 17th century. But her servants weren't particularly careful with the priceless dishes as they washed them after each party. Pieces were chipped; pieces were cracked; pieces were broken. Cochrane felt that the only way to protect her treasures was to wash them herself…but she hated the job.

Why should a rich 44-year-old woman be doing this menial job? Why wasn't there a machine that would wash the dishes for her? Well, there was—sort of. The first dishwasher was patented in 1850 by Joel Houghton. It was a wooden machine that splashed water on dishes when a hand-turned wheel was rotated. It didn't work very well, so Cochrane decided to invent a better one.

TO THE DRAWING BOARD

First, she set up a workshop in her woodshed. She measured her dishes, and designed wire racks to hold them. She placed the racks inside a wheel, then laid the wheel inside a tub. The wheel turned while hot soapy water squirted up from the bottom of the tub, falling down on the dishes. Then clean hot water squirted up to rinse them. And finally, the dishes air-dried. It worked.

But while she was busy working on the dishwasher, her ailing husband died. Mrs. Cochrane was left with little money and a lot of debt. Now she needed to follow through on this invention not for convenience, but out of necessity. She needed to earn a living.

Cochrane patented her design in 1886. A Chicago machine

In 1950, only 7% of American women dyed their hair. Today, 75% do.

firm manufactured them for her while she managed the company and marketed the product.

Although Cochrane's wealthy friends immediately ordered the "Cochrane Dishwasher" for their own kitchens, the home model did not sell well. Few homes had electricity in those days. Water heaters were rare. Most available water was hard and did not create suds well. And the price tag of $150 was huge—equivalent to about $4,500 today. Furthermore, many housewives felt that there was nothing wrong with washing dishes by hand—it was a relaxing way to end the day.

Cochrane tried changing her sales pitch to point out that the water in her dishwashing machines was hotter than human hands could stand, resulting in germ-free dishes. But it didn't matter: Her strongest potential market was not private homes, it was industry.

SUCCESS!

Cochrane got her big break when she exhibited her dishwasher at the World's Columbian Expo of 1893 in Chicago. Against heavy competition from around the world, her dishwasher received first prize for "best mechanical construction for durability and adaptation to a particular line of work." And she sold dishwashers to many of the restaurants and other establishments catering to the large crowds at the Expo. Hotels, restaurants, boardinghouses, and hospitals immediately saw the advantage of being able to wash, scald, rinse, and dry dozens of dishes of all shapes and sizes in minutes. One of the concessionaires sent her this glowing tribute: "Your machine washed without delay soiled dishes left by eight relays of a thousand soldiers each, completing each lot within 30 minutes."

Cochrane continued to improve her product, designing models with revolving washing systems, a centrifugal pump, and a hose for draining into a sink. She ignored the clergy (who claimed the dishwasher was immoral because it denied women the labor to which God had called them) and the servants (who claimed it would put them out of business). The company kept growing, pushed by Josephine Cochrane's energy and ambition until her death at age 74 in 1913. By the 1950s, the world finally caught up with Cochrane. Dishwashers became commonplace in ordinary homes... using the same design principles she had invented 70 years before.

Kiwis are the only birds that hunt by smell.

THE MAD BOMBER, PT. I

*From our Dustbin of History files, the story of a city,
a criminal psychiatrist, and a psycho with a grudge.*

SPECIAL DELIVERY

On November 16, 1940, an unexploded bomb was found on a window ledge of the Consolidated Edison Building in Manhattan. It was wrapped in a very neatly hand-written note that read,

CON EDISON CROOKS—THIS IS FOR YOU.

The police were baffled: surely whoever delivered the bomb would know that the note would be destroyed if the bomb detonated. Was the bomb not meant to go off? Was the person stupid…or was he just sending a message?

No discernable fingerprints were found on the device and a brief search of company records brought no leads, so the police treated the case as an isolated incident by a crackpot, possibly someone who had a grievance with "Con Ed"—the huge company that provided New York City with all of its gas and electric power.

WAKE-UP CALL

Nearly a year later, another unexploded bomb was found lying in the street a few blocks from the Con Ed building, this one with an alarm clock fusing mechanism that had not been wound. Again the police had no leads and again they filed the case away—there were larger problems at hand: the war in Europe was escalating and U.S. involvement seemed imminent. Sure enough, three months later, the Japanese attacked Pearl Harbor, triggering America's entry into World War II.

Shortly thereafter a strange, neatly written letter arrived at police headquarters in Manhattan:

I WILL MAKE NO MORE BOMB UNITS FOR THE DURATION OF THE WAR—MY PATRIOTIC FEELINGS HAVE MADE ME DECIDE THIS—I WILL BRING THE CON EDISON TO JUSTICE—THEY WILL PAY FOR THEIR DASTARDLY DEEDS…F. P.

True to his (or her) words, no more bombs showed up during the war, or for five years after that. But in that time at least 16 threat

---

Huh? Number of U.S. marine wildlife sanctuaries where fishing is illegal: **zero.**

letters, all from "F. P.", were delivered to Con Ed, as well as to movie theaters, the police, and even private individuals. Still, there were no bombs...until March 29, 1950.

CITY UNDER SIEGE

That day, a third unexploded bomb much more advanced than the previous two was found on the lower level of Grand Central Station. "F. P." seemed to be sending the message that he (or she) had been honing his (or her) bomb-building skills over the last decade. Still, so far none of them had exploded. And police wondered: were these all just empty threats? That question was answered a month later when a bomb tore apart a phone booth at the New York Public Library. Over the next two years, four more bombs exploded around New York City. And try as they might to downplay the threat, the police couldn't keep the press from running with the story. "The Mad Bomber" started to dominate headlines.

More bombs were found, and more angry letters—some neatly written, others created from block letters clipped from magazines—promised to continue the terror until Con Edison was "BROUGHT TO JUSTICE."

Heading up the case was Police Inspector Howard E. Finney. He and his detectives had used every conventional police method they knew of, but the Mad Bomber was too smart for them. In December 1956, after a powerful explosion injured six people in Brooklyn's Paramount Theater, Inspector Finney decided to do something unconventional.

PSYCH-OUT

Finney called in Dr. James A. Brussel, a brilliant psychiatrist who had worked with the military and the FBI. Brussel had an uncanny understanding of the criminal mind, and like everyone else in New York, this eloquent, pipe-smoking psychiatrist was curious about what made the Mad Bomber tick. But because none of the letters had been released to the press, Brussel knew very little about the case. That all changed when police handed him the evidence they had gathered since 1941.

The pressure was on: citizens were growing more panicked with each new bomb, and more impatient with the cops' inability to catch the Mad Bomber. After poring through letters, phone call transcripts and police reports, and studying the unexploded bombs, Dr. Brussel presented this profile to Inspector Finney:

> It's a man. Paranoiac. He's middle-aged, forty to fifty years old, introvert. Well proportioned in build. He's single. A loner, perhaps living with an older female relative. He is very neat, tidy, and clean-shaven. Good education, but of foreign extraction. Skilled mechanic, neat with tools. Not interested in women. He's a Slav. Religious. Might flare up violently at work when criticized. Possible motive: discharge or reprimand. Feels superior to his critics. Resentment keeps growing. His letters are posted from Westchester, and he wouldn't be stupid enough to post them from where he lives. He probably mails the letter between his home and New York City. One of the biggest concentration of Poles is in Bridgeport, Connecticut, and to get from there to New York you have to pass through Westchester. He has had a bad disease—possibly heart trouble.

GOING PUBLIC

Finney was impressed…but skeptical. His team had drawn some of the same conclusions, but even so, there had to be thousands of middle-aged men who fit that profile. What good would it do?

"I think you ought to publicize the description I've given you," suggested Dr. Brussel. "Publicize the whole Bomber investigation, in fact. Spread it in the newspapers, on radio and television." Finney disagreed. It was standard procedure to keep details of investigations away from the press. But Brussel maintained that if they handled the case correctly, the Mad Bomber would do most of the work for them. He said that, unconsciously, "he wants to be found out." Finney finally agreed. And as he left the office, Brussel added one more thing: "When you catch him, he'll be wearing a double-breasted suit, and it will be buttoned."

So the papers published the profile and the chase went into high gear. As Finney predicted, "a million crackpots" came out of the woodwork, all claiming to be the Mad Bomber, but none of them had the Mad Bomber's skill or his distinctively neat handwriting. A slew of legitimate leads came from concerned citizens about their odd neighbors, yet nothing solid surfaced. Still, Brussel was confident that the real Bomber's arrogance would be his undoing.

*Did Brussel's strategy work? Turn to
Part II on page 441 to find out.*

Neanderthals are believed to have buried their dead.

CURSES!

We've all heard of one curse or another. Usually, we laugh about them. But perhaps sometimes there's a good reason for believing.

THE CURSE OF TOSCA

Curse: Nasty things happen to actors during performances of this opera.

Origin: Unknown, but productions have been plagued with problems at least as far back as the 1920s.

Among Its Victims:

• During a production at the Metropolitan Opera in the 1920s, the knife with which Tosca "murdered" Scarpia at the end of Act II failed to retract. Singer Antonio Scotti was stabbed.

• In 1965 at Covent Gardens, Maria Callas's hair caught fire while she was singing the title role. It had to be put out by a quick-thinking Tito Gobbi, who was playing Scarpia.

• In a production in Rome in 1965, Gionni Raimondi's face was scorched during the firing squad scene.

• In 1993, Elisabeth Knighton Printy jumped off the wrong side of the stage in St. Paul, Minnesota, and plunged more than 30 feet to the ground, breaking both her legs.

Status: Ongoing. Last reported incident was in 1995, when Fabio Armiliatu, starring in a Roman production, was hit in the leg by debris from blanks fired in the execution scene. He was taken off in a stretcher. Two weeks later he returned to the stage; he fell and broke his other leg in two places while standing in the wings at the end of the first act.

THE SPORTS ILLUSTRATED JINX

Curse: If you appear on the cover of *Sports Illustrated* magazine, you're in for a slump or a defeat.

Origin: Unknown. For decades, sports stars have claimed that making SI's cover was the fastest way to a slump.

Among its Victims:

• Studying the records of 58 baseball players going back to 1955 (because there are sufficient records to check in baseball), researchers found that "there was a distinct tendency for batting performance to decline...about 50 points from immediately before appearing on the cover until three weeks after the appearance."

Status: Scientists say that if there is anything to the SI jinx, it's because it spooks players and thus is self-fulfilling. Also: "This extra attention and effort might cause more injuries, fatigue, or other interruptions to the hitter's natural flow, with the result that performance suffers."

THE OSCAR CURSE

Curse: Winning the gold statuette can ruin, rather than help, an actor's career.

Origin: Luise Rainer won back-to-back Oscars for *The Great Ziegfeld* (1936) and *The Good Earth* (1937). Two years and five horrible movies later, she was considered a has-been. Hollywood columnist Louella Parsons wrote that it was "the Oscar curse." Parsons said her Ouija board had warned, "Beware, beware, the Oscar will get you if you don't watch out."

Among its Victims:

• Rita Moreno and George Chakiris (Best Supporting Actor and Actress, 1961, *West Side Story*). Disappeared from films after winning.

• Richard Dreyfuss (Best Actor, 1978, *The Goodbye Girl*). His weight ballooned to 180 pounds, he stopped bathing, and he started bingeing on booze and drugs. (He recovered.)

• Michael Cimino (Best Director, 1978, *The Deer Hunter*). Followed Oscar with three losers: *Heaven's Gate*, *Year of the Dragon*, and *The Sicilian*.

• Linda Hunt (Best Supporting Actress, 1983, *The Year of Living Dangerously*). Last seen in the short-lived sci-fi TV series, *Space Rangers*.

Status: Considered credible in Hollywood. High expectations that can't always be fulfilled accompany an Oscar. It's also attributed to salary demands, type-casting, greedy agents or studio bosses, and stars who believe their own press and become hard to work with.

Q&A: ASK THE EXPERTS

*More questions and answers from
the world's top trivia experts.*

SEEING THINGS

Q: *What are those little squiggles you see floating on your eyes
when you look at the sky?*

A: "They're called 'floaters.' To some people they look like spots;
to others, like tiny threads. They're not on your eyes, though;
they're *in* your eyes. That's why blinking doesn't make them go
away. Floaters are all that's left of the hyaloid artery. The hyaloid
artery carried blood to your eye and helped it grow…when you
were still inside your mother's womb.

"When your eyes were finished growing, the hyaloid artery
withered and broke into pieces. But since these pieces were
sealed up inside your eye, they had no place to go. You'll see
them floating around the rest of your life." (From *Know It All!*,
by Ed Zotti)

THE COLD, WET TRUTH

Q: *Why does your nose run in cold weather?*

A: "It is not necessarily because you have a cold. If very cold air is
suddenly inhaled, the mucous membranes inside your nostrils first
constrict, then rapidly dilate as a reflex reaction. This permits an
excess of mucous to form, resulting in a runny nose or the 'snif-
fles.'" (From *The Handy Weather Answer Book*, by Walter A.
Lyons, Ph.D.)

EURASIA, EURASIA

Q: *Why are Asia and Europe considered two continents even
though they appear to be one?*

A: "The ancient Greeks thought the Eurasian landmass was divided in two by the line of water running from the Aegean Sea to the
far shore of the Black Sea. By the time they found out otherwise,
Europeans were not about to surrender their continental status."
(From *Why Things Are*, by Joel Achenbach)

Martin Scorsese played Robert De Niro's homicidal passenger in *Taxi Driver* (1976).

A BRIEF HISTORY
OF BUGS BUNNY

Who's your favorite cartoon character? Ear's ours.

IMPRESSIVE STATS
Bugs Bunny is the world's most popular rabbit:
• Since 1939, he has starred in more than 175 films.

• He's been nominated for three Oscars, and won one—in 1958, for "Knighty Knight, Bugs" (with Yosemite Sam).

• Every year from 1945 to 1961, he was voted "top animated character" by movie theater owners (when they still showed cartoons in theaters).

• In 1985 he became only the 2nd cartoon character to be given a star on the Hollywood Walk of Fame (Mickey Mouse was the first).

• For almost 30 years, starting in 1960, he had one of the top-rated shows on Saturday-morning TV.

• In 1976, when researchers polled Americans on their favorite characters, real and imaginary, Bugs came in second...behind Abraham Lincoln.

THE INSPIRATIONS
Bugs was born in the 1930s, but cartoon historians say his ancestry goes further back. A few direct antecedents:

• **Zomo.** You may not have heard of this African folk-rabbit, but he's world-famous. Joe Adamson writes in *Bugs Bunny: Fifty Years and Only One Grey Hare:*

> Like jazz and rock 'n' roll, Bugs has at least some of his roots in black culture. Zomo is the trickster rabbit from Central and Eastern Africa who gained audience sympathy by being smaller than his oppressors and turning the tables on them through cleverness—thousands of years before Eastman invented film. A con artist, a masquerader, ruthless and suave, in control of the situation. Specialized in impersonating women.

• **Charlie Chaplin.** "It was Chaplin who established that 'gestures

and actions expressing attitude' give a screen character life,"
Adamson writes. The Looney Tunes directors, all fans of Chaplin,
even stole many of his gags. For example:

> The abrupt and shocking kiss Charlie plants [on] someone who's
> getting too close for comfort in *The Floorwalker* went on to become
> one of Bugs' favorite ways to upset his adversaries. [And] the walk-
> ing broomstick in *Bewitched Bunny* does Chaplin's trademark turn,
> with one foot in the air, at every corner.

There are literally dozens of other Chaplin rip-offs. Bugs also lifted
bits from silent comedians Harold Lloyd and Buster Keaton.

• **Groucho Marx.** "Bugs uses his carrot as a prop, just as Groucho
used his cigar," points out Stefan Kanfer in *Serious Business*.
"Eventually Bugs even stole Marx's response to an insult: 'Of
course you know, this means war!' "

TIMELINE

1937: Warner Bros. animation director Tex Avery makes "Porky's
Duck Hunt." Porky Pig hunted a screwball duck named Daffy—
"who didn't get scared and run away when somebody pointed a
gun at him, but leapt and hopped all over the place like a maniac." "When it hit the theaters," recalls another director, "it was
like an explosion."

1938: Warner Bros. director Ben "Bugs" Hardaway remakes the
cartoon with a rabbit instead of a duck, as "Porky's Hare Hunt."
Says one of Bugs's creators: "That rabbit was just Daffy Duck in a
rabbit suit."

1939: Bugs Hardaway decides to remake "Porky's Hare Hunt"
with a new rabbit (as "Hare-um Scare-um"). Cartoonist Charlie
Thorson comes up with a gray and white rabbit with large buck
teeth. He labels his sketches "Bugs' Bunny."

1940: Director Tex Avery becomes the real father of Bugs Bunny
with "A Wild Hare." Bugs is changed from a Daffyesque lunatic to
a streetsmart wiseass. "We decided he was going to be a smart-
aleck rabbit, but casual about it," Avery recalled. "His opening
line was 'What's up, Doc?'...It floored 'em!...Here's a guy with a
gun in his face!...They expected the rabbit to scream, or anything
but make a casual remark....It got such a laugh that we said, 'Let's
use that every chance we get.' It became a series of 'What's Up,

Docs?' That set his entire character. He was always in command, in the face of all types of dangers."

• Bugs also gets his voice in "A Wild Hare." Mel Blanc, who did most Looney Tunes voices, had been having a hard time finding one for the rabbit...until Bugs Hardaway showed him the latest sketch for "A Wild Hare." Blanc wrote:

> He'd obviously had some work done. His posture had improved, he'd shed some weight, and his protruding front teeth weren't as pronounced. The most significant change, however, was in his facial expression. No longer just goofy, he was a sly looking rascal.

"A tough little stinker, ain't he?" Hardaway commented...and the light went on in Blanc's brain.

> A tough little stinker....In my mind I heard a Brooklyn accent.... To anyone living west of the Hudson River at that time, Brooklynites were associated with con artists and crooks....Consequently, the new, improved Bugs Bunny wouldn't say jerk, he'd say joik.

• The rabbit is now so popular that he needs a name. According to some sources, he is about to be dubbed "Happy Rabbit." Tex Avery wants " Jack E. Rabbit." But when Thorson's year-old drawing labeled "Bugs' Bunny" is turned up, producer Leon Schlessinger chooses that. Avery hates it. "That's sissy," he complains. "Mine's a *rabbit*. A tall, lanky, mean rabbit. He isn't a fuzzy little bunny!" But the name sticks.

1941: Bugs Bunny becomes competitive. Four extremely talented directors—Avery, Friz Freleng, Bob Clampett, and Chuck Jones—try to top each other with new gags and aspects of Bugs's personality. It's the key to the character's success—he's constantly growing. "As each director added new levels to this character," Adamson explains, "it was picked up by the others and became a part of the mix."

1943: Animator Robert McKimson (later a director himself), working for Bob Clampett, refines Bugs's features into what they are today. "We made him cuter, brought his head and cheeks out a little more and gave him just a little nose," McKimson says. He looks more "elfin" and less "ratlike" now.

1945: During World War II, Bugs has become a "sort of national mascot." Critic Richard Schickel writes: "In the war years, when he flourished most gloriously, Bugs Bunny embodied the cocky humor of a nation that had survived its economic crisis [in surprisingly good shape], and was facing a terrible war with grace, gallantry, humor and solidarity that was equally surprising." By the end of the war, Bugs isn't just a cartoon character, but an American icon.

BUGS FACTS

Saved by a Hare. The inspiration for the original rabbit came from Walt Disney. In 1935 Disney put out a cartoon featuring a character called Max Hare. Hardaway's rabbit looks suspiciously like Max.

Trademarks. Where did Bugs's carrot-crunching and "What's up, Doc?" come from? No one's sure, but experts have suggested they might have been inspired by a couple of popular films:

• In Frank Capra's 1934 Oscar-winning comedy, *It Happened One Night*, Clark Gable nervously munches on carrots.

• In the classic 1939 screwball comedy *My Man Godfrey*, William Powell uses the line "What's up, Duke?" repeatedly.

On the other hand, Tex Avery had a habit of calling everyone Doc—so he may have inspired the phrase. (Mel Blanc—Bugs's voice—also claims in his autobiography that he ad-libbed the line, but he seems to take credit for everything—so we don't believe him.)

Tough Act. Blanc says that recording the "What's up, Doc?" line turned out to be the most physically challenging part of doing the voice:

> "What's up, Doc?" was incomplete without the sound of the rabbit nibbling on the carrot, which presented problems. First of all, I don't especially like carrots, at least not raw. [Ed note: In another BR, we erroneously reported that he was *allergic* to carrots. Oops.] And second, I found it impossible to chew, swallow, and be ready to say my next line. We tried substituting other vegetables, including apples and celery, but with unsatisfactory results. The solution was to stop recording so that I could spit out the carrot into the wastebasket and then proceed with the script. In the course of a recording session I usually went through enough carrots to fill several wastebaskets. Bugs Bunny did for carrots what Popeye the Sailor did for spinach. How many…children were coerced into eating their carrots by mothers cooing…"but Bugs Bunny eats *his* carrots." If only they had known.

Eat Your Veggies. Actually, there were pressures to switch from

---

carrots. "The Utah Celery Company of Salt Lake City offered to keep all the studio's staffers well supplied with their product if Bugs would only switch from carrots to celery," Adamson reports. "[And] later, the Broccoli Institute of America strongly urged Bugs Bunny to sample their product once in a while....Mel Blanc would have been happy to switch...but carrots were Bugs's trademark."

Surprise Hit. To his creators, Bugs Bunny was just another character that would probably run in a few cartoons and fade unnoticed into obscurity. "We didn't feel that we had anything," Avery recounted years later, "until we got it on the screen and it got a few laughs. After we ran it and previewed it and so forth, Warner liked it, the exhibitors liked it, and so of course [the producer] ran down and said, 'Boy, give us as many of those as you can!' Which we did."

Bugs Bunny became so popular with the public that he got laughs even when he didn't deserve them. "He could do no wrong," remembers dialogue writer Michael Maltese. "We had quite a few lousy Bugs Bunnies. We'd say, 'Well we haven't got time. Let's do it.' And we'd do it, and the audience would laugh. They loved that rabbit."

*　　*　　*

REAL CANADIAN PLACE NAMES

Goobies	Mechanic	Wawa
Blow Me Down	Asbestos	Elbow
Cupids	Saint-Louis-du-	Eyebrow
Jerry's Nose	Ha! Ha!	Uranium City
Lawn	Cheapside	Head-Smashed-In
Mosquito	Ethel	Buffalo Jump
Nameless Cove	Bigger	Vulcan
Witless Bay	Porcupine	Clo-oose
Lower Economy	Swastika	Hydraulic
Malignant Cove	Swords	Spuzzum
Meat Cove	Tiny	Stoner
Burnt Church	Finger	Mayo

Odds of anyone getting hit by a meteor this year: 1 in 5 billion.

DISGUSTING FACTS

We know—with a title like this one, you can't help yourself…
you have to read them. They really are disgusting, but, well,
now you have something to share as dinner conversation.

• The average human foot has about 20,000 sweat glands and can produce as much as half a cup of sweat each day.

• Cockroaches can flatten themselves almost to the thinness of a piece of paper in order to slide into tiny cracks, can be frozen for weeks and then thawed with no ill effect, and can also withstand 126 g's of pressure with no problem (people get squished at 18 g's).

• Most of the dust in your house is made up of dead human skin cells—every day, millions of them float off your body and settle on furniture and floors.

• The average municipal water treatment plant processes enough human waste every day to fill 72 Olympic-sized swimming pools.

• According to a recent survey, over 10% of Americans have picked someone else's nose.

• Tears are made up of almost the exact same ingredients as urine.

• Most people generally fart between 10 and 20 times a day, expelling enough gas to inflate a small balloon.

• Your mouth slows production of bacteria-fighting saliva when you sleep, which allows the 10 billion bacteria in your mouth to reproduce all night; "morning breath" is actually bacterial B.O.

• Leeches have mouths with three sets of jaws and between 60 to 100 teeth.

• A tapeworm can grow to a length of 30 feet inside human intestines.

• The crusty goop you find in your eyes when you wake up is the exact same mucus you find in your nose—boogers.

• Spiders don't eat their prey; they paralyze the victim with venom, vomit a wad of acidic liquid onto them, and then drink the dissolved body.

• The average person will produce 25,000 quarts of saliva in a lifetime—enough to fill up two swimming pools.

Three out of every four creatures living on Earth are insects.

SON OF THE RETURN OF THE SEQUEL, EPISODE 2

*People complain nowadays that Hollywood just recycles
old ideas into movie series. Here's a little secret:
filmmakers have been doing it for years.*

CHARLIE CHAN: 44 FILMS. The cunning Chinese detective Charlie Chan began as the literary creation of author Earl Derr Biggers. But the character's lasting fame came from a series of movies that began with 1931's *Charlie Chan Carries On* (a title that sounds like it belongs on a sequel—possibly because it was adapted from the fifth Charlie Chan book). Chan was played by actor Warner Oland, who was Swedish, for 16 films (through 1937's *Charlie Chan at Monte Carlo*). After Oland's death in 1938, Sidney Toler (an actor from Missouri, definitely not Asian) took the role through another 11 films. When he died in 1947, Roland Winters (also not Asian) took over through the final film in the series, 1949's *The Sky Dragon*.

Interestingly, the first time a Chinese actor actually played Charlie Chan was in the 1970s when Keye Luke (who had appeared in several Charlie Chan movies as #1 Son, Lee Chan) voiced the character for a Saturday morning cartoon show.

BLONDIE: 28 FILMS. This series was based on Chic Young's popular comic strip of the same name—the one that's still running in newspapers today (more than 30 years after Young died). The series began in 1938 with *Blondie* and would last through 1950's *Beware of Blondie*. During those dozen years and 28 films, most of the cast remained the same, with Penny Singleton as Blondie and Arthur Lake as Dagwood. Even Daisy was played by the same dog for the entire run. After the series ended, Lake would reprise his role as Dagwood in a 1957 television series which, surprisingly, lasted only one season.

JAMES BOND: 22 FILMS. The Bond series of spy films has the distinction of being the longest-running film series in Hollywood—

Will Ferrell's father was a longtime keyboard player for the Righteous Brothers.

going strong for well over 40 years, dating back to 1962's *Dr. No*—and having the highest number of films in a series still in production: *Quantum of Solace*, scheduled for 2008, will be the 22nd. Sean Connery was the first, and for many, the definitive James Bond; few know that Bond author Ian Fleming originally chose Roger Moore for the role, but he couldn't sign on because he was busy with the TV series *The Saint*. After George Lazenby took a crack at the role, Moore inherited the part, followed by Timothy Dalton, Pierce Brosnan, and Daniel Craig.

THE ANDY HARDY SERIES: 15 FILMS. Diminutive actor Mickey Rooney was already a popular child film star (having starred in a long-running comedy-short series as Mickey McGuire) when, at age 17, he was cast as the spunky Andy Hardy in 1937's *A Family Affair*. Rooney seemed made for the role, and he became so popular he was awarded a special juvenile Oscar in 1938. Thirteen other Andy Hardy films would follow, through 1947—Judy Garland appeared in two, and Esther Williams made her studio debut in another. More than a decade after 1946's *Love Laughs at Andy Hardy*, MGM resurrected the character in *Andy Hardy Comes Home*, with Rooney as a grown-up Hardy, to see if the series could be restarted. It couldn't.

SHERLOCK HOLMES: 14 FILMS. There have been Sherlock Holmes films almost as long as there have been films—his first known appearance on film was in 1900. But the definitive screen Holmes is the one portrayed by British actor Basil Rathbone, who played him in a series of movies from 1939 to 1946. He first appeared as the character in 1939's *The Hound of the Baskervilles*, followed shortly after by *The Adventures of Sherlock Holmes*. Those two films had Holmes in his traditional Victorian setting, but beginning with 1942's *Sherlock Holmes and the Voice of Terror*, Rathbone's Holmes was transported to contemporary times, to battle Nazis and other 20th-century thugs. In all, Rathbone played Holmes 14 times in the film series, ending with 1946's *Dressed to Kill*. He then went on to play the sleuth in more than 200 radio performances, one of which was rumored to have been sampled in Disney's 1986 animated film tribute to Holmes, *The Great Mouse Detective*—whose hero, Basil, was named after the actor.

In Hungary, Hungary is known as *Magyar*.

SECRET INGREDIENTS

A doctor friend of ours pooh-poohs fears about chemicals in our food. "Every-thing is made up of chemicals," he says. He's right, of course, and in that spirit we offer this article, with a warning that if the idea of weird stuff being in your food bothers you, you might not want to read on.

CHICKEN McNUGGETS

Good news: a McDonald's Chicken McNugget does con-tain chicken. But it's not the main ingredient—not even close. According to Michael Pollan, author of *The Omnivore's Dilemma*, a McNugget is made up of 38 ingredients, mostly chem-icals and corn derivatives. In total, a McNugget is 56 percent corn products. But 0.02 percent is *tertiary butylhydroquinone*, a petroleum byproduct used as a preservative. TBHQ is actually butane, also known as lighter fluid.

COOL WHIP

Though it's often used as a substitute for whipped cream, Cool Whip contains no cream and no milk. The only dairy in the prod-uct is a milk protein called *sodium caseinate*. Instead of milk, Cool Whip uses a combination of ingredients, including water, corn syrup, coconut oil, and palm kernel oil, which have a much longer shelf life.

RED BULL

The main ingredient in energy drinks like Red Bull and RockStar that revs you up isn't caffeine. In fact, an 8.5-ounce can has only about as much caffeine as a cup of coffee. The "energy" actually comes from *taurine*, a stimulant much more potent than caffeine. Today taurine is synthesized in laboratories, but it was first discov-ered by German scientists in 1827, as a naturally occurring sub-stance in the bile of oxen.

VELVEETA

As milk hardens into cheese, it leaves behind a liquid byproduct called whey. Many cheese manufacturers just threw the whey in the garbage, until Kraft found a use for it. With an added stabiliz-

---

In a year, an average elevator travels the equivalent of nearly halfway around the equator.

ing agent called *carrageenin*—a derivative of Irish moss—the whey can be processed into a soft, spongy cheesy brick, better known as Velveeta.

TWINKIES
Polysorbate 60 is one of many chemical compounds in a Twinkie. One of the ingredients in polysorbate 60 is *ethylene oxide*, a highly flammable material that's toxic if consumed in extremely high amounts. It was used in grenades during the Vietnam War.

SMOOTHIES
Jamba Juice, one the country's biggest fruit-smoothie chains, offers a non-dairy option for customers who are allergic to milk. Amazingly, the second most prevalent ingredient in the non-dairy blend: nonfat dried milk.

MAGIC SHELL
A chocolate-flavored ice cream topping similar to chocolate syrup or fudge sauce, Magic Shell hardens into a thick candy shell when it's poured over ice cream. (Similar to the chocolate coating on Dairy Queen's chocolate-dipped cones.) How does the chocolate liquid harden? The effect comes from a mixture of soybean oil and paraffin wax, a petroleum product also commonly used in candles and skin cream.

DEODORANT
Deodorant isn't a food, but you do consume it every day. (Don't you?) Secret, advertised as "strong enough for a man, but made for a woman," actually contains the exact same ingredients in the exact same proportions as the popular men's deodorant Sure.

*   *   *

BUT DO THEY SELL OUT EVERY NIGHT?
Only four NBA arenas have not sold their naming rights to a corporation. They are: the Rose Garden in Portland, Madison Square Garden in New York, The Palace of Auburn Hills in Detroit, and the Bradley Center in Milwaukee.

Meatheads? NBA star Kobe Bryant's parents named him after a steak they saw on a menu.

HOAXMEISTER

Think everything you read in the newspaper or see on the news has been checked for accuracy? Think again. Sometimes the media will repeat whatever they're told...and this guy set out to prove it.

MONKEY SEE, MONKEY SAY
Joey Skaggs's career as a hoax artist began in the mid-1960s when he first combined his art training with sociopolitical activism. He wanted to show that instead of being guardians of the truth, the media machine often runs stories without verifying the facts. And in proving his point, he perpetrated some pretty clever hoaxes.

HOAX #1: A Cathouse for Dogs
In 1976 Skaggs ran an ad in New York's *Village Voice* for a dog bordello. For $50 Skaggs promised satisfaction for any sexually deprived Fido. Then he hosted a special "night in the cathouse for dogs" just for the media. A beautiful woman and her Saluki, both clad in tight red sweaters and bows, paraded up and down in front of the panting "clientele" (male dogs belonging to Skaggs's friends). The ASPCA lodged a slew of protests and had Skaggs arrested (and indicted) for cruelty to animals. The event was even featured on an Emmy-nominated WABC News documentary. But the joke was on them—the "dog bordello" never existed. (The charges were dropped.)

HOAX #2: Save the Geoduck!
It's pronounced "gooey-duck" and it's a long-necked clam native to Puget Sound, Washington, with a digging muscle that bears a striking resemblance to the male reproductive organ of a horse. In 1987 Skaggs posed as a doctor (Dr. Long) and staged a protest rally in front of the Japan Society. Why? Because according to "Dr. Long," the geoduck was considered to be an aphrodisiac in Asia, and people were eating the mollusk into extinction. Although neither claim had the slightest basis in fact, Skaggs's "Clamscam" was good enough to sucker WNBC, UPI, the German news magazine *Der Spiegel*, and a number of Japanese papers into reporting the story as fact.

All toads are frogs, but not all frogs are toads.

HOAX #3: Miracle Roach Hormone Cure

Skaggs pretended to be an entomologist from Colombia named Dr. Josef Gregor in 1981. In an interview with WNBC-TV's *Live at Five*, "Dr. Gregor" claimed to have graduated from the University of Bogota, and said his "Miracle Roach Hormone Cure" cured the common cold, acne, and menstrual cramps. An amazed Skaggs remarked later, "Nobody ever checked my credentials." The interviewers didn't realize they were being had until Dr. Gregor played his theme song—*La Cucaracha*.

HOAX #4: Sergeant Bones and the Fat Squad

In 1986 Skaggs appeared on *Good Morning, America* as a former Marine Corps drill sergeant named Joe Bones, who was determined to stamp out obesity in the United States. Flanked by a squad of tough-looking commandos, Sergeant Bones announced that for "$300 a day plus expenses," his "Fat Squad" would infiltrate an overweight client's home and physically stop them from snacking. "You can hire us but you can't fire us," he deadpanned, staring into the camera. "Our commandos take no bribes." Reporters from the *Philadelphia Enquirer*, *Washington Post*, *Miami Herald*, and the *New York Daily News* all believed—and ran with—the story.

HOAX #5: Maqdananda, the Psychic Attorney

On April 1, 1994, Skaggs struck again with a 30-second TV spot in which he dressed like a swami. Seated on a pile of cushions, Maqdananda asked viewers, "Why deal with the legal system without knowing the outcome beforehand?" Along with normal third dimension legal issues—divorce, accidental injury, wills, trusts—Maqdananda claimed he could help renegotiate contracts made in past lives, sue for psychic surgery malpractice, and help rectify psychic injustices. "There is no statute of limitations in the psychic realm," he said. Viewers just had to call the number at the bottom of their screen: 1-808-UCA-DADA. In Hawaii, CNN *Headline News* ran the spot 40 times during the week. When people called the number (and dozens did), they were greeted by the swami's voice on an answering machine, saying, "I knew you'd call." Skaggs later revealed that the swami—and his political statement about the proliferation of New Age gurus and ambulance-chasing attorneys—was all a hoax.

DETERGENT IN THE DESERT

Twenty-Mule Team Borax was America's most popular hand and laundry soap during the early and mid-1900s, and its mule team trademark is a tribute to one of the most difficult journeys ever taken.

EUREKA! IT'S...BORAX?

In 1881 prospector Aaron Winters was living near the California/Nevada border in what is now Death Valley National Park in the hopes of unearthing a vein of silver or gold. Instead, he found another "gold mine"—the hard white crystal balls he scraped away each day while mining at his claim turned out to be borax, a rare crystal used in detergents. Winters quickly capitalized on the find and sold his claim to William T. Coleman, a San Francisco businessman who created a company called the Harmony Borax Works.

Coleman hired workers to dig up the Death Valley borax. They labored in the desert heat (temperatures sometimes reached 130°) and made little money (most were paid just $1.50 a day), extracting more than 2 million tons of borax per year. All that borax then had to be transported to the nearest railroad stop, which was more than 160 miles away in the town of Mojave. Coleman employed mule teams to handle the chore. Between 1883 and 1889 (when a railway was built to access the borax mines), the mules hauled more than 20 million pounds of borax out of Death Valley.

MULE MUSCLE

Technically, these teams, called "twenty-mule teams," were made up of 18 mules and two horses. The mules—sure-footed, fast, and sturdy—supplied the muscle. The horses were the "wheelers," the animals closest to the wagon. Wheelers could weigh as much as 1,800 pounds (the average horse weighs around 1,100 pounds); they had to be heavy and tall to direct and turn the wagons.

The wagons themselves were also enormous. Each one weighed 7,800 pounds empty and was built to haul at least 24,000 pounds of borax through Death Valley's sand and rock-strewn mountain trails. The wagons' front wheels measured five feet high, and the rear wheels seven feet high; their "tires" were made of iron.

Each team pulled three wagons. The first two carried the borax, while the third carried a 500-gallon water tank and enough hay, grain, and provisions to feed the men and animals during the 10-day trip to the railroad stop, where they could again stock up on supplies. When on the trail, the wagons weighed more than 70,000 pounds.

PULLING WITH BELLS ON

The mules and horses were outfitted with thick collars and were strung together by an 80-foot chain fastened to the first wagon. A leather rope called the "jerk line" ran through the collar ring of each animal on the left side of the line. Drivers used this rope to control the team: a hard yank on the line turned the animals to the left; a series of jerks turned them right.

The mules also wore bells on their collars. This wasn't just to announce their arrival at the end of the journey; company officials thought the bells created a rhythm that helped the team walk faster. At full speed, the mules pulled the wagons approximately two miles per hour.

WANNA BE A COWBOY?

Three men worked the team: a driver, skinner, and swamper. They could each make up to $150 a month, which was a hefty sum in the late 19th century.

The driver sat atop the lead wagon; he controlled the jerk line and the brake straps. One of the most famous drivers of the time was Bill Parkinson, nicknamed "Borax Bill." Parkinson was renowned for his skill at negotiating his wagon trains through the tricky terrain, and for keeping his animals in top condition.

The skinner rode one of the wheeler horses. Also called a "teamster," it was his job to keep the wagons moving and the mules under control.

The swamper rode on the last wagon and controlled the brake when the team was going downhill. He was also the cook, black-smith, and handyman on the trip.

THE ROAD TO MOJAVE

The journey to the railroad stop took the teams over some of the West's most treacherous terrain and required 20 days for the round trip. It began in Death Valley at 190 feet below sea level, climbed to an elevation of 2,000 feet in the steep Funeral and Panamint mountains, and then descended into another desert to reach Mojave. There wasn't a single house or building along the route, and during one stretch, the teams had to walk 60 miles between watering holes. The mule teams often traveled 16 to 18 miles a day, even when ground temperatures sometimes reached 140°.

On arrival at the railroad station, workers unloaded the borax. The team rested overnight, and then set out on their return trip the next morning. Five teams of men and mules followed this schedule over the nearly six years that Coleman's company used the twenty-mule teams to extract borax from Death Valley.

TODAY

Remnants of the mine, plant, and company settlement can still be found about one mile north of the Furnace Creek visitor center in Death Valley National Park. A 3/8-mile interpretive trail circles the area and includes pictures and descriptions of life at the site when the mine was in operation. There is also one underground borax mine still operating in Death Valley National Park. It's called the Billie Mine and can be found along the road to Dante's View.

*   *   *

UNCLE JOHN'S PUZZLER

Using only one straight line, make this equation true.

$$5 + 5 + 5 = 550$$

(One possible answer is to add a line through the equal sign so it becomes a "does not equal" sign, but there is a much more clever solution than that.)

Answer:

Add a line to the first plus sign so it becomes a 4. 545 + 5 = 550

AMAZING ANAGRAMS

Over the last ten years, we've flushed out some truly amazing anagrams—words or phrases that are rearranged to form new words or phrases with (more or less) the same meaning. Here are the best of the best.

Entertainment Anagrams

TELEVISION *becomes…*
TV IS ONE LIE

BRUCE SPRINGSTEEN
*becomes…***BURSTING PRESENCE**

FRANCIS FORD COPPOLA
*becomes…***COLD POPCORN AFFAIRS**

WILLIAM SHATNER
becomes…
HI, SWELL MARTIAN!

TOM CRUISE
*becomes…***SO I'M CUTER**

JUSTIN TIMBERLAKE
*becomes…***I'M A JERK, BUT LISTEN**

JAY LENO *becomes…*
ENJOY L.A.

Around the World Anagrams

SOUTHERN CALIFORNIA
*becomes…***HOT SUN, OR LIFE IN A CAR**

WASHINGTON *becomes…*
HOGS WANT IN

THE LEANING TOWER OF PISA *becomes…*
WHAT A FOREIGN STONE PILE!

NORTH AMERICA
becomes…
MACHO TERRAIN

THE LEANING TOWER OF PISA *becomes…*
I SPOT ONE GIANT FLAW HERE

Oval Office Anagrams

THE COMING PRESIDENTIAL CAMPAIGN
*becomes…***DAMN! ELECTING TIME IS APPROACHING**

THE ASSASSINATION OF PRESIDENT ABRAHAM LINCOLN *becomes…*
A PAST SENSATION CHILLS ME, OR A FIEND SHOT IN A BARN

WILLIAM HOWARD TAFT
*becomes…***A WORD WITH ALL—I'M FAT**

Long day: In China, schools run from 7:30 a.m. to 5:00 p.m.

FOUNDING FATHERS

You already know the names—here are the people behind them.

FRANK GERBER

In 1928 his seven-month-old granddaughter, Sally, became seriously ill. The girl's physician suggested she might benefit from a diet of strained fruits and vegetables, and he put his tomato-canning factory to work on it. When Sally recovered, mothers in the area began requesting samples of the food. He started marketing the product, and within six months, Gerber Strained Peas, Prunes, Carrots, and Spinach were available across the U.S.

HERMAN FISHER AND IRVING PRICE

Together with Helen Schelle, they founded the Fischer-Price toy company in 1930 to make toys out of Ponderosa Pine. Their first big hit: Snoopy Sniffer, a "loose-jointed, floppy-eared pull toy who woofed when you pulled his wagging spring tail," in 1938. The company made its first plastic toys in 1949.

PLEASANT AND JOHN HANES

Brothers who built a tobacco business in the late 1800s, then sold it in 1900. Each invested his profits in a textile company. John's made socks and stockings; Pleasant's made new-fangled two-piece men's underwear. They were separate companies until 1962, when the families joined forces.

THOMAS JACOB HILFIGER

Born in Elmira, New York, in 1951, Tommy knew what he wanted to do from an early age: design clothing. While still in high school, he worked at a gas station, saved his money to buy used jeans, which he resold to other kids. He used the money he earned to open a chain of hip clothing stores called People's Place and got his start as a designer by telling the jeans-makers what styles would sell better. (He was right.) After working for other clothing companies for several years (Jordache fired him—they were wrong), he struck gold in 1985 with a line of urban-preppy clothing— Tommy Hilfiger.

In Canada, it is illegal to board a plane while it's in flight.

DAVID PACKARD

David Packard was an engineer with the General Electric Company. In 1938 he moved to California, where he renewed a friendship with William Hewlett. The two went into the electronics business, making oscillators that were smaller, cheaper, and better than anything else on the market. Working from a small garage in Palo Alto, the Hewlett-Packard company earned $1,000 that first year. Today the garage is a state landmark: "The Birthplace of Silicon Valley." Packard died in 1996 leaving an estate worth billions.

RUDOLF DIESEL

Born in Paris in 1858, Diesel studied mechanical engineering in college. He then dedicated his life to creating efficient heat engines, and in 1893 published his design for a new internal combustion engine. At his wife's suggestion, Diesel named the engine after himself. But the moderate fame and fortune he received from his design were short-lived. Plagued by ill health and legal battles over his patents, he lost most of his money. While traveling on a ship to England in 1913, Diesel threw himself overboard.

RICHARD REYNOLDS

The nephew of cigarette mogul R.J. Reynolds, he spent ten years working for his uncle's tobacco company, then in 1912 struck out on his own. After several setbacks, he went back to his uncle and borrowed enough money to start the U.S. Foil Company—which made foil cigarette packaging for R.J. Reynolds Co. In the mid-1930s, Richard learned of a new type of foil made from aluminum. Sensing the product's potential, he built a plant to manufacture it and began selling it as Reynolds Wrap.

GLEN W. BELL

After he got out of the Marines in 1946, Bell sold his refrigerator for $500 and used the money to start Bell's Drive-In in San Bernardino, California. San Bernardino is also the birthplace of McDonald's, and when Bell realized how well the McDonald brothers were doing, he decided it would be easier to switch to Mexican food than it would be to compete against them directly. His first restaurants were called Taco Tia. After a few name changes, he settled on Taco Bell in 1962.

Hey, tall, dark, and handsome: Female lions prefer males with dark manes.

INTERNATIONAL ELVIS

Decades after his death, Elvis is more popular than ever. He sells more records, generates more revenue, and has more fans worldwide than he did when he was alive. If you need proof, look to these Elvis impersonators.

LATINO ELVIS (Robert Lopez, a.k.a. "El Vez," Mexico)
Claim to Fame: First Mexican Elvis to think he was the *second* Mexican Elvis
Taking Care of Business: Lopez, who is famous all over Mexico and has appeared on MTV and *The Tonight Show*, grew up absolutely convinced that Elvis Presley was Mexican. "When I was a kid in the '60s, I had uncles with continental slacks and pompadours in that Elvis style," he says. "I thought Elvis looked like my uncles."

Lopez got a rude awakening when he realized that the King wasn't in Mexico even when he was *supposed* to be: "The first movie I ever saw him in was *Fun in Acapulco*. I found out later that it wasn't even filmed in Mexico, but on a sound stage." No matter—El Vez is still dedicated to emulating the King. "I don't think that you can do this unless you love and admire Elvis," he says. "This isn't just some fat-man-on-pills parody."

REFUSNIK ELVIS (Vassil Angelov, Bulgaria)
Claim to Fame: Put his life on the line by impersonating the King
Taking Care of Business: When he was a young man in the 1960s, Angelov had to hide his admiration of Elvis because sideburns and rock music were illegal in communist Bulgaria. But the communist era ended in 1990 and today Angelov runs Bulgaria's only Elvis fan club and openly tours the country imitating his idol. Someday he hopes to travel the world. "I want to look for people and places," he says, "where I can show off my God-given talent."

TOKYO ELVIS (Mori Yasumasa, Japan)
Claim to Fame: Became the first non-American to win an Elvis impersonator contest in Memphis, Tennessee, the Elvis capital of the world

---

Elvis Presley shared a bed with his mom until he reached puberty.

Taking Care of Business: Yasumasa didn't even hear his first Elvis song until he was 18, but quickly made up for lost time. It wasn't long before he had perfected an Elvis imitation and was performing on U.S. Army bases all over Japan. In 1992 he made the trip of a lifetime when he traveled to Memphis, entered the International Elvis Impersonator Contest...and won. The victory has only deepened his appreciation of the King. "Although he didn't compose or write his songs and leave any deep messages, I believe that he himself is the message," Yasumasa says. "He was using his own body and soul to convey the message of freedom to the world. This to me is really incredible."

KIWI ELVIS (Brian Childs, New Zealand)
Claim to Fame: He's living the life of Elvis...in reverse
Taking Care of Business: Elvis was a singer who collected police badges and always wanted to be in law enforcement—and Brian Childs was a New Zealand police constable who always wanted to be the King. He started out impersonating Elvis in his spare time, but his chief didn't like it and in January 2002, told him he'd have to quit his hobby. Constable Childs quit his job instead. Today he is the reigning champion Elvis Presley impersonator in neighboring Australia and is considering suing the force for wrongful dismissal.

FILIPINO ELVIS (Rene Escharcha, a.k.a. "Renelvis", Philippines)
Claim to Fame: He takes care of business—by telephone
Taking Care of Business: It's not easy to stand out from the crowd when you're an Elvis impersonator—even if you're a Filipino Elvis living in North Carolina. One of the ways Escharcha makes his mark is by whipping out his long-distance phone card in the middle of a performance and calling his cousin in the Philippines (also an Elvis impersonator) so that they can belt out Elvis tunes together, a cappella, over a speakerphone. Escharcha also keeps the King's legacy fresh by writing his own songs. In "Elvis on Terrorism," Escharcha sings, "I wonder if Elvis were here today, what would he do? I can assure you, he would do something."

Why is he so dedicated to being the King? "If you want to be somebody, you have to work at it," Renelvis explains.

THE GIMLI GLIDER, PT. I

This may be the most nail-biting story we've ever published. When Uncle John decided to make a second Best Of edition, this was the first article we said "has to be in there."

JUST ANOTHER FLIGHT

Air Canada Flight 143 on July 23, 1983, started out like any other flight. Captain Robert Pearson and First Officer Maurice Quintal had arrived ahead of time to go over the aircraft and prepare it for departure. The flight was scheduled to depart Montreal shortly before 6:00 p.m. They were going to make a quick, 19-minute hop to Ottawa to pick up more passengers before flying 1,700 miles across Canada to Edmonton, Alberta.

The plane was a twin-engine Boeing 767, one of the most sophisticated commercial aircraft of its day. It was also one of the first commercial jets with a "glass cockpit"—meaning that nearly all of the standard instruments and gauges had been replaced with a bank of computer screens displaying the same information in a digital, graphic format. (Kind of like trading up from a pinball machine to a video game.)

NEW AND IMPROVED

The 767 was so new that Air Canada owned only four of them, none of which had been in service for more than a few months. Captain Pearson, who had more than 26 years on the job, was one of only a handful of Air Canada pilots qualified to fly the plane.

The glass cockpit offered numerous advantages over traditional instruments: Fewer moving parts meant fewer instrument failures. That translated into fewer flight delays, lower operating costs, and higher profits for the airlines. And because so much information was condensed and presented in easy-to-read displays, it eliminated the need for the pilot to scan numerous tiny gauges all over the cockpit, which reduced eyestrain and fatigue.

The new 767s were so sophisticated, in fact, that only two people—the pilot and first officer (co-pilot)—were needed to fly it, instead of the usual three. The position of flight engineer had been eliminated, and the job had been divided between the

---

Is this a good thing? Helen Keller could identify her friends by their odors.

onboard computers, the ground crew, the pilot, and the first officer. Every task had been accounted for.

Or so everyone thought.

A BAD OMEN

As soon as Pearson and Quintal stepped onboard, the ground crew
told them that something was wrong with the "fuel quantity processor"—the instrument that measures the available jet fuel and displays the amount on the computer screen. Result: The fuel gauge
display was blank. And no spare fuel quantity processors were available on such short notice—the planes were too new. Captain Pearson would have to fly the plane without any fuel gauges.

But was that even permitted? In a traditional jumbo jet the
answer was no, but the 767's fuel management system was much
more sophisticated than a traditional mechanical fuel gauge. It
could measure the rate at which the fuel was being consumed,
something that had never been possible before. That meant if you
manually told the computer how much fuel was in the tanks at
the start of the flight, it could automatically subtract the amount
consumed to give a precise estimate of how much fuel was left. It
would even display the quantity in the form of a digital "estimated
fuel" gauge.

But these were only *estimates*, and they only worked if the pilot
entered the correct fuel load into the computer at the start of the
flight. If the pilot miscalculated, the information displayed in the
estimated fuel gauge would be totally off.

NOT BY THE BOOK

Understandably, Captain Pearson had reservations about flying a
jumbo jet without any working fuel gauges. Who wouldn't? So he
consulted the 767's official Minimum Equipment List, or MEL, to
see if the plane would even be cleared to fly with its fuel gauges
out. It wasn't.

But when Pearson pointed this out to one of the mechanics,
the mechanic assured him that the plane had been cleared to fly
by Air Canada's Maintenance Control division, which has the
final say—even over the MEL—as to whether an airplane is safe.
Captain Pearson still had misgivings—he didn't like reading one
thing in the MEL and hearing something else from the airline. But

the 767 *was* a sophisticated plane, so he figured that if Air Canada said it was safe to fly, it was.

MEASURE FOR MEASURE

Air Canada's four 767s were unique in another way, too: they were the first jumbo jets in the entire fleet to use the metric system instead of the traditional British "imperial" system of weights and measures. Canada began phasing in the metric system in 1979, and now Air Canada's air fleet was beginning to make the switch.

This 767's fuel was measured in kilograms, not the imperial pounds that Air Canada pilots were used to dealing with. Adding to the confusion, while the plane measured its fuel by *weight*—kilograms—the fuel truck measured its by *volume*—liters. And with the fuel quantity processor broken, all the calculations—normally done by computers—now had to be done by hand.

But whose job was it to do the math? On an ordinary jumbo jet it was the flight engineer's job to calculate fuel load. But on the 767, that position had been eliminated. As an investigation later revealed, the pilots had been told that fuel calculations were now the job of the ground crew, but since the ground crew hadn't been trained to do the calculations, then either the captain or the first officer had to be responsible for them now.

MATH PROBLEM

Captain Pearson knew that 1) he needed 22,300 kilograms of jet fuel to get to Edmonton, and 2) there were 7,682 liters of fuel in the tanks. So how many liters of additional fuel did he need to get to 22,300 kilograms? More simply put, how many liters of jet fuel are there in a kilogram? That was the question.

Pearson was used to thinking in terms of gallons and pounds, and his knowledge of the metric system was a little rusty. So he asked the guy on the refueling truck how many liters were in a kilogram. "One point seven seven," the guy answered. That sounded about right; First Officer Quintal thought so, too.

PROBLEMS MULTIPLY

How hard was it to do the math? See if you can follow along:
• If there were 7,682 liters of fuel in the tanks and 1 liter is equal

Stenophobia **is the fear of narrow spaces.**

to 1.77 kilograms, that meant the tanks contained nearly 13,600 kilograms of fuel. Thus, they had to add 8,700 kilograms to get the 22,300 kilograms they needed.

• Dividing 8,700 by 1.77 to convert back to liters, the fuel truck had to add a little over 4,900 liters of fuel to fill the tanks to roughly 12,600 liters.

• Multiply 12,600 by 1.77 and you get 22,302 kilograms—more than enough fuel to get to Edmonton.

Simple, right? Well, it's a little confusing in the best of circumstances, harder if you're just learning to master the metric system, and worse still if there's a plane full of people waiting for you to finish the math and take them where they want to go.

But just to be on the safe side, Pearson and Quintal checked and rechecked their math. Sure enough, every time they multiplied 12,600 by 1.77, they got 22,302. According to their calculations, they had enough fuel on board to make the flight, with plenty to spare.

AND AWAY WE GO
Finally satisfied, they programmed their fuel load into the computer manually, then finished their preflight checks and made the 19-minute flight to Ottawa.

During the 43-minute stopover, they had the ground crew check the fuel levels again. Pearson multiplied the remaining liters by 1.77 and concluded that he still had more than 20,000 kilograms of fuel onboard. He entered this estimate into the computer to get the estimated fuel gauge, finished his preflight procedures, and at 7:05 p.m. was cleared for takeoff.

A few minutes later, the Boeing 767 lifted into the air with 61 passengers and 8 crew members aboard. In their wildest dreams, none of them could have imagined what was about to occur.

For Part II of the story, turn to page 390.

* * *

SOARING COSTS
A used DC-9 airplane costs more today than it did when it was new in the 1970s.

An eagle's bones weigh half as much as its feathers.

MILE-HIGH COMEDIANS

Flying can be scary. That's why flight attendants and pilots sometimes try to add a little levity (get it?) to the experience. Here are some actual airplane announcements that readers have sent us.

PREPARING FOR TAKEOFF
"As we prepare for takeoff, please make sure your tray tables and seat backs are fully upright in their least comfortable positions."

"There may be fifty ways to leave your lover, but there are only four ways off this airplane."

"Your seat cushions can be used as flotation devices. In the event of a water landing, please take them with our compliments."

"To operate your seatbelt, insert the metal tab into the buckle, and pull tight. It works just like every other seatbelt, and if you don't know how to operate one, you probably shouldn't be out in public unsupervised."

"Should the cabin lose pressure, oxygen masks will drop from the overhead area. Please place the bag over your own mouth and nose before assisting children or adults acting like children."

"Any person caught smoking in the lavatories will be asked to leave the plane immediately."

"We'd also like to remind you to turn off your cellular phones, computers, video games, or any other electronic device that may interfere with the captain's pacemaker."

IN-FLIGHT GUFFAWS FROM THE PILOT
"Mornin', folks. As we leave Dallas, it's warm and the sun is shining. Unfortunately, we're going to New York, where it is cold and rainy. Why in the world y'all wanna go there I really don't know."

Most popular fruit worldwide: the mango.

"We are pleased to have some of the best flight attendants in the business. Sadly, none of them are working this flight."

"Ladies and gentlemen, we have reached our cruising altitude of 30,000 feet, so I'm going to switch off the seat belt sign. Feel free to move about the cabin, but please try to stay inside the plane until we land."

"Once again, I'm turning off the seat belt sign. I think I'll switch to autopilot, too, so I can come back there and visit with you for the rest of the flight."

"Folks, if you were with us last week, we never got around to mentioning that it was National Procrastination Day."

"The weather in San Francisco is 61 degrees with some broken clouds, but they'll try to have them fixed before we arrive."

LANDING AND DE-PLANING
After the plane touched down and was coming to a stop, the pilot's voice came over the loudspeaker: "Whoa, big fella. WHOA!"

"Sorry about the rough landing, folks. I'd just like to assure you that it wasn't the airline's fault; it wasn't the flight attendants' fault; nor was it the pilot's fault. It was the asphalt."

"We ask you to please remain seated while Captain Kangaroo bounces us to the terminal."

"As you exit the plane, please make sure to gather all of your belongings. Anything left behind will be distributed evenly among the flight attendants. Please do not leave children or spouses."

"Thank you for flying Business Express. We hope you enjoyed giving us the business as much as we enjoyed taking you for a ride."

"Thanks for flying with us today. And the next time you get the insane urge to go blasting through the skies in a pressurized metal tube, we hope you'll think of us."

"Last one off the plane has to clean it!"

A lightning bolt strikes so fast it could circle the globe eight times in a second.

MIRROR, MIRROR ON THE WALL

*Not that we're vain or anything, but we at the BRI find mirrors
endlessly fascinating. Here are some important facts about
the second-most important object in the bathroom.*

POOLS OF LIGHT

How do mirrors work? Generally speaking, by reflecting light. Most objects don't give off any light of their own. They can only be seen because light from other sources—the sun, a candle, a lightbulb—hits them and bounces off, hitting their eyes. Not all of the light bounces, though. Some is absorbed by the object and some is transmitted through the object. The part that does bounce back is the reflection. Flat shiny surfaces like water, metal, and mirrors reflect light well because very little of the light is absorbed or transmitted—most of it is reflected.

When light hits a mirror, it bounces off in the opposite direction, but at the exact same angle it came from. It appears as if the image is coming from behind the mirror, but it's not—what we see is a virtual image.

THE FIRST MIRRORS

For centuries, mankind's only mirrors were pools of water or polished metal. The first glass mirrors were made by Venetian craftsmen in the 1300s. Their method: They covered the back of a piece of glass with an amalgam of tin and mercury, rubbed flat and smooth. A piece of wool cloth would then be laid on top of the mercury and pressed with iron weights for more than a week. Then the excess mercury would be drained off. This method remained a carefully guarded secret, and for centuries Venice had a monopoly on mirrors.

In 1665 the chief minister to Louis XIV of France went to Italy and—at the risk of death—bribed 18 Venetian mirrorsmiths to move to France. Soon after their defection, the French passed a law making it illegal to import Venetian mirrors.

Three years later, a Frenchman named Louis Lucas beat the

Venetians at their own game—he invented plate glass. Venetians only knew how to make blown glass, so each mirror started out as a bottle or cylinder which was slit open and flattened while still hot. The size of mirrors was therefore very limited.

But Lucas discovered how to pour molten glass onto an iron table where it could be flattened with an iron roller. Now mirrors could be made that were much larger. Soon France became famous for its mirrors. A very pleased Louis XIV purchased 700 mirrors and lined an entire hallway at the Palace of Versailles with them in a stunning display.

UPON FURTHER REFLECTION

In 1835 German chemist Justus von Liebig discovered a way to make a better mirror. He invented a process for using silver as a backing instead of tin and mercury. He flushed the glass with silver salts and then covered it with a solution of silver nitrate. After being heated and left undisturbed for an hour, a chemical reaction caused the metallic silver to separate and adhere to the glass. Then it was coated with shellac and painted with a black backing. And that's how mirrors were made for the next 150 years.

In mirror making today, silver or aluminum is vaporized, then sprayed onto glass. For finer mirrors—such as those used in telescopes—aluminum, chromium, or gold are heated in a vacuum tank. When they reach the critical temperature, they "flash" into vapor, filling the tank with metallic gas. A film is then deposited on whatever material is inside the tank.

MIRROR FACTS AND TRIVIA

• In the 1600s, the Dutch used to cover their mirrors with curtains when not in use, lest the reflectiveness be used up!

• In ancient China, reflective pieces of polished brass were placed over doorknobs so that evil spirits would scare themselves away.

• Ben Franklin mounted mirrors outside his second-story window so he could secretly see who was knocking at his door.

• The vanity license plate "3M TA3" was banned after someone looked at it in the mirror.

• A middle school in Oregon was faced with a unique problem: A number of girls were beginning to use lipstick and would apply it in the bathroom. That was fine, but for some reason, they would also press their lips to the mirrors, leaving dozens of little lip prints. Finally the principal called all the girls to the bathroom. She explained that the lip prints were a major problem for the custodian and asked the custodian to demonstrate how difficult it was to clean one of the mirrors. He proceeded to take out a long-handled brush, dip it into the nearest toilet, and scrub the mirror. After that, there were no more lip prints on the mirrors.

• The word "mirror" comes from the Latin *mirari*, meaning "to wonder at." It's also the root word for "miracle" and "admire."

• The world's largest mirrors (to date) sit inside the twin Keck Telescopes—the world's largest telescopes—at the W. M. Keck Observatory in Hawaii. Each mirror is made of 36 hexagonal segments which work together as a single piece. Diameter: 33 feet.

• In olden days some thought that the reflection of the body in a shiny surface or mirror was an expression of the spiritual self, and therefore if anything happened to disturb that reflection, injury would follow. This was the origin of the superstition that breaking a mirror would bring seven years of bad luck.

• Trade secret: Building managers install mirrors in lobbies because people complain less about waiting for slow elevators when they're occupied looking at themselves.

• In 1994 Russian astronauts orbiting in the Mir spacecraft tried using mirrors to reflect sunlight into northern areas of their country in an attempt to lengthen the short growing season. It didn't work.

• Ever wonder if the mirror in the dressing room is a real mirror or a two-way mirror? Here's a simple test: Place the tip of your fingernail against the reflective surface. If there's a gap between your fingernail and the image, it's a *genuine* mirror. But, if your fingernail *directly touches* the image, watch out—it very well could be a two-way mirror. Remember, though, that mirror technology is always changing, so no test is 100% foolproof.

*   *   *

Word Origin: "Clock" comes from the Latin *clocca*, meaning "bell," since clock tower bells were rung on the hour. The same root gives us "cloak"—which is shaped like a bell.

...4 microns (millionths of a meter) thick. Spider webs are as thin as 1 micron.

NUDES & PRUDES

Nudity can be shocking…and so can prudery.
Which side of the fence do you fall on?

NUDE…Arne and Oeystein Tokvam, two elderly brothers living in Oslo, Norway, got the show of a lifetime when a blonde-haired woman they didn't know talked her way into their home and began stripping off her clothing. The woman, who was in her 30s, was soon joined by an older woman who also stripped naked and began dancing around the brothers' home. "The older one was the wildest of the two," Arne, 73, told a local newspaper. "We saw everything."

After about 15 minutes, the mystery women put their clothes on and left; that was when Oeystein, 80, discovered that the brothers' safe was missing, and along with it $6,600 in cash and two government checks for $1,700. "Never mind," says Arne. "It's been a long time since we had that much fun."

PRUDE…In December 2004, the city of Villahermosa, Mexico, passed a law banning nudity, even within the confines of a private home. Why the law? Because the city is so hot and humid, many people have taken to walking around nude in their homes, which many find offensive. "When people walk past their windows, you see a lot of things," says city councilwoman Blanca Pulido, who supports the new law. Penalty for being nude in your own home: 36 hours in jail or a $121 fine.

NUDE…In January 2004, Stephen Gough, 44, known as the "Naked Rambler," accomplished his goal of walking the length of the United Kingdom wearing only socks, walking boots, and a hat. His purpose: To encourage greater acceptance of the naked body. The 900-mile trip took a long time—seven months. Gough was arrested 16 times along the way and served two stints in jail for indecent exposure.

PRUDE…Satirical news anchor Jon Stewart's book *America (The Book)* spent more than 15 weeks on the *New York Times* bestseller list and was named Book of the Year by *Publishers Weekly* magazine…but that didn't stop eight southern Mississippi libraries from banning it. Reason: the satirical book contains a phony photograph of all nine Supreme Court justices in the nude. "We're not an adult bookstore," says Robert Willits, director of the Jackson-George Regional Library System. "Our collection is open to the entire public."

NUDE…In May 2004, 60 partiers on Austin's Lake Travis capsized their double-decker party barge, known as Club Fred. The cause of the accident is still under investigation. One theory: According to onlookers, the boat started to tip over when everyone aboard crowded over to one side to gawk at the sunbathers at Hippie Hollow, the only nude beach in Texas.

PRUDE…Noah Webster, well known for his dictionaries, once published a censored version of the Bible as well. "Many words are so offensive, especially for females," he explained. He changed words like *teat* to *breast*, and *stones* (testicles) to *peculiar members*. It flopped.

NUDE…When Stu Smailes died in 2002 at the age of 69, he left the city of Seattle $1 million to buy a new fountain. There's a catch—Smailes's will stipulates that in order for Seattle to claim the money, the fountain must include "one or more *unclothed*, life-size male figure(s)." Furthermore, it must be designed in "the classical style"—in other words, no cheating by making it unrecognizably abstract. "Smailes was a very funny man," said his attorney, Tim Bradbury. "He had a very strong sense of humor."

PRUDE…While campaigning for the presidency in 2007, Senator Barack Obama made a fundraising stop at the Planet Zero Art Gallery in Richmond, Virginia. And although he's campaigning on a progressive platform, one of the artworks on display was too risqué for the senator. It was a 6-by-10-foot oil painting called "Snake Charmer," which features Britney Spears (sans underwear) getting out of Paris Hilton's limo. "I wished we could have had a good dialogue about freedom of speech," said the artist, Jamie Boling, "but I understand that a politician might want to avoid being photographed in front of Britney Spears' crotch."

Strange but true: Fax machines have been around longer than telephones.

THE LAST LAUGH: <u>EPITAPHS</u>

Some unusual epitaphs and tombstone rhymes, sent in by our wandering BRI tombstone-ologists.

In Topeka, Kansas:
Tim McGrew
Here lies Sheriff Tim
McGrew who said
he would arrest
Bill Hennessy or
die—He was right.

In England:
Edgar Oscar Earl
Beneath this grassy
mound now rests
One Edgar Oscar
Earl,
Who to another
hunter looked
Exactly like a
squirrel.

In Boston, Mass.
Owen Moore
Owen Moore:
Gone away
Owin' more
Than he could pay.

In New York:
Harry Edsel Smith
Looked up the
elevator shaft
To see if the car was
on the way down.
It was.

In England:
Sir John Strange
Here lies an honest
lawyer,
And that is Strange.

In Scotland:
Stranger, tread
This ground with
gravity:
Dentist Brown is
filling
His last cavity.

In Ireland:
Tears cannot
Restore her:
Therefore I weep.

In Massachusetts:
Here lies **Ann Mann**.
She lived an old
maid
But died an old
Mann.

In England:
Mrs Nott
Nott born, Nott dead
…Here lies a woman
Who was,
And who was Nott.

In England:
Dr. I. Lettsom
When people's ill,
they comes to I,
I physics, bleeds, and
sweats 'em;
Sometimes they live,
sometimes they die;
What's that to I?
I. Lettsom.

In Arizona:
Ezikel Height
Here lies young
Ezikel Height
Died from jumping
Jim Smith's claim;
Didn't happen at
the mining site,
The claim he jumped,
was Jim Smith's
dame.

In England:
Anonymous
Stop stranger as you
pass by
As you are now so
once was I
As I am now so
will you be
So be prepared to
follow me.

Every year, about 2,500 people go to the emergency room with "toothbrush injuries."

YOUR FACE WILL FREEZE LIKE THAT!

Should you believe everything your mom said?

MOTHERLY ADVICE
From "Eat a good breakfast" to "TV is bad for you," the average mother doles out quite a few pearls of wisdom over the course of a kid's childhood. But how many of those mom rules are actually true? It turns out many scientists have studied them. Here's what they found.

"Eat your fish. It's brain food."
True. One of the fatty acids in fish, DHA, is an important component of brain cells; it aids the brain's cell-to-cell communication and nerve conduction. One study found that seniors who ate fish once a week were less likely to develop Alzheimer's.

"Don't go outside without your coat on or you'll catch a cold."
False. Colds are contagious infections usually caused by viruses. They aren't caused by cold weather or dampness, but by germs you pick up when you don't wash your hands. (So when Mom says to do that, she's right.)

"Too much TV is bad for you."
True. Too much TV means a sedentary lifestyle and lack of exercise, a major cause of obesity and a host of other health problems. And to avoid Alzheimer's, researchers suggest that you turn off the TV and exercise your brain by reading, doing crossword puzzles, playing music, and even gardening.

"If you keep making that face, your face will freeze like that!"
False. Our faces really do "freeze" into a pattern of the creases, or wrinkles, we create whenever we smile or frown. But making a silly face for a few minutes won't affect anything—except your mother's blood pressure.

"Breakfast is the most important meal of the day."
True. Many studies have found that kids who eat breakfast do better academically than those who don't. In one study, breakfast-eaters scored nearly a full grade higher on tests than those who went to school on an empty stomach.

"Eating carrots will help you see in the dark."
True. The vitamins in carrots have long been shown to improve night vision.

"Don't swallow your chewing gum or your stomach walls will stick together."
False. A popular variation on this one is "gum takes seven years to digest." Neither is true. Stomach acid is as strong as toilet bowl cleaner, and can liquefy chewing gum in a matter of minutes.

"It's important to get a good night's sleep."
True. Experiments at Harvard Medical School showed that college students who slept after they learned a new task remembered more about it the next day than students who stayed up all night after learning the same task.

"If you crack your knuckles, you'll get arthritis."
Maybe. Clinicians have found that cracking your knuckles pushes joints past their normal range of motion and puts stress on the ligaments and tendons that hold the joint together. Cracking your knuckles for a period of years could result in inflamed, arthritic knuckle joints.

"Eat slowly, and chew your food."
True. Eating too fast can lead to acid reflux disease, and many people die from choking on pieces of food. Also, chewing slowly allows you more time to taste your food, making the meal more satisfying.

"If you cross your eyes, they'll stay that way."
False. Keeping your eyes crossed for a few seconds may cause a temporary spasm of the eye muscles, but this condition usually passes shortly. The condition called "cross-eye" often begins at birth; it isn't related to voluntarily crossing your eyes.

CLASS ACTS

College isn't only about really rigorous science classes, thick textbooks, and late-night studying. As one of Uncle John's teachers put it, "College is hard—there should be some classes where you can get an easy A." That could be why most schools have "cream-puff" classes like these.

Elvis as Anthology. "Redefining the music of other performers through listening to Elvis, and watching video and movie clips." (University of Iowa)

Art and Science of Beer. "We will explore the place of beer in ancient as well as modern life, and the role beer has played in important achievements in microbiology, biotechnology and physics." (Indiana University)

Sports for the Spectator. "A study of the great American spectator sports including football, basketball, baseball, ice hockey, golf, tennis, and any others which meet the interests of the class." (Ohio State University)

Witchcraft and Politics. "Explores witchcraft, spirit possession, and cults of the dead as idioms of power and as vehicles for protest, resistance, and violent social change." (Bucknell University)

Shopping: Desire, Compulsion, and Consumption. "First we will explore the manufacturing of desire. We will then turn to historical analysis, contrasting the experience of shopping in traditional bazaars and contemporary malls. Finally, we will explore the place of shopping in our collective imaginations." (Williams College)

How to Be Gay. "Examines the notion that homosexuality is not just a desire, but a set of specific tastes in music, movies, and other cultural forms." (University of Michigan)

Star Trek and Religion. "This popular science-fiction series is set in the future, but the ideas and conflicts come from past and present debates." (Indiana University)

Campus Culture and Drinking. "The cultural understandings that motivate and shape undergraduate drinking." (Duke University)

The word *planet* is from the Greek word for wanderer. (They move while the stars remain still.)

Awareness. "Students will begin their work by designing independent learning projects, which can be anything (community service, sailing, midwifery, gardening, reading, etc.). We will answer these questions: What do you want to learn? How are you going to learn it? How are you going to know when you have learned it?" (Evergreen State College)

International Beverage Education. "The history of beverages such as wines, distilled spirits, and beers. Prerequisite: must be 21 years of age." (Oklahoma State University)

Daytime Serials: Family and Social Roles. "Analysis of the themes and characters that populate daytime serials and investigation of what impact these portrayals have on gender roles in the family and workplace." (University of Wisconsin)

The Cheerleader in American Culture. "Cheerleading is an ambiguous cultural icon. In this course we challenge the stereotypes of cheerleaders and provoke both supporters and critics to view cheerleading in a more multi-faceted light." (University of Alabama)

A FEW MORE:

- *American Golf: Aristocratic Pastime or the People's Game?* (Carnegie Mellon University)

- *Quarterstaff, Broadsword, Rapier, and Dagger Combat* (Northern Kentucky University)

- *Introduction to Leisure* (Kent State University)

- *Black Hair: The History of African-American Hairstyles* (Stanford University)

- *Underwater Fire Prevention* (University of Louisiana-Monroe)

- *Pranks: Culture Jamming as Social Activism* (St. Mary's College)

- *Relaxation Techniques* (University of Iowa)

- *History of Tupac Shakur* (University of California, Berkeley)

- *Juggling (I and II)* (University of Oregon)

- *Frisbee* (Western Connecticut State University)

- *The Social Significance of* The Dukes of Hazzard (University of Alabama)

Humans are responsible for the deaths of 30 to 70 million sharks every year.

PROJECT GREEK ISLAND, PART I

Here's the first part of our look at one of the best-kept secrets of the Cold War...or was it? It depends on how you look at it.

COOKING THE BOOKS

In 1980 a hotel executive named Ted Kleisner landed a job as the general manager of the Greenbrier, a five-star luxury resort in the Allegheny Mountains of West Virginia. The resort sprawls over 6,500 acres and includes hiking and biking trails, three championship golf courses, a hotel with over 600 rooms, more than 90 guest houses, and its own private train station. Learning to run such a large facility would have been a big job for anyone. Even so, it only took a few days for Kleisner to notice that there were some serious discrepancies in the company's books. For example:

• The resort was spending a fortune on "maintenance" of equipment that it didn't own.

• It had ordered thousands of gallons of diesel fuel that it had no need for. The fuel had disappeared without a trace.

• Every payday, dozens of paychecks were being mailed out to people whose names did not appear on the employee roster.

The deeper Kleisner dug, the more problems he found.

BENEATH THE SURFACE

Strangely, when Kleisner took his concerns to his superiors, they didn't seem that concerned...until he talked about turning the matter over to the police.

That got their attention. Not long afterward, Kleisner was instructed to report to a building in a remote section of the grounds, where a man identifying himself as a senior Pentagon official invited him into an office. "He turned up a radio very loud and shut the blinds," Kleisner recalled in a 1995 interview with

---

the London *Times*. "Then he said, 'You are about to be briefed on a top-secret government project that is part of the Greenbrier.'" After Kleisner signed a pledge of secrecy, the official let him in on one of the most sensitive secrets of the Cold War era: 65 feet beneath the West Virginia wing of the Greenbrier was a fully staffed, fully operational bomb shelter large enough to accommodate both houses of the United States Congress, plus family members and key aides, for up to 60 days in the event of nuclear war.

SHELTER SHOCK

The shelter dated back to the late 1950s and was the brainchild of President Dwight D. Eisenhower. A former five-star general, Ike knew that the Pentagon was building numerous "emergency command relocation centers" for top military leaders (including himself), to ensure that they would survive a nuclear attack by the Soviet Union and would be able to continue to oversee the defense of whatever was left of the country.

But what would happen if the military leaders were the *only* top officials to survive a nuclear war? Eisenhower worried that America might slide into dictatorship. He believed that the United States had to put as much effort into building shelters for the legislative and judicial branches of the government as it did for the military and the commander-in-chief.

HIDE AND SEEK

One of the tricks to building an effective bomb shelter, especially one designed to house top government officials, is doing it in complete secrecy—the enemy can't bomb it if they can't even find it. But how do you hide a bomb shelter large enough to accommodate more than 1,000 people, plus all the food, supplies, machinery, and equipment necessary to keep them alive for 60 days?

Eisenhower himself has been credited with being the one who came up with the idea of burying it beneath the Greenbrier resort. He had visited it a number of times over the years and liked to play golf there. The place had a lot going for it as the potential site for an important bomb shelter: It was 250 miles southwest of Washington, D.C., close enough to be accessible but far enough away to survive a nuclear strike against the city. Since it had its own train station, large numbers of people would be able to evacuate there in an emergency. Best of all, as Eisenhower learned, the Greenbrier was planning to add a giant new wing to the hotel.

At Eisenhower's request, the Architect of the Capitol approached the owners of the resort with a deal: In exchange for allowing the government to build the bomb shelter underneath the new wing *as* it was being constructed, the government would pay for the wing as well as for the bunker. Because both would be built at the same time, the thinking went, the shelter wouldn't attract much attention. Anyone who saw the work under way would naturally assume that it was all part of the hotel.

Who could pass up an offer like that? The Greenbrier's owners took the deal and work on "Project Greek Island," as the bomb shelter was code-named, began in 1958.

YOUR TAX DOLLARS AT WORK

What kind of a bomb shelter would you build if you had the unlimited resources of the federal government behind you, and no public oversight thanks to the fact that the project was a secret? The bomb shelter built underneath the Greenbrier was enormous and had everything. The size of two football fields stacked one atop the other, it was more than 60 feet underground and protected by concrete walls and ceilings 5 feet thick. It had 153 rooms, including 18 dormitories that slept 60 people each; a kitchen and a cafeteria large enough to feed 400 people at a sitting, and a full hospital suite complete with two operating rooms, an intensive-care unit, a 12-bed ward, and a "pathological-waste incinerator" large enough to serve as a crematorium if the need arose. Thirty-five doctors and nurses would have staffed the hospital if it were ever activated.

The shelter also had its own air and water decontamination facilities and a power station stocked with 42,000 gallons of fuel, enough to keep the shelter's giant diesel generators running for months on end. Giant steel and concrete blast doors protected the shelter's four hidden entrances. The largest door, which protected a tunnel large enough to drive trucks into, weighed 40 tons.

HANG IN THERE

Maintaining contact with government and military officials in other secret bunkers during a nuclear war was a top priority, as was

Pope John Paul II was an honorary Harlem Globetrotter.

broadcasting messages of hope and encouragement to any survivors fending for themselves in post-nuclear-war America. To this end the shelter was also equipped with a sophisticated communications area, complete with telephone equipment and TV and radio broadcasting studios. Who knew when nuclear war might come? The TV studio had four different pull-down backdrops of the Capitol dome, one for each season of the year, so that elected officials would look in season when speaking to their constituents back home.

AN OPEN SECRET

The bomb shelter also contained two rooms large enough to serve as House and Senate chambers. A third, even larger room, would have served as office space for the officials and their aides, and was also large enough to host joint sessions of Congress if the need ever arose.

Unlike the rest of the bomb shelter, which was concealed behind a locked and carefully guarded door marked "Danger: High Voltage–Keep Out," these large rooms were hidden in plain sight —they were open to the public and used by the Greenbrier as a basement exhibition hall. The only hint of the room's true purpose was a movable, wallpapered panel next to the corridor leading to the hotel. The panel concealed a 25-ton blast door that was normally kept open to allow access to the hall. But if a crisis ever erupted, the public would have been hustled out of the exhibition hall (the shelter was stocked with firearms and riot gear for just such an occasion); then the blast door would have been closed and locked from inside the shelter, sealing its occupants off from Armageddon and abandoning the Greenbrier and its guests and staff to their fate.

Did you ever attend an exhibit or trade show in the basement of the Greenbrier? Or maybe you saw a movie in the Governor's Hall? (The House chamber was disguised as a theater, and movies really were shown there.) If so, you were in one of the most secret bomb shelters in the world, and you didn't even know it.

What else didn't you know about the Congressional bomb shelter? For Part II of the story, turn to page 500.

In Germany, frogs say *quaak-quaak.*

ANIMALS FAMOUS FOR 15 MINUTES

When Andy Warhol said, "In the future, everyone will be famous for 15 minutes," he probably didn't have animals in mind. But even they haven't been able to escape the relentless publicity machine.

HEADLINE: *World Gets Charge from Nuclear Kittens*
THE STARS: Four black kittens—Alpha, Beta, Gamma, and Neutron—who were living at the shut-down San Onofre Nuclear Power Plant in San Diego, California
WHAT HAPPENED: How do you make a nuclear power plant seem warm and fuzzy? Find some kittens there. In February 1996, just as the owner of the San Onofre power plant was kicking off a pro-nuclear PR campaign, a worker happened to find four motherless kittens under a building. A pregnant cat, the story went, had slipped through security at the shut-down power plant, given birth to a litter of kittens, and disappeared. When the worker tried to carry them off the grounds, alarms went off. It turned out that the cute little animals were slightly radioactive...though officials explained that they were in no danger. The story was reported worldwide. *The Nuclear News*, a nuclear industry publication, called it "the biggest nuclear story in years."
AFTERMATH: Seven months later, the Atomic Kittens were pronounced "radiation-free." Offers to adopt the pets flooded in from all over the world, but workers at the plant decided to keep them.

THE HEADLINE: *O Brother, Boar Art Thou?*
THE STARS: Three male boars named Kalle, Oskar, and Willy; their mates Luise, Berta, and Sophie; and their 50 offspring
WHAT HAPPENED: In September 2003, a group called the German Hunting Protection League launched a Web site with 24-hour Web cams that let viewers watch the animals on a wildlife preserve in the Eifel Plateau in western Germany. The site didn't attract a whole lot of attention...until March 2004, when the league turned its cameras on the six adult boars and their babies. They happened to

do this at about the same time that the German version of the reality TV show *Big Brother* launched the latest installment of the series.

AFTERMATH: "Pig Brother," as the pig section of the site came to be known, was an instant hit. It attracted more than 1.5 million visitors in its first two weeks alone. Adding to the popularity: "We have microphones in the enclosure," says Anke Nuh, a spokesperson. "The mating calls are very impressive."

HEADLINE: *Nuts to Him! California Dog Wins Nutty Contest*
THE STAR: Rocky, a 100-pound male Rottweiler
WHAT HAPPENED: In 1996 a Fresno radio station ran a contest offering free Neuticles to the dog submitting the best ghost-written essay on why he wanted them. (Neuticles are artificial plastic testicles, implanted after a dog is neutered, that supposedly make the dog feel better about himself.) The appropriately named Rocky won.
AFTERMATH: The contest made national news. *Parade* magazine called it the "Best Canine Self-Improvement Story" of 1996.

THE HEADLINE: *Pet's Piano Playing No Trivial Pursuit*
THE STAR: Dinky Di, an Australian dingo
WHAT HAPPENED: Dingoes run wild in Australia and are considered pests because they prey on livestock. But when trappers caught some of the wild dogs near Jim Cotterill's roadhouse in the Northern Territory, Cotterill decided to take in one of the puppies and raise it as a pet. One night, as Cotterill's daughter was practicing the piano in the bar, the puppy began to display an unusual talent. He started howling along to the music, and soon he was jumping on the keyboard as well. "When customers came in," Cotterill says, "someone would make a noise on the piano and he would literally sing to that piano playing."
AFTERMATH: Dinky Di became the most popular attraction at the roadhouse, bringing in tourists from all over the country. In 2003 someone entered him in a nationwide contest held by Trivial Pursuit to become the subject of a question for the 20th anniversary edition of the game—and Dinky Di won. "We wanted to find Australia's most trivial person," says game spokesperson Amanda Blackhall. "We just didn't think it would end up being an animal."

Bestselling car of all time: the Toyota Corolla (over 32 million since 1966).

THE STELLA AWARDS

When Stella Liebeck's "hot coffee" suit against McDonald's made the news in 1994, many people mistakenly thought it was frivolous. It wasn't (see page 177). But it inspired Randy Cassingham's True Stella Awards, "honoring" ridiculous lawsuits. Here are some recent winners.

When Marcy Meckler left Chicago's Old Orchard Mall in 2004, a squirrel jumped out of a bush and attacked her leg. As she tried to shake the rodent loose, she fell onto the pavement, suffering cuts, scrapes, and bruises. Meckler sued the mall for $50,000, claiming the mall should have warned her that squirrels lived outside.

• Allen Heckard of Portland, Oregon, sued former NBA star Michael Jordan and Nike, for whom Jordan was an endorser, for a total of $832 million for emotional pain and suffering. Reason: Heckard says people mistake him for Jordan, causing him stress.

• In 2005 Robert Clymer of Las Vegas crashed his pickup truck while driving drunk. He sued the manufacturer of the truck and the used-car dealer from whom he bought it because he "somehow lost consciousness."

• In 2005 Barnard Lorence of Stuart, Florida, overdrew his bank account and incurred an overdraft charge. He then sued his bank for $2 million over the stress and lack of sleep he endured over the fee. (The fee was $32.)

• In 2004 Shawn Perkins got struck by lightning in the parking lot of Kings Island amusement park near Cincinnati, Ohio. Did he sue God for this "act of God?" No. Perkins sued Kings Island, claiming the park failed to warn him not to go outside during a thunderstorm.

• Michelle Knepper of Vancouver, Washington, called a dermatologist she found in the phone book about performing liposuction. After a consultation, she agreed to let him do the surgery. Sadly, he botched the job. Oddly, Knepper sued the telephone company. Why? Because the phone book ad didn't say that her doctor wasn't a board-certified plastic surgeon.

Hey! Get your own! Four Canadians have been featured on U.S. postage stamps.

THE STATE OF THE STATE OF THE UNION

Just how does the president check in with the people?

REPORT CARD
Even the authors of the United States Constitution thought that touching base was important. So they made that part of the president's job. Article II, Section 3 of the Constitution states: The president "shall from time to time give to the Congress Information of the State of the Union, and recommend to their Consideration such Measures as he shall judge necessary and expedient." In the 200-plus years since then, it's developed into an annual tradition—the TV broadcast, the joint session of Congress—that some of us watch and some of us don't. But over the years, the rituals surrounding the speech have changed. Here are a few firsts, records, and odd moments in the history of the State of the Union.

First address: In January 1790, just eight months into his first term, President George Washington delivered his address to a joint session of Congress at Federal Hall, New York City.

Shortest address: Washington's 1790 speech was also the shortest, coming in at only 833 words and clocking in at about six minutes.

Longest address: President Harry Truman's 1946 address was the longest, at more than 25,000 words. Truman, however, took pity on Congress by sending it over as a written message rather than delivering it in person.

First address in writing: In December 1801, Thomas Jefferson was the first president to send his address only as a written message to Congress. Subsequent presidents followed his example by mailing the speech for the next 112 years.

No address: William Henry Harrison (1841) and James A. Garfield

---

Don't believe us? Google it: A *googol* is the mathematical term for 1 followed by 100 zeros.

(1881) both died during their first year in office, before they could give the speech.

First modern address delivered in person: In 1913 Woodrow Wilson revived the practice of delivering the address in person before a joint session of Congress.

Only modern president never to give the speech in person: Herbert Hoover sent the address in written messages to Congress from 1930 to 1933.

First to call the speech the "State of the Union Address": Franklin D. Roosevelt, in 1935.

First to be broadcast on the radio: Calvin Coolidge's address in 1923.

First to be broadcast on television: Harry Truman's, in 1947.

First response by the opposition party: In 1966 television networks gave the Republican Party 30 minutes to respond to President Lyndon Johnson's State of the Union speech. One of the two selected speakers was Michigan representative and future president Gerald R. Ford.

First president to recognize members of the audience: In 1982 Ronald Reagan began the practice of presidents giving recognition to honored guests seated in the congressional gallery.

First address to be postponed: In 1986, when the space shuttle *Challenger* disaster occurred on the day that President Reagan was to deliver his address, the speech was rescheduled for the following week.

Most groundbreaking foreign policy mentioned: In his December 1823 message to Congress, President James Monroe spelled out his Monroe Doctrine—warning European nations not to challenge the United States in the Western Hemisphere. "The American continents…are henceforth not to be considered as subjects for future colonization by any European powers."

World's largest per-capita consumer of turkey: Israel.

Most memorable domestic policy mentioned: Lyndon B. Johnson spelled out the details of his Great Society programs in his State of the Union address in 1965. "The Great Society asks not how much, but how good; not only how to create wealth but how to use it; not only how fast we are going, but where we are headed."

Most eloquent: Abraham Lincoln's address given during the Civil War on December 1, 1862, was simple and powerful. It concluded:

> Fellow-citizens, we cannot escape history. We of this Congress and this Administration will be remembered in spite of ourselves...The fiery trial through which we pass will light us down in honor or dishonor to the latest generation...We, even we here, hold the power and bear the responsibility. In giving freedom to the slave we assure freedom to the free—honorable alike in what we give and what we preserve. We shall nobly save or meanly lose the last best hope of Earth. Other means may succeed; this could not fail. The way is plain, peaceful, generous, just—a way which if followed, the world will forever applaud and God must forever bless.

Weirdest: During Bill Clinton's 1997 address, the TV networks put Clinton on a split screen with the announcement of the verdict of the O. J. Simpson civil trial.

First to be broadcast live on the Internet: George W. Bush's speech in 2002.

*　　*　　*

BART'S BLACKBOARD

Every episode of The Simpsons *opens with Bart writing something on the blackboard. Some of our favorites:*

"Wedgies are unhealthy for children and other living things."

"I am not certified to remove asbestos."

"Nerve gas is not a toy."

"I will not hang donuts on my person."

"The Pledge of Allegiance does not end with 'Hail Satan'."

"I am not the reincarnation of Sammy Davis Jr."

"My butt does not deserve a Web site."

Q: Where was the Roman candle invented? A: China.

IT'S JUST SERENDIPITY...

The word "serendipity" means "making happy and unexpected discoveries by accident." It was coined by the English writer Horace Walpole, who took it from the title of an old fairy tale, "The 3 Princes of Serendip." The heroes in the story are always "making discoveries they are not in quest of." For example, it's just serendipity...

THAT BUBBLE GUM IS PINK

Background: In the 1920s, the Fleer Company of Philadelphia wanted to develop a bubble gum that didn't stick to people's faces. A 23-year-old employee, Walter Diemer, took the challenge. He started experimenting with different mixtures, and in a year, he had the answer. In 1928, the first workable batch of bubble gum was mixed up in the company mixing machines. "The machines started groaning, the mix started popping, and then I realized I'd forgotten to put any coloring in the gum," Diemer recalled.

Serendipity: The next day, he made a second batch. This time he remembered to color it. But the only color he could find was pink. "Pink was all I had at hand," he says. "And that's the reason ever since, all over the world, that bubble gum has been predominantly pink."

...THAT WE PLAY *BASKETBALL* INSTEAD OF BOXBALL

Background: When James Naismith invented his game in 1891, he decided to put a horizontal "goal" high over players' heads. He figured that would be safer—there would be no violent pushing and shoving as people tried to block the goal...and shots would be lobbed, not rocketed, at it.

Serendipity: As one historian writes: "The goal was supposed to be a box. Naismith asked the janitor for a couple of suitable boxes, and the janitor said he didn't have any...but he did have a couple of round peach baskets in the storeroom. So it was baskets that were tacked to the walls of the gym." A week later one of the players suggested, "Why not call it basketball?" The inventor answered: "We have a basket and a ball...that would be a good name for it."

The American goldfinch's nest is so thick-walled it will hold water....

...THAT MEL GIBSON GOT HIS BIG BREAK

Background: According to *The Good Luck Book*, "When director George Miller was looking for someone to play the male lead for his 1979 post-apocalyptic road movie *Mad Max*, he was specifically looking for someone who looked weary, beaten-up, and scarred.

Serendipity: "One of the many 'wannabes' who answered the cattle call for the part was a then-unknown Australian actor named Mel Gibson. It just so happened that the night before his scheduled screen test, Gibson was attacked and badly beaten up by three drunks. When he showed up for the audition the next morning looking like a prize fighter on a losing streak, Miller gave him the part. It launched Gibson's career as an international movie star in such films as *The Year of Living Dangerously*, *Lethal Weapon*, and the 1995 Oscar-winning *Braveheart*."

...THAT YELLOW PAGES ARE YELLOW

Background: The phone was invented in 1876, and the first Bell business directory came out in 1878. As we wrote in our *Ultimate Bathroom Reader*, it was printed on white paper. So were subsequent editions all over the country.

Serendipity: In 1881, the Wyoming Telephone and Telegraph Company hired a printer in Cheyenne to print its first business directory. He didn't have enough white paper to finish the job and didn't want to lose the company's business. So he used the stock he had on hand—yellow paper. Other companies around the country adopted it, too...not realizing it was an accident.

...THAT HOLLYWOOD STARS PUT THEIR PRINTS IN CEMENT AT GRAUMAN'S CHINESE THEATER

Background: In the early days of Hollywood, Sid Grauman's movie theater, fashioned after a Chinese pagoda, was the biggest and fanciest of its kind.

Serendipity: One day in 1927, movie star Norma Shearer accidentally stepped in wet cement as she walked in the courtyard of the theater. Rather than fill the prints in, Graumann got other stars to put their hand- and footprints in the cement. That turned it into one of Hollywood's biggest tourist attractions.

DO YOU *REALLY* NEED THAT ORGAN?

When a friend told Uncle John that she'd recently had her gallbladder removed, he wondered: What does a gallbladder do, and how can you live without it?

GALLBLADDER

Location: This four-inch pear-shaped sac sits just under the liver, below your ribs on your right side.

What It Does: It's part of the digestive system. The liver produces a substance called *bile*, which gets stored in the gallbladder before moving via a tube called the *duodenum* into the small intestine, where it digests fats.

Get It Out: The liver purifies the blood against toxins. If you eat too much cholesterol, the liver dumps some of it into the bile. During storage in the gallbladder, the cholesterol-bile sometimes hardens into gallstones: greenish, pain-causing lumps that can be as small as a grain of sand or as large as a golf ball. If the gallstones are really big and really hard, a doctor may opt to remove the entire gallbladder. But you can live without it—if you don't have a gallbladder, the liver delivers the bile directly to the duodenum.

TONSILS

Location: The almond-sized lymph nodes found on both sides of the throat.

What They Do: During infancy and childhood, tonsils prevent bacteria and viruses from entering the throat and produce antibodies to counter infections. By adulthood, your body's other defenses have fully developed, and your tonsils—now unnecessary—shrink and stop working.

Get Them Out: If an especially nasty bug goes around, a child's tonsils try to fight it off. They can end up getting so swollen and infected that swallowing becomes difficult, a condition called *tonsillitis*. Decades ago, it was cured by a tonsillectomy—surgical removal of the tonsils. The operation has become increasingly rare—75% fewer tonsillectomies are performed today than in 1970, owing to stronger antibiotics that can cure tonsillitis on their own.

Wheeeee! The first train reached a top speed of only 5 mph.

SPLEEN

Location: This purplish organ (it looks like a relaxed fist) lies under the diaphragm on the left side of your abdomen.

What It Does: As part of the immune and lymph system, the spleen is a blood filter: It produces and regulates the flow of red and white blood cells, which help to fight infectious bacteria and viruses.

Get It Out: If the spleen is ruptured (common in a severe physical trauma such as a car accident) it loses the ability to regulate, so it must be removed. This reduces the body's natural ability to fight infection, so doctors typically prescribe antibiotics, as well as immunization against flu and pneumonia.

THYROID

Location: The butterfly-shaped gland is located at the base of your neck, where it wraps around your windpipe.

What It Does: Part of the endocrine system, the thyroid disperses hormones that help regulate your body's metabolism.

Get It Out: *Hyperthyroidism* is an overactive thyroid and results in an unhealthily low weight. *Hypothyroidism*, an underactive thyroid, lowers the metabolism and, among other symptoms, frequently causes weight gain. Surgical removal of the thyroid is the treatment for the most severe cases of both conditions. Living without the thyroid is possible, but requires a lifetime regimen of oral medication.

APPENDIX

Location: The worm-shaped tube—about three inches long and one inch in diameter—is attached to your large intestine.

What It Does: Nothing—some scientists think it helped early humans digest animal bones, a need we've since evolved away from.

Get It Out: For unknown reasons, in some people the body deposits small amounts of waste in the appendix. Over time, the waste accumulates and causes the appendix to harden and swell (appendicitis) and even burst, an extremely painful and frequently life-threatening situation. The standard treatment is an appendectomy: the removal of the organ as quickly as possible. Life without an appendix proceeds perfectly normally.

NUMBER TWO'S
WILD RIDE

Uncle John feels a responsibility to "eliminate bathroom ignorance."
So for our Best of the Best of the Bathroom Reader, *we had to*
include the answer to the basic question: What happens after
you flush? (It's more complicated than you think.)

READY, SET, GO!

For you, the trip has ended. You've "done your business," (hopefully you've also had a few minutes of quality reading time), you've flushed the toilet, and you've moved onto the next thing.

But for your "business," a.k.a. organic solid waste, a.k.a. "Number Two," the trip is just beginning. Here's a general idea of what happens next.

CONNECTIONS

If you live in a rural area, your house is probably hooked up to a septic tank. We'll get to that later.

Before the 20th century, "sanitary systems" typically dumped raw sewage directly into rivers, streams, and oceans. Today, if you live in an urban area or a suburb, chances are your toilet and all of the water fixtures in your house—the sinks, showers, bathtubs, dishwasher, washing machine, etc.—are all hooked into a sewer system that feeds into a wastewater treatment plant. So the journey begins when Number Two mixes with all of the rest of the wastewater leaving your house. Then it enters the *sewer main* that runs down the center of your street (usually about six feet beneath the road surface), and mixes with the wastewater coming from the your neighbors' homes.

From there the sewer main probably joins with other sewer mains to form an even bigger sewer main. Depending on how far you are from the wastewater treatment plant, the sewer mains may repeatedly join together to form ever larger pipes. By the time you start getting close to the plant, the pipe could be large enough in diameter to drive a truck through.

Baby whales are born tail first.

PRIMARY TREATMENT

By now Number Two has a lot of company, especially if any storm drains feed into your community's system. Anything that can be swept into the the storm drains—old shoes, tree branches, cardboard boxes, dead animals, rusty shopping carts—is now heading through the giant pipes toward the treatment plant.

This floating garbage would destroy the equipment in the plant, so the first step is to remove it from the wastewater. This is accomplished by letting the water flow through a series of screens and vertical bars that trap the really large objects but let everything else—including Number Two—float through. The big stuff is then removed and disposed of, often in landfills.

THE NITTY GRITTY

Now the trip starts to get a little rough:

• The wastewater flows into a grinder called a *communitor*. The communitor is like a huge garbage disposal: It takes everything that's still in the water, Number Two included, and grinds it down into a sort of liquefied mulch that's easier to treat chemically and easier to remove. Number Two has now "become one," so to speak, with all the other solid matter still in the wastewater.

• Next this slurry flows into a *grit chamber*, where inorganic materials—stuff that can't rot, like sand, gravel, and silt—settle to the bottom of the chamber. Later, they're disposed of in a landfill.

• The wastewater then flows from the grit chamber into a closed *sedimentation tank*, where it is allowed to sit for a while so that the organic matter still in the water has a chance to settle to the bottom of the tank, where it can be removed.

• Have you ever dropped a raisin into a glass of 7-Up and watched the bubbles carry it to the top of the glass? So have the folks that design treatment plants. Some plants use a *flotation tank* instead of a sedimentation tank: They force pressurized air into the wastewater, then pump this mixture into an open tank, where the bubbles can rise to the surface. As they float up, the bubbles carry a lot of the organic matter to the surface with them (including what's left of poor Number Two), making it easier to skim from the surface and remove.

By the time the wastewater has been processed through the

What is *piperine*? The alkaloid in black pepper that makes you sneeze.

sedimentation tank or the flotation tank, as much as 75–80% of solid matter has been removed.

THE SLUDGE REPORT
So what happens to all of the organic solid matter (i.e., Number Two and all his friends) that has just been removed from the sedimentation tank? It gets turned into fertilizer.

• It goes into a *thickener*, where it's—you guessed it—thickened.

• Then it's fed into a closed anaerobic tank called a *digester*, where it's—right again—digested. Enzymes break down the solid matter into a *soluble* (dissolvable) form. Then acid-producing bacteria ferment it, breaking it down even further, into simple organic acids. Bacteria then turns these organic acids into methane and carbon dioxide gasses. The entire process of decomposition can take anywhere from 10 to 30 days, during which time it will reduce the mass of the organic matter by 45–60%.

• What's left of the digested sludge is pumped out onto sand beds, where it's allowed to dry. Some of the liquid in the sludge percolates down into the sand; the rest evaporates into the air. The dried organic material that's left can then be used as a soil conditioner or a fertilizer. (Moral of the story: wash your vegetables before you eat them.)

SECONDARY TREATMENT
That takes care of the organic matter—the part of the process known as *primary treatment*. Number Two's trip is now at an end. But what about the liquid in the sedimentation and flotation tanks? Taking care of that is known as *secondary treatment*:

• Some treatment plants pump the water through a *trickling filter*, where the water flows over a bed of porous material that's coated with a slimy film of microorganisms. The microorganisms break the organic matter down into carbon dioxide and water.

• Another process utilizes *activated sludge*—living sludge that is made up millions upon millions of bacteria cells. The wastewater is pumped into a tank containing the sludge, and the bacteria absorb any remaining organic matter.

• Finally, the wastewater is processed in something called a *secondary clarifier*, which removes the bacteria before they are discharged back into the environment.

• Some water treatment facilities don't use trickling filters or activated sludge, they just pump the water into a lagoon or a *stabilization pond*, where the water is allowed to sit while naturally occurring bacteria and other microorganisms do the same job on their own, only a little slower.

ADVANCED TREATMENT

Most wastewater that has received both primary and secondary treatment is considered safe enough to go back into the environment. But some water does require further treatment, especially if it is going to be reused by humans.

• Processes with such names as *reverse osmosis* and *electrodialysis* can remove "dissolved" solids—solids that can pass easily through other kinds of filters. Then the water is filtered and treated chemically to remove phosphorous, ammonia, nitrogen, and phosphates.

• If the water is going to be made safe for drinking, it is also treated with chlorine or disinfected by ozone.

That's it! The water is clean. (Uncle John wouldn't want to drink it, but that doesn't mean it isn't clean.)

DOWN-HOME FLUSHING

Not everyone is hooked up to a water treatment facility. If you live out in the country, you may be hooked up to a septic tank, which performs the same wastewater treatment functions, only more simply and naturally:

• The water from your toilets, bathtubs, showers, and sinks feed into a simple tank, usually made of concrete, cinder blocks, or metal.

• Solid matter settles to the bottom and the liquid remains on top.

• The liquid overflows into a system of underground trenches, often filled with rocks or gravel, where it can safely dissipate into the surrounding soil and biodegrade naturally.

• The solids settle at the bottom of the tank and break down organically. You can help the process along by adding special yeast and other treatments to the septic tank; if this isn't enough, it may have to be pumped out.

*　　*　　*

"Power corrupts. Absolute power is kind of neat."
—*John Lehman, US Secretary of the Navy*

MAKING *THE* GODFATHER, PART II

Is this part two of our story of the making of The Godfather: Part I...
or is it part one of our story of the making of The Godfather: Part II?
*Leave the gun. Take the cannoli. Read on and see for
yourself. (Part I is one page 138.)*

THE SALESMAN

If *The Godfather* had a shot at becoming a good movie, it was a very long shot indeed. Robert Evans, Paramount's vice president in charge of production, wasn't sure he wanted Francis Ford Coppola for the director's job, and Coppola was willing to do it only if he got a big enough budget to direct the film that *he* wanted to direct: a period piece, shot on location in the United States and Sicily, and faithful to the novel.

If you could boil Coppola's entire career down to the single moment that put him on the path to his future successes, it must have been the meeting he had with Evans and Stanley Jaffe, the president of Paramount, to win final approval to direct *The Godfather*. When producer Albert Ruddy picked Coppola up at the airport to take him to the meeting, he peppered the young director with all the arguments the studio heads were going to need to hear: He could finish the picture on time, he could keep within the budget, etc.

Coppola considered all this and then decided to go his own way.

REVERSAL OF FORTUNE

Rather than talk about schedules and finances, as soon as the meeting began, Coppola launched into a vivid and passionate description of the characters and the story as he thought they should be portrayed. "Ten minutes into the meeting he was up on the f*#$%ing table, giving one of the great sales jobs of all time for the film as *he* saw it," Ruddy told Harlan Lebo in *The Godfather Legacy*. "That was the first time I had ever seen the Francis the world got to know—a bigger-than-life character. They couldn't believe what they were hearing—it was phenomenal."

The average bank teller loses about $250 every year.

Evans and Jaffe were floored. "Francis made Billy Graham look like Don Knotts," Evans remembered. On the strength of that one meeting with Coppola, Evans and Jaffe abandoned the idea of a "quickie mobster flick," increased *The Godfather*'s budget to $6 million (it would later grow to $6.5 million), and announced that it would be Paramount's "big picture of 1971."

CASTING CALL

Getting Paramount to take *The Godfather* seriously would come at a price—now that the studio had so much money tied up in the film, it was determined to oversee every big decision. Take casting: Even when he was writing the novel, Mario Puzo had pictured Marlon Brando playing the Godfather, Don Corleone, and Coppola agreed that he was perfect for the part. Though he was widely considered one of the world's best actors, Brando had been in a rut for more than a decade; he had appeared in one money-losing film after another and had a reputation for being the most difficult actor in Hollywood. When he made his directorial debut in the 1961 film *One-Eyed Jacks*, his antics caused so many delays that production costs doubled and the film lost a bundle of money.

Paramount had produced *One Eyed Jacks*, and it wasn't about to make the same mistake again. "As long as I'm president of the studio," Jaffe told Coppola, "Marlon Brando will not be in this picture, and I will no longer allow you to discuss it." The studio wanted someone like Anthony Quinn to play the part; Ernest Borgnine was the Mafia's top pick for the job (according to FBI wiretaps). Rudy Vallee wanted the job; so did Danny Thomas. Mario Puzo remembered reading in the newspaper that Thomas wanted the part so badly that he was willing to buy Paramount to get it. The thought of that happening put Puzo into such a panic that he wrote Brando a letter begging him to take the part.

I'LL MAKE HIM AN OFFER HE CAN'T ACCEPT

Coppola was as determined to get Brando as Puzo was. He pushed Jaffe so hard, in fact, that Jaffe finally put him off by agreeing to "consider" Brando, but only if the World's Greatest Actor agreed to three conditions that Jaffe was certain he would never accept: Brando had to agree to work for much less money than usual, he had to pay for any production delays he caused out of his own pocket, and he had to submit to a screen test, something he *knew* Brando would see as a slap in the face.

MAKING THE MAN

Coppola gave in—what choice did he have? While all this was going on, Brando read both the book and the script and became interested in playing the part. Coppola didn't tell him about Jaffe's conditions; Coppola just asked if he could come over and film a "makeup test." Brando agreed.

At their meeting, Brando told Coppola he thought the Godfather should look "like a bulldog." He stuffed his cheeks with tissues, slouched a little, and feigned a tired expression on his face. Then he started mumbling dialog. That may not sound like much, but with these and other subtle techniques, the 47-year-old actor turned himself into an old Mafia don. The change was so complete that when Coppola brought Brando's test back to Paramount, Ruddy and the other studio executives didn't even realize it was him. The "makeup test" closed the deal—Brando not only *could* play Don Corleone, the executives decided, he *had* to play him.

GET SHORTY

Coppola also had someone in mind to play the character of the Don's youngest son, Michael Corleone. He'd recently seen a play called *Does the Tiger Wear a Necktie?*, a story about a psychotic killer, and he was convinced that the star of the play, 31-year-old Al Pacino, was just the guy for the part. Pacino was beginning to make a name for himself on Broadway, but he was still largely unknown to movie audiences.

Paramount wouldn't hear of it. Pacino was a nobody, the studio complained. The part of Michael Corleone was as big a part as Brando's, and studio wanted someone with star power to fill it. Pacino was too short, they argued. (He's about 5' 6" tall). The son of Sicilian immigrants, Pacino looked "too Italian" to play the son of a Sicilian mobster, the executives argued. Dustin Hoffman was interested, and names like Jack Nicholson, Warren Beatty, Ryan O'Neal, and even Robert Redford were also being tossed around. O'Neal and Redford didn't look anything like Italians, but they were big stars. Paramount figured they could pass as "northern Italians."

So how did Pacino land the role? Part III is on page 467.

Q: What is a *paleoscatologist?* A: An archeologist who studies ancient poop.

MAKE YOUR OWN ORIGAMI RUBBER DUCK

The Japanese art of folding paper, BRI style.

First, photocopy the pattern below onto a piece of yellow paper. Enlarging it 200% will fit it onto a standard 8½" x 11" sheet. Then cut along solid edges to make it a square. Now follow the folding steps on page 321. **Step 1:** Fold along the dashed lines as shown. **Steps 2–4:** Turn the paper over and fold under as shown. **Step 5:** Fold along the center crease, printed side out. **Steps 6–9:** Fold along the lines, then reverse the folds, pushing down while lifting up, making the tail, then the head, then the beak. Color the beak with an orange marker and *voilà*—you're done!

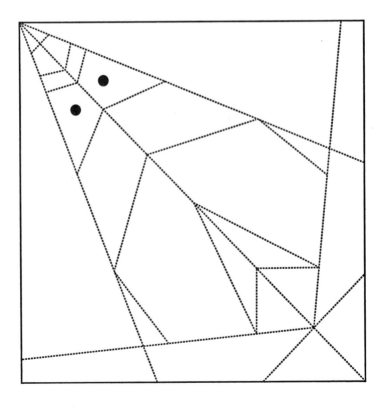

Homeland Security allotted Colchester, Vermont, $58,000 for a rescue vehicle designed to...

...bore into collapsed concrete buildings. (Colchester has no concrete buildings.)

TO THE LETTER

*Uncle John has given this page of Post Office
facts his stamp of approval.*

- The average stamp, when licked, has a tenth of a calorie.

- Stamp collecting is the most popular hobby in the world.

- The world's most-used public mailbox: at the intersection of Madison and Halsted streets in Chicago. It has to be emptied six times per day.

- First stamp design selected by vote of the U.S. public: the 1993 Elvis Presley 29¢ stamp.

- Every day the average mail carrier delivers 2,300 pieces of mail to more than 500 different addresses along his or her route.

- Zip code 12345 is assigned to General Electric in Schenectady, New York.

- For every post office in the United States, India has four.

- The islands of Antigua and Barbuda issued Elle Macpherson postage stamps in 1999.

- The U.S. Postal Service delivers more than 600 million pieces of mail a day.

- The glue on Israeli stamps is certified kosher.

- If you sent it before 1963, it didn't have a Zip code.

- Smokey the Bear has his own Zip code: 20252.

- Personal letters make up only two percent of the mail delivered by the United States Postal Service.

- Cost to mail a letter using the Pony Express: $5 per half ounce.

- Cost of mailing a letter more than 400 miles in 1816: 25¢ per letter sheet.

- The United States Postal Service handles about 46 percent of the world's mail.

- On September 26, 1970, John Kenmuir licked 393 stamps in a record four minutes.

WIDE WORLD OF WEIRD SPORTS

Tired of baseball, basketball, and football? Your worries are over—we've found some unusual alternatives for you.

CRICKET SPITTING
Where They Do It: At the Bug Bowl festival, held every April at Purdue University in Lafayette, Indiana
How It's Played: Thousands of contestants compete to see who can spit a dead, intact cricket the farthest. If the cricket loses its legs, wings, or antennae, the spit doesn't count. The world champion is Dan Capps, a mechanic at a meat-packing factory, who spit his cricket 32 feet in 1998. "It's just a matter of blowing hard," he says. "Crickets aren't very aerodynamic."

TOE WRESTLING
Where They Do It: England. The world championships are held each year in a bar in Derbyshire.
How It's Played: Rules are simple: Sit on the floor, with right foot down and left foot suspended in mid-air. Lock halluces (big toes). "Winner must force the top of the other person's foot down, similar to arm-wrestling." Note: Part of each player's bottom must always be touching the ground. According to the rules, "A player may, if the agony becomes too great, surrender by calling out the words 'Toe Much!'"

MAN VERSUS HORSE MARATHON
Where They Do It: Llanwrtyd Wells, Wales
How It's Played: Just like it sounds: people race horses, on the theory that given enough distance over twisting, uneven terrain, a man can run as fast as a horse. The 21.7-mile race (real marathons are 26.22 miles), which has been run each June for more than 25 years, grew out of a bar bet. Who won the bet? The guy who bet

---

In 1876 an English cricket player hit the ball 37 miles. (It landed on a moving railroad car.)

on the horses…at least until 2004, when a man named Huw Lobb beat 40 horses and 500 other runners to win first prize. (His time: 2 hours, 5 minutes, 19 seconds.)

REAL ALE WOBBLE

Where They Do It: Llanwrtyd Wells, Wales

How It's Played: It's a grueling 35-mile mountain bike race in the rugged terrain around Llanwrtyd Wells, with three checkpoint/watering stations along the route. The only difference between this race and a regular bike race is that the checkpoints put out cups of beer for the riders instead of water. (Bikers may consume no more than 1½ quarts of beer during the race, and if you're under 18 you need a parent's permission to enter.) "Beer gets down to the parts that you don't get down to with water," says race organizer Gordon Green. "It fortifies the cyclists."

UNDERWATER HOCKEY

Where They Do It: All over the United States

How It's Played: Teams of six players wearing fins, masks, snorkels, gloves, and helmets use 12-inch-long hockey sticks to push a puck across the bottom of a swimming pool. Most players can stay under water for about 20 seconds before they have to surface to breathe. The secret to winning is timing your snorkeling with your teammates so that you don't all swim to the surface at once, leaving the playing field wide open to the opposing team. Twenty-one teams competed in the 2005 U.S. Nationals in Minneapolis, Minnesota.

HUMAN TOWER BUILDING

Where They Do It: Barcelona, Spain, during the Festa de la Merce each September

How It's Played: Large groups climb one another to form human towers as tall as nine people high. Then, when they've stacked themselves as high as they can, a small child climbs all the way to the top to make it just a little bit taller. According to one account, "horrific collapses are common and many participants have ended up in the hospital."

LOST NAMES

When something's named after someone, we automatically assume it's an honor, and they're proud of it. But not always. Here are three examples of people who felt they'd lost their names…and wanted them back.

OLDSMOBILE

Named After: Ransom Eli Olds

How He Got It: In 1897 Olds formed a car company called the Olds MotorWorks in Lansing, Michigan. He didn't have enough money to go into production, so he gave Samuel L. Smith 95% of the Olds stock in exchange for working capital. In 1899, their factory burned down; the only thing left was one little buggy with a one-cylinder engine and a curved dashboard, called the "Oldsmobile." They concentrated all efforts on this model. It took off and became the first car in the world to be mass-produced.

How He Lost It: In the early 1900s, the "Merry Oldsmobile" was America's best-selling car. But Smith wanted to drop it to start producing a larger, heavier family car. When Olds angrily left the company to form the R.E. Olds Co., Smith sued for infringement, and won—Olds was never again allowed to use his own name in business. (He changed his company name to REO.)

SEATTLE, WASHINGTON

Named After: Chief Sealth

How He Got It: In the 1850s, Chief Sealth, a Suquamish Indian, was friendly to white settlers (who called him Seattle)—at least at first. The chief and his tribe traded flour and sugar to the whites for metal, cloth, guns, and tobacco. To make trading easier, Sealth encouraged Dr. David Maynard to open a store at the little settlement of Duwanmps. Maynard, in turn, suggested changing the name of the town to Seattle in honor of the friendly Indian chief.

How He Lost It: From Sealth's point of view this wasn't a compliment—it was an attack. It violated a tribal custom that forbade naming a place after a person who was still alive because it would offend his guardian spirit. When the townspeople refused to

---

Most popular names for U.S. high school sports teams: 1. Eagles; 2. Tigers.

change the name, Sealth asked the residents for gifts to repay him for problems that using his name would cause him in the next life. They refused that, too.

Ultimately, the Suquamish tribe was exiled from their homeland and driven onto the Port Madison Indian Reservation. Tourists can visit Chief Sealth's grave today on Bainbridge Island where the inscription on his tombstone, *I.H.S.*—Latin for "in this spirit"—was interpreted by his Indian kinsmen to stand for "I have suffered."

FAMOUS AMOS COOKIES

Named After: Wally Amos

How He Got It: Amos was a talent agent at the William Morris Agency who used home-baked chocolate chip cookies as a calling card (he found it put producers and executives at ease and in a good mood for negotiations). After awhile, some of his famous clients began encouraging him to sell the cookies. They even invested in the Famous Amos Cookie Company, which he started in 1975—making him one of the pioneers of the gourmet cookie trend. Sales of Famous Amos hit $12 million by 1982.

How He Lost It: His cookies were a success, but he was no manager, and his company started losing money. Amos had to bring in new money; from 1985 to 1988 he went through four different co-owners. Each time a change was made, Amos gave up more of his share of the pie (or cookie). By the time the Shanby Group bought it in 1988, Amos had nothing left; he even signed away his trademark rights. In 1992, when he started a new company called "Wally Amos Presents: Chip and Cookie," the Famous Amos Corp. sued him for infringement and libel.

After an acrimonious dispute, Wally Amos agreed not to use his own name or a caricature of himself on his cookies and not to badmouth the company that owns his name. Wally Amos then moved to Hawaii and started another cookie company called the "Uncle Noname Cookie Co."

*   *   *

"Names are not always what they seem. The common Welsh name Bzjxxllwcp is pronounced 'Jackson.'"

—Mark Twain

In 1862 Julia Ward Howe sold her "Battle Hymn of the Republic" to the *Atlantic Monthly* for $4.

MYTH-AMERICA

Some of the stories we recognize today as American myths were taught as history for many years. The truth might surprise you.

THE MYTH: The *Spirit of '76*, the famous painting showing a flag-carrier, a drummer, and a man playing a fife (flute), was inspired by an actual scene in the Revolutionary War.
THE TRUTH: It started off as a *Civil War* painting. Archibald Willard, a Civil War veteran himself, first painted a cartoonish version, depicting three imaginary war recruits parading around "in lighthearted fashion." It wasn't until a friend talked him into painting a more somber version that he added the revolutionary themes and gave the painting its now-famous name.

THE MYTH: Geronimo was the name of a famous Apache chief.
THE TRUTH: His name was actually Govathlay, which doesn't sound anything like Geronimo. Mexican settlers, who couldn't pronounce Govathlay, referred to the chief as "Jerome," or "Geronimo" in Spanish. And there's nothing in the historical record to suggest that Govathlay ever shouted "Geronimo!" as he jumped from a cliff into a river to escape the U.S. Cavalry. That scene was invented for a 1940 movie, which probably led directly to the legend. (World War II paratroopers *did*, however, frequently shout "Geronimo!" when they jumped out of planes.)

THE MYTH: Samuel Morse invented the telegraph in 1844.
THE TRUTH: Morse did invent Morse Code, but the telegraph itself was invented in 1831 by a Princeton University professor named Joseph Henry, who never bothered to patent it. Morse's telegraph was based largely on Henry's design. Morse "not only stole lavishly from Henry's original papers," Bill Bryson writes, "but when stuck would call on the eminent scientist for guidance. For years, Henry encouraged and assisted his efforts. Yet later, when Morse had grown immensely famous and rich, he refused to acknowledge even the slightest degree of debt to his mentor."

41% of Americans say they believe in extraterrestrials who are "much like ourselves."

SNUGL UP!

*Ann Moore made the world better for babies with
a lesson she learned from African mothers.*

VOLUNTEER OVERSEAS

In the 1960s, newlyweds Ann and Mike Moore traveled to Togo in West Africa as Peace Corps volunteers. Ann was a pediatric nurse who had taught at Columbia University and worked with refugees in East Germany and earthquake victims in Morocco. Well-educated and experienced, she was eager to share her information and expertise with mothers in a developing, poverty-stricken nation.

THE AFRICAN WAY

While Ann fulfilled her assignment teaching nutrition classes in Togo, she was surprised to find that the local women could have taught the industrialized world a thing or two when it came to raising children. African children and their mothers, she noticed, seemed to have a closer bond than most mothers and children did back in America.

Ann knew that back in the U.S., when a sick child had to go to the hospital, mother and child were separated and the medical staff took over, leaving the traumatized child alone with strangers. In Africa, mothers stayed at the hospital to be with their sick babies. Ann saw how comforting it was for suffering children to be able to rely on the presence of their mothers. And she felt that the closeness between mother and baby was of benefit to both.

Outside the hospital, Ann saw more examples of African mothers and babies staying physically close to each other. What most impressed her was the African mothers' custom of carrying their babies in fabric slings tied to their backs. In Togo, babies rarely cried and seemed remarkably contented compared to Western infants. Moore came to the conclusion that the babies were calm because being so close to their mothers made them feel secure.

IT'S NOT AS EASY AS IT LOOKS

Soon after their Peace Corps assignment was over and Ann and Mike returned to the United States, their daughter Mande was born. Wanting the best for Mande and remembering those contented Togo babies, Ann decided to carry her own daughter in a fabric sling. Unfortunately, it wasn't as easy as African mothers made it look. Mande kept slipping out of the sling.

But Ann's own mother was an excellent seamstress. She sewed a sling for her granddaughter according to Ann's design, and with Mande safely swaddled on her back, Ann (or Mike) could clean, cook, run errands, or enjoy a walk while keeping the baby close, comfortable, and secure. The Moores' baby carrier was based on an ancient idea, but it was totally new to Americans, and the soft carrier turned heads wherever they went.

Some observers warned the Moores that they were spoiling their daughter by allowing her to be constantly close to them. Mike and Ann explained their theory that making infants feel secure and loved helped create self-confident and independent children. Many loved the concept and wanted to know how to get a backpack of their own. As they began to produce more and more baby carriers for envious mothers, Mike and Ann began to feel they had a mission...and a business.

AMERICA STARTS SNUGLING

Soon Ann's mother was hiring friends to help her keep up with orders. Ann worked to improve the carrier with adjustable straps and a pouch to hold up the baby's head. Many moms wanted to be able to carry their babies on their chests, too, so Ann adapted the carrier for "front loading." By 1969 Ann had a patent on the Snugli carrier and by 1984 the company had sales of more than $6 million.

Ann's successful innovation and enterprise has brought her recognition—the *Wall Street Journal* named her one of the most influential inventors of the millennium. But she's been quick to stress that she adapted a centuries-old technique developed by African mothers. "They were really our inspiration, and it is so wonderful to think that we in America can have the same closeness with our babies."

THE WORLD'S WORST POET

Great poetry must be considered art—
It tickles the brain and stabs at the heart.
Could there be a worse poet than Uncle John?
It's all in the story that follows; read on.

ALL FIRED UP

One afternoon in June 1877, an impoverished Scottish weaver named William McGonagall fell into a funk. McGonagall was depressed because he wanted to escape the gritty industrial city of Dundee for a few days in the countryside, but he couldn't afford a train ticket. He was stuck at home, and to make matters worse, he was starting to feel a little funny. Was it a cold? The flu?

Hardly. As McGonagall later wrote in his autobiography, it was something else entirely: Divine Inspiration.

I seemed to feel as it were a strange kind of feeling stealing over me. A flame…seemed to kindle up my entire frame, along with a strong desire to write poetry. I began to pace backwards and forwards in the room, trying to shake off all thought of writing poetry; but the more I tried, the more strong the sensation became. It was so strong, I imagined that a pen was in my right hand, and a voice crying, "Write! Write!"

So McGonagall wrote. His first poem was a tribute to his friend, the Reverend George Gilfillan:

> The first time I heard him speak,
> 'Twas in the Kinnaird Hall,
> Lecturing on the Garibaldi movement,
> As loud as he could bawl.
>
> My blessing on his noble form,
> and on his lofty head,
> May all good angels guard him while he's living,
> And hereafter when he's dead.

Clawwk! A female lobster is called a *hen* or a *chicken*.

A BARD IS BORN

McGonagall showed the poem to Reverend Gilfillan, who remarked diplomatically, "Shakespeare never wrote anything like this!" Encouraged, McGonagall dropped a copy into the mailbox of the *Weekly News*, hoping they might print it. They did...and he was off on a new career.

McGonagall already had a reputation for being an eccentric: His impromptu performances of Shakespeare's plays at the factory where he worked were so bad they were funny, and his co-workers once rented a theater to watch him make a fool of himself alongside professional actors.

But it was McGonagall's poetry that cemented his fame as a local nut. He sold his poems on the street and gave readings at local pubs. And as with his Shakespeare performances, his readings were so funny that people rented halls and subsidized his performances just so they could laugh at his work. Unfortunately, they also pelted him with pies, wet towels, rotten eggs, and garbage while he read his poems. It got so bad that McGonagall refused to perform unless a clergyman sat next to him onstage to keep people from throwing things.

OUCH!

How did McGonagall cope with the abuse? Though his poetry was awful, he never doubted his own talent and refused to believe that his audiences were there to laugh at him. But it was so unrelenting that, by the early 1890s, McGonagall began threatening (in verse) to leave the city forever. Would he really leave? In 1892 the *Scottish Leader* speculated that "...when he discovers the full value of the circumstance that Dundee rhymes with 1893, he may be induced to reconsider his decision and stay for yet a year." McGonagall stayed until 1894, when he moved to Edinburgh. There he continued writing poetry until ill health forced him to lay down his pen forever. McGonagall passed away in 1902, at the age of 77, and was buried in an unmarked pauper's grave in Greyfriars Kirkyard. The grave remained unmarked until 1999, when the city of Edinburgh finally erected a plaque at the cemetery. The *Oxford Companion to English Literature* says he "enjoys a reputation as the world's worst poet," and more than a century after his death, his poems are still in print.

See for yourself: Virginia extends 95 miles farther west than West Virginia.

A MCGONAGALL SAMPLER

*So is William McGonagall the worst
poet ever? Here are selections from
his poetry to help you decide.*

ALAS! Sir John Ogilvy is dead,
  aged eighty-seven,
But I hope his soul is now in
  heaven;
He was a public benefactor in
  many ways,
Especially in erecting an asylum
  for imbecile children to spend
  their days.
      —*The Late Sir John Ogilvy*

And from the British battleships
  a fierce cannonade did boom;
And continued from six in the
  morning till two o'clock in the
  afternoon.
And by the 26th of July the guns
  of Fort Moro were destroyed
And the French and Spaniards
  were greatly annoyed.
      —*The Capture of Havana*

ALAS! Lord and Lady Dalhousie
  are dead, and buried at last,
Which causes many people to feel
  a little downcast.
      —*Death of Lord &*
      Lady Dalhousie

Ye sons of Great Britain, I think
  no shame
To write in praise of brave
  General Graham!
Whose name will be handed down
  to posterity without any stigma,
Because, at the battle of El-Teb,
  he defeated Osman Digna.
      —*The Battle of El-Teb*

Arabi's army was about seventy
  thousand in all,
And, virtually speaking, it wasn't
  very small.
      —*The Battle of Tel-el-Kebir*

Beautiful city of Glasgow,
  I now conclude my muse,
And to write in praise of thee
  my pen does not refuse;
And, without fear of contradic-
tion, I will venture to say
You are the second grandest city
  in Scotland at the present day!
      —*Glasgow*

The New Yorkers boast about
  their Brooklyn Bridge,
But in comparison to thee it
  seems like a midge.
      —*To the New Tay Bridge*

And when life's prospects may at
  times appear dreary to ye,
Remember Alois Senefelder, the
  discoverer of Lithography.
      —*The Sprig of Moss*

He told me at once what was
  ailing me;
He said I had been writing too
  much poetry,
And from writing poetry I would
  have to refrain,
Because I was suffering from
  inflammation of the brain.
      —*A Tribute to Dr. Murison*

The Roman poet Virgil spent the equivalent of $92,000 on a funeral for his pet fly.

THE "CRITIC'S CRITIC"

BRI trivia: In the bathroom of our office, you won't find a Bathroom Reader. *So what sits on our porcelain shelf? Two books of Roger Ebert's movie reviews. They make for great bathroom reading (especially when he doesn't like the film).*

"Vincent Gallo has put a curse on my colon and a hex on my prostate. He called me a 'fat pig' in the *New York Post* and told the *New York Observer* I have 'the physique of a slave-trader.' He is angry at me because I said his *The Brown Bunny* was the worst movie in the history of the Cannes Film Festival. It is true that I am fat, but one day I will be thin, and he will still be the director of *The Brown Bunny*."

"*Gone in 60 Seconds* is the kind of movie that ends up playing on the TV set over the bar in a better movie."

"Yes, I take notes during the movies. During a movie like *House of D*, I jot down words I think might be useful in the review. Peering now at my 3x5 cards, I read 'sappy,' 'inane,' 'cornball,' 'shameless,' and, my favorite, 'doofusoid.' I sigh. This film has not even inspired interesting adjectives, except for the one I made up myself."

"*Mr. Magoo* is a one-joke movie without the joke."

"*The Village* is so witless, in fact, that when we do discover the secret, we want to rewind the film so we don't know the secret anymore. And then keep on rewinding, and rewinding, until we're back at the beginning, and can get up from our seats and walk backward out of the theater and go down the up escalator and watch the money spring from the cash register into our pockets."

"I think the future of the Republic may depend on young audiences seeing more movies like *Whale Rider* and fewer movies like *Scooby-Doo 2*, but then that's just me."

"*Return to the Blue Lagoon* aspires to the soft-core porn achievements of the earlier film, but succeeds instead in creating a new genre, 'no-core porn.'"

"I hated this movie. Hated hated hated hated hated this movie. Hated it. Hated every simpering stupid vacant audience-insulting moment of it. Hated the sensibility that thought anyone would like it."
—*North*

"*Lake Placid* is the kind of movie that actors discuss in long, sad talks with their agents."

"I hope *Serendipity* never has a sequel, because Jon and Sara are destined to become the most boring married couple in history. For years to come, people at parties will be whispering, 'See that couple over there? The Tragers? Jon and Sara? Whatever you do, don't ask them how they met.'"

"I have often asked myself, 'What would it look like if the characters in a movie were animatronic puppets created by aliens with an imperfect mastery of human behavior?' Now I know."
—*Friends & Lovers*

"*Mad Dog Time* is the first movie I have seen that does not improve on the sight of a blank screen viewed for the same length of time."

"There is always the moment when the killer is unmasked and spews out his bitterness and hate and vindictive triumph over his would-be victims. How about just once, at the crucial moment, the killer gets squished under a ton of canned soup, and we never do find out who he was?"
—*Saw*

"This movie doesn't have a brain in its three pretty little heads."
—*Charlie's Angels*

"*Jack Frost* could have been co-directed by Orson Welles and Steven Spielberg and still be unwatchable, because of that damned snowman… Never have I disliked a movie character more…the most repulsive single creature in the history of special effects…To see the snowman is to dislike the snowman. It doesn't look like a snowman, anyway. It looks like a cheap snowman suit…It has a big, wide mouth that moves as if masticating Gummi Bears. And it's this kid's dad."

"If you, under any circumstances, see *Little Indian, Big City*, I will never let you read one of my reviews again."

THE SUICIDE SONG

"Gloomy Sunday" is a ballad that's been covered by dozens of performers, from Billie Holiday to Björk. But some say it's more than just a sad song... it actually causes people to kill themselves. Or is it all just a coincidence?

PIANO MAN

In 1933 Hungarian songwriter Rezso Seress was working as a piano player in a Budapest restaurant called Kispipa Véndegló. The 34-year-old was struggling to make it as a composer, but he hadn't published any songs yet.

Then his girlfriend dumped him—because, she said, he was always depressed about his dismal music career. Seress grew even more despondent about the break up, but he channeled his sadness into his songwriting. With the help of a lyricist named Laszlo Javor, Seress wrote a somber ballad called "Szomorú Vasárnap," or, in English, "Gloomy Sunday." The song was a lament about someone whose lover has died, leading the narrator to thoughts of suicide. Here's one translation:

Sunday is gloomy, my hours are slumberless.
Dearest, the shadows I live with are numberless.
Little white flowers will never awaken you,
Not where the black coach of sorrow has taken you.
Angels have no thought of ever returning you.
Would they be angry if I thought of joining you?
Gloomy Sunday.
Gloomy is Sunday; with shadows I spend it all.
My heart and I have decided to end it all.
Soon there'll be candles and prayers that are sad, I know.
Death is no dream, for in death I'm caressing you.
With the last breath of my soul I'll be blessing you.
Gloomy Sunday.

THE SONG REMAINS THE SAME

Seress added "Gloomy Sunday" to the repertoire of songs he played at the restaurant. Even though it had been gut-wrenching to write (and audience members were visibly saddened by it), Seress thought "Gloomy Sunday" was the best thing he'd ever written, and he made a serious effort to get it published by a sheet-music

---

Ouch! Hawaiians once used coconut husks for toilet paper.

company. (In Europe in the 1930s, records were available, but songs were far more popular as sheet music to be played at home on the piano.)

Seress sent the song to music publishers in Hungary, France, and England. They all turned him down, and all for the same reason. As one of the rejection letters said, "It's the terrible compelling despair about it. I don't think it would do anyone any good to hear a song like that."

Finally, in 1935, a music publisher agreed to release "Gloomy Sunday." The song became a moderate hit, providing Seress a modest income from the royalties. Things were beginning to look up.

IT'S GOT A GOOD BEAT AND YOU CAN DIE TO IT

According to the legend that has since sprung up around the song, trouble began in February 1936 when Budapest police investigated the first in a series of strange deaths. Joseph Keller, a shoemaker, was found dead with a suicide note consisting of the words "gloomy Sunday" and a request that his grave be decorated with 100 of the "little white roses" mentioned in the now-popular song. After Hungarian newspapers reported the connection between the suicide and the song, morbid curiosity made sales of "Gloomy Sunday" sheet music and recordings skyrocket.

But, eerily, so did the number of suicides allegedly related to the song:

• Two people were found in Budapest's Danube river, each clutching the sheet music of "Gloomy Sunday."

• As a band of Roma (Gypsy) street musicians performed the song, two people shot themselves.

• A man went into a nightclub and asked the band to play "Gloomy Sunday." They did, and he walked out into the street and shot himself.

• At a dinner party in a wealthy home, the song drifted from the party to the servants' quarters. Two maids heard the song and slashed each others' throats.

And, in perhaps the most bizarre twist, a Budapest woman who killed herself by drinking poison was later identified as Rezso Seress's ex-girlfriend—the inspiration for the song. Her suicide note consisted of two words: "Gloomy Sunday."

B.B. King named his guitar "Lucille" after nearly losing it in a fire...

After 18 suicides were supposedly linked to the song, Budapest police took action. They asked musicians, orchestras, and radio stations to stop playing the song and ordered stores to stop selling its sheet music and recordings, effectively banning the song.

But even the ban didn't stop the deadly effects of "Gloomy Sunday." Fueled by the controversy over what the press had begun to call "the Hungarian Suicide Song," "Gloomy Sunday" became a bestseller all over Europe. And in the next few months, it was linked to even more suicides, including a shopkeeper in Berlin who hung herself with the sheet music at her feet and a man in Rome who heard a beggar sing the song and then jumped off a bridge to his death.

ANARCHY IN THE U.K. (AND U.S.)

Curiosity about the song soon reached the United States, where a Hollywood songwriter named Sam M. Lewis composed an English translation (those are his lyrics at the start of this article). In 1936 the song was recorded by Hal Kemp and His Orchestra, one of the most popular bands of the era. It reportedly took 21 takes for them to cut the song because it upset the musicians. Unfortunately, the song's reputation had followed it from Europe, and an Ohio college student named Phillip Cooks reportedly became its latest victim: Accounts said that he listened to the song repeatedly, then took his own life in May 1936.

In 1941 Billie Holiday recorded the song—arguably the most famous version—which became a best seller in the United States and England. But her record label, fearful of more suicides, had hired Sam M. Lewis to add a third, more uplifting verse to the song. In it, the narrator says that the loss and despair were all just a dream, and that everything's actually great. The happy ending didn't help—later that year, a New York typist killed herself, leaving a request that Holiday's version of "Gloomy Sunday" be played at her funeral.

Because of all the hysteria over the song, BBC Radio in England would only play an instrumental version of "Gloomy Sunday." One day in 1941, a London policeman heard that version being played repeatedly from an apartment window. When he investigated, he found an automatic phonograph playing the

---

...started by two men fighting over a woman named Lucille.

record on repeat next to a dead woman holding an empty bottle of pills. After that, the BBC banned all versions of "Gloomy Sunday," a ban that stayed in effect until 2002.

MAYBE EUROPE IS JUST DEPRESSING

Ultimately, "Gloomy Sunday" was linked to nearly 100 suicides, a fact that troubled its songwriter, Rezso Seress, for years. He once told a reporter, "I stand in the midst of this deadly success as an accused man. This fatal fame hurts me. I cried all of the disappointments of my heart into this song and it seems that others with feelings like mine have found their own hurt in it." He never had another successful song, and became another "Gloomy Sunday" casualty when he jumped out of a Budapest window to his death in 1968.

It's been debated for years: Did people really kill themselves because one incredibly sad song destroyed their will to live? Some say no, and point out that Europe in the 1930s was not a happy place. World War II was well underway for many countries, and just around the corner for others. Fascism was on the rise, and economic depressions had crippled the continent.

And Hungary, the birthplace of the "Suicide Song," had one of the highest suicide rates in the world in the 1930s. (It still does, for reasons that would probably take an army of psychiatrists to figure out.) The song hit a sensitive nation in a sensitive spot, at just the right time. And the suicides never reached epidemic proportions in other countries—though, unfortunately, the song's reputation undoubtedly helped its sales. After the 1940s, no other suicides were linked to the song until 1997, when Scottish singer Billy Mackenzie took his own life. His band, the Associates, had recorded "Gloomy Sunday" several years earlier. It was a distant coincidence, but the Gloomy Sunday conspiracy theorists took note.

CODA

Today the song remains a favorite of musicians, both for its haunting lyrics and melody and for its dark legend. It's been covered dozens of times in recent years by artists including Ray Charles, Lou Rawls, Branford Marsalis, Marianne Faithfull, Björk, Sarah McLachlan, Sinead O'Connor, and Elvis Costello.

Longest entry in *The American Dictionary of Slang*: "vomit."

BUT WAIT!
THERE'S *STILL* MORE!

Here's Part II of the story of Ron Popeil. (Part I is on page 165.)

AMAZING SCIENTIFIC BREAKTHROUGH!
Ron Popeil wasn't particularly eager to follow in his father's footsteps—or even to be near him for that matter. Born in 1935, Ron's early childhood was spent in a boarding school (where his parents never visited). At age seven, he went to live with his grandparents, and didn't reunite with his father in Chicago until he was 16. At that point he was immediately put to work doing demonstrations of Popeil products at Sears and Woolworth's.

One day while at Chicago's Maxwell Street Marketplace, an outdoor bazaar, he had a revelation: Popeil suddenly felt he could convince total strangers to buy anything, if he were willing to give it his all. He realized he had to go into business for himself.

In 1951, at the age of 16, Popeil bought a gross of products—vegetable choppers and shoe shine kits—from his father (who sold them to Ron at normal supplier prices, making a full profit). The younger Popeil then set up a booth at the Maxwell Street market on a Sunday afternoon and hawked wildly. By the end of the day, his pockets were stuffed with cash.

He continued performing demonstrations for his father's company, set up permanently just inside the front door of Chicago's Woolworth's. At a time when the average American earned $500 a month, Popeil was making over $1,000 a week. In the summer, he even went on the county fair circuit. By dealing with customers one-on-one, he learned to anticipate what kind of objections or questions people might have to his products. Popeil honed his pitch, learning to answer those questions before they were even asked.

NOT AVAILABLE IN STORES!
In 1964 Ron Popeil went out on his own. He founded Ronco Teleproducts with his college roommate, Mel Korey. Rather than

---

The average American uses 25 barrels of oil per year. The average Japanese, about 15.

make their own products like the Popeil brothers did, Ronco contracted with other companies, avoiding the headaches and overhead of operating a factory. Popeil found a television station in Tampa, Florida, that charged $500 to produce an ad. (He made four: a 30-second, a 60-second, a 90-second, and a 120-second.) The product: the Ronco Spray Gun, a garden hose nozzle with a chamber inside to hold soap, car wax, fertilizer, or insecticide. The first commercial ran in Illinois and Wisconsin, near Popeil's Chicago base, to save shipping costs. They sold over a million Spray Guns.

Ronco's next success was London Aire Hosiery, women's nylon stockings "guaranteed in writing" not to run. Their durability was tested in the commercial, as they were subjected to a nail file, a scouring pad, and a lit cigarette. Ronco began manufacturing its own items in 1967 with the Cordless Power Scissors (they were battery-operated, but Popeil called them "cordless electric" to describe it and all future battery-operated Ronco products). All of the ads featured Ron Popeil himself. Doing his own ads saved on production costs, but it also made good business sense: Popeil had hawked so many items at fairs and stores that he was a natural salesman, and no one could sell his products better than him. He didn't even need a script. Ronco products earned $200,000 in 1964, its first year. By 1973 Ronco had annual sales of $20 million.

SUPPLIES ARE LIMITED!

Among the many Ronco gadgets of the 1970s:

• **Smokeless Ashtray** (1970). An ashtray with a cylinder above it, which houses a "cordless electric" filtering fan.

• **Pocket Fisherman** (1972). A portable, retractable fishing rod.

• **Presco-Lator** (1976). A plastic version of a French press–style coffeemaker. It bombed because it hit the market at the same time as the Mr. Coffee coffeemaker.

• **Mr. Microphone** (1978). A wireless transmitter inside a microphone. It broadcast the user's voice to any properly tuned FM radio up to 100 feet away.

• **Inside-the-Shell Egg Scrambler** (1978). An egg is impaled on the device's needle. The needle spins inside the shell to create a perfectly blended egg without having to use a mixing bowl.

- **Sit-On Trash Compactor** (1978). It worked without electricity: the user sat on a plunging platform that squished the garbage.

- **Food Dehydrator** (1979). A product of the health food craze of the 1970s, it made fruit leather, beef jerky, banana chips, and yogurt.

OPERATORS ARE STANDING BY!

But in the early 1980s, Ronco started falling apart. From 1982 to June 1983, sales dropped 31 percent. And that same year one of their biggest retailers—Woolco—closed all its stores. Then in a few months, claiming they were owed $2 million, three companies that made products for Ronco filed suit in bankruptcy court to force Ronco to sell off its assets and pay its debts. But Ronco also owed $8 million to First National Bank of Chicago and Wells Fargo Bank. (Business was so bad, Ronco had been operating on credit.) Popeil had no choice but to declare Ronco bankrupt.

The banks planned to auction off Ronco's assets, but before they could, Popeil offered $2 million of his own money to buy the company back. The banks refused and held the auction, but got a high bid of only $1.2 million, so they sold it back to Ron Popeil, who spent the next year doing what he'd done as a teenager: in-person demonstrations at department stores and county fairs.

EASY PAYMENT PLAN

The story might have ended there. But in 1984, the same year Popeil filed for bankruptcy, the FCC deregulated TV advertising. Ads no longer had to be under two minutes in length, which gave birth to a new form of advertising: the infomercial. Suddenly, products that had relied on rapid-fire pitches in short commercials (kitchen gadgets, exercise equipment, car waxes) were being pitched in half-hour advertisements designed to look like real TV programs. Broadcast and cable networks used infomercials to fill holes in their schedules, usually late at night and on weekends.

When Ginsu knives became the first major product sold this way (over $50 million in sales), Popeil realized the way to rebuild Ronco was through infomercials. "The longer you have to talk, the better chance you have of selling something," Popeil said in 1985. He went into semi-retirement in 1987, leaving day-to-day operation to others while he continued the role of TV pitchman.

Beginning with a redesigned Food Dehydrator in the early 1990s, Ronco has used infomercials exclusively. One product sold was GLH Formula #9, an aerosol can of hair-thickening powder, better known as "hair in a can" (Popeil sprayed it on his own bald spots in the infomercial). Another was the Showtime Rotisserie, a compact countertop rotisserie cooker. Popeil calls it his best invention and has sold three million units to date. But unlike the early days, Popeil now sells only items he's personally developed. "I'm an inventor first and a marketer second," he says. "Other people in our business take the spaghetti approach. They throw a lot of stuff against the wall and hope something sticks."

*   *   *

CON LETTER

An old man lived alone in the country. He wanted to plant a tomato garden, but it was difficult work, and his only son, Vincent, who used to help him, was in prison. The old man described the predicament in a letter to his son.

> Dear Vincent,
> I'm feeling bad. It looks like I won't be able to put in my tomatoes this year. I'm just too old to be digging up a garden. I wish you were here to dig it for me.
> Love, Dad

A few days later he received a letter from his son.

> Dear Dad,
> Sorry I'm not there to help, but whatever you do, don't dig up that garden. That's where I buried the BODIES.
> Love, Vincent

At 4 a.m. the next morning, FBI agents and local police arrived and dug up the entire area without finding any bodies. They apologized to the old man and left. That same day the old man received another letter from his son.

> Dear Dad,
> Go ahead and plant the tomatoes now. That's the best I could do under the circumstances.
> Love, Vinnie

Most popular flowers grown in American gardens: Sunflowers, zinnias, and impatiens.

A SEAWORTHY DESK FOR THE PRESIDENT

*The story of how a British ship made it
all the way to the Oval Office.*

JOHN-JOHN'S HOUSE

Many people remember the famous photo of young John Kennedy, Jr., in the Oval Office peeking out beneath a desk as his father, the president, works above. But less well known is the fact that the desk John-John called "My House" started out as a British ship on her majesty's seafaring service.

RESOLUTE RESCUE

In 1854 the HMS *Resolute,* a British vessel, became hopelessly trapped in Arctic ice. Surviving crew members were forced to abandon ship, but the *Resolute* stayed stuck in the ice for a year. An American whaler, the *George Henry,* was eventually able to free the *Resolute* from the ice and tow it to a port. In a gesture of international friendship, the ship was repaired and returned to Queen Victoria by President Franklin Pierce on behalf of the American people. The *Resolute* then served the British navy for nearly two decades. When the ship was decommissioned, Queen Victoria ordered that it be broken up, and some of its oak timbers were then used to make a beautiful, elaborately carved desk. Queen Victoria presented the desk to President Rutherford B. Hayes in a return gesture of goodwill between Great Britain and the United States.

Many presidents used the *Resolute* desk throughout the years. Franklin D. Roosevelt admired it, but didn't like how the open panel in the front allowed his lower body to be exposed. He ordered the kneehole to be covered with a wooden cap bearing the presidential coat of arms, reportedly to shield the braces on his legs from visitors and reporters.

When First Lady Jacqueline Kennedy embarked on a historical redecoration of the White House during the first year of her husband's administration, she discovered the historic desk with

---

Gerald R. Ford once worked as a fashion model.

Queen Victoria's original brass plaque that explained the *Resolute*'s history still attached. Mrs. Kennedy had the desk refinished and brought to the Oval Office, where she made it the centerpiece of the room. President Kennedy used it throughout his administration, along with a specially made chair to ease his chronic back pain.

Jimmy Carter loaned the desk to the Smithsonian Institution to display for a time, so the public could see and enjoy it. Ronald Reagan brought it back to the White House, but had it raised by two inches to accommodate his 6'2" frame. George H. W. Bush preferred an even larger desk and moved the piece to a private study. But George W. Bush used the Resolute desk in the Oval Office, where his predecessor Bill Clinton had returned it.

PANIC ATTACK

At some undisclosed point in time, a "panic button" was installed so the president could summon Secret Service agents in case of an emergency. The button is located at about knee level on the desk…at a height just perfect for accidental brushings. A common experience for a new president is to be startled by a rushing brigade of agents after he's inadvertently pushed the button with his leg.

*   *   *

ODD PRESIDENTIAL BEHAVIOR

- Ulysses S. Grant began each day with a breakfast of cucumber soaked in vinegar.

- Chester A. Arthur owned over 80 pairs of pants, and changed his clothes several times during the day.

- Abraham Lincoln often stored important papers inside his stovepipe hat.

- Calvin Coolidge's family communicated in sign language when they were afraid of being overheard. Herbert Hoover's family spoke in Chinese for the same reason.

JUST PLANE WEIRD

If you bought this book in an airport, you might want to skip reading this chapter until your flight is over and you're safely back on the ground.

J UICED
During the landing phase of Aeroflot Flight #2315 on May 9, 1994, over Arkhangelsk, Russia, loss of hydraulic fluid caused the landing gear system to fail; the right leg of the plane would not come down. In desperation, the crew poured every beverage they could find into the hydraulic system—soda, water, wine, milk, juice, beer, and liquor. That made it possible for the crew to lower the gear, but only partway. When the plane landed, it veered to the right and went off the side of the runway, but a serious crash had been avoided. (According to experts, in an emergency any fluid will help—even urine.)

"MR. KOTIADIS IS ON THE LINE FOR YOU."

On November 21, 2000, a Greek businessman named Nikita Kotiadis was arrested at Athens airport after phoning in a bomb threat on his own flight. Reason: Kotiadis was running late, and he wanted to delay the flight from taking off until he could get to the airport. He might have gotten away with it if he'd dialed the airport himself, but he had his secretary call, and she identified him by name before putting him on the line. Kotiadis made his threat and then raced for the airport, where he was arrested on the spot. He was later sentenced to seven months in prison for "obstructing transportation."

BLINDED BY THE LIGHT

On October 30, 1995, a Southwest Airlines flight was climbing after takeoff from McCarran International Airport in Las Vegas when a blinding beam of light swept into the cockpit. The first officer, who was piloting the aircraft, was completely blinded for 30 seconds. For another two minutes he suffered flash blindness in the right eye and after-image effects in his left eye. He was unable to focus or interpret any of the instrument readings and was "completely disoriented."

Gary Trench of Arizona once sleepwalked to work and packed toys for 3 hours before waking up.

The source of the beam: an outdoor laser light show at one of the Vegas hotels. But because so many hotels entertain guests with nightly light shows, it was impossible to determine which one was responsible. The captain (who was not affected) took over the controls until the first officer recovered.

WHERE THERE'S SMOKE...

While taxiing for takeoff in Detroit, Michigan, in April 1986, a TWA passenger saw some mist coming out of the plane's air vents. It was nothing abnormal, just condensation from an overheated air conditioner pack. But the passenger, believing that the plane was on fire, panicked and shouted, "Open the door!" The lead flight attendant responded to the emergency orders (which she thought came from the cockpit) and opened an exit door. Passengers sitting near exit doors also prepared for evacuation by opening *their* doors. Fortunately, the plane was still on the ground—21 passengers jumped off before the captain could intervene.

DYING TO FLY FIRST CLASS

On November 28, 2006, a British Airways flight took off from London headed to Boston. Three hours into the six-hour flight, a 75-year-old American passenger in business class suffered a massive heart attack. Calls for a doctor were made, there was a commotion among the flight attendants, but to no avail—a few minutes later, the man was dead. Now the question was: what to do with the body for the rest of the flight? Business class was full. So was coach. There were, however, a few empty rows in first class. Solution: move the body to first class.

Not surprisingly, this plan didn't go down well with the first-class passengers, who watched in horror as four flight attendants carried the body to an empty row. They put the man in a seat, reclined it, fastened the seatbelt, and put a blanket over his body...but not over his head, which flopped to one side. "It was a very strange and unsettling thing to experience," said one passenger, who had until then been enjoying the inflight movie, *Mission Impossible III*, when the corpse was placed across the aisle from him. Another passenger told reporters, "I felt quite uneasy. But most of the passengers were being very British about it and simply not acknowledging that there was anything wrong."

GIVES YOU STRONG MOUTH AND REFRESHING WIND

In Japan, English words are "cool"—it doesn't even matter whether they make sense, which is why they're so funny. Here are some actual English phrases found on Japanese products.

On Fresh Brand Straws: Let's try homeparty fashionably and have a joyful chat with nice fellow. Fujinami's straw will produce you young party happily and exceedingly.

Warning on a toy box: A dangerous toy. This toy is being made for the extreme priority the good looks. The little part which suffocates when the sharp part which gets hurt is swallowed is contained generously.

On Koeda brand chocolate-covered pretzels: The sentimental taste is cozy for the heroines in the town.

On a fondue set: When all family members are seated around the table, dishes are all the more tasteful. If dishes are nice, the square ceiling becomes round.

Advertisement for a restaurant: No one really goes to Aqua Bar for the drinks, but we make sure our drinks won't kill you.

On a paper coffee cup: The Art of Hot. Side by side, I'll be yours forever. Because please don't weep.

Sign for Café Miami: We established a fine coffee. What everybody can say TASTY! It's fresh, so-mild. With some special coffee's bitter and sourtaste. "LET'S HAVE SUCH A COFFEE! NOW!" is our selling copy. Please love Café Miami.

On a coat label: Have a good time! Refreshed and foppish sense and comfortable and fresh styles will catch you who belong to city-groups. All the way.

Good thing they're hauling gas: Giant oil tankers get about 31 feet per gallon.

On a package of prawn-flavored crackers: Once you have opened the packing it will be entirely impossible for you to suppress the desire to overcome such exciting challenge of your tongue. However, don't be disappointed with your repeated failure, you may continue with your habit.

In a Honda repair manual: No touching earth wire, fatal eventuarity may incur.

On a toothbrush box: Gives you strong mouth and refreshing wind!

On a package of bath salts: Humanity are fighting against tired. Charley support you.

On a washing machine: Push button. Foam coming plenty. Big Noise. Finish.

On the front of a datebook: Have a smell of panda droppings. This one is very fragrant.

On children's play microphone: Mom ma! Pap Pap! I and Lady Employees to play with it together!

On a photo developing envelope: Takes the thirst out of everyday time. A pure whiff of oxygen, painting over a monochrome world in primary colors. We all know that. It's why everyone loves fruit.

*   *   *

THE WRITING'S ON THE WALL

In Pompeii, the Roman city buried by a volcanic eruption in 79 A.D., the walls of many buildings were used as billboards on which anyone was allowed to write whatever they wanted. When the city was excavated, archaeologists found notices of upcoming plays at the theater, the schedule of games at the stadium, the price of goods in the market, and the comments of passersby. One message declared, "Everybody writes on walls but me."

The elections in Pompeii were coming up when the city was destroyed, so thousands of political ads were found, including this one: "Vote for Vatia, who is recommended by sneak thieves, the whole company of late drinkers, and everyone who is fast asleep."

Pigeons have three sets of eyelids.

PEANUTS, PART II

On page 157 we told you about the beginning of Charles Schulz's comic-strip career. Now watch as his creation takes the nation by storm.

AN UNDIGNIFIED NAME

Schulz wanted to keep the name *Li'l Folks*, but because there was already a comic called *Li'l Abner* and another called *Little Folks*, the syndicate chose a new name: *Peanuts*. Schulz hated it. "It's totally ridiculous," he said. "It has no meaning, is simply confusing, and has no dignity. And I think my humor has dignity." Nevertheless, on October 2, 1950, the first *Peanuts* strip appeared in seven newspapers. Originally, there were four main characters: Charlie Brown, his dog Snoopy, a girl named Patty, and a boy named Shermy. Back then, Charlie Brown was more of a wisecracker than a loser, and he wasn't intended to be the star of the strip. But because Shermy didn't have much of a personality and Patty was just plain mean, Charlie Brown got the best lines, becoming the protagonist by default.

Over the next three years, Shermy and Patty's roles got smaller, and two new characters—Linus and Lucy—were added to the strip. Within a year, Linus became Charlie Brown's friend and Lucy became his foil. This really opened up ideas for Schulz, especially with the addition of a Sunday strip in 1952. The now-familiar themes of the baseball team always losing and Lucy pulling the football away really struck a chord with readers...*and* newspaper editors. By 1953 *Peanuts* had expanded to over 40 newspapers, and Schulz's original salary of $90 per week had grown to $30,000 per year.

BREAKING OUT

Interestingly, it was the limitations of the format that led Schulz to focus on more character-oriented storylines. Bill Watterson, creator of *Calvin & Hobbes*, explained what Schulz was up against:

> Back when the comics were printed large enough that they could accommodate detailed, elaborate drawings, *Peanuts* was launched with a tiny format, designed so the panels could be stacked vertically if an editor wanted to run it in a single column. Schulz somehow turned this oppressive space restriction to his advantage, and

developed a brilliant graphic shorthand and stylistic economy, innovations unrecognizable now that all comics are tiny and Schulz's solutions have been universally imitated.

Schulz distilled each subject to its barest essence, and drew it straight-on or in side view, in simple outlines. But while the simplicity of Schulz's drawings made the strip stand out from the rest, it was the expressiveness within the simplicity that made Schulz's artwork so forceful.

That "expressiveness within the simplicity" made Schulz a huge hit not only with readers, but with his contemporaries as well. In 1955 the National Cartoonists Society gave Schulz the Reuben Award for "Outstanding Cartoonist of the Year." And that was only the first of many: He won the Yale Humor Award in 1956 and the School Bell Award from the National Education Association in 1960. In 1962 *Peanuts* was named "Best Humor Strip of the Year" by the National Cartoonists Society. Two years later, Schulz became the first comic-strip artist in history to win two Reuben Awards. In 1978 more than 700 cartoonists from around the world cast their votes and named Schulz "International Cartoonist of the Year."

FAMILY MAN

Meanwhile, as *Peanuts* grew in popularity, Schulz maintained a low-key lifestyle, not flaunting his riches. In 1958, at the urging of his wife, Schulz moved his family to Sebastopol, California, where he built his first studio. He made it a goal to only work from about 9 a.m. to 4 p.m. on weekdays so he could have enough time to raise his five children. That alone provided most of the "research" that he'd need to add new characters and storylines to the strip; what Schulz didn't mine from his own childhood, he mined from his children—and later from his grandchildren.

But when it was time to work, he worked. Unlike other comic-strip artists who hired a consortium to letter, color, or even draw their strips, Schulz insisted on doing every aspect of the work himself. And his process was always the same: He began with a script idea, then drew rough sketches of the scenes. Then he worked painstakingly on the wording—getting it to flow perfectly before he finalized the characters and the background.

This attention to detail in such a "simply drawn" strip added to

---

Odd fact: The average female opossum has 13 nipples.

the realism—readers felt they *knew* Charlie Brown and Snoopy. It soon became obvious that they couldn't remain confined to the borders of a newspaper comic strip for long.

PEANUTS NATION

Books were the first crossover *Peanuts* products, starting in 1952 with a hardcover collection of cartoons called *Peanuts*. No one had ever released a book of comic strips before, but it sold well enough for a second collection, called *More Peanuts*, in 1954. After that came *Good Grief, More Peanuts!* (1956), *Good Ol' Charlie Brown* (1957), and so on. Over the years, there have been hundreds of *Peanuts* collections. In fact, the abundant comic-strip books we see today owes their origins to Schulz, who almost single-handedly launched this publishing phenomenon.

For the strip's first seven years, Schulz was reluctant to give in to the many marketing opportunities presented to him. "I never even thought about licensing; all I thought about was just trying to draw the strip. But I realized this is a business, and I knew it was possible to make a lot of money at it." In 1958 Schulz finally agreed to a request from Hungerford Plastics to release a set of *Peanuts* dolls. They created six plastic characters depicting Charlie Brown and his friends, which sold very well. Over the next 15 years, fans could buy everything from Snoopy plush dolls to Charlie Brown lunch boxes to Linus wristwatches to bedsheets, T-shirts, and hundreds of other items. By 1999, there were 20,000 *Peanuts*-related products per year. While Schulz had no problem with the saturation of his characters in popular culture, he did maintain the final say over what *couldn't* be produced. Among the products he rejected: *Peanuts* ashtrays, vitamins, sugary breakfast cereals, tennis rackets, and baby wipes (for "aesthetic" reasons).

AND NOW FOR A WORD FROM OUR SPONSOR

Advertisers also understood the appeal, and many approached United Features, but Schulz relented only on a few. Kodak was the first to use *Peanuts*, placing the popular characters in their 1955 camera instruction books. In 1961 the Ford Motor Company ran a huge promotion that featured the *Peanuts* gang boasting about how economical and safe the new line of Ford Falcons were. "We got criticized quite a bit for that," Schulz recalled years later,

---

Wow! In 1986 the city of Hamilton, Ohio, changed its name to Hamilton!, Ohio.

"which is something that always puzzled me." After Ford, the *Peanuts* kids spent 15 years selling Metropolitan Life Insurance. "We also received criticism for that. A lot of people apparently hate insurance companies. Maybe they're justified."

THE BEAGLE HAS LANDED

The 1960s belonged to *Peanuts*. The optimism of the 1950s had been diminished by the looming threat of a nuclear war with the USSR, and people were scared. That may explain the appeal of *Happiness Is a Warm Puppy*, the first in a series of little square-shaped books that featured each of the *Peanuts* characters celebrating the simple things in life. In 1963 *Happiness Is a Warm Puppy* became the first book based on a comic strip to reach the *New York Times* bestseller list. And as the public mood grew even darker following the assassination of President Kennedy and the escalation of the Vietnam War, *Peanuts* became more popular, treading a thin line between innocence (the kids still play ball in the sandlot) and rebellion (a bird complains to Snoopy that no one understands his generation). Basically, *Peanuts* was *everywhere*.

• In 1965 the *Peanuts* gang made the cover of *Time* magazine.

• That same year, a Presbyterian minister named Robert Short received Schulz's permission to write *The Gospel According to Peanuts*, which presented strips from the comic as modern-day Christian parables. The book sold more than 10 million copies.

• In 1966 a rock group called the Royal Guardsmen sold three million copies of their song "Snoopy and the Red Baron."

• In 1967 *Peanuts* made their off-Broadway debut with the musical *You're a Good Man, Charlie Brown* (starring as Charlie Brown: 22-year-old Gary Burghoff, who later played Radar on M*A*S*H). The musical ran for 1,597 performances and was revived on Broadway in 1998, when it won two Tony Awards.

But perhaps the *Peanuts* kids' greatest achievement in the 1960s was when they accompanied the *Apollo 10* astronauts to the Moon in May 1969. The crew chose Snoopy as its official mascot and named the lunar module after him. The command module was called *Charlie Brown*.

For part III of the Peanuts *story, turn to page 461.*

Aloha-ho-ho! *Kanakaloka* is the Hawaiian word for Santa Claus.

REAL TOYS OF THE CIA

Uncle John loves those clever spy gadgets in the James Bond movies devised by Q. It turns out that some of them are real. Here are a few actual spy tools.

IT LOOKS LIKE: A cigarette
BUT IT'S REALLY: A .22-caliber gun
DESCRIPTION: This brand of cigarette packs a powerful puff. Intended as an escape tool, the weapon only carries a single round, but with good aim it can inflict a lethal wound from close range. To fire the cigarette, the operator must twist the filtered end counterclockwise, then squeeze the same end between the thumb and forefinger. Warning: Don't shoot the weapon in front of your face or body—it has a nasty recoil.

IT LOOKS LIKE: A pencil
BUT IT'S REALLY: A .22-caliber pistol
DESCRIPTION: Like the cigarette gun, this camouflaged .22 comes preloaded with a single shot. The weapon is fired in the same manner as the cigarette: simply turn the pencil's eraser counter-clockwise and squeeze. The only difference between the weapons is that the pencil has a greater firing distance—up to 30 feet.

IT LOOKS LIKE: A belt buckle
BUT IT'S REALLY: A hacksaw
DESCRIPTION: Fitted inside a hollow belt buckle is a miniature hacksaw. When the buckle is opened, a small amount of pressure is released from the saw's frame, exerting tension on the blade. This makes the saw a more efficient cutting machine, keeping the blade taut when sawing through, for example, handcuffs. The belt buckle saw will cut through anything from steel to concrete in about 15 minutes and will tear through rope and nylon. Don't wear belts? Buckles can be put on coats and luggage, too.

IT LOOKS LIKE: Eyeglasses
BUT IT'S REALLY: A dagger
DESCRIPTION: Concealed in the temple arms of these CIA

A one-day weather forecast requires about 10 billion mathematical calculations.

glasses are two sharp blades. Disguised as the reinforcing wire found in most eyeglass frames, the daggers are designed to be used once and broken off at the hilt, inside the victim. The lenses are cutting tools, too. The lower edges are ground to razor sharpness and can be removed by heating or breaking the frames.

IT LOOKS LIKE: A felt-tip marker
BUT IT'S REALLY: A blister-causing weapon
DESCRIPTION: Don't mistake this pen for your Sharpie, and be careful: you wouldn't want it leaking in your pocket. A little over three inches long, the marker distributes an ointment that creates blisters on the skin. In order to activate the applicator, press the tip down on a surface for one minute—then simply apply a thin coating of the colorless oil over any area, such as a keyboard or door handle. The ointment will penetrate clothing and even shoes, and will cause temporary blindness if it comes in contact with the eyes. Blisters will cover the skin wherever contact is made within 24 hours and will last for about a week.

IT LOOKS LIKE: Dentures
BUT IT'S REALLY: A concealment device (and much more)
DESCRIPTION: What could possibly fit inside a dental plate? A lot more than you'd think. Items such as a cutting wire or a compass can be placed in a small concealment tube and hidden under a false tooth. A rubber-coated poison pill can be carried in the same manner. The poison can either be ingested to avoid capture or poured into an enemy's food and utilized as a weapon. Radio transceivers can be placed in dental plates, with audio being transmitted through bone conduction. The CIA has even created a dental plate that alters the sound of one's voice. If all of these gadgets prove ineffective, then the dental plate itself can be removed and its sharp scalloped edge used for digging, cutting, or engaging in hand-to-hand combat.

* * *

James Bond: "They always said, 'The pen is mightier than the sword.'"
Q: "Thanks to me, they were right."
                                                            —Goldeneye

---

"Q" stands for *quartermaster,* a military name for the officer in charge of supplies.

THE KING OF KETCHUP

Richard Nixon smothered cottage cheese with it; Japanese eat it on rice; and one ice-cream manufacturer tried to make it a flavor. Here's the story of the man whose name became synonymous with a condiment so popular that it's found in nearly every fridge in America.

FISH FOOD

Ketchup—that humble sauce we put on everything from hot dogs to tater tots—actually got its start hundreds of years ago, in China. There, cooks used the brine from pickled fish as a dipping sauce and called it *ke-tsiap*. From China it made its way to Malaysia, where Dutch and British explorers found it and brought it back to Europe in the 1680s. The European upper classes spiced it up with local additives like pickled mushrooms, anchovies, kidney beans, and walnuts. Eventually, the British bottled it and called it "catsup."

By the late 1700s, the recipe found its way to New England, where tomatoes were added to the mix. Mid-19th-century entrepreneurs exploited the American taste for sweet food and started selling catsup made with tomatoes, vinegar, sugar, cinnamon, cayenne, and salt—a welcome addition to the dreary American diet of the time, which consisted mostly of bread, potatoes, other root vegetables, and smoked or salted meat.

A BORN SALESMAN

In the 1860s, a young boy named Henry John Heinz began selling his mother's homemade horseradish sauce door to door near Pittsburgh, Pennsylvania. Within a few years, he was farming several acres of horseradish root and had a burgeoning business.

By 1869, Heinz had branched out into pickles (relatively rare at the time), vinegar, and other condiments. Business was good enough to bring in a partner, Clarence Noble, and he and Heinz delivered their wares by horse-drawn wagons to grocers in and around Pittsburgh. By then, they owned 100 acres of garden along the Allegheny River—including 30 acres of horseradish—as well as 24 horses, a dozen wagons, and a vinegar factory in St. Louis. Within a few years, they bought 600 more acres in Illinois.

Household tip: Ketchup cleans copper. Apply it, wait a minute, and rinse. Voila!

KETCHING UP

In 1875 a banking panic forced the business into bankruptcy, but H. J., with his brother and cousin, managed to make a comeback. In the depression brought on by the banking collapse, 1876 proved to be a hard first year, but one in which a new product was introduced—Heinz sweet tomato ketchup. Next came red and green pepper sauces, then cider vinegar, apple butter, chili sauce, mincemeat (a finely chopped mixture of raisins, apples, and spices, with or without meat), mustard, tomato soup, olives, pickled onions, pickled cauliflower, baked beans, and the first sweet pickles (and sweet pickle relish) to ever hit the market.

THE PRINCE OF PICKLES

Within the next 20 years, Heinz became a household name and H. J. himself was a millionaire. How did he do it? At the 1893 Chicago World's Fair, everyone who attended the Heinz exhibit—more than a million vacationers from around the world—left the fair with a free Heinz pickle pin. Although a green plaster-of-Paris pin may not sound like much today, it proved to be one of the most effective promotional items in marketing history.

Another of Heinz's innovations was, at the time, a radical notion—that workers should be treated well on the job. In an era when long hours, poor working conditions, and low pay were the norm for urban American workers, conditions at Heinz's factories were often more pleasant than the workers had at home. The factories were also ahead of their time in sanitation and worker safety.

Heinz didn't stop at selling his food products to Americans. With his family, he visited England and brought along a bag packed with "seven varieties of our finest and newest goods." Ten years later, his first overseas office opened near the Tower of London. Heinz's products eventually became so successful in the U.K. that most British shoppers thought Heinz was a British company.

LUCKY NUMBER

The ideas kept coming. Heinz's next brainstorm proved to be another marketing success—one of the greatest in the history of retailing. The company was still in need of an easily recognizable slogan. So, while riding on a New York City elevated subway car in 1896, Heinz spotted a sign above a local store that said "21

Styles of Shoes." His own products weren't styles, he thought, but varieties. And though he had more than 60 foods in production at the time, the number 57 stuck in his mind. Several theories have circulated as to why: the numerals 5 and 7 had some significance for him and his wife; they looked good in print; or perhaps he chose them completely at random. Heinz never fully explained his reasoning, but the mystique only added to the company's success. It was a marketing move that cost Heinz practically nothing. But over the next century, millions of people have probably asked themselves, "I wonder what the 57 stands for?" That was the kind of publicity Heinz wanted.

THERE'S A PICKLE LOVER BORN EVERY MINUTE

Once Heinz was a recognized national brand, H. J. was ready to take things to the next level. With all the subtlety of a P. T. Barnum, Heinz erected a 40-foot-high flashing electric pickle—New York City's first electric sign (1900)—in the heart of Midtown Manhattan. And a 90-foot pickle at the end of a pier in Atlantic City.

That same year, there were 100 manufacturers of ketchup. But now Heinz ketchup is the standard by which other ketchups are rated, and the Heinz company owns dozens of other food brands, including Del Monte, Classico pasta sauces, Lea & Perrins, and Boston Market. The man who made it happen died of pneumonia in 1919 at the age of 75, but his name (and his ketchup) live on.

*   *   *

ON SECOND THOUGHT...

"You know, I once played Grover Cleveland in the movies."
—Ronald Reagan, 1981, commenting on House Speaker Tip O'Neill's desk, which had belonged to President Cleveland. Reagan had actually played Grover Cleveland Alexander, the baseball player

"An island of stability."
—President Jimmy Carter, 1979, describing the Shah of Iran, a few months before the Shah was overthrown

---

The first typewriter was produced by gunmakers E. Remington & Sons in 1874.

BATHROOM NEWS

Bits and pieces of bathroom trivia we've flushed out over the years.

A TRADITION IS BORN

Archaeologists exploring the tomb of a king of the Western Han dynasty (206 B.C. to 24 A.D.) have unearthed what they believe is the world's oldest flush toilet, one that predates the earliest European water closet by as much as 1,800 years. The toilet, which boasts a stone seat, a drain for running water, and even an armrest, "is the earliest of its kind ever discovered in the world," the archaeologists told China's official Xinhua news agency, "meaning that the Chinese flushed first."

ARTSY FARTSY

In 2001 a new work of art by Alphonse Gradant appeared in the Museum of European Art in Paris. Praised as "art in its rawest form…an expression of 21st-century angst, comparable to the best work of Picasso and Salvador Dali," the work later sold for $45,000. Who is Alphonse Gradant? The museum janitor.

Someone swiped one of his diagrams, had it framed, and hung it in the museum as a joke. Is it art? "No," says Gradant. "It's the layout of the men's toilet," which he colored in with red and black pens to make it easier to understand. "I needed a simple diagram that the contractor could follow," he explains. "All I was trying to do was make his work easier, not create a work of art." Museum officials refunded the $45,000. "If it was meant as a joke," says a spokesperson, "It wasn't a very funny one."

TASTES LIKE…SWITZERLAND

In February 2001, a Swiss man named Roger Weisskopf won a lifetime supply of toilet paper after he went on the German television show *Wetten Dass?* and demonstrated his unusual talent: being able to identify the name and country of origin of any brand of toilet paper…by tasting it. More precisely, by "licking, sucking, and chewing" wads of the stuff until it gives up its secrets.

No word on whether Weisskopf ate his prize. It took him a year of practice to develop his skill, which friends and loved ones

---

7% of Ireland's barley crop is used in the production of Guinness beer.

encouraged by bringing home foreign toilet paper whenever they traveled abroad. According to Weisskopf (and he would know), Swiss paper tastes the best, while Japanese paper tastes the worst. "It tastes like moth balls," he says. "It nearly turned my stomach when I was practicing." Weisskopf is now developing a singing toilet lid to cash in on his fame.

EAU DOG TOILETTE

Concerned about the estimated 500,000 tons of poop that Parisian dogs deposit on city streets each year in the French capital, Pierre Pascallon, Conservative member of Parliament, introduced a bill requiring the installation of dog toilets—to be known as *canisettes*. To pay for it, he proposed that dog owners pay a graduated tax in proportion to how much their dogs weigh.

LIKE MONEY IN THE TANK

In the 1960s, the exchange rate for Indonesian currency was 325 *rupiah* to one U.S. dollar. Distressed by the high cost and low quality of Indonesian toilet paper, some western tourists started buying *sen* notes—worth 1/100 of a *rupiah*, or 32,500 to the dollar—and using them for toilet paper.

LIKE A VIRGIN

When musicians agree to do a concert, they provide promoters and the concert hall with a list of demands called a "rider," usually food and drink requests. Madonna has an unusual item on her rider: a brand-new toilet seat at every concert venue on every stop of her tour. (It must still be wrapped in plastic to prove it's new.) After the concert, the seat is to be removed and destroyed to stop anybody from trying to sell it on eBay.

AN HISTORIC MOMENT

What was it like to be the second person to walk on the lunar surface? Astronaut Edwin "Buzz" Aldrin, who followed Neil Armstrong moments after Armstrong made his famous first step, described the experience in an interview for British television: "I held onto the near edge of the landing gear and checked my balance and then hesitated a moment....I am the first person to wet his pants on the moon."

Chew on this: Cap'n Crunch's full name is Horatio Magellan Crunch.

FOREVER MANKIND

On July 20, 1969, Neil Armstrong and Edwin "Buzz" Aldrin successfully landed the Apollo 11 *spacecraft on the moon. It was a triumph of science, humanity, and the United States. But what if Armstrong and Aldrin had ended up stranded in space…with no hope of return? President Richard Nixon's speechwriter, William Safire, prepared this speech in the event of a worst-case scenario.*

Fate has ordained that the men who went to the moon to explore in peace will stay on the moon to rest in peace.

These brave men, Neil Armstrong and Edwin Aldrin, know that there is no hope for their recovery. But they also know that there is hope for mankind in their sacrifice. These two men are laying down their lives in mankind's most noble goal: the search for truth and understanding.

They will be mourned by their families and friends; they will be mourned by their nation; they will be mourned by the people of the world; they will be mourned by a Mother Earth that dared send two of her sons into the unknown.

In their exploration, they stirred the people of the world to feel as one; in their sacrifice, they bind more tightly the brotherhood of man.

In ancient days, men looked at stars and saw their heroes in the constellations. In modern times, we do much the same, but our heroes are epic men of flesh and blood.

Others will follow, and surely find their way home. Man's search will not be denied. But these men were the first, and they will remain the foremost in our hearts.

For every human being who looks up at the moon in the nights to come will know that there is some corner of another world that is forever mankind.

Makes sense: In ancient Egyptian, the word *nile* means "water."

BANNED BOOKS

Sometimes even the most popular, critically acclaimed, and even kid-friendly books can be removed from libraries and schools.

Book: *Are You There God? It's Me, Margaret*, by Judy Blume
Banned in: Fond du Lac, Wisconsin
Reason: In 1982 concerned parents challenged this novel about a young girl dealing with puberty because it was "sexually offensive" (Margaret experiences her first menstrual cycle) and "amoral" (Margaret wonders if God is real).

Book: *American Heritage Dictionary*
Banned in: Eldon, Missouri, and Anchorage, Alaska
Reason: This dictionary used to be one of the only dictionaries that included curse words. (Who hasn't looked up dirty words in the dictionary for a cheap laugh?) Then in 1978, the Eldon public library banned it for containing 39 objectionable words. Hoping to avoid further controversy, the editors of the dictionary elected not to include the naughty words in future printings. However, in 1987 the Anchorage School Board banned the censored version because it still contained slang definitions of words, such as *knocker* and *balls*.

Book: *Little Red Riding Hood*, by the Brothers Grimm
Banned in: Two California school districts
Reason: Because the Big Bad Wolf eating people is too violent? Nope. In 1989 school officials thought the story might encourage children to drink because it shows a bottle of wine among the food Red brings to her grandmother.

Book: *Where's Waldo*, by Martin Handford
Banned in: Saginaw, Michigan
Reason: The public libraries of Saginaw tried to ban *Waldo* in 1989 because some of the pages supposedly contained "dirty things," including the bare back of a topless sunbather in a beach scene. (As if Waldo himself wasn't hard enough to find.)

Book: Mickey Mouse comics

Banned in: Italy

Reason: In 1938 Italy's National Conference of Juvenile Literature banned all materials featuring the Disney icon. The organization thought he encouraged children to be individuals, a concept that clashed with the fascist politics of dictator Benito Mussolini.

Book: *Complete Works of William Shakespeare*

Banned in: England (almost)

Reason: Though many think Shakespeare was the greatest writer who ever lived, poet Samuel Taylor Coleridge ("The Rime of the Ancient Mariner") didn't. In 1815 Coleridge attempted to ban all of Shakespeare's plays and poems throughout England because he found them crude and vulgar. Coleridge's efforts actually had the opposite effect: He didn't get the Bard banned, but the attention led to England's first real academic interest in Shakespeare.

Book: *To Kill a Mockingbird*, by Harper Lee

Banned in: Eden Valley, Minnesota

Reason: Required reading for schools across the nation, *To Kill a Mockingbird* delivers a strong message of racial tolerance. Nevertheless, Eden Valley removed it from schools in 1977, and was soon followed by schools in New York, Illinois, and Missouri. Protesters said the book's violent depiction of a hate crime actually encouraged racism.

Book: *Fahrenheit 451*, by Ray Bradbury

Banned in: Foxworth, Mississippi

Reason: In 1998 this novel about the dangers of book banning… was banned. West Marion High School in Foxworth took it off the required reading list when parents protested the book's use of the phrase "g*dd*m." (We added the asterisks because Uncle John banned the letters "o" and "a." Hppy reding and g with the flw!)

*   *   *

"There are worse crimes than burning books. One of them is not reading them."

—Joseph Brodsky

In the 1800s, people segregated their books by the sex of the author.

FACTS FOR THE ROAD

*Some auto-industry trivia to think about the
next time you're out driving around.*

• The automobile was invented in 1886. The used car lot (of 17 cars) was "invented" in 1897.

• In 1924 a new Ford cost $265.

• The first Rolls-Royce sold for $600, in 1906. Today they sell for more than $200,000.

• Whale oil was used in automobile transmission fluids as late as 1973.

• The average car has 15,000 parts.

• The first reported car theft in America took place in St. Louis, Missouri, in 1905.

• Toughest car ever: a 1957 Mercedes-Benz 180D racked up 1,184,880 miles in 21 years.

• Goodyear once made a tire entirely out of corn.

• It takes six months to build a Rolls-Royce and 13 hours to build a Toyota.

• When used to make ethyl alcohol, an acre of potatoes will produce enough fuel to fill 25 cars.

• No matter how cold it gets, gasoline won't freeze. When the temperature gets below –180°F, it just turns gummy.

• The average 1995 luxury car had more than one mile of wiring.

• The tubeless auto tire was invented by a man named Frank Herzegh. He made one dollar for it.

• It takes about two and a half gallons of oil to make a car tire.

• The right rear tire on your car will wear out before the other three will.

• More Americans have died in automobile accidents than have died in all U.S. wars.

• No butts about it: Nissan has invented an artificial butt to test car seats.

The last words Walt Disney wrote were "Kurt Russell."

LET'S PLAY NINTENDO!

Today's video game business is less about boing! and crash! than it is about ka-ching! and cash! Here's how it got that way.

N O SALE
Back in 1981, Atari was the world leader in video games. In 1983 Nintendo offered to sell Atari the licenses to their Famicom game system, but they couldn't come to an agreement, so Nintendo decided to go it alone. They renamed the American version the Advanced Video System (AVS) and in January 1985, introduced it at the Consumer Electronics Show in Las Vegas, one of the largest such trade shows in the world.

They didn't get a single order.

Nintendo's problem wasn't so much that the AVS was a bad system, but more that the American home video game industry was struggling. After several years of impressive growth, in 1983 sales of video game consoles and cartridges suddenly collapsed without warning. Video game manufacturers, caught completely off guard, lost hundreds of millions of dollars as inventory piled up in warehouses, never to find a buyer. Atari's loss of $536 million prompted Warner Communications to sell the company in 1984. Mattel sold off its version, Intellivision, the same year and shut down their entire video game division. Many other companies went out of business.

GOODBYE VCS, HELLO PC

Meanwhile, computer technology had finally advanced to the point that companies were able to manufacture and sell home computers at prices that families could afford. By 1982 a computer called the Commodore 64 could be bought for as little as $200, which was $100 less than the cost of an Atari 5200.

Why buy just a game system when you could buy a whole computer—which also played video games—for the same price or lower? Just as the video game industry had evolved from dedicated Pong-only games to cartridge-based multigame systems, game systems were giving way to the personal computer. Stand-alone video games were dead…or so most people thought.

Girl crazy: Columbia was the last Ivy League college to go coed. (It held out until 1983.)

Hiroshi Yamauchi, the president of Nintendo, didn't see things that way. His company didn't make personal computers and he didn't know much about the American market. But Famicom game systems were selling like crazy in Japan, and he didn't see any reason why they shouldn't also sell well in the United States. So what if the company didn't receive a single order at the Consumer Electronics Show? He told his American sales team to keep trying.

WORD GAMES

Nintendo's American sales team was headed by Minoru Arakawa, who also happened to be Yamauchi's son-in-law. Arakawa *had* to keep trying. He didn't have any choice—he was a member of the family.

One of the problems the AVS was up against was that retailers had been badly burned by the video game crash of 1983. They weren't about to put any more nonselling video games on their shelves. Arakawa decided that the best way to proceed was to conceal the fact that the AVS was a video game. He couldn't do that while it was still called the Advanced Video System, so he renamed it the Nintendo Entertainment System, NES for short.

He added a light pistol and some shooting games, so that he could say it was a "target game." (Guns and target games still sold well in toy stores.) Then he added the Robot Operating Buddy (ROB), a small plastic "robot" that interacted with a couple of the games played on the NES. "Technologically speaking," Steven Kent writes in *The Ultimate History of Video Games*, "ROB offered very little play value. It was mostly a decoy designed to prove that the Famicom was not just a video game."

DEJA VU

With a new name, a light gun, and a robot, Arakawa was sure the NES would sell. He rented a booth at the Summer Consumer Electronics Show and set the ROB out in front, where everyone could see it.

He didn't get a single order.

Why didn't retailers want to buy? Were consumers turned off too? Arakawa didn't know for sure, so he set up a focus group

---

A coffee pot with a sieve to strain away the grounds was not invented until 1806.

where he could watch young boys—Nintendo's target market—play NES games. Observing the scene from behind a two-way mirror, Arakawa heard for himself how much the kids disliked the NES. "This is sh*t!" as one kid put it.

ONE MORE TRY

Arakawa was ready to throw in the towel. He called his father-in-law, told him the situation was hopeless, and suggested that Nintendo pull the NES out of the U.S. market. But Yamauchi refused to hear a word of it. He didn't know much about the Consumer Electronics Show and he didn't know much about focus groups. One thing he did know was that the Famicom was *still* selling like crazy in Japan, so why couldn't it sell well in the United States? There was nothing wrong with the NES—he was certain of that.

Yamauchi told Arakawa to test it one more time—in New York City. This time Arakawa left nothing to chance. There were about 500 retailers in the city, and Arakawa and his staff visited every one. They made sales pitches, delivered the game systems, stocked store shelves, and set up Nintendo's in-store displays themselves. They made plans to spend $5 million on advertising during the Christmas shopping season, and—without permission from Yamauchi—promised retailers they would buy back any game systems that didn't sell. And they *never, ever* referred to their video game as a video game. The NES was an "entertainment system."

IS NINTENDO THE NEXT ATARI?

With the buyback guarantee, retailers had nothing to lose, so they agreed to stock Nintendo, even though they didn't think it would sell. They were wrong—more than 50,000 games sold by Christmas, prompting many stores to continue stocking the NES after the holidays. Arakawa launched similar tests in Los Angeles, Chicago, and San Francisco. The NES sold well in each city.

In 1986 Nintendo expanded its U.S. marketing push nationwide and sold 1.8 million game consoles, and from there sales grew astronomically. They sold 5.4 million consoles in 1987 and 9.3 million in 1988. By 1990 American sales of the NES accounted for 10% of the entire U.S./Japan trade deficit.

But if there's one thing that video game makers have learned the hard way, it's that *staying* ahead in the business can be a lot harder

---

During the American Revolution, patriotic brides wore red dresses to symbolize rebellion.

than *getting* ahead. For all their successes, Nintendo has made their share of blunders, too. They clung to the NES a few years longer than they should have, on the assumption that its market dominance would allow it to keep ahead of its rivals. They were wrong.

When a rival company called Sega introduced their Genesis system in 1989, Nintendo ignored it, even though the Genesis was twice as powerful as the NES. They shouldn't have—Genesis introduced a character called Sonic the Hedgehog, an edgy, anti-Mario character who appealed to older kids *and* adults the same way that Donkey Kong's Mario had appealed only to kids. In late 1991, Nintendo introduced SuperNintendo, but it was too late. Sonic's appeal, combined with six years of waiting for Nintendo to update their system, helped Sega get a toehold in the market…and outsell Nintendo.

SONY'S PLAYSTATION

But Nintendo's biggest mistake of all came in 1992. The industry was gearing up for yet another generation of game systems—using CD-ROM disks instead of cartridges. CD-ROMs were cheaper to make and stored more than 300 times more information than a Super NES cartridge, allowing for much more sophisticated graphics.

Nintendo had no experience with CD-ROMs, so they made plans to partner with Sony Corporation to make the new system. But there was a problem—Sony had already announced plans to introduce its own game system (PlayStation), and Nintendo executives were worried about revealing Nintendo's technological secrets to a competitor as large and powerful as Sony. So what did they do? For some reason, Nintendo waited until the day *after* Sony announced the partnership. Then they made an announcement of their own: they were ditching Sony and partnering with the Dutch electronics giant, Philips.

REVENGE!

Though the company had lost ground to Sega in the U.S. market, Nintendo was still the world leader in video game sales, and many Sony executives were reluctant to challenge Nintendo's dominance. The consensus: scrap the PlayStation project because Nintendo will wipe it out. But Sony CEO Norio Ohga was so furious at being humiliated by Nintendo that he almost singlehandedly forced the company to continue work on the project.

The ball that drops in Times Square every New Year's Eve is named the "Star of Hope."

The Sony PlayStation was introduced in Japan in 1994 and in the United States in 1995. Nintendo eventually scrapped its CD-ROM–based system and introduced the Nintendo 64, yet another cartridge game system.

BRAVE NEW WORLD

The Nintendo 64 was a blunder of Atari proportions. Compared to the PlayStation, it had poor sound, poor graphics...and poor sales. By August 1997, the PlayStation had surged past both Sega and Nintendo to become the industry leader. Sega, which spread their resources over too many game systems at once—Genesis, Saturn, and another one called Dreamcast—fell to a distant third and in January 2001 got out of the hardware business altogether. Today they only make game software.

Nintendo's decision to stick with cartridges for the Nintendo 64 continues to haunt them today. When Sony introduced the PlayStation 2 in 2000, they were careful to make it "backward compatible," so that virtually all 800 of the PlayStation 1 games could be played on the new console. Extra bonus: Because the PlayStation 2 used a DVD player instead of a CD-ROM player, you could also watch movies on it.

The Nintendo GameCube, introduced in 2001, was another story. It used a *mini* DVD-ROM system that didn't play movies and wasn't compatible with Nintendo 64 game cartridges. That meant Nintendo 64 owners had no incentive to buy the Game-Cube, because their old games would be just as obsolete whether they bought GameCube or PlayStation 2.

Even worse for Nintendo was the new kid on the block: the Microsoft Xbox. Considered even more technologically advanced than the PlayStation 2, Xbox gave both Nintendo and Sony a run for their money.

FORTUNE-TELLING

Who will be the next Atari? Will Nintendo's game systems fall behind Sony's and Microsoft's, or even disappear entirely? Play-Station 3, Wii, Xbox 360...what comes next?

Stay tuned—if there's one thing to be learned from the video game industry, it's that the game is *never* over.

Odds that an American worker won't tell their spouse after they receive a raise: 36%.

HERMITS OF HARLEM

Do you find it hard to part with those back issues of National Geographic?
Is your garage filled to overflowing with stuff you'll never use again?
You may be suffering from Collyer Brothers Syndrome.

THE PHONE CALL

On March 21, 1947, a telephone call came into the 122nd Street police station in Manhattan. A male voice said, "There is a dead man on the premises at 2078 Fifth Avenue." The police knew the house—it was home to the legendary and mysterious Collyer brothers. A patrolman was sent to investigate. Thus began one of the strangest tabloid stories in New York history.

THE UPPER UPPER EAST SIDE

Homer and Langley Collyer were the sons of a wealthy gynecologist from an old New York family. In the early 1900s, the family moved into a three-story brownstone mansion in Harlem, then a fashionable neighborhood. Homer became a lawyer and Langley studied engineering. All seemed right with the Collyer family.

But there were a couple of odd things about the Collyer boys. For one thing, Langley never worked. For another, the boys never moved out of their Harlem home, even after their parents died in the 1920s. In fact, it's likely they never left New York City during their entire lives.

For a while, the Collyers seemed at least seminormal. Homer, the older brother, walked the eight miles back and forth to his law office every day. Langley studied music and tinkered with inventions, like his handy-dandy vacuum for cleaning out the inside of a piano. In the meantime, Harlem went from being an upper-middle-class neighborhood to a predominantly African-American working-class enclave.

HUNKERING DOWN

As their Harlem neighborhood changed around them, the brothers gradually withdrew from the world. They stopped paying their bills and didn't object when their telephone, electricity,

Joan of Arc's actual name: Jehanne Darc. The apostrophe was added later by an English historian.

gas, and water were cut off. (For years, Langley fetched their water from a park four blocks away.) Afraid of intruders, they built barricades of junk in front of the windows and doors and booby-trapped the house by trip-wiring massive piles of newspapers and trash.

Homer was almost never seen after he suffered a stroke and became blind and paralyzed. He was cared for exclusively by Langley, who only fed him a diet of 100 oranges a week, black bread, and peanut butter, thinking it would cure his brother. He explained his prescription this way: "Remember, we are the sons of a doctor."

Langley would leave the house only at night, dressed in shabby clothes and pulling a cardboard box on the end of a long rope. He gathered food for Homer and collected things.

FAME, OF SORTS

Articles about the strange recluses began to appear in the newspapers. Once, a crowd of 1,000 gathered outside the Collyer home while Con Edison workers forced their way in to remove two old gas meters.

Then came the anonymous tip that someone had died at the house. When the police arrived, a small crowd had already gathered. The front doors were forced open, only to reveal an impenetrable wall of boxes and junk from floor to ceiling. Finally, the police entered the house through a second floor window. Inside was a junk-filled maze of tunnels. Deep inside one of them was the body of 65-year-old Homer Collyer, who'd apparently died of starvation.

WHERE'S LANGLEY?

No one had seen Langley for days. He didn't even attend Homer's funeral. In the meantime, searchers began cleaning out the house. Among other things, they found the jawbone of a horse, 14 pianos, the dismantled components of an old Model T, baby carriages, pictures of a pinup girl from 1905, plaster statues, telephone directories, tin cans, chandeliers, 13 Oriental rugs, and some unfinished knitting left by Mother Collyer in 1929. But, above all, there were old newspapers. Tons and tons of them. Langley had collected every single edition of every New York City newspaper from the year 1918 on—30 years' worth.

AT LONG LAST LANGLEY

After 18 days of junk removal, Langley's body was found hidden under a massive pile of newspapers just a few feet from where Homer died. He had apparently set off one of his own booby traps while delivering dinner to Homer and was crushed to death. The coroner said that Homer died some time after Langley. So the police figured out that when Langley was killed, Homer lost the source of his food and slowly starved to death, trapped in his house, unable to see or walk. The house had no telephone, so he couldn't call anyone—and he couldn't even reach a window to call for help.

FRONT PAGE NEWS

The story became a wild sensation; it even made the front page of The *New York Times*. Thousands of people walked or drove by the Collyer house, but they didn't stay long because of the smell. Over the next several weeks, 140 tons of junk were removed from the house, after which the house was torn down. The place where the Collyer house stood was eventually turned into a small park. In 1990, it was formally named Collyer Brothers Park.

AND THAT'S NOT ALL

One more thing that was named for the kooky Collyers was their syndrome—also known as "compulsive hoarding," a clinically recognized obsessive-compulsive disorder. When he was asked, Langley said he was saving the newspapers so Homer could catch up on the news when he regained his sight. Experts might tell you that it was a way to keep anxiety at bay—a way for the Collyers to keep their lives at 2078 Fifth Avenue safe and intact.

And though they never knew it, they'd performed an important service for the moms of America. For years after the deaths of Homer and Langley, mothers could tell their children, "Clean your room, it's worse than the Collyer brothers' house in here."

*   *   *

A TIP FROM HOWARD HUGHES

"Wash four distinct and separate times, using lots of lather each time from individual bars of soap."

Presidents Thomas Jefferson, John Adams, and James Monroe all died on July 4th.

HOMER VS. HOMER

On the left we have the wisdom of Homer, Greek poet and philosopher, who lived 3,000 years ago. And on the right we have the other Homer.

Homer the Greek

"It is the bold man who every time does his best."

"The charity that is a trifle to us can be precious to others."

"The fates have given mankind a patient soul."

"Nothing in the world is so incontinent as a man's accursed appetite."

"I detest he who hides one thing in his heart and means another."

"The man who acts the least, disrupts the most."

"A sympathetic friend can be quite as dear as a brother."

"A multitude of rulers is not a good thing. Let there be one ruler, one king."

"Never, never was a wicked man wise."

"How mortals take the gods to task! Yet their afflictions come from us."

Homer the Simpson

"I don't know, Marge. Trying is the first step toward failure."

"You gave both dogs away? You know how I feel about giving!"

"Give me some peace of mind or I'll mop the floor with you!"

"Ahh, beer…I would kill everyone in this room for a drop of sweet beer."

"But, Marge, it takes two people to lie: one to lie, and one to listen."

"It is better to watch things than to do them."

"Television—teacher, mother, secret lover!"

"I'd blow smoke in the president's stupid monkey face and all he'd do is grooooove on it!"

"I am so smart! S-M-R-T, I mean S-M-A-R-T."

"I'm not normally a religious man, but if you're up there, save me, Superman!"

Bad luck? The Confederate flag had 13 stars…but there were only 11 Confederate states.

MARATHON OF HOPE

*If you're Canadian, you've probably already heard of
Terry Fox. If you haven't, here's his incredible story.*

DETERMINATION

Terry Fox was born in 1958 and grew up in British Columbia. He was an average kid, with the exception of being very athletic—in high school he played hockey, basketball, lacrosse, and ran track. Then in 1976, shortly after graduating from high school, he was diagnosed with osteogenic sarcoma: bone cancer. A few months later, his right leg had to be amputated and Fox didn't think he'd ever be able to run or play sports again.

The night before the surgery, Fox's former basketball coach brought him a magazine article about an amputee who'd run in the New York Marathon. The story inspired Fox. He determined then and there not to let having an artificial leg prevent him from living the life he wanted to live. Fox decided to raise awareness about cancer and raise money for research by doing something nobody had ever done before: he would run across Canada.

THE RACE IS ON

For nearly two years, Fox prepared for his "Marathon of Hope." First he learned to walk with an artificial leg, then he learned to run, then he built up his endurance. Finally, on April 12, 1980, he flew to St. John's, Newfoundland, dipped his prosthetic leg in the Atlantic Ocean, and began his trek west, expecting that in a few months he'd dip it into the Pacific Ocean on the other side of the country.

The run began with almost no fanfare, but then the press picked up the story. They started detailing Fox's daily progress and suddenly all of Canada was rooting for him and bombarding his family with letters and donations. Fox's pace was staggering: every day he ran an average of 26 miles—the length of an entire marathon. Marathon runners typically train for months and spend weeks afterward recuperating. Fox was essentially running a marathon every day for months on end—with an artificial leg. Had anyone ever done something similar? No. The *Guinness Book of*

World Records lists Rick Worley as the marathon record holder: he ran 200 straight marathons, but he did it over 159 consecutive weekends, not over days as Fox was trying to do.

Then, on September 1, 1980, the Marathon of Hope ended near Thunder Bay, Ontario. The cancer had come back and spread to Fox's lungs. After running for 143 days straight, through Nova Scotia, New Brunswick, Newfoundland, Quebec, and Ontario—more than 3,300 miles—he had to abandon the quest and return home for treatment. Terry Fox died on June 28, 1981, just shy of his 23rd birthday, but his strength and determination remain beacons for an entire generation of Canadians.

FOX'S LEGACY

• During the actual run, Fox raised $1.7 million for cancer research.

• The day after the run ended, the Four Seasons hotel chain announced plans to sponsor an annual marathon in Fox's honor.

• That same week, a Terry Fox telethon raised $10 million.

• Fox was awarded the Companion of the Order of Canada (similar to a knighthood or a Presidential Medal of Freedom) and the Order of the Dogwood, British Columbia's highest civilian honor.

• In 1980 the Canadian press named him Canadian of the Year.

• An 8,700-foot Rocky Mountain peak was named Mount Terry Fox.

• A stretch of highway near the end of Fox's run was renamed the Terry Fox Courage Highway.

• Fox was memorialized on two postage stamps, had a Canadian Coast Guard ship named after him, and was named Canadian Athlete of the Decade (beating out Wayne Gretzky).

• In 1999 Terry Fox was voted Canada's greatest national hero of all time in a magazine survey.

• As of 2004, annual fund-raising Terry Fox Runs have donated more than $340 million to cancer research.

The Terry Fox Library in Port Coquitlam, B.C., houses 100,000 artifacts from Fox's life and the Marathon of Hope. One room is stacked floor-to-ceiling with boxes of letters and get-well cards. All kinds of people from all walks of life are represented, showing just how far Terry Fox reached. He only made it halfway across Canada, but he touched every corner of the country.

A musk ox is actually a sheep.

DIRECTORS' SIGNATURE SIGNS

From Hollywood's earliest days, directors have sought to leave their individual marks on their films. Some have devised small "signatures" that identify a film as their work. Can you spot them?

MAKING THEIR MARK

The French have a word for it: *auteur* (author). It's the name for a theory of filmmaking—the idea that a film director is like a book's author and is responsible for the film's vision, form, and content. Many directors' films are easily recognizable as theirs, based on the themes and style that recur in their movies. But some directors also add small signature touches or in-jokes that—if you recognize them—add to the audience's enjoyment.

FRANK CAPRA

Capra had a pet raven named Jimmy, and he found a place for him in several of his movies, starting with *You Can't Take It With You* (1938). In the Christmas classic *It's a Wonderful Life* (1946), Jimmy the raven sits on Uncle Billy's desk in the Bailey Building and Loan.

ALFRED HITCHCOCK

Probably the best-known of all director signatures, Hitchcock famously placed himself in many of his films—his unmistakable profile appears briefly in 37 out of 54 of them. To help you out, we've sniffed out Hitchcock sightings in some of his most familiar films.

Psycho: About four minutes into the film, Marion (Janet Leigh) returns to her office. You can glimpse Hitchcock, wearing a cowboy hat, through the window. Don't blink or you'll miss him—he's only on-screen for a few seconds.

Rear Window: About 30 minutes into the film, Hitchcock is winding a clock in the songwriter's apartment.

On July 4, 1776, King George III of England noted in his diary:...

Dial M for Murder: This is one of Sir Alfred's trickier cameos. Roughly 13 minutes into the film, a class reunion photo is shown. That's him on the left of the picture.

Strangers on a Train: Right at the start of the movie, Hitchcock can be seen boarding the train, carrying a double bass.

Lifeboat: Hitchcock appears briefly as the "before" and "after" pictures in a newspaper ad for a weight-loss program. Around the time of this movie's filming, Hitchcock had crash dieted and dropped 100 pounds.

QUENTIN TARANTINO

Tarantino is best known for violent films with a healthy dose of black humor. And there are several signatures to watch for: Each movie contains a "trunk shot," during which the camera is set deep in the trunk of a car so it can capture the actors as they lean in and over it. Each also has an ad for Red Apple cigarettes (a fictional brand). Tarantino almost always has one or more of his characters barefoot—it's Uma Thurman in *Pulp Fiction* and the *Kill Bill* movies.

MARTIN SCORSESE

Taking a leaf from Alfred Hitchcock's book, Scorsese appears in cameos in almost all his films. Going Hitchcock one better, Scorsese also puts many members of his family in small roles.

Cape Fear: Scorsese's mother plays a customer at the fruit stand.

The Color of Money: Scorsese is walking a dog in the casino scene. The dog was actually his own dog, and received a credit as Dog Walkby.

Goodfellas: Scorsese's mother plays Tommy's mother. The director let her ad-lib her entire scene. His father plays the prisoner who put too many onions in the "gravy" (tomato sauce).

Raging Bull: Scorsese can be seen asking Jack to go onstage. Also in *Raging Bull*, Scorsese's father is part of a mob at the Copa nightclub.

Taxi Driver: Scorsese is sitting in the background of the campaign headquarters as Cybill Shepherd walks in.

ACCORDING TO THE LATEST RESEARCH...

It seems like every day there's a report on some scientific study with dramatic new info on what we should eat...or how we should act...or who we really are. Some are pretty interesting. Did you know, for example, that science says...

AMERICANS ARE REALLY GULLIBLE

Researchers: DiMassimo Brand Advertising

Who They Studied: Friends & neighbors of 200 volunteers

What They Learned: "Americans will believe anything, as long as it comes from a friend or a neighbor." The ad company recruited 200 people to tell fibs to their friends, then polled the friends a week later. Sample results: "27% repeated the lie that 'Just Do It!' was the slogan of Ex-Lax instead of Nike; 22% believed that milk was 'the other white meat'; and 23% thought Amazon.com was a fashion Web site for large women."

GRANDMAS SMELL GOOD

Researchers: Rutgers University chemists

Who They Studied: 300 students, commenting on the underarm smells of 30 volunteers, "ranging from toddlers to 70-somethings"

What They Learned: People like the smell of older women. "The researchers collected underarm odors on gauze pads...and asked the students to assess their moods before and after sniffing the samples. 'Old women had an uplifting effect,' said Denise Chen of the Monsell Center." Smells from young men had "the opposite effect."

THERE REALLY IS A KEY TO HAPPINESS

Researchers: David Blanchflower of Dartmouth College (U.S.) and Andrew Oswald of the University of Warwick (U.K.)

Who They Studied: 100,000 people of varying ages and backgrounds

What They Learned: Blanchflower and Oswald concluded that happiness levels tend to be the lowest around age 40, and go up after that. Furthermore, "a lasting marriage brings about the same amount of happiness as an extra $100,000 in yearly income."

Composer Franz Schubert was one of Beethoven's pall bearers.

LONELY PHONE BOOTH

*In the 1960s, some miners put a phone booth in the middle
of the Mojave Desert. Long after they left, the booth
remained…waiting for someone to call.*

HELLO? ANYBODY THERE?
Miles from the nearest town, the old phone booth stood at the junction of two dirt roads. Its windows were shot out; the overhead light was gone. Yet the phone lines on the endless rows of poles still popped and clicked in anticipation—just as they'd been doing for nearly 30 years. Finally, in 1997, it rang.

A guy named Deuce had read about the booth and called the number…and continued to call until a desert dweller named Lorene answered. Deuce wrote a story about his call to nowhere, posted it on his website…and the word spread through cyberspace. Someone else called. Then another person, and another—just to see if someone would answer. And quite often someone did. Only accessible by four wheel drive, the lonely phone booth soon became a destination. Travelers drove for hours just to answer the phone. One Texas man camped there for 32 days…and answered more than 500 calls.

REACH OUT AND TOUCH SOMEONE

Someone posted a call log in the booth to record where people were calling from: as close as Los Angeles and as far away as New Zealand and Kosovo. Why'd they call? Some liked the idea of two people who've never met—and probably never will—talking to each other. Just sending a call out into the Great Void and having someone answer was reward enough for most.

Unfortunately, in 2000 the National Park Service and Pacific Bell tore down the famous Mojave phone booth. Reason? It was getting too many calls. The traffic (20 to 30 visitors a day) was starting to have a negative impact on the fragile desert environment.

The old stop sign at the cattle grate still swings in the wind. And the phone lines still pop and click in anticipation. But all that's left of the loneliest phone on Earth is a ghost ring.

So if the urge strikes you to dial (760) 733-9969, be prepared to wait a very, very long time for someone to answer.

Polite tip from etiquette experts: If no one answers the phone after 6 rings, hang up.

THE STRANGEST DISASTER OF THE 20TH CENTURY, PT. II

If you studied chemistry in high school or college, you may have solved the mystery already. If not, the answer lies just ahead. (Part I of the story is on page 90.)

CONTENTS UNDER PRESSURE

As the scientists took samples from deeper and deeper in Lake Nyos, the already high carbon dioxide (CO_2) levels climbed steadily higher. At the 600 foot depth, the levels suddenly shot off the charts. Beyond that depth, the CO_2 levels were so high that when the scientists tried to pull the samples to the surface, the containers burst from the pressure of all the gas that came out of solution. The scientists had to switch to pressurized containers to collect their samples, and when they did they were stunned to find that the water at the bottom of the lake contained *five gallons* of dissolved CO_2 for every gallon of water.

As the scientists pieced together the evidence, they began to form a theory that centered around the large amount of CO_2 in the lake. The volcano that formed Lake Nyos may have been long extinct, but the magma chamber that fed it was still active deep below the surface of the Earth. And it was still releasing carbon dioxide gas—not just into Lake Nyos, but into the surrounding environment as well. In fact, it's not uncommon in Cameroon to find frogs and other small animals suffocated in CO_2 "puddles" that have formed in low points along the ground. (CO_2 is heavier than air and can pool in low spots until the wind blows it away.)

But what was unusual about Lake Nyos wasn't that there was CO_2 in the lake; that happens in lakes all over the world. What was unusual was that the CO_2 had apparently never *left*—instead of bubbling to the surface and dissipating into the air, the CO_2 was accumulating at the bottom of the lake.

UPS AND DOWNS

In most lakes CO_2 escapes because the water is continually circulating, thanks to a process known as *convection:* Rain, cold weather, or even just wind blowing across the surface of the lake can cause the topmost layer of water to cool, making it denser and therefore heavier than the warmer layers below. The cool water sinks to the bottom of the lake, displacing the warmer, CO_2-rich water and pushing it high enough for the CO_2 to come out of the solution, bubble to the surface, and escape into the air.

STILL WATERS RUN DEEP

That's what *usually* happens, but the water at the bottom of Lake Nyos was so saturated with CO_2 that it was clear that something was interfering with the convection process. As the scientists soon discovered, the waters of Lake Nyos are among the most still in the world: Tall hills surround the lake, blocking the wind and causing the lake to be unusually consistent in temperature from the surface to the bottom. And because Lake Nyos is in a tropical climate that remains hot year round, the water temperature doesn't vary much from season to season, either. Lastly, because the lake is so deep, even when the surface is disturbed, very little of the agitation finds its way to the lake floor. The unusual stillness of the lake is what made it so deadly.

FULL TO BURSTING

There is a physical limit to how much CO_2 water can absorb, even under the tremendous pressures that exist at the bottom of a 690-foot-deep lake. As the bottom layers become saturated, the CO_2 is pushed up to where the water pressure is lower. The CO_2 eventually rises to a level where the pressure is low enough for it to start coming out of solution. At this point any little disturbance—a landslide, stormy weather, or even high winds or just a cold snap—can cause the CO_2 to begin bubbling to the surface. And when the bubbles start rising, they can cause a siphoning or "chimney" effect, triggering a chain reaction that in one giant upheaval can cause the lake to disgorge CO_2 that has been accumulating in the lake for decades.

CO_2 is odorless, colorless, and non-toxic; your body produces it and you exhale some every time you breathe. Even the air you inhale consists of about 0.05% CO_2. What makes it a killer in certain circumstances is the fact that it's heavier than air: If enough escapes into the environment at once, it displaces the air on the ground, making breathing impossible. A mixture of as little as 10% CO_2 in the air can be fatal; even 5% can smother a flame… which explained why the oil lamps went out.

SNUFFED OUT

The scientists figured that if their theory was correct, there might be other instances of similar eruptions in the past. It didn't take very long to find one, and they didn't have to look very far, either: Two years earlier, on August 15, 1984, a loud boom was heard coming from Lake Monoun, a crater lake just 59 miles southeast of Lake Nyos. In the hours that followed, 37 people died mysteriously, including a group of 17 people who died while walking to work when they came to a low point in the road—just the place where CO_2 would have settled after being released from the lake. The incident was small enough that it hadn't attracted much attention from the outside world…until now.

THE BIG BANG

In the months following the disaster at Lake Nyos, the scientists continued to monitor the lake's CO_2 levels. When the levels began to increase again, they concluded that their theory was correct.

In the meantime, they had also come up with an estimate of just how much CO_2 had escaped from the lake on August 22— and were stunned by what they found. Eyewitness accounts from people who were high enough in the hills above the lake to survive the eruption described how the lake began bubbling strangely on August 17, causing a misty cloud to form above the surface of the water. Then without warning, on August 22, the lake suddenly exploded; water and gas shot a couple of hundred feet into the air. The CO_2 had taken up so much space in the lake that when it was finally released, the water level dropped more than three feet. By measuring the change in depth, the scientists estimated that the lake had released 1.2 cubic kilometers of CO_2—enough to fill 10 football stadiums—in as little as 20 seconds. (Are you old enough to remember the huge volume of ash that Mt. Saint Helens released when it erupted in 1980? That eruption released only 1/3 of one cubic kilometer of ash—a quarter of Lake Nyos's emission.)

For the conclusion of the story, turn to page 552.

100 calories will propel a bicycle 3 miles and drive a car 280 feet.

FAMILIAR PHRASES

More origins that pack a wallop.

STUMP SOMEONE

Meaning: Ask someone a question they can't answer

Origin: Actually refers to tree stumps. "Pioneers built their houses and barns out of logs...and they frequently swapped work with one another in clearing new ground. Some frontiersmen would brag about their ability to pull up big stumps, but it wasn't unusual for the boaster to suffer defeat with a stubborn stump." (From *I've Got Goose Pimples*, by Marvin Vanoni)

EAT, DRINK, AND BE MERRY

Meaning: To feast and not worry about life's problems

Origin: "This phrase has its roots in the Bible, where, in Ecclesiastes 8:15, we read: 'A man hath no better thing under the sun, than to eat, and to drink, and to be merry.' There is a further reference in Isaiah 22:13, 'Let us eat and drink; for tomorrow we may die.'" (From *Everyday Phrases—Their Origins and Meanings*, by Neil Ewart)

TO PACK A WALLOP

Meaning: Have a powerful punch or impact

Origin: "In modern English 'to wallop' means to thrash, and in noun form, a heavy blow, but originally it...was slang for ale. The verb pack in this expression means 'to deliver.'" So, it was, literally, "deliver the beer." (From *Have a Nice Day—No Problem!*, by Christine Ammer)

TOUCH AND GO

Meaning: A risky, precarious situation

Origin: "Dates back to the days of stagecoaches, whose drivers were often intensely competitive, seeking to charge past one another, on narrow roads, at grave danger to life and limb. If the vehicle's wheels became entangled, both would be wrecked; if they were lucky, the wheels would only touch and the coaches could still go." (From *Loose Cannons and Red Herrings*, by Robert Claiborne)

Michael Caine's real name: Maurice Mickelwhite. (He took "Caine" from *The Caine Mutiny*.)

MORE AMAZING LUCK

Sometimes we're blessed with it, sometimes we're cursed with it—dumb luck. Here are some more examples of people who've lucked out…for better and for worse.

HEADIN' DOWN THE HIGHWAY

Howard Hamer had just begun his ascent from the Chiloquin airport in Oregon when his plane inexplicably lost power. Hamer searched for a place to set down his homemade Lancer 235 aircraft, and decided that an emergency landing on the northbound lane of U.S. 97 was his best option. But as he was watching for oncoming traffic while attempting to keep the plane's nose pointed up, Hamer didn't see the truck right beneath him. Apparently the truck driver didn't see him, either. When they crashed, the propeller got caught on the truck's sleeper cabin, and the tail of the plane landed on the truck's flatbed. Amazingly, both the driver and the pilot walked away unharmed.

THE UNLUCKIEST-LUCKIEST AWARD

It was bad luck when a 20-year-old Greek man accidentally shot himself in the head with his speargun while fishing off the island of Crete. A lifeguard found him floating in the water six hours later, the spear entering his jaw, going through his brain, and protruding from the top of his skull. But it was incredibly good luck when surgeons discovered that the spear had passed through one of the spaces in the brain that are nonfunctional—if it was just millimeters to the left or right, he would have suffered serious brain injury or died. They removed it in a three-hour operation that left the man with no brain damage and no health problems.

GOOSEBUMP MATERIAL

In April 2006, Carolyn Holt of St. Charles, Missouri, was driving through the city when she suffered a heart attack. Her car veered across traffic and struck a guardrail before coming to a stop. Other drivers quickly stopped to help. Luckily, two of them were nurses, and after a truck driver used his trailer hitch to smash a window and get Holt out of the car, they immediately started doing CPR.

Cheep entertainment: Some male songbirds sing more than 2,000 times each day.

But Holt didn't respond—her heart had stopped beating. That's when another stopped motorist walked over. He happened to be a defibrillator salesman...and had one of the devices in his car. The nurses used it to get Holt's heart beating, and, thanks to the improbable circumstances, she survived. One of the nurses said, "It was a true miracle that evening." The salesman, Steve Earle, said it was even more of one than they realized. "It was strange luck," he said, "because when we finish up work for the day, a lot of times we'll get in my wife's car and take it out to eat or to pick my daughter up. For some reason we just happened to get into my car."

HE WAS STUNNED
In the summer of 2000, Laurence Webbler took his eight-year-old grandson Josh on a fishing trip. But unfortunately, while they were out, Webbler suffered a heart attack. As he lost consciousness, Josh sprang into action. He picked up the electronic fish stunner his grandpa had brought and jabbed him with 5,000 volts. "That was enough to get the old ticker going again," Webbler later commented.

ANT SHE LUCKY?
In 1999 amateur skydiver Joan Murray jumped from a plane at 14,500 feet. Her main parachute failed to open, and at 700 feet her reserve chute opened briefly but then deflated. Murray hit the ground hard, landing directly on top of a fire ant hill. The ants attacked, stinging Murray again and again. Murray went into a coma, but miraculously, the ants' relentless stinging helped keep her heart beating until she was rescued. (She came out of the coma after a few weeks; she returned to skydiving two years later.)

BABY SAVES THE DAY
One afternoon in 1995 at the Kiddie Kove Nursery in Chicago, two-year-old Kolby Grinston reached up and innocently pulled the school's fire alarm. Teachers calmly filed their students outside as they had practiced many times before. Minutes later, as the children were waiting to return to their classroom, a car barreled through a red light and struck another vehicle, sending it across the nursery playground and crashing into the school. The car landed on top of a row of lockers where the children would have been standing, hanging up their jackets and sweaters before their afternoon nap, if Kolby had not pulled the fire alarm.

Disneyland, CA, and Disney World, FL, are both are located in Orange County.

CELEBRITY GOSSIP

*Here's the BRI's cheesy tabloid section—a
bunch of gossip about famous people.*

OPRAH WINFREY

After undergoing DNA tests, Winfrey proudly declared that she is a Zulu, descended from the race of warriors who once ruled South Africa. How did the modern day Zulus react? They snubbed her. African-Americans, they claim, are descended from *West* Africans. South Africans ended up in Asia and South America. Prince Mangosuthu Buthelezi, leader of the seven-million-strong tribe, said, "I hate to tell Oprah this, but she is sorely mistaken."

MARLON BRANDO

While filming the 2001 movie *The Score*, Brando refused to be on the set at the same time as director Frank Oz. Brando referred to Oz as "Miss Piggy" (Oz provided the voice of Muppet Miss Piggy many years ago) and teased him with lines like "Don't you wish I was a puppet, so you could control me." Robert De Niro was forced to direct Brando instead, with Oz giving him instructions via headset.

DONALD TRUMP

Trump once visited the Bronx's Public School 70 (located in a poor neighborhood) for the school's annual Principal for a Day event. On his way out, he dropped a $1 million bill in the bake sale cash box. (It was fake, of course—Trump's idea of a joke.)

JANIS JOPLIN

She once went on a blind date with William Bennett. He was apparently so traumatized that he became a conservative "family values" advocate...and eventually drug czar under Ronald Reagan.

PARIS HILTON

While dining at a fancy restaurant with Pamela Anderson, Hilton threw a temper tantrum when handed the menu. "I hate reading! Someone tell me what's on the menu!" Anderson told the story to GQ magazine, concluding, "I'm blonde, too. But c'mon."

Gulp! The average person swallows 295 times while eating a meal.

MICHAEL JACKSON

His opinion of other singers: Paul McCartney? Okay writer, not much of an entertainer. "I do better box office than he does." Frank Sinatra? "I don't know what people see in the guy. He's a legend, but he isn't much of a singer. He doesn't even have hits anymore." Mick Jagger? "He sings flat. How did he ever get to be a star? I just don't get it. He doesn't sell as many records as I do." Madonna? "She just isn't that good....She can't sing. She's just an OK dancer....She knows how to market herself. That's about it."

TOM CRUISE

He enrolled in seminary school at age 14 to become a priest. He dropped out when he was 15.

O. J. SIMPSON

He was originally cast for the title role in the 1984 movie *The Terminator* but was ultimately rejected because, according to a studio executive, "People would never have believed a nice guy like O. J. could play the part of a ruthless killer."

HOWIE MANDEL

The wacky comedian and game-show host was expelled from his Toronto high school. Why? For pretending to be a member of the school board and convincing a construction company to start work on an addition to the school.

JOAN CRAWFORD

She was married five times. Weird habit: Every time she remarried, she replaced all of the toilet seats in her mansion.

CORETTA SCOTT KING

Walter and Betty Roberts, a young couple in Atlanta, Georgia, gave drama lessons to the children of Coretta Scott and Martin Luther King, Jr. in the 1960s. The Robertses were white, but they welcomed black children into their home during those racially charged times. In October 1967, upon hearing the news that Betty Roberts had to go to the hospital to deliver her third child, Mrs. King paid all of the Robertses' hospital bills as a gesture of thanks. That child: Julia Roberts.

BEHIND THE HITS

Here are a few "inside" stories about popular songs.

The Artist: Nirvana
The Song: "Smells Like Teen Spirit" (1991)
The Story: Before Nirvana frontman Kurt Cobain fell for Courtney Love, he dated drummer Tobi Vail in 1991. But she eventually broke it off. One night, one of Vail's bandmates, Kathleen Hanna, was hanging out at Cobain's apartment, listening to him lament the break-up. At some point she grabbed a can of spray paint and scrawled the words, "Kurt smells like Teen Spirit" on Cobain's wall. (Teen Spirit was a deodorant that Vail wore, and her scent was still lingering on Cobain.) The phrase immediately struck him and provided the inspiration for what he later called "the ultimate pop song." "Smells Like Teen Spirit" became the first big hit from Nirvana's seminal album, *Nevermind*. It reached #6 on the Billboard charts and has since been called the anthem of a generation. Ironically, Cobain later admitted that he didn't know that Teen Spirit was a deodorant until after the song was released—he would have never knowingly put the name of a mass-produced product for teenagers into the title of one of his songs.

The Artist: Patsy Cline
The Song: "I Fall to Pieces" (1961)
The Story: Few singers conveyed emotion the way Cline did, and this anguished song about an ended love affair sounded like she'd torn her own heart out during the recording session. Truth was, she hated the tune and didn't want anything to do with it, but her record label was desperate for a hit and tricked her into believing she'd be dropped if she didn't record it. It became her first #1 single and stayed on the charts for 39 weeks. Oddly, Cline found out it was a hit after she'd nearly fallen to pieces herself. Songwriter Hank Cochran recalls, "Patsy had been in a bad car wreck. It almost killed her. She was in the hospital with her head wrapped with bandages. I told her, 'You got yourself a pop hit, girl.' I think she thought I was just fooling around. When she finally got well enough to look at the numbers, she just laid back and said, 'Damn!'"

The most flowers sold in one day in U.S. history was the day after Elvis Presley died in 1977.

The Artist: Red Hot Chili Peppers

The Song: "Under the Bridge" (1992)

The Story: After a decade as a punk-funk band little known outside Los Angeles, the Chili Peppers were possibly the unlikeliest group to score a pop hit, especially with a ballad. While recording the album *Blood Sugar Sex Magik*, the group was grasping for ideas when producer Rick Rubin discovered Anthony Kiedis's notebook and was moved by an unfinished poem the singer had written about his days as a homeless drug addict. Kiedis agreed to record it, figuring it would go nowhere. The album went on to sell 7 million copies, reach #2, and help make the Chili Peppers one of rock's biggest acts.

The Artist: The Rolling Stones

The Song: "Jumpin' Jack Flash" (1968)

The Story: One rainy winter morning, Mick Jagger and Keith Richards were in Richards's living room when Jagger suddenly jumped up, frightened by a stomping noise. Richards explained, "Oh, that's just Jack, the gardener. That's jumpin' Jack." The two laughed and Richards began fooling around on the guitar, singing, "Jumpin' Jack." Inspired by the lightning, Jagger added "Flash!"

The Artist: Sheryl Crow

The Song: "All I Wanna Do" (1994)

The Story: After years of trying to break into the Los Angeles music scene—including singing backup on Michael Jackson's "Bad" tour—Crow finally got a record deal in 1991. During a recording session, Crow wrote what she thought was a decent song...musically, anyway; she hated the words. She was stuck, so her producer ran across the street to a bookstore and bought 10 books of poetry, selected at random. He gave them to Crow, locked her in the bathroom, and told her to come out when she had something. Crow picked a poem entitled "Fun" and started singing the words, taking out some of the poet's lines and adding her own. "'All I Wanna Do' was the throwaway track of the album. It wasn't going to go on the record," she recalled. Good thing it did—the song won a Grammy and propelled Crow to superstardom. Meanwhile, an English teacher in Vermont named Wyn Cooper began receiving royalty checks for a poem he'd written 10 years earlier.

The 2½ bucks stop here: Original U.S. gold coinage included $10, $5, and $2.50 coins.

I'VE BEEN CORNOBBLED!

You won't find these archaic words in most dictionaries,
but take our word for it—they're real. And just
for fun, try to use them in a sentence.

Hobberdehoy, A youth entering manhood

Faffle, To stutter or mumble

Dasypygal, Having hairy buttocks

Cornobbled, Hit with a fish

Collieshangie, A noisy or confused fight

Wem, A stain, flaw, or scar

Calcographer, One who draws with chalk

Bodewash, Cow dung

Twiddlepoop, An effeminate-looking man

Liripoop, A silly creature

Leptorrhinian, Having a long narrow nose

Bridelope, When the new bride is "both symbolically and physically swept off on horseback" to the husband's home

Mundungus, Garbage; stinky tobacco

Chirogymnast, A finger-exercise machine for pianists

Toxophily, love of archery

Pismire, An ant

Valgus, Bowlegged or knock-kneed

Xystus, An indoor porch for exercising in winter

Jumentous, Having a strong animal smell

Saprostomous, Having bad breath

Balbriggan, A fine cotton used mainly for underwear

Atmatertera, A great-grandfather's grandmother's sister

Anisognathous, Having the upper and lower teeth unlike

Whipjack, A beggar pretending to have been shipwrecked

Spodogenous, Pertaining to or due to the presence of waste matter

Crapandina, A mineral such as toadstone or bufonite said to have healing properties

Galligaskin, Baggy trousers

What's for dinner, honey? A hive of honeybees eats up to 30 pounds of honey over the winter.

GIMLI GLIDER, PART II

*Here's the second installment of our story about the little
jumbo jet that could. (Part I starts on page 283.)*

LITTLE THINGS MEAN A LOT

To understand what happened aboard Flight 143, we need to revisit the math. It turns out that Captain Pearson made a slight error in his calculations. When you multiply liters by 1.77, you convert them into *pounds*, not kilograms (to convert a liter to a kilogram, you multiply by 0.8). Flight 143 had 20,302 *pounds* of fuel in its tanks when it left Montreal, not 20,302 kilograms. And since 1 pound weighs less than half of 1 kilogram, Flight 143 had less than half the fuel it needed to get where it was going.

Normally Captain Pearson and First Officer Quintal would have known long in advance that they were running low on fuel—the gauges would have triggered a little red warning light. But not in this case. Since Pearson and Quintal's original estimate was so far off, the low-fuel light never came on. The estimated fuel gauge showed plenty of fuel left…even as the last drops were being sucked from the tanks.

BEEP! BEEP! BEEP! BEEP!

The first hint of trouble came just minutes before the engines quit, about two hours into the flight. Four quick audible beeps sounded in the cockpit and a warning light came on, indicating that one of the two fuel pumps in the left wing was reporting low pressure. That's not unheard of, and at first Captain Pearson assumed that there was something wrong with the fuel pump. But moments later four more beeps sounded and the *second* fuel pump in the left wing reported low pressure. What are the odds that two pumps would fail at the same time? Captain Pearson concluded it couldn't be the pumps. It had to be the fuel.

He decided to divert Flight 143 to Winnipeg, the nearest major airport. Whatever the problem was with the left fuel tank, he wanted it fixed before they flew any farther. He took the plane down from 41,000 feet to 28,000 feet, and made plans to land with only one engine, if it came to that.

More people on the West Coast prefer chunky peanut butter; East Coasters, creamy.

TANKS FOR NOTHING

About five minutes after the first alarm sounded, four *more* beeps sounded and two *more* lights came on. Then *another* four beeps and *another* four lights. Now the two fuel pumps in the right wing tank, as well as the two fuel pumps in the center tank, were reporting low pressure. (The pumps themselves were fine—they were reporting low pressure because the fuel tanks were empty and pumping nothing but air.)

Nine minutes after the first beeps, a loud *bong!* sounded in the cockpit. The left engine, completely starved of gas, sputtered out. Pearson and Quintal, still trying to figure out what was going on, prepared to land the 767 at Winnipeg with only one engine. It was an emergency situation, but it was something the plane was designed to do and something they had been trained to handle.

Then, three minutes later, the right engine ran out of fuel and quit. Pearson and Quintal hadn't been trained to land a 767 with both engines out. Nobody had—jumbo jets aren't supposed to run out of gas.

FROM BAD TO WORSE

In a normal aircraft with conventional mechanical instruments, the instruments keep working even if all the engines quit. But as Captain Pearson quickly realized, glass cockpits are different. They get their power from electrical generators powered by the jet engines. When both engines fail, the generators quit producing electricity…and all the computer screens go dark.

In an instant, Pearson lost the digital instruments that displayed the plane's airspeed, altitude, and heading. He lost his transponder, which gives the plane's location, speed, and altitude to air traffic controllers, and he lost his vertical speed indicator, which told him how fast the plane was losing altitude. He didn't even have a clock.

There was more. The hydraulic system, which controls the landing gear and rudders, is also powered by the engine. So as the engines were quitting and the cockpit was going dark, Pearson felt his control yoke (similar to a steering wheel) and his rudder pedals stiffen and become unresponsive.

He had no fuel, he had almost no instruments, and he was quickly losing his ability to control the aircraft.

FOR EMERGENCY USE ONLY

Airplanes are designed with many redundancies built in, so that if a piece of equipment fails, there's usually a backup and the plane can fly and land safely. Quintal flipped the switch to activate the auxiliary power unit (APU), which is designed to provide backup electricity and hydraulics. There was just one problem: like the generators, the APU was powered by jet fuel. The hydraulic system and the glass cockpit flickered to life for a moment, then went dark again when the APU sputtered out.

That was it for the digital instruments—there was no other source of power for them. But there *was* one more backup system to power the hydraulics.

SECOND WIND

Did you ever stick a pinwheel out the window of a moving car when you were a kid? The Boeing 767 has a device called a ram air turbine (RAT), located near the right wheel well. It's a propeller on a long arm and in an emergency it can be manually extended out into the airstream, just like a kid's pinwheel. When the RAT hits the airstream, the propeller spins, generating just enough hydraulic pressure in the process to power basic flight controls.

As Captain Pearson wrestled with the controls, Quintal engaged the RAT. Then he grabbed the 767's emergency procedures manual and started looking for the section that told them what to do when both engines failed. There was no such section. So many redundancies had been built into the 767 that its designers never bothered to plan for the ultimate failure—no fuel in the tanks. They figured that all of the other redundancies and alarms would prevent such a thing from ever happening. The planes weren't supposed to run out of fuel—not in the air, not on the ground, not ever.

And because the 767 had never been flight tested with both engines off, nobody knew how the jet would perform as a "glider," or what amount of altitude it would lose for every mile traveled. Pearson knew that the plane was at about 28,000 feet when the second engine failed. But how far could it glide before it hit the ground? Were nearby airports close enough for the plane to glide to, or would it crash before they got there? He just didn't know.

A fashion model's career lasts, on average, about six years.

CHANGE OF PLANS

Thankfully, Flight 143's radios had a backup battery, so *they* still worked. With help from Winnipeg Air Traffic Control, Quintal was able to estimate that the plane was losing about 5,000 feet of altitude for every 10 miles traveled. That wasn't good news. By now they were only about 35 miles away from Winnipeg, but according to Quintal's calculations, if they stayed the course they would crash about 12 miles short of the runway. They had to find a closer place to land.

The air traffic controllers suggested the old Canadian Air Force base in Gimli, Manitoba, about 50 miles north of Winnipeg. The base had been closed since 1971, but one of the two parallel landing strips was still used by civilian aircraft. Each one was more than twice as long as the one at Winnipeg, and long runways are a nice thing to have when you're trying to land a 300,000-pound aircraft without any power. More importantly, Quintal was already familiar with the airport, because he had trained there when he was in the Air Force.

Flight 143 was going to Gimli.

For Part III, turn to page 562.

* * *

FORECAST: CHANCE OF TOAD-CHOKER

Arizonans have their own slang when it comes to rain. A few samples.

Dust-Settler: A teaser. Enough rain to do just that—settle the dust.

Turd-floater: This happens when it rains so much that the ground and everything on it gets completely saturated, lifted from its place of deposit, and transported to a lower elevation.

Tank-filler: This is the next best kind of rain—enough to fill the livestock water tanks, saving the ranchers from having to haul it in. Tank fillers are usually heavy rains that come after a turd floater.

Toad-choker (or frog strangler): Lots of rain in a short time. Result: drowned amphibians on the open range.

Gully-washer: This type of rain can be deadly. It happens when rain falls faster than it can be absorbed into the ground, turning gullies and just about any other low spot into a temporarily raging river.

The whistling swan has the most feathers of any bird, about 25,000.

HAPPY HOLIDAYS

*Time to celebrate with some little-known
trivia about some very big days.*

LABOR DAY

In 1893 amid growing labor unrest, President Grover Cleveland sent 12,000 federal troops to stop a strike at the Pullman train car company in Chicago. The strike was broken, but two men were killed and many more were beaten. For Cleveland and the Democrats, the move backfired—the pro-business brutality only served to bolster the growing union movement.

To win back constituents, Congress passed legislation the following year making the first Monday in September a national holiday honoring labor. It was a presidential election year, so President Cleveland promptly signed the bill into law, hoping it would appease American workers. It didn't. Cleveland was defeated… but Labor Day was established for good.

GROUNDHOG DAY

February 2, the midpoint between winter solstice and spring equinox, has been celebrated for eons. The Celts called it *Imbolc* ("in the belly"—for sheep pregnant with lambs); Romans had *Lupercalia,* a fertility celebration. For other cultures, too, the day was marked by rituals of "rebirth" and hope for a bountiful new growing season.

According to Irish tradition, a snake emerges from "the womb of Earth" and tests the weather to see if spring has arrived. The Germans had a similar tradition, except that they watched for badgers waking from hibernation. If the day was a sunny, shadow-casting day, more winter weather was to come. No shadow meant an early spring.

When German settlers came to Pennsylvania in the 1700s, they brought the custom with them…but there were no badgers, so they substituted another hibernating animal: the groundhog.

~~COLUMBUS~~ AMERICAN INDIAN DAY

Attempts to designate a national day honoring Native Americans have been made—unsuccessfully—for nearly a century. In 1914 Red Fox James, a Blackfoot Indian, rode 4,000 miles on horseback in support of a national day of recognition for Native Americans. He ended the journey in Washington, D.C., where his proposal for the holiday was adopted by 24 state governments. The state of New York became the first to officially designate an American Indian Day, in May 1916.

While it has yet to be recognized as a national holiday, several states, South Dakota being the first, have officially changed another time-honored holiday to American Indian Day: the second Monday in October—Columbus Day.

MERRY MITHRAS

The Bible doesn't say when Jesus was born, but many historians think it was in April. So why is Christmas celebrated on December 25? One possible reason: *Mithras*. Mithras was a Persian deity known as The Conquering Sun, and his birthday was traditionally celebrated at the winter solstice in late December. Mithraism and Christianity were both becoming popular in the Mediterranean region at about the same time. But early Christians were determined to prevail, so they adopted December 25 as the date of the Nativity. By the third or fourth century A.D., the already popular day was firmly entrenched as Christmas.

*   *   *

THIS AIN'T NO PARTY

In April 2002, a Veterans of Foreign Wars group in Utah issued a resolution demanding that the date of Earth Day be changed. Why? April 22 is former Soviet leader Vladimir Lenin's birthdate. The group refused to celebrate on the birthday of "the godless master of manipulation, misinformation, and murder."

Not only that, members claim the day was chosen intentionally and that former Wisconsin senator Gaylord Nelson, founder of Earth Day, is a communist sympathizer. "He voted against funding the Vietnam War," said one post commander.

The 86-year-old Nelson said it was a coincidence. "Several million people were born on any day of the year. Does the VFW want to change it to another day on which, undoubtedly, some really evil person was born? Hitler? Mussolini? Genghis Khan?"

Another April 22 birthday: St. Francis of Assisi.

LITTLE THINGS MEAN A LOT

*"The devil's in the details," says an old proverb. It's true—
the littlest things can cause the biggest problems.*

THE WORD 'PLEASE'

In 1995 Pacific Bell Telephone told its 4,500 directory assistance operators to answer calls with either: "Hi, this is _____, what city?"or "Hi, I'm _____, what city?" According to Pac Bell, these new greetings take 1.2 seconds to say, compared to 1.7 seconds when "please" is used. The phone company calculated that shaving half a second off of each call makes it possible for operators to handle 135,000 more calls per hour.

A PIECE OF TAPE

In the early morning of June 17, 1972, an $80-a-week security guard named Frank Wills was patrolling the parking garage of an office complex in Washington, D.C., when he noticed that someone had used adhesive tape to prevent a stairwell door from latching. Wills removed the tape and continued on his rounds...but when he returned to the same door at 2:00 a.m., he saw it had been taped *again*. So he called the police, who discovered a team of burglars planting bugs in an office leased by the Democratic National Committee. This "third-rate burglary"—and the coverup that followed—grew into the Watergate scandal that forced President Richard M. Nixon to resign from office in 1974.

A FEW WASHERS

The $1.6 billion Hubble Space telescope was launched into orbit on April 24 1990, and immediately needed repairs. Cost of the rescue mission: $86 million. Cause of the problem: a few 25¢ washers that technicians used to fill in a gap in an optical testing device. No one noticed they were there...until they shook loose.

Geologically speaking, we live in the Cenozoic era, which began 65 million years ago.

SUPERPREDATORS OF THE DEEP

Built-in lights, electrical sensors, flotation devices: Sharks have more ways to kill than an international spy. Here are some of their secrets.

THEY'RE EVERYWHERE!

Over the past 400 million years, sharks have evolved into nature's perfect killers. As anyone who saw *Jaws* can tell you, sharks can attack silently and with great bursts of speed. Their jaws can snap a sea lion in half, and their enormous throat can swallow both pieces whole.

And if that's not enough to haunt your nightmares, there are nearly 400 species of sharks, ranging from about six inches to 50 feet long, inhabiting every oceanic corner of the globe. The good news is that most of them don't have the least interest in humans. Some, like the polka-dotted whale shark (weighing in at 13 tons), are perfectly happy with plankton and schools of small fish. The most common shark, the dogfish, lives mainly on fish, crabs, octopus, and squid. In fact, instead of eating people, the reverse is true. These sharks, among others, are more likely to appear on *our* dinner tables.

ARMORED AND DANGEROUS

All the same, sharks have to be respected as dangerous predators with millions of years of evolution on their side. The shark's torpedo-shaped body can shoot through the water at speeds of over 30 mph. Their skeletons are made of lightweight cartilage rather than bone, which gives them great flexibility in battle. Even the shark's liver helps it catch prey. Rich in oils and lighter than water, the liver works like a flotation device to keep a shark buoyant, cruising along easily while it hunts for food.

JAWS

Then there are the actual jaws. The biting strength of some sharks is a crushing 6.5 tons per square inch. The great white slashes at

---

The dwarf shark is no bigger than your hand; the whale shark is as big as a bus.

its victims with over 3,000 teeth. (Most sharks have at least four parallel rows of teeth—if one tooth breaks or is knocked out, another tooth moves forward to replace it.) And a shark's teeth aren't all in its mouth. Its skin is covered with thousands of tiny teeth called placoid scales. These sharp, pointy scales are covered with enamel, just like teeth, and make shark skin so abrasive that it becomes a weapon. A shark can tear at its prey just by brushing against it. Scared yet? There's more.

SENSING THEIR SUPPER

You can swim from hungry sharks, but you can't hide. Their eyes have what's called a *tapetum*, a reflecting layer behind the retina that enhances vision. Sharks' eyes are so sensitive to individual flickers of light that they can pick up the slightest movement. Lantern sharks, which live in dark water 6,000 feet deep, have phosphorescent lights embedded on their bellies to help them see in the dark. But if a shark decides to kill, it doesn't have to rely on sight alone. Sound travels nearly five times faster in water than in air, and a shark can pick up the sounds of prey from a distance of 3,000 feet. They're primed to hear low-frequency sounds, like the sound of contracting muscle tissue in an injured, struggling fish—or human.

A shark's sense of touch is enhanced by a strip of sensory cells along each side of its body that can feel the vibrations of prey moving through the water. And if by some chance a shark doesn't see, hear, or feel its prey, the hunt isn't over. Its sense of smell is so acute that some sharks can smell one drop of blood diluted in one million drops of seawater.

And if five powerful senses aren't enough, sharks have an astounding *sixth* sense. All animals, including human beings, emit electrical signals, which a shark detects with a special system of gel-filled pores around its head and mouth. In dark, deep water or sandy shallows, these electrical sensors allow a hunting shark to position its head and mouth, then close in on a victim that it can't even see.

LIGHTNING STRIKES VS. SHARK ATTACKS

With all that deadly equipment, it's not surprising that sharks sometimes kill humans. But shark attacks on humans are rare—in fact, it's often reported that the average human is far more likely to get hit by lightning than attacked by a shark. But why is that, when so many people swim in the ocean? Probably because we taste bad. Sharks cruise near swimmers every day without bothering them, and many people have survived shark attacks because the shark bit them, then spit them out.

The 1970s movie *Jaws* terrified the world with its story of a great white shark devouring swimmers and boaters on the Atlantic coast. But the great white and other large sharks aren't mindless demons with an overwhelming desire for human flesh—they happen to feed in the shallows where humans like to swim. Researchers now believe that attacks often occur when a shark, in murky water, mistakes a swimmer for a school of fish or a threatening enemy. And a diver in a wetsuit can resemble the great white shark's favorite meal: a tasty seal or sea lion.

SHARK KILLS GO OVERBOARD

Peter Benchley, author of *Jaws*, has said that if he rewrote the story today, the great white shark would be a victim, not a villain. Sharks existed before the first dinosaurs appeared, but in the past two decades—partly because they seem so threatening—millions of sharks have been slaughtered by humans. Now some species (including the great white) are in danger of extinction. When sharks disappear, other sea life does, too. Lobsters, for example, become endangered when there aren't enough sharks to control the lobster-eating octopus population. Today naturalists are waging an ongoing battle to save these magnificent underwater killers...and warning that the world will suffer if the shark can't do its lethal job.

* * *

SHARK ATTACK!

• Sharks can be dangerous even before they're born. While examining a pregnant sand tiger shark, a scientist was once bitten by the shark's embryo.

• Four species—the great white, tiger shark, bull shark, and hammerhead—are responsible for 85% of all shark attacks.

...The offspring of both are called calves.

THE WORST BUSINESS DECISION IN U.S. HISTORY

The worst decision in history? A bold claim, especially when you consider how many bad decisions people make every day (except Uncle John). Still, have you driven a Daisy lately? No, and you never will, either. Here's why.

TILTING AT WINDMILLS

In the early 1880s, a Plymouth, Michigan, watch repairman named Clarence J. Hamilton came up with the idea of making windmills from metal instead of wood. Farmers used windmills to pump water for crop irrigation, and in those days most of them built the windmills themselves. Hamilton thought that if he could design a better, sturdier windmill made from iron and sell it at a low enough price, farmers would line up to buy them. So in 1882 the Plymouth Iron Windmill Company opened for business.

It turns out Hamilton was wrong—farmers in the 1880s were loathe to spend money on anything they could make themselves, even if his iron windmills were better. After six years in business, the Plymouth Iron Windmill Company was still struggling, so Hamilton invented something else that he thought would help boost windmill sales: a toy rifle that used compressed air to shoot industrial ball bearings —"BBs" for short—instead of bullets. It wasn't the first BB gun ever invented, but this one was made of metal, which made it sturdier and a better shot than competing guns, which were made of wood. His idea was to give a free BB gun to every farmer who bought a windmill.

FLOWER POWER

Hamilton showed the air rifle to the company's general manager, Lewis Cass Hough, who shot at the trash can in his office and then went outside and shot an old shingle from 10 feet away. "Boy!" he said. "That's a daisy!" The name stuck…but Hamilton's idea of giving away free BB guns with every windmill didn't— farmers wanted the guns, not the windmills. So the Plymouth Iron Windmill Co. changed its name to the Daisy Manufacturing Co. and started making BB guns full time.

The city of Tsuenchen, China, was designed to resemble a carp when viewed from above.

BB KING

In 1891 Lewis Hough hired his nephew Charles Bennett and made him Daisy's first salesman. Smart move. Thanks to Bennett's hard work, by the turn of the century, Daisy was manufacturing 250,000 air rifles a year.

By 1903 Bennett was president of the company and a pillar of the Plymouth business community. To celebrate his success, that spring he made a trip into nearby Detroit to buy an Oldsmobile, the hottest-selling car in the country.

But before he took his test drive, Bennett happened to stop at a tailor shop to buy a suit, and while there he mentioned he was going to buy a car. A man named Frank Malcomson happened to overhear him, and as Bennett was leaving, Malcomson introduced himself. He explained that his cousin, coal merchant Alex Malcomson, had started his own auto company with the help of a business partner. So far they'd managed to build only one test car, but Malcomson told Bennett that he should really take a ride in his cousin's car before he signed the papers on the Oldsmobile. Bennett agreed to go for a ride that very afternoon.

About an hour later, Alex Malcomson's business partner, a relatively unknown engineer named Henry Ford, pulled up in the test car, which he called the Model A. Bennett hopped in, they went for a drive, and by the time they were through, Bennett had given up his plans to buy an Oldsmobile. The Model A was a better car, he told Ford, and he was willing to wait until it came on the market.

But how long would that take? And how much would it cost? Ford said he wasn't sure and that Alex Malcomson was a better person to ask. So he drove Bennett to Malcomson's office, dropped him off, and then sped off to parts unknown. "He probably had someone else that he was taking for a ride," Bennett reminisced many years later.

RISKY BUSINESS

Would the Model A ever come to market at all? The *car* may have been impressive, but the company behind it, if it could even be called a company, was a mess. Ford & Malcomson, soon to evolve into the Ford Motor Company, was having trouble coming up with the cash it needed to begin production. Henry Ford deserved

When a person is dying, hearing is the last sense to go. Sight is the first.

a lot of the blame: in less than two years he'd wrecked one auto company and gotten himself thrown out of another. He had a bad habit of sneaking off to tinker on race cars when he should have been designing regular cars to sell to the public. And in the process he'd burned through nearly $90,000 of his investors' money—about $1.8 million today—while managing to build only about a dozen cars.

Malcomson was hardly better. He was the largest coal dealer in the area, but he'd built up his business by borrowing huge sums of money from nearly every banker in Detroit. He was so overextended, in fact, that he had to hide his interest in the Ford company so that his bankers wouldn't know what he was up to.

When Ford and Malcomson made the rounds of Detroit's wealthiest investors to raise funds for yet another auto company, few took them seriously. The two men were reduced to cajoling money out of relatives, suppliers, Malcomson's attorneys, his coal company employees, his landlord, and anyone else they could think of…including Charles Bennett.

DEAL OF A LIFETIME

When Bennett went into Malcomson's office to talk about buying a car, Malcomson offered him a chance to buy a stake in the company. A *huge* stake in the company. Reports vary as to exactly how much he was offered, but it was at least 25% and may have been as much as 50%—for as little as $75,000.

A 50% stake would have made Bennett the largest individual shareholder, with Ford, Malcomson, and the others dividing up the other 50%. Bringing Bennett into Ford made a lot of business sense: Associating with such a successful businessman would make the Ford Motor Company seem viable, too, making it easier to attract other investors and to borrow money from bankers no longer willing to lend money to Malcomson alone.

Bennett knew a good product when he saw one, and he wanted in. There was only one thing stopping him—he didn't have $75,000. But the Daisy Manufacturing Company did. So when he got back to Plymouth, Bennett told his business partner Ed Hough (Lewis Hough's son) that he was going to invest some of Daisy's money in a car company.

SLOW DOWN, PARDNER

That was when Daisy's attorneys informed Bennett that the company charter forbade investing its funds in other companies. The reasoning was logical. What would happen if Ford & Malcomson went under like so many other auto companies had? Daisy would lose its investment. And if it merged with the automaker (another idea Bennett was toying with), it might even have to make good on that company's losses. Besides—kids were always going to want BB guns for Christmas. Would anyone still be interested in automobiles five years from now? Maybe cars were just a fad.

"Bennett's fellow directors at Daisy balked at the proposal, on the grounds that there was no reason to diversify from air rifles into something as whimsical as the automobile," writes Douglas Brinkley in *Wheels for the World*.

THANKS, BUT NO THANKS

Bennett tried everything he could think of to get Daisy's directors to agree to invest in the auto company, but nothing worked—and Daisy never did buy in. Instead of getting half of the company, Bennett had to settle for buying a 3.3% stake for $5,000, which was all he could personally afford.

To be fair, there's a good chance that even if Daisy had been willing to buy half of what would soon become the Ford Motor Company, Henry Ford might not have allowed it. Ford was determined to be his own boss, and when the investors in his earlier auto companies tried to assert themselves, he just walked away, leaving them holding the bag. That as much as anything had caused him to fail. It's questionable whether he would have allowed anyone other than himself to own such a huge stake in the new company.

Plus, there was talk that if Daisy got involved with the new company, Bennett might want to give a BB gun away with each car sold, or even worse, that he would insist the new car be called a Daisy. According to Brinkley, Henry Ford "was not about to see his latest creation named after a flower or a gun."

DUMB DECISION #2

Bennett owned 3.3% of Ford, so when the company introduced the Model T in 1908 and grew into the largest auto manufacturer on Earth, Bennett became stinking rich, right? Wrong. After he and Malcomson took sides against Henry Ford in a power struggle (never a good idea) and lost, Bennett sold his Ford shares. That was in 1907—the year *before* the Model T changed the world. Bennett got $35,000 for his shares.

GO AHEAD AND CRY

Had Bennett held onto his 3.3% stake in the Ford Motor Company until 1919—for 12 more years—when Henry Ford bought out the last of the other shareholders and assumed full ownership, he would have earned $4,750,000 ($47 million today) in dividends. His stock would have been worth $12.5 million ($123 million today). Not a bad return on a $5,000 investment.

Had Daisy bought 50% of the company in 1903 (and had Henry Ford not run the company into the ground, as he had done with earlier ventures when he wasn't allowed to call the shots), their half of the Ford Motor Company would have been worth at least $125 million ($1.24 *billion* today), and possibly as much as $500 million ($4.95 *billion* today).

"The original investors in the Ford Motor Company had received the largest return on risk capital in recorded business history," Robert Lacey writes in *Ford: The Men and the Machine*. Thanks to one bad decision, Daisy's investors didn't get a penny of it.

*   *   *

SMART CROOKS (for a change)

How do you make sure the police won't interrupt your burglary? Fix it so they can't even leave their headquarters. That's what happened in 2001 in the Dutch town of Stadskanaal. Thieves simply padlocked the front gates of the high fence that surrounds the police compound, then robbed a nearby electronics store. That set off a burglar alarm in the police station, but there was nothing police could do about it—they were all locked in. As the crooks made off with TVs and camcorders, Stadskanaal cops had to sit and wait for reinforcements to arrive from the next town. A police spokesman said, "It's a pity all our officers were at that moment in the police station. Normally most of them are on patrol." They've since taken precautions to make certain it never happens again.

There are 71 known moons in our solar system (so far).

SMELLS LIKE...MURDER

Premature death seems almost like an occupational hazard among
rock stars. But that doesn't make fans—or conspiracy theorists—
any less suspicious, particularly in the case of suicide.
And this one seems more suspicious than most.

The Deceased: Kurt Cobain, leader of Seattle grunge band
Nirvana. Gained notoriety with the 1991 angst-filled
anthem "Smells Like Teen Spirit."

How He Died: On April 8, 1994, an electrician spotted Cobain's
dead body lying on the floor of a greenhouse room above the
detached garage at the musician's Seattle residence. Police determined that Cobain had injected himself with heroin, then stuck a
shotgun into his mouth and pulled the trigger. Near the body they
found a "suicide note." According to media reports, Cobain's wallet, open to his driver's license, was next to the body, ostensibly to
make identification easier after the blast to the head.

To the police (and most of the media), it looked like a clear case
of another rock star destroyed by his demons. But did the police
overlook evidence that might have pointed to a different conclusion?

SUSPICIOUS FACTS
• At the time Cobain was shot, he had three times the lethal dose
of heroin in his blood. According to experts, even an addict like
Cobain would be comatose with that level of the drug in his body,
incapable of positioning a gun and pulling the trigger. Cobain had
two fresh needle marks, one on each arm. Did he inject himself
twice? If he was intent on committing suicide, why didn't he just let
the overdose do its work? Or were the second injection and the
shotgun blast the work of someone else?
• There were no legible fingerprints on the shotgun that killed
Cobain. (The gun wasn't even tested for fingerprints until nearly a
month after his death.) Fingerprints can be wiped off a gun, but is
that what happened here? If so, who wiped the gun clean, and why?
• Only part of the "suicide note" found by Cobain's body sounds like
he planned to kill himself—the last four lines—and some experts

---

So *that's* why we bail water: The handle of a bucket or a kettle is called the *bail.*

question whether those lines are in his handwriting.

Most of the note is an anguished apology to his fans for his lack of enthusiasm and seems more about his resignation from the music industry than suicide. (Shortly before his death he decided not to headline the Lollapalooza tour.) Only the last four lines are addressed to his wife and daughter. Was suicide an afterthought, or did he actually have no intention of killing himself?

• The driver's license by the body wasn't left there by Cobain—the first police officer on the scene found Cobain's wallet nearby and displayed the license by the body for photographs.

• Someone attempted to use Cobain's credit card until just hours before the body was discovered, even though, according to the coroner's report, Cobain had died four days earlier. Cobain himself had last used the card to buy a plane ticket from Los Angeles to Seattle on April 1. The card was not found in his wallet.

WHAT REALLY HAPPENED?

If suicide seems unlikely, accidental death looks next to impossible. How could Cobain, a hardened addict, so seriously misjudge his heroin dose? After such a dose, could he have accidentally positioned the shotgun on his chest and pulled the trigger? And if suicide and accident are ruled out, that leaves only…murder. But who would have wanted to kill Cobain and make it appear a suicide?

THE LOVE CONNECTION

Cobain's wife, rock star Courtney Love, was in the L.A. area at the time Cobain's body was discovered. But according to Tom Grant, an L.A. private investigator, Love may have been involved in a conspiracy to kill her husband, possibly with the aid of Michael Dewitt, the male nanny who lived at the Cobain residence. Possible motives according to Grant:

✔ Cobain may have told Love he was leaving her; if the pair divorced, Love would get half of Cobain's estate. With a suicide she would get it all.

✔ Cobain's record sales would increase after a suicide, giving Love even more money.

✔ Her own career would benefit. (Love's band, Hole, headlined the Lollapalooza tour in place of Cobain and Nirvana.)

IS THIS LOVE?

Grant has a unique perspective—Love hired him to find Cobain after Cobain escaped from a drug rehab center just a few days before he died. Grant continued his investigation after the body was found and was disturbed by the inconsistencies and contradictions in Love's behavior:

✔ Love phoned in a missing persons report on April 4, the day Cobain died, according to the coroner's report. Claiming she was Cobain's mother, Love told Seattle police he had bought a shotgun and was suicidal. But a receipt found on Cobain's body showed that his best friend Dylan Carlson bought the gun for him almost a week earlier, *before* Cobain entered rehab. According to Carlson, Cobain wanted the gun for protection, not suicide. By phoning in the report, was Love trying to plant the idea that Cobain was suicidal?

✔ Love directed Grant to look for Cobain in a number of Seattle hotels and to check out his drug dealers. Even though Dewitt, the nanny, had told Love he'd talked with Cobain at their residence on April 2, Love did not tell Grant he'd been seen there. Was Love trying to keep Grant from finding Cobain too soon?

✔ When Grant visited the Cobain residence with Carlson the day before Cobain's body was found, there was evidence that Dewitt had been there recently. (Neither Grant nor Carlson looked in the greenhouse.) Later that day Dewitt told friends he was leaving for Los Angeles. Grant says he had the feeling Dewitt was avoiding him.

✔ The electrician who found Cobain's body was hired by Love to check the security system at the residence and, according to Rosemary Carroll, Love's entertainment lawyer, she specifically told him to check the greenhouse. Was she setting him up to find the body?

FADE AWAY

In the note found beside Kurt Cobain's body, his last words, before the disputed last four lines, were "...it's better to burn out than to fade away." Did he think shooting himself was the only way out of his apathetic malaise, or did he simply plan to leave the music scene near the peak of his popularity to avoid becoming just another mass-marketed rock star, ultimately drifting into irrelevance? The police investigation is closed...so we'll probably never know.

Study: Surgeons who listen to music during operations perform better than those who don't.

IT'S SERENDIPITY

*On page 309, we told you that the word "serendipity"
means "making happy and unexpected discoveries
by accident." Here are a few more examples.*

THE FIRST SYNTHETIC FIBER

In 1854 a devastating silkworm epidemic struck the silk industry in France, wiping it out, and in 1865 the renowned French scientist Louis Pasteur was asked to study the disease. One of his assistants, a young chemist named Hilaire de Chardonnet, became convinced that France needed some kind of artificial substitute for silk. Unfortunately, he had no idea how to find one.

In 1878 Chardonnet was working in a darkroom with some photographic plates when he knocked over a bottle of a photographic chemical called *collodion* (cellulose nitrate). He didn't bother to clean it up right away, and by the time he got around to it, much of the spill had evaporated. What was left? A sticky mess that produced "long, thin strands of fiber" as he wiped it up. The strands reminded him so much of silk fibers that he spent the next six years experimenting with the substance. Finally he invented what he called "artificial silk." In 1924 the name was changed to Rayon. It was the first commercially viable synthetic fiber, and paved the way for the entire synthetics industry.

THE FIRST ARTIFICIAL SWEETENER

In 1879 Constantin Fahlberg, a chemist at Johns Hopkins University, put in a long day at the lab. Then he washed up and went home for dinner. As he sat at the dinner table, Fahlberg noticed that the bread was surprisingly sweet. Then he realized that it wasn't the bread at all—it was something on his hands...and even his arms. He went back to the lab and tasted every beaker and basin he'd worked with that day (chemists weren't as cautious about poisoning themselves then). He finally found the source of the sweetness—a chemical called *ortho-sulfobenzoic acid imide*, which is 200-700 times as sweet as granulated sugar. Fahlberg patented the substance—the world's first artificial

---

Half of the body's water is lost and replaced every ten days.

sweetener—in 1885 under the name saccharin, from *saccharum*, the Latin word for sugar.

A FEW POP ICONS

A Classic Movie: When Frank Capra's *It's a Wonderful Life* was released in 1946, it was dismissed by critics as sappy and sentimental; by the 1950s it was largely forgotten. In the mid-1970s the movie's copyright lapsed and nobody remembered—or bothered—to renew it. That made the film "public domain"—i.e., legally, TV stations could broadcast it for free. That's why so many stations started showing it every holiday season…which is what turned it into the "Christmastime classic" it is today.

A Popular Radio Show: In 1977 the Program Director at Boston's public radio station WBUR invited five Boston-area mechanics to sit on a panel for a call-in talk show about cars. Two of the mechanics he asked were brothers Tom and Ray Magliozzi, owners of the Good News Garage in Cambridge, Massachusetts. Ray was busy, but Tom accepted the offer…and turned out to be the *only* person who showed up. He answered callers' questions so well that he was asked to return the next week. The week after that, he brought Ray along—and they've been doing "Car Talk" together (as Click and Clack, The Tappet Brothers) ever since.

A Movie Star: In 1983, Martha Coolidge, director of a film called *Valley Girl*, was angry with the casting director, who kept auditioning "pretty boys" for the lead role. So Coolidge went to the reject pile, pulled the first photo off the top, held it up and said. "Bring me someone like this." The picture was of Nicolas Cage, and he got the part. It was his first lead role.

…AND EVEN WORLD WAR I

"Private Henry Tandey had the man in his rifle sights at point-blank range. It was September 28, 1918, on the French battlefield of Marcoing…and Tandey's courage in battle that day would earn the young soldier [a medal]. Yet when Private Tandey realized the German corporal he was aiming for was already wounded, he couldn't bring himself to pull the trigger. Only years later did he realize that the object of his mercy was none other than Adolf Hitler." (*Bizarre* magazine)

Good news! A karaoke singing of "We Are the World" burns 20.7 calories.

FOR WHAT ALES YOU

It's not just for breakfast anymore! We've discovered that beer has many inventive and unlikely uses around the home and beyond. (Uncle John's never had so much fun researching an article.)

• Beer is slightly acidic, making it useful for cleaning copper pots. Throw a small amount of beer in the pot, let it sit for a few minutes, and then wipe it out.

• Beer adds shine and luster to hair. Boil one cup of beer until it's reduced down to ¼ cup. Let it cool and mix with your regular shampoo.

• After a beer shampoo, try a beer conditioner. Mix three tablespoons of beer with half a cup of warm water. After washing your hair, rub in the beer solution, leave it in for a couple minutes, then rinse. The beer reportedly makes flat hair bouncier.

• Beer kills pesky garden slugs. Fill some wide-mouthed jars a third of the way full with beer. Bury them about 15–20 feet from your garden, with the rims level to the soil. Slugs love beer. They'll smell it, try to drink it, then fall into the jars and drown.

• A bath of ice-cold, extra-bubbly beer soothes tired feet.

• If drinking too much beer got you lost, beer can also help you find your way back home. Put some in a bowl and let it go flat. Magnetize a needle by stroking it against a piece of silk, then put it in the bowl of beer and it will point north/south.

• Spray organic beer on the brown patches in your lawn. The grass will absorb the fermented sugars, which stimulate growth.

• Flat beer cleans wooden furniture. Wipe some on a soft cloth, clean the furniture, then wipe dry with another cloth.

• Try this only at your own risk, but beer can shine gold. Pour the beer onto a cloth, rub it gently over the gold (but *not* any gemstones) and wipe clean with a towel.

• Beer even removes coffee stains from rugs. Pour the beer directly over the stain, then rub it into the fibers. (Disclaimer: Try this one only at your own risk, too.)

The alcohol content of a can of beer and a shot of whisky are virtually identical.

SPY HUNT: GRAY DECEIVER, PART II

Here's the second part of our intriguing tale of espionage, money, and politics. (Part I is on page 201.)

TO TELL THE TRUTH

The map of dead drops (places where spies and their handlers exchange money and secret documents) that the FBI found in CIA agent Brian Kelley's home was pretty incriminating, but it wasn't enough to secure a conviction, so the Bureau decided to trick Kelley into taking a lie detector test. They arranged for him to be transferred to a "new assignment," debriefing a non-existent Soviet defector. To be approved for the new assignment, Kelley's CIA superiors explained to him, he had to take a polygraph test.

The results of the test stunned even the seasoned FBI mole hunters—Kelley passed with flying colors. There wasn't a flicker of a guilty response anywhere on the test. Fooling a lie detector test so thoroughly takes a lot of skill. This guy was *good*.

KNOCK KNOCK

Next, they set up a "false flag" operation: an FBI agent masquerading as an SVR agent knocked on Kelley's door and warned him that he was about to be arrested for spying and needed to leave the country. The agent then handed Kelley a written escape plan and told him to be at a nearby subway station the following evening. Then the man disappeared into the night…and the FBI waited to see what Kelley would do. If he made a run for the subway station, that would in effect be an acknowledgement that he was indeed a spy—people who aren't spying for the SVR don't need help fleeing the country.

The next morning Kelley went to work as usual and reported the incident to the CIA. He even gave an accurate description of the "SVR agent" to a sketch artist. Once again the FBI was astonished by Kelley's skill under pressure. Somehow he must have detected that the SVR guy was a fake and was not taken in by the

---

"Bubble gum" flavor originally was a combination of wintergreen, vanilla, and cinnamon.

trick. He was so cool and collected that the investigators gave him a new nickname—the "Iceman."

IN YOUR FACE

The FBI still lacked enough evidence to get a conviction and was running out of options. They made a last-ditch attempt at tricking Kelley into incriminating himself. On August 18, 1999, he was called into a meeting at CIA headquarters and confronted by two FBI agents who told him that they knew everything about his spying, even his SVR code name, KARAT. Kelley professed astonishment and denied everything, so the FBI agents pulled out Kelley's handwritten map. "Explain this!" one of them said.

"Where did you get my jogging map?" Kelley asked.

The interview did not go as the FBI had hoped. Kelley didn't crack—he even offered to answer questions without his lawyer present and to take another polygraph test. The agents turned him down: if Kelley could fake one lie detector test, he could fake two.

After questioning him for more than seven hours, the agents gave up. Kelley was stripped of his CIA badge and security clearances, placed on paid administrative leave, and escorted out of CIA headquarters. But he wasn't arrested or charged with spying—there still wasn't enough evidence. He spent the next 18 months on leave while the FBI built a case against him. The mole hunters confronted his daughter, also a CIA employee, and told her that her father was a spy. She claimed to know nothing about her father's spying. Neither did Kelley's other children when they were confronted, nor did his colleagues and close friends when they were interviewed. No one had suspected a thing. Kelley was that good.

SHOPPING

By the spring of 2000 the FBI had compiled a 70-page report recommending that the Justice Department charge Kelley with espionage, which is punishable by death.

While the Justice Department considered the matter, the FBI expanded its search for evidence against Kelley to the former Soviet Union. They tracked down a retired KGB officer who they thought might have some knowledge of the case and lured him to the United States for a "business meeting." Then, when the officer arrived in the United States, the FBI made its pitch—it was willing to pay him a fortune in cash if he would reveal the identity of the mole. The ex-KGB officer made a counteroffer: he had the mole's entire case file in his possession and was willing to sell it outright to the FBI. He added that the file even contained a tape recording of a 1986 telephone conversation of the mole talking to his Russian handlers, so there was no question that the FBI would have the evidence it needed to win a conviction.

VOICE RECOGNITION

The FBI eventually agreed to buy the file for $7 million. It also agreed to help the KGB officer and his family to relocate to the United States under assumed names. The money changed hands, and in November 2000 the file slipped out of Russia and arrived at FBI headquarters. There was enough material in it to fill a small suitcase—hundreds of documents, dozens of computer disks, a cassette tape, and an envelope with the words "Don't Open This" written on it.

The FBI was convinced it finally had the evidence it needed to convict Brian Kelley on spying charges and to put him to death. All the agents had to do was read the files, listen to the recorded conversation on the tape, and build their case. They put the cassette in a tape recorder, pushed PLAY, and waited to hear Kelley's voice. Their long campaign to bring him to justice was at an end.

AN UNEXPECTED DEVELOPMENT

Or was it? It quickly became obvious that the voice the FBI heard talking to the KGB agent wasn't Brian Kelley's. Once again, the FBI agents were in awe of Kelley's abilities as a spy. Even when talking to his KGB handlers, he had had the good sense to protect his identity by having an intermediary—a "cut out," as they're known—make his call for him.

One of the FBI agents, Michael Waguespack, recognized the voice, but couldn't place it. Meanwhile another agent, Bob King, had started reading through some of the spy's correspondence with his Russian handlers and had come across an unusual expression that sounded familiar: in two different places, the spy quoted World War II General George S. Patton telling his troops, "Let's get this over with so we can kick the $#%@ out of the purple-piss-

---

Who cut the tofu? Soybeans produce more flatulence than any other bean.

ing Japanese." Bob King remembered his supervisor in the Russian analytical unit, an agent named Robert Hanssen, repeatedly using the same quote in conversation.

Huh?

"I think that's Bob Hanssen," he told the other agents. Waguespack knew Hanssen, too, and he went back to listen to the tape again. Sure enough—the voice was Robert Hanssen's.

OFF THE HOOK

It took a minute for the mole hunters to realize it (and probably longer than that for them to admit it), but they had been on the trail of the wrong man, an employee of the wrong intelligence agency, for more than three years.

Brian Kelley wasn't a master spy at all—he was an innocent man. The searches and electronic surveillance hadn't found anything because there wasn't anything to find. He passed the polygraph test because he was telling the truth. He reported the "false flag" sting to his superiors because he had nothing to hide. His jogging map really was a jogging map. The "dry cleaning" at Niagara Falls? He was there on official CIA business and the mole hunters tailing him happened to lose him in traffic. Shopping at the same mall as the SVR? A coincidence—everybody shops somewhere.

With his time in the Air Force and the CIA, Kelley had served his country with honor and distinction for 38 years; yet all he had to show for it was a 70-page FBI report to the Department of Justice recommending that he be tried for espionage and executed.

BAD LUCK, GOOD LUCK

What are the odds that a retiring KGB officer would have taken Robert Hanssen's file with him when he retired, and that the FBI would have been successful in tracking him down? Or that they would have been willing to cough up $7 million for the file? To this day, Kelley, his family, and his friends all wonder what would have become of him had the FBI been unable to get (or unwilling to pay for) Hanssen's KGB file.

Now that the FBI had Hanssen's file, how would
they catch this elusive master of espionage?
Part III of the story is on page 536.

THE SIXTH PASSENGER

The harrowing tale of a man who made the ultimate sacrifice.

DISASTER
A horrific scene unfolded on one frigid January day in 1982. In the midst of a snowstorm, a passenger jet carrying 79 people crashed into Washington D.C.'s 14th Street bridge. The plane hit seven cars, then ripped through 20 feet of guardrail before plunging into the icy waters of the Potomac River. Yet amid all the sorrow and chaos that resulted from this terrible accident was an incredible story of selflessness.

Because of the severity of the storm, it took rescue teams near-ly 30 minutes to get to the scene. When they arrived, only the tail of the plane remained above water—and six survivors were cling-ing to it for their lives. As the news cameras rolled, the heavy snowfall and blustery winds made the rescue attempt difficult for the police helicopter, but the skilled pilot was able to keep the air-craft steady enough to start sending down lifelines.

THE RESCUE BEGINS
The first man to grab the rope seemed more alert than the others, and instead of taking the line for himself, he helped secure it to a badly injured woman who was then carried to shore. A few min-utes later the helicopter returned, lowering the line again. And again the man passed the line to someone more in need. When the chopper next returned, two lines were lowered, along with a shout from one of the rescuers: "We need all of you on these lines *now*—the tail is sinking fast!"

The "sixth passenger," as the press would later call him, helped secure two people to the first line, then tied the other line around the last injured survivor. But there was no room left on the line for him. Once again he waved for the helicopter to go on without him. It had nearly reached the riverbank when the two people on the single line lost their grip and fell back into the water. It took an agonizing few minutes for rescuers to get them to shore, but with the help of a bystander who jumped into the water, they did.

Downsizing? Americans spend about $30 billion per year trying to lose weight.

Sadly, by the time the helicopter was able to get back to the downed plane, it was too late—both the tail section and the sixth passenger had been swallowed by the icy river.

REMEMBERING A HERO

The "sixth passenger" was later identified as Arland Williams, a 46-year-old bank examiner from Atlanta. Many paid tribute to his selfless act—saving five lives at the cost of his own. Williams was posthumously awarded the U.S. Coast Guard's Gold Lifesaving Medal. Williams's alma mater, The Citadel in South Carolina, created the Arland D. Williams Society "to recognize graduates who distinguish themselves through community service." And the 14th Street bridge—up until then called the Rochambeau Bridge—was renamed the Arland D. Williams, Jr. Memorial Bridge. But the most apt tribute came from the pastor at Williams's funeral:

> His heroism was not rash. Aware that his own strength was fading, he deliberately handed hope to someone else, and he did so repeatedly. On that cold and tragic day, Arland D. Williams, Jr., exemplified one of the best attributes of human nature, specifically that some people are capable of doing anything for total strangers.

*　　*　　*

PAPER OR PLASTIC?

Some items and prices from a 1961 grocery store flyer.

5-piece Wrench Set: 97¢

Men's Cotton Pajamas: $1.00

Deluxe Rubber Bathmat: 58¢

Ladies Socks: 25¢

Asparagus: 29¢/bunch

Good 'N' Rich Cake Mix: 7¢

Waldorf Toilet Tissue: 35¢

Kellogg's Corn Flakes: 2 for 25¢

Pillsbury Flour, 5 lbs: 39¢

Corn: 5 ears for 29¢

Coffee: 57¢/lb.

Rib Roast: 69¢/lb.

Bumble Bee Tuna: 3 cans for $1

Hydrox Cookies: 39¢

Wisk, ½ gallon: $1.39

Celery: 17¢/bunch

Haddock Fillet: 38¢/lb.

Chuck Roast: 34¢/lb.

Philadelphia Cream Cheese: 29¢

Kosher Salami: 69¢/lb.

Chicken: 25¢/lb.

Tomatoes: 2 cartons for 25¢

Highest temperature ever recorded at the South Pole: 8°F.

THE RISE AND DEMISE OF ULYSSES S. GRANT

You've seen Grant on the $50 bill; you know that he was a president and also the general who won the Civil War. Here are some things you probably didn't know about him.

SCHOOL OF HARD KNOCKS

In 1839 an Ohio tanner named Jesse Grant managed to obtain an appointment to the U.S. Military Academy for his son, Ulysses. Ulysses wasn't the slightest bit interested in a military career, but Jesse didn't think his son had much of a head for business. West Point was free, and it offered Ulysses his best chance for a good education. So off he went.

Ulysses graduated from West Point in 1843, fought in the Mexican War, and remained in the military until 1854, when he resigned and became a civilian again.

Ulysses promptly proved his father's suspicions correct: he had no head for business. He took up farming and failed at it; then got a job in real estate and failed at that, too. By 1860 Grant, a graduate of West Point, was back working as a clerk in his father's store. He was 37, and a failure. But the Civil War was about to save him.

The first shots were fired at Fort Sumter, South Carolina, on April 12, 1861. The fort fell to the Confederacy the following day, prompting President Abraham Lincoln to call for troops. Grant returned to the army and was quickly promoted to brigadier general. "Be careful, Ulyss, you are a general now," Jesse Grant wrote him after learning of the promotion. "It's a good job, don't lose it!"

ITCHING FOR A FIGHT

In the early months of the war Grant was assigned mostly defensive tasks, but he wanted to go on the offensive. In February 1862 he won approval for a plan to attack two key Confederate strongholds: Fort Henry, on the Tennessee River, and Fort Donelson on the Cumberland. Grant, with 17,000 troops and the assistance of gunboats commanded by Commodore Andrew Foote, planned to attack the forts.

This page is about 500,000 atoms thick.

Fort Henry fell after just a few hours of fighting; the attack on Fort Donelson began a week later and raged for two days. By February 15, defeat was imminent.

As was the custom in 19th-century warfare, the fort's commander, General Simon Bolivar Buckner, sent a message to Grant proposing a truce so that the two men could negotiate terms of surrender. Buckner had served with Grant in the Mexican War and had even lent him money, but if he was expecting generous terms from his old friend, he was soon rebuked. Grant's reply was swift and blunt: "No terms except an unconditional and immediate surrender can be accepted." Buckner, complaining that he had no choice but "to accept the ungenerous and unchivalrous terms," gave in.

Capturing the two forts marked the first major Union victories in the war, and turned "Unconditional Surrender" Grant, as his admirers nicknamed him, into a national figure. He was promoted to major general. And "purely by accidental circumstance," as Grant himself later put it, the campaign caused him to pick up the habit that would eventually claim his life—cigars.

THE SPOILS OF WAR

Up to this point, Grant had smoked a pipe, but only occasionally. When Commodore Andrew Foote was wounded in the assault on Fort Donelson, he asked Grant to confer with him aboard his ship, and offered him a cigar. Grant was still smoking it on his way back to his headquarters when a staff officer informed him that Confederate soldiers were attacking. Grant recalled in 1865:

> I galloped forward at once, and while riding among the troops giving the directions for repulsing the assault I carried the cigar in my hand. It had gone out, but it seems that I continued to hold the stump between my fingers throughout the battle. In the accounts published in the papers I was represented as smoking a cigar in the midst of the conflict; and many persons, thinking, no doubt, that tobacco was my chief solace, sent me boxes of the choicest brands from everywhere in the North. As many as 10,000 were soon received. I gave away all I could get rid of, but having such a quantity in hand, I naturally smoked more than I would have done under ordinary circumstances, and I have continued the habit ever since.

STILL SMOKIN'

Inundated with free cigars, Grant was soon addicted. In March 1864, he was promoted to lieutenant general and given command of all the Union armies. By then he was smoking his first cigar of the day right after breakfast as he stuffed the pockets of his uniform with another two dozen. When he accepted General Robert E. Lee's surrender in 1865, Grant was still puffing away. And after the war the gifts of free cigars and related paraphernalia—ashtrays, cigar holders, cigar stands, and so on—only increased.

Even in those days people had an idea that smoking was unhealthy, and in 1866 Grant tried to cut back on the stogies. "I am breaking off from smoking," he told a newspaper reporter. "When I was in the field I smoked eighteen or twenty cigars a day, but now I smoke only nine or ten." (One large cigar can contain as much tobacco as an entire pack of cigarettes.) Grant was elected president in 1868 and reelected in 1872. He smoked his way through both terms; though he still tried to quit on occasion, he never managed to cut back much.

WHAT GOES AROUND...

Grant was still smoking heavily in the summer of 1884 when he experienced throat pain while eating a peach. Doctors found a small cancerous growth in the soft palate of his mouth; at the time of discovery it may still have been small enough to be surgically removed, but by the time Grant got around to having it treated in the fall, the mass had grown to the point that it was inoperable.

Grant struggled with the disease for about a year before dying on July 23, 1885. The man who never wanted a military career and never smoked more than an occasional pipe before the Civil War, died a war hero...from smoking.

*   *   *

WHERE THERE'S A WILL

• The world's longest will was 95,000 words and took more than 20 years to complete.

• The world's smallest will was written on the back of a postage stamp. It included the required signatures of two witnesses.

Let it be: One of every three insects in the world is a beetle.

LOONEY LAWS

Believe it or not, these laws are real.

It's illegal to ride an ugly horse down the street in Wilbur, Washington.

Virginia law prohibits "corrupt practices or bribery by any person other than candidates."

You can't carry an ice cream cone in your pocket in Lexington, Kentucky.

It's illegal to spit against the wind in Sault Sainte Marie, Michigan.

Goats can't legally wear trousers in Massachusetts.

Oregon prohibits citizens from wiping their dishes. You must let them drip-dry.

It's illegal to swim on dry land in Santa Ana, California.

If you're in Arkansas, don't mispronounce "Arkansas." It's against the law.

It's illegal in Hartford, Connecticut, to educate your dog.

It's against the law to anchor your boat to the train tracks in Jefferson City, Missouri.

If you tie an elephant to a parking meter in Orlando, Florida, you have to feed the meter just as if the elephant were a car.

It's against the law to pawn your wooden leg in Delaware.

Kentucky law requires that every person in the state take a bath at least once a year.

While on horseback in Washington, D.C., it's illegal to catch fish.

In Birmingham, Alabama, it is illegal to drive a car while blindfolded.

In Hawaii no one may whistle in a drinking establishment.

It's illegal to fish for whales in an Ohio stream, river, or lake.

In Marblehead, Massachusetts, each fire company responding to an alarm must be provided a three-gallon jug of rum.

In Minnesota it is illegal to dry both men's and women's underwear on the same clothesline.

A mouse's heart is smaller than an M&M.

OUTSIDER MUSIC

"Outsider music" is experimental, musical art created by nonmusicians (often self-taught) for their own enjoyment or as a means of self-expression. It's usually recorded at home, and frequently disregards common musical structures, sounds, rhythm, and even melody. If you like your music weird, adventurous, unique—and oddly compelling—listen up.

BACKGROUND

Since 1975, Irwin Chusid has been a disc jockey on WFMU, a New Jersey radio station that plays underground—and often strange—music. In the late 1970s, a friend gave Chusid an LP called *Philosophy of the World* by a group called the Shaggs. Chusid had never heard anything like it: the band banged on their instruments without melody or rhythm and didn't seem to be playing in unison. Chusid thought it was baffling, terrible…and charming. As bad as it was, he thought it was undeniably earnest. Ever since, Chusid has combed flea markets and yard sales for what he calls "outsider music."

So what's the difference between outsider music and just plain bad music? According to Chusid, "passion, soul, idiosyncratic ideas, sincere self-expression, and guilelessness." More specifically, it's music created by people who lack the talent, tunefulness, or knowledge of musical structures found in mainstream popular music. Much of it is self-recorded and the results are bizarre and startling.

In 2000 Chusid wrote a book about outsider music titled *Songs in the Key of Z*. Here are some of his top picks.

THE SHAGGS. In 1966 four New Hampshire sisters (Betty, Dorothy, Helen, and Rachel Wiggin) were given used instruments by their father, who pulled them out of school and told them to become a rock band. They had only a few basic lessons before they made their album *Philosophy of the World*. The result: dissonant noise played by musicians who sound like they're playing their instruments for the first time (and independently of each other). It became a cult hit with fans of weird music—Frank Zappa called it one of the best albums ever made.

Carly Simon's father is the Simon of publishing giant Simon & Schuster.

WESLEY WILLIS. He recorded over 1,000 songs, almost all accompanied by the same demo track played on a cheap keyboard. Most of Willis's songs are about concerts he attended, and the lyrics usually follow the same pattern: "This band played at the Rosemont Horizon. About a thousand people were at the show. The jam session was awesome. It really rocked the (name of animal)'s (part of animal's anatomy)." Then he screams the band's name a few times, then sings another verse, adds in some keyboard sound effects, and ends with a popular advertising catchphrase, such as "Wheaties, breakfast of champions!"

LANGLEY SCHOOLS MUSIC PROJECT. In 1976 Hans Fenger was hired to teach music at five elementary schools in rural Langley, British Columbia. To interest the kids in music, he had them sing songs by the Beach Boys, the Eagles, and David Bowie. The kids were so enthusiastic that Fenger recorded them (arranged into a giant choir) in a school gym and handed out LPs of the recordings to their parents. Critics say the familiar songs performed by children in an echo-drenched gym are haunting and moving. "It touches the heart in a way no other music ever has, or ever could," said critic and jazz musician John Zorn. A CD of the performance was released in 2001.

JANDEK. Since 1978, Jandek (real name: Sterling Smith) has released more than 50 albums of folk, blues, and "noise rock." He goes through phases: He'll record acoustic songs on several records, then several records' worth of noisy experimental music, leading fans to believe that he records hundreds of songs at a time in one feverish session. The recordings vary from spoken word and a cappella singing to scream-filled electric guitar noisefests to stark acoustic folk songs, and Jandek plays all the instruments.

THE LEGENDARY STARDUST COWBOY. In the 1960s, this performer (real name: Norman Odom) invented a new kind of music that combined rockabilly with extremely fast hard rock. (It later came to be called "psychobilly.") His best-known song is the 1968 single "Paralyzed," in which Ledge (as he likes to be called) furiously strums on an acoustic guitar, then growls, snarls, and makes other noises, occasionally yelling out "Paralyzed!" The song cracked the Billboard Top 100 in 1968.

A standard CD is 4.7 inches in diameter.

THAT'S AMORE?

When the moon hits your eye like a big pizza pie, it hurts.

In 2005 Ahmed Salhi, 24, was sentenced to nine months home arrest in Ferrara, Italy, for violating immigration laws. He begged the judge to change the sentence to nine months in *prison*...because he couldn't bear his wife's nagging. "I need some peace," he said.

• A couple in Aachen, Germany, had been sleeping in separate beds for months when the wife finally woke the husband up in the middle of the night and demanded he fulfill his "husbandly duties." He refused. She called the police and demanded they make him do it. "The officers did not feel able to resolve the dispute," a police spokesman said, "let alone issue any kind of official order."

• A woman in Newport, Arkansas, was arrested after she pulled a gun on Larry Estes, a preacher who had just started the service in his church. The woman was Tammy Estes, the preacher's wife. Witnesses later reported that Mrs. Estes was upset over text messages that she'd found from her husband to another woman. After holding Rev. Estes at bay for two hours, she surrendered to police.

• During the 1950s, a couple in Kuligaon, India, had an argument that resulted in the husband moving out of the house...and into a nearby treehouse. As of 2006, the 83-year-old was still living there. "We quarreled over a tiny issue," his wife told reporters. "I've tried to get him to come back, but he has refused all the time."

• In September 2005, Mark Bridgwood, 49, of Dartmouth, England, noticed a classified advertisement in his local paper for a yacht. It was *his* yacht. His estranged wife, Tracy, was secretly selling it for less than half its $180,000 value. "Any quick cash offer considered," the ad said. The fuming husband nixed any possible sale by taking an ax to seawater valves under the vessel's waterline. The 53-foot yacht went down immediately. "It was a beautiful boat," said Tracy, who works as a waitress. "And he sank it."

Coffee should be black as hell, strong as death, and as sweet as love. —Turkish proverb

THE LADY OF THE LINES

If you've ever heard of the Nazca lines, you have this woman to thank for preserving them for posterity. And if you've ever doubted that one person can make a difference, think again...

HELP WANTED

In 1932 a 29-year-old German woman named Maria Reiche answered a newspaper ad and landed a job in Peru, tutoring the sons of the German consul. After that, she bounced from job to job and eventually found work translating documents for an archaeologist named Julio Tello.

One day she happened to overhear a conversation between Tello and another archaeologist, Toribio Mejia. Mejia described some mysterious lines he'd seen in a patch of desert about 250 miles south of the capital city of Lima, near the small town of Nazca. He tried to interest Tello in the lines, but Tello dismissed them as unimportant. Reiche wasn't so sure. She decided to go to Nazca and have a look for herself.

MYSTERIOUS LINES

Gazing out across the desert floor, Reiche was amazed by what she saw: More than 1,000 lines crisscrossing 200 square miles of desert, some as narrow as footpaths, others more than 15 feet wide. Many ran almost perfectly straight for miles across the desert, deviating as little as four yards in a mile.

The lines were made by early Nazca people, etched into the desert floor between 200 B.C. and 700 A.D. They had created the lines by removing darkened surface fragments (known as "desert varnish") to reveal the much lighter stone underneath.

But why?

WAITING FOR SUNDOWN

An American archaeologist and historian named Paul Kosok had a theory. At first he thought the lines might be irrigation ditches, but they weren't large enough or deep enough to transport water. Then he started to wonder if they might have some kind of astronomical significance. So, on June 21, 1941, the southern hemi-

---

Dressed to kill: During the French Revolution, a woman named...

sphere's winter solstice, he went out into the desert and waited for the sun to set.

Sure enough, when the sun set, it did so at a point on the horizon that was intersected by one of the Nazca lines. The line seemed to serve as an astronomical marker, telling the Nazca people that the first day of winter had arrived.

BIG BIRD

Kosok had also observed that while most of the Nazca lines were straight, some were curvy. But it wasn't until he plotted one on a piece of paper, then looked down to see that he'd drawn the outline of a giant bird, that he realized that some of the lines were *drawings*. The drawings were so large that they could not be made out by anyone looking at them from the ground.

With the discovery of the solstice line and the giant bird, Kosok became convinced that the Nazca lines were an enormous astronomical calendar, or, as he put it, "the world's largest astronomy book," with each line carefully laid out to correspond to something in the heavens above. Maybe, he speculated, the giant bird represented a constellation in the night sky. He offered Reiche a job helping him survey the lines so that he could prove his theory.

LIFELONG PASSION

She took the job, and after a few months of tramping across the desert each day with little more than a canteen of water and a pencil and paper to record her observations, she found what she was looking for: a line that intersected with the sun on the southern hemisphere's summer solstice, December 21. That was all it took—Reiche was convinced that Kosok's theory was correct. And she would spend the rest of her life trying to prove it.

At first Reiche could afford to visit the Nazca lines only occasionally, and because she was German she was not allowed to work at the site at all during World War II. By 1946, however, she was living in Peru year-round and spending nearly all of her waking hours in the desert trying to unlock the secret of the lines. When Kosok left Peru in 1948, she continued without him.

Studying the lines wasn't as simple as it sounds. In those days, many of them were so obscured by dirt, sand, and centuries of new desert varnish that it was barely possible to find them. That they were distinguishable at all was thanks only to the fact that they were etched a few inches into the desert floor.

CLEAN SWEEP

Reiche decided to "clean" the lines so that they could be more easily seen. First she tried using a rake. When that didn't work, she switched to a broom. It's estimated that over the next 50 years, she swept out as many as 1,000 of the lines by herself, carefully mapping the location of each one as she went along, and returning to the same lines at different times of day and in all lights to be certain that she was following their true courses.

In the process Reiche discovered—and *uncovered*—as many as 30 drawings similar to the giant bird that Kosok had found, including numerous birds, two lizards, four fish, a monkey, a whale, a pair of human hands, and a man with an owl-like head. The scope of her work is astonishing: When you look at an aerial photograph of the Nazca lines—any photograph of any of the lines or ground drawings—there's a good chance that Reiche swept those lines herself. Mile after mile after mile of them, using only one tool—an ordinary household broom.

LOST IN SPACE

Just as Reiche was almost single-handedly responsible for restoring the Nazca lines, she was also the first to bring them to public attention. Her 1949 book *Mystery on the Desert* helped to generate worldwide interest in the lines.

But what really put them on the map was a 1968 book written by a Swiss hotelier named Erich Von Daniken. His book *Chariots of the Gods* proposed that some of the lines were landing strips for alien spacecraft. According to Von Daniken's theory, aliens created the human race by breeding with primates, then returned to outer space. The early humans then etched the drawings into the desert floor, hoping to attract the aliens back to Earth.

JOIN THE CROWD

Chariots of the Gods was an international bestseller, and its success prompted other people to write books of their own with more theories about the origin of the lines. One speculated the lines were ancient jogging tracks; another claimed they were launch sites for

Nazcan hot-air balloonists. These books turned the Nazca lines into a New Age pop culture phenomenon, helping to attract tens of thousands of tourists to the site each year.

As a result, the Nazca lines began to suffer from overexposure—more and more tourists went out into the desert on foot, on dirt bikes, and in dune buggies, doing untold damage to the lines in the process.

Reiche did what she could to protect them. For years she lived in a small house out in the desert so that she could watch over the lines herself, and she used the profits from her writing and lecturing to pay security guards to patrol the desert. By the end of her life she was crippled by Parkinson's disease, but she continued to study the lines and was known to chase intruders away in her wheelchair. By the time of her death in 1998 at the age of 95, she was nearly deaf and almost completely blind. Not that it really mattered to her—"I can see every line," she said, "every drawing, in my mind."

FINAL IRONY

Though Reiche devoted most of her life to proving that the Nazca lines are a giant astronomical calendar, that theory has been largely discarded. Researchers now believe that while a few of the lines may indeed point to astronomical phenomena such as the summer and winter solstices (with more than 1,000 lines running across the desert floor in all directions, even *that* may be a coincidence), most of the lines are processional footpaths linking various sacred sites in the desert. The ground drawings, they believe, are artwork the Nazcans made for their gods.

*　　*　　*

FOSSIL FUELS

When locomotives were first used in Egypt in the 19th century, wood and coal were scarce. So what did they use for fuel? The one thing they had plenty of: human mummies—millions of them.

Famous forgotten female: Diane Crump—1st woman to ride in the Kentucky Derby (1970).

WALKEN TALKIN'

Tim Burton on Christopher Walken: "You look at him and you know there's a lot going on, yet you have no idea what."

"I've always been a character actor, although I'm not quite sure what that means."

"I think I'm strange. I'm happy being strange."

"I don't have a lot of hobbies. I don't play golf. I don't have any children. Things that occupy people's time. I just try to take jobs. I basically work so much because I'm lazy."

"When you're in a scene and you don't know what you're gonna do, don't do anything."

"People are completely mysterious to me. Even in my own family I have no idea what any of them are thinking."

"I don't need to be made to look evil. I can do that on my own."

"I used to be prettier than I am, but I think I look better now. I was a pretty boy. Particularly in my early movies. I don't like looking at them so much. There's a sort of pretty thing about me."

"I think that when I play these villains, maybe what is different is that the audience sees me play these and they know that that's Chris and he's having fun and he knows that and you know that and everybody knows that."

"I make movies that nobody will see. I've made movies that even I have never seen."

"How great would it be if actors had tails because tails are so expressive. I have cats and you can tell if they're annoyed. If they're scared, they bush their tail. If I had to play scared in a movie, all I'd have to do is bush my tail. I think that if actors had tails it would change everything."

"I am a solitary person, as an animal. There are animals who live alone and animals who live in groups, there are aggressive ones and the ones that are like the lilies of the field."

"Bear costumes are funny. Bears as well."

Doe! There are more than 520,000 deer-related traffic accidents every year in the United States.

ACTING LIKE ANIMALS

Ever wonder about those animal stars in the movies?
Well, here's a bit of trivia on some of them.

BART THE BEAR

Called the John Wayne of Bear Actors, 9-foot-tall Bart was a star. Usually cast as "The Bear", Bart appeared in 16 films; his best-known role was the bear who mauls Brad Pitt's character in the 1994 drama *Legends of the Fall*. He's costarred with well-known actors like John Candy, Dan Aykroyd, Steven Seagal, Anthony Hopkins, and Alec Baldwin. Bart has even been a presenter at the Oscars: in 1999 he helped Mike Myers present the award for best sound effects. Bart, who was huge for his sub-species of Kodiak bear (1,700 pounds), died of natural causes in 2000 at the ripe old age of 23. But his legacy lives on in his son (also named Bart), who appeared in *Dr. Dolittle 2* (2001) and *Without a Paddle* (2004).

BANDIT THE RACCOON

This feisty critter starred with Marilyn Monroe is the 1954 Western *River of No Return*. During a shoot in a giant indoor studio with 200 pine trees, Bandit became frightened and hid somewhere in the maze of the fake forest. Monroe helped Bandit's trainer look for him by crawling on her knees through the spiderwebs, dust, and wooden struts of the set's support structure. Bandit was found safe and sound.

CASS OLÉ

This Arabian stallion, the star of *The Black Stallion* and *The Black Stallion Returns*, was found in San Antonio, Texas, after a world-wide search. The horse learned to act a bit—pulling back his ears to show anger and pulling back his lips to show affection. But for the climactic scene at sea, Cass Olé didn't learn to swim; it was considered too dangerous. So a swimming horse, a breed specifically developed to swim in the ocean, was imported from France for the scene. Cass Olé became a star, met presidents Carter and Reagan, and sired more than 130 foals before his death in 1993.

The first choices for the leads in *The African Queen*: John Mills and Bette Davis.

CANDY-MAKING SQUIRRELS

Charlie and the Chocolate Factory (2005) faithfully adapted the famous "nut scene" from Roald Dahl's original book: the movie shows a room full of squirrels who crack nuts and sort them on a conveyor belt. What viewers might not know is that those big-screen squirrels are real. Director Tim Burton founded a "school for squirrels" where 200 of the rodents spent 19 weeks learning to sit on stools, and to crack and sort nuts—just for that short scene.

PENGUIN ARMY

Tim Burton had another group of animals trained for 1992's *Batman Returns*, where the supervillain Penguin uses a flock of armed penguins to try to take over Gotham City. Burton went to every extreme to make sure the birds were comfortable on the set; they had their own refrigerated trailer, their own swimming pool, and fresh fish every day. The set was kept at freezing temperatures to keep the birds comfortable (and the actors very chilly). The live penguins were joined on set by robotic look-alikes, some of which looked so real that the real penguins snuggled up to them.

HERBIE THE DUCK

The lead duck in the 1961 comedy *Everything's Ducky*, Herbie, was known to defecate every time he quacked. When Herbie was on the set, the frustrated crew members had to watch where they stepped to avoid constantly slipping and sliding. But luckily for them, Herbie had three doubles for *Everything's Ducky*. They all looked like him: pure white with yellow-orange bills. Their names: Burp Adenoids, Duster, and Flops.

FREDDIE THE LION

Star of the 1965 movie *Clarence, the Cross-Eyed Lion*, Freddie really was cross-eyed. For a time, his wranglers tried their best to fix his eye problem, even going so far as getting him a pair of prescription sunglasses, to no avail. Freddie was known for his mild-mannered personality and was good with children. He was so calm that he let his animal costar, Judy the chimpanzee, climb on his back whenever she wanted. But because of his sweet nature, producers had to get another lion to act as his double during the snarling scenes in the movie.

The world's first skateboard park was built in Port Orange, Florida, in 1976.

THE ÜBER TUBER

Oh, the poor potato—a symbol of laziness (couch potato) and unhealthy eating (cheese fries). But it deserves much better. Here's how the lowly potato altered the course of human history.

SPUDS OF THE INCAS

For at least 4,000 years, potatoes have been cultivated in the Peruvian Andes. The Incas called them *papas*, and although the flowers are toxic (they're members of the deadly nightshade family), the part that grows underground—the tuber— is one of the healthiest foods humans have ever cultivated. Consider this: The average potato has only 100 calories, but provides 45% of the U.S. Recommended Daily Allowance of vitamin C; 15% of vitamin B6; 15% of iodine; and 10% of niacin, iron, and copper. Potatoes are also high in potassium and fiber, with no fat and almost no sodium.

But the papas that the Incas cultivated looked more like purple golf balls than today's potatoes. More than 5,000 different varieties grew in the Andes, and there were more than 1,000 Incan words to describe them. The potato was so integral to Incan culture that they buried their dead with potatoes (for food in the afterlife) and measured time based on how long it took a potato to cook.

THE EDIBLE STONE

When the Spanish conquistadors invaded the New World in the 1500s, they resisted this strange new food at first, not wanting to lower themselves to eating anything so "primitive." But when their own food stores ran low, the Spaniards were forced to eat potatoes. They liked them so much that they brought some tubers back to Europe in 1565.

Europeans balked at what they called the "edible stone." It was dirty, had poisonous leaves, and tasted horrible when eaten raw (which led to indigestion). The Catholic Church condemned potatoes as "unholy" because there was no mention of them in the Bible. Farmers started growing them, but only to feed livestock. It's amazing that potatoes ever caught on, but thanks to a few key events, that's exactly what happened.

KING'S EDICT: JUST EAT IT

The potato's first big boost in Europe came from Frederick the Great, ruler of Prussia. In the 1740s, Prussia was mired in a war against Austria. Faced with the prospect of his nation's crops (and food supply) being trampled by invading armies, Frederick urged his farmers to grow potatoes. Why? Because potatoes grow underground. A potato field could be marched over or even burned, and survive, where wheat and barley fields would be devastated.

But the Prussian people didn't understand why the king wanted them to eat animal fodder, and most refused. So Frederick sent his personal chefs out to travel the countryside and distribute potato recipes to his subjects. When that didn't work, he issued an edict that anyone who refused to eat potatoes would have their ears cut off. Potatoes caught on relatively quickly in Prussia after that.

PRISON FOOD

But they didn't in France. Along with most other French people, King Louis XVI reviled the potato. "It has a pasty taste," wrote an 18th-century French historian. "The natural insipidity, the unhealthy quality of this food, which is flatulent and indigestible, has caused it to be rejected from refined households."

During the Seven Years War (1756–1763), a French pharmacist named Antoine Parmentier was imprisoned in Germany, where he was fed the same food as the pigs: potatoes. But when he was released, he felt stronger and healthier than before his imprisonment. He credited his health to the potato and became its biggest advocate. Granted an audience with the king, Parmentier told his prison story and urged him to fund a series of potato farms to feed the hungry. Louis was intrigued, but not enough to carry out Parmentier's grand scheme. Instead, he donated a few acres of the worst possible land near Paris. Historically, nothing would grow there— nothing, that is, until Parmentier grew potatoes. They thrived.

But how would Parmentier convince his fellow citizens to eat them? Knowing that people usually want what they can't have, Parmentier devised a plan. First, he positioned soldiers around his field in order to "protect" the valuable crop from theft. Second, he instructed the soldiers to take bribes and allow peasants to sneak in at night to steal the spuds. The plan worked, and within a few decades, potato farms became as common as wineries in France.

The Choctaw Nation donated $710 to the Irish during the Potato Famine.

In 1767 Benjamin Franklin traveled to Paris, where he attended a banquet hosted by Parmentier consisting of nothing but potato dishes. Franklin was instantly won over by their taste and versatility and took some seedlings home to the Colonies, where he gave them to his friend, Thomas Jefferson. Jefferson, too, was enthusiastic about the vegetable and urged every farmer he knew to grow it. Yet even with the statesman's endorsement, the potato didn't catch on quickly in the Colonies. The Old World cultural and religious stigmas against it were still too strong.

THE BLIGHT

It was a different story in Ireland. The potato, first brought there around 1590, quickly became one of the country's main crops. The Irish climate and soil—in many areas too poor to grow grain—were perfect for growing potatoes. In addition, potatoes could go straight from the earth to the kitchen without having to be refined at a mill, which made the crop very appealing to the poor. The potato is actually credited with saving Ireland from famine…but no one knew how devastating Ireland's reliance on it would become.

For all of its attributes, the potato has one major drawback: it is susceptible to potato blight. Caused by a funguslike organism called *Phytophthora infestans*, which travels in airborne spores, an outbreak can destroy every potato plant for hundreds of miles. Even today, scientists have not found a cure.

In 1845 Ireland was hit hard with blight, and the country's entire potato crop failed. As food stores dwindled, Ireland begged neighboring England, which ruled them at the time, for help. But the British did nothing. When the blight hit again the following year, the British sent soldiers and farmers to help out, but by then there was little anyone could do—tens of thousands of acres of potato fields were dead or dying. When the crops failed yet again in 1847, families that relied on their potato crops to pay rent were evicted from their land, causing a mass exodus from Ireland. Result: About a million people died, and millions more fled to Europe and the Americas (including the families of John F. Kennedy and Henry Ford).

Before the Potato Famine, Ireland was on its way to becoming a major political force in the West: High-yielding potato crops were boosting the country's economy, and its eight million citizens

Where did Harry Lillis Crosby get the nickname Bing? From the comic strip *The Bingsville Bugle.*

were close to gaining independence from England. Within three years, however, the population was cut almost in half and the land was scarred from repeated attacks of blight. Many Irish held their English rulers responsible, claiming that they waited too long before helping. The Irish Potato Famine only intensified the bad blood between the two nations that continues to this day.

THE BIRTH OF THE MODERN POTATO
The potato blight hit North America as well, but because the United States also grew corn, oats, wheat, and barley, Americans were able to compensate for it. Besides, even with Franklin's and Jefferson's endorsements 50 years earlier, the potato was still primarily used as livestock feed.

The potato did have its advocates in America, though—none more important than horticulturist Luther Burbank. Burbank spent 55 years developing more than 800 new varieties of fruits, vegetables, nuts, and grains. His goal was, simply, to feed the world. Burbank's greatest achievement came in 1871 when he developed a hybrid potato—the Burbank—that produced twice as many tubers per crop and was much larger than any potatoes that had existed before. Most importantly, this new potato showed more resistance to blight than previous varieties. Burbank sent some tubers to Ireland to help rebuild the potato crop, which, even 20 years later, was still suffering the effects of the famine.

Thanks to Burbank's advances, the potato started to catch on in North America. Once it did, it didn't take long for chefs to learn how versatile the vegetable is. Potatoes can be boiled, baked, or fried; they can be mashed, sliced, or powdered; they can be used to make sauces thicker and stop ice crystals from forming; and they can be used to make pasta and baked goods. After hundreds of years of distrust and suspicion, by the beginning of the 20th century, the potato had become one of America's staple crops.

THIS SPUD'S FOR YOU
In the 1920s, Idaho was emerging as "The Potato State." Why Idaho? Because of its altitude, the days are warm and the nights are cool, creating the perfect growing climate. There is also plenty of irrigation water to soak tubers submerged in the porous volcanic soil. And because few people lived in Idaho at the time, millions

of acres of land were available for potato farms.

The most successful of the farmers was J. R. Simplot. He started working on a potato farm in Declo, Idaho, when he was just 14. With a keen mind for business and understanding of distribution, Simplot became the potato baron of Idaho and the main supplier of potatoes to the western United States, as well as to the U.S. Armed Forces in the 1930s and '40s. (Simplot now has annual revenues of $3 billion—he is McDonald's #1 potato supplier.)

Through the Great Depression and into World War II, potatoes thrived as an inexpensive, easy-to-grow crop that could easily feed the masses—and the troops. This was crucial during wartime. Most crops only grow in specific climates or terrains, which means that they have to be cultivated in one place and delivered to another. Ships carrying fresh produce overseas were always in danger of being sunk by the enemy. Potatoes, on the other hand, could be grown almost anywhere. In Europe and the Americas, thousands of farmers grew nothing else during those years. By the end of World War II, the all-American meal was simply "meat and potatoes."

The vegetable that was first revered by the Incas, then used as pig feed in the Western world, is now a $100 billion-a-year business.

POTATO FACTS

• Potatoes produce 75% more food energy per acre than wheat and 58% more than rice.

• Potatoes can also be used to make ethyl alcohol (ethanol). "There's enough alcohol in one year's yield of an acre of potatoes," said Henry Ford, "to drive the machinery necessary to cultivate the fields for one hundred years." Potatoes are used in manufacturing medicines, paper, cloth, glue, and candy.

• It's the only vegetable that can be grown in desert regions and in mountains above 14,000 feet.

• The average American eats about 80 pounds of potatoes a year, but that has health advocates worried. Why? Because they're usually deep fried or buried under butter and cheese. The skin of the potato—which contains half its fiber—is usually discarded.

• In 1995 potatoes became the first vegetables grown in space. In the future, NASA plans on using spuds as the main crop to feed space travelers on long voyages.

What do the hummingbird, the loon, and the kingfisher have in common? They can't walk.

THE STRANGE TALE OF PHINEAS GAGE

A gruesome accident and its strange aftermath: the birth of a controversial medical procedure.

A HOLE IN ONE

Phineas Gage considered himself a lucky man. At the age of 25, he had a well-paid job as construction foreman for the Rutland and Burlington Railroad in Vermont. On September 13, 1848, as Gage was packing a load of explosives into the ground, the charge exploded without warning. The iron rod he was using to tamp the explosives into the earth flew into the air with the force and speed of a rocket, hitting Gage directly in the head. The 3'7" rod, which weighed 13 pounds, entered his left cheek, careened straight through his skull and brain, and exited out of the top of his head like a yard-long bullet.

Gage's co-workers loaded him into an ox cart and took him—still conscious—to a hotel, where some local doctors treated him. They never expected him to live; he was bleeding horribly and was blind in his left eye. But he was still able to walk and talk, and he returned home just 10 weeks after his accident. But Gage wasn't unscathed, not by any means. The iron bar had virtually destroyed the front left lobe of his brain...and had irrevocably changed his personality.

LIKE A NEW MAN

A few months after the accident, Gage was feeling well enough to return to work. But his old boss refused to hire him back at the same position because, even though Gage was almost back to normal physically, emotionally, and mentally, he was a changed man. Before the accident, he'd been efficient, capable, kind, and polite; now he was foul-mouthed, rude, and easily annoyed.

Gage never worked as a foreman again. He drove coaches and cared for horses in New Hampshire and, later, in Chile. He

---

Jellyfish are over 95% water and have no heart, blood, brain, or gills.

exhibited himself (along with the rod) as a curiosity at P. T. Barnum's Museum in New York. He lived for 13 years after the accident until 1860, when he died after a series of epileptic seizures.

Gage's skull and the rod are now on display at Harvard Medical School, where they've been studied intensively over the years by neuroscientists.

FIRST THE GOOD STUFF

To the neurologists of the day, Gage's abrupt personality changes were a clue to the fact that certain portions of the brain corresponded with personality functions. And in fact, Gage's case made the very first brain tumor operation possible in 1885. After studying what had happened to Gage, the operating physician concluded that lesions or tumors located in the frontal lobes of the brain didn't affect the brain's ability to take in sensory information. Nor did they have an impact on physical movement or speech. However, such localized lesions or tumors did produce highly characteristic and unusual personality changes like Gage's.

In 1894 that same surgeon removed a tumor from a patient's left frontal lobe. The patient had complained his thinking was becoming increasingly slow and dull. Seeing the similarities between this patient's mental faculties and Gage's, the doctor successfully removed the tumor that lay, just as he expected, in the left frontal lobe of the brain.

THE BIRTH OF THE LOBOTOMY

Gage's case put scientists on alert. Now they knew that certain areas of the brain were responsible for certain functions. In 1890, after a German scientist discovered that dogs were tamer and calmer after their temporal lobe was removed—a procedure known as a lobotomy—the attending doctor at a Swiss insane asylum performed similar surgery on six of his patients in 1892. The patients who had been hard to handle, restless, and even violent, seemed much calmer after the surgery. Lobotomies fell out of favor for a time, but were revived in the 1930s. Suddenly, a sort of lobotomy frenzy overtook the American psychiatric world.

"Never insult seven men when all you're packing is a six-shooter." —Zane Grey

THE ICE PICK TRICK

Along came enterprising physician and neurologist Walter Freeman, later known as the "Lobotomy King," who performed over 3,000 lobotomies from the 1930s to the 1960s. Impatient with the slowness of other brain surgery methods, Freeman even created the superquick ice-pick lobotomy. Instead of surgically opening a hole in the patient's head, he put his patients under local anesthesia and plunged an ice pick through the skull and into the brain. Once in, Freeman would swing the ice pick swiftly back and forth, severing the prefrontal lobe. An ice pick lobotomy took only a few minutes. The lobotomy-happy Freeman would set up production lines at mental hospitals, operating on as many as 10 patients in a single afternoon.

EVERYBODY'S DOING IT

Lobotomies were the psychiatric cure-all of choice in the 1940s and '50s. They were used not just on uncontrollable patients, but homosexuals, political radicals, "troublesome" personalities, and other so-called undesirables who veered from established norms. Even amateur surgeons got into the act; they performed hundreds of lobotomies without first performing psychiatric evaluations. Joseph Kennedy ordered a lobotomy on his "difficult" daughter Rosemary in 1941 without consulting anyone else in the family. Playwright Tennessee Williams was devastated to find in 1937 that his schizophrenic sister Rose Williams had been lobotomized, altering her personality utterly and permanently. The movie *Frances* is the true story of fiercely independent actress Frances Farmer (as played by Jessica Lange), who, after her lobotomy, is a tragic picture of blandness.

LOBOTOMY TODAY?

Lobotomies are now outlawed in most countries, although they're still occasionally performed to control violent behavior in Japan, Australia, Sweden, and India.

Even though Phineas Gage needed that 1848 accident like a, well, like a hole in the head, his case revolutionized brain surgery—in good ways and bad.

Laser stands for Light Amplification by Stimulated Emission of Radiation.

MYTH-CONCEPTIONS

*"Common knowledge" is frequently wrong. Here are
some examples of things that many people believe...
but that according to our sources, just aren't true.*

Myth: Watching TV in a dark room is bad for your eyes.
Fact: As Paul Dickson and Joseph C. Goulden write in
Myth-Informed, "The myth was created in the early
1950s by an innovative Philadelphia public relations man named
J. Robert Mendte, on behalf of a client who manufactured lamps."

Myth: Flamingos are naturally pink.
Fact: Flamingos are grey when chicks. They turn pink as adults
because the sea creatures they eat turn pink during digestion. The
pigment is then absorbed by the bird's body and colors its feathers.
If flamingos are fed a different diet, they're white.

Myth: Tonto's nickname for the Lone Ranger, Kemo Sabe, means
"faithful friend."
Fact: In Apache, it means "white shirt," and in Navaho it means
"soggy shrub." But *Lone Ranger* creator George Trendle didn't know
that. He took the name from a summer camp he went to as a boy.

Myth: The artist Vincent Van Gogh cut off his entire ear.
Fact: The famous episode followed two months of hard work, hard
drinking, and an argument with his friend, Paul Gauguin. Van
Gogh was despondent and cut off only a small part of his earlobe.

Myth: Crickets chirp by rubbing their legs together.
Fact: They rub their wings.

Myth: The largest pyramid in the world is in Egypt.
Fact: The Quetzalcoatl pyramid southeast of Mexico City is 177'
tall, with a base covering 45 acres and a volume of 120 million
cubic feet. Cheops, the largest in Egypt, though originally 481'
tall, has a base covering only 13 acres and a volume of only 90
million cubic feet.

Actress Mia Farrow is the biological or adoptive mother of 15 children.

Myth: The captain of a ship at sea can perform weddings.
Fact: U.S. Navy regulations—and those of the navies of many other nations—actually prohibit ships' commanders from joining couples in marriage.

Myth: Your hair and nails continue to grow after you die.
Fact: They don't. Your tissue recedes from your hair and nails, making them appear longer.

Myth: You should never wake a sleepwalker.
Fact: There's no reason not to wake a sleepwalker. This superstition comes from the old belief that a sleepwalker's spirit leaves the body and might not make it back if the person is wakened.

Myth: Shaving your hair makes it grow in faster and thicker.
Fact: The rate of your hair's growth is determined by hereditary factors. Shaving will have no effect on the rate of its growth.

Myth: Ticks are insects.
Fact: Insects have six legs and three body parts. Ticks, on the other hand, have eight legs and two body parts, which classifies them as arachnids, not insects.

Myth: Julius Caesar was a Roman emperor.
Fact: In Caesar's time, Rome was a republic and had no emperor. The Roman Empire didn't exist until 17 years after Caesar's death.

Myth: Lightning comes out of the sky and strikes the ground.
Fact: Scientists now believe that the lightning bolt we see is actually moving from the ground up to the sky.

Myth: The lion is the king of the jungle.
Fact: The lion doesn't live in the jungle; it lives on the plains, where it can run and chase its prey.

Myth: The sky is blue.
Fact: The sky is black. Dust particles and droplets of moisture in the air reflect the sun's light and make it appear blue.

The largest chicken egg on record measured 12.25 inches around and weighed 12 ounces.

THE MAD BOMBER, PT. II

When we left the case of the Mad Bomber (page 257), Dr. James Brussel, the original "profiler," had just released his theories to the press, setting the game afoot. Here's how it played out.

FOUND OUT

The Mad Bomber's response to his case being made public: he took his terror a step further. The bombs kept coming and the letters got more brazen. "F. P." even called Brussel on the telephone and told him to lay off or he would "be sorry." Brussel had him exactly where he wanted him.

The final clue came when police received a letter revealing the date that began the Mad Bomber's misery: September 5, 1931—almost 10 years before the first bomb was found. Brussel immediately ordered a search of Con Ed's personnel files from that era. An office assistant named Alice Kelly found a neatly written letter from a former employee named George Metesky who had promised that Con Edison would pay for their "DASTARDLY DEEDS."

I WILL make THE CON Edison sorry ·· I WILL Bring them before the bar of Justice - PUBLIC OPINION will condemn them – for BewArE I will PLACE MORE bombs under Theatre SEATS IN THE Near future.

The police traced Metesky to what neighborhood children called the "crazy house" on Fourth Street in Waterbury, Connecticut, just beyond Westchester County, New York. When they arrived, George Metesky was wearing…pajamas. He greeted them warmly and freely admitted to being the Mad Bomber. He even showed them his bomb-making workshop in the garage.

They told him to get dressed for his trip to the station. He returned wearing…a double-breasted suit, buttoned.

Misnomer? *Judo* translates to "the gentle way."

DEDUCTIVE REASONING

So how was Dr. Brussel able to provide such an accurate description?

• It was pretty evident that the Mad Bomber was a man. In those days, very few women would have had the knowledge necessary to make bombs. Bomb-making is, moreover, a classic behavior of paranoid males.

• Because 85% of known paranoids had stocky, muscular builds, Brussel added it to the profile. Metesky had a stocky, muscular build.

• Male paranoiacs have difficulty relating to other people, especially women, and usually live with an older, matriarchal-type woman who will "mother" them. Metesky lived with his two older sisters.

• Another clue to Metesky's sexual inadequacy, Brussel claimed, was his lettering. His script was perfect except for the "W"s—instead of connecting "V"s that would have been consistent with the rest of the letters, Metesky connected two "U"s, which Brussel saw as representing women's breasts.

• Brussel concluded that Metesky was between 40 and 50 years old because paranoia takes years to develop, and based on when the first bomb was found, Metesky had to have already been well down the road. Brussel was close—Metesky was 54.

• What led Brussel to believe that Metesky did not live in New York City was his use of the term "Con Edison"—New Yorkers call it "Con Ed."

• Metesky's language identified him as middle European, too. His use of "dastardly deeds," as well as some other phrases, was a sign of someone with Slavic roots. There was a high concentration of Poles in southern Connecticut, and Brussel connected the dots.

• Paranoids believe that the world conspires against them, so Brussel knew that something traumatic must have happened to Metesky. He was right. On September 5, 1931, Metesky was injured in a boiler explosion at a Con Ed plant. He complained of headaches, but doctors could find no sign of injury. After a year of sick pay and medical benefits, Metesky was fired. A failed lawsuit sent him over the edge, and he began plotting his revenge.

• Brussel also predicted that the Bomber would have a debilitating

---

One species of moth lives entirely on cow tears.

heart disease. He was close: Metesky suffered from a tubercular lung.

• How did Brussel know what kind of suit Metesky would be wearing when he was arrested? Simple: Paranoids are neat freaks, as was apparent in his letters and bombs. He would wear nothing less than the most impeccable outfit of the day—a double-breasted suit, buttoned.

AFTERMATH

George Metesky proudly explained everything to the police. In all, he had planted more than 30 bombs, but miraculously, no one was killed. Metesky said that that was never his intention. "F. P.", he explained, stood for "Fair Play."

On April 18, 1957, George Metesky was found mentally unfit to stand trial and was committed to the Matteawan Hospital for the Criminally Insane. In 1973 he was deemed cured and was released. Metesky lived out the remainder of his days in his Waterbury home, where he died in 1994 at the age of 90. Dr. Brussel gained celebrity status for his role in the case; today he's considered the father of modern psychological profiling in criminal investigations.

TRAGIC LEGACY

Although Metesky's bombs never killed anybody, it was more because of strange luck than "Fair Play." (Police called it a "miracle" that his theater bombs—planted inside the seats—never took any lives.) Even worse, Metesky may have helped pave the way for others who were more successful in their terrible exploits. According to investigators, both the "Zodiac Killer," who killed at least six people—some with bombs—in the San Francisco area in the 1970s, and Ted "Unabomber" Kaczynski, who killed three people in the 1980s and '90s with package bombs, were inspired by George Metesky, New York City's Mad Bomber.

*   *   *

"One thing I can't understand is why the newspapers labeled me the Mad Bomber. That was unkind."

—George Metesky

U.S. city that consumes the most ketchup per capita: New Orleans.

LET ME WRITE SIGN—
I SPEAK ENGLISH GOOD

When signs in a foreign country are written in English, any combination of words is possible. Here are some real-life examples.

"Guests are prohibited from walking around in the lobby in large groups in the nude."
—*Havana hotel*

"If this is your first visit to the USSR, you are welcome to it."
—*Moscow hotel*

"It is forbidden to enter a woman even if a foreigner is dressed as a man."
—*Seville cathedral*

"Visitors two to a bed and half an hour only."
—*Barcelona hospital*

"All customers promptly executed."
—*Tokyo barbershop*

"We highly recommend the hotel tart."
—*Torremolinos hotel*

"I slaughter myself twice daily."
—*Israel butcher shop*

"Because of the impropriety of entertaining persons of the opposite sex in the bedroom, it is requested that the lobby be used for this purpose."
—*Colon restaurant*

"All vegetables in this establishment have been washed in water especially passed by the management."
—*Sri Lanka restaurant*

"Gentlemen's throats cut with nice sharp razors."
—*Zanzibar barbershop*

"Very smart! Almost pansy!"
—*Budapest shop*

"Swimming is forbidden in the absence of the savior."
—*French swimming pool*

"Dresses for street walking."
—*Paris dress shop*

"Go away."
—*Barcelona travel agency*

Hunter S. Thompson missed his high school graduation ceremony because he was in jail.

BARBIE'S MOM

The Barbie doll has come in many incarnations—a teacher, a singer, a flight attendant, and even an astronaut—but never a mother. Too bad, since her creator was one of the world's most successful entrepreneur moms.

IMMIGRANT ROOTS

Barbie's creator had few toys when she was growing up in Denver, Colorado. Ruth Mosko was born in 1916 to Jewish immigrants who'd fled persecution in Poland. As the youngest of 10 children, Ruth had a difficult childhood. Her mother was illiterate and in such poor health that Ruth had to leave home to live with her older sister.

When she was in high school, Ruth fell for a man named Elliot Handler. She eventually moved to California and the two were wed in 1938. Though she married young, Ruth's relationship with Elliott turned out to be not only a long-lasting marriage (63 years), but also a strong business partnership. Elliot became an expert at creating giftware, while Ruth had a talent for marketing and merchandising his products. By 1944 the successful couple were living in a house that Elliot designed, and they had two children: Barbara (nicknamed "Barbie") and Kenneth (nicknamed "Ken").

In 1945 Ruth and Elliot, along with business partner Matt Matson, formed a company that would become one of the largest toy companies in the world—Mattel ("Matt" + "Elliott"). The first Mattel products were wooden picture frames, but the company soon branched out into toys when Elliot started making dollhouse furniture from leftover frame scraps. Over the next decade, Mattel grew exponentially, with Elliot and Matt creating toys and Ruth marketing them.

UNLIKELY INSPIRATION

As a mother in the late 1940s and early '50s, Ruth noticed that her daughter Barbara didn't have many types of dolls to play with—mostly baby dolls, dolls that looked like little girls, and paper dolls. Ruth noticed that Barbara preferred the paper dolls, which looked like fashionable young women and had a variety of

---

Learning the hard way: In Bangladesh, kids as young as 15 can be jailed for cheating on final exams.

gorgeous outfits that could be changed frequently. This observation gave Ruth an idea. She wanted Mattel to create a teenaged doll or a career-woman doll for girls to play with. But Mattel's male executives discouraged her, and she gave up on the idea.

A BARBIE IS BORN

Then in 1956, the Handlers went on a European vacation. In a small store in Lucerne, Switzerland, Barbara saw a molded plastic doll that interested her. It was a Lilli doll made in Germany. A mature German lady, Lilli had an alluring female shape and face. She was actually created as a takeoff on a bawdy comic strip character, and had been designed to appeal to the male bar crowd. But Ruth bought her for Barbara—and the little girl loved her. Based on that reaction, Ruth became convinced that this idea for a new type of doll would be a runaway success.

Ruth used Lilli as a prototype for a new doll, and decided to name it Barbie. With a Barbie doll, Ruth figured, a little girl could act out the fantasy of growing up and having beautiful clothes. "My whole philosophy of Barbie was that through the doll, the little girl could be anything she wanted to be," Ruth wrote in her autobiography. "Barbie always represented the fact that a woman has choices."

BARBIE TAKES OFF

Ruth presented her idea to the executives at Mattel. At first they resisted the doll's curvaceous figure. They didn't think any mother would buy a doll with, well, large breasts. But Ruth insisted that the doll would sell, so Barbie made her first appearance at the 1959 Toy Fair in New York City, wearing a zebra-striped bathing suit and costing $3. The male buyers didn't care for the doll, but the little girls who saw her did. Mattel was deluged with orders and sold more than 350,000 dolls that year.

Five years later, Barbie was a million-dollar product, and Ruth did everything she could to keep Barbie current and on top of the latest trends. As women took on more varied careers, Barbie took them on too, including becoming an astronaut in 1965. Barbie's social circle began to expand with the introduction of the Ken doll. Then came Midge and Skipper. And eventually Stacie, Todd, and Cheryl were added, named for Ruth's grandchildren.

SHE'S UNREAL

Despite the doll's worldwide success, Barbie's figure remained controversial. The National Organization for Women argued that Barbie gave girls an unhealthy body image. If she were 5'9" instead of 11" inches tall, Barbie's measurements would be "unrealistic," top heavy and wasp-waisted—an ideal that, if girls actually tried to emulate it, would probably lead to anorexia. An academic expert once calculated that a woman's likelihood of being shaped like Barbie was less than one in 100,000. Mattel bowed to the criticism, and redesigned Barbie in 1997 to have a slightly smaller bustline and wider waist. But working in Barbie's favor was the fact that her creator—who by then was a grandmother—had become one of the top executives in the male-dominated toy industry. Ruth Handler liked to point out that successful women—and feminists—would often admit to her that they'd loved to play with Barbie when they were kids.

Today a new Barbie doll is sold approximately every three seconds. Barbie is a $1.5 billion business for Mattel, so tomorrow's young girls will probably have Barbies to play with as well. And Ruth Handler's unusual idea for a doll has become an icon of American life.

*　　*　　*

CHAMPIONS OF BREAKFAST

Remember Flutie Flakes, *the cereal promoted by NFL quarterback Doug Flutie? Here are some other real athlete cereals. (Most are just Honey Nut Cheerios or Frosted Flakes with flashy packaging.)*

- Slam Duncans (Tim Duncan, basketball)
- Slammin' Sammy's (Sammy Sosa, baseball)
- Warner's Crunch Time (Kurt Warner, football)
- Lynn Swann's Super 88 (Lynn Swann, football)
- Jeter's (Derek Jeter, baseball)
- MarinO's (Dan Marino, football)
- Moss's Magic Crunch (Randy Moss, football)
- Elway's Comeback Crunch (John Elway, football)
- Jake's Flakes (Jake Plummer, football)

Bears live in *dens,* badgers live in *setts,* and squirrels live in *dreys.*

DR. YESTERYEAR

Uncle John loves reading about ancient treatments for common illnesses.
But he never tries them…and hopefully neither will you.

• Doctors in ancient India closed wounds with the pincers of giant ants.

• The world's first recorded tonsillectomy was performed in the year 1000 B.C.

• Sixteenth-century French doctors prescribed chocolate as a treatment for venereal disease.

• Leprosy is the oldest documented infection— first described in Egypt in 1350 B.C.

• Among the "treasures" found in King Tut's tomb: several vials of pimple cream.

• Acne treatment, circa A.D. 350: "wipe pimples with a cloth while watching a falling star."

• The Hunza people of Kashmir (India and Pakistan) have a 0 percent cancer rate. Scientists link it to the apricot seeds they eat.

• Oldest form of surgery in the world: trepanning (drilling holes into the skull).

• In the Middle Ages, Europeans "cured" muscle pains by drinking powdered gold.

• In medieval Japan, dentists extracted teeth with their hands.

• Doctors in the 1700s prescribed ladybugs, taken internally, to cure measles.

• England's Queen Victoria smoked marijuana to treat her cramps.

• Between 1873 and 1880, some U.S. doctors gave patients transfusions of milk instead of blood.

• During World War I, raw garlic juice was applied to wounds to prevent infection.

• People in ancient China would swing their arms to cure a headache.

Hey, shorty! The length of a single human DNA molecule, when extended, is 5'5".

DUMBEST CROOKS

More proof that crime doesn't pay.

TAKE THE MONEY AND...?

"Jeffrie Thomas, 35, walked into a Signet Bank in Baltimore, Maryland, in April 1997 and handed the teller a note demanding money. When police arrived and asked which way he went, employees pointed to a man counting cash near a teller's station. It was Thomas, adding up the take, police said. Thomas, who was unarmed, was taken into custody."

—*Baltimore Sun*

HOW DID YOU KNOW?

"MacArthur Wheeler, 46, was sentenced to 24 years in prison in Pittsburgh, Pennsylvania, in 1996, a conviction made possible by clear photography from the bank's surveillance camera. Wheeler and his partner did not wear masks and, in fact, were not concerned about the camera at all, because they had rubbed lemon juice all over their faces beforehand, believing the substance would blur their on-camera images."

—*Medford* (Oregon) *Mail Tribune*

BLESSINGS FROM ABOVE

"A Tampa, Florida, burglar who decided to rob a 24-hour convenience store didn't know the store was open 24 hours. He cut a hole in the roof, then fell through and landed on the coffee pot just as a police officer was buying some coffee."

—"The Edge," *The Oregonian*

HOW 'BOUT A BREAKFAST BURRITO?

"The Ann Arbor News reported that a man failed to rob a Michigan Burger King because the clerk told him he couldn't open the cash register without a food order. So the man ordered onion rings, but the clerk informed him that they weren't available for breakfast. The frustrated robber left."

—*A Treasury of Police Humor*

GOLF "FASHION"

*Why does down keep a duck up? Why are there five windows
at the bank, but only two tellers? Why do golfers wear
such strange clothes? To some questions, there are no
answers. (Except for the one about golf clothes.)*

THE FORMAL ERA

1400s: Golf is beginning to be played in Scotland. Golf clothes are ordinary Scottish clothes—elaborate and colorful kilts, scarlet waistcoats, and tams—woolen caps with wide circular crowns and a pom-pom in the center. The loose-fitting garments (especially those breezy kilts) allow for free movement.

1500s: Golf becomes a sport of royalty, with James IV of England being the first known royal golf addict. Golf wear becomes the very formal wear of "lord" and "lady" golfers.

1700s: The first private golf clubs are founded by gentlemen golfers in eastern Scotland. The Royal Burgess Golfing Society of Edinburgh, one of the earliest, has a strict dress code for members: red jacket, white shirt, trousers, and club-issue tie, all to be worn while golfing.

1800s: European women golfers wear bustles and large hats, either tied on or pinned. Their play is restricted mostly to putting, partly due to their cumbersome clothing, but also because it is against social decorum to swing a club above shoulder height. The middle of the century sees the first golf professionals, who aren't upper class but are rather from the lower class—mostly caddies and craftsmen. Their attire is still formal, but in a much less expensive way. (And they're not allowed to be members of golf clubs.)

1888: Scotsman John Reid opens one of the first American golf clubs, New St. Andrews, in Yonkers, New York. With it comes the strict European dress code, including the red jacket. Most British and American clubs are now issuing jackets, and members can be fined for wearing improper attire on the course.

1890s: Women golfers get a little breathing room—literally—as they are now allowed to wear long skirts, buttoned-up boots,

---

billowy blouses, and straw hats. But showing ankle during play is forbidden.

1910s: At both private golf clubs and newly emerging public courses, standard dress for American men is a woven dress shirt with a stiff collar, slacks, a coat, and a tie. Women wear expanding pleats down the sides of their tweed jackets to prevent clothes from ripping mid-swing. The tweed golf sweater becomes the first casual golf garment and is worn off the course as well.

1920s: Professional golfers (the lower-class golfers) begin to take over from the gentlemen at the clubs—but they still have to play at the clubs. The flamboyant Walter Hagen sets new trends during the equally flamboyant Jazz Age. Hagen wears plus-fours—knee-length knickers that got their name from the extra four inches of fabric that billow around the knees—two-tone shoes, a sleeveless argyle sweater, and a loose-fitting blazer. One journalist comments that the sight of Hagen "was enough to make the flappers choke on their gum."

1940s: The postwar era sees the colors fade, as drab, though still elegant, comfort wear comes in. *Esquire* magazine calls it "the grey flannel world of golf." Ben Hogan rules the golf world in dark gray slacks, a light-colored shirt, a cashmere sweater, and his ever-present white cap.

1960s: Color TV is in—and color comes to golf as never before. Doug Sanders earns the nickname "Peacock of the Fairways" for his purple pants and turquoise sweaters and is named *Esquire* magazine's "Best Dressed Athlete." Tony Jacklin wears all purple (including a turtleneck) when he wins the British Open in 1969. Gary Player sticks out by not sticking out, dressing head to toe in solid black.

1970s: Former pro (and current broadcaster) David Feherty shares some painful memories:

> I can't help but think that the decades of the 1970s and '80s were the lowest point in golf fashion…High-waisted, beltless slacks infested our pro shops, making it impossible to retrieve a scorecard from the hip pocket, unless you went for it over your shoulder. The white patent belt was almost compulsory and shirt collars were so long and pointed they became extremely dangerous in high winds. They could put your eye out, for heaven's sake! The only solace I could find was in the fact that my teammates looked equally absurd.

There are more insects in 10 square feet of a rain forest than there are people in Manhattan.

PGA player Johnny Miller defines the era with his countless pairs and varieties of plaid pants, tight at the waist and flared—almost belled—at the bottom.

1980s: Greg "the Shark" Norman defines golf's new (and cool) look with comfortably loose slacks and colorful polo shirts. And he always wears his trademark straw Panama hat. Polo shirts, also called "golf shirts," become immensely popular off the course. Payne Stewart straddles the traditional and modern, matching his polo shirts with retro wear—plus-fours, argyle socks pulled up to the knees, and a tam.

1990s to present: What's worn on the course become largely indistinguishable from the casual look worn in office buildings around the country. Today, golf wear has become almost a billion-dollar business with designers such as Tommy Hilfiger and Ralph Lauren introducing entire lines of golf clothes. You can also get Arnold Palmer, Jack Nicklaus, and Greg Norman golf wear, as well as the biggest seller: Nike's Tiger Woods Collection, featuring Tiger's undeniable contribution to pro golf fashion, the baseball cap. (Swedish golfer Jesper Parnevik is one of the era's mavericks, appearing at PGA events in a rainbow of brightly colored, skintight pants.) Still, to keep golf wear from becoming *too* casual, many golf clubs enact strict dress codes, banning denim, sleeveless shirts, T-shirts, and sweatshirts.

*   *   *

A JACK ATTACK

"In 1994 actor Jack Nicholson allegedly jumped out of his car at an intersection and attacked motorist Robert Blank's Mercedes-Benz with a golf club when Blank cut him off in traffic. After smashing the car's windshield and denting its roof, Jack allegedly got back into his own Mercedes and drove away. Nicholson was later charged with misdemeanor assault and vandalism; Blank sued him, claiming assault and battery. But the civil suit was settled out of court, and the criminal case was dropped. Jack later said, in his defense, that a friend of his had just died, and that he (Jack) had been up all night playing a maniac in a movie."

—*Hollywood Scandals*

It was once a custom in England to pass a newly born baby through the rind of a cheese.

THE "AMERICAN SYSTEM"

In Part 1 of our story (page 223), we told you how Eli Whitney's invention of the cotton gin in 1792 built the pre-Civil War Gone-with-the-Wind South. Here's the story of Whitney's other invention—the one that destroyed it.

LIKE MONEY IN THE BANK

Even before Eli Whitney ginned his first handful of upland cotton, he believed that he was on his way to becoming a wealthy man. "Tis generally said by those who know anything about [the cotton gin], that I shall make a Fortune by it," Whitney wrote in a letter to his father. His friend Phineas Miller certainly agreed—Miller became Whitney's business partner, providing money that Whitney would use to build the machines. They would both grow rich together...or so they thought.

COPYCATS

Things didn't work out quite as planned. There were two problems with Whitney and Miller's dreams of grandeur:

First, just as Whitney had intended, his cotton gin was so simple and so easy to make that just about anyone who was good with tools could make one. So a lot of planters did, even though doing so violated Whitney's patent.

Second, Whitney and Miller were too greedy for their own good. They knew that even if they had enough cash to build a cotton gin for every planter who wanted one (they didn't), the planters didn't have enough cash to buy them. So rather than build gins for sale, Whitney and Miller planned to set up a network of gins around the South where *they* would do the ginning in exchange for a share of the cotton they ginned. A *big* share—40%, to be exact. That was more than the planters were willing to part with, least of all to a Yankee. The planters fought back by ginning their cotton in machines they made themselves or by buying illegal copycat machines made by competitors.

And there were rumors: that Whitney himself had stolen the idea for the cotton gin from a Southern inventor; that the copycat gins were actually "improved" models that didn't infringe on

Whitney's patents; and, worst of all, that Whitney's machines damaged cotton fibers during the ginning process. That last rumor stuck: By the end of 1795, the English were refusing to buy cotton ginned on Whitney & Miller machines; only cotton ginned on illegal (and usually inferior) machines would do. "Everyone is afraid of the cotton," Miller wrote in the fall of 1795. "Not a purchaser in Savannah will pay full price for it."

COURT BATTLES

Whitney and Miller spent years battling the copycats in court and convincing the English textile mills that their cotton was still the best. The stress may have contributed to Miller's death from fever in 1803, when he was only 39. Whitney carried on, and finally won his last court fight in 1806. But the victory came too late to do any good, because the patent on the cotton gin expired the following year. Now copying Whitney's cotton gin wasn't just easy, it was also perfectly legal.

So how much money did Whitney make on the invention that created huge fortunes for Southern plantation owners? Almost none. In fact, some historians estimate that after his several years of legal expenses are taken into account, he actually *lost* money.

The cotton gin would clothe humanity, but in the process of inventing it, Whitney had lost his shirt. "An invention can be so valuable as to be worthless to the inventor," he groused.

THIS MEANS WAR

But Whitney was already working on another invention—one that would establish his fortune and transform the world again...even more than the cotton gin had.

In March of 1798, relations between France and the United States had deteriorated to the point that it seemed a war might be just around the corner. This presented a problem, because France was the primary supplier of arms to the United States. Where would the country get muskets now?

Congress had established two national armories beginning in 1794, but they had produced only 1,000 muskets in four years, and the government estimated that 50,000 would be needed if a war with France did come. Private contractors would have to supply the rest. Whitney, facing bankruptcy, was determined to be one of them.

ONE THING AT A TIME

Until then, all firearms were made by highly skilled artisans who made the entire weapon, crafting each part from scratch and filing and fitting them by hand. Each part, and by extension each musket, was one of a kind—the trigger made for one gun wouldn't work on any other because it fit only that musket. Broken muskets could only be repaired by expert craftsmen. If the weapon broke in the middle of a military campaign, you were out of luck. Armorers capable of such skill were scarce, and new ones took forever to train, which was why the U.S. arsenals were having such a hard time making muskets.

IF YOU'VE SEEN ONE, YOU'VE SEEN THEM ALL

Whitney proposed a new method of making muskets, one he'd been thinking about since trying to speed up production of his cotton gins:

• Instead of using one expert craftsman to make an entire gun, he would divide the tasks among several workers of average skill. They'd be easier to train, and easier to replace if they quit.

• Each worker would be taught how to make one part. They would use special, high-precision machine tools, designed by Whitney.

• The tools would be so precise that the parts would be virtually identical to each other. Each part would fit interchangeably in any of the muskets made in Whitney's factory.

• Once the pieces for a musket had been made, assembling them into the finished weapon would be—literally—a snap.

• Ready-made interchangeable spare parts would make it possible for any soldier to fix his musket himself.

BETTER LATE THAN NEVER

On June 14, 1798, Whitney signed a contract with the U.S. government to deliver 10,000 muskets within two years. But the war with France never came. Good thing, too, because Whitney missed his deadline by eight years. Supply shortages and yellow fever epidemics disrupted the schedule, so it took him longer to make his machine tools than he originally thought.

Whitney's reputation as a genius helped him to get extensions

The average shopping-center Santa weighs 218 pounds and has a 43-inch waist.

and advances against his government contract. But more than anything, what gave Whitney freedom to take the time necessary to perfect his new system was a demonstration he gave to President-elect Thomas Jefferson and other high officials in 1801. Dumping a huge pile of interchangeable musket parts onto a table, Whitney invited them to pick pieces from the pile at random and assemble them into complete muskets. For the first time in history, they could.

THE AMERICAN SYSTEM

It may not sound like a big deal, but it was. Whitney had devised a method of manufacturing more muskets of higher quality, in less time and for less money, than had ever been possible before. And he did it without the use of highly skilled labor. Once again, Whitney had invented something that would change the world.

What worked with muskets would also work with clothing, farm equipment, furniture, tools, bicycles, and just about anything else people could manufacture. Whitney called his process "the American system." Today it's known as *mass production*. In time it would overshadow even the cotton gin itself in the way it would transform the American economy.

Only this time, the transformation would be felt most in the North…and it would bring the South to its knees.

For Part III of the Eli Whitney story, turn to page 518.

*   *   *

Q&A: ASK THE EXPERTS

Q: *How do those luminous light sticks work?*
A: "You mean those plastic rods full of liquid chemicals that are sold at festivals and concerts, and that start glowing with green, yellow, or blue light when you bend them, and that gradually lose their light after an hour or so? When you bend the stick, you break a thin glass capsule containing a chemical, usually hydrogen peroxide, that reacts with another chemical in the tube. The reaction gives off energy, which is absorbed by a fluorescent dye and reemitted as light. As the chemical reaction gradually plays itself out because the chemicals are used up, the light fades." (From *What Einstein Told His Barber*, by Robert L. Wolke)

Not b-a-a-a-d: According to scientists, sheep can remember 50 faces for two years.

RANDOM ORIGINS

A few more beginnings of everyday things.

TRAVEL AGENCIES

In 1841 a Baptist missionary named Thomas Cook chartered a train to take 570 temperance campaigners from Leicester, England, to a rally in Loughborough, 11 miles away. In exchange for giving the business to the Midland Counties Railway, Cook received a percentage of the fares. The success of that trip inspired him to organize many more. Eventually he expanded beyond the temperance movement and began booking trips for tourists. Cook has been credited with inventing not only the travel agency, but modern tourism, as well. Today the company that bears his name is one of the world's largest travel agencies.

MAIL-ORDER CATALOGS

In September 1871, a British major named F. B. McCrea founded the Army & Navy Cooperative in London to supply goods to military personnel at the lowest possible price. Its first catalog was issued in February 1872...six months before an American named Aaron Montgomery Ward put his first catalog in the mail.

THE CINEMA MULTIPLEX

Invented by accident by theater owner Stan Durwood in 1963, when he tried to open a large theater in a Kansas City, Missouri shopping mall. The mall's developer told Durwood that the support columns in the building could not be removed to build a single large theater...so Durwood built two smaller theaters instead. He showed the same movie on both screens—until it dawned on him that he'd sell more tickets if he showed two different films. It was a huge success; the national attention he got spurred a "multiplex boom" in other cities.

WALLPAPER

It wasn't long after the Chinese invented paper more than 2,000 years ago that they began gluing pieces of it to the walls of their homes. Wallpaper was also popular in medieval Europe, where it

---

Population explosion: From fertilization to birth, a baby's weight increases by 5 billion times.

was a cheap alternative to tapestries and murals. But these early examples were only imitations of the tapestries and murals they replaced. It wasn't until about 1688 that wallpaper as we know it came into being: That was when Jean Papillon, a French engraver, invented the first paper with repeating patterns that matched on every side when the sheets were pasted next to each other.

CONTROL-ALT-DELETE

David Bradley was on the team that developed IBM's first personal computer, or PC, in 1981. Given the assignment of coming up with a way to restart the computer (simply turning it off and turning it back on damaged the hardware), he came up with what he called "the three-finger salute": the computer would restart if the "control," "alt," and "delete" buttons were all pressed simultaneously. Why those three buttons? Bradley figured it was nearly impossible to press that combination of keys by accident.

TUXEDO RENTALS

Charles Pond made his living entertaining at London parties in the 1890s. He couldn't afford a formal suit of his own, so he borrowed them from his friend Alfred Moss, who ran a clothing store. Eventually Moss got tired of Pond's mooching and started charging him a small fee to rent a suit overnight. Today, Moss Bros. is the largest formalwear rental chain in the U.K.

GPS (GLOBAL POSITIONING SYSTEM)

Not long after the Soviet Union launched *Sputnik* in 1957, a team of American scientists monitoring the satellite's radio transmissions noticed that the frequency of its signal increased as it approached and decreased as it traveled away from them—a classic example of the "Doppler" effect. They realized they could use this information to pinpoint *Sputnik*'s precise location in space; conversely, if they knew the satellite's location, they could use it to determine their own location on Earth. This principle served as the basis for the U.S. military's NAVSTAR GPS system, which became operational in 1993. The U.S. intended to restrict the system to military use, but when the Soviets shot down a Korean Airlines flight in 1983 after it wandered into Soviet airspace, President Ronald Reagan announced that the system would be made available for public use.

When Harper Lee won the 1961 Pulitzer Prize for *To Kill a Mockingbird*, she broke out in hives.

ONE GIANT MISQUOTE FOR MANKIND

Here's the story behind one of the most famous quotations of all time.

MAN ON THE MOON

Neil Armstrong knew the world would be listening to the first human words spoken on another world, so he thought long and hard about what he would say before he placed his foot on the surface of the Moon. After much deliberation, the *Apollo 11* astronaut decided on these words: "That's one small step for a man, one giant leap for mankind."

On July 20, 1969, with an audience of half a billion people, Armstrong hopped off the ladder of *Apollo 11*, took a step on the moon, and attempted his quotation, which was beamed back to Earth, 250,000 miles away. But what exactly did he say? Here is what the world heard: "That's one small step for man, one giant leap for mankind."

Big difference. Without the word "a" before "man," the quote made little sense. He essentially said: "One small step for mankind, one giant leap for mankind."

TO "A" OR NOT TO "A"

"Damn, I blew the first words on the Moon, didn't I?" Armstrong lamented to NASA officials when he got home...except he wasn't entirely sure he *had* botched his famous line. Inside his helmet, he could hear the same static-drenched audio feed that was beamed back to Earth and couldn't remember if he said the "a"—or if it had been drowned out by static.

For nearly 40 years, Armstrong deflected criticism of his goof, citing the distinct possibility that he had said the "a." Few believed him, but no one could argue that the sentiment wasn't there; everyone knew what he was trying to say. "Certainly the 'a' was intended," he explained, "because that's the only way the statement makes any sense." Official quotation books acknowledged the "a" by placing it in brackets, but it still bothered

---

Absentee ballot? Astronaut John Blaha became the first American to vote from space, in 1997.

Armstrong. He wanted to know the truth—the most famous words of the 20th century were still in question.

MODERN SCIENCE TO THE RESCUE

One man who also wanted to know the truth was an Australian computer expert named Peter Shann Ford. In 2006 Ford obtained the NASA recording of Armstrong's feed and ran it through a sophisticated sound-editing software system. After careful review, Ford picked up a nearly undetectable acoustic vibration after the word "for." He slowed it down, scrutinized the vibration, and concluded that it was a vocal utterance lasting only 35 milliseconds. It was, undoubtedly, Armstrong's missing "a." It seems that the astronaut—who had been awake for 24 hours when he said the famous words, and was nervous and excited to be the first person on the Moon (who wouldn't be?)—had hurried through his speech so quickly that the "a" got lost in the static.

Ford presented his results to NASA. "I find the technology interesting and useful," a relieved Armstrong told reporters. "And I find his conclusion persuasive."

*   *   *

[Audible] Quotes from the Moon Landings

"The surface is fine and powdery. I can kick it up loosely with my toe. It does adhere in fine layers, like powdered charcoal, to the sole and sides of my boots. I only go in a small fraction of an inch, maybe an eighth of an inch, but I can see the footprints of my boots and the treads in the fine, sandy particles. There seems to be no difficulty in moving around, as we suspected."

—**Neil Armstrong**

"Magnificent desolation."

—**Buzz Aldrin**

"Whoopee! Man, that may have been a small one for Neil, but it's a long one for me!"

—**Charles "Pete" Conrad,** *Apollo 12* **commander, third man on the moon, and the shortest Apollo astronaut**

"To be proud with knowledge is to be blind with light." —Benjamin Franklin

PEANUTS, PART III

Our story of Charles Schulz continues with the tale of a low-budget holiday special that became a classic. (Part II is on page 349.)

READY FOR PRIMETIME

In 1964 a San Francisco television producer named Lee Mendelson made a documentary about baseball legend Willie Mays that garnered some pretty good reviews. Having honored the world's greatest baseball player, he later recalled, "now I should do the world's worst baseball player, Charlie Brown." So Mendelson approached Schulz with the idea of making a documentary about *Peanuts*. Schulz had seen the Willie Mays show and was very interested. The two had just started work on the documentary *Charlie Brown & Charles Schulz*, which focused on Schulz's troubled childhood, when the Coca-Cola company approached Mendelson about making a *Peanuts* Christmas special for 1965. "I said, 'Absolutely!'" recalled Mendelson. "I phoned Sparky and told him that I had just sold a Charlie Brown Christmas show. He asked which show and I told him, 'The one we're going to make an outline for tomorrow.' And we literally did the outline in one day."

With the story worked out, Schulz hired Bill Melendez, the animator that Ford had used on the *Peanuts* commercials. (Melendez's impressive resume included such Disney films as *Bambi* and *Fantasia*, and many classic Bugs Bunny and Daffy Duck cartoons for Warner Bros.) The three men would end up working together on dozens of *Peanuts* specials and films over the next 30 years.

ON A SHOESTRING

But their first project turned out to be the most difficult. For one thing, they had a tiny budget to work with, which resulted in very choppy animation, even by 1960s standards. There were other problems, too: CBS wanted to hire adult actors to voice the children, *and* they wanted a laugh track. By this time, Schulz was powerful enough to get what he wanted, and he wanted actual children's voices with no laugh track. (He cringed at the idea of telling people when they should be laughing.) CBS gave in, but had another demand—they didn't want Linus reciting a Bible verse. "The whole thing is about the true meaning of Christmas!" Schulz argued. "Take that out and there's no show!" After some hard-fought negotiations, the network finally relented, as they also did about using jazz music in the soundtrack. CBS executives didn't understand it; they were expecting the special to flop.

A TRADITION IS BORN

Airing on Thursday, December 9, 1965 (in *Gilligan's Island*'s regular time slot), *A Charlie Brown Christmas* became an overnight sensation. More than half of the televisions in the United States tuned in. While Schulz, Mendelson, and Melendez cringed at some of the low-budget technical aspects of *A Charlie Brown Christmas*—the static speaking style of the kids (especially Sally, who was voiced by a little girl too young to read, so she had to be fed her lines phonetically)—they felt that they had created something unique. The critics agreed. They lauded its simple message that Christmas means more than crass commercialism (even though the special *was* sponsored by Coca-Cola). The public agreed, too. *A Charlie Brown Christmas* won an Emmy and a Peabody Award and became a Christmas tradition.

More animation followed, most notably *A Boy Named Charlie Brown* in 1969 (the first *Peanuts* feature film) and two more well-received holiday specials: *It's the Great Pumpkin, Charlie Brown* in 1966 and *A Charlie Brown Thanksgiving* in 1973. In all, the team of Schulz, Mendelson, and Melendez produced more than 40 primetime specials over the next three decades. (Melendez also provided the squeaky voices of Snoopy and Woodstock.)

HEAVY BURDENS

But as the years went on, Schulz devoted less and less of his time to these outside projects, leaving most of the screen work to Mendelson and Melendez. In the early 1970s, Schulz's home life started to deteriorate, leading to a divorce in 1972. "I didn't think she liked me anymore," he said, "and I just got up and left one day." A year later, while skating at a local ice rink, Schulz met Jeannie Clyde. The two hit it off and were married in 1973. They remained together for the rest of Schulz's life.

With a renewed spirit and more time to work on the strip, Schulz spent the rest of the 1970s perfecting the characters he'd been fleshing out over the previous 20 years. Only a few new characters were added; instead, he focused more on extended story lines such as Peppermint Patty's troubles at school, Snoopy's campus adventures as "Joe Cool," and Charlie Brown's first-ever win at a baseball game (he walked with the bases loaded). But even though *Peanuts* remained popular, it was obvious that it had peaked in the 1960s. That was fine with Schulz—the fewer promotional appearances and outside projects he had to deal with, the better.

LOSING ITS EDGE

By the 1980s, Schulz found himself in the odd position of being the "old timer." Suddenly it was no longer "*Peanuts* and everything else." A new crop of humor cartoonists, all inspired in some way by *Peanuts*, were making their own marks on the daily comics page—Lynn Johnston's *For Better or For Worse*, which Schulz loved, Jim Davis's *Garfield*, which Schulz loathed, and Gary Larson's *The Far Side*, which Schulz never said much about... although he probably wasn't too pleased to see Larson's depiction of Charlie Brown buried up to his neck in the sand (by Indians) awaiting an army of oncoming ants. Yet that's the kind of cutting-edge humor that was catching people's attention in the early 1980s. Charlie Brown and Snoopy's antics seemed passé next to, say, the political volatility of Garry Trudeau's *Doonesbury*. For the first time, *Peanuts* was no longer leading the way.

To compete with the new strips, Schulz was urged by his syndicate to modernize the look of *Peanuts*—or at least make the kids start commenting on current events. Schulz refused both requests and stubbornly kept *Peanuts* locked in the same innocent setting where it began. "I could never be a political cartoonist," he said in 1988, "because I refuse to blast people I don't know. I suppose that's why they say *Peanuts* is no longer on the cutting edge. That's absurd. What's 'cutting edge,' anyway? Insulting the president? Delighting in meanness? If that's cutting edge, then I don't want it." One of Schulz's strongest advocates was up-and-coming comic strip artist Bill Watterson, creator of *Calvin & Hobbes*. In 1987 he came to Schulz's defense:

> Every now and then I hear that *Peanuts* isn't as funny as it was or it's gotten old. I think that what's really happened is that it

changed the entire face of comic strips and everybody has now caught up to him. I don't think he's five years ahead of everybody else like he used to be, so that's taken some of the edge off it. I think it's still a wonderful strip in terms of solid construction, character development, and the fantasy element. Things that we now take for granted—reading the thoughts of an animal, for example—there's not a cartoonist who's done anything since 1960 that doesn't owe Schulz a tremendous debt.

HEART PROBLEMS AND INTO THE WOODS

Schulz's struggles with keeping the strip timely only increased when his health started to deteriorate in the early 1980s. For one, it made the demands of a daily strip more difficult to keep up with. Normally, Schulz had a three-month lead time, meaning the comic he drew today would run in the newspapers 90 days later. That gave him ample time to develop new stories. But in 1981, the 59-year-old cartoonist suffered a heart attack, prompting an emergency quadruple-bypass. As he recovered, he saw his lead times shrink down to a few weeks. And he hated working under pressure. Worse yet, he developed Parkinson's disease, which caused his hands to shake. "It's just annoying," Schulz said in 1988. "It slows me down, and I have to letter very carefully. After my heart surgery, it was intolerable, and then I wracked up my knee playing hockey. That was worse than the heart surgery; it just took all the life out of me. I remember one day I came back, and I was so weak I finally had to quit. I just couldn't hold that pen still. Am I supposed to sit here the rest of my life drawing these things while all my friends are dying or retiring?"

Rather than pack it in, however, Schulz invented new story lines in the 1990s to help him cope. He focused heavily on Snoopy's adventure as a Beagle Scout—following the dog and his bird friends into the forest. "Hiking, camping, and roasting marshmallows over an open fire can revive a writer's dampened spirit," Schulz said.

THE END OF AN ERA

Schulz had planned to draw the strip well into his 80s…until he suffered a stroke and was diagnosed with colon cancer in November 1999. Yet he still refused his syndicate's insistence that he bring in ghostwriters. "Everything has to end," he said. "This strip is my excuse for existence. No one else will touch it." (Schulz was always saddened to see one of his cartoonist friends retire or die, only to have their syndicate hire other artists to keep the strip going.) But with his health failing, on December 14, 1999, Schulz, now 77, reluctantly announced his retirement. He died on February 12, 2000, the same day the last original Sunday *Peanuts* strip ran. It was a montage of classic scenes, along with a note that came straight from Snoopy's (and Sparky's) typewriter:

> Dear Friends, I have been fortunate to draw Charlie Brown and his friends for almost 50 years. It has been the fulfillment of my child-hood ambition. Unfortunately, I am no longer able to maintain the schedule demanded by a daily comic strip. My family does not wish *Peanuts* to be continued by anyone else, therefore I am announcing my retirement. I have been grateful over the years for the loyalty of our editors and the wonderful support and love expressed to me by fans of the comic strip. Charlie Brown, Linus, Lucy...how can I ever forget them...

YOU'RE A GOOD MAN, CHARLIE SCHULZ

Schulz was buried in Sebastopol, California, with full military honors. Fittingly, four Sopwith Camel biplanes (Snoopy's plane from his battles with the Red Baron) performed a flyover. A few months later, nearly 100 of Schulz's fellow cartoonists showed their appreciation with *Peanuts*-themed comic strips.

According to Robert Thompson, a professor of popular culture at Syracuse University, *Peanuts* may be the "longest story ever told by one human being." He pointed out that the 50-year journey of the *Peanuts* gang is longer than that of any epic poem ever writ-ten, and dwarfs any Tolstoy novel or Wagnerian opera. One of Schulz's heroes and best friends, a World War II cartoonist named Bill Mauldin, summed up Sparky's impact: "I rank Schulz with Gandhi in the scope and influence on people in the 20th century. Sure, Gandhi spoke to multitudes, but has anybody counted Schulz's circulation? And the same message is conveyed: Love thy neighbor even when it hurts. Love even Lucy."

If you're like us, you can never get enough of the Peanuts characters. For their individual stories, check out the Peanuts Gallery on page 568.

A common housefly carries some 1,941,000 bacteria on its body.

SOUTHPAW TRIVIA

We wouldn't be in our right minds if
we left out these left-handed facts.

• If you're left-handed, you're definitely outnumbered. Lefties make up only 5 to 15 percent of the population.

• If you're a female southpaw, you're even more unusual—there are roughly 50 percent more left-handed males than females.

• The artwork found in ancient Egyptian tombs portrays most Egyptians as right-handed. But their enemies are portrayed as left-handers, a sign they saw left-handedness as an undesirable trait.

• Ancient Greeks never crossed their left leg over their right, and believed a person's sex was determined by their position in the womb—the female, or "lesser sex," sat on the left side of the womb.

• Roman customs dictated that they enter friends' homes "with the right foot forward"...and turn their heads to the right to sneeze. Their language showed the same bias: the Latin word for left is *sinister* (which also means evil or ominous), and the word for right is *dexter* (which came to mean skillful or adroit). Even the word *ambidextrous* means "right-handed with both hands."

• Lefties are more likely to be on the extreme ends of the intelligence scale than the general population: a higher proportion of mentally retarded people and people with IQs over 140 are lefties.

• Why are lefties called *southpaws*? In the late 1890s, most baseball parks were laid out with the pitcher facing west and the batter facing east (so the sun wouldn't be in his eyes). That meant left-handed pitchers threw with the arm that faced south. So Chicago sportswriter Charles Seymour began calling them southpaws.

• What did traditional Christians believe was going to happen on Judgment Day? According to custom, God blesses the saved with his right hand—and casts sinners out of heaven with his left.

MAKING *THE GODFATHER*, PART III

Here's the third installment of our story on how the most popular novel of the 1970s ended up as one of the greatest films of the 20th century. (Parts I and II are on pages 138 and 317.) Salud!

THOSE EYES

Coppola had his heart set on Al Pacino for the role of Michael Corleone, and, as he had with Marlon Brando, he just kept pushing until he finally got his way. Paramount forced him to test other actors for the part, and every time he did he had Pacino come in and do another screen test, too. Robert Evans got so sick of seeing Pacino's face that he screamed, "Why the hell are you testing him again? The man's a midget!"

But Coppola would not back down, not even when Pacino grew discouraged filming test after test after test for a part that he knew the studio would never give him. Ironically, it may have been that very frustration that got Pacino the part—in some of the screen tests he appears calm but also seems to be hiding anger just below the surface. This moody intensity was an accurate reflection of his state of mind, and it was just the quality he needed to convey to be successful in the role.

Did the screen tests convince Paramount that Pacino was right for the part, or did Coppola finally just wear them down? Whatever it was, Pacino got the job. "Francis was the most effective fighter against the studio hierarchy I've ever seen," casting director Fred Roos told one interviewer. "He did not do it by yelling or screaming, but by sheer force of will."

YOU LOSE SOME, YOU WIN SOME

By the time Paramount finally got around to approving Pacino for the role, he'd signed up to do another film called *The Gang That Couldn't Shoot Straight*. To get him out of that commitment, Coppola made a trade: He released another young actor from appearing in *The Godfather* so that he could take Pacino's place in *The Gang That Couldn't Shoot Straight*. The actor: Robert De Niro—

The famous "horse's head" seen in *The Godfather*...

he'd been cast as Paulie Gatto, the driver and bodyguard who betrays Don Corleone. Losing the part may have been disappointing to De Niro at the time, but it also cleared the way for him to play the young Vito Corleone in *The Godfather: Part II*, the role that won him his first Oscar, for Best Supporting Actor, and made him an international star.

FAMILY PROBLEMS

As if fighting Paramount wasn't bad enough, Coppola also had to contend with the real-life Mafia, which wasn't too pleased with the idea of a big-budget Italian gangster movie coming to the screen. Joe Colombo, head of one of the *real* "five families" that made up the New York mob, was also the founder of a group called the Italian-American Civil Rights League, an organization that lobbied against negative Italian stereotypes in the media.

The League had won some impressive victories in recent years, successfully lobbying newspapers, broadcast networks, and even the Nixon Justice Department to replace terms like "the Mafia" and "La Cosa Nostra" with more ethnically neutral terms like "the Mob," "the syndicate," and "the underworld." The League was at the height of its powers in the early 1970s, and now it set its sights on *The Godfather*.

I'M-A GONNA DIE!

How would you deal with the Maf…er, um…the "syndicate" if they were trying to stop the project you were working on? Albert Ruddy, the producer, decided to face the problem head on: He met with Colombo in the League's offices to discuss mutual concerns, and he even let Colombo have a peek at the script. Colombo's demands actually turned out to be fairly reasonable: He didn't want the film to contain any patronizing Italian stereotypes or accents—"I'm-a gonna shoot-a you now"—and he didn't want the Mafia identified by that name in the film. Ruddy assured Colombo that Coppola had no plans to use that kind of speech, and he even promised to remove all references to "the Mafia" from the script.

Colombo didn't know it at the time, but removing the word "Mafia" from the script was an easy promise to keep because it wasn't in there to begin with—guys who are in the Mafia don't sit around discussing it by name.

In effect, Colombo had agreed to end the Mob's opposition to the film and even to make some of his "boys" available for crowd control and other odd jobs, and had gotten next to nothing in return. (In 1971, during filming of *The Godfather,* Colombo was gunned down in a Mob hit and lingered in a coma until 1978, when he finally died from his wounds.)

LASHED TO THE MAST

One of the nice things about winning so many battles with studio executives is getting to make the film you want to make; the bad thing is that once it becomes your baby, if things start to go wrong it's easy for the studio to figure out who they need to fire—*you.*

Filming of *The Godfather* got off to a rough start—Brando's performances in his first scenes were so dull and uninspired that Coppola had to set aside time to film them again. Al Pacino's earliest scenes didn't look all that promising, either. His first scenes were the ones at the beginning of the film, when he's a boyish war hero determined to stay out of the family "business." Pacino played the scenes true to character—so true, in fact, that when the Paramount executives saw the early footage, they doubted he'd be able to pass as a Mafia don.

For a time the set was awash with rumors that Coppola and Pacino were both about to be fired. How true were the rumors? Both men were convinced their days were numbered—that was one of the reasons Coppola cast his sister, Talia Shire, as Don Corleone's daughter, Connie: He figured that if he was going to lose his job, at least *she'd* get something out of the film.

FAIR-WEATHER FRIENDS

More than 30 years later, it's difficult to say how true the rumors were, especially now that the film is considered a classic—the executives who would have wanted to fire the pair back then are now more likely to take credit for discovering them. But the threat was real, and Marlon Brando saved Coppola by counter-threatening to walk off the job if Coppola was removed from the film.

Al Pacino saved his own skin when he filmed the scene where he murders Virgil Sollozzo and Captain McCluskey (Al Lettieri and Sterling Hayden) in an Italian restaurant. That was the first scene in which he got the chance to appear as a cold-blooded

---

You gotta start somewhere: Jack Nicholson once had a job answering Tom and Jerry's fan mail.

killer, and he pulled it off with ease. Finally, Paramount could see that he could indeed play a Mafia don.

PUTTING IT ALL TOGETHER

Once these early problems were resolved, the production made steady progress and remained more or less on schedule and on budget. Marlon Brando behaved himself on the set and delivered one of the greatest performances of his career; the other actors gave excellent performances as well. As Paramount executives reviewed the footage after each day of shooting, it soon became clear to everyone involved that *The Godfather* was going to be a remarkable film.

In 62 days of shooting, Coppola filmed more than 90 hours of footage, which he and six editors whittled down to a film that was just under three hours long. (Paramount made Coppola edit it down to two and a half hours, but that version left out so many good scenes that the studio decided to use Coppola's original cut.) By the time they finished—and before the film even made it into the theaters—*The Godfather* had already turned a profit: So many theaters rushed to book it in advance that it had already taken in twice as much money as it had cost to make.

LARGER THAN LIFE

The advance bookings were the first sign that *The Godfather* was going to do really big business; another sign came on March 15, 1972, the day the film premiered in the United States. That morning when Albert Ruddy drove into work, he saw people waiting in front of a theater that was showing *The Godfather*. It was only 8:15 a.m., and the first showing was hours away, but the fans were already lining up around the block—not just at that theater, but everywhere else in America, too.

The long lines continued for weeks. As *The Godfather* showed to one sold-out audience after another, it smashed just about every box-office record there was: In April it became the first movie to earn more than $1 million in a day; in September it became the most profitable Hollywood film ever made, earning more money in six months than the previous record holder, *Gone With the Wind*, had earned in 33 years. In all, it made more than $85 million during its initial release. (How long did it hold the record as

Hollywood's most profitable film? Only one year—*The Exorcist* made even more money in 1973.)

Nominated for 10 Academy Awards, *The Godfather* won for Best Actor (Brando), Best Adapted Screenplay (Coppola and Puzo), and Best Picture.

The Godfather revived Marlon Brando's career and launched those of Francis Ford Coppola, Al Pacino, Robert Duvall, Diane Keaton, James Caan, Talia Shire, and even Abe Vigoda (who later starred in TV's *Barney Miller* and *Fish*), whom Coppola discovered during an open casting call. "The thing that I like most about the film's success is that everyone that busted their hump on this movie came out with something very special—and good careers," Albert Ruddy said years later. "All of these people came together in one magic moment, and it was the turn in everybody's careers. It was just a fantastic thing."

SERENDIPITY
Two memorable scenes in The Godfather *came about only by chance:*

• Luca Brasi Memorizes his Speech
It wasn't unusual for real-life wiseguys to hang out around the set during location shoots; one day during filming in the Little Italy neighborhood of New York, a mobster visited the set with an enormous bodyguard in tow. The bodyguard, a onetime professional wrestler named Lenny Montana, was 6'6" and must have weighed over 300 pounds. Albert Ruddy spotted him and pointed him out to Coppola, who cast him on the spot as Luca Brasi, the hit man who is garroted early in the film and ends up "sleeping with the fishes."

Montana had no acting experience, and in his scene with Marlon Brando he was so nervous that he kept stumbling over his lines. Rather than replace him with someone who could act, Coppola made Montana's fumbling a part of the story by creating the scene where Luca Brasi rehearses and repeatedly flubs the few words he wants to say in his meeting with Don Corleone at Connie and Carlo's wedding. For the meeting with the Don, Coppola used one of Montana's actual blown takes.

• The Don's Death Scene
On the day that Coppola was supposed to film the scene in which

Don Corleone dies while playing with his grandson, they were having trouble getting the young boy playing the grandson to perform his part. Brando mentioned a trick that he liked to use with his own small children: He would cut up the peel of a slice of orange into teeth, stuff it into his mouth, and play "monster" with his kids. Coppola liked the sound of it, so he tossed the script aside and filmed Brando playing monster with the boy. That was the scene that ended up in the movie.

THREE BITS OF *GODFATHER* TRIVIA

• **Foreboding fruit:** One of the best-known uses of foreshadowing in all three *Godfather* films is the use of oranges to hint at upcoming scenes of violence and death. The Godfather buys a bag of oranges just before he is gunned down; later in the film, he dies while playing "monster" with his grandson with an orange peel stuffed in his mouth. The character Sal Tessio (Abe Vigoda), who betrays Michael and is murdered at the end of the film, is introduced at the beginning of the movie playing with an orange. According to production designer Dean Tavoularis, oranges didn't start out as symbolic of anything. Cinematographer Gordon Willis, who worked on all three *Godfather* films, is known as "the Prince of Darkness" because he likes to film in low light, so Tavoularis put oranges in some sets for contrast—just to brighten scenes that would otherwise have been extremely dark and devoid of color.

• **Hits:** The scene where Sonny Corleone beats up his brother-in-law, Carlo Rizzi, contains a famous blooper that has become known as "The Miss": Sonny takes a swing at Carlo and obviously misses, but there's a sound effect, and Rizzi still reacts as if he's been punched. (Ever notice that Rizzi is wearing an *orange* leisure suit?) The entire fight sequence, including The Miss, was reenacted in a 2003 episode of *The Simpsons* titled "Strong Arms of the Ma."

• **Name game:** Francis Ford Coppola was named after his grandfather, Francesco Pennino. Where'd the "Ford" come from? The Ford Motor Company. They sponsored a radio show that employed his father, Carmine Coppola, as a conductor and musical arranger.

First movie to earn $100 million: *Jaws* (1975). First movie to earn $200 million: *Jaws* (1975).

DO-IT-YOURSELF JELLO

In previous editions of Uncle John's Bathroom Reader, *we told you how to make shrunken heads and atomic bombs. Those are pretty tough acts to follow...but we think this comes close.*

WHAT YOU'LL NEED
A few pounds of animal remnants (see Step 1), a sharp knife, a surgical-grade bone saw, a colander or strainer, a power washer, an aluminum cauldron, a roasting pan, two huge plastic vats, 20 gallons of lime, 20 gallons of a 4% hydrochloric-acid solution, distilled water, a microwave, cheese-cloth, a food dehydrator, a food processor, Kool-Aid mix...and about a week.

1. Gather up any cow, sheep, or horse bones, hooves, skin, or any random body tissue you might have lying around. Don't have any? Don't worry: Call a local slaughterhouse and ask for "raw pre-processing waste." But make *sure* that the bones and skin they give you are fresh—no more than a day old.

2. Carefully inspect the body parts. Discard any pieces that smell foul or look rotten. Overly decayed bits of bone and flesh produce stringy and inconsistent gelatin. (And besides, they're gross.)

3. Cut the parts into small, five-inch-wide pieces. Use a sharp paring or serrated knife on the skin and tissue. For the bones, you're probably going to have to use a top-of-the-line electric carving knife, power saw, or surgical bone saw.

4. Place the small pieces in a large colander or strainer. Take it all into the backyard and thoroughly wash all of them off with a high-pressure hose or power washer. This will free them of any unwant-ed animal debris, such as leftover blood or gristle.

5. Throw the clean pieces of bone, hoof, and tissue into a big pot and soak them in boiling water for about five hours. (The power-washing got rid of the blood and gristle, but a boiling bath gets rid of almost all of the fat.) After five hours of boiling, the fat will be floating at the top of the pot. Skim it off and throw it away.

6. Preheat your oven to 200°F. Place the clean, fat-free bones, skin, and other tissue in a roasting pan and bake them for 30 minutes.

7. Back to the backyard. Get a huge plastic vat, fill it with lime, and toss in the animal chunks. This semi-decomposes the materials, removing unwanted minerals and organic body chemicals from the cow parts. Let it all soak in the lime for about two days.

8. Get another plastic vat and fill it up with a mixture of 96% water and 4% hydrochloric acid (available in any scientific-supply store or on the Internet). This facilitates the release of collagen from the animal material, which is the bouncy, "gelatinous" element of gelatin. Leave the pieces in the vat for three days.

9. After removing them from the acid bath (wear gloves!), take the pieces back inside and throw them into an aluminum cauldron and boil them in *distilled*—not tap—water. Using a slotted spoon, carefully skim off any gooey chunks that rise to the surface. This is waterlogged gelatin, and it's what you've been after for the past week.

10. Next, the liquidy gelatin chunks have to be sterilized. In gelatin-processing plants, they go into a high-heat flash heater for four seconds. If you don't have an industrial flash heater, put the goopy bits in the microwave on a ceramic plate (it's soak-proof) for about 10 seconds.

11. Strain the chunks through fine cheesecloth to filter out any tiny remnants of bone, skin, or meat that remain attached to the gelatin.

12. Separate the semi-solid gelatin from the liquid by drying it out. Processing plants use the industrial flash heater for this, too, but you can substitute a home food dehydrator or beef-jerky maker lined with wax paper. Let it sit for about 24 hours.

13. You're almost done! Scrape the dry (but slightly sticky) gelatin out of the dehydrator and put it all in a food processor. Grind it into a powder. Mix in some powdered flavorings—Kool-Aid mix works pretty well. Add in the hot water and let it stand in the fridge for a few hours. Alternative: Go to the store and buy a box of gelatin dessert mix for 59 cents. Follow the directions on the box.

Shakespeare's *A Midsummer Night's Dream* takes place in spring.

OOPS!

Everyone's amused by tales of outrageous blunders—probably because it's comforting to know that someone's screwing up even worse than we are. So go ahead and feel superior for a few minutes.

PLANK YOU VERY MUCH

"A woman came home to find her husband in the kitchen, shaking frantically with what looked like a wire running from his waist toward the electric kettle. Intending to jolt him away from the deadly current, she whacked him with a handy plank of wood, breaking his arm in two places. Until that moment, he had been happily listening to his Walkman."

—Associated Press

WHAT A CLOWN

"On its July 30 'Family Fun' page, the *Kansas City Star* ran a blurb on National Clown Week. Accompanying the text, naturally enough, was a photo of a clown. But the editor selecting the file photo neglected to look at the flip side, which would have revealed that the clown in question was John Wayne Gacy, a Chicago serial killer (and onetime clown) executed five years ago for killing 33 boys and young men. The *Star* apologized the next day in an editor's note."

—Brill's Content

NAKED AMBITION

"Thirty-one-year-old stripper Roberto Pamplona suffered a broken nose and multiple injuries after performing his act in Milan, Italy. He was supposed to be stripping for a party in one room, but showed up next door...where the Catholic Mothers Against Pornography were meeting. The innocent mix-up angered the 'Mothers' and Pamplona's act erupted into a riot halfway through the show."

—"The Edge," Oregonian

THE LIGHTS ARE ON, BUT...

"Police in Oakland, California, spent two hours attempting to sub-

---

The other *Gong Show:* People who once cleaned out cesspits were known as *gongfermers.*

due a gunman who'd barricaded himself inside his home. After firing 10 tear gas canisters, officers discovered that the man was actually standing right beside them, shouting pleas to come out and give himself up."

—*Bizarre News*

SUB-CONTRACT

"To make a few extra bucks, Canada sold two old navy destroyers, the *Kootenay* and the *Restigouche*, to Richard Crawford of Florida. However, they inadvertently transformed him into a military power because they forgot to remove a 10-foot-tall, eight-barreled anti-submarine launcher from one of the ships. Embarrassed Defense Department officials announced that Crawford wouldn't be allowed to leave Canadian waters until he turned in his guns."

—*In These Times*

PROVING THEIR POINT

"English supermarket chain Somerfield has apologized after it said Easter eggs were to celebrate the 'birth' of Jesus. Ironically, the public relations slip-up came as it sought to publicize a survey suggesting a high level of ignorance about Easter's religious significance."

—BBC News

STICKIN' IT TO 'EM

"One of Britain's most prestigious art galleries put a block of slate on display, topped by a small piece of wood, in the mistaken belief it was a work of art. The Royal Academy included the chunk of stone and the small bone-shaped wooden stick in its summer exhibition in London. But the slate was actually a *plinth*—a slab on which a pedestal is placed—and the stick was designed to prop up a sculpture. The sculpture itself—of a human head—was nowhere to be seen. The Academy explained the error by saying the parts were sent to the exhibitors separately. 'Given their separate submission,' it said in a statement, 'the two parts were judged independently. The head was rejected. The base was thought to have merit and was accepted.'"

—*Telegraph* (U.K.)

There are 4,570 tons of gold at Fort Knox. (New York's Federal Reserve Bank has 5,000 tons.)

THE TWO GRAVES OF MAD ANTHONY WAYNE

*Historians tell many stories about heroes who are so
beloved that everyone wants a piece of them. In
the case of this man, they mean it literally.*

WHAT'S IN A NAME

Great generals frequently earn descriptive nicknames: "Blood and Guts" Patton, "Black Jack" Pershing, and "Stonewall" Jackson, to name a few. Revolutionary War hero "Mad Anthony" Wayne got his nickname for his bravery in battle—he was bold, he took big risks...and he won. His forces smashed the British in a surprise attack on Stony Point, New York; he led the American victory at Monmouth, New Jersey; and he prevented a disastrous rout at Brandywine in Pennsylvania. Washington's reports repeatedly praised Major General Wayne for his leadership and valor, and the Continental Congress awarded him a special gold medal celebrating the victory at Stony Point.

Wayne was born near Philadelphia on New Year's Day, 1745. He grew up to be a surveyor, then took over as manager of the family tannery until the Revolutionary War began. When the war ended, Wayne returned to civilian life, but his fighting days weren't over yet. In 1792 President Washington called him out of retirement for one last combat mission.

BACK IN ACTION

The British were arming and sponsoring a coalition of the Miami, Shawnee, Delaware, and Wyandot Indian tribes in Ohio, hoping to protect the British-held Northwest Territory by blocking further westward expansion by the United States. Wayne was given command of the Legion of the United States, with the mission of driving the British out and destroying the coalition.

General Wayne spent almost two years recruiting and training his command, then went into action. On August 20, 1794, the U.S. Legion destroyed the tribal army at the Battle of Fallen Timbers, near present-day Toledo. The Treaty of Greenville was signed

---

The world's smallest park—452 sq. inches—is in Portland, OR. (It was designed for snail racing.)

August 3, 1795, opening the Northwest Territory to American settlement.

His mission accomplished, Wayne headed home...but never made it. He fell ill en route and died of complications from gout on December 15, 1796, at the age of 51. His body was buried in a plain oak coffin near Erie, Pennsylvania, almost 300 miles west of his family home in Radnor, near Philadelphia. There he rested for 13 years, until his family decided they wanted to bring their hero's body home for a proper funeral. His son, Isaac, was given the task of bringing the general's remains back to the family.

CARRY ME BACK

Isaac Wayne made the long journey to Erie in a one-horse sulky—a two-wheeled cart more suitable for carrying light loads in urban areas than for carrying a heavy casket all the way back to Radnor. When his father's body was exhumed, it was remarkably well preserved, but there was no way it could bear bouncing along rutted dirt roads for 300 miles. It was a dilemma for the son. He couldn't return empty-handed—he had to find another solution. So he asked Dr. Wallace, who had cared for his father during his final illness, to dismember the body. (He refused to watch the operation, saying he wanted to remember his father as he looked in life.)

Next, the body parts were boiled in a large iron pot. Wallace and four assistants then carefully scraped the flesh from the bones, which were reverently placed in a wooden box and presented to the old soldier's son. The flesh was returned to the original oak casket and reburied in the original grave.

THE OTHER FINAL RESTING PLACE

Isaac returned home with his precious cargo, and, after the long-delayed funeral, the bones of "Mad Anthony" Wayne were finally interred in St. David's Episcopal Church Cemetery in Radnor, giving the Revolutionary War hero two graves.

But that's not the end of the story. Today, Radnor is connected to Erie by paved freeways instead of rutted dirt roads. There is a legend that some of the bones were lost on the grueling trip home ...and the ghost of "Mad Anthony" haunts the freeways, searching for his lost leg.

WAYNE'S WORLD

• **Have you every been to...**Wayne City, Illinois; Waynesville, North Carolina; Fort Wayne, Indiana; Wayne, Michigan; Waynesboro, Virginia; Wayne, Waynesburg, or Waynesboro, Pennsylvania; Waynesfield or Waynesville, Ohio; or Wayne Township, New Jersey?

• **Did you attend...**Wayne State University in Detroit, Michigan; Wayne High School in Huber Heights, Ohio; Wayne Middle School in Erie, Pennsylvania; Wayne High School in Fort Wayne, Indiana; Anthony Wayne Middle School in Wayne, New Jersey; or General Wayne Elementary School in Paoli, Pennsylvania?

• **Did anyone in your family...**perform military service at Fort Wayne in Detroit, Michigan?

• **Did you ever...**picnic in Anthony Wayne Recreation Area in Harriman State Park, New York, or drive across the Anthony Wayne Suspension Bridge near downtown Toledo, Ohio?

• **Have you ever driven on...**Anthony Wayne Drive in Detroit, Michigan; Wayne Avenue in Ticonderoga, New York; or Anthony Wayne Avenue in Cincinnati, Ohio?

• **Did you ever...**see a film at the Anthony Wayne Movie Theater in Wayne, Pennsylvania; get your hair cut at the Anthony Wayne Barber Shop in Maumee, Ohio; or fish on the Mad River in Dayton, Ohio?

They're all named after Mad Anthony Wayne.

MORE MAD-NESS

• In 1930 actor Marion "Duke" Morrison was about to get his first starring role, in director Raoul Walsh's Western, *The Big Trail*. But Fox Studios didn't like the name "Duke Morrison"—it wasn't American-sounding enough. So Walsh suggested changing it to "Anthony Wayne," after the general. The film's producer thought that Anthony Wayne sounded "too Italian," and that Tony Wayne "sounded like a girl." So they changed his name to John Wayne.

• According to many pop-culture historians, the comic book character Bruce Wayne—better known as Batman—was named after Scottish patriot Robert the Bruce...and Mad Anthony Wayne.

GANDER

*Far too few people know the heartwarming story about what
happened in a small town on a remote island in the North
Atlantic on September 11, 2001. Canadian air traffic
controller (and BRI member) Terry Budden told us
about it, and we decided to share it with you.*

THE TOWN OF GANDER

Gander is located in Newfoundland, Canada's easternmost province. The town is central to Newfoundland Island, and the home of Gander International Airport. The decision to build an airport on Gander was made in 1935 because aircraft couldn't make the long flight from New York to London without stopping to refuel. Newfoundland falls on the Atlantic Ocean right under the flight path between these two points, making it the ideal stopover location. The town itself formed around the airport and was mostly populated by people who worked in support of the aviation industry. They referred to Gander as "the crossroads of the world."

Today, of course, aircraft can fly farther without refueling, making Gander an unnecessary stop. With the exception of local and cargo flights, very little international traffic stops there anymore. Gander has since become a quiet town. Until September 11, 2001.

GROUNDED

Less than an hour after the terrorist attacks of September 11, the U.S. Federal Aviation Administration grounded all flights and closed their airspace for the first time in history. Transport Canada (Canada's equivalent to the FAA) followed suit, ordering all aircraft to the ground. There were approximately five hundred planes arriving over the east coast of Canada with nowhere to go. Air traffic controllers quickly started directing these flights to the closest airports. Before long, 38 planes were parked wingtip to wingtip on Gander's taxiways and runways—and more than 6,500 passengers and crew suddenly found themselves stranded.

The Trans-Canada Highway is the world's longest national highway (6,699 miles).

THE LOGISTICAL NIGHTMARE

Town officials and coordinators immediately scrambled to assess the situation thrust upon them, still reeling from the images on CNN. The Emergency Coordination Center at the airport and the Emergency Operations Center at the town hall were activated, and the situation was discussed. Gander has many contingency plans for all sorts of different situations—there is even a contingency plan for an emergency space-shuttle landing at the airport—but no plan for accommodating and feeding so many people for an undetermined amount of time. The town's 500 hotel rooms were no match for 6,500 unexpected visitors.

Des Dillon of the Canadian Red Cross was asked to round up beds. Major Ron Stuckless of the Salvation Army became the coordinator of a mass collection of food. Murray Osmond, the only Citizenship and Immigration officer on site, began the arduous task of processing thousands of passengers. "There was also the issue of security," Osmond told reporters. "We didn't know which planes out there might have individuals aboard like the ones who attacked the World Trade Center." He worked with a planeload of U.S. soldiers who had arrived to help maintain order.

While airport officials made preparations to process everyone, the passengers had to remain on board—some for as long as 30 hours—worried, confused, and cut off from the outside world. They couldn't see the attacks that kept the rest of the world glued to their televisions and still had no idea why they had been forced to land. Before long, though, passengers with cell phones and portable radios began spreading the word that the United States was under attack. If so, what would be the passengers' fate? Were they war refugees? How long would it be until they saw home again?

JUST PLANE FOLKS

When the passengers finally disembarked, they received a warm welcome. Although Newfoundland is the poorest province in Canada, everyone helped out:

• It was quickly decided that the majority of the rooms would go to the flight crews so they would be well rested and ready to travel on short notice. The decision as to where to house everyone else had to be faced next: the town of Gander, even with all its residents, churches, schools, and shelters opening their doors, could handle only about half of the stranded passengers. The rest would have to be transported to the surrounding communities of Gambo, Lewisporte, Appleton, Glenwood, and Norris Arm. But transporting these people seemed to be a problem as well—the local bus drivers had been on strike for weeks. They weren't for long: the striking bus drivers put down their picket signs and manned 60 buses to drive the passengers to their destinations.

• Families were kept together. Many places set up special rooms for families with babies and small children where portable cribs were assembled, and boxes were filled with toys and games. Diapers, bottles, and formula were provided, all free of charge.

• When calls went out for food and bedding, people emptied their cupboards, refrigerators, and closets and went to the airport. "They were there all night long, bringing food and standing at the tables, passing it out," said Captain Beverly Bass from American Flight 49. Asked who was manning the tables, a passenger from Air France Flight 004 responded, "They were the grocer, the postman, the pastor—everyday citizens of Gander who just came out."

• The passengers weren't allowed to take their luggage off the flights; they were there with just the clothes on their backs. So, responding to radio announcements, the residents and businesses of Gander supplied deodorant, soap, blankets, spare underwear, offers of hot showers and guestrooms—even tokens for the local laundromat and invitations to wash their clothes in people's homes.

• A lot of the guests didn't speak English and had no idea what was happening. Locals and U.S. soldiers were put to work as translators.

• The local phone company set up phone banks so that all the passengers could call home. They strung wires and cables so those staying in schools, churches, and lodges would also have access to television and the Internet. Passengers participated, too—those who had cell phones passed them around for others to make calls until the batteries ran dead.

• Hospitals added extra beds and sent doctors to the airport, just in case. Anyone with a medical background worked with the local doctors and pharmacies to tend to those with special needs. People in need of prescriptions received what they required at no cost.

• Residents of Twillingate, a tiny island off the northeast coast of

Newfoundland, prepared enough sandwiches and soup for at least 200 people, then delivered them to the mainland.

• To keep their spirits up, the passengers were given a choice of excursion trips, such as boat cruises of the lakes and harbors, while others went to see the local forests and memorials. Whale and iceberg watching were also popular activities. Newfoundlanders brought in entertainers who put on shows and grief counselors to talk to those who needed it.

After the airspace reopened, with the help of the Red Cross the passengers were delivered to the airport right on time. Not a single person missed a flight. Many of the "plane people," as they were sometimes called, were crying and sharing stories with each other. Passengers and locals exchanged phone numbers and addresses with their newfound friends.

THE AFTERMATH

Many travelers have since shown their thanks with donations to local churches, libraries, and charitable organizations.

• Lufthansa Airlines was so moved by the townspeople's reaction that they named one of their new aircraft after the town, an honor never before given to any place outside of Germany.

• The passengers from Delta Flight 15 started a scholarship fund and raised more than U.S. $30,000 for the school that housed them.

• The Rockefeller Foundation, which had used a small computer lab at a school in Lewisporte as the nerve center for their philanthropic activities, supplied the school with a brand new state-of-the-art computer lab.

• Gander Academy, which housed the passengers of Sabena Flight 539, Lufthansa Flight 416, and Virgin Flight 21, has received $27,000 in donations from the passengers that stayed there. The school is using the funds to finance a new six-year global peace awareness program.

• On the one-year anniversary, Canadian Prime Minister Jean Chretien traveled to Gander to honor the townsfolk. "You did yourselves proud," he told a crowd of 2,500 people who had gathered on the tarmac. "And you did Canada proud."

For a little more on the Gander story, turn the page.

In a typical diamond mine, you have to dig 23 tons of ore to find a single one-carat diamond.

A NOTE FROM GANDER

*Continuing our Gander story (page 480), here's a great letter
we found posted on the Internet from Gander resident
Scott Cook, reprinted with his permission.*

"It's been a hell of a week here in Gander. The stories are amazing. We had 38 aircraft with a total of 6,656 people drop by for coffee. They stayed for three or four days. Our population is just under 10,000, so you can imagine the logistics involved in giving each of these people a place to sleep and a hot meal three times a day.

"Many of us spent our time bringing people home so they could get a shower or, once the rain started on the third day, driving them to the mall or sightseeing to relieve their boredom. The diversity of the people who have been in my car and in my shower over the past few days is pretty wild.

"You should have seen the look on my little girl's face when three Muslim women came home with me for a shower. With their robes, she could only see their faces, hands and feet. Their hands and feet were covered with henna paint and two of them didn't speak English. There was a king from the Middle East here, a British MP, the Mayor of Frankfurt, Germany, etc., etc.

"There were also immigrants from all over the world, some of whom didn't have two pennies to rub together. They all slept side by side in schools and church halls. Except the Irish, of course! A flight from Ireland was put up at a couple of local drinking establishments! The Royal Canadian Legion and the Elks Club. One woman here gave a driving tour to a fellow from the U.S. When she brought him back to his gymnasium cot, they exchanged cards. She looked at his and said, 'So you work with Best Western?' He replied, 'No, I own Best Western.'

"You should have been here, but of course, there wouldn't have been room."

"We make a living by what we've got, but we make a life by what we give." —Winston Churchill

THE SCIENCE OF MOVING PICTURES

Here's the story of how one man's curiosity—and another's tenacity—forever altered the way we view the world.

THE CHALLENGE

When a horse is running or trotting, do all four hooves ever leave the ground at the same time? That was the basis of the wager that Leland Stanford, former governor of California and founder of Stanford University, made with some friends in 1872. The question was a hot topic in horse racing circles at the time. Most people believed that a horse always had one hoof in contact with the ground, but Stanford thought otherwise. Because a horse's legs move so fast, it was impossible to tell just by looking, so Stanford needed a way to slow down the movement so it could be studied.

Later that year, Stanford offered Eadweard Muybridge, a world-famous landscape photographer, $25,000 to find the answer. Muybridge had no idea if he could successfully set up and perform an experiment to settle the dispute, but he figured he'd give it a go.

THE EQUIPMENT

In most 19th-century cameras, a picture was taken when the photographer removed the lens cap for several seconds in order to expose the film and capture an image. The subject had to remain perfectly still during this time, or the resulting photograph would be blurred. In order to capture fast action like a galloping horse, the exposure time would have to be very short.

Muybridge invented a fast shutter mechanism that relied on a small piece of wood with a hole drilled in it that slid past the lens. The wood was positioned so that a pin held it in place, covering the lens. When the pin was removed, gravity would cause the wood to drop and as the hole moved past the lens, the film was exposed for a fraction of a second.

Beeswax and fish scales are common lipstick ingredients.

THE PROCESS

The first time Muybridge tried taking a photograph as a horse ran by, he didn't get much of an image at all. He tried various methods of making the shutter move faster and faster to shorten the exposure time, and as he did the quality of the image began to improve. Finally he hit upon the idea of using two pieces of wood and slipping them past each other so quickly that he could achieve an exposure time of about 1/500th of a second. That solved the problem of capturing a reasonably clear image of a horse at a gallop, but he still had to settle the bet.

THE SHOOTER

In 1874 Muybridge's work was interrupted by a bizarre scandal. During a confrontation with a man he believed was his wife's lover and the father of one of their children, Muybridge shot and killed the man. Muybridge was imprisoned until his trial in February 1875, and was finally acquitted—thanks to the lawyer that Stanford had hired for him. But after the trial, he decided to leave the country and dropped his experiments until he returned to California in 1877. He then resumed his work on increasing the shutter speed until he'd reduced the exposure time to less than 1/2000th of a second.

THE TRIGGER

Once Muybridge was satisfied with the quality of the images, he had to figure out a way to capture several images in sequence. He decided to place several cameras in a row all pointing in the same direction and to trigger them in sequence as the horse galloped past. He attached strings to all the camera shutters and stretched them across a track, so that as the horse passed by, it would touch each string in turn, and the cameras would take their pictures one at a time and in sequence.

In 1878, after years of experiments, Muybridge got what he wanted: a sequence of 12 images, with one of them clearly showing that all four of the horse's hooves were off the ground at the same time. It was the first successful photographic representation of a sequence of movement, and it made Muybridge internationally famous—and prosperous. He collected his well-earned $25,000 from Stanford.

Dry ice is used to seed clouds and produce rain.

THE NEXT STEP

In 1879 Muybridge invented the zoopraxiscope, a device with counter-rotating discs that projected the images sequentially. Now an observer could actually see the horse galloping—and the effect was truly stunning. After a public showing in San Francisco, a reporter gushed, "Nothing was wanting, but the clatter of hoofs upon the turf and the occasional breath of steam to make the spectator believe he had before him the flesh-and-blood steeds."

Muybridge continued his experiments using more cameras and photographing the motions of other animals and later did extensive studies of human movement. He eventually published his photographs in a portfolio called *Animal Locomotion* (1887) and two books: *Animals in Motion* (1899) and *The Human Figure in Motion* (1901). The latter created quite a stir at the time for its use of nude male and female models.

THE CREDIT

Thomas Edison is usually credited with creating the first motion pictures in 1889, but it was actually the work of Muybridge—and the $25,000 bet—that provided the foundation for Edison's invention and the evolution of movies.

*   *   *

WHAT'S IN YOUR CANDY BAR?

In 1972 the Oregon Health Department discovered that the chunks in Hoody Chunky Style Peanut Butter were not peanuts, but rat droppings. Company executives were sentenced to 10 days in prison for health violations, and the U.S. Food and Drug Administration issued strict new guidelines on the amount of foreign matter permissible in packaged foods. They include:

1. No more than 50 insect fragments or two rodent hairs per 100 grams of peanut butter.

2. No more than 10 fruit fly eggs in 100 grams of tomato juice.

3. No more than 150 insect fragments in an eight-ounce chocolate bar.

—*Wrong Again!*

Japanese high-speed trains use magnets to "float" over the tracks so they can go faster.

THE KING

Elvis facts have entered the bathroom.

- Elvis Presley was nearsighted. He owned $60,000 worth of prescription sunglasses when he died.

- On an average day, four people call Graceland and ask to speak to Elvis.

- According to *Billboard*, the number-one single of the 1950s was "Don't Be Cruel," by Presley.

- Boris Yeltsin's favorite Elvis song: "Are You Lonesome Tonight?"

- Elvis Presley got a C in his eighth-grade music class.

- The least Elvis ever weighed as an adult was 170 pounds in 1960, following his discharge from the U.S. Army. The heaviest was at the time of his death: 260 pounds.

- Elvis's favorite amusement park ride was the bumper cars.

- Elvis had a pet monkey named Scatter.

- The U.S. Post Office sold a record 123 million Elvis Presley commemorative stamps when they were first issued in 1993.

- The Elvis Presley hit "Hound Dog" was written in about 10 minutes.

- One of Elvis's favorite meals was a pound of bacon—and nothing else.

- Elvis auditioned for a spot on the 1950s TV show *Arthur Godfrey's Talent Scouts* but didn't make the cut. Neither did Buddy Holly when he tried it.

- Elvis is the top-earning dead celebrity in the world. His estate took in $45 million in 2004, 28 years after his death.

- Graceland is the second-most-visited house in the United States. The first is the White House.

- Seven percent of Americans believe Elvis is still alive.

A *Variety* critic's review of the 1978 film *Movie Movie*: "Awful Awful."

LUCKY FINDS

Ever found something valuable? It's a great feeling. Here's a look at a few people who found really valuable stuff... and got to keep it. You should be so lucky.

THE CASE OF THE MISSING LIST

The Find: A famous list

Where It Was Found: In a suitcase in Germany

The Story: When a Stuttgart couple found an old suitcase in their parents' loft after they died in 1999, they didn't think much of it—until they saw the name on the handle: O. Schindler. Inside were hundreds of documents—including a list of the names of the Jewish slave-laborers and their fake jobs that factory owner Oskar Schindler gave to the Nazis during WWII. The bold move saved 1,200 Jews from extermination and inspired the movie *Schindler's List*. Apparently, friends of Schindler's had used the loft as a storage space decades earlier and then forgot about it. The couple gave the suitcase and all the documents to a newspaper, but asked for no money in return. It now resides in Yad Vashem Holocaust Museum, in Jerusalem.

TREASURE IN THE TRASH

The Find: The $200,000 grand prize–winning cup in a Wendy's Restaurant fast food contest

Where It Was Found: In the garbage

The Story: In 1995 Craig Randall, a 23-year-old trash collector in Peabody, Massachusetts, noticed a Wendy's contest cup sitting in some garbage he was collecting. "I won a chicken sandwich the week before," he told reporters, "and I figured, hey, I'd get some fries to go with it." Instead, when he peeled off the sticker he saw: "Congratulations. You have won $200,000 towards a new home." The fact that he *found* the cup didn't matter; Wendy's gave him the money anyway. "I have no idea where it came from," he said. "It was just sitting there."

FLEA MARKET TREASURE

The Find: A copy of the Declaration of Independence, printed on the evening of July 4, 1776

The secret to his success? Napoleon carried chocolate with him on all of his military campaigns.

Where It Was Found: Inside a picture frame

The Story: In 1989 an unidentified "middle-aged financial analyst from Philadelphia" paid $4 for a painting at a flea market. He didn't even like the painting, but liked the frame, so he took the picture apart...and when he did, a copy of the Declaration of Independence fell out. "It was folded up, about the size of a business envelope," says David Redden of Sotheby's Auction House. "He thought it might be an early 19th-century printing and worth keeping as a curiosity."

A few years later, the man showed the print to a friend, who suspected it might be valuable and encouraged him to look into it. He did, and learned that only hours after finishing work on the Declaration in 1776, the Continental Congress had delivered the handwritten draft to a printer with orders to send

> copies of the Declaration...to the several Assemblies, Conventions & Committees...and the Commanding Officers of the Continental troops, that it be proclaimed in each of the United States & at the head of the Army.

This was one of those original copies. No one is sure how many were printed that night; today only 24 survive, and most are in poor condition. But the one in the picture frame was in mint condition, having spent the better part of two centuries undisturbed. In 1991 it sold at auction for $2.4 million.

GARAGE SALE TREASURE

The Find: Two Shaker "gift" paintings

Where They Were Found: Inside a picture frame

The Story: In 1994 a retired couple from New England bought an old picture frame for a few dollars at a garage sale. When they took the frame apart to restore it, two watercolor drawings—dated 1845 and 1854—fell out.

A few months later, the couple was traveling in Massachusetts and noticed a watercolor on a poster advertising the Hancock Shaker Village Museum. It was similar to the two they'd found. Curious, they did some research and found out the works were called "gift paintings."

It turns out that the Shakers, a New England religious sect of the 1800s, did not allow decorations on their walls; Shaker sisters, however, were permitted to paint "trees, flowers, fruits and birds...to depict the glory of heaven." The paintings were then "gifted" to other sisters and put away as holy relics. And one of the couple's paintings was signed by the most famous of all "gift" artists, Hannah Cohoon.

They called a curator of the Hancock Museum with the news, but he didn't believe them. Only 200 Shaker "gift" paintings still exist...and very few are of the quality they described. Moreover, all known paintings were in museums—none in private hands. Nonetheless, in January 1996, the couple brought the paintings to the museum, where they were examined and declared authentic. A year later, in January 1997, Sotheby's sold them for $473,000.

HOLY GRAIL

The Find: A first edition copy of a book called *Tamerlane*

Where it was Found: In a New Hampshire antique shop

The Story: In the winter of 1988, an antique dealer named Robert Webber paid $500 for a large collection of musty old books at another dealer's estate auction.

One of the books was titled *Tamerlane and Other Poems*, and was dated 1827. "It was an awful looking thing," Webber recalled. The slim brown book had a ring stain from a drinking glass. Its edges were faded and the printing was poor. Even if the book had been new, it wouldn't have looked pretty. "By a Bostonian" was all it said about the author.

Webber put a price tag of $18 on it. "My wife wanted to keep it and read it," he said. "But I said, 'What do you want that dirty old thing for?'" It sat there for a few days in his antique bar, with a pile of pamphlets on fertilizer and farm machinery. A man came into the store, saw the book and the $18 price tag, and offered $15 for it. Sold.

The customer was either really cheap or just slow to realize what he'd bought. *Tamerlane* is nicknamed "the black tulip" by book collectors because it is the rarest and most valuable book in American literature. "A Bostonian" was Edgar Allen Poe and *Tamerlane* was his first book of poetry, a self-published failure. Eventually, the man who bought the book (his identity is secret) notified Sotheby's of his find; they picked it up in an armored truck and later auctioned it for $198,000.

The religion of the Todas people of India forbids crossing bridges.

(BAT) BOMBS AWAY!

*Here's a batty bit of World War II history
you may not have heard before.*

BAT MAN

In the days and weeks following the bombing of Pearl Harbor on December 7, 1941, a lot of people wrote letters to President Roosevelt. Some wrote to express their sympathy with the victims or their outrage at the attack; others made suggestions about how to fight back against Japan.

One man, a dentist from Irwin, Pennsylvania, wanted to talk about bats. His name was Lytle S. Adams, and he had recently been to the Carlsbad Caverns in New Mexico, home to one of the largest bat colonies in North America. When Adams learned of the attack on Pearl Harbor, his thoughts returned to the bats he'd seen—could they be useful to the war effort? He was convinced they could.

COM-BAT

In his letter to the president, Adams explained that bats are capable of carrying more than their own weight in flight. In many species, for example, the mother bat carries two or even three of her young as she searches for food. If bats could carry their children, Adams reasoned, why couldn't they carry tiny bombs?

The dentist's plan went further: Bats hate sunlight, so if bats carrying time-delayed incendiary devices could be released over a Japanese city shortly before dawn, as the sun rose, the bats would seek refuge from the light. Many would roost in the eaves and attics of buildings—a great number of which were made of flammable materials like wood, bamboo, and paper soaked in fish oil. When the firebombs detonated, thousands of tiny fires would start in buildings all over the city.

Not only that, bats typically hide out of sight in hard-to-reach places, and that would make the fires difficult to detect. By the time they were discovered, the fires would be well established but still small enough at first (each bat would weigh less than half an ounce, so the bombs would have to be small, too) that people would have a fighting chance to escape. Casualties would be lower than with conventional firebombs, which weighed hundreds of pounds and engulfed entire buildings on impact, giving occupants no warning and no chance to escape. For all their destructive power, Adams believed that "bat bombs" could be a more humane weapon of war than regular firebombs.

How many fires could be started with bats? "Approximately 200,000 bats could be transported in one airplane," Adams wrote, "and still allow one-half the payload capacity to permit free air circulation and increased gasoline load. Ten such planes would carry two million fire starters."

ASSAULT AND BAT-TERY

Perhaps the most impressive feature of bat bombs was not their destructive power, but the psychological impact they could have on the Japanese. The bats would be dropped by planes before dawn, and by the time the bombs went off, the planes would be long gone. Entire cities would ignite spontaneously and burn to the ground...with no warning and no explanation.

"The effect of the destruction from such a mysterious source would be a shock to the morale of the Japanese people as no amount of ordinary bombing could accomplish," Adams wrote to Roosevelt. "It would render the Japanese people homeless and their industries useless, yet the innocent could escape with their lives."

How flammable were Japanese cities? When a woman living in Osaka, Japan, knocked over her hibachi-type cookstove in 1911, 11,000 homes burned to the ground. And it was *raining*.

TO THE BAT CAVE!

President Roosevelt forwarded Adams's letter to Colonel William J. Donovan, who would soon head the Office of Strategic Services, forerunner of the CIA. "It sounds like a perfectly wild idea but is worth looking into," FDR wrote. "This man is *not* a nut."

Dr. Adams got the go-ahead to assemble a 20-person staff and begin working out the details on how such a weapon might be built. What species of bats would be best? What kind of firebomb would be used? How would the device be attached to the bat? How would the bats be dropped over cities? There was a lot to figure out. Here's what they came up with:

The Bats

The researchers decided early on that they would use a species called the Mexican free-tailed bat. They weighed about half an ounce but were capable of carrying a load of as much as three-quarters of an ounce. Tens of millions of them made their summer homes in caves in Texas and other southwestern states. Just as important, these bats hibernated in the winter. That meant they could be put into artificial hibernation so that the bombs could be attached, then kept in cold storage until they were ready to be released over Japan.

The Incendiary Bombs

One of the researchers assigned to the project was an incendiary bomb specialist—a chemist named Louis Fieser. He devised a tiny bomb that weighed a little over half an ounce and consisted of a timer and a thin plastic capsule measuring three-quarters of an inch in diameter by two inches long, filled with a jellied gasoline he'd invented, napalm.

Initially the designers planned to attach a bomb to each bat's chest with a piece of string and a surgical clip that mimicked the way baby bats latched onto their mother's fur with their claws. But that turned out to be too complicated, so they switched to a simple adhesive and just glued the bombs to the bats.

The "Bombshell"

If you just threw a bunch of hibernating bats out of an airplane, their fragile wings would break the moment they hit the airstream at 150 mph or else they would fall all the way to the ground—and die on impact—before they could emerge from hibernation. So the researchers designed a protective bomb-shaped canister to put the bats into. The "bombshell" was cigar-shaped and had fins, just like a regular bomb—except that it was filled with bats and was poked full of holes so they could breathe.

Inside the canister, the hibernating bats were packed into cardboard trays similar to eggshell cartons, and these cartons were stacked one on top of the other. Each bombshell held 26 cardboard trays, each of which held 40 bats. That meant each bomb would contain 1,040 bats.

HOW IT WORKED

• The bombshell was designed so that when it was dropped from a plane, it would free-fall to an altitude of 4,000 feet, at which point a parachute would deploy, slowing its descent.

• When the parachute opened, the bomb's outer shell would pop off and fall away. The stacked cardboard trays, which were tied to one another with short lengths of string, would then drop down and hang from the parachute about three inches apart, like rungs on a rope ladder.

• As the cardboard trays dropped into position, a tiny wire would be pulled from the incendiary device attached to each bat. Just like pulling a pin from a hand grenade, when the string was pulled, the firebombs would be armed and set to go off in 30 minutes, 60 minutes, or whatever interval the bombers chose.

• The bats, now exposed to the warm air and floating slowly to earth, would have enough time to warm up, emerge from their hibernating state, climb out of their individual egg-carton compartments, and fly away to seek shelter.

• When time ran out, the incendiary device glued to their chest would explode into flames, incinerating them instantly and setting fire to whatever structure they had taken refuge in.

BAT-TLE GROUND

A bombshell filled with bats and tiny firebombs sounded clever, but would it really work? Dr. Adams's team built a prototype, loaded it with 1,040 bats fitted with dummy bombs, and dropped it from a plane in a remote region outside Carlsbad Air Force Base in New Mexico. The test went off nearly without a hitch: the parachute deployed, the trays dropped open, and the bats awakened from hibernation and flew off in search of shelter from the sun.

The only snafu was that the researchers misjudged how far winds would carry the bat trays. Instead of landing in the middle of nowhere (the project was top secret, after all), the bats ended up flying to a ranch and roosting in the barn and ranch house. The researchers caught up with the creatures half an hour later and collected them as the mystified rancher looked on (he never did learn what the bats were carrying or what they were for).

BAT REVENGE

But the real proof of the power of bat bombs came later that day when Louis Fieser, the incendiary specialist, wanted some film footage of a bat armed with a live incendiary bomb actually exploding into flames. He took six hibernating bats out of cold storage and set their bombs to detonate in 15 minutes, figuring that in such a short time, the bats would still be hibernating and wouldn't fly away.

What Fieser failed to take into consideration was that on a hot New Mexico afternoon, the bats would come out of hibernation quickly. All six bats woke up within 10 minutes, escaped, and roosted in the rafters of various buildings of the airfield where the test was being conducted. Five minutes later the bombs went off, and every building on the airfield—the control tower, barracks, offices, and hangars—burned to the ground.

BAT TO THE DRAWING BOARD

Believe it or not, bat bombs were found to be *more* effective than conventional firebombs. One study concluded that a planeload of conventional firebombs would start between 167 and 400 fires, whereas a planeload of bat bombs would start between 3,625 and 4,748 fires.

So how many bats died in combat during World War II? Not even one. After spending 27 months and $2 million looking into the feasibility of bat bombs, the Pentagon canceled the program in March 1944. The military claimed that the bats were too unpredictable to be useful, but Jack Couffer, a research scientist who worked on the project, has a different theory. Couffer speculates in his memoirs that the government knew the Manhattan Project was making steady progress toward the world's first atomic bomb, and the military decided to focus on that instead.

Which explanation is true? Only the U.S. government knows for sure. Sixty years later, the reasons for the cancellation of the program, like the blueprints to the incendiary device itself, are still classified.

*   *   *

A weapon is an enemy even to its owner.
—**Turkish proverb**

SAY UNCLE!

Uncle John would like to take a few minutes to talk about some of the other famous "uncles" in American history.

UNCLE SAM, *a symbol of the United States*
Birth: Sam Wilson owned a meat-packing plant in Troy, New York. When the War of 1812 broke out, the government contracted him to supply meat to troops stationed nearby. He started stamping crates for the army with a big "U.S." But when a government inspector visited the plant and asked a worker what the initials meant, the worker shrugged and guessed it stood for his employer, "Uncle Sam."
Everyone's Uncle: The nickname spread among the soldiers. Soon, all army supplies were said to come from "Uncle Sam." Then a character called Uncle Sam began showing up in newspaper illustrations. The more popular he got, the more patriotic his outfit became. In 1868, Thomas Nast dressed Uncle Sam in a white beard and Stars-and-Stripes suit for a political cartoon. Nast borrowed the look from a famous circus clown named Dan Rice.

UNCLE TOM, *title character of* Uncle Tom's Cabin
Birth: Harriet Beecher Stowe wanted the title character of her novel, Uncle Tom's Cabin, to be "simple, easygoing and servile"…but also "noble, high-minded, and a devout Christian." She found inspiration in conversations with her cook, a free woman who was married to a slave in Kentucky. As Stowe explained in an 1882 letter to the *Indianapolis Times*, the cook said her husband

> was so faithful, his master trusted him to come alone and unwatched to Cincinnati to market his farm product. Now this, according to the laws of Ohio, gave the man his freedom, *de facto*. But she said her husband had given his word as a Christian, his master promising him his freedom. Whether he ever got it, I know not.

Everyone's Uncle: The book was published in 1852 and quickly became one of the best-selling novels of the 19th century. It played an important role in arousing anti-slavery passions that resulted in the Civil War. When Lincoln met Stowe, he greeted

---

According to legend, there's a Superman in every episode of *Seinfeld.*

her by asking, "Is this the little woman whose book made such a great war?" Over time, "Uncle Tom" became a derogatory term to African-Americans, referring to someone too servile, or who cooperated too closely with whites—not entirely fair, since Uncle Tom was ultimately flogged to death by slave owner Simon Legree after he refused to reveal the hiding place of two female slaves.

UNCLE REMUS, narrator of a popular series of folk tales

Birth: Joel Chandler Harris grew up in the South after the Civil War listening to folk tales told by former slaves. As an adult, he began collecting them and publishing them. One of the most helpful people he talked to was an elderly gardener in Forsyth, Georgia, called Uncle Remus. Harris made him the narrator of his books.

Everyone's Uncle: In the enormously popular *Uncle Remus: His Songs and His Sayings* (published in the late 1800s), Uncle Remus, a former slave, entertains his employer's young son by telling him traditional "Negro tales" (believed to have come from Africa) involving Brer Rabbit, Brer Fox, and Brer Wolf. Harris' books preserved the tales in print form and introduced them to a worldwide audience. Disney's animated *Song of the South* made Uncle Remus a part of modern American pop culture (Zip-a-dee-doo-dah!).

UNCLE FESTER, *crazed character from the* Addams Family *TV series*

Birth: The ghoulish family in Charles Addams's *New Yorker* cartoons was never identified by (first) name—so it was never clear exactly who the bald fiend in the family portraits was. But in 1963, Addams agreed to let ABC make a TV sitcom out of his characters. All he had to do was give the characters names and family relationships. The bald guy officially became Morticia's Uncle Fester.

Everyone's Uncle: The TV show was a Top 20 hit in 1964-65. Fester was brought to life by Jackie Coogan, who had been the first child star of the silent film age. In 1923, he was the biggest box office star in the country, but his appeal faded as he got older. By 23 he was broke and out of work. After a tragic life that included arrests for drugs and booze, Coogan made a comeback. He showed up for the *Addams Family* audition with a huge walrus mustache and hair on the sides of his head. Told that Fester was hairless, he returned the next day shaved completely bald and got the part.

Polar bears can eat 50 pounds of meat in one sitting.

THIS *IS* MY OTHER CAR

*Our readers have sent us hundreds of great bumper stickers
over the years. Here are some of our favorites.*

*We are born naked, wet, and
hungry. Then things get worse.*

**HORN BROKEN.
WATCH FOR FINGER**

Yes, this is my truck.
No, I won't help you move.

*I feel like I'm diagonally
parked in a parallel universe*

*Very funny, Scotty.
Now beam down my clothes.*

IF YOU CAN READ THIS,
I'VE LOST MY TRAILER

Don't believe
everything you think.

SUBURBIA: Where They
Tear Down the Trees and
Name Streets After Them

MY OTHER VEHICLE
IS IN ORBIT.

Honk if anything falls off.

**Just keep staring—
I may do a trick.**

*Forget World Peace—Visualize
Using Your Turn Signal!*

I Doubt, Therefore I Might Be

*We Have Enough Youth, How
About a Fountain of "Smart"?*

**Meandering to a
different drummer.**

*Why am I the only person on
Earth who knows how to drive?*

*Earth is the insane asylum
of the universe*

Officer, will this bumper sticker saying

**SUPPORT LAW
ENFORCEMENT**

save me from getting a ticket?

Buckle up—it makes it
harder for the aliens to
snatch you from your car.

*If I Had a Life, I Wouldn't
Need a Bumper Sticker.*

I may be slow, but
I'm ahead of you.

*a PBS mind trapped
in an MTV world*

**I have no idea
where I'm going.**

Gene Kelly had a 103° fever when he danced to the title song in *Singin' in the Rain.*

PROJECT GREEK ISLAND, PART II

It's still one of the best-kept secrets of the Cold War—a bomb shelter large enough to house the entire U.S. Congress. Here's Part II of our story of your tax dollars at work. (Part I starts on page 299.)

TRY NOT TO THINK ABOUT IT

For all its amenities, the bomb shelter was still a *bomb shelter*, after all, one designed to be used at what would probably have been the end of the world. The designers put a lot of thought into managing the psychological stresses the shelter occupants would undoubtedly be under if nuclear war ever came. Each of the 18 dormitory rooms had its own lounge stocked with books, magazines, an exercise bicycle, and a TV to provide distractions (though it's unclear what people would have watched on postapocalyptic TV). To make the shelter seem less like an underground tomb, the walls of the cafeteria had fake "windows" that looked out onto painted landscapes. The pharmacy was stocked with plenty of antidepressants, and there was an isolation chamber to contain anyone who went completely nuts under the strain.

OPEN FOR BUSINESS

In all the shelter cost more than $10 million to build, and the hotel wing on top of it cost another $4 million. Both projects were completed in October 1962—just in time for the shelter to be activated during the Cuban missile crisis, the only time in the shelter's 30-year history that it went on full alert. At one point during the crisis the Senate and House of Representatives (and numerous crates of top-secret documents) came within 12 hours of relocating to the Greenbrier. That was as close as Project Greek Island ever came to actually being put to use.

But just because the shelter was never *put* to use doesn't mean that it wasn't kept *ready* for use. For the next 30 years, 12 to 15 retired military personnel with high security clearances were

---

In ancient Egypt, warm donkey droppings were prescribed to alleviate sore eyes.

always stationed at the Greenbrier, where they posed as TV repairmen working for a shell company called "Forsythe Associates." To make their cover story believable, the "repairmen" really did spend as much as 20 percent of their time repairing TVs at the resort.

KEEPING IT FRESH

The rest of the time, they and a few dozen trusted Greenbrier employees who had been sworn to secrecy were down in the bunker maintaining equipment, replacing burned-out lightbulbs, changing bedsheets, restocking expired food and other supplies, and cleaning the 110 showers, 187 sinks, 167 toilets, and 74 urinals that were never used. They rotated the magazines and books in the lounges to keep the reading material fresh, and they kept the pharmacy stocked with the prescription medications of all 435 members of the House and Senate.

Once a year, they replaced outdated medical equipment so that the hospital kept up with advances in medicine. Because bed space in the dormitories was assigned by seniority, after each election the workers changed the name tags on the bunk beds as older politicians left office (or died) and younger ones moved up the ranks. They even turned the pages on the daily calendars scattered throughout the facility so that they would always show the correct date. If at any time in those 30 years the House and Senate had been forced to evacuate to the Greenbrier, it would have seemed as if the bomb shelter had just opened for business that morning.

SHHH!

So how secret was the bomb shelter? It depends on what you mean by secret. As far as anyone can tell, the people who signed secrecy pledges did honor their commitment. Not that they had much choice—they faced stiff fines and prison time if they talked. But you just can't build a facility that big without it attracting *some* attention, if from no one else then at least from the construction workers who watched as 4,000 loads of concrete, more than 50,000 *tons* in all, were hauled up to the site and poured to make five-foot-thick walls and ceilings in a "basement" that was 65 feet underground. How many hotel basements are 65 feet underground?

How many have five-foot-thick walls and ceilings? Even if the workers didn't know *what* they were building, they knew it was *something* unusual, and by the time the project was finished the entire valley buzzed with gossip and speculation.

At one point the government became so concerned about how much the locals might have pieced together about the site that they sent two agents who knew nothing about it to the area posing as hunters to see how much information they could pry out of the locals. According to one version of the story, they returned with so much information about the bomb shelter that the government had to give them top-secret security clearances.

One thing that helped to keep the secret from traveling outside of the area was the fact that with more than 1,500 employees, the Greenbrier wasn't just the largest employer in the valley, it was pretty much the only one of any significance in the entire county. Even if you didn't work there you knew someone or were related to someone who did. People gossiped about the facility with each other (and with the occasional nosy hunter), but somehow the story never got much farther than that. The world outside Greenbrier County remained almost completely in the dark.

BLAME IT ON THE MEDIA

Project Greek Island remained a secret (if you can call it that) until May 1992, when the *Washington Post* revealed its existence in an exposé. By then the Cold War had been over for several months—the Soviet Union passed into history on Christmas Day 1991—and the bomb shelter had fulfilled its purpose. Rather than deny the *Post* story, the Pentagon acknowledged the shelter's existence…and then promptly shut it down. Ownership of the facility reverted to the Greenbrier, which converted half of it into a data-storage facility and opened the rest to public tours…for now, anyway: At last report the resort was thinking about turning it into a casino with a James Bond theme.

DOWN UNDER

The United States isn't the only country that sank a lot of time and money into holes in the ground for top government officials: The British government built an entire underground city, com-

---

The Quecha language of Peru has about 1,000 words for "potato."

plete with two train stations, 60 miles of road, and one pub in a rock quarry 70 miles outside of London. Canada built a network of seven "Diefenbunkers" (nicknamed in honor of Prime Minister John Diefenbaker, who had them built) outside of major cities around Canada.

WHITE ELEPHANT

When the Cold War ended, these countries learned the same lesson that the U.S. did: It's a lot easier to build giant underground facilities with five-foot concrete walls than it is to figure out what to do with them when you're done with them. The British site has been for sale since 2005 (so far, no takers); the Canadians did manage to sell off one Diefenbunker in Alberta, but when rumors spread that the new owner was thinking about reselling it to a biker gang, the government bought it back and demolished it.

And even though the Cold War has long been over, the threat of a nuclear attack on Washington, D.C., remains. Chances are there's another hi-tech, high-luxury bunker located somewhere on the outskirts of the nation's capitol...that hopefully will never have to be put to use.

*　　*　　*

FAMOUS PEOPLE AND
WHAT THEY COLLECT(ED)

Brad Pitt: chairs

Richard Simmons: dolls

Dustin Hoffman: antique toys

Janet Jackson: porcelain pigs

Winston Churchill: hats

Penelope Cruz: coat hangers

Tom Hanks: antique typewriters

Claudia Schiffer: dried insects

Quentin Tarantino: board games based on TV shows

Marilyn Manson: Kiss dolls and prosthetic limbs

Kim Basinger: inflatable ducks

IT'S A WEIRD, WEIRD WORLD

More proof that truth really is stranger than fiction.

DIRTY POLITICS

"The African country of Swaziland has been thrown into a political crisis after Mgabhi Dlamini, the speaker of parliament, stole a piece of royal cow dung out of the royal corral. Dlamini's opponents say he wanted to use the stuff in a ritual that would improve his standing with the king. The theft was detected by witch doctors who had foreseen it in a vision. Dlamini admits to having taken a handful of dung but insists he did not intend to use it for personal profit."

—The Telegraph (U.K.)

IN COLD BLOOD

"When Chamlong Taengniem's 13-year-old son died in a motorcycle accident, she had no idea he would revisit her. As a lizard. The Thai mother claims a lizard followed her home after her son's cremation and sleeps in his mattress and drinks his favorite drinks. Flocks of people have journeyed to the woman's home to catch a glimpse of the lizard, even stroking its stomach in the hopes of finding clues to future lottery numbers."

—"The Edge," The Oregonian

CAGEY PROPOSITION

"In Halberstadt, Germany, an organist kicked off a performance of the late, radical composer John Cage's 'Organ 2/ASLSP' (an acronym somehow derived from 'as slow as possible'), which was written for 20 minutes, but thanks to technology and imagination, will be performed over a period lasting 639 years. The first six months will be devoted to creating the organ's first note. The purpose of the performance is to contrast the piece with the frenzied pace of modern society."

—Medford (Oregon) Mail Tribune

WHITE ON!

"A University of Northern Colorado intramural basketball team has been inundated with T-shirt requests since naming itself 'The Fightin' Whites.' The team, made up of Native Americans, Hispanics, and Anglos, chose the name because nearby Easton High refused to change *its* nickname from 'Reds' and drop its American Indian caricature logo. The team plans to donate profits from the shirts to an American Indian organization. The shirts show a 1950s-style caricature of a middle-aged white man with the phrase 'Every thang's gonna be all white!'"

—USA *Today*

TYRANNOSAURUS RETCH

"London's Natural History Museum, home to an animatronic *Tyrannosaurus rex*, decided to re-create the exact odor that would have come out of T-Rex's mouth, a mixture of dead flesh and rotting meat. One problem: 'The smell was found to be so offensive it would have put people off,' says a museum spokesperson. 'So we've gone for a smell that was found in the environment instead.'

"Officially named *Maastrichtian miasma*, the reformulated scent is a concoction of jaguar urine, cesspit, boiler room, brewery, wild stag, machine oil, garbage, Thai curry, smoked fish, and ozone. Bottles of dinosaur smell are available for purchase in the museum gift shop."

—*The Times* (London)

HI-HO, HI-HO, IT'S OUT OF WORK WE GO

"Snow White had to make do with just four dwarfs due to cost-cutting at a theater in the German town of Stendal. The Altmark Stendal theater said it could afford only six actors for its Christmas rendition of *Snow White and the Seven Dwarfs*, which led to protests from theater-goers from the nearby city of Hanover who wanted to see all seven dwarves.

"The theater attached two puppets in dwarf outfits to a background wall to give the production six dwarfs. And the actor playing the prince was supposed to double as the seventh, but only made one brief appearance on stage. 'That dwarf wasn't on stage the whole time,' theater spokeswoman Susanne Kreuzer said, 'because he was stuck down in the mine working overtime.'"

—*Gold Coast Bulletin* (Australia)

Weigh yourself; multiply it by 0.0028. That's how much salt (by weight) you have in your body.

UNSCRIPTED

When actors have to come up with their own lines…

"I have no experience, but I guess they're different from dogs and horses."
—**Bo Derek, on children**

"If I'm androgynous, I'd say I lean toward macho-androgynous."
—**John Travolta**

"I loved making the movie *Rising Sun*. I got into the psychology of why she liked to get tied up in plastic bags. It has to do with low self-esteem."
—**Tatjana Patitz**

"The only happy artist is a dead artist, because only then you can't change. After I die, I'll probably come back as a paintbrush."
—**Sylvester Stallone**

"Good looking people turn me off. Myself included."
—**Patrick Swayze**

"There is no capital of Uruguay, you dummy—it's a country."
—**Lorenzo Lamas, to Jon Stewart on *The Daily Show***

"I feel my best when I'm happy."
—**Winona Ryder**

"Sure the body count in this movie (*Die Harder*) bothers me, but it's what everybody likes. At least it's not an awful body count—it's a fun body count."
—**Bonnie Bedelia**

"In an action film you act in the action, in a drama film you act in the drama."
—**Jean-Claude Van Damme**

"You can hardly tell where the computer models finish and the real dinosaurs begin."
—**Laura Dern, on *Jurassic Park***

"I think that the film *Clueless* was very deep. I think it was deep in the way that it was very light. I think lightness has to come from a very deep place if it's true lightness."
—**Alicia Silverstone**

"He's the chief, right? What else is there to say? It's not bad sleeping with Einstein."
—**Lara Flynn Boyle on then-boyfriend Jack Nicholson**

"My main hope for myself is to be where I am."
—**Woody Harrelson**

Scientists say: Gesturing with your hands while speaking improves your memory.

THE TALLEST MAN IN THE WORLD

You may think being the tallest guy in the room is a great thing.
Here's the story of a man who probably wouldn't agree.

TALL TALE

On February 22, 1918, Addie Wadlow gave birth to an 8½-pound baby boy in the town of Alton, Illinois. She and her husband, Harold, named him Robert.

The boy was normal-sized at birth, but he didn't stay that way for long: by the time he was six months old, he weighed 30 pounds (twice as much as a typical six-month-old weighs). By 18 months, he weighed 62 pounds. In the first two years of Robert's life, his parents—and apparently even his doctors—didn't think there was anything particularly odd about the rapid growth. They just thought he was a naturally big kid who was growing earlier than most kids. Sooner or later, they figured, his growth would slow down and his peers would catch up.

BIG KID

That notion could not have lasted long. By the time Robert was five years old, he stood 5'4" tall, just seven inches shorter than his father, and wore clothing made for a 17-year-old. He passed his father in height before he turned eight, and by nine Robert could carry his dad up the stairs of the family home.

What was it that caused Robert to grow at such an astonishing rate? Ironically, it was caused by one of the smallest organs in the human body: the pituitary gland, a pea-sized organ located in the center of the skull, just beneath the brain. Robert's pituitary gland was producing too much growth hormone. Today pituitary abnormalities can be treated with surgery and hormone therapy, but in the early 1920s things were different. When Robert was 11, a doctor told the family that attempting such surgery would probably kill the boy, so the Wadlows gave up on that idea and focused on giving their son as normal a childhood as possible.

Patriotic fact: Bald eagles can swim.

THE BIG TIME

As a young boy, Robert naturally turned heads wherever he went. (He once terrified a department store Santa when he ran after him to tell him what he wanted for Christmas.) But he remained virtually unknown outside the small community of Alton until 1927, when he visited St. Louis with his father and caught the eye of some newspaper reporters. The reporters measured and weighed the third-grader (he was 6'2½" and 180 pounds) and published several photos in the *Globe-Democrat*.

The pictures were picked up by the Associated Press and published in newspapers all over the country, and Robert became one of the most famous kids in the United States. Visitors began trekking to Alton in the hopes of catching a glimpse of the world's biggest little boy. People would park their cars outside his elementary school just to watch him walk home from school. When he passed their car they'd drive down a few hundred feet, park the car, and watch Robert walk by again. Some people followed him all the way home.

SMALL WORLD

From his earliest memories, Robert towered over his peers—he never knew people his own age who were his size. By the start of his teenage years he'd grown taller than all of the adults he knew. By his mid-teens, Robert entered a new phase of his life: he literally began to outgrow the world around him. Until then his hobbies had included photography and playing the guitar, but his hands grew so large that operating a camera or playing his favorite instrument became impossible.

By his 16th birthday, Robert stood more than 7'10" tall and weighed 370 pounds, making him the tallest person in the United States. Even the largest-sized clothing didn't fit him anymore; from now on everything he wore would have to be tailor-made, using three times as much cloth as normal-sized clothing. His shoes had to be made by hand, too (the machinery that mass-produced footwear was designed to make shoes only up to about a size 15, and Robert's feet would one day top out at size 37). And because Robert's feet never stopped growing, he had to order his shoes a few sizes too large so they would still fit by the time they arrived.

Columbus's ship the *Santa Maria* weighed less than the *Titanic's* rudder.

TAKING ITS TOLL

Robert's rapid, uncontrollable growth was more of a handicap than you might think: he needed to take long walks and participate in other regular exercise to keep up the muscle strength that support- ed his enormous frame. But his rapidly growing bones couldn't get all the calcium they needed, so they were weak and prone to injury. He didn't have much sensation in his feet, either, which made walking more difficult. As Robert got older his body became increasingly frail and unsteady; falls became more dangerous. By his late teens he was walking with a cane.

When Robert entered college in 1936 at the age of 18, he was 8'3½" tall and less than an inch away from becoming the tallest human in recorded history. Rather than walk to school as he had in high school, he now had to take a cab. Too large to sit upright in a normal-sized car, he had to crouch on his hands and knees across the backseat. When he arrived at school, he shoved one leg backward out the door, then the other, and backed his way out of the cab.

IF THE SHOE FITS

College proved to be too much of an ordeal for Robert. He could not sit at a normal desk. Fountain pens and notebooks were tiny and unwieldy in his hands, making note-taking during lectures almost impossible. He had trouble working the microscope in his biology class and drawing diagrams of the organisms he was study- ing in his lab notebook. Even going up and down stairs was a chal- lenge—Robert's 18-inch-long feet were too big to fit on the steps. And because he didn't fit in—literally—with the other students, he was frequently lonely.

Robert finished his first year of college but didn't return for a second. Instead, he decided to open a shoe store. To do that he needed money, of course, and he knew how to get it: in the past he and his dad had made occasional promotional tours for the International Shoe Company. Now that Robert was finished with school, he talked his dad into quitting his job and traveling with him full-time until he had enough money to open his own shoe store in Alton.

By now Robert was so large that travel by train or airplane was pretty much out of the question—sure, if the railroad or the airline agreed to remove a row or two of seats, there might be room enough for Robert to sit, but he could no longer squeeze himself into the tiny train and plane bathrooms. So he and his dad bought a car that was big enough to seat seven people, ripped out the middle row of seats, and hit the road—Dad did the driving, and Robert sat in the back (he was too tall to drive).

In the summer months, Robert made appearances in northern states; in the winter Robert and his dad headed south. They would stay out for a few weeks at a time, typically visiting two towns every day. Robert drew huge crowds wherever he went, and it soon proved to be impractical to greet so many people inside the shoe stores. So they began working with an advance man who arranged for either a large truck or a platform to be set up outside each store.

Most of the people who came to see Robert were polite, but he had to put up with the same old jokes ("How's the weather up there?") at every stop, and some people even pinched his legs through his trousers or kicked him in the shins to see if he was walking on stilts. Robert took it in stride—but if the pincher or kicker was wearing a hat (and nearly everyone did in the 1930s), he playfully retaliated by grabbing it and putting it someplace high where the person couldn't easily get it back.

GENTLE GIANT

In all, Robert and his dad visited more than 800 towns in 41 different states between 1937 and 1940, traveling more than 300,000 miles in the process. On July 4, 1940, they were scheduled to ride in a parade in Manistee, Michigan. Robert wasn't feeling well, but he decided to go ahead with the parade anyway.

The parade lasted more than two hours, and in that time Robert's condition deteriorated until he could barely hold his head up. By the time he made it back to the hotel he had a fever of 101°F. The hotel doctor looked Robert over and found the source of the problem: an infected blister on Robert's ankle, caused by a poor-fitting metal brace. The brace had been fitted a few weeks earlier to strengthen his ankle. (By his early 20s, Robert had very little feeling left in his feet; if he had noticed the blister at all, he didn't realize how serious it was.) When doctors couldn't find a hospital nearby that was equipped to handle a patient as large as

Robert—he was too big to fit in a hospital bed—they decided it would be better to treat him right there in the hotel room.

Over the next several days, the infection worsened and Robert's condition deteriorated. Had it happened just a few years later, Robert could have been treated with penicillin and might have made a full recovery. But penicillin had not yet come into widespread use, and once an infection got established there was little that could be done to stop it. At 1:30 a.m. on the morning of July 15, Robert passed away in his sleep. At the time of his death he was 8'11", making him a full seven inches taller than the previous record holder, an Irishman who died in 1877.

He never did get to open his own shoe store.

Robert's body was returned to Alton, where it was buried in a 10'9"-long, 1,000-pound casket, carried by 12 pallbearers and eight assistants. The big man got a big send-off as every business in Alton shut down on the day of the funeral. More than 40,000 people filed past the casket before it was laid to rest.

LEGACY

If you're lucky enough to find a shoe store that Robert Wadlow visited on one of his publicity tours, it might still have a pair of his shoes on display—he left a pair at every stop. And, if you visit Alton, Illinois, you can see his lifesize bronze statue, erected in 1985. The town museum has a display of some of Robert's personal possessions.

During his lifetime Robert resisted being exploited for his size, and he feared that his remains might be exploited, too. So before he died, Robert asked his father to do everything he could to prevent his body from being abused after his death. Accordingly, Harold Wadlow refused to allow a postmortem exam, and he had his son buried under eight inches of reinforced concrete to protect against grave robbers. The family also destroyed Robert's clothing and most of his oversized personal possessions, to prevent them from being displayed in freak shows.

"We treated Robert after death just as he would have wanted us to," biographer Frederic Fadner quotes Harold Wadlow saying in his book *The Gentleman Giant*. "I am sure that he died with complete confidence in us. We could not and did not betray that confidence after he was gone."

FAMOUS LAST WORDS

If you had to choose your last words, what would they be?

"I am about to, or, I am going to die. Either expression is used."
—**Dominique Bouhours, grammarian**

"Don't let it end like this. Tell them I said something."
—Pancho Villa

"O.K. I won't."
—**Elvis Presley, to his girl-friend's request that he not fall asleep in the bathroom**

"Monsieur, I beg your pardon."
—**Marie Antoinette, to her executioner, after stepping on his foot**

"Never felt better."
—Douglas Fairbanks, Sr.

"I don't need bodyguards."
—Jimmy Hoffa

"Curtain! Fast music! Lights! Ready for the last finale! Great! The show looks good!"
—**Florenz Ziegfeld, Broadway producer, hallucinating on his deathbed**

"Does nobody understand?"
—James Joyce

"Bless you, sister. May all your sons be bishops."
—**Brendan Behan, author, to his nurse, a nun**

"That was the best ice cream soda I ever tasted."
—Lou Costello

"No."
—**Alexander Graham Bell, in sign language, to his deaf wife, who pleaded, "Don't leave me."**

"Yeah."
—**John Lennon, to the cop in the ambulance, who asked, "Are you John Lennon?"**

"Why not? Why not?"
—Timothy Leary

"Napoleon…"
—Josephine Beauharnais

"Josephine…"
—**Napoleon Bonaparte (even though divorced, the two still loved each other)**

"Either that wallpaper goes, or I do."
—Oscar Wilde

THE STRANGE FATE OF TED'S HEAD

Ted Williams's lifelong dream was to be known as "the greatest hitter who ever lived." It's sad, then, that today many people know him as "that baseball player who got cryonically frozen."

HEADING FOR HOME

In the summer of 2001, some old friends went to Hernando, Florida, to pay a visit to Ted Williams, the legendary Red Sox slugger and the last major league player to bat over .400. The "Splendid Splinter" was 83 years old and in poor health; in recent years he'd battled heart disease, strokes, and a broken hip. Now nearly blind, Williams required round-the-clock nursing care and could only get around with the aid of a walker. But his spirits were high as he visited with his friends, and when one of them pointed to a photograph of Slugger, a beloved Dalmatian that had died in 1998, Williams told them that he was saving the dog's ashes so that when he died, they could be scattered together in the waters at one of his favorite fishing spots.

The old ballplayer's health deteriorated further over the next year, and on July 5, 2002, he died. Just as he'd told his his friends, his will instructed that his remains "be cremated and sprinkled at sea off the coast of Florida where the water is very deep."

COLD STORAGE

It wasn't to be. Even as Williams lay dying, a "standby team" dispatched by an organization called the Alcor Life Extension Foundation was at his bedside, waiting patiently for him to breathe his last. Within moments of his being declared dead at 8:49 a.m., the team sprang into action, pumping his body full of blood thinners and packing it in a body bag filled with dry ice for the trip to a nearby airport, where a chartered jet stood by to take it to Alcor headquarters in Scottsdale, Arizona. By 11:30 p.m. Williams's body was stretched out on the Alcor operating table. There, in a procedure lasting 37 minutes, a surgeon decapitated the corpse so that head and body could be frozen separately in "dewars," high-tech steel thermoses filled with liquid nitrogen. Over the next several days, his head and body were slowly chilled to -320°F, and they've been floating in what Alcor calls "long-term storage" ever since. Williams's head reportedly sits in a dewar on a shelf; the rest of his body floats in a much larger dewar several feet away.

CRYONICS 101

The purpose of freezing bodies "cryonically," as advocates call it, is to halt decay and preserve the body in as intact a form as possible, in the hope that someday medicine will be able to cure the dead person's illnesses and reverse the aging process. When that day comes, the person can be thawed out, resuscitated, and restored to a second youthful, vigorous life.

The cryonics movement has been dismissed by mainstream scientists as a hopeless, pseudoscientific pipe dream. Even if cryonic freezing is perfected at some point in the future, critics argue that modern techniques are so primitive and toxic, and inflict so much irreversible damage, that resuscitation of people frozen today will likely never be possible. Even Alcor requires clients to sign forms acknowledging that resuscitation may never happen…but that hasn't stopped more than 800 living people from signing up to be cryonically frozen when they die. As of 2007, approximately 80 of them have died and been put into long-term storage at Alcor's facilities in Scottsdale. Scores more have signed up for similar procedures at other cryonic organizations in the United States and Europe. Worldwide, it's estimated that fewer than 500 people have been cryonically frozen so far, but thousands more customers are ready to go the moment their "first life cycle," as cryonics enthusiasts put it, comes to an end.

SON OF A GUN

So how did Ted Williams end up at Alcor? We'll probably never know for certain whether he changed his mind in the final months of his life and opted for cryonic preservation without updating his will, as his son John-Henry Williams claimed, or if John-Henry, acting as his father's power of attorney, had the old man frozen against his wishes.

John-Henry, who was 33 at the time of his father's death, was Ted's middle child and only son, one of two children he fathered with Dolores Wettach, his third wife. For most of John-Henry's life, he and his father had not been close. Ted and Dolores divorced when the boy was only four, and he and his sister Claudia were raised by Dolores on her family's farm in Vermont. Father and son began to grow closer in the early 1990s when John-Henry, fresh out of college, stepped in to manage his father's business affairs after Ted, then in his mid-70s, was swindled out of millions of dollars by a business partner who turned out to be a con man.

WHO'S IN CHARGE?

Over the next few years, John-Henry gradually took control over nearly every aspect of the old ballplayer's life, shutting out many friends, family, and loved ones in the process. He turned his father into a one-man sports memorabilia franchise, badgering him to spend hours a day autographing photos, jerseys, baseballs, bats, and other merchandise—entire cases of the stuff, day in, day out, even after Ted's health began to fail. John-Henry also filled his father's schedule with more paid public appearances at card shows and other events than Ted had ever attended before.

At the time, Ted was one of the biggest names on the card show circuit—photos signed by him routinely sold for $300, baseballs went for $400, bats for $800, and jerseys for $1,000. John-Henry claimed that pushing his father to sign hundreds of signatures a day was therapeutic, and that it kept the old man's mind on baseball. Ted's home-care nurses thought he was being abused, but when they spoke out John-Henry fired them on the spot.

HANDS OFF

When the old slugger was hospitalized in January 2001 for complications from open-heart surgery, John-Henry gave strict instructions that the nurses not insert IVs into his right arm or do anything else that might impair that arm's range of motion.

Then, when Ted was released and began to receive physical therapy at home, "all of the exercises, all of the work, were being done to restore strength and mobility to his right hand," Leigh Montville writes in *Ted Williams: The Biography of an American Hero*. Why focus so much attention on the right hand? "So he'll be able to sign autographs again," John-Henry explained.

Something to sweat about: The 10 hottest years on record have all occurred in the last 2 decades.

ANOTHER BRIGHT IDEA

It was at about this time that Ted Williams's oldest daughter, Barbara Joyce (Bobby-Jo) Ferrell, says that her half brother John-Henry came to her with an idea of how to keep the income flowing in long after their father was no longer able to sign his name. "Have you ever heard of cryonics?" she says John-Henry asked her. "Wouldn't it be neat to sell Dad's DNA? There are lots of people who would pay big bucks to have all these little Ted Williamses running around." Bobby-Jo recoiled at the thought and called John-Henry "insane." Her concerns did not diminish when John-Henry assured her, "We don't have to take Ted's whole body. We can just take the head."

LIKE DAUGHTER, LIKE FATHER

Leigh Montville describes how a home-care nurse overheard John-Henry pitching cryonics to his father more than a year before the old man died. "You're outta your %@#&! mind," Ted reportedly told his son. "What about just your head?" John-Henry asked. Ted's angry response, as he walked back to his room: "%@#& you!" (That nurse was fired in May 2001.)

It isn't clear whether John-Henry really did manage to sell his father on the merits of cryonics in the last year of his life, or if Ted's wish to be cremated and scattered at sea were simply ignored. Ted Williams never met with Alcor representatives, and he never signed their Consent for Cryonic Suspension form, either. John-Henry, acting as power of attorney, signed it for Ted after his death, even though his power of attorney ended when Williams died.

The only written evidence that John-Henry ever presented to support his claim that his father had opted for cryonic freezing was an oil-stained note, handwritten in block letters, that he produced three weeks after Ted's death. The note read:

> 11-2-00 JHW, Claudia and Dad all agree to be put into bio-stasis after we die. This is what we want, to be able to be together in the future, even if it is only a chance.
>
> John-Henry Williams
> Ted Williams
> Claudia Williams

Does the similarity end there? The balanced diet for a human is about the same as that of a rat.

SOMETHING FISHY

John-Henry's detractors were suspicious of the note. While Ted usually signed his autographs as "Ted Williams," he always signed legal documents as "Theodore S. Williams." They didn't doubt it was Williams's signature, only where it came from. Whenever he was getting ready to autograph baseball memorabilia, Ted commonly signed his name on a few blank pieces of paper to warm up. Bobby-Jo and others believe that John-Henry faked the note by writing the text onto a piece of paper that already had one of Ted's warm-up signatures on it. But when Claudia vouched for her signature in an affidavit, the executor of the estate accepted the note as a genuine expression of Ted's wish to be cryonically frozen.

By now Bobby-Jo had spent more than $87,000 from her own retirement fund on lawyers to have her father taken out of deep-freeze and cremated according to the instructions in his will, but with her money running out and Claudia Williams vouching for the authenticity of the note, she gave up the fight. Ted's head and body remain frozen to this day.

Alcor billed John-Henry $136,000 for services rendered; he sent them an initial payment of $25,000 and defaulted on the rest. As of August 2003, he still hadn't paid, though by then it wasn't clear if there was any money left to spend. During the last years of Ted's life, John-Henry had apparently used his power of attorney to raid his father's assets and use them to bankroll an Internet startup company. When the dot-com bubble burst in 2000, the company filed for bankruptcy, nearly $13 million in debt. By the time Ted died, most of his assets had been sold off or mortgaged to the hilt.

THE END?

John-Henry must have worked out some kind of arrangement regarding his father's Alcor bill, because when the younger Williams died from leukemia in 2004 at the age of 35, his body was shipped to Alcor, too. Is he floating in the same tank as his dad? They're big enough to hold four people, but Alcor isn't talking. The only thing that can be said for certain is that if the two men are thawed out and brought back to life, John-Henry will sure have a lot of explaining to do.

In Elkhart, Indiana, it's against the law for a barber to threaten to cut off a child's ears.

THE COTTON WAR

Here's Part III of our story on Eli Whitney.
(Part II starts on page 453.)

NOT GONNA HAPPEN
Eli Whitney's cotton gin played a pivotal part in creating the pre–Civil War south as an economic power. Cotton had transformed the South from an underdeveloped, underpopulated wilderness into the home of America's largest cash crop. It enriched not only the South, which grew it, but also the North, which had its own fledgling textile industry, and whose merchants shipped it to England.

One of the ironies of the invention is that the wealth it helped create ultimately led to the Civil War and doomed the South to defeat. King Cotton gave Southerners a false sense of security. The North *needed* cotton, the thinking went, so how could it go to war against the South?

THE BRITISH ARE COMING...AGAIN
And what about England, which imported 90% of its cotton from the South? Cotton fueled its economy too, and Southern leaders like Jefferson Davis (who would become president of the Confederacy in 1861), were convinced that if war did come, England would side with the South. England would have little choice but to use the Royal Navy to keep Southern ports open, so that its access to cotton would be guaranteed. The North knew this as well, the Southerners reasoned, and that made it even less likely that the Northern states would ever go to war over slavery. Fighting the South was one thing; fighting England *and* the South was another.

"You dare not make war upon our cotton," South Carolina Senator James Henry Hammond proclaimed in 1858. "No power on Earth dares make war on it. Cotton is King."

But when the war finally did come in April 1861, England didn't hesitate—it immediately declared its "strict and impartial neutrality" and then sat on the sidelines. Why? England didn't have to worry about cotton—the long, slow buildup to the Civil War had given English mills plenty of time to stockpile extra cotton. When that ran out, they would make do with what they could buy from countries like Egypt and India. And unemployment resulting from cotton shortages was tolerated, because many English textile workers opposed slavery and were willing to go without jobs to help end it.

SLIP-SLIDING AWAY

Another nail in the coffin: The South's failure to expand its economy beyond a single cash crop left it vulnerable. The invention of the cotton gin had encouraged cotton cultivation not just in the southern United States, but all over the world, and as cotton plantations sprang up in other countries, the price of cotton began a long, steady slide throughout the 1850s.

For decades, Southern planters had reinvested their profits into expanding cotton production instead of diversifying into factories, textile mills, or anything else. As the price of cotton fell, plantations lost money. By the late 1850s, there was little cash available to diversify the Southern economy, even if the South had wanted to. It was too late.

MASS PRODUCTION

In the North, things were different. Manufacturers of everything from doors and windows to nuts, bolts, shoes, plows, and grandfather clocks had adopted the principles of Eli Whitney's "American system," and were now using machine tools to mass-produce their wares. Soaring profits encouraged further investment and growth; from 1840 to 1860, the 100-mile-long region between Delaware and New York was the most rapidly industrializing region on Earth.

With the growth of industry came increased economic and military strength. By the start of the Civil War, factories in the North were producing goods at a rate of 10 times that of the South. For every ton of iron produced in the South, the North produced 15; for every firearm the South produced, the North manufactured 32. Northern states had more than twice the population of Southern states, and three times the wealth.

And though the South grew 24 times as much cotton as the North, the North had 14 times as many textile mills. So when war

Q: How bad was the smog in London in 1952?...

came in April 1861, it was the Union soldiers, not the Confederates, who were best outfitted for battle. Though the Civil War dragged on from 1861 to 1865, its outcome was a virtual certainty from the very beginning.

ELI WHITNEY'S LEGACY

For a person who had never discovered a continent, never commanded an army, and never served as president, Eli Whitney had about as big an impact on American history as anyone. And unlike his fellow inventors Henry Ford and Alexander Graham Bell, *two* of his inventions altered the course of history, not just one.

Cotton gave the South its wealth and strengthened the institution of slavery, sparking the tensions that would lead to the Civil War. At the same time, cotton convinced Southerners that if war did come, its importance guaranteed that the South would never lose. And that made the South all the more willing to fight.

With the invention of mass production, Whitney gave the North the military might and economic strength that it used to destroy the South that the cotton gin had built.

"If Whitney's cotton gin enabled the slave-system to survive and thrive," writes historian Paul Johnson, "his 'American System' also gave the North the industrial muscle to crush the defenders of slavery in due course....He is a fascinating example of the complex impact one man can have on history."

*   *   *

SPECIAL DELIVERY

"Rome post-office workers were confronted by a group of men delivering a very big package, too big for the security hole that packages are normally slipped through. Ignoring security rules, employees asked the group to go to a service window behind the counter. As soon as they brought the package inside, a robber burst out of the carton, waved a gun, and shouted, 'It's a holdup.' The criminals escaped with 115,000 lira."

—*Townsville Bulletin* (Australia)

TOOTLE THE HORN

When signs in a foreign country are written in English, any combination of words is possible. Here are a few our favorites.

On the grass in a Paris park: "Please do not be a dog."

Outside a Hong Kong dress shop: "Ladies have fits upstairs."

In a Tokyo barbershop: "All customers promptly executed."

Outside an Athens shop: "Park one hour. Later dick dock goes the money clock."

In a Tokyo rental car: "When passenger of foot heave in sight, tootle the horn. Trumpet him melodiously at first, but if he still obstacles your passage then tootle him with vigor."

In a Nairobi restaurant: "Customers who find our waitresses rude ought to see the manager."

In a Spanish shop entrance: "Here speeching American."

Detour sign in Japan: "Stop: Drive Sideways"

In a Sri Lanka restaurant: "All vegetables in this establishment have been washed in water especially passed by the management."

In a Copenhagen airport: "We take your bags and send them in all directions."

In an Austrian ski lodge: "Not to perambulate the corridors in the house of repose in the boots of ascension."

In a Hong Kong supermarket: "For your convenience, we recommend courteous, efficient self-service."

In a Finland hostel: "If you cannot reach a fire exit, close the door and expose yourself at the window."

On a Viennese restaurant menu: "Fried milk, children sandwiches, roast cattle and boiled sheep."

In a Swiss mountain inn: "Special today—no ice cream."

Your tongue can detect sweetness in a solution of 1 part sugar to 200 parts water.

TOILET TECH

Better living through bathroom technology.

• **Toilet "Landing Lights."** Invented by Brooke Pattee of Lake Forest, California, this lighting system illuminates the inside of your toilet bowl when you lift or lower the lid, allowing you to take care of business without blinding yourself in the middle of the night by turning on the bathroom light. An automatic timer turns the lights off after several minutes.

• **The Strap-on Animal Waste Collector** is designed for dogs owned by people too squeamish to use a pooper-scooper. Invented by Angela Raphael of New York City, it looks kind of like a pet harness, only backward with two add-ons. One waste receptacle attaches beneath the dog's tail, and one attaches beneath the dog to capture urine. Extra bonus: Both receptacles are disposable.

• **The Automobile Urinal.** Invented by Aston Waugh of East Orange, New Jersey, it consists of three parts: a hanging water tank, a miniature padded toilet bowl that the driver sits on while driving, and a waste storage tank that stows neatly beneath the driver's seat. After use, the driver flushes the device by opening a valve; water from the hanging tank flows through a tube into the toilet bowl, and from there into the storage tank underneath the seat. "For privacy," the inventor advises, "the user may wrap a large towel around him or herself from the waist to the knees before undoing the clothing to facilitate urination." (Not recommended for use while operating a cell phone.)

• **The Versatile Interactive Pan (VIP)** lets your toilet do the shopping. Created by Twyford, a toilet manufacturer in Cheshire, England, it analyzes your urine and stool samples for dietary deficiencies, compiles a shopping list of needed nutritional items, then e-mails your local supermarket to order the foods. "If, for example, a person is short on roughage one day," says Twyford spokesperson Terry Wooliscroft, "an order of beans or lentils will be sent from the VIP to the supermarket and delivered the same day." The toilet can also e-mail a doctor if it detects health problems. Added bonuses: The seat is voice activated and the toilet flushes automatically.

• **The Flatulence Filter Seat Cushion.** From UltraTech Products of Houston, Texas, the foam cushion contains a hidden "super-activated" carbon filter that absorbs unfortunate odors as soon as they are created. The filter is hidden inside the cushion's gray tweed fabric, so no one has to know it's there—for all anyone knows, it's just another seat cushion. The company also makes a smaller filter pad that you can wear inside your underpants, "for protection when you are not at your seat."

• **Urilift.** During the day when it's in the closed position, the Urilift looks like a manhole cover. But at night, when the bars are open, a city worker points a remote control at the manhole cover, and voila! Up out of the ground pops an open-air, *pissoir*-style urinal that's about six feet tall and can accommodate three people at a time. Then in the morning when the bars are closed and respectable people don't want to look at a public urinal, the Urilift sinks back into the ground and disappears out of sight.

• **Universal Clean Seat.** A toilet seat that is perfectly circular instead of the traditional oval shape, if the Universal Clean Seat is dirty, you just wave your hand over a special sensor. A cleaning tool then pops out of the back of the seat, makes contact with the toilet seat ring and spins it like a phonograph record for 15 seconds, during which time it washes, disinfects, and dries the seat.

• **Toilet Snorkel.** In 1982 William Holmes received a patent for a device designed to access a source of fresh air during fires in high-rise buildings, where help may be slow to arrive. Snake this slender breathing tube down through any toilet and into the water trap, and access fresh air from the sewer line's vent pipe. At the user end, the breathing tube is connected to a strap-on mask. Good news: The Toilet Snorkel comes with an odor-eating charcoal filter.

• **Tilt-A-Roll.** Should the toilet paper roll over the roll, or under the roll? The Tilt-A-Roll lets you have it both ways: it's a toilet paper holder mounted on a swivel so that if you don't like the way the roll is rolled, spin it 180° and it's just the way you like it.

Most common speed limit sign in the United States: 25 mph.

THE NIAGARA FALLS MUMMY

Canada has never had a king or queen of its own...but did it have a pharaoh? Here's the story of a famous missing mummy.

WHO'S THAT GIRL?

Have you ever heard of Nefertiti? After Cleopatra, she's probably the most famous queen of ancient Egypt. Nefertiti was the wife of Akhenaton, who ruled from 1353 to 1336 B.C. A famous limestone bust of her is on display at the Egyptian Museum in Berlin, and because of this she is a popular historical figure in Germany.

Queen Nefertiti's mummy has been missing for more than 3,000 years...or has it? In 1966 a German tourist named Meinhard Hoffmann paid a visit to the Niagara Falls Museum, a cheesy tourist museum and freak show on the Canadian side of the falls. He looked at their famous Egyptian mummy exhibit, which had been displayed alongside two-headed calves, five-legged pigs, and other fascinating oddities for nearly 150 years. One mummy in particular caught his attention: It was unwrapped—removing a mummy's linen bandages had been common practice in the 19th century—and the body was partially covered by a shroud. Hoffmann wondered if the mummy might actually be Nefertiti, but how could he prove it? He couldn't—there was no way to verify his suspicion. Still, he took plenty of pictures of it before returning to Germany.

CROSS MY HEART

A decade passed. Then one day in 1976 Hoffmann read in an article that Egyptian queens of Nefertiti's era were mummified with their left arm, but not their right arm, folded high across the chest. He remembered that one arm had been folded across the naked mummy's chest, and when he dug out his photographs, he saw that it was indeed the left arm. *Could it be Nefertiti?* He couldn't tell whether the right arm was also folded across the chest, because it was obscured by the shroud.

Hoffmann got a photograph of the Nefertiti bust in the Egyptian Museum and compared it to his photographs of the mummy. Sure, the mummy's face was shriveled and wrinkly, while the face on the bust was pristine and beautiful. Even so, Hoffman thought they were astonishingly similar.

ON SECOND THOUGHT...

Having convinced himself that the mummy was Nefertiti, Hoffmann set out to convince others as well. Over the next several years he gradually developed his case, and in 1985 he managed to persuade a TV producer at Germany's Channel Two that he'd found the lost mummy. The producer made plans to do a TV special on the subject and flew Hoffmann and a camera crew to the Niagara Falls Museum. There an Egyptologist would remove the shroud and examine the mummy to confirm that it was the mummy of a queen, and most likely that of Nefertiti.

The examination got no further than the removal of the shroud—as soon as the Egyptologist removed it, it was clear that *both* arms were folded across the chest, not just one, which pretty much ruled out the possibility of the mummy being a queen. It was also clear that the naked mummy was anatomically a male, which ruled out the queen theory for sure.

LOOK ON THE BRIGHT SIDE

That was a pretty big letdown after such a huge buildup, but it was here that Hoffmann demonstrated a remarkable capacity for optimism. Not a queen? Not a problem—"It must be a pharaoh!" he exclaimed.

Hoffmann actually had a point: Kings of the period *were* mummified with both arms folded high across the chest. That (and their male anatomy) was what distinguished them from the mummies of queens. But kings weren't the only people in Egypt who were embalmed with their arms folded that way: About 1,300 years after Queen Nefertiti passed from the scene, Egypt was annexed by the Roman Empire and it then became fashionable for commoners to be embalmed with their hands folded high across their chest. This made it difficult to tell an ancient king from a newer commoner. The two had been confused many times in the past, especially by amateurs and wishful thinkers like Hoffmann.

BACK TO SQUARE ONE

The suspicion that the mummy was a Roman-era commoner seemed to be confirmed when the mummy was X-rayed and dark masses were seen inside the chest cavity. Mummies from Nefertiti's era had their organs removed and their chest cavities stuffed with linen to retain their natural shape. During the Roman Era, on the other hand, the organs were wrapped in linen and placed back in the chest cavity. The dark masses in the X-rays appeared to be organ packets, which led the group to conclude that the mummy was that of a commoner of the Roman Era.

Who wants to watch a TV show about a mummified commoner? Channel Two cancelled the special—it never aired.

DEJA VIEW

That's where things stayed until the late 1980s, when an Egyptology student named Gayle Gibson began visiting the museum in Niagara Falls to study four well-preserved coffins that were part of the Egyptian collection. She noticed the folded arms on the mummy and wondered about it, too, but the idea of a royal mummy lying undiscovered in such tacky surroundings for so many years seemed too farfetched to be true.

Then, in 1991, Gibson brought a mummy expert named Aidan Dodson, who was visiting from the U.K., to look at the collection. As soon as Dodson laid eyes on the mummy and saw its exquisite condition, the obvious skill of the embalmers, and of course the position of the arms, he, too, began to seriously suspect that the mummy might be a pharaoh. The next step was to try to get a scientific estimate of the mummy's age using carbon dating. In 1994 the museum agreed to allow the mummy to be tested, and scientists gave it a date of somewhere between 800 and 1500 B.C.—far too old to have been embalmed during the Roman Era. This mummy was no commoner.

HEADING SOUTH

So who was it? Given the mummy's age, the chances that it was indeed that of a king increased considerably. But events still moved slowly; it wasn't until after the Niagara Falls Museum closed in 1998 and the entire Egyptian collection was sold to Emory University in Atlanta (for $2 million) that further testing

---

Last song the Beatles played in concert: "Long Tall Sally." Last song they recorded: "I Me Mine."

was done. Researchers at the university submitted the mummy to a battery of sophisticated tests that had not been available previously, including CT scans and computer imaging. This enabled them to get a much better look at the dark masses in the chest, which turned out not to be organ packets after all. They were tightly wound rolls of linen, which have been found in other royal mummies of the period.

The piece of evidence that had been thought to rule out a royal connection now seemed to confirm it, as did a CT scan of the skull. It showed that the skull cavity contained a large amount of tree resin, a precious and very rare material in ancient Egypt—further evidence that the mummy was indeed that of a king.

THE CANDIDATE

But *which* king? As researchers unlocked the mummy's secrets, mounting circumstantial evidence pointed increasingly away from other missing pharaohs and toward a single candidate: Ramses I, founder of the 19th Dynasty, which ruled Egypt from 1291 to 1183 B.C. On the throne for less than two years, he was the grandfather of Ramses II, or Ramses the Great, whose 66-year reign was the second longest in Egyptian history.

Ramses I's body was believed to have been removed from a tomb containing several royal mummies in the mid-19th century, at about the same time that a collector representing the Niagara Falls Museum was touring Egypt acquiring the mummies that ended up in the collection. He bought it for £7, or about $34.

LIKE FATHER, LIKE SON

Ramses I's mummy had been missing from Egypt for more than 140 years, but those of his son, Seti I, and his grandson Ramses the Great are both in the Egyptian Museum in Cairo. Their faces bear a striking resemblance to the mummy from the Niagara Falls Museum, and that similarity was backed up when X-rays of the mummy's skull was compared to X-rays of all of the Egyptian Museum's royal mummies, taken in the 1960s. The shape of a human skull is hereditary, so if the mummy was related to Seti I and Ramses II, measurements of his skull were likely to be similar to theirs. Sure enough, the measurements of the Niagara Falls mummy matched those of Seti I and Ramses II more closely than those of any other royal mummy in the Egyptian Museum.

The case for the mummy being Ramses I is based entirely on circumstantial evidence, but there's so much of it that there is now very little room for doubt: The Niagara Falls mummy is almost certainly that of a king, and most likely that of Ramses I.

A BARGAIN AT TWICE THE PRICE

Scooping up the Niagara Falls Museum's entire Egyptian collection for $2 million seemed to be a pretty good bargain—the mummy of Ramses I is a priceless treasure. But rather than keep it, as soon as the mummy's identity was established to everyone's satisfaction, Emory University announced that they were giving the mummy to Egypt. In October 2003, Ramses was flown back to his home after an absence of 150 years.

"There was never any question about whether the mummy would be returned to Egypt if it proved to be a royal," the university museum's curator, Peter Lacovara, told *National Geographic*. "It was simply the right thing to do."

DELAYED GRATIFICATION

So who gets credit for finding Ramses I in his hiding place at Niagara Falls? Meinhard Hoffmann thinks it should go to him. Even when "experts" assured him that the mummy was a commoner, he was so convinced it was a pharaoh that he documented his claim in writing and hired a lawyer to notarize it. In the document, Hoffmann even suggested three possible identities for the mummy: Aye, Horemheb…and Ramses I.

"Here's the real reason I did that," says Hoffmann. "Because if all of a sudden you come out and say, 'Oh, I knew all that 20 years ago,' people will doubt you and say you're nothing but an opportunist."

*   *   *

FLUSH LIKE AN EGYPTIAN

The birthplace of the toilet seat (and the human litter box) was the ancient Egyptian city of Akhetaten. There is archaeological evidence that around 1350 B.C., "seats" made of wood, stone, and pottery were commonly placed over large bowls of sand.

WORD ORIGINS

*Ever wonder where these words came from? Here
are the interesting stories behind them.*

PAPARAZZI
Meaning: Photographers who follow celebrities
Origin: "From a character in the 1960 Federico Fellini film,
La Dolce Vita, a photographer named Signor Paparazzo. When
Fellini was growing up, one of his classmates was a boy who was
always squirming and talking fast. A teacher gave him the nickname *Paparazzo*, an Italian dialect word for a mosquito-like insect
that is always buzzing around in the air. When Fellini was writing
La Dolce Vita, he gave his classmate's nickname to his fictitious
photographer, a character who constantly flitted around the rich
and famous. Before long the real-life photographers who follow
celebrities everywhere began to be known as *paparazzi*, the plural
of paparazzo." (From *Inventing English*, by Dale Corey)

ALCOHOL
Meaning: An intoxicating beverage
Origin: "The word comes from Arabic *al-kuhul*, a powder used as a
cosmetic. Borrowed into English, *alcohol* came to mean any distilled substance. Alcohol of wine was thus the 'quintessence of
wine'...by the middle of the 18th century *alcohol* was being used
on its own." (From *Dictionary of Word Origins*, by John Ayto)

FEISTY
Meaning: Spunky, quarrelsome
Origin: "A 'fart' word. First appeared in the 13th century meaning
'a breaking of wind' or 'to break wind.'" (From *Take My Words*, by
Howard Richler)

KILL
Meaning: To cause the death of a person or animal; to abruptly
end something
Origin: "The word may seem age-old, but it evolved in its present

sense in the 14th century out of the Old English *cyllan*, meaning 'strike' or 'beat.' A 14th-century poem in the West Midland dialect has the gruesome word in this sense: 'We kylle of thyn heued' (we strike off your head), and it is easy to see how this could develop in the modern sense, with *kill* first meaning 'put to death with a weapon,' then 'put to death' in general." (From *Words About Words*, by David Grambs)

BLESS

Meaning: To consecrate or invoke divine favor

Origin: "A gracious word with a grisly history. Its forefather was Old English *bledsian*, a word that meant 'to consecrate with blood,' this, of course, from the blood sacrifices of the day. In later English, this word turned into *blessen*, and the term finally came to mean 'consecrated.' So today when we give you the greeting, 'God bless you,' we are actually saying, 'God bathe you in blood.'"
(From *Word Origins*, by Wilfred Funk)

ASSASSIN

Meaning: One who carries out a plot to kill a prominent person

Origin: "In the 11th and 12th centuries, the *Hashashin* ("hashish eaters") were a secret murder cult of the Ismaili sect of Muslims. Their leader, Hasan ben Sabah, offered them sensual pleasures, including beautiful maidens and hashish, so that they supposed they were in heaven. He then sent them on gangland-style missions to rub out prominent targets, assuring them of a quick trip to paradise if things went sour. The Hashashin survived in our word *assassin*."
(From *Remarkable Words with Astonishing Origins*, by John Train)

EXPLODE

Meaning: Burst or shatter violently

Origin: "This word has a history in the theater, where its meaning was once quite different than it is today. Originally 'explode' meant to drive an actor off the stage by means of clapping and hooting. It is made up of the Latin prefix *ex-* (out) and *plauder* (to applaud). The word still retains the sense of rejection, such as in the act of exploding a theory—exposing it as false—and, in general use, there is still noise associated with things which explode." (From *Dictionary of Word and Phrase Origins*, *Volume II*, by William and Mary Morris)

In the 1570s, the Spanish were defeated by a Dutch army on ice skates.

(NOT) MADE IN CHINA

Economists estimate that as much as 90% of all retail goods available in the United States are made overseas, particularly in China. These products include stereos, plastic toys, cups, belts, TVs, shoes, T-shirts, backpacks, telephones, coffee makers, toasters, and even religious memorabilia, just to name a few. Even though so many things are made in China, the things you might assume come from China probably don't.

• **Fine china.** Most fine china plates are bone china, a high-quality porcelain. The majority of the world's china is made not in China, but in England, Italy, and the United States.

• **Tea.** The phrase "not for all the tea in China" is misleading—India is the world's largest grower of black tea, accounting for a third of the world's supply. China, where tea originated, produces 10%.

• **Opium.** Ever seen an old movie with a scene of Chinese men relaxing in an opium den? Opium isn't Chinese. The British smuggled it into China from India.

• **Rice.** Rice is closely associated with Chinese food. But China isn't the world's largest exporter. Not even close. Thailand shipped 7.5 million tons of rice in 2002. China exported only 2 million.

• **Chinese restaurants.** There are 73 Chinese food restaurants in China's capital city, Beijing. In New York City, there are more than 300.

• **China dolls.** They were *never* made in China. Germany, France, and Denmark began making these porcelain dolls in the 1840s.

• **Fortune cookies.** They were invented in 1914 at San Francisco's Japanese Tea Garden. While there are now fortune cookie factories in China, most are made by the Wonton Food Company in New York—they churn out 2.5 million cookies daily.

• **Chinese checkers.** Based on Halma, an earlier game played on a square board. Pressman Brothers created a star-shaped game board in 1928 and called it Chinese Checkers to capitalize on the popularity of mah-jongg.

According to the experts, 75% of people wash their stomach first when showering.

BAD HISTORY! BAD!

*Or, eight reasons why you shouldn't get
your history from Hollywood.*

THAT'S ENTERTAINMENT

A night at the movies is a fine way to amuse yourself and support America's $6 billion-a-year film industry, but it's a bad way to learn anything useful about history. Even when you throw out the "historical" comedies or special-effects extravaganzas, the supposedly more "accurate" genre of historical drama is still full of bad history…or history "reedited" to make the story less confusing, more exciting, or more compatible with Mel Gibson. Even Oscar-winning films are replete with inaccuracies that would make your history teacher tear his hair out. As proof, here are a few recent historical dramas that have played fast and loose with the past.

Pearl Harbor (2001): Before the attack on Pearl Harbor in the film, Japanese Zeros are shown flying low over wholesome American kids playing baseball. But the kids would have to have gotten up pretty early to play ball, since the attack occurred just before 8 a.m. Commander-in-Chief of the Pacific Fleet Admiral Husband Kimmel is likewise shown golfing, as if to emphasize his utter unpreparedness for the attack. In fact, he was nowhere near the greens when the attack occurred. (Kimmel, the Navy's fall guy, was relieved of command after the attack; he's since been exonerated.)

Movie heroes Ben Affleck and Josh Hartnett are shown taking flight and doing battle with attacking Japanese Zeros; in the real world, it was Army pilots Kenneth Taylor and George Welch who managed to get into the air. Later, Affleck and Hartnett fly in Doolittle's raid over Tokyo; no actual pilots flew in both battles. Affleck is also shown serving in Britain's Eagle Squadron. While the squadron did include Americans, they were all civilians.

Final small inaccuracy: In one scene a sailor displays a dollar bill with the word "HAWAII" on it; those bills, introduced in Hawaii so they could be declared illegal if the Japanese invaded, came out in July 1942—long after the Pearl Harbor attack.

During WWI, Germany offered Arizona, New Mexico, and Texas to Mexico to change sides.

Thirteen Days (2000): The film in which Kevin Costner averts nuclear war during the Bay of Pigs, with a little help from President Kennedy. Most historians and participants of the event suggest that Costner's character, JFK adviser Kenny O'Donnell, was not nearly as pivotal a character in the crisis as he's shown to be. Indeed, several critical scenes in the film show O'Donnell doing things he never did in real life—taking Bobby Kennedy to meet the Soviet ambassador, giving pep talks to pilots before they over-fly Cuba, and having a moment with JFK himself before a Kennedy television address.

Gladiator (2000): This Oscar-winning toga flick is a historical mess right down to the Latin inscription chipped into the Coliseum. First off, there is no historical general to match Russell Crowe's Maximus. There was of course a real Marcus Aurelius, whose son was named Commodus. However, Commodus didn't smother Marcus Aurelius to death when he learned he wouldn't be chosen as emperor, if for no other reason than he already was emperor (or more accurately, co-emperor) when his father died in A.D. 180. Moreover, while Commodus did in fact enjoy prancing about as a gladiator, much to the scandal of the higher classes, he was not killed by a revenge-crazed former general during gladiatorial battle. His real death in 192 is even weirder: He was strangled by a champion wrestler hired as an assassin by his advisers.

Also, the Roman Empire didn't become a republic again after Commodus's death, as intimated in the movie. Commodus was succeeded as emperor by one Publius Helvius Pertinax, who lasted only three months before his assassination.

The Patriot (2000): Neither Mel Gibson's character Benjamin Martin nor the chief baddie William Tavington are actual historical characters, but both are based loosely on real people: Francis "Swamp Fox" Marion and British Lieutenant Colonel Banastre Tarleton, respectively. The operative phrase here is "loosely," since Francis Marion owned slaves and loved a good fight (a far cry from Gibson's Martin, who was reluctant to go to war and paid free black citizens to work on his plantation).

Tarleton, while earning the nickname "Bloody Ban," didn't set fire to churches while the parishioners were still in them. He also didn't die in the film's climactic Battle of Cowpens; he lived until 1833.

The Battle of Cowpens, it should be noted, didn't have nearly the amount of heavy firepower as is portrayed in the film. There were only two light cannons, brought by the British. Other than that, it was muskets and swords—still bloody enough. Incidentally, British commander Lord Cornwallis, portrayed in the movie as a somewhat stuffy older man, was actually only 42 at the time of the battle, in which he did not take part. The British forces were led by Tarleton, who led badly—he lost 600 out of 1,500 men, while the colonists lost a mere 72.

U-571 (2000): You know that part in the movie when the crack team of U.S. soldiers launches a surprise attack on a German submarine and steal the sub's Enigma code generator? Never happened. The U.S. had no part in capturing the naval Enigma machine; that honor belongs to the British, who climbed aboard the German sub U-110 on May 9, 1941, to recover a working Enigma machine, its cipher keys, key books, and other cryptological records.

The Germans subsequently made their naval Enigma machines more complicated, requiring the Brits to perform the same maneuver again on October 30, 1942, when British sailors boarded the U-559. Two soldiers drowned in the attempt to bring up the sub's Enigma machine, but the signal key books were retrieved, which allowed the Allies to crack the naval Enigma code again. Americans did board the German sub U-505 in 1944, retrieving sensitive papers and maps, and earning the leader of the boarding crew, Lt. Albert David, the Congressional Medal of Honor.

There *was* a German submarine with the designation U-571 that patrolled the waters off the U.S. Eastern shore, sinking several merchant ships between 1942 and 1943. It sank in the North Atlantic on January 28, 1944, after an Allied aircraft dropped depth charges around it. All hands were lost.

Elizabeth (1998): Lots of people in this film are in the wrong place at the wrong time, or simply shouldn't be there at all. Bishop Stephen Gardiner, shown leading the Catholic Church opposition to Queen Elizabeth, died three years before she was crowned. Sir William Cecil was not an old man when Elizabeth came to the throne, as he is in the film, but a spry 38; he remained one of the queen's closest advisers until his death in 1598. Sneaky Francis Walsingham, portrayed as two or more decades older than the queen, was in fact only one year older. Robert Dudley, Elizabeth's fallen lover in the film, never really fell, but rather remained one of the queen's closest friends until his death in 1588. Other time-slip issues include Elizabeth's excommunication by the pope, which happened far later, in 1570.

Amistad (1997): While the majority of the characters in this retelling of the famous slave ship rebellion are based on real-life people, Theodore Joadson, played by Morgan Freeman, is not. The *Amistad* is shown making port in the winter; in the real world, it made port in August 1839. (Interestingly, in 1839 slavery was still legal in Connecticut, where the *Amistad* made port; a general emancipation in the state was not enacted until 1848. The film rather conveniently doesn't bring up the fact of a northern state still allowing slavery.) The film also shows the leader of the Africans, Cinque, peppering his lawyers (who included former president John Quincy Adams) with legal questions and helping create the defense. But there's no real evidence that he did this.

Braveheart (1995): There's a lot to complain about here, but for the sake of brevity, let's focus on the film's portrayal of the relationship between William Wallace (hunky Mel Gibson) and Princess Isabella (sultry Sophie Marceau). In the movie, she's seen negotiating with Wallace for English king Edward I before she eventually jumps his bones and ultimately (one assumes) places his child on the English throne as Edward III.

Wallace was captured by the English and very messily executed (the movie got that right) in 1305. Isabella was born in 1292, making her 13 at the time of Wallace's death. She didn't wed Edward II until 1308—by which time, incidentally, he was already king. (Isabella would, however, play a primary role in deposing her husband in 1327.) The movie fiddles with the death of Edward I, who died in 1307, not immediately after Wallace's death, and certainly not due to panic over the idea of a Scotsman one day gaining his throne. Also, it should be noted that Edward I wasn't in the habit of throwing his son's gay lovers out of windows.

SPY HUNT: GRAY DECEIVER, PART III

Here's part III of our story on one of the biggest mole hunts in FBI history. (Part II is on page 411.)

FINGERED

The FBI mole hunters had never suspected Robert Hanssen of spying before, but all residual doubt that he was their man disappeared when the KGB officer who sold them Hanssen's file began to interpret the file's contents.

What about that mysterious sealed envelope marked "Don't Open This"? The FBI waited until the retired KGB officer arrived to open it. The officer explained that when the spy left documents and computer discs at a dead drop, he wrapped them in two plastic garbage bags to protect them from the elements. The envelope contained one of the spy's garbage bags. The KGB officer explained that only he and the spy had touched the bag; if Hanssen was the spy (and wasn't wearing gloves when he wrapped the package), it would likely contain his fingerprints.

The agents took the bag to the lab and succeeded in lifting two fingerprints from the bag. As they expected, the prints were Hanssen's. Every piece of evidence in the KGB file pointed to him and him alone. He even had a thing for diamonds and strippers, just as Russian sources had been reporting for years.

GRAYDAY

The investigators put aside their investigation of GRAY DECEIVER, gave Hanssen the nickname GRAYDAY, and started investigating him. They arranged for Hanssen to be promoted to a new job at FBI headquarters, where he could be closely watched by hidden cameras. Then they tapped his office phone and searched his laptop computer. They couldn't bug or search his house—his wife and two of his six kids still living at home were never gone long enough—but when a house across the street from Hanssen's was put up for sale, the FBI bought it, moved in, and began watching Hanssen from there. Whenever Hanssen left home, undercover

---

An Australian company makes eco-friendly coffins out of recycled newspaper.

FBI agents secretly followed him.

This time, the mole hunters' work paid off: after about three months of constant surveillance, on the afternoon of February 18, 2001, Hanssen was caught red-handed leaving a package of computer discs and classified documents in a dead drop in Foxstone Park near his home in Vienna, Virginia. A payment of $50,000 in cash was retrieved from another dead drop in a nature center in Arlington, Virginia.

The evidence against Hanssen was overwhelming, and he knew it. He confessed immediately and later agreed to a plea bargain in which he was spared the death penalty in exchange for cooperating fully with the FBI investigation into his crimes.

Hanssen admitted that he'd been spying off and on for more than 20 years. He started in 1979, quit in 1981 when his wife caught him (a devout Catholic, she made him go to confession but never turned him in), started again in 1985, quit when the Soviet Union collapsed in 1991, and started again in 1999. He continued spying until his arrest in 2001.

GRAYBOOB

The FBI had long assumed they were hunting a master spy, someone who knew how to cover his tracks and would be very hard to catch. They formed that impression over time as they failed to collect any incriminating evidence against Kelley (other than his jogging map), even though they were certain Kelley was the spy.

But as the investigation into Hanssen continued, the mole hunters realized just how wrong they'd been. Hanssen was smart enough not to tell the Russians his real name, but he was no master spy—in fact, he could have been caught years earlier if the people around him had been paying attention and doing their jobs. Over the years Hanssen left so many clues to his spying that he practically glowed in the dark.

✔ He used FBI phone lines and answering machines to communicate with his KGB handlers in the 1980s.

✔ When the KGB paid him cash, Hanssen sometimes counted the money at work, then deposited it in a savings account *in his own name*, in a bank less than a block from FBI headquarters in Washington, D.C.

Native to Indiana? A species of spider, *Calponia harrisonfordi*, is named for Harrison Ford.

✔ At a time when he made less than $100,000 a year, Hanssen kept a gym bag filled with $100,000 in cash in his bedroom closet. One time he left $5,000 sitting on top of his dresser. His brother-in-law, Mark Wauck, also an FBI agent, saw the unexplained cash and reported it to his superiors, also noting that Hanssen had once talked of retiring to Poland, which was then still part of the Soviet bloc. An FBI agent retiring to a Communist country? The FBI never investigated the incident.

THE PERSONAL TOUCH

✔ The FBI, and even the KGB, had assumed that Hanssen never met with any Russian agents, but they were wrong. Hanssen launched his spying career in 1979 by walking right into the offices of a Soviet trade organization that was known to be a GRU (the military version of the KGB) front and offering his services, even though he knew the office was likely to be under surveillance. When he made his first contact with the KGB in 1985, he did so by sending a letter through the U.S. mail to a known KGB officer who lived in Virginia. Both approaches were incredibly foolhardy, but Hanssen got away with it both times.

✔ In 1993 Hanssen botched an attempt to resume spying for GRU when he walked up to a GRU officer in the parking lot of the man's apartment building and tried to hand him a packet of classified documents. The officer, thinking it was an FBI sting, reported the incident to his superiors at the Russian Embassy, who lodged a formal protest with the U.S. State Department. The FBI launched an investigation—which Hanssen closely followed by hacking into FBI computers—but the investigation was unsuccessful.

In 1992 Hanssen hacked into a computer to gain access to Soviet counterintelligence documents. Then, fearing he might be caught, he reported his own hacking and claimed he was testing the computer's security. His colleagues and superiors believed his story and were grateful to him for pointing out the weakness in the system. The incident was never investigated.

AT THE STATE DEPARTMENT

But perhaps the most inexplicable breach of security came in 1994, when Hanssen was transferred to an FBI post at the State Department's Office of Foreign Missions. As the Justice Department later described it, Hanssen was "wholly unsupervised" by either the State Department or the FBI for the next six years. In that time he didn't receive a single job performance review. Hanssen spent much of his time out of the office visiting friends and colleagues; when he did go to the office he spent his time surfing the Internet, reading classified documents, and watching movies on his laptop. Then he resumed spying for the Russians.

✔ In 1997 Hanssen asked for a computer that would connect him to the FBI's Automatic Case Support System (ACS) and got it, even though his job didn't call for it. Soon after he got the computer, Hanssen was caught installing password breaker software that allowed him to hack into password-protected files. When confronted, Hanssen said he was trying to hook up a color printer. His story went unchallenged and the incident was never investigated.

✔ Using the ACS systems, Hanssen downloaded hundreds, if not thousands, of classified documents and gave them to the Russians. At the same time, he repeatedly scanned the FBI's files for his own name, address, and the locations of his various dead drops to check whether the FBI was onto him.

✔ He also stumbled onto the FBI's investigation of Brian Kelley. Assuming that Kelley, too, was a mole, he warned the Russians about the investigation. Then he did what he could to keep the FBI focused on Kelley, so that he could continue his own spying.

SUMMING IT UP

In the years that Hanssen spied for the Russians, he handed over thousands of America's most important military and intelligence secrets. He revealed the identities of scores of secret Russian sources, at least three of whom were executed, and he caused hundreds of millions of dollars in damage to American intelligence programs. Hanssen also sold computer software to the Russians that allowed them to track CIA and FBI activities. Someone in Russia then sold it to Al-Qaeda, which may have used it to track the CIA's search for Osama Bin Laden.

Hanssen was paid $600,000 for his efforts (and promised that another $800,000 was waiting for him in a Russian bank). He is the most damaging spy in FBI history and possibly in the history of the United States.

FAILING GRADE

After Hanssen's arrest, the inspector general of the Justice Department launched an investigation into how the mole hunt had gone so wrong and how Hanssen had been able to spy for so long without attracting suspicion.

In August 2003, the inspector general issued a scathing report condemning the FBI mole hunters for focusing on the CIA without seriously considering the possibility that the mole might be in the FBI, especially since most of the biggest secrets known to have been compromised had come from the FBI. (The mole hunters' explanation for how CIA agent Brian Kelley could have known so many FBI secrets: they thought he was seducing female FBI employees and selling *their* secrets to the Soviets.)

THE HONOR SYSTEM

The inspector general's report also faulted the FBI for "decades of neglect" of its own internal security. Before Hanssen's arrest, the Bureau operated on what was effectively the honor system: in his 25-year career, Hanssen never once had to take a lie detector test or submit to a financial background investigation, which might have turned up the KGB cash he was depositing in banks near FBI headquarters in his own name.

Hanssen had virtually unlimited access to the FBI's most sensitive material—over the years he handed over thousands of original, numbered documents to the Soviets and no one had noticed they were missing. He also had unrestricted, unmonitored access to the ACS computer system, which gave him access to thousands more documents. The ACS software did have an audit feature that would have revealed Hanssen's searches for classified information or for references to himself, but the audit feature was rarely, if ever, used. Hanssen knew it and felt secure enough to conduct thousands of unauthorized and incriminating searches over the years.

AFTERMATH

• **The FBI.** No one involved in the Kelley/Hanssen mole hunt was disciplined or fired from the FBI, although several agents were promoted. The FBI says it has tightened security since the Hanssen arrest. The Bureau's ACS computer system was scheduled to be replaced by a new $170 million software program called Virtual

Case File in 2003. As of January 2005 only 10 percent of the system was in place, and the system was so flawed that the FBI was weighing whether to scrap the entire project and start over again.

• **Robert Hanssen.** On July 6, 2001, Hanssen pleaded guilty to 15 counts of espionage, conspiracy to commit espionage, and conspiracy; he was sentenced to life in prison without the possibility of parole. He was supposed to cooperate with U.S. investigators, but he flunked a lie detector test when he was asked, "Have you told the truth?" So instead of being sent to a high-security prison, where he would have had some freedom of movement, he was assigned to a "supermax" prison in Florence, Colorado, where he is confined to his soundproof 7' x 12' cell for 23 hours a day.

• **Bonnie Hanssen.** Because she cooperated with investigators and passed a lie detector test that showed she had no knowledge of her husband's espionage after 1981, Bonnie Hanssen was allowed to collect the widow's portion of her husband's pension and to keep their three cars and family home.

• **Brian Kelley.** After Hanssen's arrest, Kelley was completely exonerated. He returned to the CIA and received an apology from the FBI. He did, however, lose his covert status when his identity was revealed by an investigative reporter writing a book about the Hanssen case. At last report he was still working at the CIA, teaching spy catchers how to avoid making the same mistakes that were made when he was targeted by the mole hunters.

After Kelley's identity was revealed in 2002, he went public with his concern that nothing had changed at the FBI and that the same mistakes could happen again. The mole hunters "were so overzealous, so myopic," he told the *Hartford Courant* in 2002. "If these abuses happen to us, what chance does the average citizen have to protect their civil liberties?"

*　　*　　*

A Sandwich Is Born. During World War II, Americans soldiers stationed in Europe found three items in their ration kits: peanut butter, jelly, and bread. One day, legend has it, some soldier put the three together. Proof? There is no written record of the PB&J sandwich before the war, and after the war sales of peanut butter and jelly skyrocketed in America.

The Pacific Ocean holds about 6,000,000,000,000,000,000,000 gallons of water.

GOLF TREK

Space: the final back nine. These are the voyages of astronaut Alan Shepard. His primary mission: to seek out new lies, new par-3s—to boldly golf where no man has golfed before!

STARDATE: FEBRUARY 6, 1971

The *Apollo 14* crew had been on the Moon for nearly 36 hours. At the end of the second extravehicular activity assignment, 47-year-old astronaut Alan B. Shepard, Jr. revealed that he'd smuggled on some extra equipment for the mission: the detachable head of his six-iron and two golf balls. The following transcript comes directly from official NASA records:

Shepard: Houston, while you're looking that up, you might recognize what I have in my hand as the handle for the contingency sample return. It just so happens to have a genuine six-iron on the bottom of it. In my left hand, I have a little white pellet that's familiar to millions of Americans. I'll drop it down. Unfortunately, the suit is so stiff, I can't do this with two hands, but I'm going to try a little sand-trap shot here. [His first swing misses.]

Ed Mitchell: You got more dirt than ball that time.

Shepard: Got more dirt than ball. Here we go again. [His second swing pushes the ball about three feet.]

Mission Control: That looked like a slice to me, Al.

Shepard: Here we go. Straight as a die. One more. [His third swing finally connects and sends the ball off-camera.]

Shepard: Miles and miles and miles...

Mission Control: Very good, Al.

EPILOGUE

So in addition to being the first American in space (he made his first flight in 1961), Alan Shepard was, and still is, the only human to play golf on the Moon. Actual estimates of how far his ball went—and remember this is a golfer talking—were about 300 yards. Shepard brought the club back to Earth, where it is now on display at the USGA Hall of Fame in New Jersey. The golf ball, as far as we know, is still on the Moon.

Golf lingo: a "Captain Kirk" is a shot that goes "where no man has gone before."

IT'S GREEK TO ME

Εϖερ ηεαρ σομεονε σπεωινγ φαργον ανδ ωονδερ "Ωηατ τηε ηελλ αρε τηεψ ταλκινγ αβουτ?" Σο ηασ Υνχλε ϑοην. ΗερεΠσ α παγε φορ ανψονε ωηοσε εϖερ σαιδ "ΙτΠσ Γρεεκ το με."

Γαρβαγε: 400,000 πουνδσ οφ "πιζζα σλυδγε" (φλουρ, τοματο παστε, χηεεσε, πεππερονι, ετχ.)
Λοχατιον: Ωελλστον, Οηιο
Σουρχε: Α ϑενο'σ, Ινχ., φροζεν πιζζα πλαντ
Προβλεμ: ϑενο'σ προδυχεδ σο μυχη ωαστε ιν τηειρ πιζζα φαχ–τορψ τηατ τηε λοχαλ σεωαγε σψστεμ χουλδν'τ αχχομμοδατε ιτ. Τηεψ χουλδν'τ βυρψ ιτ ειτηερ, βεχαυσε ενϖιρονμενταλ εξπερτσ σαιδ ιτ ωουλδ "μοϖε ιν τηε γρουνδ" ονχε τηεψ πυτ ιτ τηερε. Τηεψ ηαδ το τρυχκ ιτ ουτ.

Γαρβαγε: 27 ψεαρσ' ωορτη οφ ραδιοαχτιϖε δογ ποοπ
Λοχατιον: Υνκνοων
Σουρχε: Δεπαρτμεντ οφ Ενεργψ εξπεριμεντσ. Φορ αλμοστ τηρεε δεχαδεσ, τηε ΔΟΕ στυδιεδ τηε εφφεχτσ οφ ραδιατιον βψ φεεδινγ 3,700 βεαγλεσ ραδιατιον–λαδεν φοοδ. Εαχη ατε τηε φοοδ φορ α ψεαρ ανδ α ηαλφ, ανδ ωασ τηεν λεφτ το λιϖε ουτ ιτσ λιφε.
Προβλεμ: Νο ονε αντιχιπατεδ τηατ ωηιλε τηε εξπεριμεντ ωασ γοινγ ον, τηε δογ–δοο ωουλδ βε δανγερουσ ανδ ωουλδ ηαϖε το βε τρεατεδ ασ ηαζαρδουσ ωαστε. Τηεψ σαϖεδ ιτ φορ δεχαδεσ… and φιναλλψ τοοκ ιτ το α ηαζαρδουσ ωαστε φαχιλιτψ.

Γαρβαγε: 1,000 πουνδσ οφ ρασπβερρψ γελατιν ανδ 16 γαλλονσ οφ ωηιππεδ χρεαμ
Λοχατιον: Ινσιδε α χαρ ιν Προϖο, Υταη
Σουρχε: Εϖαν Ηανσεν, α στυδεντ ατ Βριγηαμ Ψουνγ Υνιϖερ–σιτψ. Ηε ωον α ραδιο χοντεστ φορ "μοστ ουτραγεουσ στυντ" βψ χυττινγ τηε ροοφ οφφ α στατιον ωαγον ανδ φιλλινγ τηε χαρ ωιτη τηε δεσσερτ.
Προβλεμ: Ηανσεν χουλδν'τ φινδ α ωαψ το γετ ριδ οφ τηε ϑελλ–Ο. Ηε φιναλλψ δροϖε το α μαλλ παρκινγ λοτ, οπενεδ ηισ χαρ δοορσ, ανδ δυμπεδ ιτ δοων α δραιν. Ηε ωασ φινεδ $500 φορ ϖιολατινγ Υταηϖσ Ωατερ Πολλυτιον Χοντρολ Αχτ.

Forgotten fad: Ancient Greek women wore cicadas on golden threads in their hair.

THE MAN WHO SAVED A BILLION LIVES

Ever heard of Norman Borlaug? Most people haven't,
yet he's credited with a truly amazing accomplishment:
saving more lives than anybody else in history.

THE POPULATION BOMB

In his 1968 best seller, *The Population Bomb*, author and biologist Paul Ehrlich wrote that "the battle to feed all of humanity is over." Ehrlich's chilling book predicted that a rapidly growing world population would soon lead to massive worldwide food shortages, especially in third-world countries. World population was just over 3.5 billion at the time and was increasing at a faster rate than food production. "In the 1970s and 1980s," Ehrlich wrote, "hundreds of millions of people will starve to death." Most experts agreed with Ehrlich's dire predictions...but they hadn't anticipated Dr. Norman Borlaug.

FARM BOY

Borlaug was born in 1914 and grew up on a farm in Saude, Iowa. In 1942 he graduated from the University of Minnesota with PhDs in plant pathology and genetics. In 1944 he was invited by the Rockefeller Foundation, a global charitable organization, and the Mexican government to head a project aimed at improving wheat production in Mexico. His assignment: to develop a more productive strain of wheat that was also resistant to stem rust, a fungal disease that was becoming a major problem in Latin America.

Borlaug chose two locations with an 8,500-foot altitude difference for his testing. He grew and crossbred thousands of different strains of wheat, and worked with the latest fertilizers, looking for plants that could grow in both environments. Reason: they had to be able to grow anywhere.

Over the next several years Borlaug was able to develop hardy, highly productive strains, but he found that the tall wheats he was using would not support the weight of the added grain. So he crossed the tall wheats with dwarf varieties that were not only

Church Street? The main street of Barbotan, France, runs through the town's church.

shorter but had thicker, stronger stems. And that was his break-through: a semi-dwarf, disease-resistant, high-output wheat. He worked incessantly to get the seeds distributed to small farmers throughout Mexico, and by 1963 Borlaug's wheat varieties made up 95 percent of the nation's total production, with a crop yield that was more than six times greater than when he'd arrived. Not only could Mexico stop importing wheat, they were now an exporter—a huge boost to any nation's nutritional and economic health, but especially to an underdeveloped one. And now Borlaug wanted to take his high-yield farming global. He wanted, he said, to secure "a temporary success in man's war against hunger and deprivation."

ANOTHER VICTORY

In 1963 the Rockefeller Foundation sent Borlaug to Pakistan and India, two nations with severe hunger and malnutrition problems. Borlaug's help was resisted at first; there was cultural opposition to new farming methods. But when acute famine struck in 1965 (1.5 million people would die by 1967), the barriers came down. And the results were incredible: by 1968 Pakistan, which just a few years earlier relied on massive grain imports, was entirely self-sufficient. By 1970 India's production had doubled and it too was getting close to self-sufficiency.

At four o'clock in the morning one day in 1970, Margaret Borlaug got a phone call. She raced out to the fields and informed her husband, already hard at work, that he had won the Nobel Peace Prize. "No, I haven't," he said. He thought it was a hoax. But he had indeed won it for having saved the lives of millions—perhaps hundreds of millions—of people in India and Pakistan and for the message it had sent to the world. "He has given us a well-founded hope," the Nobel committee said, "an alternative of peace and of life—the green revolution."

NOTHING ESCAPES CONTROVERSY

Borlaug had also been working on other grains, such as corn and rye, and in the 1980s began developing more productive strains of rice to increase production in China and Southeast Asia. He was setting up similar programs in Africa, but ran into a major hurdle: environmentalists opposed his methods. Among their charges: spreading the same few varieties of grains all over the planet is

The Latin word for "dust" is *pollen*. (It can also mean "fine flour.")

harming biodiversity; huge farms are benefiting from his techniques and killing off the small farmer; inorganic fertilizers used in the Borlaug method are harmful to the environment; and genetically engineered food is unnatural and potentially dangerous.

"Some of the environmental lobbyists are the salt of the earth," Borlaug said, "but many of them are elitists. If they lived just one month amid the misery of the developing world, as I have for fifty years, they'd be crying out for tractors and fertilizer and irrigation canals and be outraged that fashionable elitists back home were trying to deny them these things." He admitted that he would rather his work benefited small farmers, but added, "Wheat isn't political. It doesn't know that it's supposed to be producing more for poor farmers than for rich farmers." Supporters argue that Borlaug's high-yield method has actually been a boon for the environment, saving hundreds of millions of acres of wild land from being turned into farms. The controversy continues, but none of it has stopped Borlaug from his mission.

KEEP ON PLANTING

In 1984, with the help of Japanese philanthropist Ryoichi Sasakawa, Borlaug set up the Sasakawa Africa Association (SAA), training more than a million farmers throughout Africa. Result: using Borlaug seed and methods, cereal grain yields have increased from two- to four-fold.

As of 2005—at the age of 91—Norman Borlaug is still at it. He continues to work with Mexico's International Maize and Wheat Improvement Center, still heads the SAA, runs research programs, teaches young scientists, gives lectures, and, of course, still works in the field. Over his 50-plus-year career he has been credited with saving as many as a billion people from starvation, and has received numerous international awards. In May 2004, he was presented with another: at St. Mark's Episcopal Cathedral in Borlaug's college town of Minneapolis, he was shown their new "Window of Peace." The *Minneapolis Star Tribune* described the event: "He gazed upward to see the sun shining through a 30-foot-tall stained glass window. There—along with depictions of Mother Teresa, Mahatma Gandhi, and other modern-day peacemakers—was a life-size likeness of Borlaug, holding a fistful of wheat."

In 1876 every building in Jaipur, India, was painted pink for a visit by the Prince of Wales.

SO LONG, NEIGHBOR

One thing that nearly all Americans born after 1965 have in
common is that they grew up watching Mr. Rogers. He was
one of the true pioneers of children's television. We haven't
written much about him before, and when he passed
away in 2003 we decided it was time we did.

HOME FOR THE HOLIDAYS

In 1951 a college senior named Fred McFeely Rogers finished school in Florida and went home to stay with his parents in Latrobe, Pennsylvania. He wasn't exactly sure what he wanted to do with his life. For a while he wanted to be a diplomat; then he decided to become a Presbyterian minister. He'd already made plans to enroll in a seminary after college, but as soon as he arrived home he changed his mind again.

Why? Because while he was away at school, his parents had bought their first TV set. Television was still very new in the early 1950s, and not many people had them yet. When Rogers got home he watched it for the very first time. He was fascinated by the new medium but also disturbed by some of the things he saw. One thing in particular offended him very deeply. It was "horrible," as he put it, so horrible that it altered the course of his life.

What was it that bothered him so much? "I saw people throwing pies in each other's faces," Rogers remembered. "Such demeaning behavior."

KID STUFF

You (and Uncle John) may like it when clowns throw pies and slap each other in the face, but Fred Rogers was appalled. He thought TV could have a lot more to offer than pie fights and other silliness, if only someone would try. "I thought, 'I'd really like to try my hand at that, and see what I could do,'" Rogers recalled. So he moved to New York and got a job at NBC, working first as an associate producer and later as a director.

Then in 1953, he learned about a new experimental TV station being created in Pittsburgh. Called WQED, it was the country's first community-sponsored "public television" station. WQED

The squiggle over the "n" in mañana is called a *tilde*.

wasn't even on the air yet, and there was no guarantee that an educational TV station that depended on donations from viewers to pay for programming would ever succeed. No matter—Rogers quit his secure job at NBC, moved to Pittsburgh with his wife, Joanne, and joined the station.

"I thought, 'What a wonderful institution to nourish people,'" Rogers recalled. "My friends thought I was nuts."

LOW-INCOME NEIGHBORHOOD

When Rogers arrived at WQED in 1953, the station had just four employees and only two of them, Rogers and a secretary named Josie Carey, were interested in children's programming. The two created their own hour-long show called *The Children's Corner* and paid for all of the staging, props, and scenery (mostly pictures painted on paper backdrops), out of their own meager $75-a-week salaries.

Because *The Children's Corner* had to be done on the cheap, Rogers and Carey decided that much of the show would have to revolve around showing educational films that they obtained for free. Rogers was in charge of hustling up the free films and playing the organ off camera during the broadcast; Carey would host the show, sing, and introduce the films.

LUCKY BREAK

That was how *The Children's Corner* was *supposed* to work, but the plan fell apart about two minutes into their very first broadcast. The problem wasn't that Rogers couldn't scrounge up any free films, it was that the films he *did* manage to get were so old and brittle that they were prone to breaking when played. Sure enough, on the first day of the show, on WQED's first day on the air, the first film broke.

Remember, this was before the invention of videotape, when television shows were broadcast live—so when the film broke, the entire show came to a screeching halt. *On the air.* In the broadcast industry this is known as "dead air"—the TV cameras are still on, and the folks at home are still watching, but there's nothing happening onscreen. Nothing at all.

PAPER TIGER

At that moment Rogers happened to be standing behind a paper

---

backdrop that had been painted to look like a clock. He quickly looked around and spotted "Daniel," a striped tiger puppet that the station's general manager, Dorothy Daniel, had given him the night before as a party favor at the station's launch party.

"When the first film broke, I just poked the puppet through the paper," Rogers remembered years later, "and it happened to be a clock where I poked him through. And he just said, 'It's 5:02 and Columbus discovered America in 1492.' And that was the first thing I ever said on the air. Necessity was the mother of that invention, because it hadn't been planned."

The puppet worked and the old films didn't, so *The Children's Corner* became an educational puppet show. Daniel Striped Tiger, who lives in a clock, remained a fixture on Rogers's shows for the rest of his broadcast career. Numerous other characters, including King Friday XIII, Lady Elaine Fairchilde, and X the Owl all made their debut on *The Children's Corner*.

NEIGHBORHOOD WATCH

The Children's Corner stayed on the air for seven years; then in 1963 Rogers accepted an offer from the Canadian Broadcasting Corporation to host a 15-minute show called *Misterogers*, the first show in which he actually appeared on camera. (That year he also became an ordained Presbyterian minister.)

By 1965 *Misterogers* was airing in Canada and in the eastern United States, but it had the same problem that *The Children's Corner* had—not enough money. *Misterogers* ran out of funds and was slated for cancellation...until parents found out: when they learned the show was going off the air, they raised such a stink that the Sears Roebuck Foundation and National Educational Television (now known as the Public Broadcasting Service, or PBS), kicked in $150,000 apiece to keep the show on the air.

Lengthened to a full half hour and renamed *Mister Rogers' Neighborhood*, the show was first broadcast nationwide on February 19, 1968.

INNER CHILD

Very early in his broadcasting career, Rogers drew up a list of things he wanted to encourage in the children who watched his show. Some of the items on that list: self-esteem, self-control, imagination, creativity, curiosity, appreciation of diversity, cooperation, tolerance for waiting, and persistence. *How* Rogers encouraged these things in his young viewers was heavily influenced by his own childhood experiences:

• **His grandfather.** Many of the most memorable things Rogers said to children were inspired by things his own grandfather, Fred Brooks McFeely, said to him. "I think it was when I was leaving one time to go home after our time together that my grandfather said to me, 'You know, you made this day a really special day. Just by being yourself. There's only one person in the world like you. And I happen to like you just the way you are,'" Rogers remembered. "That just went right into my heart. And it never budged." (Rogers named Mr. McFeely, the show's Speedy Delivery messenger character, after his grandfather.)

• **The Land of Make-Believe.** Fred Rogers was a sickly kid who came down with just about every childhood disease imaginable from chicken pox to scarlet fever. He spent a lot of time in bed, quarantined on doctors' orders. To amuse himself, he played with puppets and invented imaginary worlds for them to live in. "I'm sure that was the beginning of a much later neighborhood of make-believe," Rogers said.

• **Explanations.** Like most children, when Rogers was very little, he was frightened by unfamiliar things—being alone, starting school, getting a haircut, visiting a doctor's office, etc. "I liked to be told about things before I had to do them," he remembered, so explaining new and unfamiliar things became a central part of the show. (On one episode he even brought on actress Margaret Hamilton, who had played the Wicked Witch of the West in *The Wizard of Oz*, to explain that she was just pretending and that kids didn't need to be afraid.)

• **Sweaters.** Rogers got most of his sweaters from his mother, who knitted him a new one every year for Christmas. He wore them all on his show.

• **Sneakers.** Those date back to his days on *The Children's Corner*—"I had to run across the studio floor to get from the puppet set to the organ," Rogers explained. "I didn't want to make a lot of noise by running around in ordinary shoes."

Do you know how long it takes the Earth to go around the sun? 46% of Americans don't.

GOODBYE, NEIGHBOR

Rogers taped nearly 900 episodes of *Mr. Rogers' Neighborhood* over its more than 30 years on the air. They're still broadcast by more than 300 public television stations around the United States as well as in Canada, the Philippines, Guam, and other countries around the world. Videotapes of the show are used to teach English to non-native speakers (singer Ricky Martin credits Mr. Rogers with teaching him to speak English).

Rogers retired from producing new episodes of the show in December 2000, and the last new episode aired in August 2001. He came out of retirement briefly in 2002 to record public service announcements advising parents on how to help children deal with the anniversary of the September 11th attacks. He made his last public appearance on January 1, 2003, when he served as Grand Marshal of the Tournament of Roses Parade and tossed the coin for the Rose Bowl Game. Mr. Rogers passed away from stomach cancer two months later.

THOUGHTS FROM MR. ROGERS

• "The world is not always a kind place. That's something children learn for themselves, whether we want them to or not, but it's something they really need our help to understand."

• "Anything we can do to help foster the intellect and spirit and emotional growth of our fellow human beings, that is our job. Those of us who have this particular vision must continue against all odds."

• "People don't come up to me to talk about the weather. I've even had a child come up to me and not even say hello, but instead say right out, 'Mr. Rogers, my grandmother's in the hospital.'"

• "So many people have grown up with the *Neighborhood*, I'm just their dad coming along. You know, it's really fun to go through life with this face."

*　　*　　*

INCENTIVE TO WIN?

At the end of every New York Yankees home game, the P.A. system plays the song "New York, New York": the Frank Sinatra version if they win...and the Liza Minelli version if they lose.

The French Poodle isn't French and the Great Dane isn't Danish. They're both from Germany.

THE STRANGEST DISASTER OF THE 20TH CENTURY, PT. III

Natural disasters aren't uncommon. Unfortunately, we often read about devastation caused by floods, hurricanes, and earthquakes. But how often do you hear about death and destruction caused by a giant burp? (Part II of the story is on page 379.)

CLOUD OF DOOM

Cattle herders graze their animals on the hills above Lake Nyos, and after the lake disgorged as much as 80% of its massive store of CO_2 in one big burst, dead cattle were found as high as 300 feet above the lake, indicating that the suffocating cloud shot at least that high before settling back onto the surface. Then the gas poured over the crater's edge into the valleys below, traveling at an estimated 45 miles per hour.

For people living in the villages closest to the lake, death was almost inevitable. A few people on hillsides had the presence of mind to climb to higher ground; one man who saw his neighbors drop like flies jumped on his motorcycle and managed to keep ahead of the gas as he sped to safety. These were the lucky few. Most people didn't realize the danger until they were being overcome by the gas. Even if they had, it would have been impossible to outrun such a fast-moving cloud.

CURIOSITY KILLED THE CAT

In villages farther away from the lake, people had a better chance of survival, especially if they ignored the noise the lake made as it disgorged its CO_2. Some survivors said it sounded like a gunshot or an explosion; others described it as a rumble. But people who stepped outside their homes to see where the noise had come from, or to see what had caused the rotten egg smell (a common smell "hallucination" associated with CO_2 poisoning) quickly collapsed and died right on their own doorsteps. The sight of these first victims passing out often brought other members of the household to the door, where they, too, were overcome...and killed.

People who were inside with their windows and doors shut had a better chance of surviving. There were even cases where enough CO_2 seeped into homes to smother people who were lying down asleep, but not enough to kill the people who were standing up and had their heads above the gas. Some of these survivors did not even realize anything unusual had happened until they checked on their sleeping loved ones and discovered they were already dead.

AN OUNCE OF PREVENTION

The disaster at Lake Nyos was only the second such incident in recorded history—the 1984 incident at Lake Monoun was the first. To date, scientists believe that only three lakes in the entire world, Nyos, Monoun, and a third lake called Lake Kivu on the border of Congo and Rwanda, accumulate deadly amounts of dissolved CO_2 at great depths.

It had taken about a year to figure out what had happenend at Nyos. Then, when it became clear that the lake was filling with CO_2 again, the government of Cameroon evacuated all the villages within 18 miles of the lake and razed them to prevent their inhabitants from coming back until the lake could be made safe.

Scientists spent the next decade trying to figure out a way to safely release the gas before disaster struck again. They eventually settled on a plan to sink a 5½-inch diameter tube down more than 600 feet, to just above the floor of the lake. Then, when some of the water from the bottom was pumped up to the top of the tube, it would rise high enough in the tube for the CO_2 to come out of solution and form bubbles, which would cause it to shoot out the top of the tube, blasting water and gas more than 150 feet into the sky. Once it got started, the siphon effect would cause the reaction to continue indefinitely, or at least until the CO_2 ran out. A prototype was installed and tested in 1995, and after it proved to be safe, a permanent tube was installed in 2001.

RACE AGAINST TIME

As of the fall of 2006 the tube was still in place and releasing more than 700 million cubic feet of CO_2 into the air each year. That's a little bit more than enters the lake in the same amount of time. Between 2001 and 2006, the CO_2 levels in Lake Nyos dropped 13%.

But the scientists who study the lake are concerned that 13% is too small an amount. The lake still contains more CO_2 than was released in the 1986 disaster, and as if that's not bad enough, a natural dam on the north side of the lake is eroding and could fail in as little as five years. If the dam collapses, the disaster of 1986 may prove to be just a small taste of things to come: In the event of a dam failure, 50 million cubic meters of water could pour out of the lake, drowning as many as 10,000 people as it washes through the valleys below. That's only the beginning—releasing that much water from the lake would cause the level of the lake to drop as much as 130 feet, removing the water pressure that keeps the CO_2 at the bottom of the lake and causing a release of gas even more catastrophic than the devastation of 1986.

SOLUTION

Scientists and engineers have devised a plan for shoring up the natural dam with concrete, and it's believed that the installation of as few as four more siphon tubes could reduce the CO_2 in the lake to safe levels in as little as four years. The scientists are hard at work trying to find the funding to do it, and there's no time to waste: "We could have a gas burst tomorrow that is bigger than either [the Lake Monoun or the Lake Nyos] disaster," says Dr. George Kling, a University of Michigan ecologist who has been studying the lake for 20 years. "Every day we wait is just an accumulation of the probability that something bad is going to happen."

*　　*　　*

THIRSTY?

Pete Conklin worked as a lemonade vendor for the Mabie Circus in the 1850s. One hot day, business was so brisk he had to make a batch in a hurry and used a bucket of water from a nearby tent. When he poured his first glass, he noticed the lemonade was pink. Conklin immediately began selling his mistake as "strawberry lemonade." So what made it pink? A circus performer's red tights had been soaking in the bucket of water Conklin had used.

The Arctic tern flies as far as 10,500 miles when it migrates.

BANJO RISING

When you hear banjo picking, images of mountains and barn dances come to mind. It may surprise you, then, to learn that this seemingly most "American" of instruments began as an African folk instrument ...and came to the New World aboard slave ships.

FIRST CONTACT

While traveling through the Gambra River area of West Africa in 1620, British explorer Richard Jobson noticed some local people playing musical instruments he'd never seen before. He wrote about one of them in his journal:

> That which is most common in use is made of a great gourd, and a necke thereunto fastned, but they have no manner of fret, and the strings they are either such as the place yeeldes, or their invention can attaine to make, being very unapt to yeeld a sweete and musi-call sound, notwithstanding with pinnes they winde and bring to agree in tunable notes, having not above six strings upon their greatest instrument.

Although that "great gourd" was the first written mention of the banjo in the Western world, nearly every ancient culture had a musical instrument made of a hollow drum (a gourd or turtle shell) attached to a neck (a stick), with strings across it. In Africa, these instruments were known by many similar names: *banjar, banjil, banza, bangoe,* and *banshaw.*

Of all the early drum-and-string instruments that the Africans played, the most likely direct ancestor of the American banjo was the *akonting,* which originated near Gambia. Many early North American slaves came from Gambia and, according to music historians, the bamboo used to make the akonting's neck was called *bangoc,* pronounced "ban-joo."

SPREADING THE SOUND

While the akonting may have been the banjo's predecessor, it's doubtful that any of them made their way to North America. Most African slaves arrived in the New World with few or no possessions, so they constructed new instruments the same way they had for centuries—with whatever materials they could find. In

Cole Porter's original lyrics to "I Get a Kick Out of You" referenced the Lindberghs....

America, they often used a bowl-shaped calabash gourd with the top half sawed off and the skin of a groundhog, goat, or cat stretched tightly around it to make a drum. The final touch was a fretless wooden neck that held three or four strings, usually made from gut, twine, or hemp.

To the white colonists, the banjo was an exotic oddity, but many were drawn to its music in spite of its reputation as a "slave instrument." In time, slaves taught many white people to play it. By the mid-1700s, white banjo players had become popular entertainers in traveling music shows.

THE SWEENEY MINSTRELS
The first acclaimed American banjoist was Joel Walker Sweeney. When he was 13 years old, he learned how to play the banjo from slaves on his father's farm in the Virginia town of Appomattox Court House. A gifted musician and natural showman, Sweeney traveled around Virginia and North Carolina in the 1830s, putting on shows and charging a few pennies for admission. He could sing, dance, imitate animal sounds, and, legend has it, play the fiddle and banjo at the same time. Eventually, Sweeney began wearing blackface (made from the ash of burned cork) and performing in minstrel shows—troupes of white performers who sang and played songs, performed skits, and did magic tricks. And always at the heart of his minstrel show was the banjo. In the 1840s, the Sweeney Minstrels spread the banjo sound even farther when they toured New York City, England, Scotland, and Ireland. Sweeney also popularized the rhythmic "clawhammer" playing style that the slaves had taught him—hitting the strings hard with the fingernails on the downstroke, then strumming with the thumbnail on the upward motion. Clawhammer would be the standard playing style for the next 50 years.

FOUR STRINGS OR FIVE?
Sweeney is often credited with another innovation that's still in use: the five-string banjo. Most early banjos had only four strings, but Sweeney added a fifth string to his instrument to get a fuller sound. The result was something like the modern banjo: four strings that went all the way from the bridge to the end of the neck, and a shorter, high-pitched "drone" string that ran to a tuning peg only

halfway down the neck. In the 1840s, Sweeney contracted with a Baltimore drum maker named William Boucher to build the first five-string banjos available for sale. The modern banjo was beginning to take shape: The gourd was replaced with an open-backed drum, and steel strings took the place of gut, producing a louder, brighter sound. But two more ingredients for the modern banjo—the resonator and the fretted neck—were still many years away.

A BANJO CULTURE

Another of Sweeney's lasting legacies was his enthusiastic work as an instructor: He taught the banjo to scores of people, some of whom became famous players themselves. Billy Whitlock, a Sweeney student, led the Virginia Minstrels (along with Dan Emmet, who wrote "Dixie") to great success in New York City, where Sweeney soon followed and found a built-in audience. Whitlock, in turn, taught Tom Briggs, who soon became a famous picker, but more importantly published the *Briggs Banjo Instructor*, the instrument's first instruction book (still in print today).

By the time the Civil War broke out, banjo playing was so popular that many army regiments had their own minstrel groups to keep up morale. Sweeney's own son, Sam, made a name for himself as Confederate General Jeb Stuart's personal banjo player, and performed shows for the Army of Northern Virginia. And Sweeney's students—now much in demand as entertainers—all added their own style to the banjo, creating a staggering array of strumming patterns and tunings. Banjo music was growing more diverse every year.

"THE DEPTH OF POPULAR DEGRADATION"

After the Civil War ended, the instrument's popularity continued to spread, but mainly in rural areas. Most of high society shunned the twangy banjo, preferring the guitar, which had a fuller sound and was easier to play because it had only one standard tuning, while the banjo could have dozens. Once associated with slaves, the banjo had become a symbol of the poor and uneducated. Soon, even the press was scorning it. The *Boston Daily Evening Voice* linked the banjo to "the depth of popular degradation fit only for the jig-dancing lower classes of the community."

Trying to bring the instrument more respectability, many players

Experts say pounding grain was probably the first intentional rhythm created by humans.

cut back on the rhythmic clawhammer styles and developed more refined fingerpicking techniques similar to those of the guitar. Instead of playing in restaurants, saloons, and train stations, the banjo players of the late 1800s played in people's homes, leading to the fad of "parlor music" and to what some have called the banjo's "classical period." (Before the phonograph and the radio, parlor music was the only way for nonmusicians to hear music at home.)

One parlor musician, Henry C. Dobson, made his mark on the music world by asking a banjo builder to add the last pieces to the modern banjo: frets for more precise intonation, a resonator for amplification, and a tone ring—a metal shell in the banjo's body that helped balance the sound. Now the banjo could do anything a guitar could do...almost.

STEWART'S BANJEAU

As the banjo's popularity began rising again, some players thought that the instrument belonged in one place it hadn't yet been: the classical orchestra. Leading the charge was Samuel Swain Stewart, a Philadelphia instrument maker who had built thousands of banjos. Stewart believed that the banjo should be taught to educated musicians via sheet music, unlike the learn-by-ear method of the early minstrels and slaves. So he distributed banjo sheet music and instruction manuals to music and book stores all over the country. He also published a magazine, *Stewart's Banjo and Guitar Journal*, which included articles like "The Banjo Philosophically: Its Construction, Its Capabilities, Its Evolution, Its Place as a Musical Instrument, Its Possibilities, and Its Future." Stewart even tried to change the spelling to "banjeau" in an attempt to make the instrument sound more refined.

Stewart also used his considerable wealth to sponsor many of the 19th century's greatest banjo players, including Horace Weston, a freeborn black man from Connecticut. A virtuoso player, Weston started in minstrel groups, but later found great success as a parlor musician—so much, in fact, that he became the first African American musician to headline a show in Europe when he toured with a production of *Uncle Tom's Cabin* in 1873.

AIN'T GOT THAT SWING

By 1900 the banjo was nearly as popular in America as the guitar,

Oldest female artist with a #1 song on the Billboard Hot 100: Cher, age 52, with "Believe" (1999).

and its repertoire of music was diverse enough to please almost any audience. But the clawhammer strumming style that had started it all was now nearly extinct. A 1915 article in the *New York Clipper* pulled no punches: "The banjo playing of the old-timer was something that would not be tolerated at present. It was banging and twanging and plunketty plunk, used probably for plantation songs of a hilarious or noisy order." Clawhammer style was *supposed* to be noisy, to help the banjo project over a band. But the style had outgrown its usefulness: The new plectrum banjo (designed to be played with a guitar pick), along with resonators and steel strings, had made the instrument loud enough to be heard in dance bands. And the widespread use of fingerpicks, which made the clawhammer style obsolete, was pushing the instrument to the peak of its popularity.

If the banjo was so popular 100 years ago, why is it a niche instrument today, associated primarily with country and bluegrass music? Mostly because of jazz. When jazz bands became popular in the 1920s and '30s, the guitar, with its lighter-gauged strings, proved better than the banjo for creating the complex rhythms needed. And the guitar blended better with the jazz sound compared to the twang of the banjo, which tended to overwhelm other instruments. That isn't to say there weren't banjo players in early jazz bands—there were. But they were steadily being replaced by guitarists. In order to survive, the banjo had to travel a different road.

BLUEGRASS

By the time of the Great Depression in the 1930s, the banjo craze had all but ended. And when factory closures halted the production of steel strings, it nearly disappeared altogether. It wasn't until the postwar boom of the 1940s that the banjo would make yet another resurgence.

That resurgence came mainly from the work of one man: Earl Scruggs. Born in North Carolina in 1924, Scruggs grew up playing hillbilly songs in a musical family, and was taught a three-finger banjo technique by a North Carolina picker named Snuffy Jenkins. Scruggs took this style and sped it up, creating his own specialty, now called "Scruggs style." In the 1940s, Scruggs and his new style led to a new genre of music. In traditional old-timey music, every

---

The first European instrument to reach China was a harpsichord presented...

instrument takes the melody and supports it. If there is a solo, it's usually performed by one player, only once in a song. In jazz, however, the players trade off—one instrument takes the lead while the rest take the melody, and every player gets at least one solo in any given song. Scruggs fused the sound of old-timey music with the style of jazz by making the banjo a lead instrument. And voilà—modern bluegrass was born.

Although the bluegrass genre can be traced back to 1939 with the formation of Bill Monroe and his Blue Grass Boys, the style took off when Scruggs joined the band in 1945. He proved that when let loose, the banjo is a formidable instrument for soloing. Scruggs became the 20th century's most famous banjo player and has influenced scores of pickers after him.

KEEP ON PICKIN'

Shortly after it found a new home in bluegrass, the banjo became the center of another popular subgenre in the late 1950s: folk music. Pete Seeger, a Harvard dropout, helped start the folk movement in the 1940s, and he did it on the banjo. Seeger favored "roots" music, pre-bluegrass slave and minstrel styles such as clawhammer. Combining these old-style sounds with pop-song structures and socially conscious lyrics, Seeger wrote or cowrote such folk classics as "Where Have All the Flowers Gone?" and "If I Had a Hammer," and adapted the spiritual hymn "We Shall Overcome"—which later became the unofficial anthem for the civil rights movement.

In the 1960s, the banjo branched into another genre when a New York teenager named Béla Fleck first heard Earl Scruggs's banjo playing on the theme song to *The Beverly Hillbillies*. By the 1970s, Fleck was hooked, and became a banjo virtuoso by his mid-twenties. He would go on to combine bluegrass with jazz fusion, and is one of today's best-known banjo players, introducing the instrument to a whole new generation.

BACK HOME AND BEYOND

All through its fragmented and tumultuous history, one place where the banjo never went out of style was the South. "The banjo fit in perfectly with the Southerners' love of homemade music," writes Mike Seeger, one of the 20th century's most prolific banjo pickers (and half-brother of Pete Seeger). "Banjo playing became a fad in the North, but in the South this robust expression of African American tradition became a vital part of Anglo American music."

Today, the banjo is as versatile as ever, picking its way into many musical genres, from rock (Beck) to blues (Taj Mahal), and even to eclectic "world" music (Kaleidoscope). In recent years, there's been a resurgence of African American banjo pickers: Players such as Otis Taylor, Alvin Youngblood Hart, Don Vappie, the Ebony Hillbillies, and Guy Davis are bringing the instrument full circle, proving that the "great gourd" with the humble origins is alive and well.

*　　*　　*

RANDOM ORIGINS OF ROCK BAND NAMES

THE B-52'S. They weren't named after an Air Force jet. "B-52" is a Southern term for a tall bouffant hairdo, which the women of the band wore early in the group's career.

GENESIS. Named by record producer Jonathan King, who signed the band in 1967. He chose the name because they were the first "serious" band he'd produced, and his signing them marked the official beginning of his production career.

CREAM. Eric Clapton, Jack Bruce, and Ginger Baker considered themselves the cream of the crop of British blues musicians.

THEY MIGHT BE GIANTS. Named after an obscure 1971 B-movie starring George C. Scott and Joanne Woodward.

RADIOHEAD. They were originally called On a Friday (because they practiced on Fridays). But the EMI execs who signed them in 1992 feared that On a Friday might be confusing to some, so the band quickly chose a new name. Their inspiration: an obscure Talking Heads song called "Radio Head."

DAVID BOWIE. David Robert Jones changed his last name to Bowie to avoid being mistaken for Davy Jones of the Monkees. He chose Bowie after the hunting knife he'd seen in American films.

Ice Cube's real first name is O'Shea. He was named after O.J. Simpson.

GIMLI GLIDER, PART III

Here's the final installment of our story on the world's largest unintentional glider. (Part II starts on page 390.)

MEANWHILE, BACK IN COACH
So how were the passengers holding up while all this was going on? Surprisingly well. One of the nice things about this new Boeing 767 was that its engines were so quiet and the cabin so well insulated for sound that few passengers were even aware at first that both engines had stopped.

It wasn't until the flight attendants began preparing everyone for an emergency landing that passengers realized the situation was serious. People were instructed to remove their eyeglasses, dentures, and any sharp objects from their pockets and to fasten their seatbelts low and tight around their hips. Then they were told to assume the "crash position"—arms crossed, hands holding the top of the seatback in front of them, head resting on their arms—and prepare for a rough landing. In the galley, flight attendants were tossing silverware, coffee pots, food trays, liquor bottles, and any other loose items into the trash to keep them from becoming deadly projectiles.

Meanwhile, the air traffic controllers in Winnipeg had already called ahead to the Gimli police and fire departments, and they were racing to the old Air Force base as Flight 143 headed in for a landing. People on the ground got their first hint that something unusual was happening when a strangely silent jumbo jet suddenly sailed into view, flying very low over buildings and the local golf course. Terrified Gimlians scattered in all directions.

LOOK OUT BELOW

Had anyone other than Captain Pearson been flying the plane, there's a good chance that Flight 143 would have already crashed. But, on top of being one of Air Canada's best jet pilots, he was also a licensed glider pilot with more than 10 years experience. It turned out that he needed every minute of that experience as he tried to wrestle the blind, crippled jumbo jet safely to the ground.

Pearson had a few mechanical backup instruments to help him, including a magnetic compass, an artificial horizon (to help him keep the plane level) an altimeter (which gives the altitude), and an airspeed indicator. But since gliding a 767 to a landing had never been attempted before, what Pearson had to rely on more than any instrument...was his own judgment.

He knew that if he came in too fast, he'd send the plane hurtling off the end of the runway into whatever lay beyond. Coming in too slow was even worse—the 767 could stall and nosedive straight into the ground. He had to glide in at just the right speed. But what *was* the proper glide speed? He had no way of knowing...he was going to have to guess.

The normal landing speed for a 767 is between 115 and 153 knots (between 130 and 175 mph), depending upon the total weight of the aircraft including the passengers, cargo, and fuel. Pearson finally settled on 180 knots (about 205 mph). Coming in that fast was likely to blow out tires on the landing gear, but he decided he couldn't risk coming in any slower.

UH...ABOUT THE LANDING GEAR

As Pearson approached the Gimli landing strip, he suddenly realized he was coming in too high. He had to slow the plane down, which would cause it to lose altitude. Otherwise he risked overshooting the runway. To increase drag and slow the plane down, he told Quintal to lower the landing gear. Quintal pulled the lever to the down position and...nothing happened. The landing gear was powered by the hydraulic system, but the RAT (the pinwheel thingy) wasn't generating enough hydraulic pressure to lower them.

Luckily there's an emergency method: a switch that pulls the pins out of the landing gear doors. The landing gear then drops down and slams into the locked position. Quintal flipped the switch, and he and Pearson listened as the left and right landing gears noisily dropped and locked. But what about the nose gear? Suddenly another warning light came on in the cockpit—the nose gear had not locked into place, and there was no time to fix it.

SPIN CONTROL

Remember how the RAT propeller spins as the air rushes past it? Well, there's a catch—as the airplane comes in for a landing, the air speed drops, the propeller spins slower, and less hydraulic pressure is generated. That's why the landing gear didn't come down when it was supposed to, and it's also why the control yoke and rudder pedals were becoming increasingly stiff and unwieldy just when Captain Pearson needed them most.

More bad news: even with the landing gear down, Pearson was still coming in too fast. He wrestled the plane into a glider maneuver called a sideslip: he whipped the control yoke hard to the left, as if he were preparing to make a left turn, and practically stood on the right rudder pedal as if he were turning right. The effect of this maneuver was to greatly increase the drag, reducing airspeed. But it also caused the left wing to dip dangerously low to the ground. Witnesses say Pearson held this position until the wingtip was about 40 feet off the ground...*traveling at 180 knots.*

NO PLACE FOR A PICNIC
Could anything else go wrong? Yes. As you'll remember, Gimli Air Force Base had two parallel runways, 32 Left and 32 Right, one of which was still used by private aircraft. Captain Pearson didn't know which was which but he had to pick one, so he picked 32 Left. He held the 767 in the tilted position until the very last second, then leveled off the jet and prepared to land.

He had no power, no instruments, and hardly any brakes; the plane was coming in too fast; the controls were stiff, the nose gear was not locked into position; and some of the tires on the landing gear were certain to burst on impact. So what did Pearson see at the far end of the runway just moments before touching down? Race cars. Lots of race cars.

Winnipeg Air Traffic Control had told him that one of the runways was still used for aircraft, but what they didn't tell him (because they probably didn't know) was that the other runway—the one he was trying to land on—had been converted into the straightaway of an auto club racetrack. The Winnipeg Sports Car Club had held a race earlier in the day. The race was over, but the drivers, their families, and their cars—plus campers, tents, coolers, and barbecues—were all at the end of the runway. They were having a cookout.

Pearson didn't see the cars or the people until the very last minute, and because the 767 was coming in so silently, surprisingly few people saw the plane. Many who did see it coming in—tilted with its left wing nearly scraping the ground—were too stunned to move. But it didn't matter: there was no way everyone could have cleared the runway in time. Pearson was going to have to land the plane in a much shorter distance than he'd planned.

TOUCHDOWN!

Sure enough, when the 767 hit the runway, two tires on the right landing gear burst. But enough of them remained intact for Pearson to maintain control of the aircraft. He literally stood on the brake pedals, throwing his own weight into slowing down the plane.

Jet aircraft land on the rear wheels first; then, as the plane loses speed, the nose drops and the nose gear touches down. As Pearson had feared, when Flight 143's unlocked nose gear hit the runway, it buckled and collapsed, and the nose of the plane slammed onto the runway.

But that equipment failure may have been a blessing in disguise. The fuselage of a jumbo jet is engineered to be tough enough to land on its belly if necessary, and that's exactly what happened: the plane skidded and scraped down the runway, throwing up a cloud of sparks and smoke. But it also slowed the aircraft dramatically.

BRAKE DANCING

The plane was down, but Pearson still had to steer it to keep it centered on the runway. Normally you steer with the nose wheel, but since that was out of commission, he steered by shifting his weight from one brake pedal to the other, braking hard left when the plane veered to the right, and hard right when it veered to the left. Suddenly he noticed a metal guardrail off to one side. He headed for it. The 767 made a heck of a racket as it sheared one guardrail post after another, but the maneuver helped slow the plane even more.

The 767 finally came to a halt about halfway down the runway, 500 feet away from the auto club. The terrifying glide into Gimli lasted for what must have seemed an eternity, but only 29 minutes had passed since the first amber warning light came on in the cockpit. The time was 8:38 p.m. Had Flight 143 been scheduled for just an hour later, it would have been too dark to land.

A painting of a guide dog leading a blind man was found in Pompeii dating from 79 B.C

TERRA FIRMA

The nose-down landing kicked up so many sparks that some insulation in the belly of the plane caught fire, but members of the race car club ran over with their fire extinguishers and put it out. Meanwhile, the flight attendants were working to evacuate the plane as quickly and safely as possible. Evacuating from the front of the plane was a snap—passengers just had a short jump onto the tarmac. The drop from the emergency exits at the rear was much longer, and a few people suffered minor injuries as they escaped the plane. Amazingly, they were the only people injured on Flight 143.

BLAME GAME

Air Canada's preliminary investigation into the disaster determined that the flight crew and the ground crew were ultimately responsible. Captain Pearson was demoted to first officer for six months, First Officer Quintal was suspended with pay for two weeks, and three members of the ground crew were suspended without pay for 10 days.

Critics immediately accused Air Canada of blaming its employees in order to protect its own reputation, and the ensuing public outcry prompted a much larger investigation, which lasted more than a year. *That* investigation blamed the accident on the airline's poor training and poor procedures, and questioned the wisdom of introducing a metric aircraft into an imperial air fleet.

The report not only exonerated Pearson and Quintal but also credited them with saving the passengers against very long odds. "The consequence would have been disastrous had it not been for the flying ability of Captain Pearson with valuable assistance from First Officer Quintal," the final report read.

THE REAL CULPRIT

But what had caused the fuel quantity processor to fail in the first place? Investigators took it apart to find out. The culprit: a single bad solder joint—a poor electrical connection that caused the system to send a weak signal to the fuel quantity processor instead of a strong one. It was actually worse than no connection at all.

The fuel quantity processor knew how to handle a *complete* loss of signal: it was programmed to switch to a backup signal if the first signal failed. But the processor didn't know how to respond to a *weak* signal, so rather than switch to the backup signal that was functioning properly, it shut down altogether and the fuel gauges went blank.

LESSON LEARNED

In the aftermath of Flight 143, Air Canada updated its procedures and improved its training. Most importantly, it assigned the task of calculating the fuel load to one individual who is qualified to do it even if the computers aren't working. The "Gimli Glider" experience has not been repeated, at least not at Air Canada. (In August 2001, an Air Transat Airbus A330 with a fuel leak ran out of fuel over the Atlantic Ocean. It glided some 60 miles to a safe landing at an airport in the Azores Islands.)

What happened to the 767? After the emergency landing, several mechanics were dispatched to Gimli to repair the jet enough so that it could be flown to Winnipeg for more extensive repair work. Believe it or not, their van ran out of gas on the way. The mechanics eventually made it to Gimli, and the plane made it back to Winnipeg. The damage was duly repaired, and the Gimli Glider was restored to the Air Canada fleet. It's been flying without incident ever since.

At last report the plane is still in service. Are you reading this on an Air Canada flight? A 767? Ask the flight attendant if you're riding on the Gimli Glider.

On second thought, maybe it's better to wait until you're back on the ground.

*   *   *

TECHNO-QUIZ

If you owned a model Mark IV FM, what would you have?

    a. A new SUV.   **c.** A top-of-the-line radio.
    b. A DVD player.   **d.** A nuclear weapon.

Answer:

d. You'd have the atom bomb that was dropped on Nagasaki in 1945. The bomb was designated "Mark IV FM" on its blueprints.

When electric eels meet, they change frequencies so their electrical fields don't interfere.

THE *PEANUTS* GALLERY

Over 50 years, Charles Schulz created more than 60 different characters for Peanuts. *He consistently added new ones, wrote others out, and allowed the ones he kept to grow. On page 157 we told you about the* Peanuts *story. Now here's a look at the cast.*

CHARLIE BROWN

- First appearance: October 2, 1950. Charlie Brown started out around four years old, but aged to six in 1957, and later to eight years old.
- While Charles Schulz was teaching at the Art Instruction School in the late 1940s, he fell for a "red-haired girl"—an accountant named Donna Johnson. His heart was broken when she chose another man shortly before he was going to propose to her. As he did with so many other aspects of his life, Schulz used it in the comic strip. Over the course of the strip's run, an unseen "red-haired girl" is the object of Charlie Brown's unrequited love. Another of Johnson's characteristics showed up in *Peanuts*, too: Like Charlie Brown, she often wore a pale yellow shirt with a black, horizontal zigzag going across it.
- Schulz was often asked if Charlie Brown was bald. "He's got hair," he responded. "It's just so light you don't notice it."

"I wonder what would happen if I walked over and asked the little red-haired girl to have lunch with me. She'd probably laugh right in my face. It's hard on a face when it gets laughed in."
—**Charlie Brown**

SNOOPY

- First appearance: October 4, 1950. "Originally he was to be called Sniffy," recalled Schulz, "but I was walking uptown one day and saw a comic magazine about a dog named Sniffy. On my way back to my job, I remembered that my mother had said, 'If you ever have another dog, you should name him Snoopy.' I thought, hey, why didn't I think of that before?"
- Snoopy communicated (via a thought balloon) for the first time in 1952 and walked on two legs for the first time in 1956.
- On December 12, 1958, Snoopy first attempted to sleep on the

top of his doghouse, but he fell off, and thought to himself, "Life is full of rude awakenings." That awakening was great for Schulz, who made Snoopy's doghouse a *Peanuts* character in its own right. He never showed it from any other angle but the side, and never showed the inside. (It's said to be very roomy.)

• Over the decades, Snoopy's various fantasy characters included Joe Cool, the World War I Flying Ace, Foreign Legionnaire, Beagle Scout, and the Literary Ace, whose first written words were: "It was a dark and stormy night." In all of *Peanuts* history, Snoopy has taken on more than 150 different personas.

"My life has no purpose, no direction, no aim, no meaning, and yet I'm happy. I can't figure it out. What am I doing right?" **—Snoopy**

LINUS VAN PELT

• One day while Schulz was still teaching at the Art Instruction School in the early 1950s, he drew a little baby with wild hair and showed it to a friend named Linus Maurer. Maurer thought the kid looked funny, so Schulz decided to work him into the *Peanuts* strip, and call the boy Linus. He first appeared on September 19, 1952, as Lucy's happy baby brother, but aged quickly as Schulz realized Charlie Brown needed a friendly ear.

• Seeing his own kids drag their blankets around the house, in 1956 Schulz gave one to Linus. Even though Linus "grew up" to school age, he never lost the need for it. Schulz was always proud of having introduced the term "security blanket" into the lexicon.

• Linus represented Schulz's spiritual side, as the boy often quoted the Bible. As a young man in Minneapolis, Schulz was involved in the Church of God, but grew disillusioned with organized religion. Late in life he described himself as a "secular humanist."

• Linus's infatuation with the Great Pumpkin first played out around Halloween of 1959. "Linus, who is bright but very innocent," explained Schulz, "got one holiday ahead of himself and confused Halloween with Christmas."

"Dear Great Pumpkin, I am looking forward to your arrival on Halloween night. I hope you will bring me lots of presents. Everyone tells me you are a fake, but I believe in you. Sincerely, Linus van Pelt. P.S. If you really are a fake, don't tell me. I don't want to know." **—Linus**

Nothing to sneeze at: A cough travels at 600 mph.

LUCY VAN PELT

• First appearance: March 3, 1952. Lucy was originally a baby, but her self-centered streak was there from the beginning. "Lucy comes from the part of me that's capable of saying mean and sarcastic things," Schulz said. She was originally modeled on Schulz's daughter Meredith, whom he once described as a "fussbudget."

• Nearly every autumn, Schulz would dedicate a Sunday strip to Charlie Brown's attempt to kick a football held by Lucy, who invariably pulls it away at the last second—something that Schulz's friends often did to him when he was a kid.

"I'm worried about a little boy who sits in front of me at school. He cries every day. This afternoon I tried to help him. I whacked him one on the arm. There's nothing like a little physical pain to take your mind off emotional problems."
—Lucy

SCHROEDER

• First appearance: May 30, 1951. Early in the strip, as a lark, Schulz wanted to show Charlie Brown singing the melody to Beethoven's Ninth Symphony, so he copied the actual notes—clef and all—into the strip. He loved the way it looked, and searched for a way to keep using the musical staff. He thought of the toy piano that his young daughter liked to play and decided that one of the *Peanuts* cast should play one, too. So he chose his newest character, a baby he called Schroeder, who was named after a boy Schulz used to caddy with at a golf course in St. Paul.

• Although Schulz's favorite composer was Brahms, he chose Beethoven to be Schroeder's hero because the name "Beethoven" is intrinsically funnier than "Brahms." (It also explains why Schroeder is so adamant about turning down Lucy's advances: Beethoven was a lifelong bachelor, so Schroeder has to be one, too.)

Lucy: *Schroeder, do you think a pretty girl is like a melody?*
Schroeder: *I can't say…I've never known any pretty girls.*

SALLY BROWN

• Charlie Brown's little sister first appeared on August 23, 1959, as a baby, but quickly grew up to kindergarten age. Over the years, her main role has been to offer her (and Schulz's) cynical opinions on the state of modern education, most notably the "new math."

Movie director John Waters is a crime junkie; he had seats at the Watergate and Manson trials.

- Another victim of unrequited love in the *Peanuts* world, Sally is infatuated with her big brother's best friend, Linus. In Sally's eyes, Linus can do no wrong (she calls him her "sweet babboo").

"I worry about getting old...who wants to be nine?"   —Sally

PATRICIA "PEPPERMINT PATTY" REICHARDT

- Peppermint Patty debuted on August 22, 1966. It started when Schulz looked at a bowl of candy in his kitchen and was intrigued by the name "Peppermint Patty." He decided to use the name for a character before another cartoonist did.

- Schulz liked Peppermint Patty—the way she didn't understand that Snoopy was a dog (she called him "that funny-looking kid with the big nose," and his dog house is "Chuck's guest cottage"). He worked her into numerous story lines, giving her an outsider's perspective, and believed she could "carry a strip all by herself."

- Because of Peppermint Patty's penchant for sleeping through school, in the 1980s researchers at Stanford University asked Schulz to send her to a narcolepsy clinic to help raise people's awareness of the disorder. (She did go, but it was determined she was falling asleep in class because she stayed up too late at night.)

- Peppermint Patty's troubles with schoolwork echoed Schulz's. Both would rather draw, look out the window, sleep—anything that didn't involve studying. She got a "D-minus" on just about every school project she attempted.

"That was a hard test, Marcie. I didn't know if it was an essay test, true or false, or multiple choice. I just put down 'Not Guilty.'"

—Peppermint Patty (she got a D-minus)

MARCIE

- Named after Schulz's friend Marcie Carlin, Marcie joined the gang at summer camp in 1971, where she met Peppermint Patty.

- Some readers wondered if Marcie was gay, not only because of her boyish appearance, but because she also called her friend, Peppermint Patty, "Sir." So is she? Schulz never commented on it, but did say that "if Marcie and Peppermint Patty ever have a falling out, it's likely to be over Charlie Brown, who they both secretly love."

The latrine at a Roman fort near Hadrian's Wall in Britain had room for 20 to sit side-by-side.

Peppermint Patty: *How come you're always calling me "Sir" when I keep asking you not to? Don't you realize how annoying that can be?*
Marcie: *No, Ma'am.*

WOODSTOCK
• On April 4, 1967, a bird that resembled Woodstock haphazardly flew up to Snoopy's doghouse and landed on his nose. Over the next four years, a series of birds regularly visited Snoopy and complained about various things, including the state of affairs for young people, Schulz's nod to the growing Hippie movement. He was finally named in 1970 in honor of the Woodstock music festival.
• "I've held fast with Woodstock's means of communication," said Schulz, "though it has been tempting at times to have him talk. I feel it would be a mistake to give in on this point."

"iii iiii iii ii ii iii!"   —Woodstock

FRANKLIN
• The first African-American kid in the *Peanuts* neighborhood, Franklin first appeared on July 31, 1968. It was the height of the Civil Rights movement, leading many fans to see it as a statement on desegregation. But Schulz said he never meant it that way. "I simply introduced Franklin as another character, not a political statement." Schulz recalled an editor from the South who said, "I don't mind you having a black character, but please don't show them in school together." Schulz ignored the request.
• Often playing the straight man, most of Franklin's humor comes from his deadpan reactions to Peppermint Patty, who sits behind him at school, and to the other kids in Charlie Brown's neighborhood, who are a bit too weird for his tastes.

"My grandfather says that once you're over the hill, you begin to pick up speed."
        —Franklin

PIG-PEN
• First appearance: July 13, 1954. Pig-Pen never really evolved beyond just being a complete mess, and Schulz, never wanting to force anything, gradually worked him out of the strip. The character did, however, have one lasting influence on society: When

---

What's *fulgerite*? Fossilized lightning, occurring when a bolt melts soil into glass.

scientists discovered that every kid really does have their own individual "pollution cloud," they termed that cloud the "Pigpen effect."

"I have affixed to me the dirt and dust of countless ages. Who am I to disturb history?"
                                                                —**Pig-Pen**

PATTY AND VIOLET

• Patty, not to be confused with Peppermint Patty, was there from the beginning; Violet first appeared as her best friend on February 7, 1951.

• Although the two girls shared Lucy's snobbery and her disdain for Charlie Brown, Schulz never really fleshed them out. "Some characters just don't seem to have enough personality to carry out ideas," he said.

• Interestingly, it was Violet who first pulled the football away from Charlie Brown in 1950. Lucy took over the following year.

Violet: *"Charlie Brown, it simply goes without saying that you are an inferior human being!"*
Charlie Brown: *"If it goes without saying, then why did you say it?"*

RERUN VAN PELT

• Linus and Lucy's younger brother first appeared as a baby in 1972, and Schulz really didn't know what to do with him…until he put Rerun on the back of his mother's bicycle in 1974.

• When Schulz became a grandfather, he had a new crop of young ones to mine for character traits, so he applied them to Rerun.

• Like the kids of the 1970s, Rerun was more cynical than Linus, and therefore easier for Lucy to identify with. It allowed Schulz to show Lucy's softer side as she sort of became Rerun's protector.

Lucy: *Okay Rerun, let's work on our counting again. Now, how many fingers do you see?*
Rerun: *All but the thumb.*

GROWN-UPS

Why are there no adults shown in the *Peanuts* comic strips? "Well," answers Schulz, "there just isn't any room for them. They'd have to bend over to fit in the panels. If you added adults, you'd have to back off and it would change the whole perspective."

Longest recorded flight of a champagne cork: 177 feet, 9 inches.

WORDS OF WISDOM

We hope you enjoyed our Best of the Best of the Bathroom Reader. *We leave you with thoughts both witty and wise gleaned from our two quotation books.*

"Humor is a reminder that no matter how high the throne one sits on, one sits on one's bottom."
—**Taki**

"Go to bed in your fireplace. You'll sleep like a log."
—**Ellen DeGeneres**

"An escalator can never break; it can only become stairs."
—**Mitch Hedberg**

"When birds burp, it must taste like bugs."
—**Calvin,** *Calvin & Hobbes*

"I believe in looking reality straight in the face...and denying it."
—**Garrison Keillor**

"The way I see it, if you want the rainbow, you gotta put up with the rain."
—**Dolly Parton**

"Well done is better than well said."
—**Benjamin Franklin**

"Don't dig for water under the outhouse."
—**cowboy proverb**

"Victory goes to the player who makes the next-to-last mistake."
—**Savielly Tartakower, chessmaster**

"Education is what you get when you read the fine print; experience is what you get when you don't."
—**Pete Seeger**

"There's only one corner of the universe you can be certain of improving, and that's your own self."
—**Aldous Huxley**

"Just because something doesn't do what you planned it to do doesn't mean it's useless."
—**Thomas Edison**

"When choosing between two evils, try the one you've never tried before."
—**Mae West**

"Don't compromise yourself; you're all you've got."
—**Janis Joplin**

"In three words I can sum up everything I've learned about life: it goes on."
—**Robert Frost**

Dolly Parton once lost a Dolly Parton look-alike contest.

Also available
from *Uncle John's
Bathroom Reader!*

THE LAST PAGE

FELLOW BATHROOM READERS:
The fight for good bathroom reading should never be taken loosely—we must do our duty and sit firmly for what we believe in, even while the rest of the world is taking potshots at us.

We'll be brief. Now that we've proven we're not simply a flush-in-the-pan, we invite you to take the plunge: Sit Down and Be Counted! Become a member of the Bathroom Readers' Institute. Log on to *www.bathroomreader.com*, or send a self-addressed, stamped, business-sized envelope to: BRI, PO Box 1117, Ashland, Oregon 97520. You'll receive your free membership card, get discounts when ordering directly through the BRI, and earn a permanent spot on the BRI honor roll!

If you like reading our books...

VISIT THE BRI'S WEB SITE!

www.bathroomreader.com

- Visit "The Throne Room"—a great place to read!
  - Receive our irregular newsletters via e-mail
    - Order additional *Bathroom Readers*
      - Become a BRI member

Go with the Flow...

Well, we're out of space, and when you've gotta go, you've gotta go. Tanks for all your support. Hope to hear from you soon. Meanwhile, remember...

Keep on flushin'!